**By the Same Author**

*Jutland. The Unfinished Battle*
*The Last Days of the High Seas Fleet. From Scapa Flow to Scuttle*
*George Jellicoe, SAS and SBS Commander*

## What the Reviews Said

***Jutland. The Unfinished Battle***

*Closely reasoned, fair-minded and thoroughly readable.* (included in 'Six of the best First World War reads', *The Sunday Times*)

*A lively and engaging analysis of the controversial fleet action that combines new material with the sympathetic but not uncritical perspective of the British C-in-C's grandson.* (Rear Admiral James Goldrick, RAN)

*The best narrative account of the battle currently available.* (Prof Eric Grove, *Navy News*)

*A compelling and dramatic account scrupulously accurate and fair.* (Robert Massie, Pulitzer Prize-winning author, *Castles of Steel, Dreadnought*)

*Thoroughly researched and absorbing … an excellent addition to the vast array of literature about the epic clash.* (*Warships, International Fleet Review*)

*A superb analysis … A balanced, measured and yet nuanced account of the greatest sea battle of World War I.* (Prof Holger Herwig, author, *Luxury Fleet*)

*The best account I have read about this greatest of sea battles.* (Capt Don Walsh, USN retd)

*His description of the battle itself is a masterpiece of historical writing.* (Prof Dr Michael Epkenhans, Bundeswehr Military History)

***The Last Days of the High Seas Fleet. From Scapa Flow to Scuttle***

*Jellicoe's book makes a unique contribution to the historic record of what was the final act of Imperial German Sea Power.* (*The Northern Mariner*)

*Using detailed research, particularly from German sources and eye-witness accounts, Nick Jellicoe has produced another highly enjoyable read on a fascinating episode.* (*Warship World*)

*Superbly illustrated, the book combines an engaging narrative with penetrating analysis.* (*The Naval Review*)

*As usual Jellicoe is fair and empathetic to his subjects and writes an accessible account of a complex situation, again perhaps the best available.* (*Navy News*)

***George Jellicoe, SAS and SBS Commander***

*A hugely powerful tale of one of the most revered and inspirational Special Forces commanders of WWII.* (Damien Lewis, bestselling author, *SAS. Band of Brothers*)

*An exceptionally informative and enjoyable tribute to an important pioneer of Britain's world-famous Special Forces.* (*The Guards Magazine*)

*A fascinating read.* (Julie Peakman, author, *Hitler's Island War*)

*well told and enjoyable to read … provides applicable historical lessons for modern military leaders.* (*International Journal of Naval History*)

# JELLICOE'S WAR

To the memory of Rear Admiral James Goldrick, RAN, and Captain Don Walsh, USN. Both submariners, both taken too early. And to all who have perished at sea, their watery graves known only to God.

# JELLICOE'S WAR

## The U-boat Threat in World War One and the Question of Convoy

Nicholas Jellicoe

Seaforth
PUBLISHING

First published in Great Britain in 2024 by
Seaforth Publishing
An imprint of Pen & Sword Books Ltd,
George House, Beevor Street, Barnsley S71 1HN

www.seaforthpublishing.com
Email info@seaforthpublishing.com

*British Library Cataloguing in Publication Data*
A CIP data record for this book is available from the British Library

ISBN 978-1-0361-0902-8 (Hardback)
ISBN 978-1-0361-0904-2 (ePub)
ISBN 978-1-0361-0906-6 (PDF)



Pen & Sword Books Limited incorporates the imprints of Atlas, Archaeology, Aviation, Discovery, Family History, Fiction, History, Maritime, Military, Military Classics, Politics, Select, Transport, True Crime, Air World, Frontline Publishing, Leo Cooper, Remember When, Seaforth Publishing, The Praetorian Press, Wharncliffe Local History, Wharncliffe Transport, Wharncliffe True Crime and White Owl.

Typeset and designed by Mac Style
Printed and bound in Great Britain by CPI Group (UK) Ltd, Croydon, CR0 4YY

FSC www.fsc.org MIX Paper | Supporting responsible forestry FSC® C013604

## Contents

# Foreword

As a submarine officer with forty years of active service in the United States Navy, I was thrilled to be asked by Nick Jellicoe to write the foreword for *Jellicoe's War: The U-boat Threat in World War One and the Question of Convoy*. This book is about the rise of the German Submarine Force in the First World War and the implementation of convoy operations to disrupt German efforts to interdict Allied sea lines of communication (SLOCs). Jellicoe's account is meticulously researched and, unlike other attempts to simply document the tonnage achieved by the 'Dark Knights of the Atlantic Corridor' – German U-Boat commanders – this book weaves together hundreds of stories of both cruelty and bravado on the high seas. As a campaign which almost brought the Allies to their knees, it is well worth your time to delve into the First Battle of the Atlantic.

Not since reading Theodore Roscoe's comprehensive history of US submarine operations in the First World War as an ensign aboard my first submarine in 1982, have I enjoyed a book dedicated to the art of submarine warfare this much. Roscoe's voluminous tome was on board every submarine on which I served. During annual Submarine Birthday Balls, after the tolling of the bells, it was there to tell our story: the CO or XO would read of a daring mission, a harrowing approach or an attack in the Atlantic or Pacific theatres of the Second World War. During the readings, there was deafening silence on the mess decks as the crew listened to the accomplishments of those who sailed before us, in arduous conditions, and on boats that had none of the creature comforts of the nuclear-powered submarines of today. And during every dolphin awards ceremony I ever attended, citations were read.

I also had the great honour and fortune of meeting some whose exploits were detailed in Roscoe's book. Some of the most memorable were Medal of

Honor winners like RADM Dick O'Kane, CO, USS *Tang*; RADM Eugene 'Lucky' Fluckey, CO, USS *Barb*, the 'Galloping Ghost of the China Coast'; and VADM Lawson P. 'Red' Ramage, CO, USS *Parche*. Likewise, it was my pleasure to get to know Captain Edward L. Beach, another submarine hero of the Second World War, CO of USS *Piper* and later, the nuclear-powered submarine USS *Triton*, the first nuclear-powered boat to circumnavigate the Earth. Beach was Naval Aide to President Eisenhower before he retired, and later one of the most influential authors at the US Naval Institute in Annapolis, Maryland. His book, *Run Silent, Run Deep* (1955), was on *The New York Times* bestseller list for months before becoming an acclaimed Hollywood movie starring Clark Gable and Burt Lancaster. I think Beach would have enjoyed reading Nick Jellicoe's latest book.

*Jellicoe's War* chronicles Admiral Jellicoe's journey from a young naval officer to command of the Grand Fleet which engaged the German High Seas Fleet in the Battle of Jutland in 1916, a battle Nick Jellicoe has written about in another very informative work: *Jutland: The Unfinished Battle*. Nick Jellicoe is forthright about the battle's outcome, which I have often thought to be a Pyrrhic victory for both sides. In this book, Nick Jellicoe opines:

> Jutland's outcome turned out to be bitterly disappointing for a British public constantly fed expectations of another Trafalgar by its national press, and for many Royal Navy officers who saw a guaranteed victory snatched by foul weather, faulty British ship design, underperforming munitions and erratic leadership … Much contemporary press reporting portrayed Jellicoe as a vestige of a bygone age, an officer moulded by the the Victorian strictures of his upbringing. That picture was nurtured by political enemies and naval rivals.

The question of victory or defeat at Jutland perpetuates the ongoing debate by navalists and maritime strategists. Nick Jellicoe professes that much has been written about Jellicoe and Jutland, but less so about the emerging threat in the undersea domain – the German Submarine Force. *Jellicoe's War* attempts to fill that void; and in my estimation, his vivid account succeeds.

Early on, the author credits the French for recognising the value of the submarine in a *Guerre de Course* that overshadowed the Mahanian decisive battle at sea. It is interesting that, while neither the British nor German High Commands appreciated the impact the submarine would have, originally it was the French who asserted the submarine's asymmetric advantage.

The author provides an insightful quote from noted navalist Richard Hough on British disdain for submarines at the start of the war as follows:

> Most senior naval officers viewed this new weapon with hostility and suspicion. Submarines were on the one hand criticized for their limited powers, being considered mainly for defence of harbours and anchorages and quite incapable of working at sea against a fleet; and, contradictorily, for being such a potential threat to the battleship, in which the country had invested more than any other two nations in the world, that to encourage its development was to hazard the country's security.

It is one thing to develop a weapon of war with such enormous destructive potential but quite a different challenge to train officers and crews needed to take a submarine to sea, putting themselves in harm's way in order to inflict enormous damage on an enemy. Unlike any other nation of this era, Germany had both the weapon capable of mass destruction and the trained crews to man it, many of whom operated with unmatched ruthlessness and drive to send as many Allied ships as possible – regardless of whether they were warships, passenger liners or hospital ships – to the bottom of the sea.

When criticising the Germans for their conduct in unrestricted submarine warfare, one cannot throw stones in glass houses. After the attack on Pearl Harbor on 7 December 1941, the United States was not well prepared. Inexperience and timidity reigned in many of our commanding officers, who had up to this point been peacetime sailors. In a leadership shakeup, Admiral Charles A. Lockwood took command of the Pacific Submarine Force and shook things up by putting aggressive young officers on our deploying submarines.

I never met the legendary skipper, LCDR Dudley W. 'Mush' Morton of USS *Wahoo*. Before she was lost with all hands, she sank 55,000 tons of Japanese shipping in four war patrols. Some testified that Morton authorised the shooting of Japanese prisoners in the water after the *Buyo Maru* was sunk. His XO, Dick O'Kane, denied that Morton gave any such orders, but it's doubtful we will ever know the truth; in the fog and friction of war, sometimes the rules are skewed. For this reason, in today's professional force, we have extensive training on authorised use of military force (AUMF) and rules of engagement (ROE). Based on Jellicoe's well-researched accounts of the conduct of German submarines at sea, this kind of ROE was clearly absent in the First World War. In fact, among some very successful U-boat commanders, a wide divergence in standards of behaviour and ethical conduct at sea existed.

In my opinion, this is where the author's research is most interesting, at least to this former submariner. Many of the Dark Knights were accomplished tacticians, ship drivers, warriors and leaders. Take Otto Weddingen, for example; revered by his men, he played by the rules of war, though he lobbied the kaiser for unrestricted submarine warfare, which was never granted in his lifetime. Weddingen sank four British warships, earning him the highest order of the Knight's Cross and Pour Le Mérite from Imperial Germany.

Another commanding officer – also an advocate of unrestricted submarine warfare – Hans Rose, was also known for his skill as a submariner, with eighteen ships sunk and seven disabled to his credit. *U-53*'s skipper was noted for the compassion he showed his victims.

The most chivalrous of German submariners was undoubtedly Germany's top submarine ace, Lothar von Arnauld de la Perière, who preferred his deck gun to the torpedo. De la Perière regularly surfaced *U-35* to issue an ultimatum to 'abandon ship' before opening fire. His record of 194 ships sunk (454,000 tons) remained unmatched throughout the First World War and Second World War. Confident of his and his crew's abilities, de la Perière proved that one could play by the rules of war and still be dealt a winning hand.

Finally, Austrian submariner Georg von Trapp sank eleven merchant ships and two Allied warships (60,000 tons). Von Trapp was also an advocate for unrestricted submarine warfare, but he drew the line at collaboration with the Nazis in the Second World War and fled to Switzerland with his family, then to America, where he and his second wife, Maria, and his children were made famous by Hollywood in the movie *The Sound of Music*.

Contrast this behaviour with that of the man most responsible for the catalyst that eventually brought the United States into the war on the side of the Allies. As CO of *U-20*, the boat that sank the *Lusitania* in May 1915, Walter Schwieger was responsible for the deaths of 1,198 passengers from a total of 1,951 on board; 128 were American.

Revered by his crew and regarded as a thoughtful and caring commanding officer, Schwieger showed little compassion for *Lusitania*'s innocents. Conspiracy theories abound; the author writes that, coincidentally, Schwieger's patrol orders have disappeared from the archives. One might assume that the *Lusitania* was purposely targeted. At the time, the German High Command was not of one mind in supporting unrestricted submarine warfare for fear of risking America's aiding of the Allies. President Woodrow Wilson and his Cabinet, however, had no desire to get entangled in a European war, preferring to remain isolationist and put their trust in Wilson's League of Nations approach to solving problems.

Schwieger later claimed that he didn't know it was a passenger liner and thought it to be carrying war materiel. Despite Germany's denials that the ship was purposely targeted, the minter Karl Goetz quickly struck a coin commemorating the sinking, which created an international backlash. In response, Great Britain struck an identical coin to raise money for the victims of the sinking but also exploited the occasion to decry the loss of life on the high seas and the German government's collusion with its navy in whitewashing such a crime. Many years ago in London, I purchased one of these coins in Covent Garden; I have it displayed in my library as a reminder of the lethality of unrestricted submarine warfare.

Part of the problem was in the lack of clear orders and consistency in the chain of the German High Command. Reading Jellicoe's book compelled me to take two volumes of the first edition of Alfred von Tirpitz's memoirs off the shelf in my study and examine his position on unrestricted submarine warfare during the First World War. In his preface to the 1919 edition, Tirpitz expresses his lamentations as a leader of a defeated power and attributes Germany's failure to political interference and overzealousness:

> The despair that seized upon all patriotically minded Germans when the empire which we had thought invincible collapsed has also wrecked many people's faith in our nation and in the continuity of its historical development. It seemed to me that my duty therefore is to write down my reminiscences, because I can show proofs that the old structure of our state was not antiquated and rotten but was capable of any development and moreover that the political legend of a ruthless autocracy and a bellicose military caste having let loose this war is an insult to truth. The Kaiser, in particular, did not want the war but did his utmost to prevent it when he realized the danger.[1]

As Jellicoe maintains, it was not just the British Admiralty that doubted the effectiveness of the submarine but also the German High Command and Tirpitz himself. Nonetheless, in reflection after the fact, Tirpitz alludes to a late realisation as to the value of the submarine and a waffling throughout the war as to how to employ this valuable asset:

> In addition, the effect of submarines in battle, having regard to the high speed of the fighting ships, was almost entirely a matter of chance; indeed, their real value was rather that they rendered tracts of the sea unsafe, somewhat after the fashion of a movable minefield, and in the danger created by them for any ships that might be rendered incapable of movement.[2]

Tirpitz admits that Germany made a mistake in both delaying the start of and then rescinding the order to conduct unrestricted submarine warfare. As evidence, he cites a compilation of contradictory orders, both condoning and condemning attacks on Allied shipping:

> Such are the impressions from the fleet. Order, Counter-order, Disorder! When one reviews these commands and counter-commands, which in

> part were quite impossible to carry out, and when one remembers further that they had to pass through the different commands to the individual commanders, one can well understand what confusion and irritation must have been caused to commanders by this perpetual and often self-contradictory interference of the political authorities and the Cabinet.[3]

As a result of the German Cabinet's procrastinations, Tirpitz submitted his resignation more than once until it was finally accepted by the kaiser in March 1916. By the new year of 1917, Scheer issued orders to the High Seas Fleet to commence the submarine commerce war, a period which Nick Jellicoe describes as adding 'a new ferocity to the submarine war'.

The German Submarine Force executed the new orders with a vengeance. Some of the atrocities that occurred were avoidable. After successfully torpedoing her, William Werner pulled *Torrington*'s survivors on deck, stripped them of their lifejackets and then submerged his boat, men still left topside. A few days later, the crew of the *Toro* met the same fate, and Paul Wagenfuhr copied Werner's brutal tactic with the crew of the *Belgian Prince*. In my humble opinion, all were war crimes, even if unlikely to be prosecuted after the war.

The Second Battle of the Atlantic in the Second World War offers some interesting perspectives. After the successful attack on the RMS *Laconia* in September 1942, *U-156*'s commander, Hartenstein, realised that there were over a thousand Italian POWs on board. He manoeuvred to rescue as many as possible, calling for help and risking the safety of his own boat. In response, Fleet Admiral Donitz, himself a First World War submarine commander, issued the 'Laconia Order': only commanding officers and engineers could, henceforth, be rescued; luckily for them, their intelligence value was high. The order was used as evidence at Donitz's trial at Nuremberg. Remarkably, US Fleet Admiral Chester Nimitz testified under oath (remotely) and offered that the policies of the German Submarine Force were no different than the US Navy Submarine Force in the Pacific theatre regarding Japanese survivors of submarine attacks. Possibly as a result, Donitz received a ten-year sentence instead of the death penalty.

As the new unrestricted campaign unfolded, an increasing number of American citizens suffered the mortal consequences. President Woodrow Wilson, his confidant Colonel Edward M. House and Secretary of the Navy Josephus Daniels were on edge. Daniels was ill-prepared to be a wartime secretary and had never served in uniform. Neither he, nor other members of the President's Cabinet, understood the far-reaching implications of unrestricted submarine warfare in the European theatre, let alone its impact on supply chains.

As Jellicoe points out, after the revelations of the famous 'Zimmerman Telegram', Wilson had finally had enough and broke off diplomatic relations with Germany. Admiral Sims was sent to London to work with the Allies in the defence of trans-Atlantic SLOCs. With him came the promise of a US destroyer presence, so when he arrived in London, he was greeted warmly by Admiral Jellicoe despite the marked difference in rank. Sims ranked the lowest of thirty-one USN admirals; possibly an indicator as to the level of control that the US government wanted to maintain over the relationship. What Washington may not have anticipated was that Sims quickly ingratiated himself and was considered a valued partner and friend by the British Admiralty. Sims left his ego at the door: rank did not matter. He focused on brainpower and application of good strategy and tactics. He even acquiesced to putting US Navy units under direct Royal Navy command and control. He also disagreed with Daniels, who preferred protection for troop transports, whereas Sims saw more value in protecting trade and the SLOCs.

The resulting working relationship between Sims and Jellicoe became the model for Allied cooperation and interoperability and carries on today in the NATO Alliance. Fortuitously, I had the pleasure of attending the symposium on 'Sea Control and Foreign Policy' at the US Naval War College in April 2017. Like *Jellicoe's War*, forums like this are important, and I was quoted during the conference as having lent my support to it as Director, Navy Staff:

> First of all, this provides a forum for a debate on the direction that the Navy is going in the 21st century … This forum combines active-duty military along with diplomats who are all important when we talk about the Navy and diplomacy.[4]

To examine the reasons for Sims's position, on the 100th anniversary of his arrival in London, the War College facilitated a panel at the conference entitled 'Echoes of the First World War in the 21st Century'. Instead of having traditional academics debate the idiosyncrasies of unrestricted submarine warfare or the convoy system in the First World War, the College invited the grandsons of both of these Great War leaders – Dr Nathan Sims and Nick Jellicoe – to take part. It was the first time the two had met and led to a fascinating discussion.[5]

Before departing the conference, I was quoted on the value of this, and other symposia like it, to understanding the value of sea power and sea control:

> While a lot has changed in how we build ships, man ships, and train our sailors, the strategy of sea control has remained a constant throughout the history of maritime strategy.[6]

What I find amazing is the clear lack of understanding of the root cause of German interdiction of Allied SLOCs, and moreover, what to do about it? Neither Lloyd George and his War Cabinet, including the Admiralty, nor Wilson and his Secretary of the Navy could agree on the German centres of gravity and how to defeat or mitigate them. The German Submarine Force was one of them, and remarkably, as Tirpitz testified in his memoirs, not even the German High Command could agree that it had a game-changing asymmetric weapon that could have turned the tide of the war against the Allies as early as 1915. Thankfully, it did not.

On the question of what to do about it, Nick Jellicoe provides a bird's-eye view of both American and British thought on the value of convoy operations, and to a certain extent refutes allegations that Admiral Jellicoe's reticence to employ convoys earlier in the war was a 'disgrace'. On the contrary, in my reading of the book, Admiral Jellicoe was a deep thinker and a deliberate decision-maker.

Before he committed huge resources to convoy operations which he, Beatty and others worried would strip the Grand Fleet – the very force needed for the ultimate decisive battle at sea – of its escorts, Jellicoe had to be sure. Even if, with the tie that occurred at Jutland, one might have concluded that the time and place for that decisive battle had passed. As strong opposition to convoys still remained in the Admiralty, Jellicoe continued to hesitate on a trial, and received additional criticism from Lloyd George and his Cabinet. Finally, the first trial of the convoy system set off from Gibraltar to Plymouth on 10 May 1917, over ten days at an excruciatingly slow 6.5 knots. All seventeen ships made it to Plymouth! From then on, convoys started to sail regularly from the US to Europe and vice versa.

On the question of convoys, Jellicoe's frosty relationship with Lloyd George and the War Cabinet was unhelpful. From the author's notes, after the war, Jellicoe maintained that one of the limiting factors in getting convoy operations going forward was the lack of escorts; the US Navy's entry into the war addressed the problem. Another mitigating factor was, in Jellicoe's own words, the 'gargantuan task' that implementing convoy operations would mean. Without the benefits of modern-day communications, unified command and control to enable the common operating picture that navies enjoy today, I would agree with Jellicoe's assessment in 1917.

Did the convoy system work? Admiral Donitz maintained that it did: 'The German submarine campaign was wrecked by the introduction of the convoy system.' While the precipitous drop in losses of ships under convoy marked a huge success, Jellicoe adds two caveats: convoy did not significantly increase German submarine losses, nor did it prevent the sinking of ships proceeding to or from the rallying points. Although U-boats did not operate more than a few hundred nautical miles from land, and were not as much of a threat in the open ocean of the Atlantic, vulnerabilities still occurred before marrying up with the escorts. Indeed, the first risk faced by merchant mariners participating in convoy operations was getting to the rallying point. I understand these vulnerabilities because I participated in the seventy-fifth anniversary of convoy operations at a rallying point in Reykjavik Harbour, Iceland, in 2018, during Exercise Trident Juncture – the largest NATO Live Exercise for reinforcement of Iceland and Norway since the end of the Cold War.

November 1917 witnessed first blood to the Americans, with USS *Fanning* sinking its first U-boat. Now there could be no more excuses – the USN was thoroughly engaged and willing to risk its own losses for the war effort.

Despite the relative success of the convoys, Admiral Jellicoe continued to have issues with Lloyd George and his War Cabinet. He was dismissed as First Sea Lord during Christmas 1917, an act which does not seem fair, given all that Jellicoe had been through and after his long service to the country. Replacing him did not solve all the challenges that the Royal Navy was facing in new naval construction, repair and supply chain issues. In fact, it might have somewhat hindered progress.

Throughout 1918, Germany remained an empire in decline; Scheer was forced to reprioritise his forces with the homeland's defence. At the war's end, according to the terms of the Armistice, Germany was compelled to turn over its surviving submarines, amounting to half of the force for a total of 176 boats. Another 178 had perished during the war.

Men like Jellicoe and Sims played a hugely important role in the defeat of Imperial Germany. Unfortunately, the Armistice would last only two decades before war in Europe broke out again. Sadly, the earlier lessons learned from unrestricted submarine warfare had to be relearned the hard way in the Second Battle of the Atlantic, hence the value of Nick Jellicoe's work in bringing forward the documented truth for future generations of naval officers.

Admiral James G. Foggo, USN (ret.)<br>Dean of the Center for Maritime Strategy<br>Navy League of the United States

# List of Illustrations

*Between pages 150 and 151*

*Unless otherwise credited, all illustrations are public domain*

## Illustrations in the text

### U-boat Commanders



### Thematic text boxes



### Other graphics, maps and tables

# Acknowledgments

The idea for this book was born in Cobh, Ireland, in 2017 when I was speaking at a conference on 'The Submarine War in Irish Waters', a guest of Professor Commander David Kohnen USN (ret'd) of the John Hattendorf Foundation at the United States Naval War College.

Cobh was a fitting place. Here were buried many of *Lusitania*'s victims after her sinking by *U.20*. It was here I met with Dr Nat Sims, the grandson of Admiral William Sowden Sims USN. From Cobh, then known as Queenstown, the newly arrived American destroyers immediately went into action under the operational command of a foreigner, Admiral Sir Lewis Bayly RN. Together, we concocted the idea of this book, originally to be written by Nat, Reinhard Scheer-Hennings (Admiral Reinhard Scheer's adopted great-grandson) and myself. While the idea proved too ambitious, the book still bears testimony to much of the help they have since given me.

Over the years, I have received help from near and far. Gert Normann Anderson at The SeaWar Museum in Thyborøn, Denmark, has been a constant source of support since our first meeting in 2015, planning for the Jutland Centenary. I accompanied Gert as a guest on two archaeological expeditions and he also made his extremely extensive archives completely accessible to me. Gert's friend, the journalist and historian Knud Jacobsen, has been a great additional source of deep knowledge.

I owe special thanks for their advice and thoughts to Dr Iain Balantyne, author of *The Deadly Trade*, Prof Chuck Steele (US Air Force Academy) and Andrew Jampoler (author of *Hard Aground: The Wreck of the USS Tennessee and the Rise of the US Navy*) for patiently tackling some of my early drafts. John McCarthy, as in my earlier books, has continued to generously lend his sharp eye. His editing suggestions are always appreciated. Italian historian Enrico

Cernuschi, with whom I share common interests ranging from Jutland to the Second World War in the Aegean Islands, gave me the benefit of his many deeply knowledgeable insights, as did Dr James Smith of King's College. Susan Scott, from the Cayzer Family Archives, corrected many of the references to Clan Line ships and the Cayzer family. Andrew Gillard, as with previous books, helped me with digitally reading the old scripts in many of the German texts, allowing me an easier task of translation.

A friendship that now goes back more than ten years with Prof Dr Michael Epkenhans, former head of the Bundeswehr's Zentrum fur Militarigeschichte und Sozialwissenschaften, helped identify contradictions and errors galore before it was too late. I am grateful for his great tact and patience.

Sadly, some close friends who were involved in the book are no longer with us. Two have been lost to cancer: Rear Admiral James Goldrick RAN (ret'd), in early 2023, and Dr Stephan Huck, with whom I worked on the Deutsche Marinemuseum's Jutland Exhibition, 'Schlacht ohne Siegern'. Stephan, who taught me much about how history should be curated and communicated, became a close friend. His tragic loss at the early age of 53 was felt by many. James was a retired submariner and a specialist in ASW. I met Captain Don Walsh, USN (ret'd), when I was working at Rolex. In 1960, Don dived the bathyscape, *Trieste*, 7 miles down to the bottom of the Mariana Trench. His record dive remains unmatched. (In 2012, James Cameron respectfully stopped a few metres short to allow Don to keep his extraordinary record.) As a submariner, I had so very much wanted Don's thoughts on what I had written. He'd taken the manuscript with him on what I think was his last expedition.

Some visits left lasting impressions: one was at the invitation of Karl Decaluwé, Governor of West-Flanders, to attend the Zeebrügge commemorations. My wife and I stayed, as his guests, in the same building Admiral Schröder had used in 1915 as the Headquarters for the Flanders Flotilla.

I first met Admiral James Foggo III USN (ret'd) at a US Naval War College alumni meeting in southern Germany in 2016. My wife and I were graciously entertained by he and Cynthia at his Washington Navy Yard's quarters the very next year. It was a memorable dinner, attended also by the then CNO John Richardson and Sam Cox, head of the US Navy's History and Heritage Command. I am deeply honoured he agreed to write the Foreword.

I remain indebted to Rob Gardiner of Seaforth Books for his support of my literary efforts from my very first book, *Jutland: The Unfinished Battle*. A good editor is worth their weight in gold. My thanks too to Tony Walton, who stepped into the breech to give my book its final polish. Any mistakes that are still here are entirely of my own making. Every effort has been made to confirm that photographic copyright has been respected.

As always, my family's patience has been keenly tested! Many thanks to Francesca, for her help with the maps and graphics; to Zoë, for her editorial thoughts; and last but never least, my wife Trish, who very bravely accepts the mountains of naval memorabilia that seem to have overwhelmed our family's home.

# Dramatis Personae

**American**

Benson, Admiral William S., Chief of Naval Operations, 1915–1919
Bryan, William Jennings, Secretary of State, 1913–1915
Daniels, Josephus, Secretary of State for the Navy, 1913–1921
Gerard, James, Ambassador to Germany, 1913–1917
Lansing, Robert, Secretary of State, 1915–1920
Page, Dr Walter, Ambassador to Court of St James from March 1913
Sims, Vice Admiral William S., Commander US Naval Forces in Europe, 1917–1918
Taussig, Cdr Joseph Knefler, Commander Destroyer Division 8, 1917
Wilson, Woodrow, President, 1913–1921

**British**

Asquith, Herbert H., Prime Minister, 1905–1916
Bacon, Vice Admiral Reginald, SO Dover Patrol, 1915–1918
Bayly, Vice Admiral Sir Lewis, SO Coast of Ireland, 1915–1919
Beatty, Admiral Sir David, Commander-in-Chief Grand Fleet, 1916, First Sea Lord, 1919–1927
Carson, Sir Edward, MP and First Lord of the Admiralty (1916–17)
Cayzer, Sir Charles, owner of Clan Line Shipping
Churchill, Sir Winston, First Lord of the Admiralty
Consett, Captain Montagu, Naval Attaché, Stockholm
Denniston, Alastair, Member of OB40
Dreyer, Captain Frederic, Asst Director, Anti-Submarine Division (ASD), 1916, DNO, 1917
Duff, Rear Admiral A.L., Director ASD, 1916–1918
Fisher, Admiral Sir John, First Sea Lord, 1904–1910, 1914–1915, Chairman BIR

Geddes, Sir Eric, Controller, Admiralty, 1917, First Lord of the Admiralty, 1917–1919
Grey, Sir Edward, British Foreign Secretary, 1905–1916
Hankey, Sir Maurice, Cabinet Secretary, 1916–1922
Henderson, Cdr Reginald, ASD, 1917*
Jackson, Admiral Sir Henry, First Sea Lord, 1915–1916
Jellicoe, Admiral Sir John, Commander-in-Chief Grand Fleet, 1914–1916, First Sea Lord, 1917
Keyes, Rear Admiral Sir Roger J., Commodore, Submarine Services, 1912, SO Dover, 1918
Leslie, Norman, Ministry of Shipping, Admiralty Liaison
Lloyd George, Sir David, Prime Minister, 1916–1922
Madden, Admiral Sir Charles, Chief of Staff, Grand Fleet, 1914–1916, 2iC Grand Fleet, 1916
Manisty, Fleet Paymaster Cdr H Eldon, Organising Manager of Convoys
Oliver, Vice Admiral Sir Henry, Director Naval Intelligence Division
Ryan, Cdr Cyril P., Head of Hawkscraig Hydrophone Research Station
Wemyss, Vice Admiral Sir Rosslyn, First Sea Lord, 1917–1919

**German**

Bachmann, Admiral Gustav, Head of the Admiralstab, 1915
Bernstorff, Count Johann Heinrich, Ambassador to the United States
Bethmann-Hollweg, Staatsekretär Theobald von, Chancellor, 1907–1919
Capelle, Admiral Eduard von, Head of the RMA (Reichsmarineamt), 1916
Erzberger, Matthias, Head of Catholic Centre Party, Signatory to Armistice, 1919
Hipper, Vice Admiral Franz von, Befehlshaber (Commander-in-Chief) High Seas Fleet, 1918
Ingenohl, Friedrich von, Befehlshaber High Seas Fleet, 1914–1915
Michelsen, Andreas, Befehlshaber der U-Boote
Müller, Admiral Georg Alexander, Chief of the Naval Cabinet
Pohl, Admiral Hugo von, Befehlshaber, High Seas Fleet, 1915–1916
Scheer, Admiral Rheinhard, Befehlshaber, High Seas Fleet, 1916–1918
Tirpitz, Großadmiral Alfred von, architect of Kaislerliche Marine, RMA Chief until 1916

**Other**

Holland, John Phillip, inventor of the Holland submarine
Le Bon, Admiral, Chief of Staff, French Navy

* In the April 1917 Admiralty organisation, Cdr Henderson worked as one of Rear Admiral Duff's immediate assistants when the was head of the Anti-Submarine Division. In May 1917, Captain William Fisher replaced Duff as head of the ASD when Duff became ACNS (Assistant Chief of the Naval Staff).

# Key Dates in the U-Boat War

**1914**

| | |
|---|---|
| 9 Aug | *U.15* sunk by HMS *Birmingham*, first U-boat sunk in the war |
| 20 Aug | 1st Order in Council (OIC) introducing Blockade |
| 13 Sept | HMS P*athfinder* torpedoed by *U.21*, first warship to be sunk by a submarine in the war |
| 22 Sept | Sinking of HMS *Aboukir*, *Cressy* and *Hogue* by Weddigen's *U.9* |
| 3 Oct | British lay first Channel minefield |
| 15 Oct | Sinking of HMS *Hawke* |
| 20 Oct | SS *Glitra*, first merchant ship destroyed by a submarine's crew, leading to 2nd OIC redefining absolute and conditional |
| 26 Oct | SS *Amiral Ganteaume* narrowly escapes torpedo attack |
| Nov | British declaration of North Sea a War Zone |
| 21 Dec | Tirpitz interview alluding to Germany's submarine blockade |

**1915**

| | |
|---|---|
| 1 Jan | HMS *Formidable* sunk by *U.24* |
| 4 Feb | Unrestricted submarine campaign announced (19th in Channel, 22nd Mediterranean) |
| 12 Mar | *U.29* (Weddigen) sunk by HMS *Dreadnought* |
| 7 May | RMS *Lusitania* torpedoed |
| 27 Jun | *U.40* first U-boat to fall prey to a decoy trawler towing a submerged submarine |
| 19 Aug | SS *Arabic* torpedoed by *U.24* |
| Oct | intensification of U-boat war in Mediterranean |

**1916**

| | |
|---|---|
| 22 Mar | First successful depth charge (*U.68*) by *Farnborough* |
| 24 Mar | SS *Sussex* torpedoed |
| 4 May | *Sussex* Pledge signed |
| 31 May | Battle of Jutland |
| 19 Aug | North Sea Submarine Trap |
| 7 Oct | *U.53*, first Atlantic crossing by a military submarine |
| 28 Nov | Jellicoe leaves Grand Fleet to become First Sea Lord |
| 12 Dec | German peace proposals |

**1917**

| | |
|---|---|
| 9 Jan | Unrestricted submarine warfare declared |
| 6 Apr | US Declaration of War on Germany |
| July | *U. Deutchland* arrives in Baltimore |
| 18 Aug | Scheer's North Sea submarine trap |
| 24 Dec | Jellicoe forced out of Admiralty |

**1918**

| | |
|---|---|
| 23 Apr | Zeebrügge raid |
| 29 Aug | *UB.109*, last submarine to be sunk in the straits of Dover, blown up by shore-controlled mines |
| 28 Oct | *UB.116* sunk in Scapa Flow, last submarine sunk in the war |
| 9 Nov | HMS *Britannia* sunk, last battleship sunk in the war |
| 11 Nov | Armistice signed |
| 20 Nov | Surrender of first U-boats at Harwich |

# Phases of the Submarine War

**1. Initial Naval Focus (Aug 1914–Jan 1915)**
NORTH SEA: Focus on Grand Fleet's superiority rather than anti-commerce role. First submarine patrol (6 Aug) ends with sinking of 2/11 boats. *Pathfinder* (*U.21*, Aug), *Aboukir*, *Cressy*, *Hogue* (*U.9*, 22 Sept), *Hawke* (*U.9*, 15 Oct), HMS *E3* (*U.27*, 18 Oct), *Formidable* (*U.24*, 1 Jan 1915).

MEDITERRANEAN: Focus against French blockade of Otranto – *Jean Bart* (*U.12*, 21 Dec), *Léon Gambetta* (*U.5*, 27 Apr)

**2. Unrestricted U-Boat Blockade (18 Feb–18 Sept 1915)**
NORTH SEA, CHANNEL & IRISH SEA: Declaration of Submarine War Zone effective 18 Feb. Enemy vessels in zone to be attacked, neutrals at risk. *Lusitania* sinking (*U.20*, 7 May) leads to three US diplomatic notes: right of Americans passengers (13 May), defence of British Blockade (9 Jun, Sec State Jennings resigned in protest) and warning that future sinkings to be considered 'deliberately unfriendly' (21 Jul). Start of Channel mining (*UC.5*, 21 Aug). *Arabic* sinking (*U.24*, 19 Aug) leads to restriction that liners can be sunk only after warning (28 Aug), imposition of restrictions (1 Sept) and withdrawal of U-boats (18 Sept).

**3. Mediterranean Commerce War (Oct–Apr 1916)**
MEDITERRANEAN: War Zone effective 22 Feb 1915. Steadily reinforced after operations surrounding Britain curtailed. *U.33* and *U.35* reinforced by *U.38*, sailing to Cattaro base and new *UB.II* boats being assembled at Pola. Dec 1915 Mediterranean tonnage was more than 50 per cent of all theatres.

Sinking of *Ancona* (*U.38*, 8 Nov) with loss of American life led to suspension of 'sinking without warning' (Apr 1916).

**4. Supporting Naval Operations (1916)**

NORTH SEA, CHANNEL & IRISH SEA: While pre-Jutland coastal picket line failed and no submarines took part in the battle, Scheer's submarine trap (18 Aug) caused major strategic change in limiting Grand Fleet operations to the northern end of the North Sea. USW resumed in Channel (4 Nov).

MEDITERRANEAN: Operations continued against a background of weak Allied ASW (poor performance of Otranto Barrage and little inter-Allied naval cooperation). Half 1916 tonnage losses in the Mediterranean.

AMERICAS: German submarine 'reach' demonstrated by successful blockade running operations of *U.Deutchland* and the visit of *U.53* to Newport (7 Oct).

**5. Full Unrestricted Warfare (1 Feb 1917–War's End)**

22 Dec Pleß presentation by Holtzendorff results in 31 Jan declaration by kaiser that campaign will start 1 Feb. US sever diplomatic relations (3 Feb), Congress declares war as an 'Associated Power' (6 Apr), RADM Sims arrives (9 April) and first elements (DD-8) arrive in Queenstown (7 May). Introduction of convoy system (June), improved ASW weapons and tactics reduce losses to 300,000 tons/month after disastrous April losses of 860,000 tons. Von Jagow replaced by hardliner Zimmermann (24 Nov). Jellicoe resigns (24 Dec). U-boat operations extended to American shores with militarisation of U-kreuzers and to the Azores and W. African coast. U-boats recalled (24 Oct 1918). First twenty-four U-boats surrender at Harwich (20 Nov).

# Abbeviations and Definitions

| | |
|---|---|
| *Aal* | Eel, slang for a torpedo (Ger) |
| ADM | Admiral |
| Admiralstab | Imperial German Naval Staff |
| AFB | Allgemeinefunkspruchbuch (Ger), replaced in 1917 by the HVB |
| AMC | Armed merchant cruiser |
| Ashcan | slang (US). Depth charge |
| A/S | Anti-submarine |
| ASD | Anti-Submarine Division |
| Asdic | A term usually defined as 'Allied Submarine Detection Investigation Committee', but 'Anti-Submarine Division-ic' also suggested |
| ASW | Anti-submarine warfare |
| BdU | Befehlshaber der U-Boote (Ger), Chief of U-Boats (title established 5 June 1917 by Michelsen) |
| BuOrd | Bureau of Ordnance (USN) |
| CID | Committee for Imperial Defence |
| CNO | Chief of Naval Operations (US) |
| CNS | Chief of Naval Staff (from 1917, a position held by the First Sea Lord) |
| Controlled Sailings | Protection given to the shipping lanes rather than the individual or groups of ships within a lane |
| Convoy | Group of ships sailing together under common command and under armed escort (Ger, *das Geleitsystem*) |
| COS | Chief of War Staff |
| CPO | Chief Petty Officer |

| | |
|---|---|
| DDNS | Deputy Director of the Naval Staff |
| D/F | Direction Finding |
| DID | Director of Intelligence Division of the Naval Staff; renamed Director of Naval Intelligence Division (DNI) |
| DNI | Director, Naval Intelligence Division |
| DNS | Director of the Naval Staff |
| DOD | Director, Operations Division of the Naval Staff |
| DSC | Distinguished Service Cross |
| DSM | Distinguished Service Medal |
| DSO | Distinguished Service Order |
| DTD | Director, Trade Division of the Naval Staff |
| E. Dienst | Entzifferungsdienst (German Naval Decoding Service) |
| Explosive Sweep | Explosive charges attached to a line towed astern of a ship that could be electrically detonated over a submarine |
| FdL | Führer der Luftschiffe (Ger), SO, Airships |
| FdU | Führer der Unterseeboote (Ger), SO, Submarines (title used until 5 June 1917 by Bauer) |
| FFB | Flottenfunkspruch (Ger lit. 'Fleet Radio language book'); replaced SKM (Signalbuch der Kaiserlichen Marine) in 1917 |
| FHMS | French submarine |
| HMS | His Majesty's Ship |
| HMHS | His Majesty's Hospital Ship |
| Hochseeflotte (HSF) | The High Seas Fleet |
| HVB | HandelVekehrsBuch (Ger), code book issued to all German merchant ships to be used in wartime |
| Holland Boat | One of the first submersibles, named after its inventor, J.P. Holland |
| ID | Intelligence Division of the Naval Staff |
| Indicator Net | A net which was suspended from highly visible buoys which would 'indicate' the presence of an enemy submarine enmeshed; on later developments, the buoy would light up |
| Kaleu | Shortening for Kapitänleutnant (Ger) |
| K-brot | Kriegsbrot (Ger), lit. 'war bread' |
| MID | Mentioned in Dispatches |
| NCB | Naval Consulting Board (US) |
| OHL | Oberste Heeresleitung (Ger), Army High Command |
| Paravane | A device that would be towed underwater, attached to each side of a ship at the bow to cut the cable of mines in its path |

| | |
|---|---|
| PO | Petty Officer |
| Q-ship | Merchantman disguised to carry ASW weapons – mostly artillery and depth charges (also known as Special Service ships or Trap ships, Ger: U-boot-Fallen) |
| RMA | The Imperial Navy Office (Ger: Reichsmarineamt) |
| RMS | Royal Mail Ship |
| RNR | Royal Naval Reserve, formed from officers and men of the Merchant Navy |
| RNVR | Royal Naval Volunteer Reserve, formed from civilian captains |
| RSW | Restricted submarine war (Ger: eingeschränkten U-boot Handelskrieges) |
| *Schnorkel* | Originally designed by the Dutch, the Schnorkel was perfected by the German Navy in the Second World War; a tube extends from the submarine above water to allow the diesel engines to 'breathe' |
| SecNav | Secretary of the Navy (US) |
| SMS | *Seine Majestäts Schiff* (Ger), His Majesty's Ship |
| SS | Steamship |
| SSB | Secret Service Bureau |
| SM U. | *Seine Majestäts U-boot* (Ger), His Majesty's U-boat; note that the same U-boat could carry two designations if serving in the Mediterranean under Austro-Hungarian 'command' – *UB.49*, for example, was designated *U.CXXX* |
| Sonar | Sound Navigation and Ranging (US designation for asdic) |
| U-boat | *Unterseeboot* (Ger), lit. 'under water boat' |
| USW | Unrestricted submarine war (Ger *uneingeschränkten U-boot Handelskrieges*) |
| VB | *Vekehrsbuch* (Ger), Imperial German naval code, used in communications between naval attachés, warships, consuls and Flag Officers |
| War Zone | The area around the British Isles considered as a zone of military operations in which civilian ships would be treated as valid targets (Ger. *Sperrgebiet*) |
| Y-gun | Two-barrelled deck mortar used to launch depth charges in two opposite directions. |
| Y-stations | Stations set up to intercept, record and pass on enemy signals traffic. Y-Service was known as the Intercept Service |

# Introduction

John Jellicoe remains a controversial admiral. In the public mind, Admiral Sir John Jellicoe's career, as Commander-in-Chief of the Grand Fleet, is most associated with one day, 31 May 1916, *Skagerrakschlacht*, the long-awaited meeting of two huge rival fleets in an ultimate feat of arms, a decisive battle. Jutland's outcome turned out to be bitterly disappointing for a British public constantly fed expectations of another Trafalgar by its national press, and for many Royal Navy officers who saw a guaranteed victory snatched by foul weather, faulty British ship design, underperforming munitions and erratic leadership. The battle left the Royal Navy badly divided for almost a century.

Much contemporary press reporting portrayed Jellicoe as a vestige of a bygone age, an officer moulded by the Victorian strictures of his upbringing. That picture was nurtured by political enemies and naval rivals.

Jellicoe himself was not the kind of man to invest in his image, spin stories for his own benefit or take critical and complex decisions under pressure without due consideration and caution. In many ways, that proved his undoing, although historically much of the record has been rebalanced in his favour.

His time as First Sea Lord is, I think, different. It is remembered for one thing, and one thing alone: the long-delayed implementation of the convoy system, or, as some would have it, his apparent role as an opponent. By the end of 1916, finding a solution to the growing U-boat menace had become a key challenge for the Royal Navy. Maybe, without intending to, Jellicoe put himself forward as the man for the job.

It wasn't surprising that few in the Royal Navy were prepared: naval thinking was dominated by the conviction that one great 'decisive' battle', what the Germans called the *Entscheidungsschlacht*, would decide the fate of nations in the war at sea. As the weeks turned to months, the months to years, and as the hopes and frustrations of Jutland faded, it was clear that its leading proponent, Alfred Thayer Mahan, had not been infallible after all.[1] A war on commerce was also seen by others who shared Mahan's views on the primacy of the battle fleet (the Colomb brothers[2] and Sir Julian Corbett[3]) as a weapon of the weak and an 'indecisive' strategy. They believed the defence of commerce was a distraction from the Fleet's main purpose: the defeat of the enemy's fleet.

Nor is it surprising that a wide range of differing opinions existed within Germany's navy about how the U-boat war would be waged: naval supreme command was fundamentally fragmented. It was designed to be: the kaiser had always wanted to keep a controlling hand. Complicating everything was the constant wavering by the politicians and by the army. Unlike Britain, as a land power, Germany's army was its Senior Service. The army was 'the foundation of the State'.[4] The kaiser had created an almost impossible mechanism to channel the guidance and advice of his senior politicians, military and navy. Throughout the war, these tensions boiled over time and again, regarding how the submarine weapon should be best used. The divisiveness often verged close to insubordination. Those who favoured moderation included the Chancellor, Theobald von Bethmann-Hollweg, and Admiral Georg Alexander von Müller, head of the Imperial Marine Kabinett. Others, like the first two wartime High Seas Fleet commanders, Friedrich von Ingenohl and his successor, Hugo von Pohl, were more 'hawkish'. Then there were those who 'sat on the fence', all too easily influenced by the kaiser's own opinions. One, von Tirpitz, was always testing the political waters, to the point where his opinions lacked credibility. Another was Erich von Falkenhayn, the army's Chief of Staff (Oberste Heeresleitung/OHL), described by an American diplomat, James Gerard, as a 'courtier'.[5] Others would gradually be won over to a more aggressive submarine war by the army facing stalemate in the trenches. Such was the evolution of the thinking of Henning von Holtzendorff, head of the German Imperial Naval Staff, the Admiralstab. Strong supporters of the principle, Rear Admiral Adolf von Trotha and Reinhard Scheer, both felt such warfare would be better launched at a later date when Germany had the number of submarines necessary to conclude a successful war against the British.[6]

Destroying submarines was not as easy as it might appear. In 1917, the available weapons were minimal. Few had believed the submarine to be the serious threat to the dominance of the Royal Navy that it would become, hence little had been done to understand the submarine's true potential or to find the weapons and develop the tactics to counter them.

Jellicoe's approach was to keep an open but disciplined mind before giving preference to and supporting the development of weapons, tactics and systems that showed likely results.

The most effective weapon turned out to be the mine, in combination with anti-submarine nets. With no effective mine immediately available, Jellicoe took the most expeditious approach: he copied the proven design of the enemy mine and pushed for as high a production schedule as could be managed. The employment of a barrage only partially answered the question.

In homage to the legacy of Nelson, the Royal Navy has always exhibited a deeply imbued preference for the offensive. In the context of convoys, seen above all as a defensive tactic, the Royal Navy's response was to try to bring the attack to the enemy, to hunt out U-boats, rather than protect merchant ships.

The trouble with this approach was that this only worked when a U-boat was a visible surface target. Once submerged, the British found themselves at a loss as to how to locate targets accurately enough to make a hit with a weak countermeasure, the depth charge. While huge strides were made in hydrophone-aided location, no effective search capability was at hand until the development of asdic in the Second World War. While again progress was made in the development of the depth charge, the inaccuracy of locating a target meant that only saturation depth-charging might produce results, and such an approach was not possible with the very small numbers of depth charges made available to either British or American ships before the end of the war.

In the past, Britain had successfully used convoys to protect merchant ships at sea. Civilian members of the Cabinet, notably the Prime Minister, David Lloyd George, and the Cabinet Secretary, Sir Maurice Hankey, pushed the Admiralty to institute what seemed to be an obvious solution: the convoy system. While the underwater threat was a new danger to convoys, Jellicoe was cautious of moving to support it until he knew he had the resources available and the right logistics structure to make it work.

The Royal Navy relied on its destroyer flotillas to protect its battle squadrons; any re-tasking of those assets had significant implications for the use and freedom of action of the Grand Fleet, considered the backbone of Britain's naval supremacy.

The unease was made worse because Admiralty planners grossly overestimated the number of ships needing protection. When the embarrassingly obvious methodological mistake was identified, it alleviated one concern. In parallel, before America entered the war, little could be done on the American side of the Atlantic to organise inbound convoys or supplement worn-out British naval escorts with additional cruisers and destroyers.

The charge that has been levelled against Jellicoe, that he was slow on the uptake of convoys, is thus a reasonable one. What is unreasonable is that he actively opposed their implementation. Furthermore, once the principle was agreed upon, the design and implementation of the convoy system was achieved without major errors. Only in the Mediterranean theatre, where the difficulties of a fragmented command structure made progress difficult, was implementation unacceptably long.

The implementation of convoys was far more complex than is made out. It was not only that the submarine threat made the principle of convoy defence one that should be considered apart from historical experience; its implementation, once considered the correct course of action, was equally complex. It was not just about the lack of destroyers, Commander Reginald Henderson's discovery of the 'real figures', the escort-to-convoy ratio, etc; it also involved the complete appropriation by the state of the nation's transportation system and economic management. It also involved the airing of the Young Turks' generational grievances against the institutions at the very core of the Royal Navy and the ideological impasse between Mahanian battle fleet officers and those wanting to turn the focus to the protection of trade. It involved new concepts, strategies and tactics whose efficacy and viability evolved with time and with how their components were mixed. Like so much of what we see all around us today in an age of fake news, ideological confrontation and political radicalism, how the story of the naval war has been told has suffered from these influences.

After Britain's declaration of war, Sir John Jellicoe, the newly appointed Commander-in-Chief of Britain's Grand Fleet, prepared for a war at sea that would be decided by the powerful guns of the great dreadnought fleets. At this point, he did not grasp – few did – that the threat would come from below the surface, against a new foe, the U-boat.

As the first few months of the war unfolded, preconceptions and beliefs surrounding the use, value and potential of the submarine were challenged to their core. It was not just Otto Weddigen's sinking of the three old, armoured cruisers HMS *Aboukir*, *Cressy* and *Hogue* that shattered accepted thinking, it was the brutal awakening to a new reality by the avalanche of 'firsts'.

Operating ranges were completely rethought when U-boats were spotted in the Firth of Forth and then at Scapa, and finally by Otto Dröscher's circumnavigation of the British Isles in *U.20*. Even so, all the Navy seemed to be able to come up with was to increase cruising speeds by introducing zigzagging. In October 1914, the SS *Glitra* was stopped by *U.17* and sunk by scuttling charges. The event should have sent alarm bells ringing. Even though Prize Rules – the rules of war at sea – were respected, its sinking foreshadowed a new kind of war.[7] As an anti-commerce role had not been planned, initial U-boat targets were mostly naval; when civilian ships were targeted, Prize Rules were, in large part, respected. Of the 116 merchantmen sunk in the war's first three months, ninety-four were lost under such restrictions.[8]

Over the next four years, submarine warfare twisted and turned as new technologies allowed longer patrols, neutrals exerted diplomatic pressure and the Western Front inexorably became the war of attrition in the trenches. Depending on the circumstances, what was allowed to be sunk changed: sometimes neutral shipping, other times armed merchant ships; at some points American and Italian ships were exempted (but at other times not), and sometimes passenger liners too if they were thought to be transporting troops or at night in the Channel. The flying of a neutral flag guaranteed no safe passage: indeed, it could invite death by the unseen silence of a torpedo rather than being boarded under Prize Rules. It meant that the difference between 'restricted' and 'unrestricted' warfare could never easily be construed as a binary proposition. Different rules applied to different circumstances, making a U-boat commander's challenge of command the more stressful.

The U-boat war was as different as the geography it spanned. In the Mediterranean, German U-boats racked up higher-than-expected tonnage, both because Allied command was fragmented and there existed a decreased risk of sinking American shipping. It was a successful submarine war waged with civility – 80 per cent of the sinkings happened with prior warning. It was also cost-effective – 75 per cent of the sinkings were made with deck artillery rather than torpedoes. What's more, the Mediterranean proved to be the most efficient U-boat theatre – Allied Mediterranean losses amounted to 40 per cent of the total, with the Germans only employing 20 per cent of their U-boat resources. With better and longer patrol conditions, a commander such as von Arnauld de la Perière was able to become Germany's leading ace with almost half-a-million tons to his credit, almost all sunk respecting Prize Rules.

In the Western and Southern Atlantic, the Allies were shocked by *U. Deutschland*'s 10,000-mile return trip to Baltimore in June 1916 and Hans Rose's Newport (Rhode Island) visit the following October. It sent the British scuttling to protect what had previously been outlying zones of conflict, such as the Azores, and the Americans to fear for their own safety, should they enter the European conflict, now that their own coastline was in range.

Through 1915 and much of 1916, the conduct of the submarine war was a muddled affair. The fallout from the sinking of the RMS *Lusitania* in May 1915, the resulting pledge from Germany after the *Arabic* attack to cease such attacks and the renewed fears after the *Sussex* incident a year later in March, created confusion among Germany's submariners. However, while American public opinion was incensed, it would still take an unwilling President a full two years to declare war. American diplomatic efforts to force a cessation of German submarine warfare in return for the British ending their blockade came to nothing. This was partly because of the lack of political control of the German Navy: with Schneider's sinking of the 15,801-ton White Star liner, SS *Arabic*, on 19 August and Schwieger's attack on the RMS *Hesperian* in September, orders had been flagrantly disobeyed and seemingly made a mockery of the combined attempts by the German Chancellor and the US Government to calm the situation.

Finally, in 1916, Admiral Reinhard Scheer, the third Commander-in-Chief of Germany's Hochseeflotte (High Seas Fleet) and early believer in multidimensional fleet tactics, started to use his surface ships in conjunction with airships above and submarines below. He redirected the naval focus in preparation for what would culminate in the meeting of fleets at Jutland and the integral use of U-boats as part of a combined surface–submarine trap in August in which two British 5,400-ton light cruisers, HMS *Falmouth* and *Nottingham*, were sunk. If Jutland had seemed to change nothing, Scheer's 18 August sortie changed everything: Jellicoe (with the full agreement of Vice Admiral Sir David Beatty, still commanding the Battlecruiser Fleet) decided to keep the Grand Fleet out of the southern reaches of the North Sea.

> The loss of those two warships was manageable, but the morale of the Grand Fleet was not. The lack of a true ASW doctrine gave the German submarines an exaggerated, but sinister fame of invulnerability.[9]

While indecision reigned in Berlin, some of the more aggressive U-boat commanders like Walter Schwieger (*U.20*) took matters into their own hands at the start of 1915, attacking hospital ships such as the *Asturias* in open defiance of the wishes of the political-military leadership. Other submarines – *U.19* and *U.21*, for example – successfully sank shipping respecting Prize Rules. After pressure from the navy's Chief of Staff, Gustav Bachmann,[10] and Großadmiral Alfred von Tirpitz, von Pohl was finally able to persuade an indecisive kaiser to declare submarine war on 4 February 1915, only exempting American and Italian merchant shipping. Between May and August 1916, however, the war on commerce was reined in, particularly when it came to neutral shipping.

Germany used Britain's blockade as its justification. Many saw Britain's actions as a unilateral interpretation of the Treaty of London, one that was exacerbated by their decision to remove the distinctions between *absolute* and *conditional* contraband. *Handelskrieg*, a true commerce war, was announced as starting on 18 February. Even neutral vessels were now at risk: 'attacks intended for hostile ships might affect neutral ships also'.[11] The Germans justified this again using the actions of the British: their merchant ships and liners often sailed under the protection of neutral flags, an action the Admiralty fully endorsed (but had not proactively recommended). Germany was cleverly appealing directly to the sensibilities of the largest neutral nation, America.

Almost immediately, however, the kaiser waivered and specifically excluded ships flying neutral flags and hospital ships from his new campaign.

With the debate in the German Cabinet unresolved, 1916 started with ambiguity. Since the *Arabic* Pledge, there had been few successful attacks without warning in the Channel, the North Sea and the Western Approaches. On 24 March, the cross-Channel ferry, the *Sussex*, was severely damaged by a Flanders-based submarine, *UB.29*. Even though there were no Americans among the fifty dead, Americans were still injured and the incident reignited international censure of Germany, adding fuel to America's 20 April threat to sever diplomatic relations.

At the end of 1916, the man to whom Britain turned for an answer was Admiral Sir John Jellicoe. Churchill had famously said, talking of his command of the Grand Fleet at Jutland, that he was 'the only man on either side who could have lost the war in an afternoon'. He was now being tasked with a similarly heavy burden: to find a way to protect Britain's oceanic lifelines from the ravages of Germany's U-boats. Upon his shoulders lay the nation's fate.

With the failure of Germany's Christmas 1916 peace proposals and the army's change of position, the kaiser's wavering ended. Germany's highest command was coming to the realisation that while there might be a chance of *peace* with continued restrictions, *victory* was out of the question without unrestricted submarine warfare of the harshest kind; a war built on terror, not just military practicality.

On 1 March 1917, the damning contents of Foreign Minister Arthur Zimmermann's telegram – with Germany promising Mexico the return of territories lost almost a century before if it declared war on the USA – came to light and were made public. The text was confirmed by the German Foreign Minister in front of the American press, further weakening Wilson's ability to continue evading the European war. On 4 April, a limited declaration of war was finally made against Germany (Austria-Hungary was only later included on 7 December). One month later, on 4 May, the first US naval elements, Destroyer Division 8, arrived in Queenstown (today's Cobh), southern Ireland. By 1 July, twenty-eight units – from a total of fifty-two units in the USN – were in European waters.[12] The conclusion that 'the submarine had a greater impact on the troubled history of this century than any other weapon' is a fair one: it was responsible for bringing America into the war.[13]

While the actual direct contribution to sinkings might have been minimal, the American presence was of unquestionable psychological and deterrent value, not to mention the massive ongoing benefits of her industrial and financial support. In no small way, it laid the solid foundations on which future Anglo–American naval cooperation was born.

This phase of the submarine war introduced a new level of ferocity not seen before; by April 1917, 64 per cent of sinkings were being made with no warning given (in 1915, 21 per cent; 1916, 29 per cent).[14] Holtzendorff's defence of the naked violence and terror initially worked: neutral traffic quickly declined. In the first two months of 1917 there was a 25 per cent decrease of port entries into neutral harbour compared with the previous year, and by April, losses reached a staggering 860,000 tons.[15] It was the blackest month of Britain's war at sea.

Losses fell off as U-boats went home to refuel and rearm, and then the convoy system, coupled with the increased availability of newer, American destroyers, nascent hydrophone technology, better mines, deeper minefields and barrages slowly – very slowly – started to even the score. With decreased success against arriving Atlantic convoys, the Germans switched focus both to longer-range operations off the Azores and, in the second half of 1917, to increased inshore patrolling. At the end of the year, however, the surface threat to the convoys that many, including Jellicoe and William Sims, had feared finally materialised, with two fatal attacks on Scandinavian convoys, one in September and another in December.

January 1918 came with both great success and avoidable loss for the Allies in the Channel: three submarines were sunk in the Dover Strait, but a nighttime attack by German destroyers sank seven trawlers, the sinking of two more hospital ships continuing the slaughter. The Strait claimed more submarines between April and May, but the great raid on Zeebrügge, while an enormous morale booster for the Navy, did little to impede German operations.

In men and materiel, the cost of fighting the U-boat was enormous. The German Navy had started the war with twenty-eight, built a further 344 and lost 192 (by action or scuttling). More than 12 million tons of Allied merchant shipping was sunk by German submariners during the war at a human cost, to Germany, of 4,472 of their submariners.[16] When peace finally came, the submarines were the only forces in the High Seas Fleet that technically surrendered.

Neither Jellicoe, former First Sea Lord Sir John Fisher nor Louis Battenberg, Director of the Naval Intelligence Division, were invited to Beatty's orchestrated ceremony at Rosyth (or Harwich, for that matter) at the end of the war. History very often forgets when and how the foundations for victory have been laid.

# 1

# War in an Industrial Age

For centuries, nations have traded across land and sea, but with the advent of the Industrial Revolution, the resources needed to sustain a nation's economy grew exponentially.

**Trade Dependency**

Jackie Fisher always maintained that 'it's not invasion that we have to fear if the navy is beaten, it's starvation'.[1] Even if Britain possessed 40 per cent of the world's shipping, her dependency on food imports was a major vulnerability.[2] In 1914, 'almost 60 per cent of the food consumed in Britain was imported from overseas, about two-thirds by crude weight and more than half by value'.[3] In some categories, this figure was even larger: 100 per cent of Britain's sugar was imported, 79 per cent of her grain.[4] Equally important, 90 per cent of British trade was carried on British merchant ships under a British flag.

*1909–1913, Britain's Share of Imports*

| Category | Per cent |
|---|---|
| Wheat and Flour | 78.7 |
| Cereals and Pulses | 56.2 |
| Meat | 35.7 |
| Butter | 43.4 |
| Cheese | 74.2 |

Source: Dunn, *Bayly's War*, p.26

Germany's foodstock vulnerability was not as bad. Around 25 per cent of Germany's food was imported, but the problem was more in distribution and pricing controls. Local authorities were allowed to set price ceilings to control the inflationary effects of hoarding. These measures were deeply resented by farmers, who reacted by looking elsewhere for higher prices. While initially the resulting food deficit was addressed by slaughtering livestock – in early spring 1915, a mass slaughter of pigs (*Schweinemord*) took place – it then caused a pork glut. In the raw materials of industrial production – iron ore, certain metals like copper, rubber, etc – Germany was dependent on imports.

The speed of economic growth in Germany accelerated urbanisation and the growth of a new middle class. In war, both had significant impact: the rural labour force, already flowing into the cities, was now stripped more by mobilisation at a time when agricultural production had to become more efficient to feed the cities. There, new buying power created new tastes, new patterns of consumption and increased 'luxury' imports.

**Sea and Land Power**

Unlike Germany, a continental land power, Britain's power rested on the seas. Her strength derived from her navy and its ability to project power across the globe, developing and protecting a colonial empire, nurturing the economy. Britain 'based her strength and foreign policy on the ability of the Royal Navy to protect the seaborne commerce that sustained Britain's economic growth and Great Power status'.[5]

That role had continually put Britain at odds with seaborne challengers – the Dutch, Spanish, Portuguese and the French. The Royal Navy was there to protect the passage of goods along its coasts and across oceans that divided continents.

While Britain considered herself more a global colonial power than a European one, Germany, by contrast, was almost wholly a European land power, whose growing industrial might was making more demands on overseas resources. Otto von Bismarck's departure signalled the beginning of the end of European stability. Now, without the firm guiding hand of his experienced Chancellor, Wilhelm II strove to build a navy: not just a coastal defence and colonial force, but a true battle fleet that increasingly defined the nature of the nation's new challenge to Britain. On the diplomatic front, the British bolstered relations with France; on the military front, Fisher pivoted Britain's naval strength out of the Mediterranean and the Far East to Gibraltar to prepare for a North Sea focus. In 1907, Russia too, the traditional enemy of the Great Game, was appeased by a Convention over Persia.

Britain's strategy in the First World War was not a long-planned programme, but a conditioned reflex: to use her navy to slowly strangle an enemy's economy. Britain, expecting the war to be a short one, agreed to send a small expeditionary force to the continent, more as a symbolic gesture to the French.

No imports could come by sea to feed her economy or people. As the leading continental land power in Europe, Germany 'expected to win the war on land before sea power could be a factor, [and] it was initially of little import to them that their strategic naval position was markedly inferior'.[6] Reinhard Scheer, the third wartime Commander-in-Chief of the High Seas Fleet, would later echo Alfred von Tirpitz's disappointment with his fellow countrymen. Germany, he wrote after the war, never understood the importance of sea power:

> If only we had realized from the start that the influence of England's sea power on the course of the war would be as great as it turned out to be later, to our disadvantage, a higher importance would have been attached to this question at the outset.[7]

As the nineteenth century closed and a new century opened, Britain had recognised new challengers: across the oceans there was the United States and Japan, but in Europe the most immediate threat was Germany.

War is the subjugation of an enemy by all available means. Military conflict is only one means to that end; the slow erosion of an enemy's will or physical ability to fight can be as important. The destruction, impairment or blocking of food supplies has been a standard of military activity for centuries.

Aggressive German mining and submarine attacks against merchantmen carrying food to Britain claimed significant success. The quantity of foodstuffs lost at sea was huge: in 1917, the crisis year, 46,000 tons of meat and 85,000 tons of sugar was destroyed at sea.[8]

### Blockade as an Instrument of Economic War

The strangulation of an adversary's economy by a global naval assault on its supply chain, following it to its overseas sources, was quintessentially Mahanian. He 'felt that it was clear that overseas commerce, overseas political relationships, and commercial maritime routes would dominate as "the primary objects of external policy of nations"'. It was only logical that 'the instrument for the maintenance of policy directed upon these objects is the Navy'.[9]

Nevertheless, Britain's strategic weapon of choice – the Royal Navy's centuries-old tradition of blockade – was a blunt cudgel impacting non-belligerent neutrals and enemies. It had to be used with caution and often put the nation's navy at odds with her diplomats. In the context of 1914, Britain's Foreign Secretary, Sir Edward Grey, had to find a way for the country to 'wage economic war without making the United States an enemy'.[10]

The employment of blockade – the interdiction of the movement of goods between producing and consuming countries – became how Britain used sea-power to achieve her goals. Traditionally, the Navy used what was termed 'close blockade', but by 1914, the decision was taken to form a *distant* blockade. Being 'close' meant being able to place ships close inshore, within visible distance of an enemy's harbour, so that ships attempting to enter could be physically interdicted. The threat of defensive torpedo boats and submarine defence or minefields increasingly made this approach too dangerous, hence assets forming the blockade were pulled back to form a more 'distant' watch. With the advent of these new weapons, to operate on an enemy's coastline was seen as increasingly dangerous, even if the distant waging of war would feel like it 'was developing more and more into a passive waiting for the enemy, a lurking along the British coasts'.[11] After 1910, the evolution of strategy was rapid: the 1911 war plans were replaced in 1912 by the notion of an 'observational blockade', which by July 1914 was also replaced with the concept of 'distant blockade'. That shift strongly underlined the geographic importance of Britain's northern naval base in the Orkney Islands: Scapa Flow. The new policy did not favour Germany: '[T]heir plans traditionally had rested on the prospect of a close blockade, which would afford opportunities for their light craft.'[12]

The task of the Grand Fleet, based off Scotland's north-eastern coast at Scapa Flow, was to seek battle with Germany's own battle fleet, prevent invasion and offer protection to the means of blockade, the 10th Cruiser Squadron. In 1917, Jellicoe, nevertheless, was not convinced that blockade would deliver the desired results by itself. He warned Beatty, now commanding the Grand Fleet, that he was 'quite wrong in assuming that the blockade will ever cause the enemy to give in'. At most, he asserted, it would only cause them a great deal of suffering. Was Jellicoe merely reflecting his frustration with the seemingly counter-productive efforts of Grey's Foreign Office, or was this a bigger issue?[13]

## The Legal Framework of the War at Sea

An attempt to establish an international Prize Court was made at the Second Hague Peace Conference in 1907. The British objected to some of the principles that would be applied by the court and lobbied for a new conference, the International Naval Conference, to be held in London at the end of 1908. On 26 February 1909, the court's proposed rules were published as part of the Declaration of London, signed by all the powers involved in its development (Britain, Germany, Austria-Hungary, France, Japan, Russia and the United States). The British Government backed a bill modifying British law to comply with the Prize Court conventions. It successfully passed through the House of Commons but was rejected by the upper house, the House of Lords. Without Britain's ratification of an international court, the others (except the United States) withdrew their support.

The declaration essentially governed how naval warfare could be legally undertaken: that blockade had to be 'effective' to be legal, how trade goods (contraband) could be defined as absolute or conditional, that submarines were required to surface to take account of the safety of passengers and crews, neutral rights and the treatment of unarmed merchant ships, and their arming. So-called 'Cruiser Rules' set forth the principle that naval vessels stopping an enemy merchant ship must vouch for the safety of the crew before the ship could be sunk or taken into custody: the difference between restricted and unrestricted submarine warfare is essentially the respect for, or the rejection of, Cruiser Rules. When not respected, conditions of unrestricted submarine warfare are said to exist.

Sir Julian Corbett, the British naval strategist, was firmly opposed to the limitations on seizure which he outlined in a 1907 essay, 'The Capture of Private Property at Sea'. He saw the restrictions on 'general capture' of an enemy's commerce as neutralising one of the main weapons in Britain's war chest, her navy. The fact that Britain never ratified the declaration is ironic; after all, it was the British who proposed the convention in the first place. Both Britain and Germany ignored it, while the United States kept pushing for it to be the basis for the rules of the war at sea.

Historically, the link between commerce war and piracy was sometimes an embarrassment for a state sponsor that discouraged its practice:

> Commerce warfare was for centuries sustained and made possible by privateers – that is, private individuals authorized by the state to seize enemy shipping in exchange for a portion of the spoils, more politely known as 'Prize money'".[14]

Providing a legal framework diminished the embarrassment. Rules established earlier and embodied in the 1856 Treaty of Paris stipulated that for 'blockades to be binding, they must be real, that is to say, maintained by a force sufficient to prevent access to the coast of the enemy'. A belligerent could fall back on a rules-based framework if their blockade was not 'effective'.

Blockade was a legal minefield:

> Legally, Britain had to decide whether to abide by the Declaration of London. If she did, and declared a distant blockade, it was restricted to a policy of contraband control, though definitions of contraband were open to interpretation. If she ignored the Declaration and ruthlessly asserted belligerent rights, it risked a damaging clash with neutral powers, above all the United States, determined to exercise its rights to Freedom of the seas.[15]

In the event of blockade, rules covering what could or could not be carried as cargo were needed. There were also provisions for neutral merchant shipping which, if found to be carrying cargoes that were of material assistance to an enemy, could be boarded and taken to an allied port for more thorough inspection. There, if found to fall under certain provisions, a cargo could be seized, i.e. taken as a 'prize'. If the ship could not be taken to a port, then she could be scuttled if provisions for the safety of the crew were made.

These rules were consolidated into the 1909 Declaration of London, designed to allow 'the free passage of food and other non-military cargoes' on the seas. Under the treaty – ironically named, as it was never ratified by the British – cargoes were divided into three broad categories:

1. Absolute contraband covered any war materials of an exclusive 'military nature', regardless of whether the materials were being shipped directly or indirectly to an enemy, i.e., being trans-shipped through a neutral country like the Netherlands or Sweden. Guns and explosives were thus considered as 'absolute contraband'.
2. Conditional contraband included goods with 'an indirect effect on the enemy war effort such as foodstuffs, fuel, clothing, bullion, etc' and were liable to seizure if going through an enemy port. To avoid excessive conflict with the United States, Britain later agreed to pay for any cargoes they seized.
3. Free List items, goods which could not be used for military purposes (raw cotton, oil, rubber), were exempt from seizure, even though a vessel could still be seized if over half the goods carried consisted of absolute contraband materials.

Defining what constituted contraband was difficult. Even among the Allies there was little agreement. Countries refused to include some of their more important exports on the list – Canadian nickel, British tin and French aluminium.[16] Britain's Foreign Office also wanted the exclusion of some dual-purpose materials. Nitrates, for example, are a key ingredient for both explosives and fertiliser. While the diplomats focused their arguments on its more humanitarian, agricultural usage, the real reason was Chile's importance as a trading partner.

The role of neutrals added a hugely complicated consideration to the conduct of commerce control: Germany often purchased goods directly from neutrals, for example Swedish iron ore in exchange for coal or essential foodstuffs shipped through Denmark and Norway.

The Americans complained about British contraband restrictions. However, it is doubtful whether these really had such a negative effect; maybe the opposite. Grey pointed out that while US exports had declined by $126 million in the seven months before the start of war, by the end of 1914, exports had exceeded those of the previous year. On an annualised basis, they had increased by around $20 million over the first four months of the war.

Waging economic war, therefore, had to be a careful balancing act. Britain had to recognise the importance of neutrals while meeting its own interests: either sources of finance to fight the war (principally from the United States) or commodities important for war production or to sustain its population (from around the globe but, for the importance of this issue, principally the United States and Scandinavia or the Netherlands). Britain had to find ways to limit Germany or other Central Powers from benefiting, even if the 'Protection of British trade and reduction of the enemy's were [sometimes] two sides of the same coin.'[17]

Preventing the free movement of goods to or from a belligerent may not always deliver the desired benefit. This has been the case for the total import bans on Russian oil and gas that was imposed in 2022, which caused extensive debate among European partners because of their differing levels of dependence.

**Protection of Trade or Battle Fleet Engagement**

After several fleet exercises, in early 1914, Fisher voiced his growing concerns to Churchill: '[T]he submarine is the coming type of war vessel for sea fighting.' He was particularly concerned that the traditional British strategy of blockade would be fundamentally compromised. The capability of German submarines would mean that 'surface ships can no longer either maintain or prevent blockade', and of particular note was that 'the power to obtain the command of narrow seas' would be 'increasingly difficult'.[18] Not only did the submarine threaten the existing rules of war, it would challenge Britain's traditional naval strategy: '[T]he whole foundation of our naval strategy, which served us so well in the past, has broken down! The foundation of that strategy was blockade.'[19] As usual, Fisher's forebodings were well-grounded.

While the submarine might not have had a decisive impact on Britain's superiority at sea, it quickly exhibited its potential, profoundly affecting the Grand Fleet's freedom of movement. Following the debacle of 22 September 1915, with the sinking of three British warships, Jellicoe wrote to Churchill saying it was 'suicidal to forego our advantageous position in big ships by … taking them into waters infested with submarines'.[20]

Temple Patterson observed that Jellicoe was only copied in the correspondence, but concludes that 'it is difficult to avoid the assumption that his own anxieties and eventual pessimism on this subject owed something to the views of his mentor'.[21] Small wonder that Jellicoe was strongly against Churchill's pre-war planning to seize the island of Borkum off the Ems estuary.[22]

Blockade did not appeal to many naval officers, and while the Grand Fleet's presence guaranteed the work of the blockading force, Admiral Dudley de Chair's 10th Cruiser Squadron, the role of Britain's Navy was not linked primarily to protecting its own commerce. What would the Navy's role be?

At the start of the twentieth century, the influence of writers like Alfred Thayer Mahan (*The Influence of Sea Power upon History, 1660–1783*, written in 1890) deeply affected thinking in the great naval powers, not only Britain and Germany, but also the navies of Japan, the United States, France and Italy. Most of the naval thinkers of the day were battleship men. Influenced by his writings, most naval officers could not imagine that anything other than a 'decisive battle' waged by great dreadnought navies could be the way to win a war at sea.

War on an enemy's trade was little considered, with the protection of trade subsumed to secondary consideration. The Royal Navy's strategic thinking was well summed up in 'War Plans and Distribution of the Fleet', a publication that in 1907 'estimated that attacks on British Commerce had the lowest priority in the German scheme for War at Sea'.[23] The superiority of British sea-power was thought capable of reducing any such attempt by a rival fleet to 'simple pinpricks'.

One of the Royal Navy's high-profile thinkers was Kenneth Dewar. This iconoclastic officer, later to become a harsh critic of Sir John Jellicoe, was demanding, rebellious, intellectually brilliant and outspoken, a leading member of the Royal Navy's Young Turks. In a gold-medal essay written for the Royal United Services Institute (RUSI), he highlighted the magnitude of Britain's dependency on imports but concluded, 'the destruction of the enemy's naval forces, is of course, the most effectual method of protecting trade'. The idea of the convoy system, later recognised as one of the critical success factors in the submarine war, was 'scarcely mentioned'.[24]

A similar point of view was expressed by Henderson of the ASD, who maintained that Britain's 'naval strength will be frittered away in trying to protect our commerce instead of striking effective blows against the enemy'. Like Dewar, Henderson merely reflected the quasi-obsessive focus of naval officers on defeating an enemy's battle fleet at sea in a decisive action. The protection of a nation's commerce was seen as a distraction from the navy's primary role. Henderson's point of view was widely held. Commander Carlyon Bellairs MP, also one of Jellicoe's later critics, wrote a rebuttal to Colonel Hozier, the Secretary of Lloyds, who had at least considered convoying for slower vessels. It was out of the question: it would be 'a waste of naval force defending the Convoys'. Moreover, 'the safety of commerce is in the superiority of our fighting forces in the face of the enemy's force'.[25]

The submarine was distinctly un-Mahanian, but then, to paraphrase one of Fisher's comments to Lord Selbourne, 'history is nothing more than the erosion of established truths'.[26] Individual thinkers like Jackie Fisher, who were brave enough to stand against the accepted orthodoxy of the day, were rare.

# 2

# Fisher's Apprentice: Crafting the Tactics and Weapons of War

Two weapons haunted John Jellicoe: mines and torpedoes. The mine was already many years in development; the torpedo, a relative newcomer. For both, the war dramatically accelerated their testing, development and use.

Jellicoe's naval career and name is less associated with the war against the submarine than with one battle, Jutland (known in Germany as the *Skagerrakschlacht*). In fact, they were different sides of the same coin: the struggle for sea-power, one waged on the surface, the other below the waves. Much has been written about Jellicoe and Jutland, less about his eventual struggle with the submarine threat.

At Jutland, Jellicoe's battle line faced both the reality of surface torpedo attack as well as the imagined threat of mines and submarines. Prior to Jutland, the Royal Navy had already lost one dreadnought and eight pre-dreadnoughts to either mines or torpedoes. That the latter was non-existent at Jutland is not that important; Jellicoe's fears proved to be just as powerful in influencing his actions as the former. A year later, however, Britain faced the far greater threat of the unrestricted submarine war on commerce.

After the war, Jellicoe wrote at length about the impact of these new weapons: first in 1920 in *The Crisis of Naval War*, followed a year before his death in *The Submarine Peril*. As he wrote in 1934, 'all the information which we now possess on the subject was not then available'. The book, however, was also a defence of his own war record against persistent attacks by Lloyd George and others. The subject matter was vitally important for the naval record, but Jellicoe's writing was full of statistics, unengaging and dry.

Despite his proximity to 'Jackie' Fisher, Jellicoe wasn't intimately involved with British submarine development or the development of active countermeasures to German submarines before the war. Sir John Fisher was the man who created Britain's modern Royal Navy, much of his most well-known work carried out while First Sea Lord between 1904 and 1910. While Tirpitz was creating Germany's new navy, 'Jackie' Fisher was reinvigorating an old one. Like Jellicoe, he had a modest background and rose in the Navy through professionalism, carefully nurtured sponsors and remarkable strategic vision. Anticipating Britain's future struggle with Germany, he pivoted the Royal Navy from the Mediterranean to the North Sea, drove forward his revolutionary ship design in the dreadnought and the battlecruiser, championed the strategic choice of oil over coal and cut the fat out of the Royal Navy's bloated inventory of ships to push for efficiency and meritocracy over legacy and seniority. Jellicoe's perspective on, and involvement with, the submarine was always tied to the fleet he would command, more focused around the impact of the submarine on dreadnought construction and Grand Fleet tactics rather than on submarine or anti-submarine warfare. The war would quickly change that outlook.

In 1907, as a young rear admiral, Jellicoe received a copy of Commander Sueter RN's new book, *The Evolution of the Submarine Boat, Mine and Torpedo*. His copy now sits on my own bookshelves with some of his other books.[1] The fact that Germany's *U.1* was only launched in December 1906, months before his book was gifted to Jellicoe, makes Sueter's insights more impressive. The book is a compendium of sorts, a global history of submarine development and the state of play at that moment in the world's major navies. With prescient foresight (if we are to include the submarine as a 'torpedo craft'), Sueter talked about the future:

> ...there can be little doubt that in the next European struggle Germany will rely not so much on her massive battleships, but more largely on torpedo craft and minelayers for carrying out the maximum amount of destruction at a minimum outlay.[2]

By 'torpedo craft' he meant both the surface torpedo boat as well as the submarine. A submarine was essentially nothing more than a submersible torpedo boat which, following the Italian doctrine, could either be '*sottomarini*' (designed to mainly operate underwater) or '*sommergibili*' (designed to mainly operate on the surface but capable of diving and moving at a slow 2–3 knots for a few days). Sueter foretold Germany's use of Belgian harbours as its naval front line in a future war, following what had happened in the Napoleonic Wars. He also foresaw the eventual role of the Flanders Flotilla. It was the type of naval engagement that Tirpitz had sought, close to German waters, where such craft could best be used.

In 1907, outside of innovative naval thinkers like Jackie Fisher or civilians such as Sir Arthur Conan Doyle, few could have imagined the submarine's strategic evolution.[3] It would start the war doing static sentry duty but end it with the wholesale destruction of commerce. Fisher abhorred those who thought that winning wars was about parade-ground presentation, scrubbed decks and polished brass. His brutal realism stands in stark contrast to the sentiments in David Hannay's wishful conclusion in *The Fire Ship*:

> Victory has never so far gone to those who fight by evasion, by concealment, by striking in the dark, by waiting for the unguarded moment – points they may score, but they have never won in the end.[4]

So accurate were Conan Doyle's predictions that he was attacked by many who, with the benefit of hindsight, said that it was he who gave the Germans the idea of submarine warfare, even forcing him to issue an apology:

> I need hardly say that it is very painful to me to think that anything I have written should be turned against my own country. The object of the story was to warn the public of a possible danger which I saw overhanging this country and to show it how to avoid that danger.[5]

### The Advent of the Submarine as a Weapon of War

So how did the submarine emerge as such a powerful weapon? In the space of a quarter-century, the submarine evolved from being seen as the weapon of choice for weaker navies to a formidable fighting machine with its own place alongside the most powerful of fleets. After the *Lusitania* sinking,

> it seemed as if the U-boat, the unwanted stepchild of the von Tirpitz era, had become the only offensive weapon the Imperial Navy possessed.[6]

In its early years, the submarine's role was restricted by its limited development: in speed, operating range, diving depth and armament. The submarine, at the turn of the twentieth century, was only a hint of what it would become within the next few, let alone fifty, years. Initially, for the Royal Navy, its role was basically an anti-access role, for coastal and harbour defence and reconnaissance. Its role was never imagined as anything more than defensive.

As it developed, the submarine was seen 'more as an adjunct to the battle fleet than as a weapons system on its own'.[7] It was a very misleading characterisation. The submarine would eventually be most effectively used by Germany as a weapon in commerce war, a task to which is was not ideally suited: surfacing to stop and search rendered it vulnerable and her small crew made the idea of reducing it further to man a prize crew impracticable. As the Allies retained surface command, their reliance on submarines was proportionately reduced.

The first navy to really focus resources on the development of the submarine was the Marine Française. Early vessels were known as 'submersibles', not 'submarines', since they were designed as surface vessels with a capability to go below the surface, not as vessels that worked primarily underwater.

Before Mahan, a new school of naval thinking had developed in France opposed to the sole reliance on big-ship thinking. The *Jeune École* argued the notion that 'mosquito fleets' made up of torpedo boats and submarines were the way war at sea would be waged in the future, targeting trade and commerce rather than seeking a decisive big-fleet battle. Two of the leading lights of the school were Admiral Aube and a journalist, Gabriel Charmes. In 1886, the latter wrote that France should prepare for a *Guerre de Course* ('war on commerce') with these new weapons. The aims of the *Jeune École* and what later emerged as the submarine strategy was very different: one was to bombard coastal towns to 'panic the British into ceasing hostilities; the German plan on the other hand, was literally to starve the opponent into submission'.[8] So it was clear, as far back as 1906, that in a trade war, the submarine could have a role. It was the moral issue – 'the constraints of a civilised society' – which 'blinkered' the British.

> The use of the phrase 'weapon of the weak' suggests also that the submarine was seen in certain quarters as being morally weak. It was felt that the battleship encapsulated the British character.[9]

This is how the British felt. During the 1900 Naval Estimates debate, George Goschen (First Lord of the Admiralty, 1895–1900) characterised the submarine as 'eventually a weapon for Maritime powers on the defensive … the arm of a weaker power'.[10] At the same time, he left some wriggle room, saying that their role could easily be expanded or 'be useful to us in many places, like torpedo boats'.[11]

A submarine branch was established in France in 1888, the same year the 30-ton, electric-motor-powered *Gymnote* was commissioned.[12] Within five years, the vessel's displacement increased nearly tenfold in the new 266-ton *Gustav Zédé*, named after one of *Gymnote*'s designers. In January 1898, a series of well-publicised sea trials by the *Gustav Zédé* showed her successfully launching another new weapon, the torpedo (she was armed with two), at a training-battleship, the *Magenta*, in a training exercise.[13] The newspaper *Le Matin* organised an equally effective public appeal for funds, raising 2 million

Francs to speed its development, and in 1900 the French parliament voted for a construction budget of £4.75 million to build 150 submarines and torpedo-boats.[14] Admiral Hyacithe-Laurent-Théophile Aube understood that the submarine was a weapon that could 'combine offense and defence in the highest degree'.[15]

At the 1899 Hague Conference, Russia proposed outlawing the new weapon and Germany (like Britain) was willing to back the proposal if other powers joined them. In the end, however, France and some lesser powers withheld their support.

In the United States, another navy was equally hard at work, pushed on by an unusual Irishman, John Philip Holland, whose first submarine, the *Holland I*, 'took after a pencil, sharpened at both ends'.[16] In 1899, Holland successfully sea-trialled a 75-ton vessel, the *Holland VI*, designed primarily for harbour and littoral defence, and the United States Navy decided to buy its first model, the *SS-1*. 'The purchase was made over the objections of most of the navy hierarchy and without help from the navy's professional bureaucracy.'[17] It was the United States Navy's sea trials that caught Lord Charles Beresford's attention:

> When a common-sense level-headed nation like that of the United States has tried and adopted submarine boats, it would appear probable that such craft must have some value in warlike operations.[18]

Sir Arthur Wilson initiated discussions with the American Electric Boat Company, and an arrangement was reached whereby Vickers was licensed to build the first five Holland submarines for the Royal Navy. That October, the debate on the basic role of the submarine started in earnest. Wilson clearly positioned the new British submarines more as defence against possible French developments.

Despite Wilhelm Bauer's 1850 *Brandtaucher* or the designs of the Swedish *Nordenfelt* forty years later, Germany was slow to throw her hat into the ring: its first U-boat, the *U.1*, was only launched in December 1906, 'well after every other major navy in the world, including even Portugal and Turkey'.[19] Despite that, the submarine had not established a strong following.

Managing the navy's budget took the genius of a man like Tirpitz in Germany: the senior service was the army, after all, not the navy. The May 1906 draft *Novelle* provided a small amount for German U-boat development, although Alfred Tirpitz was not a supporter of submarines, derisively calling them pieces of '*altes Eisen*' – old iron. Young officers serving with the new submarines found their navy did little but cold-shoulder them. Others, like Lothar Persius, would be dismissed because of their support for submarines.[20]

Tirpitz would even rib officers such as Georg-Günter von Forstner (later commander of *U.28*): 'Ach! My dear, give it up! The bottom of the ocean is for fishes, and the sky is for birds.'[21] At the start of the war, a future ace, Max Valentiner, talked of his own doubts and that the submariners were laughed at:

> Had Tirpitz been right in thinking the submarine was only a peacetime weapon? Were all the young women right, the ones on the dancefloors in Kiel, who would laugh out loud whenever a submariner asked them to dance?[22]

The first submarines that the industrial powerhouse Krupp built were not even for Germany: three – the *Karp*, *Karas* and *Kambala* – were constructed for the Russian navy, each with a single bow tube capable of launching three 457mm torpedoes. It wasn't until two years later, on 3 December 1904, that the company received its first German order. The *U.1* was 139ft long, displaced 238 tons on the surface and, again, only carried a single bow tube. Her Körting kerosene engine was, however, a 'far less dangerous animal' than the 16-cylinder Wolsey petrol engine in British counterparts.[23] In 1908, two years after she was completed, *U.1*'s 600-mile journey through the Skagerrak from Heligoland to Kiel provided a taste of things to come.

It was the submarines built for Russia and the *U.1* that got Tirpitz thinking. He had not been at all keen and had resisted any investment, explaining that he had 'refused to throw money away on submarines so long as they could only cruise in home waters'.[24] In the 1905–06 naval estimates, around £70,000 was earmarked 'for experiments connected with submarines'.[25] Within three years, the submarine budget would be increased to 5 million marks, and in 1910 orders were placed for eight submarines, twenty-one by 1914.[26] In submarines, Germany was outspending most of the established naval powers except for the French, even if a more independent role was still not being talked about.

In the early years, few were thinking of using submarines as the underpinning for a *guerre au commerce*. The idea that submarines and destroyers were the weapons of choice for a second-rate naval power was fast gaining acceptance. If one could not directly seize mastery of the oceans, one could at least deny it to a foe. But before the First World War's outbreak, even the Germans had little idea of what a powerful weapon they held in their hands – 'U-boats were designed and their crews trained exclusively to attack enemy warships', and, I should add, harbours and coastal defence.[27] An exception was Vice Admiral von Schleinitz, writing in the *Deutsche Revue* in August 1908, although it was Nordmann, the first commander of *U.1*, who 'got the ball rolling' by asking for a strategic study on how many submarines would be needed for such a war.[28] In May 1914, such a study was made in Germany for the Kiel Submarine Inspectorate by Kapitänleutnant Ulrich-Eberhard Blum. The study, sent to Tirpitz for his approval, recommended a commerce war waged by 222 U-boats stationed at forty-eight key blockade points around Britain.[29] Tirpitz rejected the proposal; his focus on the battle fleet was questioned by few. One critic was a retired admiral, Karl Galster, who published a pamphlet in 1907 promoting the idea of a defensive fleet built around torpedo boats, mines and submarines.[30] Focus on U-boat development took a positive step in 1913 with the creation, on 13 December, of the Inspektion des U-Bootwesens (UI) in Kiel.

The submarine performed well in the 1912–13 naval manoeuvres the next year, despite Tirpitz opposing their inclusion: Otto Weddigen's *U.9* 'sank' three battleships in the spring exercises. That summer, during the final peacetime naval manoeuvres before the outbreak of war, Weddigen demonstrated torpedo reloading while submerged. Johann Spiess, Schwieger's First Officer on the *U.9*, commented on the pace of development:

> The practice and manoeuvres of the U-boats now increased to feverish intensity. The dark shadow of war was drawing ever closer … and we could not tell how soon those mimic battle operations of diving and torpedoing might become the real thing.[31]

The replacement of the old Körting kerosene engines with the diesel engine in *U.19* was the real revolution, allowing a U-boat to radically extend its range into the North Sea.

Before the full potential of the submarine became apparent, many opposed its possible role as a commerce raider. In October 1914, even Pohl expressed his opinion to Bauer that this role would constitute a 'severe violation of international law',[32] and Tirpitz rejected Blum's idea of building a fleet of 222 submarines for this purpose.

But as its potential emerged, a rationale for the legality of its operations was given strong support by what the British had initiated with the Orders in Council. Hermann Bauer, appointed the first Führer der U-Boote three weeks after the outbreak of war, a very experienced U-boat commander in his own right who had served on ten different U-boats, took this point of view.[33] He wrote: '[T]he thought of cutting England off from her sea supply by means of submarines had received little consideration, since such a submarine war against English sea trade would not have been in conformity with the [1909] London Declaration.' However, Bauer immediately followed that up by saying that it was 'only when the English government systematically eliminated these regulations, insofar as they hindered it, through its Orders in Council and blocked Germany from the world ocean by Blockade, did Germany also feel compelled to defend itself and retaliate'.[34]

### Submarine Development in the Royal Navy

The development of British submarines (and later anti-submarine warfare) was hampered by an inevitable ideological debate within the Royal Navy as to whether submarine technology should be supported at all.

> Most senior naval officers viewed this new weapon with hostility and suspicion. Submarines were on the one hand criticized for their limited powers, being considered mainly for defence of harbours and anchorages and quite incapable of working at sea against a fleet; and, contradictorily, for being such a potential threat to the battleship, in which the country had invested more than any other two nations in the world, that to encourage its development was to hazard the country's security.[35]

Jackie Fisher's vision of the submarine was stark and turned out to be accurate. 'The submarine,' Reginald Bacon wrote, 'was Lord Fisher's child and his dynamic energy overrode all naval and departmental obstruction.'[36] Even Churchill and Tirpitz couldn't find the same clarity of understanding, although Fisher made out that he and Tirpitz shared the exact same position so far as the submarine was concerned. Just months before Jutland, he would write to 'Dear old Tirps' saying that he 'didn't blame [him] for the submarine business' and that he would 'have done the same [himself], only our idiots in England wouldn't believe it when [I] told them'.[37]

In championing the submarine, Fisher was like a dog with a bone. He would not let up. Writing to the then DNI, Rear Admiral Louis Battenberg, he implored:[38]

> Drop a battleship out of the programme (it is necessary on account of financial necessities) but at any cost double the output of submarines … if we don't double our output of submarines and go ahead with the Whitehead [torpedo] there will be such an uprising in the country bye & bye as never yet known in the British Empire.[39]

Already there was a young naval officer, Captain Reginald Bacon, who had been appointed in May 1901 as Inspecting Captain of Submarine Boats by Lord Walter Kerr, Fisher's predecessor.[40] His task was to develop – with the six submarines he had – the book on submarine tactics.[41] Within weeks, he had persuaded the Admiralty that submarines, rather than mines, could provide a better defence of ports. Without help from Fisher, whom he regarded as 'an ardent supporter', the road might have been considerably bumpier.[42] Described by Halpern as a 'brilliant, if somewhat difficult, officer', Bacon would have his work cut out for him:[43] 'Between 1901 and August 1914 there were sixty-eight serious submarine accidents, including twenty-three collisions, seven battery explosions and twelve fuel explosions.'[44]

Even so, Fisher was cautious about whether Britain should 'lead the way'. Writing to Lord Selbourne in 1900, he said: '[I]f we built as quickly as we ought to build, we ought always to commence after they are well advanced and have the more powerful vessel afloat beforehand.'[45] He also knew that as a commerce raider, because of its size and limited crew, the submarine would be unlikely to be able to follow the established rules of war at sea.

Submarine *No.1* was launched in April 1902. Bacon's early assessment of HMS *A.1* (actually ordered as *Holland No.6*) was that it would be a 'fair weather craft', 'too small to operate in anything but the calmest of weather'.[46] The submarines, which would mainly be used for harbour defence, were hopelessly problem-ridden: *A.1*, *A.3*, *A.4*, *A.5*, *A.7* and *A.8* all developed major problems but were used as sources of learning. The same year, the Admiralty committed to building ten submarines a year. At least at the top, the importance of the submarine was recognised.[47]

In 1902, Kerr had already recognised the need to develop anti-submarine warfare tools and the torpedo school, HMS *Vernon*, was engaged to spearhead the research. In a precursor to William Sims's later comments in *The Victory at Sea*, Bacon soon realised that efforts should be better focused on detection. He had little interest in developing evasive surface tactics, so concentrated more on attack. In the latter he persuaded the Admiralty of the real role submarines could play in protecting British harbours, even though the use of the word 'defence' was almost forbidden in Royal Naval tactical discussion. British naval culture was always more prone to support all things 'offensive'.

Already, in 1904, Fisher wanted to see a solid submarine-building programme launched. It was during his fifteen months as Commander-in-Chief Portsmouth, a post he took up on 31 August 1903, that he 'turned serious attention to the submarine'.[48] It was natural: he had developed a very deep interest in the Whitehead torpedo and thence an interest in vessels that could serve as launch platforms. The torpedo boat was the answer for surface delivery; the submarine, after 1899, eventually for an effective subsurface option.

> The Whitehead torpedo can be carried with facility in Submarine boats, and it has now attained such a range and such accuracy … that even at two miles' range it possesses a greater ratio of power of vitally injuring a ship in the line of battle than does the most accurate gun … There is this immense fundamental difference between the automobile torpedo and the gun – the torpedo has no trajectory; it travels horizontally and hits

> below the water, so all its hits are vital hits; but not so the gun – only in a few places are gun hits vital, and those places are armoured.[49]

Early in 1904, Fisher invited the Prince and Princess of Wales to come see his 'toys' in Portsmouth.[50] He had also been working on the king and had very thoroughly briefed him before the two had dinner with Bacon. Ponsonby noted that before Bacon arrived,

> the King knew a great deal … but he listened attentively to all that Captain Bacon said when he practically repeated all that Fisher had told him.[51]

As her husband descended into the depths aboard the HMS *A.1*, the princess was heard to stage-whisper: 'I shall be very disappointed if George doesn't come up again.'[52] The fear was very real; the prince had visited the submarine in dry-dock, being repaired. She'd been rammed by mistake and had sunk with eleven crew still aboard in a collision off the Isle of Wight with HMS *Juno*. Three years later, in June 1908, the *A.8* would sink off Plymouth Sound with all fifteen hands on board after a 'suspected battery explosion'.[53]

While it seems clear that Fisher took every opportunity to promote awareness of the submarine, it might also be fair to say that the submarine fell victim to Fisher's Dreadnought battleship and battle-cruiser programme. Any over-promotion of the submarine could have proved problematic, potentially losing support among the more Mahanian, 'big ship' Royal Navy officers. While Fisher believed that his 'beloved submarines are going to magnify the naval power of England seven times more than at present', naturally there was a resistance to change.[54] So much so that he once declared in exasperation:

> It is astonishing to me, perfectly astounding, how the very best amongst us fail to realize the vast impending revolution in Naval warfare and Naval strategy that the submarine will accomplish.[55]

Fisher faced strongly entrenched opposition. He was ridiculed by his great political rival, Lord Charles Beresford, who called the submarine 'Fisher's playthings'.[56] In parts of the Admiralty, there was a similar sentiment: Captain Herbert Richmond, for instance. As Assistant Director of Operations on the Naval Staff, a 'brilliant' naval officer, his opinions on the convoy system would influence Lloyd George's Cabinet Secretary, Sir Maurice Hankey, in 1917. In July 1914, he wrote scathingly about the weapon, admittedly in the context of a commerce war:

> [T]he submarine has the smallest value of any vessel for the direct attack upon trade. She does not carry a crew which is capable of taking charge of a prize, she cannot remove passengers and other persons if she wishes to sink one. Therefore, she will not affect direct action in attack, which must be made by cruisers and other surface travelling vessels.[57]

Appearing in the *Naval Review* in 1914 (in an article titled 'The Submarine and the Surface Vessel'), Richmond went on to say that this precluded the submarine from commerce war 'unless the ordinarily accepted rules of warfare are radically altered'.[58] Others have taken this to mean that Richmond understood that the submarine could *only* operate in unrestricted mode. Unsurprisingly, he was decidedly pessimistic about being able to persuade the Admiralty of his ideas:[59]

> Satan disguised as an angel of Light wouldn't succeed in persuading the Admiralty or the Navy that in [the] course of some few years the Submarines will prevent any fleet remaining at sea continuously either in the Mediterranean or in the North Sea.[60]

It was natural that a defence against any future attack on commerce would be surfaced. A second article in the *Naval Review* ('Protection of Trade in Past Wars') came down on the side of the convoy rather than 'the cruising system': 'the reason is obvious. The convoy system is the most economical use of force.'[61] In view of his later position, it's interesting to note that another contributor to the *Naval Review* ('The Influence of Commerce in War') that year was Kenneth Dewar. While 'remarkable for anticipating the strategy adopted by the Admiralty in the war', he nevertheless only thought in terms of the surface threat to convoys.[62]

Admiral Sir Arthur Wilson did not seem to immediately grasp the significance of the 1904 exercise in which five British Holland submarines successfully war-gamed the defence of Portsmouth harbour, 'killing' four battleships in the exercise. It was Wilson who famously called the submarine 'a damned un-English weapon'. Although he said that 'they'll never be any use in war … [he intended to] get the First Lord to announce that we intend to treat all submarines as private vessels in wartime and that we'll hang the crews'.[63] In fact, Wilson clearly understood the potential threat of the submarine, even if he publicly downplayed its importance. He 'recognized the potentialities of the submarine but the Navy as a whole was still suspicious or indifferent'.[64] It was more that he found the submarine morally repugnant. At the very least, the submarine needed to be tested, even if he found the idea of submarine warfare abhorrent. He and Churchill shared the same moral ground. He proclaimed that 'no other type of vessel has assumed suddenly so vast an influence over the daytime operations of an enemy'. In 1910, Wilson's assessment of the submarine threat was closer to that of Fisher than his contemporary caricature would suggest: 'The really serious danger that this country had to guard against in war is not invasion but the interruption of our trade and destruction of our merchant fleet.'[65]

Some listened to Fisher. Lord Esher, for example, set up an important sub-committee of the Committee for Imperial Defence, tasked with defining the reforms needed in Britain's armed forces.

> If he is right, and his argument appears unanswerable, it is difficult to exaggerate the vast impending revolution in naval warfare and naval strategy that the submarine will accomplish.[66]

Of course, there were technically minded officers, such as Sir Henry Jackson, whose ears had pricked up on hearing some of the developments by foreign navies, for example when the *Gustave-Zedé* torpedoed the training-battleship *Magenta* in the 1898 exercises. The first successful underwater torpedo launch had only been carried out the previous year.

In his book *The Crisis of the Naval War*, according to Peter Hore, Jellicoe seems 'to have written Fisher out of the (submarine) debate altogether'.[67] As Matthew Seligman noted, 'anticipating' the importance of the submarine and 'having a solution' are not the same thing.

It was also Wilson who, after hearing about two D-class submarines 'sinking' two cruisers off the west coast of Scotland in an exercise in 1910, decided to appoint 'a young sea-going captain of forceful character', Roger Keyes, as Inspecting Captain of Submarines.[68] While Keyes also had a strong supporter in Churchill, who thought him 'a brilliant officer' who had 'more knowledge and feeling for war than almost any naval officer I have ever met', Fisher, maybe more realistically, did not think highly of him.[69] In January 1915, he scathingly wrote: 'There never was such a mistake as putting Keyes in charge of submarines, who had not the faintest idea how to employ them!'[70] Nevertheless, Keyes did understand his shortcomings. He realised that he would need strong technical advisors and he put together a Submarine Advisory Committee, to which he made some notable appointments.

Fisher had even thought of towing submarines into an enemy harbour to lie in wait before the declaration of war. It was very like his pre-war thinking on a pre-emptive Copenhagen-like strike. Six months before war broke out, he wrote to Prime Minister Herbert Asquith confidently predicting the role submarines would play in the coming war. Asquith, however, stopped Fisher's

Cabinet paper from wider circulation as he 'thought it fantastic that any civilized people would resort to such ruthless tactics'.[71]

Fisher had no doubt that a submarine war would be a fundamentally different one. In January 1914, in a note to Churchill, he wrote that the submarine

> cannot capture the merchant ship; she has no spare hands to put a prize crew on board; little or nothing would be gained by disabling her engines or propeller; she cannot convoy her into harbor; and, in fact, it is impossible for the submarine to deal with commerce in the light and provisions of international law.

It begged the question:

> Under these circumstances, is it presumed that the hostile submarine will disregard such law and sink any vessel heading for a British commercial port? ... This is freely acknowledged to be an altogether barbarous method of warfare [but] the essence of war is violence, and moderation in war is imbecility.

Churchill, appointed First Lord of the Admiralty at the end of 1911, agreed: he did 'not believe this [commerce raiding] would ever be done by a civilised power. If there were a nation vile enough to systematically adopt such methods, it would be justified and indeed necessary to employ the extreme resources of science against them.'[72]

By 1912, even the Admiralty was starting to wake up:

> No other class of vessel yet designed belongs more naturally to the defensive than the submarine; but the German development of the submarine tends to turn even this weapon of defence into one of offense, by building not the smaller classes which would be useful for the defence of their limited coastline, but large submarines capable of sudden and offensive operation at a distance from their base across the sea.[73]

Indeed, it was feared that, 'For the first time, the enemy could be lurking anywhere at any time.'[74] The Admiralty started to take a quiet, but keen, interest in submarine development:

> Each design has been carefully examined and sufficient experiment has been made in each case to ascertain its probable value. It has been quietly dropped with the result of delaying the development of the submarine boat for about 20 years.[75]

Duncan Redford floats the idea that the absence of any submarine from the 1902 *Naval Review* 'could be taken to mean that the Admiralty was predisposed to sideline submarines', but he very quickly dismissed its likelihood.[76] The Admiralty, or at least its more conservative elements, always disliked the *Review*. Jellicoe even thought it a mechanism that dangerously distributed the collective intelligence of younger naval officers useful to the enemy in wartime.

Germany's first submarine, *U.1*, was only launched in 1906, and neither Captain (later Sir) Richard Webb, the Director of the Admiralty Trade Division, nor the 'War Plans and Distribution of the Fleet' mentioned submarines.[77] The construction of German submarines was first stipulated in the 1912 *Novelle*, but only twenty-eight were ready by August 1914, and of these only ten were so-called HochSee-U-Boote built for longer endurance (by comparison, Britain had sixty-eight submarines, of which eighteen were longer-endurance models). It was also in 1912 that submarines, contrary to Tirpitz's orders, took part in fleet manoeuvres.

Few understood the potential seriousness of a German submarine threat. In 1911, Sir Julian Corbett warned that Britain's trade was an obvious focal point of enemy strategy, but he did not make the connection:

> Anything, therefore, which we are able to achieve towards crippling our enemy's finance is a direct step to his overthrow, and the most effective means we can employ to this end against a maritime State is to deny him the resources of sea-borne trade.[78]

Nor had Webb: he had talked of a possible loss of seventy-seven ships a week to German *surface ships*, with four cruisers and twelve armed liners in the Atlantic.

Fisher was particularly nervous about the effect of submarines in the narrow waters of the Channel, and had even warned that 'there will be no place for any great ship in the North Sea'. Jellicoe confidently wrote at the time – 1909 – that Germany needed another eight years before she 'had enough submarines truly to menace the North Sea'.[79] He was right. Eight years later, he would be facing the harsh reality of German submarine war, not only in the North Sea but in the Atlantic and Mediterranean as well. Nevertheless, he was deeply worried and could be equally pessimistic about the danger of a lurking submarine trap:

> The situation is a difficult one: it is quite possible that half our battle fleet might be disabled by underwater attack before the guns opened fire at all.[80]

As First Sea Lord, Fisher knew he had to radically accelerate submarine development. One of his great achievements was to scrap the monopoly that Vickers Maxim at Barrow-in-Furness had enjoyed up to that point. Britain, like Germany's reliance on Krupp until 1914, was overly exposed to Vickers. Fisher's actions possibly resulted from a visit with Roger Keyes. While Keyes might not have been endowed with an excess of intellect, he did see the Vickers monopoly as a brake on innovation (and, just as important, output) and promptly got rid of it. The latter recalled a visit Fisher made to see the *D.1*, when Fisher, 'looking at me very sourly asked me why we had not built more submarines'. Keyes 'replied hotly that Fisher's own policy of concentrating on the smaller type of purely defensive craft, which would be of very limited value in war, was largely to blame and went on to criticise the monopoly in submarine building given by Fisher to Vickers, Ltd'.[81] Keyes would later admit that 'we all discarded' Fisher's logic as 'impossible and unthinkable'.[82]

Britain started the conflict with more submarines than any other navy, seventy-four in all.[83] Germany, by contrast, 'did not have the numbers to match [her] aspirations' and could only show twenty-eight built or in the process of being built.[84] Fisher's support, however, had at least helped Britain's submarine development keep abreast: in 1906, only 5 per cent of the naval budget was spent on submarines; by 1914, with seventy-five boats, it possessed the largest fleet.[85] Yet numbers don't always tell the whole picture: Britain had fewer long-range submarines than Germany, only eighteen of the total afloat. The longer-range D- and E-class designs were still on order and undelivered.

Fisher's task in supporting the development of a thoroughly new form of warfare demanded his kind of leadership; he would never get what he wanted

> unless the whole engineering and shipbuilding resources of the country are enlisted in the effort, and the whole of the peace paraphernalia of red-tape routine and consequent delay are brushed on one side.[86]

He thought it not unreasonable to have a submarine built in nine months; in the end, 'a dozen more were actually delivered in five months'.[87] Taking a page out of the Dreadnought experience, he thought that additional engines should immediately be ordered, as 'we know from experience that it is in the machinery parts that defects and failures occur'.[88]

In 1904, Jackie Fisher had been appointed First Sea Lord. He knew what he wanted – 'the five best brains in the Navy below the rank of Admiral and … two other brains for the consideration of the types of the future fighting vessels'.[89] Along with Captains Henry Jackson, Reginald Bacon, Charles Madden and Wilfrid Henderson were William Henry Gard and Alexander Gracie. John Jellicoe was appointed Director of Naval Ordnance, where he was intimately involved in the supply of HMS *Dreadnought's* main armament and the development of Director Fire Control. In this position, he maintained a continued contact with William Sims, who had served as the USN's Inspector of Target Practice from 1902–05 and had visited the yards where *Dreadnought* was being built. Their paths had crossed physically in China in 1900; they would work together closely to counter the submarine threat in 1917. In Tom Hone's words, Sims was 'intelligent, extremely energetic, intolerant of personal and professional sloppiness, a good writer and a gifted off-the-cuff speaker, and had proved to be an unusually happy and successful teacher while a young officer'.[90]

As part of the 'Fishpond', Jellicoe shared much of his mentor's thinking,[91] but certainly not all. Fisher was, for the most part, complimentary about Jellicoe's support for the submarine, congratulating him in December 1913 for his 'splendid pushing'.[92]

But time ran out and in December 1914, from his cabin in *Iron Duke*, Jellicoe wrote to Fisher saying as much: '[I]t has all come true, even to the sinking of merchant ships, in which no one believed at all.' This war was going to be a different kind of war.

### Anti-Submarine Warfare in the Early Royal Navy

Submarines 'become vulnerable once they disclose their presence by attacking'.[93] Any success depends on being undetected, and once detected, attacking and escaping with speed. Active measures against submarines – anti-submarine tactics – were almost entirely limited to surface response: gunnery and ramming, defensive netting and explosive drags. No dropping bomb, or depth charge, existed. And there was nothing to help locate a submarine except visual discoloration if the submarine happened to be close to the surface.

Before taking command of the Grand Fleet in 1914, Jellicoe held key positions at the heart of the Royal Navy: in 1905 as Director of Naval Ordnance and in 1908 as Third Sea Lord and Controller (3SL), a position which not only oversaw Naval Ordnance but also Naval Construction, naval dockyards as well as the Navy's scientific departments. In preparation for higher command, at the end of 1910, Fisher promoted him to Commander-in-Chief Atlantic Fleet, where he gained vital operational experience in the management of a dreadnought fleet. Then in 1911, after advancement to vice admiral, he was made 2iC in the Home Fleet.

Some of John Jellicoe's earliest dealings with submarines were focused on their likely impact on battleship design and tactics. One issue that came up in1910, roughly when Jellicoe had been 3SL, concerned the composition of the battle line. At that point, most senior British naval officers thought that the line should exclusively consist of battleships. It was Admiral William May who set the ball rolling, saying that there were two possible approaches to protecting the battle line from torpedo attack, 'either to employ divisional tactics or to attach scout cruisers and destroyers ... to ward off hostile torpedo craft'.[94]

The submarine's relatively slow speed meant that its inclusion in the battle line was unlikely in the immediate future, so contemporary tactical development, which revolved almost exclusively around the role of the Battle Fleet, left the submarine aside when it came to deterrence. Submarines' 'lack of speed, which prevented them from accompanying a battle fleet, meant that the threat posed by such warships in a general engagement was probably regarded as negligible, at least for the time being'.[95]

The opposing position was that the battleship's armament should be augmented with secondary quick-firing guns. Eventually, this position prevailed and 6in guns were added to British battleships. Before accepting McKenna's offer of the post of 3SL, Jellicoe stated his position:

> [I]t will be necessary for this country to lay down three or four battleships a year for some little time to come (completing them in two years) if we are to retain the two-power standard in this class of vessel. A strong programme of destroyers and a moderate one of small cruisers will also be necessary.[96]

Jellicoe supported Bridgeman's[97] opposition, which was based on the concern for additional weight added in armament being better directed to added underwater blister protection, external water-filled bulges waterline-mounted on a battleship, designed to absorb the effects of a torpedo exploding by pre-detonation outside of the hull structure.[98] He felt that, while engaged, a battleship might have to compromise its manoeuvring to allocate fire away from an enemy battle line towards an attacking torpedo force. Reginald Bacon added his point of view: the 6in gun might better be mounted on auxiliary vessels, 'but not until late 1912 did the Royal Navy begin to build such vessels: which became known as light cruisers'.[99] Another battleship improvement, which came under the heading 'improved underwater protection', was the fitting of three engine rooms abreast of each other, as 'with the centre engine-room alone intact ships thus fitted should be able to steam at considerable speed'.[100]

### The Submarine at the Outbreak of War

*Kieler Woche* takes place annually in June.[101] As the ships' crews from the Royal Navy's visiting squadron bid their German hosts farewell, Rear Admiral George Warrender sent out a final message of friendship, one sailor to another: 'Friends now, friends forever.' Within a month, the officers and men who had feted each other during *Kieler Woche* would be at war.

Across the Atlantic, within days of war being declared, John Phillip Holland died. The moustachioed Irish inventor, seen in one photo emerging from the hull of a submarine wearing his bowler hat, was arguably the genius, the real father of the modern-day submarine. For more than fifty years, he'd worked on its development. He had invented a weapon that, far from helping end war, would now conjure up a new picture of brutality to the war at sea. After he died on 12 August, *The New York Times* wrote:

> [A]lthough he was interested in submarines, Mr. Holland was opposed to war, and his idea of submarines was to incapacitate warships and not to destroy them and kill the men on them.

In Germany, Tirpitz quickly made it known that he thought that Germany's senior naval commanders had 'under-estimated' the potential of the U-boat, but the new position was probably just as much influenced by his wanting to ride on the wave of success as any personal conviction. As Vice Admiral Albert Hopman remembered it:

> The almost fabulous success of *U.9* has brought about the greatest joy in the entire headquarters and has done much good for the reputation of the Navy. The State Secretary naturally emphasizes again how this war is making the importance of the submarine ever clearer and speaks of future fleets that consist only of ocean cruisers and submarines.[102]

However, Tirpitz also found Weddigen's early success – torpedoing three armoured cruisers from his submarine, *U.9* – problematic: 'It [the submarine's potential] is now exaggerated as a result of the success of *U.9*.'[103] Its success even surprised its supporters: 'we never dreamed that they would so successfully take the first role as our most effective weapon in naval warfare,' Forstner admitted.[104] He added that Allied armies 'depend for their sustenance and supplies upon the freedom of the seas. The trade routes of the world constitute the arteries which feed the muscles of these armies. Germany is endeavouring to cut these arteries by the submarine.'[105]

The U-boat quickly evolved in functionality, range, killing power and independence of action. In October 1916, Admiral Jellicoe found himself writing that the German submarine threat was 'a very serious and ever-increasing menace' which was 'by far the most pressing question of the present time'.[106] Elsewhere, he reiterated the sentiment: it was the 'most serious menace the Empire has ever faced'. The new war was frighteningly cost-effective for Germany: 'for each U-boat lost, 32 merchant ships had been sunk – 5,708 ships in all, or a quarter of the world's tonnage.'[107]

# 3

# Operational Command: Jellicoe as Commander-in-Chief Grand Fleet

On 4 August 1914, 55-year-old 'Silent Jack' Jellicoe took command of the Grand Fleet at Scapa Flow. Raising his Flag in HMS *Iron Duke*, Grand Fleet officers were initially taken aback by the suddenness of the change in command. To replace an experienced Commander-in-Chief such as Sir George Callaghan on the outbreak of hostilities seemed to border on recklessness.

John Jellicoe shared these concerns. It was a career move that he found particularly difficult because of his friendship with Sir George. As he turned over his duties at the Admiralty on 30 July, he was under the impression that he was to be Sir George's 2iC, not his replacement. He got a hint of what might be in the offing the next day when, speaking with Battenberg and Churchill, it was made clear that there *might* be circumstances in which he would succeed Sir George more immediately.

As he prepared to travel north to join the fleet, he was handed an envelope to be opened in Sir George's presence if war was declared. Jellicoe clearly knew what was going on and was worried: Callaghan had the loyalty of the Grand Fleet. He had also been a close friend of Jellicoe's and would remain one, becoming one of my father's godparents when he was born in April 1918. Jellicoe tried to persuade Churchill to change his mind. Over the next few days, a steady stream of telegrams was exchanged, Jellicoe's responses getting 'perilously close to impertinence' for his stubborn resistance to Churchill's direct, written orders.[1]

Nevertheless, Callaghan and Jellicoe worked out a smooth transfer of flags to be formally executed at 0830hrs on 4 August, after which the Grand Fleet, 'the most powerful fleet that had as ever yet sailed', finally put to sea under its new commander.[2] Its purpose was to support the imposition of a distant blockade on Germany. Its strength was impressive: twenty-one dreadnoughts and eight pre-dreadnoughts, escorted by waves of cruisers and destroyers. One group, the 10th Cruiser Squadron, was responsible for closing the gap between the Shetlands and the Norwegian coast. Also known as the Northern Patrol, its first wartime commander, Rear Admiral Dudley de Chair, would report to Jellicoe until March 1916.[3]

### The Execution of Pre-planned Orders

With war declared, British plans went into immediate effect: German cable lines were cut, the Grand Fleet was sent to Scapa Flow, the mining of the Strait of Dover was put in motion and more than 1,200 German ships in British-controlled ports were seized.[4]

Germany's use of undersea cables for communications made it vulnerable. Within hours, the first clandestine operation took place. A decision was made in 1911 by a small sub-committee of the Committee for Imperial Defence that, in the event of war, actions would be taken to either cut Germany's undersea cables or, where communications went through unsecure commercial operations, to monitor them. Cutting the cables would encourage a move towards either wireless-telegraphy (W/T) or cables run from a neutral territory.

Instructions were sent out and, at around 0315hrs on 5 August, the cable ship *C.S. Alert* started dragging the bottom of the Channel, hooking one of the five cables connecting Emden, on the North German coast, to Britain, France, Spain, America and Africa. When the Germans lodged a diplomatic complaint, the lines were temporarily restored but promptly re-cut.[5]

In Cornwall, the cables carrying traffic across the Atlantic came ashore in the small village of Porthcurno. On 4 August, a single man – known as a 'Secret Censor' – sent a curiously enigmatic message to London: 'Fixity London, fixed.' Around the world, other 'Secret Censors' did the same. Between 400 and 580 individuals in over 120 countries – 180 alone in the UK – were now monitoring and copying all enemy signals traffic. Over the next four years, 'in all, 80 million messages would be subject to censorship'.[6]

Germany also reacted quickly, with every one of the approaches to Britain's North Sea ports mined on 5 August.

### Economic War by Executive Order

Sir Edward Grey would play a crucial role in the war. The Foreign Secretary's aims were clear. 'The object of diplomacy,' he wrote, 'was to secure the maximum of blockade that could be enforced without a rupture with the United States.'[7] The blockade against Germany had to be as tough as it could be without being counter-productive in its repercussions from European neutrals like the Netherlands, Denmark or Norway, and particularly not from its largest international member, the USA.

Even if Americans would be somewhat more favourable to the British, sentiment was strongly regional: the East Coast was largely pro-British, the West Coast strongly anti-Japanese and the Mid-west 'certainly not pro Ally'. The experience of her colonial past was still a powerfully emotive memory. In the 1910 census, 10 per cent of Americans used German as a first language, and besides, both the Irish and Russians were far more likely to side with the Central Powers than with Britain. The anti-English sentiment of many Irish had been stoked by centuries of what appeared to many as little more than an occupation. Addressing this issue, an Admiralty assessment commented:

> [A]ny project of twisting the tail of the British lion invariably finds cordial and traditional support among the majority of heterogeneous nationalities which compose the United States of America.[8]

Diplomatically, Grey had met with President Wilson's most trusted and influential advisor, Colonel Edward M. House, shortly before the war in July 1913. House was an important sounding board as 'he fancied himself in the role of *éminence grise*'.[9] Masterfully, in seemingly warm and friendly conversations, Grey coaxed House to paint a picture of what America's position might be on some of the key diplomatic issues. Wilson, it was said, 'found himself still in a world about which he knew very little', and Grey understood that, to influence Wilson, he had to influence House.[10] For the reclusive President, House was vital: he was his 'second personality. He is my independent self. His thoughts and mine are one.'[11]

Grey, therefore, went to great lengths to nurture the friendship, gifting the colonel books on fishing and procuring invitations for him to stay in grand English country houses. 'He preyed on House's ego by utilising flattery to disarm the inexperienced diplomat.'[12]

House also visited Germany and met with Tirpitz. He found the meeting confusing: the old admiral was strongly anti-British. Later, in 1914, he 'spoke of England, Germany and the United States being the "only hope of advancing Christian civilization"'.[13] House did not grasp the opportunities for leverage which Grey certainly would have. On the day war was declared, Wilson announced his willingness to advance the United States as a mediator for Europe's belligerents. It was a very difficult moment for Wilson, for some not so obvious reasons: his wife, Ellen, was terminally ill and died two days later. The President, as he usually did, disappeared behind closed doors and distracted himself by reading detective stories.

It was only at the insistence of his first Secretary of State, William Jennings Bryan, that President Wilson was persuaded to declare that the guiding principle for all belligerents in the war at sea should be the 1909 London Declaration. On 19 August, Germany announced her agreement, while Britain not only had not signed the Treaty, she also refused it any consideration. Germany's move was carefully designed to paint the British into a corner. However, in London, America's man on the ground, Ambassador Walter Page, 'frequently informed Grey that he did not support the avenue that the United States had taken'.[14] It was an extraordinarily unprofessional position for a diplomatic representative. On 26 August, Page outlined the British position to Washington. No immediate response was forthcoming, although two days later Washington put forward a seemingly naïve demand that Britain release all those ships that had been at sea when the war started. Congress even debated the possibility of America purchasing those interned in US ports, which – not wanting to see German war coffers replenished – Grey was strongly against.

Starting with a first Order in Council (OIC) on 20 August, Britain sharpened its stance. Essentially an executive order, the series of Orders that would be rolled out over the year with escalating economic and diplomatic impact, aimed at tightening an economic noose around Germany.

Seven important dates marked these decisions: 20 August 1914, 29 October 1914, 11 and 23 March 1915, 26 April 1915, 31 May 1915 and, exactly one year after the first Order in Council, the seventh on 20 August 1915. Not every Order in Council produced entirely new concepts; mostly, each built on previous Orders. Through these Orders, Britain defined the terms of its blockade – what goods were covered and why, which trade routes were restricted, how neutrals could trade and how Britain intended to enforce its policy. Britain reserved the right to seize goods which it deemed to be aiding Germany. After the 11 March OIC, the British escalated their response: rather than 'confiscating' goods, they would now completely prevent ships reaching neutral or German ports.

Britain also introduced the principle of 'Continuous Voyage', allowing its ships to seize unconditional contraband which it believed to be 'destined for the enemy, regardless of the port it was delivered to'.[15] Britain reserved the right to seize conditional contraband no matter the port of delivery if Germany was to be the final destination.[16] If the search on the high seas was felt to be inadequate or too difficult, a ship would be sent to an allied port for inspection, but before that, a prize crew would board to make sure no papers or materials were destroyed. It was not always straightforward to either classify the goods or be sure of their final destination.

On this key issue, however, Grey countered much of America's economic argument by pointing out that no detained cargoes had been confiscated, rather they had been 'sold at full value with no loss to the exporter'. He had thus succeeded in moving the discussion 'from the strict legality of the Order in Council to how the American public would perceive it'.[17] American exporters would still receive the financial benefits.

A second Order followed two months later, on 29 October. It would be nine days after the first merchant ship had been sunk.[18] Under the rules of the day, it first had to identify its target and remove the crew to safety before any act of destruction could be carried out. The Order included a modification to checks on trans-shipment and now put the onus on the shipper to produce the proof. It also redefined the contraband list by outlining what was considered 'Absolute' or 'Conditional', the first of which covered goods that were considered of direct military value to Germany and which would, therefore, be subject to immediate seizure while retaining due consideration towards 'Conditional' goods. Certain items were also reclassified from 'Conditional' to 'Absolute'.[19] These were often dual-purpose items like lead, glycerin, copper, petroleum, rubber, iron ore and even barbed wire, aluminium and sulphuric acid.

Copper was included as it was directly used in munitions manufacture, but it was inevitably contentious; half-a-million Americans worked in mining copper. Here, however, Grey managed to demonstrate that the Americans themselves had caused the fall in copper output, done before the war to maintain high prices.

The following year, with two Orders in March (the 11th and 23rd), Britain went even further: the first 'wiped out' the distinction between the first two contraband categories entirely. The idea of Continuous Voyage now declared that any prohibited goods that were ultimately destined for any of Britain's enemies aboard neutral ships would be termed contraband and subject to seizure, while also allowing for the inspection of cargoes in neutral ports to discourage ongoing shipment.

Beginning with the fifth Order (26 April), the British approach significantly hardened by redefining foodstuffs as potentially contraband. The rulings gave Germany a solidly exploitable moral case that she used to stir worldwide opinion against Britain in any disruption of the food supply that would inevitably impact civilians.

By the winter of 1915–16, fat, sugar and bread were being rationed in Germany, and as winter ended, potato stocks were low. Fat and meat stocks were the same because of the 'great swine massacre' that spring. Blockade was a gift to German propogandists – Britain's inclusion of medicines and baby foods certainly caused some indignation for many Americans – but much more serious was Britain's ruthless suppression of the Irish Easter rebellion. The great famine was still a living memory and there were large and vocal Irish communities in many of America's north-eastern cities, as well as in Illinois and Ohio.

The final 1915 Orders (31 May and 20 August) expanded and refined the existing blacklist of neutral companies, vessels and individuals that were suspected of sanction-busting. The last Order represented outlined the potential use of force against blockade runners. The blacklist could now benefit from a full year's experience. Opportunities for diplomatic error multiplied.

Meanwhile, within the German submarine service, pressure was building for commerce raiding without restrictions: on 8 October, Korvetenkapitän Hermann Bauer wrote to the Hochseeflotte Commander-in-Chief, von Ingenohl, formally requesting permission. Like some of his counterparts in the Royal Navy, or even from officers like Hermann Bauer, Ingenohl 'considered their use against merchantmen uncivilized'.[20] Nevertheless, on 20 October, two days after HMS *E.3* became the 'first submarine to fall victim to one of its own kind', the SS *Glitra* became the first merchant ship to be sunk by a U-boat. Finally, on 2 November, the British declared the North Sea a militarised 'war zone', which meant that all neutral shipping headed for neutral Scandinavian countries or the Netherlands now had to pass through the English Channel, making seizure by the British infinitely easier.

Five days later, von Pohl was lobbying for a counter-blockade, and within two months Germany retaliated: Berlin also declared a similar war zone, a *Sperrgebiet*, in the waters that surrounded the British Isles: 'From February 18 onward, every merchant ship met in this war zone will be destroyed, nor will it be possible to obviate the danger with which passengers and crew are thereby threatened.' Furthermore, an ominous warning was added advising neutrals that it 'may not always be possible to prevent the attacks meant for hostile ships from being directed against neutral ships'.[21] Any ship – be it neutral or Allied – was now considered as a valid target within specified zones of operation.

Therein lay the difference between the British approach of 'blockade' and the German 'war zone': blockade respected much of the legal backing of law for war at sea. The German approach lacked discrimination. Through the Orders in Council, Britain made every effort to define what constituted contraband goods and what did not.

## The Blockade in Operation

Most German trade had to pass through the continental northern ports, the Baltic or the English Channel. The first and the last were natural 'choke points', where Germany's enemies could tighten their control on the flow of her goods.

The gap between the Shetland Islands and the Norwegian coast controlled northern access to the Atlantic trade routes. Churchill agreed with Jellicoe's recommendations that ships of the Grand Fleet should support the 10th Cruiser Squadron to close this 610-mile gap – 'for all practical purposes the blockade had arrived right at the center of the British maritime strategy'.[22] The Northern Patrol comprised the 10th Cruiser Squadron, its ships sailing 'at slow speed west in the day against incoming traffic and east at night, stopping for an hour at daylight and dusk' in constant patrol.[23]

> One might in truth say that whilst the forces under the immediate command of Admiral Jellicoe made up the Grand Battle Fleet, it was the squadrons under Admiral de Chair, which formed a Grand Examination Fleet. The latter, relying on the former's protection, though miles away, was able to be the Battle Fleet's executive: to put into application the massed sea power, to chase, stop, examine and even arrest, not merely any merchant ship of Germany, but any neutral suspected of carrying cargoes or passengers on Germany's behalf.[24]

At the southern end, of course, blocking any exit from the English Channel, was the Dover Patrol, the nucleus of which was a force of twelve Tribal-class destroyers. As its role grew in importance under the command of Horace Hood, Reginal Bacon and Roger Keyes, additional strength was added: monitors, armed trawlers, minesweepers, motor launches (MLs), submarines and seaplanes.

Between March 1915 and December 1916, the average weekly number of vessels stopped numbered 286. On top of that was a monthly average of another 150 fishing and coastal vessels.[25] Despite this, daily life on the Northern Patrol could be decidedly boring. Surgeon Probationer James Shaw, from one of the 'live bait' ships, the armed cruiser *Changuinola*, complained that 'we see nothing but sea and sky'.[26] Brian de Courcy-Ireland, based out of Kirkwall in Orkney on the rather aptly named HMS *Relentless*, talked about how the men would try to spice up the daily routine:

> We used to find that if you really wanted to get a bit of a move on, we used to drop a depth charge which they thought was a submarine in the vicinity, you see, and up would go the smoke from their funnels and they'd belt on for a bit.[27]

The work was unglamorous, repetitive and frustrating: the 'failure to hold so many of the ships perilously brought in for investigation at Kirkwall' instantly stirred constant tensions between the Royal Navy and the Foreign Office:[28]

> The fate of the detained ship was decided in London ... The difficulties with which the Foreign Office was faced in regard to neutral susceptibilities was naturally not so apparent in the Fleet as to the Authorities in London.[29]

## The Unseen Threat of Germany's U-boats

Germany started the war with only thirty-six submarines that had little defined purpose. Only six months before, Blum's proposal for a larger submarine fleet had been presented to, and rejected by, Tirpitz. Although nine more (including the first two Type-*UB*s) were to be added by February 1915, Germany would close 1914 with only twenty-one U-boats operating in the North Sea, but of these, 'only three or four could be maintained on patrol'.[30]

In both navies, what role the submarine could play was confused, even though both agreed on harbour and littoral defence. The very first use of Germany's submarines was to patrol off Heligoland as 'buoyant sentry boxes' guarding the sea lanes to Wilhelmshaven and the Kiel Canal.[31] They were literally tethered in one spot to buoys, and every evening they would return to the safety of harbour. Uncertainty thus surrounded the submarine. As Premsel noted, 'In the first year of the war there was a large amount of uncertainty about the possible uses of submarines in naval warfare.'[32] In an offensive role, the submarine's intended targets were warships, not merchant ships. It would take much trial and error, and political to-and-fro, to shape the real potential of the submarine.

The British made much of merchantmen being defenceless, but the problem, as the Germans saw it, was that 'they provided the means to make war. They might be defenseless, but they were certainly not harmless.'[33] Ironically, it was the British measures of self-defence that changed the game. Arming a merchant ship against submarine attack forced the submarine to fire first and ask questions later: it 'was the first step in removing the submarine's invisibility'.[34] Later tactics, like those of Q-ships disguised as innocent and defenceless merchantmen, made the adoption of more aggressive submarine tactics both understandable and inevitable.

Jellicoe was surrounded with threats; the submarine would be the most challenging. His own thinking and that of Battlecruiser Fleet Commander Vice Admiral Sir David Beatty were very much aligned, although, true to his character, Jellicoe at heart was a realist:

> Our principal dangers are mines and submarines, and I think in time we shall be able to manage them satisfactorily.[35]

Submarines had already influenced Jellicoe's thinking on ship construction, deployment and defence. The question, however, of how the Grand Fleet should meet the threat had hardly been addressed. Jellicoe was more focused on its meeting with the HSF (Hochseeflotte, the High Seas Fleet) rather than any trade protection role. Besides, the U-boat had not yet shed its sheep's clothing.

From the start, German submarines significantly impacted a wide range of operational and tactical considerations that included safety and security of fleet anchorages, training and freedom of movement – the safety of gunnery ranges, the increased need for protective screening and the decreased freedom of movement in southern North Sea waters. Such considerations determined how Jellicoe would seek a northern North Sea battle and his anticipation of German Fleet tactics.[36]

### SEA MINES

On the second day of war, German mines claimed their first victim: the British cruiser HMS *Amphion* was sunk 30 miles off the coast of Suffolk with the loss of 151 lives.[37] Mines accounted for around '23 per cent of the 78 battleships and cruisers lost between 1914 and 1918, 57 per cent of the 120 destroyers lost, 27 per cent of the 170 submarines'.[38] For the British, it was 'responsible for a minimum of 48 U-boat sinkings'.[39] British minelaying forces were significantly increased in 1917. In January, the force consisted of 'four merchant ships and one flotilla leader'. By the year's end, another twelve cruisers and twelve destroyers (or flotilla leaders), plus three submarines, had been added.[40]

The Germans did not initially mine their own harbour approaches, 'for fear of catching their own capital ships'.[41] Sea mines needed to account for ships passing overhead at high and low tide. But nor did they 'systematically' mine Scapa Flow's approaches.[42] Both quickly recognised the effectiveness of the submarine for the task.

At the end of 1915, there were two British standard mines, both using hydrostatic pistols at 40ft and 80ft settings: the Type D, which contained 300lbs of Amatol, and a smaller Type D* with 120lbs of HE. The former was available in January 1916 but was in such short supply that most A/S vessels were only allowed two mines. Instability was another problem – two exploded on the deck of the cruiser HMS *Blonde* as she was sub-hunting off Scapa. Another type of A/S weapon was the 'explosive sweep', explosive charges attached to a line towed astern of a ship and electrically detonated over a submarine. With design improvements, relatively small, 80lb mines could be strung along the wire. By the end of 1915, a more sophisticated version was made with the destroyer paravane. The explosive version only claimed one victim: *UB.69*, sunk on 9 January 1918 by the escort sloop *Cyclamen*.

The mine's use in ASW wasn't anticipated: Bacon explained that 'our mines were designed for use against ships'.[43] As a result, minefields were initially laid at depths far too shallow for submarines. With low water, German submariners were able to navigate around mines, clearly visible on the surface like 'caviar on toast'.[44] If a captain decided not to wait, he could go through a minefield, trying to avoid snagging a mooring cable which pulled the mine down towards his hull. Despite hearing the sound of the cables grating along the hull being an unnerving experience, in 'virtually every instance the cable parted'.[45] How mines were laid varied; they could be anchored to the sea floor, attached to static nets or to sweeps, and laid both by surface and subsurface craft.[46] The 'Indicator Net' was suspended from buoys which would 'indicate' the presence of an enemy submarine enmeshed by obvious movement, or released a buoy which would light up a flare. Some versions could be towed behind a drifter at very slow speed: 'the most effective use for these nets was found to be in conjunction with electro-contact mines' ('E.C. Mine nets').[47]

The British developed a new mine based upon the German *Horn* mine, the 'H' mine, copied 'nut for nut and bolt for bolt'.[48] Orders for 100,000 H2 mines were placed, the first 1,500 being ready in September 1917.[49] Writing to Sims, Jellicoe said that he'd ordered them before tests had even been concluded because the need was so great and 'as [he] expected success'.[50] Five hundred of the September delivery were sown in the Heligoland Bight, and over the next three months 10,389 were laid there and at Dover.[51] The mine 'changed the contempt of the enemy for British mines into a wholesome fear and respect'.[52] Submarine sinkings 'rose dramatically from two to sixteen between the first and second half of 1917, compared to four losses overall in 1916'.[53] One important casualty was *U.20*'s Walther Schwieger, now commanding *U.88* and trying to run the Horns Reef barrier on 7 September. The explosion was so large that speculation had it that one of the new H2 mines probably detonated its bow torpedo load. In October, other submarines were caught in barrage nets: on 3 October, *UC.14* was sunk by a mine off Zeebrügge, and on 9 October, *U.106* was trapped in the Bight.

## HMS *Birmingham* Claims the First U-boat

When no British fleet appeared in southern waters, the Germans planned a submarines sortie. Ten vessels set off into the North Sea: 'They fully realized for the first time they had their chance to prove what a submarine could do under wartime conditions.'[54] On 6 August, the U-boat's leash was untethered.

The first operation proved disappointing. *U-9* turned back with engine problems, while the others – *U.5*, *U.7*, *U.8*, *U.13*, *U.14*, *U.15*, *U.16*, *U.17* and *U.18* – continued spaced out in a patrol line 7 miles long. *U.13* was lost; her fate, following her last contact on 12 August, is unknown.[55] *U.16* ran aground in Lerwick harbour but eventually managed to get free.

*U.15* came across three potential targets – HMS *Ajax*, *Orion* and *Monarch*. Kapitänleutnant Richard Poehle launched one of her six 17.7in torpedoes at *Monarch* but missed.[56] This abortive attack was probably 'the first torpedo ever to be fired in anger' in the First World War, and, significantly, at a naval vessel.[57]

That same evening, 9 August, a periscope was spotted from both HMS *Iron Duke* and HMS *Dreadnought*. They hunted the submarine, but it was hopeless. A few hours later, HMS *Birmingham* reported a submarine 'either on the surface or breaking the surface in the heavy swell', close to Fair Isle, Shetland.[58] It was Poehle's *U.15*, apparently repairing her engines on the surface. It was reported that banging noises were heard from inside the closed hull, but that would have been highly unlikely.[59]

On Captain Duff's orders, the cruiser swung around, guns opening fire, and at full steam bore down on a target a tenth of her own size, the 512-ton submarine. Even though they had little in the way of tactics or equipment designed for the purpose, the attack was successful:

> She turned quickly and rammed, striking the submarine aft, a glancing blow. The enemy boat came up astern, showing her number *U.15* and appeared to be turning towards the *Birmingham* to attack. The *Birmingham* opened fire with all 6-inch guns that would bear, turned and rammed the submarine amidships at full speed, cutting her in half. The submarine sank at once and no bodies came to the surface.[60]

Arthur Duff's actions accounted for the deaths of the twenty-three German submariners on board.[61] She went down with all hands, '*untergegangen mit Mann und Maus*'.[62] Ironically, 'Eight weeks earlier, the 5,440-ton *Birmingham* was a welcome guest at the Kiel Regatta.'[63] Her attack was met with disbelief and Jellicoe had been taken completely by surprise; the German base was 450 miles distant. All three incidents occurred north of the 58th parallel, and,

> it seemed incredible (at the time) that enemy submarines could be operating so far from home … the Commander-in-Chief concluded that the enemy submarines must be operating from an advanced base, possibly on the Norwegian coast.[64]

In September, another series of attacks on Scapa Flow had everyone on edge again. After HMS *Falmouth* signalled a sighting around 1800hrs, she and HMS *Vanguard* started firing at what was thought to be a periscope. Jellicoe sent two units, the 11st Light Cruiser Squadron (LCS) and 2nd Destroyer Flotilla, to join the search. When HMS *Drake* also 'spotted' a submarine, Jellicoe ordered the whole fleet to weigh anchor. It showed the Royal Navy's lack of preparation, both in building adequate defences for the principal northern base and in the lack of suitable active countermeasures.

Around 2100hrs, the Grand Fleet left the anchorage in 'exceedingly thick' weather. Jellicoe felt that 'protection against submarine attack was an absolute necessity, as the Fleet could not remain at a base that was open to this form of attack'.[65] What now transpired was a 'naval form of the shell game', moving the fleet from one location to the next.[66] Late afternoon on 4 September, the Grand Fleet's dreadnoughts arrived at a new base, Loch Ewe, on Scotland's north-west coast just north-east of Skye: 'The fact that the great battleship [HMS *Iron Duke*] was anchored in Loch Ewe and not at Scapa Flow was in itself testimony to the power of the submarine threat.'[67] They would remain there for seventeen days.[68] A month later, a submarine was sighted and the fleet moved yet again.[69]

Security concerns dominated the war's opening months. The *Royal Oak*'s loss in the opening months of the Second World War is sufficient proof of the potential threat that submarines could represent, even if in the First World War no British dreadnought was ever successfully torpedoed, but 'it was not until the middle of 1915 that the base [Scapa Flow] could be considered reasonably safe'.[70] Jellicoe was critical of the slow progress on the installation of A/S defences:

> [I]t is, I regret to say, entirely erroneous to imagine that submarine-proof-harbours will be completed by the middle of November. The situation at Scapa Flow is that only about 300 feet of obstruction has at present been laid out of a total length of about four miles and only a length of about one mile has actually arrived in the port.[71]

Jellicoe would use the intervening months to close off insecure channels by sinking blockships and by adding defences to Hoxa Sound, where batteries were built on either side of the Channel. The added strain was only alleviated when he could spend more time with an old friend, Sir Stanley Colville, recently promoted to vice admiral commanding the Orkneys and Shetland.

Churchill probably shared Jellicoe's frustration, as he was trying to persuade him to move the Grand Fleet to Rosyth. One of his arguments was that 'the inner line of anti-submarine defences has been completed and is thoroughly satisfactory; [while] the outer line is almost completed'.[72] Jellicoe needed little persuading:

> There is no doubt that strategically Rosyth has the greater advantages. I have constantly recognised this point in communications with the Admiralty.[73]

Another 'plus' for Rosyth was the 'wear and tear' on warships steaming further north to Scapa, as well as the trains taking coal to the northernmost point of the British Isles. In May 1916, Jellicoe expressed these same thoughts: moving the Grand Fleet south would bring it 30 miles closer to Denmark and 130 miles closer to the Dutch coast, 'the two possible places where a battle might take place'.[74] Consolidating the two fleets at one base would probably also better leverage the Grand Fleet's limited destroyer and smaller A/S resources. At a meeting with Beatty and the Sea Lords on 25 June, he agreed to the use of a common base at Rosyth for both the Battle Fleet and the Battlecruiser Fleet.

### HMS *Pathfinder* – The First Successful Submarine Torpedo Attack

Further south, Kapitänleutnant Otto Hersing was operating off the Firth of Forth's May Island, where, on 5 September at 1545hrs, the 2,490-ton cruiser HMS *Pathfinder* was torpedoed by *U.21*. It was the first time a modern warship had been sunk by a submarine.[75] She sank so fast that only one of her lifeboats was lowered and 256 men from a crew of 268 were lost. The kaiser proclaimed Hersing's success 'a ray of light'.[76] Among some British officers, it was scarcely believable a submarine could have done this: 'the report that the *Pathfinder* was sunk by a submarine, and not a mine, is completely untrue and a fabrication', wrote one midshipman, at the time serving on HMS *Crescent*, part of Dudley de Chair's Northern Patrol.[77]

#### KAPITÄNLEUTNANT OTTO HERSING (1885–1960)

While Otto Hersing doesn't rank as one of Germany's top ten aces, he was a formidable U-boat commander who came to be known as the *Zerstörer von Schlachtschiffen* (destroyer of battleships).

After serving in the Mediterranean, Hersing returned to the North Sea. In August 1917, attacking a fifteen-ship convoy south-west of Ireland, he changed tactics to take *U.21* very close to make depth-charging more dangerous for the escorting destroyers and increasing their risk of damaging their own transports.

Hersing sank a total of forty ships or 113,580 GRT, including two pre-dreadnought battleships (*Triumph* and *Majestic*) and two cruisers (*Pathfinder* and the *Amiral Charnier*).

The day before, *U.21* had silently sneaked directly past where Commander Ryan was stationed at Inchkeith. He was working on early ideas of what would eventually become asdic.[78] It was also supremely ironic that the torpedo that struck *Pathfinder* was a 19.69in Type G Whitehead. Its designer, Robert Whitehead, was an Englishman from Bolton.

Hersing was always confident of the submarine as a new weapon. Alone, he had tried to break up the passage of the British Expeditionary Force (BEF) to France, and while ultimately unsuccessful, he still brought back valuable intelligence. A second vessel, Werner Fürbringer's *U.20*, accompanied Hersing and also 'returned empty handed'.[79] That October, *U.20* was ordered to attack Canadian transports disembarking troops at Boulogne. After having successfully found a way through the mined barrage, no ships showed up.

A week or so later, on 3 October, Britain moved to protect what it thought an obvious threat to BEF supply lines. Thirteen submarines from Roger Keyes's Harwich-based forces were ordered to provide a screen, spread along a picket line from the North Goodwin Sands to Ruytingen Shoals. At the same time, a new minefield east of the Dover–Calais line was to be laid; the German Navy had lost an extraordinary opportunity.

## Scapa Flow's Undefended Refuge

As the Commander-in-Chief, Jellicoe witnessed first-hand the poverty of available ASW against the initial threat in the Grand Fleet's major anchorages. At Scapa, nervous sailors and an epidemic of 'periscopitis' led to a significant increase in reported submarine sightings.

> As long as he could keep his fleet at sea, the Commander-in-Chief felt he could cope with the submarine menace for he had adequate destroyer screens to protect his battle fleet.[80]

Scapa Flow had nine different routes which vessels could use, 'three of which were considered navigable by the largest ships'.[81] The 1 September incident had already prompted Jellicoe to move the Grand Fleet from Scapa Flow to Loch Ewe, but after a second incident on 16 October, he decided to steam even further south-west to Lough Swilly in Northern Ireland.[82] The second incident – probably the result of a seal being mistaken for a periscope – caused panicked firing into the waters of the Flow and jokingly became known as 'The First Battle of Scapa'. After a U-boat had been reported in the late afternoon, the fleet returned to Lough Swilly, with some squadrons assigned to Loch na Keal on Scotland's western isle of Mull, a little south of Loch Ewe.[83] Swilly was thought a safe location, as its relatively shallow waters made navigation difficult for submarines and because soldiers based at Fort Dunree added extra security as they could watch the lough entrance. Beatty was despondent, writing to Churchill that 'we have no place to lay our heads ... we must have a place where we can stop for four or five days now and then to give the engineers a chance. Such a place does not exist.'[84] The Grand Fleet did not return to Scapa until 9 November.

On 17 November, Jellicoe moved the Grand Fleet across to Scotland's west coast, the battlecruisers dropping anchor in Loch na Keal. Beatty's Flag Captain, Ernle Chatfield, could not hide his damaged pride:

> Here was a pretty kettle of fish. The great Fleet was homeless and insecure, like American colonists chased by stealthy Red Indians.[85]

The great dreadnoughts, the colossal fighting machines on which the fortunes of a nation had been spent, were now threatened by a lesser naval power's submarines.

A week later, *U.18*, on her third mission, was successfully rammed and was scuttled. After an encounter with a trawler badly damaged the submarine's periscope, Hennig surfaced to make repairs on the bilge pump. All twenty-two crew members except one were picked up. The very next day, Bruno Hoppe tried a second time to penetrate Scapa Flow's defences, but *U.22*'s engine was playing up, not giving him enough power to fight the dangerously powerful currents of the Pentland Firth.

Hennig was captured, and with him stayed the secret of Scapa Flow's shockingly ineffective defences. He was unable to radio any details of the vital discovery. Even if the German Navy was not aware of Scapa's weaknesses, these encounters made Jellicoe deeply anxious. It would not be until the Second World War that Whitehall really grasped the danger. Funds and resources to build a proper defence of the Flow only came about when the Churchill Barriers were built by Italian POW labour following the *Royal Oak*'s sinking. Jellicoe had similar misgivings about Invergordon at Cromarty and Rosyth on the Firth of Forth. This episode was just another nail in the coffin.[86]

Again, on 3 December, in an eerie premonition of *U.47*'s audaciously successful attack on the *Royal Oak* twenty-five years later, using the same access through the Holm channel, a German submarine penetrated the Flow's eastern entrance. Luckily, even though she escaped, *U.47* was spotted by a guard destroyer, the *Garry*.[87]

### The Shock Wave of a Triple Sinking – HMS *Aboukir*, *Cressy* and *Hogue*

Although one opportunity was lost, another was grasped: on 22 September, cruising off the Hook of Holland, Kapitänleutnant Otto Weddigen managed to sink three British warships, the *Cressy*, *Aboukir* and *Hogue*.

The three British ships were 'steaming in formation, two miles apart, 10 knots'.[88] The old armoured cruisers were first spotted by Johann Spiess, Weddigen's First Officer (or the 'Heinrich', as all watch officers were fondly nicknamed). On a U-boat at sea, a disciplined watch was fundamental. Especially when a target was sighted, all watch officers had to maintain a rigorous focus on their assigned quadrant – 'too often has it happened that when everyone is staring at the object of interest, the U-boat has been caught unawares'.[89] Weddigen was below having breakfast, but he decided to attack even though the batteries had not yet fully charged.

The first to be hit, at 500 yards, was *Aboukir*, *U.9*'s torpedo slamming into her starboard beam just after 0720hrs. At the same instant *U.9* fired her 'Eel' and the boat 'porpoised', raising her bow above water with the sudden adjustment in weight. *Aboukir*'s bow 'was high and the ram stuck above the surface of the sea'.[90] The crew thought she'd hit a mine.

A little later, at 0755hrs, Weddigen sent two more torpedoes on their way, this time aiming at the *Hogue*, only 300 yards distant. She immediately sank to a depth of 15 metres. Weddigen used the time to reload, although *U.9* was having a tough time in the swell and was pitching heavily up and down. As the submarine 'bumped', he ordered the crew to run to the stern, stopping the rapid lift which threatened to break the surface. Having succeeded, the bow now posed the same problem. Despite her own mortal damage, *Hogue*'s guns opened fire as the *U.9* broke the surface. Spiess recalled the scene:

> The periscope revealed a fearful picture. The giant with four funnels turned slowly over to port. Men climbed like ants over her side and then, she turned turtle completely, they ran about on her broad flat keel until, in a few minutes, she disappeared beneath the waves.[91]

Within five minutes, *Hogue*'s quarterdeck was awash; within another ten, she had joined the *Aboukir*. Two stern torpedo shots put paid to the third ship, *Cressy*. The first missed – by 20ft – but the second exploded on her port beam. To be sure, Weddigen swung the submarine, now almost completely out of electrical power, around 180 degrees and launched another bow shot at the stricken cruiser. Weddigen paid tribute to his adversary. Talking of the *Cressy*, he spoke with professional admiration: 'Her men stayed at their guns looking for their … foes. They were brave [and] true to their country's sea traditions.'[92]

It was a stunning achievement. The 493-ton submarine had just claimed three cruisers, each displacing more than 12,000 tons, even if Spiess later said that 'the minimizing effect of the single-lens periscope had caused us greatly to underestimate the size of our prey'.[93] In total, 1,460 British sailors went down with their ships. It was a horrendous loss of life – 'two-thirds more than the

### KAPITÄNLEUTNANT OTTO WEDDIGEN (1882–1915)

Otto Weddigen became a household name. On 11 March 1915, when taking the surrender of a merchant ship, the *Aden-wen*, one of her crew fell overboard and he sent over dry clothes. After sinking the French steamer *Auguste Conseil*, he asked the master 'to present his compliments to Lord [*sic*] Churchill' (Gray, *Captains*, p.38). On 12 March 1915, after sinking three British merchant ships, he stayed surfaced for three hours to make sure that the crews were able to get to their boats and then stopped a French sail ship to ask them to take the merchant crews on board. Once he broke his arm, diving into the North Sea to rescue one of his crew members.

Weddigen joined the submarine service in 1910 and was part of, along with eight other officer trainees, the crew that managed to escape from the *U.3* when she sunk in Kiel Harbour on 17 January 1911. Twenty-eight men managed to squeeze through the 17.7in diameter torpedo tube when she was raised and held in position by a crane. Three officers did not make it – two were dead when the hatch was opened, while the third died before reaching hospital. Two years later, in May 1913, he managed to successfully 'hit' three battleships in a four-torpedo training salvo.

Awarded Germany's highest decoration, the *Pour le Mérite*, his second command, *U.29*, was sunk by HMS *Dreadnought*. Weddigen died with all hands.

number Nelson lost at Trafalgar'.[94] Among the dead were thirteen boys who had just arrived from Dartmouth Training College, the youngest of whom was just 14. In an unusually fair commentary, the *Daily Mail* wrote: 'It would be idle to deny that the exploit reflects the greatest credit on the German submarine service.'[95]

One poor sailor was three times unlucky: Wenman 'Kit' Wykeham-Musgrave had been on the *Aboukir*, then had swum to the *Hogue* only to find that she was next and finally ended up on *Cressy*. The only good luck he had was that he was picked up by a Dutch ship, *Titan*. Extraordinarily, the 15-year-old midshipman went on to serve again in the Second World War.

Weddigen was awarded the Iron Cross, 1st and 2nd class, his entire crew the Iron Cross, 2nd class. The medal's design became Weddigen's *U.9*'s conning tower crest; every subsequent *U.9* was allowed the same privilege. Three months later, the French Navy's 25,000-ton battleship, the *Jean Bart*, was torpedoed by the Austro-Hungarian submarine, *U.XII*, in what was described by one writer as 'the Austro-Hungarian navy's "Weddigen moment"'. The sinking was celebrated the same way as in Germany.[96] The submarine would sink a year later while attempting to enter the heavily guarded waters around Venice's *Arsenale*. The bodies of her crew remain buried in the Venetian lagoon cemetery island of San Michele. Like Germany's Weddigen, Ergon Lerch became a national hero and was awarded the Knights Cross of the Order of Leopold, and his entire crew was decorated.

### The Loss of HMS *Hawke*

The presence of U-boats, sighted off Aberdeen, was signalled by the sinking of the 7,350-ton Edgar-class cruiser HMS *Hawke,* now part of Dudley de Chair's 10th Cruiser Squadron. Her name embraced a proud tradition previously associated with five other naval ships. It was also associated with her collision, in 1911, with *Titanic*'s sister ship, the *Olympic,* off the Isle of Wight, following which her stern section had to be replaced.

On 13 October, the *U.9* left Wilhelmshaven, along with *U.18*, bound for Scapa Flow. Technical problems led to her switching places with Johannes Feldkirchner's *U.17.* Just off Aberdeen, she spotted cruisers protecting troop transports with around 30,000 Canadian troops on board. However, it was impossible for Weddigen to keep up, let alone find a suitable firing solution, as the British had now started using zigzag as an effective evasive manoeuvre:

> They continually altered course; they varied their speed, sometimes moving at 7 knots and sometimes spurting up to 14 knots. They were infinitely more difficult targets since the whole problem of approaching and attacking them changed from minute to minute.[97]

The tactic seemed to work; Spiess and Weddigen 'gave up all hope and went below'.[98] The Grand Fleet's tactics had changed fundamentally:

> Before it became clear that the submarine was a true sea going threat and that it could attack at anytime and anywhere in the open sea, big ships could maintain relatively low speeds – the Grand Fleet's battleships pottered around at no more than 10 knots in the opening weeks of the war and sometimes less than that. This not only reduced fuel consumption in itself, it allowed something even more important. Coal bunkers were distributed around the ship … the physical constraints were such that it was later estimated that at 14 knots or more – the cruising speed of the Grand Fleet during the war – at least 25% of the coal was inaccessible.[99]

Around 0930hrs, *Hawke* briefly stopped to pick up the mail from a sister ship, HMS *Endymian*. The trailing German submarine observed a small cutter being lowered:

> I gazed at the little picture on the upper ocean. The distant three cruisers (*Hawke*, *Endymion* and *Theseus*) were some wide space apart, but were converging, and were steering for a point, and that point was apparently in the vicinity where we lay. No wonder the Commander thought they must want a torpedo … we steered at full speed for the point toward which they were heading, our periscope showing only for a few moments at a time.[100]

After the pick-up, *Hawke* left to retake her position. She held back another fifteen minutes to recover the cutter but now only steamed at a leisurely 13 knots and without zigzagging. She might have been going even more slowly: according to Alexander Scrimgeour, then a young midshipman on HMS *Crescent*, her captain, Hugh Williams, had requested that the ship stay an additional two days to repair her engines, which would only give him 10 knots. It was a sign of her age that when she was launched in 1891, *Hawke* had been able to make a full 20 knots. The normal procedure for ships in the Moray Firth was to run at 17 knots because of the danger of submarines. Supposedly, the admiral in question – de Chair – refused the request. Williams was leaving the *Crescent*'s quarterdeck and was overheard muttering to his 'Flags': 'It is pure murder sending the ship with over 500 officers and men on board to sea in this state.'[101] Scrimgeour recalled that since the account of the incident was 'strictly confidential', he had to remain silent, on pain of 'dismissal from the service'.[102] Only too late, the submarine was spotted, manoeuvring to line up a shot.

At 1050hrs, *U.9* was able to launch a bow shot at 500 yards. The track was seen: 'I was on the bridge in the forenoon watch when an Able Seaman said to me, "I don't like the look o' that." And then we saw the bubbles … Oh, the bubbles.'[103] The ship was hit 'abreast of the fore funnel', destroying her engine room and giving her no chance to raise any steam. According to a stoker:

> Those on deck, for an instant immediately after the explosion, saw the periscope of submarine which showed above the water like a broomstick.[104]

Seen through the periscope, *Hawke*

> manoeuvered for a shot … she nearly ran us down. We had to dive deeper and let her pass over us, else we would have been rammed. Now we were

> in a position for a stern shot at an angle, but she turned. It was a fatal turning, for it gave us an opportunity to swing around for a clear bow shot at 400 metres ... We dived beyond periscope depth, ran underwater for a short distance, and then came up for a look ... The *Hawke* had already disappeared. She sank in eight minutes. Only one boat was in the water. It was the mail dory that had been lowered before the torpedo explosion.[105]

Another survivor, lamenting the loss of life, wrote:

> We were struck right amidships between the two funnels, quite close to one of the magazines. All hands were on deck, and it was a terrible explosion. The vessel immediately took a heavy list to starboard. I have never been on a ship so well equipped with life-saving apparatus, but the way the vessel heeled over made it almost impossible to get the boats out. The boat in which I was saved had a narrow escape from being taken down with the suction. We were struck about 11 o'clock in the forenoon, and just as we got away from the *Hawke*, we distinctly saw the periscope of the enemy's submarine come to the surface. We thought he was going to ram us, but apparently he was on the lookout for any other rescuing vessels. Prior to the accident the *Hawke* was cruising about zigzag fashion, and we never saw the submarine until we felt her. It was beginning to get hazy when we were almost run down by the Norwegian steamer which picked us up. This boat, after affecting the rescue, cruised about in search of the rafts, but nothing was seen.[106]

Some press reports said that she sank in between four or five minutes; the submarine's own log reported the 7,890-ton 'protected' cruiser sank in eight minutes. No matter the actual time, her death came so fast that she couldn't fight back; 'an attempt to man the guns was made but, owing to the extra acute list of the vessel, it was found impossible to train them on the submerged craft.'[107] When a fuel tank exploded, fire spread rapidly; the fight was over.

No one noticed her absence until they turned back. At 1320hrs, Feldkirchner went after *Hawke*'s sister ship, HMS *Theseus*. *U.17*'s torpedo missed and she nearly paid for her impudence with her life, Feldkirchner admitted: 'A second more and we would have got the full murderous impact of the ram bow.'[108]

Five hundred and twenty-four men were lost on Hawke. About seventy were saved; fifty-two of them (including three officers) were picked up by a Norwegian steamer, the *Modasta*, and later transferred to a trawler, the *Ben Rinnes*. The Lord Mayor of Hull awarded her captain, Isak Swedswig, a gold watch and each of her crew £2.[109] After racing out from Scapa, a destroyer, HMS

*Swift*, found another twenty men and one officer. Hugh Williams, her captain, was among the dead. Like the September triple-ship sinking, there were many young cadets on board, and because *Hawke* had spent time training based in Queenstown, County Cork, forty-nine of her dead were Irish.

Come November, the Edgar-class cruisers were finally replaced by 'armed liners'.[110] Many had been badly damaged in a storm, but it was clear that they were simply too old to do the job.

### The Loss of HMS *Audacious*

On 27 October, HMS *Audacious*, only commissioned in 1913, hit a mine near Tory Island and sank as she was being towed back to an anchorage in Northern Ireland's Lough Swilly. Jellicoe ordered a news blackout, but his decision to withhold the ship's fate was widely criticised. Some justification came later, after the war, when the third Commander-in-Chief of the German High Seas Fleet, Reinhard Scheer, wrote:

> In the case of the *Audacious* we approve of the English attitude of not revealing a weakness to the enemy, because accurate information about the other side's strength has a decisive effect on the decisions taken.

After the losses, however, Jellicoe wrote to Churchill:

> I *long* for a submarine defence at Scapa; it would give such a feeling of confidence … if a submarine did get in, she practically has the British Dreadnought Fleet at her mercy up to the number of her torpedoes.[111]

Beatty was equally disturbed, saying that it 'was only Divine Providence that has saved us from an appalling disaster'.[112]

Elsewhere, Jellicoe commented:

> [T]he German mind could not believe that we would be such fools as to place our Fleet in a position where it was open to submarine or destroyer attack … If the Germans had half a dozen men of the stamp of our submarine commanders, we should now be a German colony.[113]

Before the year was out, in the English Channel, the submarine would again show the risks awaiting warships: on 31 October, *U.27* successfully torpedoed another old cruiser, the 5,600-ton *Hermes*. Two weeks later, on 11 November, just off Deal, the 810-ton gunboat HMS *Niger* was also sunk by *U.2*, the first submarine to use the new Flanders base. There were only seventy-seven survivors.

### *Glitra* – The First Attack on Merchant Shipping

On 20 October 1914, an 866-ton British steamer, the SS *Glitra*, carrying almost 2,000 tons of coal, coke and oil for Stavanger, became the first merchant ship to be sunk by a U-boat. Kapitänleutnant Johannes Feldkirchner was aboard *U.17* off the Norwegian coast, returning from the earlier sortie with Weddigen. He spotted the British merchant ship and pulled up alongside 7 miles off the Norwegian coast after having given a series of signals: 'Heave to immediately otherwise I will shoot' and 'Abandon ship immediately'.

A prize party with three crewmen was sent across and, as *U.17* did not have a deck gun, mounted a light machine gun on deck. *Glitra*'s crew was given ten minutes to disembark and Captain H.E. Johnston was ordered, at pistol point, to lower the British flag. Claims that Feldkirchner tore up the flag, then trampled on it in a fit of pique, seem likely fabricated. Other reports that she carried sewing machines and whisky made her cargo appear innocent and commonplace. After her sea cocks were opened, she sank in fifteen minutes. The submarine then towed her passengers and sixteen crew in two lifeboats towards the Norwegian coast.[114] German reports say that the boats were released when two pilot boats were seen approaching.[115] So confusing were the rules, that Feldkirchner was worried 'he might get a court martial for an unauthorized sinking'.[116] Just the opposite: when he got back, every man in the submarine's crew 'breathed easier when the Commander-in-Chief of the Fleet expressed his agreement with his conduct'.[117]

Following the mining of HMS *Audacious* on 3 November, the British declared the North Sea a military zone, making it look like a reaction to German mining. This allowed them to lay their own minefields. It also prompted von Pohl to seriously start thinking about a retaliatory *Handelskrieg*. He had originally been 'lukewarm' and 'felt that it would be a serious violation of international law' as it was 'not yet justified by the infringements of that law already committed by England'.[118] Jellicoe felt that between Pohl and von Ingenohl, Pohl 'has the greater experience', even if he found him 'not very healthy, always very white and transparent looking'.[119] Writing to Beatty, he was not above poking some fun at his 'taciturn' counterpart: the German, he wrote, 'looks as if he had lost half-a-crown and found sixpence'.[120]

The *Glitra* sinking had shown that the submarine *could* be used against merchant ships while respecting Prize Rules. It was 'a model demonstration of compliance with the rules of war', even if it heralded a new phase in the war at sea, '*einen Wendepunkt in der Geschichte des Seekrieges*'.[121] It was, nevertheless, surprising that Feldkirchner succeeded in getting the *Glitra* to come to a stop, given that *U.17* wasn't equipped with a deck gun.

Very soon, *U.21* and *U.17*'s actions were followed by others – *U.5*, *U.11*, *U.12* and *U.24*. Feldkirchner's restraint contrasted starkly with a fellow commander, Kapitänleutnant Rudolf Schneider. On 24 October, he attacked the 4,950-ton French steamer, *Amiral Ganteaume.* Despite 2,500 Belgian refugees being on board, Schneider attemped to torpedo her without warning, claiming after the ensuing outcry that he thought her a troopship.[122] At first, a mine was blamed for the explosion.[123] Schneider's actions would have complied with the London Declaration if she had been carrying troops.[124] *Glitra*'s name is remembered, as she was the first merchant vessel 'sunk' by a U-boat (scuttled by charges), but the attempted torpedoing of the *Amiral Ganteaume* sounded a far more ominous warning. More than forty civilians were killed, many from the ensuing panic. Around fifteen passengers were drowned; some had been seen swimming away from another ship, the *Queen*, coming to her rescue. Many had been pushed overboard by their fellow passengers uncontrollably surging forward. 'One woman, carrying a small child, jumped at the wrong moment, fell between the two ships and they too were crushed.'[125] In 1919, King George V awarded an MBE to her captain, Robert Carey. They'd met two years earlier and the king realised that there was a 'gap in the honour system' that failed to recognise the courage of non-combatants.[126]

In October, Kapitänleutnant Otto Dröscher secretly circumnavigated the United Kingdom around the northern coast of Scotland in *U.20.* The achievement's significance would become clear when the Dover Strait route became too dangerous. Dröscher's successor as commander of the ill-reputed *U.20*, Walther Schwieger, would attain an altogether different reputation, being remembered in history as the man who sank the *Lusitania.*

On 3 November, Hersing's *U.21* forced another French steamer, the *Malachite*, to a stop. After the ship's papers had been examined and the crew taken off, *U.21*'s deck-mounted 37mm gun sank her close to Le Havre. The U-boat threat in the Channel was mounting. Three days later, again respecting Cruiser Rules, *U.21* sank another merchantman, the collier SS *Primo.*

On 19 November, the first U-boat entered the Zeebrügge docks. The arrival of Walter Forstmann's *U.12* marked a significant day. On 29 March 1915, more boats followed, and within three months a full flotilla would be based there. The new base gave U-boats 'an average savings of two-and-a-half days on all distant operations'.[127]

### Testing the Waters – The Tirpitz Interview

After the war, authoritative commentators such as Karl Spindler and Reinhard Scheer both denied any pre-war planning for submarines to attack merchant ships. Scheer even protested that 'such aggressive ideas were quite foreign to our naval policy', and that it was only later that the policy of *a guerre de course* was adopted 'under the necessity of defending ourselves and when we recognized the magnitude of the disaster which England had planned for us'.[128]

By the first winter, the British blockade was starting to bite. It was also clear that the war was going to be considerably more challenging.

In an exclusive interview on 21 December 1914 with the Berlin representative of 700 Americans, newspaper journalist Karl von Wiegand, Tirpitz tested the waters by putting forward the idea of launching a submarine war on British shipping. Tirpitz was asked by Wiegand if Germany was considering the same methods (of blockade) that they had been subject to. Tirpitz was succinct:

> Why not? England wants to starve us. We can play the same game, surround England, torpedo any English ship or any of its allies that come near any port in England or Scotland, and thereby cut off the greater part of the food supply.

He added: 'In larger submarines we are superior to England'.[129]

According to Tirpitz, the severity of the British blockade was adequate justification for Germany's counter-blockade, an unrestricted submarine war against British commerce. Published a few days later, Tirpitz's interview was a direct attack on Chancellor Bethmann-Hollweg's public position and significantly encouraged stronger German public support for an aggressive submarine war. Not surprisingly, the interview annoyed the same people who might have been allied to his cause. Pohl found it 'extremely unfortunate that our military plans have been disclosed' and found himself siding with Bethmann-Hollweg:[130]

> Is it wrong to make the public aware of our intentions now without us being certain that our military resources are sufficient to carry out a submarine war against England?[131]

The kaiser was 'very upset' and tried to get Pohl to discount the whole episode as some kind of mistake. Pohl couldn't do this, as the scenario was likely to happen. Since Bethmann-Hollweg had some forewarning of the interview, he might actually have 'turned a blind eye' and used it as a means of testing American public opinion: 'the chancellor allowed Tirpitz to do the dirty work'.[132] It might have been the case that the Foreign Ministry 'blunderingly failed' to abort the interview: 'its publication could have been stopped'.[133]

The problem was that the interview gave real power to the public – the voters who would influence Woodrow Wilson and German policymakers – and thus restricted the politicians, painting them into a corner. As von Pohl put it:

> Publicly, the enemies were advised to prepare for a U-boat blockade; publicly, the German people were made aware of their possession of an infallible weapon. From this point on, it was impossible to tear the submarine from the heart of the nation.[134]

On 2 February, Arthur Zimmermann met with the American Ambassador, James Gerard, and, raising the issue of German civilians starving, said that it was quite possible that Germany might retaliate with its own blockade. He apparently added that the situation could be escalated if Germany blockaded France's northern and western ports, to cut off British troops and supplies from reaching the Western Front.

### Jellicoe's Initial Reappraisal of the U-boat Threat

Jellicoe thought 'it was courting disaster' to base British capital ships at Scapa Flow as long as it remained undefended.[135] The German submarine had evolved speedily into a highly effective offensive weapon. The Germans had significantly rethought the definition of the submarine's theatre of operations: with no significant use of British warships in German coastal waters, the submarine's coastal defence role was shelved. The improvements in range and endurance had taken Jellicoe and many fellow officers by surprise. After the initial shock of Weddigen's triple cruiser attack, the *Hawke* episode proved the U-boat's ability to operate effectively in northern waters.

After the 16 December raid on Hartlepool and Scarborough, Jellicoe 'express[ed] his astonishment that the Germans had not used the submarines in joint operations to cause the enemy forces to run into a trap'.[136] Furthermore, *U.21*'s bombardment of Barrow-in-Furness at the end of January 1915 highlighted the equal vulnerability of the west coast of England.

German submarines had also demonstrated that British submarines were equally valid targets. On 18 October, a U-boat sunk a British submarine off the German coast. Wegener's *U.27* had crept up on HMS *E.3* and successfully torpedoed her, after he had initially misidentified her conning tower number as '83' rather than 'E.3'. *U.27* stalked *E.3* for two hours, coming up on her 'up sun', where her two bridge lookouts had their backs turned. Two G6 torpedoes were launched. Wegener could see survivors in the water but, as he suspected other British submarines might be near, had to dive. When he returned, no survivors remained. All twenty-eight crew members had disappeared.

By October, Jellicoe had started to draw conclusions as to the submarine's impact on a future fleet action. On the 30th, he wrote to both Churchill and the Admiralty, concluding that since the Germans 'will endeavour to make full use of these weapons [submarines, mines and torpedoes] in a fleet action' he would aim 'to fight … in the northern portion of the North Sea' to push the endurance of these types of vessels to their limits and to his advantage. He noted his intention of refusing to follow an enemy that might 'turn away from an advancing fleet', as he felt this would represent a risk of being drawn over German mines and submarines.[137] Another concern was that minesweepers would only slow the fleet, making ships more vulnerable to torpedo attack. As a countermeasure, he recommended that battleships should never proceed at less than 12 knots and should vigorously zigzag, three points to either side. To the ever-cautious Jellicoe, the submarine put his dreadnoughts at risk, but, surprisingly, did not seem to worry him unduly so far as trade protection was concerned:

> It is suicidal to forego the advantageous position in the big ships by risking them in waters infested by submarines. The result might quite easily be such a weakening of our battle fleet and battlecruiser strength as seriously to jeopardise the future of the country by giving over to the Germans the command of the open seas. After all the submarine has a very limited sphere of action. *They can't hurt our over-sea commerce* [author's italics], nor can they help theirs to get in. So long as we retain our superior Sea-going Fleet they are powerless. Therefore, there seems to me to be no question whatever as to what course we should pursue. We have strangled German trade, and we could do this more effectively if we devoted ourselves entirely to it by using the Battle Fleet well up north spread to intercept trade … Only we must give up the idea – whilst so employed – of Southerly Battle Fleet movements … *We should not risk heavy ships till the submarine menace has been minimised* [author's italics].[138]

Jellicoe gives a very clear outline of much that would dictate his future actions, but some of his assumptions are very ill-informed about the 'over-sea commerce' threat that was developing. Equally, the talk of 'minimising' the submarine threat is accompanied by no *new* thinking as to how. He only mentions 'profitably' employing cruisers in submarine hunting.

### The Loss of HMS *Formidable*

As dawn broke on 1 January 1915, the lives of 547 hands were claimed from the complement of HMS *Formidable*. Flying the flag of Vice Admiral Sir Lewis Bayly, the 14,500-ton pre-dreadnought was in a tight formation of eight battleships escorted by two cruisers, 'holding an unswervingly straight course at a steady 10 knots' down the Channel.[139] Her slow speed courted disaster.

Rudolf Schneider missed his first opportunity at 0150hrs, but was soon handed another when the column reversed track back to Portland harbour.

*U.24* was waiting on the surface. At 0225hrs, a second torpedo was fired, this time hitting the last ship in the line, quickly flooding her boiler room. On *U.24*, one of the crew started up an old gramophone but was told to shut it off; it was too early to celebrate.[140] As *Formidable* began to settle, boats were lowered. At 0315hrs, Schneider's third 'eel' delivered the *coup de grâce*, but then he ran into trouble, *U.24* crashing into the sinking wreck and ending up on the seafloor 47 metres below. It was later discovered that the boat's two periscopes were both bent back at right angles. Despite her mortal wounds, it took the leviathan another seventy minutes before rolling over. Only 201 men survived; among the dead being Captain Loxley and thirty-four of his officers.[141] With the amount of time that had passed between the first strike and her sinking, it was extraordinary that the toll was so high. Eventually arriving back at Zeebrügge, Schneider and his crew were personally met and congratulated by Admiral Ludwig von Schröder of Marinekorps Flandern.

Reputedly, one of *Formidable*'s lifeboats had come ashore at Zeebrügge and was promptly put into the submariner's 'museum'. It was a grim artefact of the disaster. Forstner described another item in the same museum: a bronze propeller that had been embedded in a submarine's conning tower. Bayly, however, would have his revenge: two years later, he would become, with Jellicoe's support, the leading figure in the defence of the Western Approaches, with the help of William Sims and the first naval resources from the United States Navy. At Dover, the attack led to a renewed energy to strengthen the port's defences. Within weeks, a 17-mile-long barrage of indicator nets, guarded by armed drifters, was laid, and a new minefield was sown in the Channel off Deal.

**1915, Neutrality Challenged**

The war at sea knew no national boundaries; mines sank both friend and foe. Increasingly, the enforcement of the blockade brought the same outcome. With both countries separately declaring war zones, non-belligerent ships – including the men, women and sometimes children aboard – faced the same risks.

In 1915, the submarine war took a turn for the worse. It covered a wider area and now also included *any* civilian merchant shipping. Increasingly, the Royal Navy was seen to be failing and could no longer be counted upon for protection at sea.

While Americans viewed 'Freedom of the Seas' – the principle by which the natural 'law of the sea' protecting neutral vessels from sinking or seizure is respected – as an article of faith, their protests over British behaviour in the North Sea produced few results. They were rankled by apparent British high-handedness. Britain's merchant fleet was dominant – 'approximately half the merchant tonnage of the world'.[142]

## The Complexity of German Naval Command

Germany's various naval and political factions broke apart into opposing camps when it came to the question of how to conduct the naval war, particularly planning for the U-boat's role.

It did not help that the kaiser purposefully kept his senior naval command, unlike that of the army, fragmented. 'The kaiser acted as the sole conduit through which information passed from the military to the political sector and from the political sector to the military.'[143] It maintained his control. The kaiser wanted

> to be his own Commander-in-chief … [he] could not allow Tirpitz the power to unify command of the navy; he therefore placed Admiral Pohl in the position of Chief of the Naval Staff, making him the chief advisor to the kaiser on naval matters. Tirpitz's role as Secretary of State for Naval Affairs was therefore reduced to that of an operational advisor.[144]

In March 1899, Kaiser Wilhelm restructured his naval command, dissolving the old Oberkommando der Marine (OKM) and creating two new reporting structures. The Imperial Admiralty Staff (Admiralstab), whose primary role was planning and intelligence, survived in a subordinated role to Wilhelm and was kept small by Tirpitz so as not to pose too much competition. Tirpitz became head of the Naval Office (the Reichsmarine Amt, or RMA). In Germany's peacetime navy, the RMA was responsible for the navy's administrative running: its budgeting, design, construction needs, supply and manning, and was answerable to both the emperor and to the Chancellor. The Admiralstab and the RMA constantly intrigued against each other. In wartime, operational authority was split between the navy's Inspector-General and regional commanders and the head of the Admiralstab. Initially, no Fleet Commander-in-Chief was appointed, the role being held by the kaiser himself with the intention that the position would be filled annually for fleet exercises only. Not unnaturally, critical functions supporting army–navy liaison were non-existent.

In wartime, Admiral Georg Alexander von Müller, head of the Marine Kabinett, was responsible for personnel appointments and promotions, which put him in a very powerful position that 'eventually turned him into the worst kind of courtier'.[145] His proximity to the centre of power gave him the kaiser's ear and he acted as a political gatekeeper.

For some specific units, operational command created its own ambiguity: the Flanders Flotilla, for example, had one reporting line to the Navy Office, but the High Seas Fleet and those operating in the Mediterranean had different ones. In fact, the Flanders Flotilla was sometimes even half-jokingly labelled 'Tirpitz's private navy'.[146]

*German Navy Command Structure 1914–18*

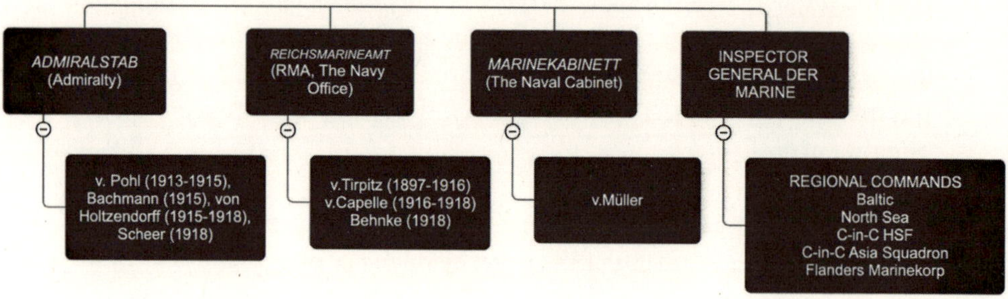


It's ironic that 'the man most associated with unrestricted submarine warfare, both within Germany and internationally, had no voice in the timing of its introduction'.[147] In Tirpitz's absence, it was primarily Hugo von Pohl, as head of the Admiralstab, who pushed the kaiser to consider the submarine campaign against British trade. This, despite Bauer's estimation that he could only count on four U-boats when seven were needed to be 'continuously on patrol'.[148]

Those who understood the nuanced complexity of submarine warfare felt a deep sense of frustration with their country's political leadership. Germany had to make a choice: either to employ a conventional counter-blockade or to aggressively pursue commerce war.

The Chancellor, Bethmann-Hollweg, and the Secretary of State for Foreign Affairs, Gottlieb von Jagow, were both supported in their opposition to unrestricted submarine warfare by von Müller. The Chancellor's fear was that the same terror that made it so successful would ultimately turn world opinion, *particularly* American public opinion, against Germany. From the very beginning, Bethmann-Hollweg kept the kaiser in check, supporting a more conciliatory approach to submarine warfare. The proponents of a stronger, more ruthless approach were powerful and included Tirpitz, the senior commanders of the High Seas Fleet, Friedrich von Ingenohl and, later, Hugo von Pohl. Ingenohl, for example, strongly supported torpedoing hospital ships, despite its obvious illegality. The Admiralstab, however, accepted that a blockade using U-boats might not be legally supportable: even 'our own Prize courts would judge this blockade to be ineffective'.[149]

Depending on the situation on the ground, the army's High Command weighed in to either support or oppose submarine warfare in its various forms. In the early days, the army Chief of Staff, Erich von Falkenhayn, found himself in the Bethmann-Hollweg–Müller camp, while in the latter part of the war, Ludendorff and von Hindenburg gravitated to a more aggressive form of U-boat warfare.[150] Falkenhayn only later switched camps when he saw the war evolving into one of attrition, hoping that unrestricted submarine warfare would bring German victory. Others would vacillate. Henning von Holtzendorff, for example, opposed aggressive submarine warfare in the early years, arguing that Germany did not yet possess sufficient U-boats, the bases from which to operate or even sufficient operational experience. Both von Trotha and Scheer would later be firm supporters, but at this point thought that 'the first half-hearted attempts at submarine warfare were a profound mistake as they gave notice to the British Admiralty to prepare for future eventualities'.[151]

### The Politics of the Submarine Debate

The heated debate around the submarine and its future role became a convenient rallying cry for thinkers of the *Jeune École* school.

> Early U-boat successes supplied the advocates of a commercial war with ammunition for a new assault on Tirpitz's battleship strategy.[152]

The visible successes of the U-boat, in stark comparison to the caged inactivity of the High Seas Fleet, 'brought a new threat to the primacy of RMA in naval circles'.[153] Small wonder that troublemakers like Persius were dealt with so swiftly. Tirpitz's leadership was in question and, after his short-lived advocacy of unrestricted submarine warfare in 1914, his integrity increasingly questioned. He was, after all, the quintessential battleship man.

Von Pohl was replaced at the Admiralty by a Tirpitz supporter, Gustav Bachmann, whose fortunes were closely tied to the Großadmiral. After the instability of 1915 caused first by the *Lusitania* sinking, then that of the *Arabic*, Tirpitz's star had started to fade. He lost his position on the General Headquarters Staff on 30 August, and the very next day Bachmann was replaced by Holtzendorff, called out of retirement 'partly because he agreed to Bethmann-Hollweg's line on the U-boat war'.[154] He asserted that a U-boat war against Britain would do little: 'Believe me gentlemen, you will not scratch the whale's [Britain's] skin with your U-boat war.'[155] With Tirpitz now pushing for a resumption of unrestricted submarine warfare, on 17 March 1916, the kaiser finally accepted his resignation. With the resumption of restricted warfare on 20 April, Scheer recalled his boats. As Weir put it, he 'questioned the value of remaining on station with a restricted hunting license'.[156]

Although his successor, Eduard von Capelle, defended his predecessor, the RMA's power was in decline. Admiral Paul Behnke noted:

> The opinions of the state secretary hold no weight among the people. In the navy, the position of the RMA has become purely administrative, it no longer plays a leading role.[157]

Real political power would not be recovered until Reinhard Scheer built the Seekriegsleitung (SKL, Marine Warfare Command) at the end of 1917 along the lines of the Oberste Heeresleitung (OHL, Army High Command). Holtzendorff's power was hobbled by Bethmann-Hollweg throughout much of 1916. It would only be in the wake of the Somme, with the new perspectives of Hindenburg and Ludendorff, that the submarine lobby started to recover, albeit too late.

## Putting Intelligence to Work

By early 1915, intelligence employed in the naval war did not just include the now famous work of Room 40, it comprised all and every means of consolidating a constantly updated picture on the tactics, men and material of Germany's navy.

As the war progressed, the role and importance of intelligence was increasingly appreciated. The British naval intelligence community mushroomed from fifty individuals in 1914 to 'several thousand' personnel by 1918. The enormous increase in the volume of decrypted traffic can be illustrated by three actions: Scarborough, Dogger Bank and Jutland.[158] During the six days of Jutland, there were over 600 decrypts, compared to fifty for the Scarborough action and eighty for Dogger Bank.[159] A number of writers, including Patrick Beesly, Jason Hines and more recently Andrew Boyd, have tackled in detail the use of intelligence in the naval war. At Jutland, Boyd, like Beesly, underlined the failure to translate decrypted intelligence into operational value even if, in the end, he doubted whether Jellicoe could have capitalised on it fast enough to turn the hoped-for resumption of operations on 1 June into anything close to a victory. By the end of the day, visibility was reduced to 4 miles, ending any possibility of a renewed fleet engagement.

Much of the Allied success, either in sinking or damaging enemy submarines and, later, managing convoys to avoid submarine traps, resulted from improved intelligence and more effective management of intercepted communications.

The idea that the Germans were somehow unaware of the capabilities of British intelligence persists, despite what some of their senior commanders said at the time: 'We could be perfectly certain from the behavior of British submarines that the enemy had an amazingly accurate knowledge of the passages we had cleared through our minefields.'[160] Both sides, in fact, might have ended up equally sophisticated in gathering intelligence, but the Germans had a distinct geographic disadvantage for Direction Finding (D/F) operations, with less available coastline and, at least until 1916, no concerted effort to manage intelligence in the way OB40 (the Admiralty's cryptanalysis section) was doing:

> In many ways, the newly formed *E-Dienst* was the antithesis of Room 40. Whereas Room 40 became a centralized organization by the Fall of 1915 with a clear mission and under the direct control of the Admiralty, the *E-Dienst* had become centralized only in 1916. However, any benefits brought by centralization were effectively neutralized by the dual tasking forced on the *E-Dienst* by the High Seas Fleet's requirement to monitor German fleet communication while carrying out the *Admiralstab*-directed collection of British signals.[161]

Following the operations at the start of the war to cut or monitor German cable traffic, messages started to arrive at the Intelligence Division. Since it was coded, Vice Admiral Sir Henry Oliver, DID (Director of Intelligence Division), was going to need help.[162] The 48-year-old officer, in the post since November 1913, was 'a workaholic, who rarely left his office and taciturn to the point of rudeness'.[163] Because of this 'extreme taciturnity', he was known as 'Dummy' Oliver.[164] He was anything but.

On the war's first day, Oliver met with an old friend, Sir Alfred Ewing, at the time Director of Naval Education (DNE), who asked him 'to take charge of a department to unravel the German ciphers'.[165] Oliver was on his way to lunch and, by chance, bumped into Ewing on his way across Horse Guards Parade, near Admiralty Arch. Ewing, 'a gently spoken Scotsman who was always dressed in an immaculate grey suit', immediately agreed as he was 'rather at a loose end', he said.[166] Even if he had no doubt, however, that 'the chance of success was small', Ewing immediately went to work to teach himself everything he could about ciphers:[167]

> [I]n the first few days I visited Lloyd's, the General Post Office and the British Museum to see their collection of code books … Admitted into the Great Library behind the British Museum, conducted to the appropriate shelves and left to prowl among dusty code books, I was able to glean from them certain general notions about how codes were or might be built up.[168]

In October 1914, Room 40 was established, and, on 8 November, a charter agreed with the First Lord of the Admiralty, Churchill.[169] It came to be known as OB40 or 40OB, as its location was in the Admiralty's Old

Building and to specifically help protect its security, situated nowhere near the Intelligence Division.

Ewing's immediate tasks were to not only help the decoding of signals but to also set up a network of W/T Intercepting and Direction Finding stations around the country. He was able to quickly attract interesting talent: his position as DNE gave him access to Osborne and Dartmouth naval colleges.[170] One new recruit, 'the most significant', was a 33-year-old teacher of German, Alastair Denniston, a fellow Scot and Olympic field-hockey player, who'd been educated both at the Sorbonne and in Bonn and taught German at Osborne. Denniston would 'dominate British SIGINT [signals intelligence] for the next thirty years'.[171]

In October 1914, a former captain of HMS *Queen Mary* took over the Intelligence Division from Oliver. Admiral Sir William Reginald Hall was a formidable DID: 'In a conflict from which the Admiralty does not in general emerge well, Hall's work was the outstanding exception.'[172] Hall had a pronounced facial twitch, caused by one eye which would 'flash like a Navy signal lamp', hence his nickname 'Blinker'.[173] His genius, one writer proclaimed, 'lay not only in organising the admirable service which deciphered these compromising messages but in knowing by instinct how most effectively to use them'.[174] The American Ambassador, Walter Page, held him in high esteem, saying that he 'could read any man's soul'. He had a 'shrewd penetrating glance and a quick mode of speech'.[175] Hall would remain in the position until January 1919, when Wemyss, Jellicoe's successor as First Sea Lord, 'got rid of him, rather abruptly and without full recognition of the service had had rendered'.[176]

## Breaking the German Naval Codes

From the start, the British had in their possession some very valuable information: much of the code on which German naval communications were based. At the war's outset, a priceless gift fell into Allied hands: in August 1914, the Russians found three copies of SMS *Magdeburg*'s code books when the light cruiser ran aground in bad visibility on the Estonian coast. The crew was in the process of transferring to a destroyer, SMS *V.26*, when the fog lifted. Two Russian cruisers caught her and opened fire, prematurely setting off her precautionary demolition charges. Ewing's biographer included a colourful account of the circumstances, even saying that 'the Russians found the body of a drowned signalman, still clasping in his arms the highly confidential signal book of the German navy'.[177] On 13 October, the Russians gave OB40 a copy of what they'd found: the *Signalbuch der Kaiserlichenmarine* (SKM, sometimes simply referred to as SB, *Signalbuch*[178]), as well as 'the current key, a copy of the German naval grid chart for the Baltic, the bridge log and the ship's war diary'.[179] The SKM was a massive book, 6in thick, containing all the major operational codes for the navy. Given that the *Magdeburg*'s captain was responsible for losing the German Navy's critical code books, his name, Habenicht, was rather apt (literally, it means 'don't have').

Two copies were kept by the Russians and a third picked up by HMS *Theseus*, sent by Jellicoe to collect the vital intelligence.[180] On 13 October, Churchill received his copy, which was then passed to the fleet paymaster, Charles J.E. Rotter, who was able to break its secrets within a month. Like Denniston, Charles Ehrhardt Rotter was a German specialist. He realised that some of the SKM codes were being 'superenciphered: once encoded, the letters had been switched according to a key to yet another set of letters'.[181] Although he 'died in the years after the war, no obituary notice paid tribute to what he had done'.[182] The SKM would continue to be used until May 1917, when it was replaced by the more complicated FFB (*Flottenfunkspruchbuch*).

In October, the British also obtained a copy of a general code book used by naval and commercial vessels, as well as Zeppelin traffic, known as the *Handelsverkehrsbuch* (HVB).[183] The materials had been uncovered on 11 August by an enterprising Australian naval captain, John Tracy Richardson, on the German steamship, the SS *Hobart*. Disguised as civilians, he and a group of sailors had managed to get aboard the steamer and, once aboard, to seize her. The captain had clearly hidden his code books, so Richardson snuck away in his cabin, where he waited until the German ship's Master and a crew member reappeared that night to retrieve the confidential materials. It was immediately offered to the Admiralty, who initially didn't even bother to reply, so the offer was repeated on 7 September. Even if German intelligence knew the books had fallen into the wrong hands, 'bizarrely it remained unchanged till 1916', when it was replaced with the *Allgemeinefunkspruchbuch* (AFB).[184]

Finally, at the end of November, the safe from a German destroyer, SMS *S.119*, fouled a British trawler's nets and was brought to the surface. It had been sunk off Texel in October 1914. Inside was a copy of the Substitution Book (known as VB, for *Vekehrsbuch*, the find was quickly dubbed 'the miraculous draught of fishes').[185] Each was an incredible catch; together, they laid bare most of German naval communications.

## D/F, Directionals and Intercepts

After her cables infrastructure had been destroyed, Germany increasingly used W/T. At the start of the war, there was only one British 'long-range listening station', which was at Stockton-on-Tees. The network grew with an almost comically 'can-do' amateurishness. A barrister-cum-radio buff, Russell Clarke, along with a close friend, Colonel Hippisley, 'tuned into German naval signals for fun'.[186] Clarke persuaded Ewing, whom he knew well and counted as a friend, to set up a shorter-wave station at Hunstanton on the Norfolk coast.[187] Marconi then agreed to set up three more in Britain and overseas, in Malta, Ancona and at the Strait of Otranto. By 1917, 'complete coverage' of the North Sea was achieved, although coverage in the Baltic and the Mediterranean was 'more limited'.[188] After Stockton, new listening stations were established at Lowestoft, Lerwick, Aberdeen, York, Flamborough Head, Birchington, Murcar and another five in Ireland under Lewis Bayly's direct command. The intercepted signals by what would at the end amount to Y-Service's network of fourteen stations would then be sent on to OB40 for decryption.

Everyone recognised the value of Ewing's work. To the public, he might have been caricatured as 'Eavesdropping Ewing' or 'The Navy's Nosey Parker', but Jellicoe acknowledged his work, saying he knew its 'immense value' and how 'exceedingly helpful it was to [him] in the Grand Fleet'.[189]

The British were in a geographically superior position than the Germans to set up a large-scale triangulation network needed for D/F. The German equivalent D/F stations were located at Nordholz (near Cuxhaven) and on Borkum in the Frisian Islands, under construction in 1915 to support Zeppelin activities. That July, German naval intelligence opened their own operation in Brügge, and this became one of the stations under the overall command of the Neumünster HQ when it became operational in February 1916.

The system was primitive but usually worked to give the approximate position (quoted rather over-ambitiously as 'somewhere within the radius of about two miles') of a surface ship or U-boat. Each signal would give 'the direction or bearing of the source' at 'the point at which the signal strength was most marked'.[190]

### U-BOAT SIGNALS PROTOCOL

U-boats frequently needed to signal Germany: covering details of an enemy vessel's sinking, enemy warship sightings, whether the submarine was coming home and, in that case, if help was needed getting through 'friendly' minefields. When Otto Bock, a submarine telegraphist, was interrogated by Bernard Trench, 'the top interrogator of U-boat prisoners', interesting details emerged.[191] His own U-boat, *UC.61*, would listen each day to messages from Brügge at 0100, 0500, 1000, 1500 and 1800hrs GMT, at 1100hrs to Nauen, the Admiralty's station, and at 1700hrs to the fleet-wide messages that came from SMS *Arcona* in the Ems estuary. Other stations included Norddeich and Neumünster.

Every twenty-four hours, the Germans changed the code, but they alerted the British by always transmitting the word 'Silence' before a change was about to take place. The first three letters of a call sign revealed a submarine's identity. When an 'ace' was identified and was being tracked, Q-ships in the vicinity were warned to be on the lookout. They also found the encryption key and another important piece of information was how the German Navy divided the North Sea into box grids for faster communication of locations.

With a sizeable force at sea, the picture was much more complex than at first imagined: 'The busiest month of all was June 1917. During that month the first of the big U-cruisers put to sea. There were 27 boats of all types working in the North Sea, 13 in the Channel, 15 in the Mediterranean, 3 in the Baltic and 2 in the Black Sea.'[192]

Progressively, the application of the new technology helped bring the hunters closer to their prey. While 'wireless intercepts and direction-finding could only give a rough location in which to search', surface and aerial search brought it closer still, and finally, hydrophone and magnetic anomaly measurement helped close the remaining detection gaps.[193]

'Directionals' became the basis for what was later termed TA (Traffic Analysis), then simply known as Wireless Intelligence (W/T Intelligence). TA looked at, among other things, an enemy's networks, procedures and call signs. Sometimes just the volume of signals was more reliable than signals interpretation:

> Macro-level data interpretation proved useful in tracking enemy forces at sea in real time by following the volume and location of their [German] wireless traffic, without decoding individual messages.[194]

It was a mistake to think that the Germans weren't also mining similar intelligence, but 'it [the HSF] remained oblivious to its [own] cyphers' vulnerability', while the British response was 'incomplete, focusing on radio silence at sea rather than developing cyphers that would be more difficult to break'.[195] Lloyd George blamed many of the woes faced by merchant ships on the lack of wireless discipline, claiming

> wireless instructions to merchant vessels – about rendezvous points with escorts – were intercepted by the Germans, decrypted and tip-offs sent to U-boats. The merchant vessels 'found not a guide, but a pirate waiting their arrival … In fact, by this egregious plan, our ships were in effect often shepherded into the abattoir where the slaughterers lay in wait for them'.[196]

Sometimes, a German submarine would even send out a false SOS signal in the hope of luring rescue vessels to the area and into a trap.

## The Missing Piece – Intelligence Analysis

What the British missed, however, was the *integration* of analysis with decryption. This was probably Churchill's fault: he had ensured that 'SIGINT would be managed and conducted *in isolation* [author's italics] from the existing Intelligence Division which was its logical home'.[197] The separation put Ewing's and Hall's organisations into direct competition. There was little love lost between OB40 and the Navy's established intelligence gathering: academics and scientists rarely found mixing with the military, or in this case with RN officers, easy. Room 40 staff were often belittled for their lack of understanding of naval terminology, procedure and customs. Maybe this was the reason why Clarke's characterisation of Jackson was so strongly negative. It often meant that many operational opportunities from SIGINT were lost, even if it is true that the codes gave the British 'security'. Without the raw information about the movements of the HSF, Oliver maintained that Britain 'would [have been] compelled to keep a large proportion of [its] scouting forces constantly at sea, with all the liability of damage by torpedo or mine, and the consequent wear and tear on personnel and material'.[198]

Elaborate measures were taken to cover the real source of information. As was the case at Jutland, there was an 'acute fear of compromising the precious SIGINT source'.[199] Relaying intelligence to operational commanders would usually only happen if it was possible to imply that the source was D/F.

Another avenue was disinformation: creating the idea in German intelligence that the British had a formidable espionage network and that HUMINT (human intelligence) was the real source of their intelligence. A French diplomat introduced himself to German intelligence by presenting himself at the German Embassy in Madrid, offering to sell secrets. The German Ambassador, Prince Ratibor, was eventually convinced he was bona fide. He was, in fact, a double agent. However, the Secret Service Bureau's (SSB) most successful agent, designated TR16, was a former German naval engineer, Karl Krüger, who became 'its most important source'.[200] Having professional access, he gleaned valuable information directly from the shipyards – in April 1915, for example, on U-boat construction, and following Jutland, a very detailed report on 27 June which was 'described by Hall as 100 per cent', even if earlier reports had contained errors.[201]

## The Dogger Bank Action

Intelligence gave the British an opportunity to intercept important raids. One such occasion occurred on 23 January, when Beatty was ordered to sea in anticipation of one of Hipper's Aufklärungsgruppe's reconnaissance missions. Beatty planned to lay in wait behind the enemy after their ships had passed north, placing him in a blocking position between them and, on their return, their home base. The 3rd Battle Squadron, the 'Wobbly Eight', would be sent from Rosyth and Jellicoe's ships would join from Scapa.

As the trap closed, the British sank the cruiser SMS *Blücher*, but, because of an unfortunate series of signals from Beatty, failed to catch the main force. His own flagship, HMS *Lion*, was severely damaged and, at a critical moment, lookouts reported a submarine on his starboard bow. A later naval intelligence report concluded that what had been seen was more likely to have been a torpedo, fired by SMS *V.5*, surfacing after a long run. At the time, however, Beatty concluded it was a submarine trap and reported that '[he] personally observed the wash of a periscope, two points on our starboard bow'.[202] It was the squadron's subsequent turn to port that opened the range with ships in Hipper's rear.

## Political Indecision Leads to Unilateral Naval Action

While the kaiser fumbled over his policy options, surrounded by internal conflict and overwhelmed by contradictory opinion, others took matters into their own hands. Three submarines (*U.19*, *U.20* and *U.21*) were sent on missions designed to create more pressure on the waverers. While *U.19* and *U.21* might have respected Prize Rules, *U.20* certainly didn't.

On 30 January, *U.20* – now under a new commander, Walther Schwieger – torpedoed three merchant ships without warning, and worse still, on the night of 31 January, tried the same tactic on the large 12,002-ton hospital ship *Asturias*. She had been running at 14 knots under full illumination. The submarine's own log confirmed that the ship had been 'clearly identified' as a hospital ship, with large red crosses painted on her white hull, but that, because she was running at night, she was sunk. Luckily, she actually escaped (the torpedo had failed to detonate), but fell victim to another submarine in March 1917. Over the month, of the seven merchant ships sunk, three were without warning: 'the navy was waging its own, separate war'.[203]

## The U-boat Counter-blockade

The new High Seas Fleet commander, Hugo von Pohl, had to wait for the right moment to catch the kaiser's ear; it was difficult without first having to go through von Müller. On 2 February, the kaiser visited Kiel to welcome the new head of the HSF. It was the opportunity Pohl had been waiting for, and as the two men were being ferried around in the admiral's barge – without Müller – Pohl made his move.

Afterwards, of course, each had his own version of events. Müller made out that, far from being left out of the critical decision, he'd already agreed to the important policy change. The kaiser later said that he had agreed to nothing as he could hardly hear what Pohl had said. It was clear that the kaiser was frustrated. Kurt Riezler, Bethmann-Hollweg's private counsellor, described what he saw:

> He is fed up with his lies. Tirpitz has been pushed aside in the naval management by the vain Pohl; he does nothing but talk big and stir up trouble. His dismissal is impossible, though, because of his popularity with the simple people.[204]

Bachmann and Tirpitz chose to weigh in on Pohl's side, arguing that they were 'convinced that Great Britain will end the blockade six weeks after the new commercial war begins'.[205] It was a wildly over-optimistic promise, bound to backfire. Finding himself without Tirpitz's support, Bethmann-Hollweg now turned to the army's Chief of Staff, von Falkenhayn, and built an alliance on a common concern: America. Pohl was convinced that the '*mere threat* [author's italics] of submarine warfare would scare off neutral shipping thus allowing Germany to strangle Britain without having to worry of a negative reaction'.[206] He managed to calm some of the Chancellor's fears of further alienating the most powerful neutral by falsely claiming that German U-boats would easily identify American ships.

The waverers were outmanoeuvered. The new submarine campaign was presented 'as a reply to the British starvation blockade' to avoid it being seen 'as a deliberate abandonment of the principles of international law'.[207] Germany claimed that Britain's unilateral interpretation of the Treaty of London and removal of the distinctions between *absolute* and *conditional* classes of contraband had been illegal. The submarine counter-blockade was therefore presented as a justifiable breech of international law. British actions – its maritime blockade of Germany, the arming of merchantmen and the mining of the North Sea – necessitated her response.

There were three main components to the announcement:

> First, the waters around Great Britain and Ireland, including the whole of the English Channel, are hereby declared to be a War Zone [*Sperrgebiet* or *Kriegsgebiet*]. From February 18 onwards every enemy merchant vessel encountered in this zone will be destroyed, nor will it always be possible to avert the danger thereby threatened to the crew and passengers. Secondly, neutral vessels also will run a risk in the War Zone, because in view of the hazards of sea warfare and the British authorisation of January 31 of the misuse of neutral flags, it may not always be possible to prevent attacks on enemy ships from harming neutral ships. Lastly, navigation to the north of the Shetlands, in the eastern parts of the North Sea and through a zone at least thirty nautical miles wide along the Dutch coast is not exposed to danger.[208]

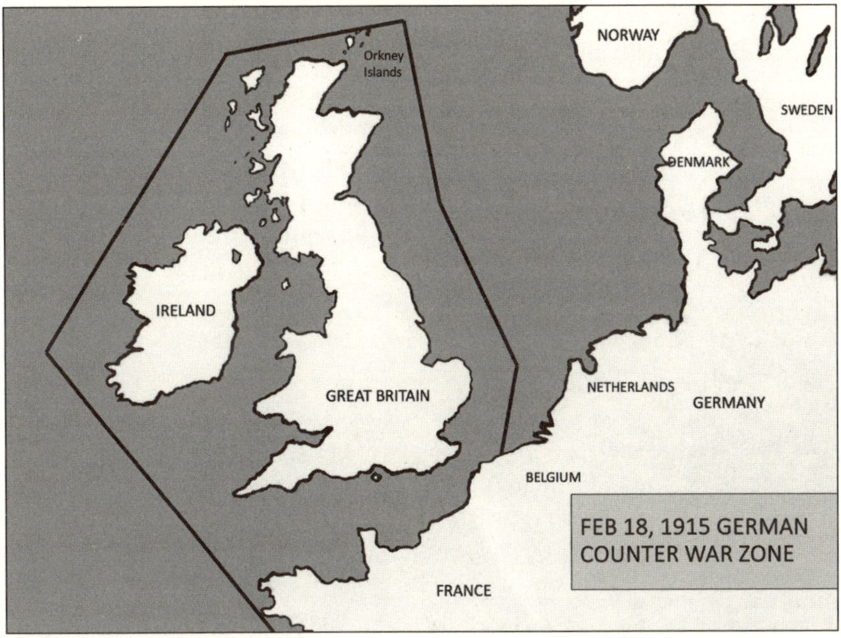


The protection of Prize Rules was to be discarded: *within the war zone*, merchant ships were liable to submarine attack without warning. Neutral flags no longer offered any guarantee of safety.

For a decision with such a profoundly unpredictable outcome, it's extraordinary that the briefing given to submarine commanders – generally young officers – was so ambiguous. In the light of the later diplomatic furore caused by the *Lusitania*, *Arabic* and *Sussex* incidents, the briefing appeared to be little more than a carte blanche for younger, more aggressive officers, keen to make a mark for themselves in the 'tonnage league'. How Scheer put it, meant they could act with impunity:

> The first consideration is the safety of the U-boat. Consequently, rising to the surface in order to examine a ship must be avoided for the sake of the boat's safety, because, apart from the danger of a possible surprise attack by enemy ships, there is no guarantee that one is not dealing with an enemy ship even if it bears the distinguishing marks of a neutral. The fact that a steamer flies a neutral flag, and even carries the distinguishing marks of a neutral, is no guarantee that it is actually a neutral vessel. Its destruction will therefore be justifiable unless other attendant circumstances indicate its neutrality.[209]

Small wonder that on 12 February, both the United States and Italy vigorously complained, prompting an urgent signal to the fleet two days later.

1. For urgent political reasons send orders by wireless to U-boats already dispatched for the present not to attack ships flying a neutral flag, unless recognised with certainty to be enemies.
2. As indicated in the announcement on February 2, HM the Emperor has commanded that the U-boat campaign against neutrals to destroy commerce, as indicated in the announcement of February 4, is not to be begun on February 18, but only when orders to do so are received from the 'All Highest'.[210]

It was a very public *volte-face.* Pohl was incensed; he felt that his U-boats were being needlessly put at risk.

**The False Flag Issue**

The second point of Germany's three-point announcement was significant: while Britain held the world's largest commercial fleet, it was a relatively common practice in war to fly the flag of a neutral, 'so long as no hostile act was committed while the false flag was flying'.[211] Under this convention, British decoy Q-ships were, therefore, legally obliged to fly their own colours before opening fire. With some justification, the Germans maintained that the practice made it more dangerous for neutral ships. Forstner noted: 'Of course, many neutrals had to suffer from the deceptions practiced by the English.'[212] As Jameson put it,

> The Germans were understandably annoyed by an Admiralty order which made incidents with neutrals more likely and was thus clearly advantageous to the Allied cause.[213]

Germany held that the British had abused international law by declaring the use of neutral flagging a legitimate *ruse du guerre.* The position was a clever exploitation of Britain's use of neutral flags. It made the British appear as the aggressor: it was Britain's fault that neutral shipping could no longer avoid being targeted. But both sides were stretching the facts to make their case. The Admiralty had not, as they made out, 'initiated or encouraged the *general use* of neutral flags [author's italics]'; it had only issued instructions for merchantmen to fly 'neutral flags, preferably American … in the Channel approaches'.[214] Nevertheless, though it denied any intentional outcome, Britain had 'stirred the pot'.

The Americans were particularly incensed that their flag had been used and demanded that it no longer be employed in these circumstances. Around the same time, 6 February, Wilson's confidant and advisor, Colonel House, arrived in London and met with Britain's Foreign Secretary the next day. He would undertake long discussions with Grey at the latter's Eccleston Square house, loaned to him by Churchill. He had crossed the Atlantic at the end of January on Cunard's *Lusitania*, her captain, Dow, flying the American flag (as she would when torpedoed in May). He had told passengers the reason why he'd done so was that 'he had been greatly alarmed the night before … and expected to be torpedoed'.[215] House stayed until May, only making a brief trip to Berlin before returning dismayed that the talks there had not been 'favourable for any discussion looking towards peace'.[216]

Grey proposed that Britain could lift the food embargo if the Germans reinstated restrictions. This should have been taken up. The fact that Tirpitz immediately changed Germany's demands damaged the strong moral stance that had been established. Demanding, instead, the release of all impounded German ships, the initiative fell apart. Both sides had overplayed their hands.

On 12 February, US diplomatic notes were delivered to both belligerents: to the British, complaining about the use of false flags; to the Germans, questioning the legality of their submarine blockade unless effectively maintained, claiming that it was 'an indefensible violation of neutral rights' and that the United States would 'hold the German Government to strict accountability'.[217] The wording, however, of the American note to Germany was significantly tougher. While trying to maintain the semblance of impartiality, Wilson clearly felt stronger ties to the British:

> The real difference between blockade and submarine in Wilson's view was not that the former took property and the latter took lives, but that the former was British and the latter was German.[218]

The notes 'sent a subtle message to Grey as to where the United States stood' on the issue of the British blockade.[219] On 16 February, Germany replied: Britain was being allowed to mine the North Sea with impunity while America was profiting from supplying war materiel.

For the Allies, Germany's new campaign had been 'a gift from heaven'.[220] The aggressive moves were easily leveraged by British propaganda and the Cabinet finally felt that it could institute stricter measures towards the neutral governments. Relationships with the neutrals demanded a delicate balancing act: Britain had an interest in maintaining some imports from Scandinavia but felt it could now turn up the pressure. On 11 March, the British announced, as a 'retaliatory measure', an Order in Council tightening controls on all materials with Germany identified as the possible ultimate destination, doing away with the distinction between the first two contraband categories. Addressing the concerns of the neutrals, Asquith made the following announcement:

> If, as a consequence, neutrals suffer inconvenience and loss of trade, we regret it, but we beg them to remember that this phase of the war was not initiated by us.

**Running the Dover Barrage**

While talks were still in progress, *U.16* sailed. Her captain was under orders to sink ships that gave 'the impression of being transports'. On the 15th, she sank the *Dulwich*, and four days later torpedoed a Norwegian tanker, the *Belridge*, which nevertheless managed to make Folkstone. *U.30* had sailed on 10 February to the Irish Sea and sank the 3,112-ton *Cambank* without warning ten days later. In many ways, the *Belridge* attack was as significant an event as the *Glitra* or the *Amiral Ganteaume*: she was the first neutral ship nearly torpedoed in the First World War.

Between the attack on the *Belridge* and 1 June, another three Norwegian, two Dutch and one American ship (a tanker) were sunk without warning in the same area.[221] Not only was there now a pattern of sinkings without warning, but neutral vessels were also under threat.

On the first day of the new campaign, *U.8* tried to pass through the Dover Barrage by running deep, trying to get under the belt of steel. Her commander, Alfred Stoss, got caught and, try as he might, couldn't seem to shake his submarine free: 'the brightly painted buoys on the surface danced wildly as the U-boat struggled to tear free'.[222] He finally succeeded, however, and went about his business, sinking five steamers over two days off Beachy Head (totalling 16,000 GRT); all without warning.

Three days later, Stoss was joined by another four submarines (*U.6*, *U.9*, *U.20* and *U.27*). Initially, *U.6* seemed doomed: she was spotted by a lookout on the 500-ton *Thordis*, who ran her down, smashing one periscope, bending the other and damaging the conning tower. The master of the *Thordis*, Captain John Bell, was awarded a prize of £500 for being the 'first mercantile captain to sink a U-boat'. Below the surface, however, *U.6*'s commander, Oberleutnant z.S. Rheinhold Lepsius, succeeded in repairing the injured boat and getting her home.

Of the others, one, *U.9*, had to be taken back home by Spiess with mechanical problems, while *U.20* had little luck finding targets; Schwieger had been out for twenty days and only managed to sink a collier off Liverpool. On 4 March, Alfred Stoss was out again and tried to pass under the Dover Strait in *U.8*. After the submarine was spotted, he was fired on by the destroyer HMS *Viking* and again become entangled in one of the indicator nets. A drifter, *Roburn*, spotted the telltale movements on the cable from the surface and immediately called in more destroyers.[223]

This time, Schwieger's luck ran out: a second explosive sweep from HMS *Gurkha* was set off when it touched the submarine's hull:

> Every lamp in the U-boat was smashed, and water began to pour in through several holes; a short-circuited switchboard caught fire, and all the motors stopped. Tanks were blown as chlorine gas, smoke, and water began to fill the boat.

The submarine finally had to surface, where *Gurkha* and her sister destroyer, *Maori*, were waiting. There was nothing left but surrender. Before leaving, however, German sailors opened the boat's sea cocks and she went down in waters 17 fathoms deep.

Stoss and his crew were at first treated as war criminals, rather than as POWs. It was a clear violation of the rules of war:

> The flagrant illegality of the German methods and the contempt shown by the German Government and commanders for legitimate neutral interests rendered it difficult for neutrals to protest against the adoption by the Allies, as measures of reprisal, of steps which if taken earlier in the war would undoubtedly have been met by the strongest opposition on the part of interested third parties.[224]

### The Polite Pirate – Otto Weddigen's death

Otto Weddigen was now operating off the Scilly Isles in his new command, the *U.29*. He had always respected the Prize Rules when attacking merchant shipping and came to be known in *The Times* as 'the Polite Pirate' as he had never fired on a passenger liner despite orders to do so.[225] In order that his conduct not be held against him, he would often find a suitable excuse to dive his boat, letting the crew sleep while a surface target passed overhead. It meant that more harmless, but defenceless, surface traffic might continue in safety.

When *U.29* first appeared on 12 March, Weddigen promptly disposed of four ships with the submarine's larger 19.7in torpedoes. On each occasion, he allowed the crews sufficient time to abandon ship. Taking the northern route around Scotland to Germany, he surfaced the submarine on the night of 17 March to recharge his batteries, when his watch officer spotted warships: 'It's the whole bloody Grand Fleet!' Weddigen's first shot was aimed at HMS *Neptune*, but missed. With her five twin 12in turrets, the 19,680-ton battleship was a tempting target. Her zigzagging, however, put off his aim. With attention focused elsewhere, he failed to see another ship.

On HMS *Dreadnought*, the watch officer, Lt-Cdr Piercy, had spotted *U.29*'s periscope wake off the starboard bow. Her periscope, as well as her torpedo (passing 30 yards astern of HMS *Neptune*), had been spotted from HMS *Marlborough* around 1218hrs. Ten minutes later, *U.29* was again spotted, this time off *Dreadnought*'s port bow at around 1,500 yards. Captain Alderson swung the massive battleship around, joining her to start the chase, bearing down on the submarine at 17½ knots, with a sister ship, HMS *Temeraire*, at 18 knots. At 600 yards, they opened fire from one of the 12pdrs, missing the submarine by only 50 yards. Frustratingly, the gun then jammed. After a seven-minute chase, the 20,000-ton *Dreadnought* successfully rammed her 867-ton prey, a mere minnow by comparison: 'She passed aft, slowly becoming more vertical until just clear of our stern she disappeared.'[226]

It would be *Dreadnought*'s only contribution to the war. She would never see action again. One of her escorting destroyers, HMS *Blanche*, found nothing on the spot where *U.29* had been hit, only clothing and 'much oil and bubbles on the surface'.[227] In a final tribute, Koerver wrote: 'No U-boat in the First World War ever got as close to the British Grand Fleet as Weddigen's.'[228] Now, along with thirty-two of his crew, he was in the cold embrace of a watery grave.

Jellicoe congratulated *Dreadnought*'s crew on their 'seamanlike handling', but, as he had previously done with *Audacious*, urged secrecy. Instigating a new policy of strict silence surrounding the fate of U-boats after the ramming of *U.29*, he felt that it could only increase German unease not knowing the fate of U-boats, their commanders or crews: 'It must be very disconcerting to the enemy when [a] submarine disappeared and [the] cause of loss [is] not known.'[229]

Two weeks later, on 29 and 30 March, he and Beatty made a sweep of the North Sea. He 'complained strongly' to the Admiralty that the sortie had exposed the Grand Fleet to 'needlessly grave risks of submarine attacks'. Temple Patterson commented that Jellicoe seemed to be more concerned about the menace to the Grand Fleet than the submarine's threat to commerce. The sortie was late in the planning: Jellicoe's dreadnoughts were 'insufficiently screened', with the only destroyers available at Scapa – just sixteen of them.[230]

### Increased Sinkings in the Strait

U-boats were getting caught in the British nets, although usually only momentarily: on 6 April, *U.33* managed to get free, as did *U.35*, which was only stuck for several hours before also wriggling free.

*U.37*, a new submarine, didn't make it back. It was concluded that she had been sunk by a mine. After 10 April, the Dover Strait were declared off-limits. The longer northern route used up valuable time better reserved for active hunting. For the men it was also an added strain, and for the boats a heavier maintenance toll. Additionally, Pohl 'insisted' on keeping six U-boats back for 'defensive patrols in the Heligoland Bight'.[231] It meant that

> the *average* number of submarines which could be kept on station at the only point which could vitally affect Britain's economy would be less than two for the remainder of the year![232]

## MARINEKORPS FLANDERN
### The Brügge, Zeebrügge and Ostend bases

With the capture of Flanders at the end of 1914, 'the kaiser entrusted the Belgian coast to his navy'. The Marinekorps Flandern was established under the command of Admiral Ludwig von Schröder, nicknamed *der Löwe von Flandern*, and officially opened on 29 March 1915, with the appointment of Korvettenkapitän Karl Bartenbach as the unit's first commanding officer, 'an able and energetic commander'.[233] Flanders became one of the most successful German submarine bases: its submarines sunk 2,554 vessels (around 4.5 million BRT, *Bruttoregistertonne* – gross register tonnage), or 'twenty-three per cent of the Allied shipping losses, not counting vessels sunk by mines', according to Scheer.[234] The base would 'ultimately bear the brunt of Germany's aspirations'.[235]

In early 1915, work started in earnest: 14,000 workers helped build submarine pens and drydocks. The three main bases – Oostend, Zeebrügge and Brügge – were connected by a series of canals and protected by a system of coastal artillery employing 5,000 German technical personnel. Leaving their protected base, the submarines would often have an air escort from the seaplanes of Zeebrügge's Seeflugstation Flandern. Architecturally, the submarine flotilla headquarters in Brügge was unique: 'the Jesuits had built the place and it looked like it; it was a curious, charming old stone building with mullioned windows that overlooked a narrow, crooked, cobble-stoned street.'[236] Just outside the town, German officers used a chateau as their country club.

The submarine complement was built up with the arrival of *U.24*, *U.28*, *U.31*, *UB.5*, *UB.15*, *UB.13* and *UB.6* in April 1915, and in May the first Type-*UC* boat, *UC.11*. When *UC.2* was recovered on 2 July 1915, the British understood Flanders was basing minelaying submarines. The base steadily built up:

| | | |
|---|---|---|
| 1915 | October | 16 boats operational |
| 1916 | September | Delivery of new *UC.II* boats |
| 1917 | January | 22 |
| | March | 38 |
| | June/September | Arrival of new Type-*UB.III* (*UB.54* – *UB.57*) |
| | 1 October | 2nd U-Flotille Flandern |

One of the reasons for the success was, undoubtedly, the radio discipline of the Flanders U-boat captains: 'This unit of the German navy had instituted a strict policy of radio silence of its boats at sea. This rendered extremely difficult any attempts by NID at tracking the movements of the boats by direction-finding or cryptographic means.'[237]

By spring 1915, Brügge was operating with a small group of *UB*-boats. The submarines typically were the new Type-*UB*. The small 92ft versions – each displaced only 127 tons surfaced – were 'ideal vessels for the shoals and narrows of the Thames Estuary and the Dover Strait.'[238] Dover was just 285 miles away.

Neutral shipping was increasingly the target of U-boat actions. The Dutch steamer, *Medea*, torpedoed off Beachy Head, exemplified their plight: all she had on board when she sank was a cargo of oranges and tangerines. Her sinking resulted in a vitriolic legal battle between the Netherlands and Germany, even if her cargo, conditional contraband, would have been liable to seizure.

Flags were of little consequence, even white ones. On 10 April, the 5,940-ton steamer *Harpalyce*, clearly painted in bold wording COMMISSION FOR BELGIAN RELIEF in huge white letters on her hull, was torpedoed without warning. Seventeen members of her forty-four-strong crew were killed. Despite the German outrage at British use of false flags, acts like these gave Britain's propaganda effort everything it needed. In London, at a dinner party, American Ambassador Walter Page reported that while there was 'little or no denunciation … it was universally accepted that America would enter the war within the month'.[239]

### The Sinking of the RMS *Lusitania*

At Scapa, Jellicoe was writing to Beatty that 'the submarines seem to have gone to bed for the moment'.[240] On 30 April, however, Kapitänleutnant Walther Schwieger left Emden aboard the *U.20*. Nothing seemed unusual about the mission, but it would become one of the most significant of the war.

In the same way that much of the British documentation is not easily found, Schwieger's sailing orders similarly can no longer be located in the German naval archives, yet there is much circumstantial evidence to suggest that, not only did his specific orders include the sinking of the *Lusitania*, but that he also knew and recognised that the ship spotted by his submarine on the eventful morning of 7 May was Cunard's RMS *Lusitania*. Norddeich had already informed him on the evening of 6 May that *Lusitania* 'leaves Liverpool for New York on May 15th', meaning that she was on schedule for a departure to New York and would soon, therefore, be in the vicinity of his submarine's patrol area.[241] Schwieger also had aboard someone with special knowledge of White Star ships: the pilot, Lanz, had worked for them before the war. Nevertheless, on the morning of 7 March, *U.20* was on a homeward course for Wilhelmshaven.

*Lusitania* was sailing in a declared German war zone. Liners had already been used by the British as troop transports. *Lusitania* was, however, in a slightly different category: the fast liner carried a number of 5.2cm and 12cm guns on her reinforced decks, she had reinforced munitions storage facilities and was not only registered as a British Fleet Reserve ship, but was carrying military cargo on the day.[242]

Despite warnings in American newspapers placed directly below Cunard's own schedule information, emphasising the danger of sailing, they were almost completely ignored. Placed by the Imperial German Embassy, the notice stated that 'vessels flying the flag of Great Britain, or of any of her allies, are liable to destruction in those waters, and that travelers sailing in the war zone or ships of Great Britain or her allies do so at their own risk'. Despite everything, people simply did not believe that Germany would resort to torpedoing such a renowned passenger liner.

In Queenstown, the American Consul, Wesley Frost, read of the German warnings but seemed unperturbed:

> The reference to *Lusitania* was obvious enough but personally it never entered my mind for a moment that the Germans would actually perpetrate an attack upon her. The culpability of such an attack seemed too blatant and raw for an intelligent people to take upon themselves.[243]

Indeed, in the Admiralty, the concern seemed to be more for their own ships than a liner like *Lusitania*. After being informed of new, heavy U-boat activity,

### WALTHER SCHWIEGER (1885–1917)

Schwieger came from an old Berlin family and was already 32 when the war started. His most famous command was *U.20*, the submarine that sank the RMS *Lusitania*. Today, *U.20*'s conning tower can be seen at the Sea War Museum in Thyborøn, Denmark.

In 1916, *U.20* was grounded on the west coast of Denmark. After she had been lost, Schwieger took command of *U.88*, also lost with all hands on 5 September 1917. With over thirty-four war patrols, Schwieger was responsible for sinking forty-nine ships totalling 183,883 GRT.

Schwieger was much admired by his men. Zentner wrote that 'he was the soul of kindness towards the officers and men under him'. In the portrait, he is seen wearing Germany's highest decoration, the *Pour le Mérite*.

Jellicoe ordered HMS *Orion*, which had been undergoing a refit, to delay her departure from Devonport. HMS *Gloucester* and *Duke of Edinburgh* were alerted by Admiral Oliver, and HMS *Jupiter* told to take the North Channel route with an escort of destroyers. The channel was also open to commercial traffic, but Webb at the Trade Division, for reasons unknown, did not pass the information on to *Lusitania*.

Only OB40 seemed cautious. They informed Jellicoe that on 30 April, 'Four submarines sailed yesterday from Heligoland' (*U.35*, *U.36*, *U.39* and *U.40*). Another two immediately followed from Emden; one was *U.20* (on 3 April), the other *U.27* (on 4 May). The latter had been easy to track – her radio operator 'repeated the boat's position fourteen times in twenty-four hours'.[244] As the *U.20* passed Queenstown, HMS *Juno* was spotted steaming back to harbour. The passenger liner's cruiser escort had been called back– rather mysteriously – owing to 'U-boat danger'.

On *Lusitania*'s bridge, her 58-year-old captain, 'Bowler Bill' Turner, gave orders for the final approach to Liverpool to be carried out at a leisurely 18 knots.[245] He had reduced speed from 21 knots, as he 'wanted to arrive at Liverpool Bar without stopping, and within two or three hours of high water'.[246] Turner was a 'careful man' and had at least taken some precautions. He knew he was in dangerous waters: as he entered St George's Channel, 'he had the lifeboats swung out, the watertight doors closed, and the number of lookouts doubled'.[247] But, crucially, he neither increased speed nor zigzagged.

*U.20* surfaced in dense fog. Gradually, the heavy blanket lifted and at around 1320hrs, a ship was spotted: *U.20*'s chief mechanic, Obermachinist Friedrich Sellmer, had the duty watch. Through her periscope, the ship's details were noted; *U.20*'s periscope had a lever on the right side between a high-powered lens and one that gave a wider picture of the horizon.[248] Visible were 'four funnels and masts of a steamer at right angles to our course'.[249]

Just thirty minutes before, as *Lusitania* steered to the Old Head of Kinsale, Turner had ordered the ship to turn to starboard. It was all Schwieger needed, bringing his target 'exactly into the *U.20*'s path'.[250] He carefully lined up a shot, then at 1410hrs, with the target barely 700 metres distant, with a shout of '*Los!*' let loose a single torpedo, running true at a depth of 9ft. When its wake was spotted from the bridge, Turner didn't even have time to walk over to the helmsman before it hit.

Schwieger did not need to fire again; a massive secondary explosion was seen through the scope. Initially, its cause was put down to coal dust, but later a possible link was made to the munitions stored in her cargo holds. *Lusitania*'s screws could not be reversed; the massive 31,500-ton ship kept ploughing ahead, increasingly listing, unable to lower her lifeboats. When it finally became possible, many were overturned. Turner himself stayed on his bridge until the very last moment and literally floated off, holding on to a chair.

As the great ship was coming to her last resting place, she 'suddenly stopped dead in her dive and quivered throughout her length. Her bow had hit the rocky bed of the sea.'[251] Only eighteen minutes had passed. All around, survivors struggled in the water. An English nanny, Alice Drury, was in one of the few usable boats. In her own words, she had become 'a bit hysterical' before she finally jumped:

> The suction of the liner was pulling us back. Every time the oars went forward, we were going as if we were going to be drawn under. Eventually, we got away and I saw the funnels disappearing. I saw all those lifeboats – the lifeboat I was in was the only one saved on that side. There was a submarine on the surface watching us. I saw the sailors watching all those bodies of people and wreckage. The sea was as calm as a pond. I don't think anyone would be alive now if it hadn't been a lovely calm day.[252]

One thousand, one hundred and ninety-eight of her 1,951 passengers and crew died in the disaster.[253] Ninety-four were children. But it was the fact that 128 of the 159 Americans listed aboard were among the dead that caused the ensuing diplomatic storm.

In retrospect, it now seems clear that Captain Turner was targeted by senior British officials as the fall-guy. Fisher and Churchill were after his blood. They had much to lose: the *Lusitania* had been carrying substantial quantities of military supplies – mainly ammunition.[254] The ship was also registered as part of the British Fleet Reserve and was sailing in a declared war zone. Much would be made of the fact that the liner's decks had been reinforced for weapons and that her speed represented a threat.[255] Churchill and Fisher maintained that Turner had disobeyed direct orders to zigzag his ship (new orders would be transmitted to commercial ships on 13 May, a week following the disaster).[256]

Historian Diana Preston addressed the question that conspiracy theorists have bandied about: namely, that Churchill somehow engineered *Lusitania*'s sinking as a means of bringing America into the war.[257] Having dismissed the idea of a 'deliberate' act, she concluded that 'any credible conspiracy' would only be 'through acts of omission rather than commission'. OB40's behaviour raised suspicions (for Patrick Beesley, among others) that the liner had been purposefully 'sacrificed'.[258] Churchill had even voiced such thoughts; in February 1915, he had written to a member of the British Chamber of Commerce:

> To allow neutral ships to call at our coasts in the hope of bringing the United States into conflict with Germany in particular because we need

> the trade for ourselves and if some of the ships affected get into trouble, so much the better.

While Preston admits that Fisher and Churchill were both quite capable of being 'ruthless enough to be credible conspirators', all the circumstantial evidence she presents is too weak to support a conspiracy argument.[259]

Edward Grey was very careful in his dealings with America. The Foreign Secretary clearly did not want to tip the balance by too-aggressive blockade measures, but by the same token probably agreed wholeheartedly with Sir Cecil Spring-Rice's 9 May telegram:

> As our main interest is to preserve US as a base of supplies, I hope the language of our press will be very guarded.[260]

It was not necessarily in Britain's interests to have the United States enter the war: it would give her leverage in post-war European policy, something which later did occur and did, indeed, irritate both France and Britain.

In Washington, Wilson, 'true to his personal style … mulled over his options for several weeks'. Ambassador Page and Colonel House, at the time in London, both let it be known that the President might have to declare war 'if the United States wanted to maintain respect in the world'.[261] A further round of diplomatic notes was prepared. However, did Americans, outside of the East Coast establishment, really care? Probably not: *The San Francisco Chronicle* even wrote that the sinking was Germany's 'largest individual triumph in the war on British commerce'.[262]

Woodrow Wilson asked Germany to specifically exclude American passenger liners from submarine attack. The Germans replied with 'unusual Teutonic subtlety', going back to their earlier position that this was possible only if the 'United States made an agreement with Great Britain allowing the free importation of food supplies into Germany'.[263] The inclusion of passenger liners, however, clearly provided a certain logic to the terror of the submarine war. Bachmann at the Admiralstab wrote to Pohl in no uncertain terms:

> It is in the military interest to make submarine warfare as effective as possible. Do not shy away from sinking enemy passenger liners. Their loss will cause the greatest impact.[264]

Maybe it was not immediately evident, but Germany had succeeded in losing one of the critical encompassing factors for success in the U-boat war: opinion of the neutrals. At the diplomatic level there was a sharp intake of breath, but while Müller at the Marine Kabinett speculated on 'War with America?', Tirpitz went on the offensive:

> In the interest of the state, it is of absolute necessity to now stand firm against the neutrals, and especially against the United States. Our legal position must be that *Lusitania* was an auxiliary cruiser and had a cargo of ammunition aboard.[265]

There were, however, no immediate or substantive changes in German submarine policy towards neutrals. In Germany, Schwieger was even publicly hailed the returning hero, the sinking described as 'an extraordinary success' by the *Frankfurter Zeitung*. Pohl sent his congratulations: 'To Captain and crew my warmest appreciation of success achieved of which HSF is proud and my best wishes for return.' It was in stark contrast to the kaiser's express wishes to U-boat commanders in February that they should 'let the crew disembark before sinking if possible'.[266] Privately, the kaiser is said to have reprimanded Schwieger.

A Munich medalist, Karl Götz, produced a commemorative coin depicting Death selling tickets to passengers, below which was provocatively inscribed 'Business Above All'. So quickly did he want to get his coin into the hands of customers that he mistakenly dated it 5, not 7 May.

In Britain and America, Schwieger was portrayed as a murderer. In Britain, any shop with a German-sounding name was burnt down. In this atmosphere, the First Sea Lord, Prince Louis of Battenberg, felt obliged to change the family name to Mountbatten. Jellicoe, privately, I believe, would have been appalled at the tarnishing of a whole nation because of the actions of one individual. He had so many friendships from his days in China – von Usedom, von Holtzendorf, von Trotha, as well as Prince Heinrich (younger brother of Kaiser Wilhelm II and future Commander-in-Chief of Germany's Baltic Fleet during the First World War), to name a few.[267] Götz's coin was a gift to Allied propaganda: the medal was mass-produced. Inside the box, with a copy of the original coin, was a note describing the meaning of the *Lusitania*'s sinking:

> This indicates the true feeling the War Lords endeavour to stimulate, and is proof positive, that such crimes are not merely regarded favourably, but are given every encouragement in the land of *Kultur*.

Not surprisingly, Schwieger's fellow officers felt he merely followed orders. The instructions issued in February 1915 stated that 'hostile merchant ships are to be destroyed', that neutral flags offered no guarantee of identity or purpose and that submarine commanders must put the safety of their ship and crew first.[268] In the end, Schwieger's actions were written up as if the attack had been a case of mistaken identity.

On 10 May, Count Johann Heinrich Bernstorff, the German Ambassador, made a personal visit to the State Department to express his 'deep regret … to the loss of so many American lives'. In retrospect, it was clear that Schwieger 'had sown the seed, slow germinating as it might be, which would eventually grow into America's entry into the war'.[269] Two days after the sinking, Bethmann-Hollweg succeeded in persuading the kaiser to agree that neutral shipping would no longer be targeted. He also wrote to the US Ambassador, Gerard, saying that the incident was a regrettable mistake for which Germany would pay full compensation.

A series of diplomatic notes followed, and on 13 May a renewed demand for a general cessation of unrestricted submarine war was lodged. To avoid being labelled the wrongdoer, Grey 'flattered Wilson in his role as mediator', even communicating that Britain was now 'considering' finishing the blockade in return for a cessation of submarine war. It successfully deflected the discussion away from *Lusitania*'s dubious cargo manifest. Germany responded clumsily: food was not the issue; it was the embargo on raw materials that they wanted lifted. The emotional appeal of hunger had been replaced by an appeal to American commercial interests, minimising the pain that was being suffered by German civilians. The change in direction lost Germany much of the world's moral support that would surely have continued had the script of innocent civilians as the victims been maintained.

Gustav Bachmann recorded his impressions of the discussions in early June 1915. He provides some insight into the complex manoeuvrings of the submarine war's key players. One after the other, Bethmann-Hollweg, Tirpitz, Müller, von Treutler, von Falkenhayn and Bachmann presented their arguments. Bachmann emphasised that, since the spring, the situation had been made more difficult for U-boats following the British Admiralty's

> instruction to merchant ships to use neutral flags and markings … secret instruction from the British Admiralty from February came into our hands, in which it is stated directly that the shipowners and captains should … use all means to confuse English ships with neutral ones.[270]

Despite neutrals being warned of the dangers of entering the war zone, 'neutral shipping in the war zone had unfortunately increased extraordinarily'. All that Bachmann could recommend was that the kaiser's orders, underlining the importance of treating neutral ships, particularly American-flagged ships, be again emphasised.

Both Tirpitz and Bachmann felt that it was better to end the submarine war completely rather than make concessions. To Bachmann, that 'would be deeply regrettable, as it would deprive our navy of its only currently effective weapon against England'.[271] The kaiser felt he had no choice but to bow to international pressure, saying that the 'continuation of the submarine war in the current manner (in particular the torpedoing of neutral ships) would increase the likelihood of declarations of war on us by neutral powers'.[272] The idea of a declaration of war by the Netherlands 'would be particularly unpleasant for us at the moment from a military point of view'.[273] Bachmann was put in an unenviable situation when the kaiser framed his own position: 'He doesn't even demand that the submarine war should stop completely. The Navy just has to guarantee that nothing happens that could turn the neutrals – especially America – against us.'[274] To many, that consideration only emasculated the effectiveness of the submarine, but Bachmann and Tirpitz kept pushing the compromise. Over dinner, the kaiser accepted the argument, so much so that he wanted the order sent immediately.

On 1 June, after Bachmann had reviewed the proposed text with the Chancellor, a message was sent out to submarines that 'merchant ships are only to be attacked if quite convinced that they are hostile'. The very next day, however, Bethmann-Hollweg was able to obtain an edict saying that passenger liners were to be spared. As Bachmann put it, 'the release of enemy passenger steamers was neither demanded at the earlier meeting at Pleß, nor would I be in a position to agree to it, as this would actually render the submarine war ineffective'.[275] The kaiser's order to protect passenger liners was never sent, a fact that Pohl tried to hide by maintaining that the submarines were out of radio contact. The order 'was not allowed to be disseminated outside of the navy'.[276] Bachmann put it bluntly: 'Since such a restriction seemed unacceptable to me from the outset, I did not take it into account for the order to be issued.'[277] Such behaviour was described by the German naval historian, Hans Joachim Koerver, as 'insubordination'.

But it was also the proximity of officers like von Müller to the kaiser that acted, in Bachmann's words, as a 'rubber wall', constantly reversing positions. By 5 June, the Pleß 'clan' had succeeded in undermining the position taken by Tirpitz and Bachmann: 'The Kaiser regrets that the issue of large passenger steamers was omitted from the June 1st order on submarine warfare and orders an immediate corresponding addition.'[278] He added an important qualifier – 'at least during the pending negotiations'. The outcome of Müller's behind-the-scenes manoeuverings were answered on 6 June by a combined response from Capelle of the RMA, Tirpitz, Bachmann and Behncke:

> Through such an order, Germany loses its last weapon against England and suffers a loss of military reputation among its enemies and the neutral powers that can never be repaired. In general, this order, which cannot remain secret, will be seen as an apology for the *Lusitania*. It can only be interpreted by our opponents, by the neutrals, by our own people and in our own navy, as a dangerous sign of weakness.[279]

That evening, Bachmann drew up his letter of resignation.

The navy hardliners were not happy: These restrictions, they thought, would merely weaken any continued campaign: '[I]f the U-boat War was continued but passenger ships were to be spared, this would so effectively impair the prosecution of the U-boat War as to render it meaningless.' In his diary, Franz Hipper noted a similar comment: 'KptzS [Kapitän zur See] von Levetzow advised me that this was the end of the U-boat war.'[280] As a submarine commander, Hashagen felt that the kaiser's insistence on Prize Rules being applied to submarine warfare 'was as good as to renounce it'.[281] Many of his fellow officers agreed.[282]

Wilson increased the pressure. Writing to Count Bernstorff on 2 June, he again demanded a complete end to submarine war. A week later, the note was sent to Berlin. It was too much for some of the hardliners, and on 6 June Tirpitz submitted his resignation (along with Bachmann's), only to have the gesture rejected by the kaiser.

The emperor decided to wait until 25 June, when he could meet with Bachmann, Tirpitz and Müller in person. He was prepared to offer Germany's cessation of submarine warfare on condition that Britain lift her blockade. It was an endless – and pointless – tit-for-tat, a 'dance around the Maypole', one that would never find agreement. The exercise seemed purely and uniquely designed to appeal to public opinion rather than offer any substantive solutions to end the deadlock.

American Ambassador Gerard even went as far as to personally draft the basis of the German response. It was unprecedented. The German note, which promised their submarines would make every effort not to endanger American lives, was received on 12 July. Wilson backed down; America wanted to avoid war. On 19 July, Müller wrote in his diary: 'The navy wants to continue to sink all enemy liners, while the Chancellor wants to postpone this until the negotiations with America are completed.' The need for a cessation of the submarine war was dropped. All he now asked for was agreement to respect Prize Rules.

The Admiralty's regard for Wilson was not high – 'having been elected on a peace ticket he prefers to deal by force of typewriters than a force of arms'.[283]

**Looking for Answers**

Jellicoe's remedial approach to the submarine threat was hardly innovative: it was merely to strengthen anti-submarine patrols. His immediate concerns were for the safety of the Grand Fleet, so he asked that 'some more effective means of harassing and destroying hostile submarines' be found. He listed his recommendations. The principal problems the patrols faced included their slow speed, lack of effective communications, minimal firepower and the need for centralised coordination. He wanted patrols 'stiffened by destroyers'. The resources in the north at Aberdeen and in the Orkney Islands were increased.

Like Jellicoe, Beatty's frustration was welling over, but neither he nor the Commander-in-Chief were thinking beyond offensive patrols:

> I am greatly disturbed at this attitude of the Admiralty on the submarine menace. It is growing daily in intensity … In fact, our failure to grasp the nettle and organize a force to deal with them *now* [emphasis in original] during the long days when we have some chance of success will be bitterly repented later when the conditions are not so favourable.[284]

### AUXILIARY HUNTING PATROLS

The British grouped together collections of every type of small boat – yachts, motorboats and even trawlers – under the command of RNVR officers into 'Auxiliary Patrols'. At the end of 1914, approximately 750 vessels were involved; by the war's end, 3,100. Alone, they were ineffective; working together with other more purpose-built ASW assets, the APs proved themselves 'moderately useful'.[285]

Faster patrols critically needed the support of destroyers, and much effort was made to increase the Royal Navy's inventory. Each successive Admiralty Board ordered the building of large quantities of destroyers (Churchill: ninety-three and nine destroyer leaders; Balfour: thirty-four and four). Shipyard capacity, however, faced significant production problems: orders couldn't be met. Consequently, Jellicoe (and later Beatty) resisted efforts to strip the Grand Fleet of destroyers for ASW duties. Patrolling, supported by those naval officers who wanted more 'offensive' ASW, was an extraordinary drain on resources, offering only minimal returns: 'It was extremely rare for patrols to be in the right place at the right time in the right force to repel an attack on a merchant ship, still less to find the enemy before he attacked.'[286] Patrolling was 'fundamentally unsound', for it 'left the initiative to the elusive enemy'.[287] In the last fifteen months of the war, out of forty U-boats destroyed by surface action, twenty-four were destroyed by convoy escorts. Hunting forces only accounted for one U-boat.[288] (See Appendix B, 'Method of Destruction')

The training of Patrol Boat officers was very different to that of other naval officers – they were either RNR or RNVR. They had, in Marder's words, 'never looked at it in the military light of destroying the submarine'.[289] Most of the work was done by 'over-age' destroyers or craft designed for different work.[290]

Despite the strong indications of success from convoys, in March 1918 the 'anti-convoy lobby … was calling for the escort force to be reduced by 30 per cent to return more ships to offensive patrols'.[291]

Beatty, however, also recognised that 'our system of hunting him [German U-boats]… has not been very productive', even if it might 'have had the effect of nullifying his efforts'. He was clearly thinking that depth-charge development was necessary, as the 'underwater explosion is the only answer to the underwater vessel'.[292] Earlier in the month, he had asked Admiral Sir William Pakenham, 'Paks', of the 2nd Battlecruiser Squadron to look closely at measures for 'Counter-attack Against Enemy Submarines'. Monetary prizes were offered for innovative ideas.

Jellicoe had, for some time, been pushing the Admiralty to find a single 'energetic officer' under whom anti-submarine patrols could be coordinated. In July, the Admiralty accepted his recommendation that Vice Admiral Sir Lewis Bayly be that person.[293] On 17 July, Coke was replaced at Queenstown by Bayly to oversee the Western Approaches as C-in-C Coast of Ireland. Although not a central Admiralty position, the appointment was a first, important step to a coordinated strategy to counter the U-boat.[294] Bayly's performance would surpass the confidence Jellicoe placed in him.

At first, Bayly's patrols were 'not very successful, since the submarines on the whole work effectively outside the limited range of his patrols'.[295] Almost immediately, however, information started to be fed to him about specific submarines that might be passing through his area. For example, on 27 July, he was told that *U.36* was coming south from Cape Wrath after sinking French steamer *Danae*, and on 7 August that two more submarines heading for the Mediterranean would pass through his area within two days, based on their current speed.

## A Second Diplomatic Crisis: The *Arabic* Sinking and the Pledge

Schneider's latest attack on a British passenger liner nearly 'threw a spanner into the works' during the careful diplomatic exchanges following *Lusitania*'s sinking.

With 423 passengers and crew onboard, the White Star liner ss *Arabic* was just starting her journey to New York when she was spotted by *U.24*. She was barely 40 miles from where the *Lusitania* had gone down, 60 miles from Liverpool, around 50 miles south of the Kinsale Head. For more than ten years, she had safely sailed the same route. This day, 19 August, she briefly diverted to help rescue survivors from Schneider's first victim of the day, the ss *Dunsley*. He had finished her off with deck artillery.

After a short, forty-second run, *U.24*'s torpedo slammed into the 15,801-ton *Arabic*, exploding about 30 metres from her stern, destroying her radio room. Her 21-year-old radio operator had only managed to send one signal before further communications were impossible. The one signal, however, got the ship's position wrong. The ship sank in seven minutes, leaving behind forty-four dead, among whom two were American.[296]

When the news of the sinking broke, any further diplomatic progress on the *Lusitania* reparations negotiations were frozen. Almost immediately, Bernstorff acknowledged the impact to American diplomats: 'I know that you do not wish to discuss the *Lusitania* question till the *Arabic* incident has been definitely and satisfactorily settled.'[297] *U.24* had dramatically reignited *Lusitania*'s smouldering powder keg.

Arriving back in Emden, Schneider was met by Bachmann, who, apparently, suggested he publicly declare that *Arabic* had been trying to ram his submarine. At first, Schneider reputedly refused, saying it had been another case of mistaken identity. Needless to say, the ramming version became the official line. Bernstorff's diplomatic note said that, according to Schneider's action report,

> she [the SS *Arabic*] was recognised as an enemy vessel, as she did not fly any flag and bore no neutral markings. When she approached, she altered her original course, but then again pointed directly toward the submarine. From this the commander became convinced that the steamer had the intention of attacking and ramming her.[298]

It was not very convincing. Only later did he admit seeing 'many lifeboats' on the 'fat goose', a strong clue to his having recognised her as a passenger ship, with the boats swung out and ready.[299]

Once again, Wilson found himself in a difficult position. The attack had reopened old wounds and ignited an angry debate in America. The President continued to waver, making it clear in his address to Congress that 'the people of this country count on [him] to keep them out of the war'.[300] At home he was made to look weak, even though internationally it was a 'watershed' moment in Anglo-American relations. The sinking had turned the tide of opinion against Germany:

> Until that fateful afternoon, the United States, steering a carefully neutral path between the two warring nations, had complained with almost equal bitterness to both belligerents.[301]

Behind the scenes, German diplomats were struggling with Schneider's story. Ambassador Gerard was quietly told of the political infighting in Berlin. Bethmann-Hollweg was being challenged by the navy to protect officers like Schwieger and Schneider. As a result, he could do little else but refuse Washington's demand for reparations.

Bethmann-Hollweg was astonished to find out that the navy had disobeyed the kaiser's instructions. While Tirpitz, Pohl and Bachmann continued to argue for aggressive submarine action, Bethmann-Hollweg was obliged to ask for a clarification of the orders in force: 'Please confirm whether the Imperial orders to spare large liners was recently lifted.' He repeated the request and demanded that another signal be sent to submarine commanders asking that they 'Remember the limitations ordered by the All Highest'.[302] It's quite incredible to think that he had to do so. Two days later, on 26 August, supported by Bethmann-Hollweg and Falkenhayn, the kaiser repeated his instructions to Tirpitz, and on 30 August another message was sent out to the submarine forces: 'Henceforth, passenger steamers may only be sunk after warning has been given and the passengers and crew have been saved.'

Orders went out for the submarines to return to base. Pohl, angered by the kaiser's continual interference, had taken the decision; Scheer would do the same in late 1916. Only days earlier, on 15 August, the kaiser had argued that 'Germany would not allow its submarine policy to be dictated by the Americans'. His words now seemed empty. To minimise the danger implicit in an order 'almost impracticable for a U-boat to obey', several submarines were redeployed from the Western Approaches and the Channel to the Mediterranean, where there was less risk of sinking American shipping.[303] Jellicoe incorrectly concluded that the reduction of local activity was due to crews receiving increased training, 'possibly in anticipation of unrestricted warfare'.[304]

In Berlin, Müller wrote about the 'fighting mood' of many submarine officers.[305] Kapitänleutnant Max Valentiner, who had lost both his cousin, Bernd Wegener, and his close friend, Klaus Hansen (*U.41*), to Q-ship attacks, was furious.[306] Tirpitz was 'full of wounded vanity'. He was 'seething with rage and wants to submit a new letter of resignation'.[307] In Washington, Robert Lansing, the 'trim and elegant' US Secretary of State, hawkish as ever, was breathing down the President's neck.[308] Germany was told that she could only avoid war with the United States if unrestricted submarine tactics were ended. With the loss of American life, even if only a small number, the British Foreign Office 'at last felt able to court the wrath of the US South by placing cotton on the absolute contraband list'.[309] In 1914, Grey had earlier strongly resisted French pressure to do so. A lot was at stake: if Germany could be persuaded to abandon unrestricted warfare, it would be Britain that would be seen to be the violator of neutral rights. The moral ground would be lost.

Bowing to the kaiser's conciliatory tone, the German Ambassador now pledged that 'passenger liners will not be sunk without warning and without ensuring the safety of the non-combatants aboard providing that the liners do not try to escape or offer resistance'. The pronouncement angered many

Germans and deepened the breach between Germany's political and naval leadership, what Hough called a kind of 'internecine conflict' between the Naval High Command, the Chancellor, the Foreign Minister and the kaiser.[310]

The kaiser's assurance, which came to be known as the *Arabic* Pledge, was broken almost as soon as it had been made.[311] On 4 September, Schwieger torpedoed the 10,920-ton liner RMS *Hesperian* 80 miles from the Fastnet Rock. Two days later, under tow to Ireland, she sank. From a complement of 650, eight died in the explosion and thirty-two more were drowned when one of the port-side lifeboats overturned while being lowered. One of the crew who died turned out to be an American. Even though the night sky had been clear and the torpedo attack made from only 300 yards, Schwieger protested his target had just been a 'big dim shadow'.[312] The German Foreign Office denied that she had been torpedoed ('much more likely the boat ran on a mine'), though tell-tale fragments from the torpedo were found on deck.[313]

Canadian philanthropist Frances Stephens was on her final way home. In an extraordinarily cruel twist of fate, the ship, now carrying her corpse on its last journey home, was torpedoed by the same man, Walther Schwieger, who had originally caused her death on the *Lusitania*.

Bachmann was relieved the same day, 4 September, and replaced by Henning von Holtzendorff, a relative of Müller and no friend of Tirpitz. Jellicoe knew Holtzendorff from his China days. It's ironic that it would be he who would unleash Germany's most aggressive period of unrestricted submarine warfare in 1917. The mood in Berlin was changing. Falkenhayn, the army's Chief of Staff, now thought that the war was becoming 'a battle for sheer survival', a war of attrition, and that in those circumstances the use of any weapon, including the U-boat – with all the risks of alienating the neutrals – was the only way forward. In December, he parted ways with Bethmann-Hollweg, saying: 'So, I am very sorry, but I have to distance myself from you on the question of the U-boat war.'[314] The constant reconfiguration of alliances between colleagues was bewildering.

The *Arabic* Pledge ended 'the respite in diplomatic tensions that followed Wilson's third *Lusitania* note'.[315] Even if it would still take more than a year, Wilson was moving slowly towards war. On 22 September, Colonel House wrote of him saying as much:

> Much to my surprise, he said he had never been sure that we ought not to take part in the conflict and if it seemed evident that Germany and her militarist ideas were to win, the obligation upon us was greater than ever.[316]

Germany's U-boat war was 'petering out from lack of numbers'.[317] The number operational in August was half that of June, and in September only five U-boats put to sea 'for commerce raiding'. With the Type-*UB* craft mostly being used for shallow coastal waters, the Type-*UC* minelayers became the backbone of the submarine war in British waters.

On 19 September, Scheer ordered HSF submarines in the North Sea to return. The U-boat campaign 'west of Britain and in the English Channel' was discontinued. The moves launched a deep internal debate on how to continue the submarine war.[318] After American protests, 'mining operations were seen as more useful'.[319] Some submarines which had previously only used torpedoes were now 'partially equipped with mines which could be fired out of the torpedo tubes', a move the BdU Andreas Michelsen described as an 'unsatisfactory half-measure' because mining was so uncertain in its eventual victims.[320]

## The Increasing Threat in the Mediterranean

An immediate result of the *Arabic* attack was to shift the focus of German submarine operations south to the Mediterranean and Adriatic. The waters were characterised by numerous 'choke points' – Malta, Gibraltar, Suez and Crete. Only there, where 'there were few passenger steamers and travelling Americans, could the submarine campaign be continued without excessive weakening'.[321] It was also in August 1915 that a dangerous milestone was passed: for the first time in the war, monthly sinkings outpaced shipbuilding and replacement. Britain's merchant fleet was being slowly, but surely, whittled away.

The Mediterranean had its own rules. Italy was not yet in the war, and a distinction had to be made between U-boats that were under German command and those of the Austro-Hungarian navy. West of Cape Matapan, U-boats flew Austrian flags and ships could be sunk without warning.

Four large submarines were sent from Germany in August to reinforce the Austro-Hungarian fleet at Cattaro in the Adriatic. Claus Rücker, Waldamar Kophamel, Konrad Gansser and Walter Forstmann brought the submarines (respectively, *U.34*, *U.35*, *U.33* and *U.39*) through the Gibraltar narrows. Max Valentiner, wanting to join earlier, arrived later with the larger *U.38*. His request had been rebuffed by Holtzendorff, concerned about the transit time and the slim pickings en route ('None of the four boats had had any luck on the way'), but the weather was better than in the North Sea and operations could be carried out for longer periods.[322] Valentiner got his way, telling Holtzendorff that he would 'sink 50,000 tons on the journey'.[323] Later, in his memoirs, he rather vainly wrote about his pushiness. He had been wrong, he wrote:

> In 1915, I should never have gone to the Mediterranean; back then, I was the most feared U-boat commander in the North Sea.[324]

On 23 October, Kophamel attacked a troopship off Salonika, sinking the 7,000-ton *Marquette* with one torpedo. When he saw that ten nurses had been among the victims, 'the humanitarian skipper was greatly distressed'.[325] It was Kophamel who, in one of the war's more bizarre episodes, brought back two camels to Pola, gifts to the kaiser from a Senussi tribal leader, aboard the narrow confines of *U.35*. The crew stank of camel dung so badly that they were totally shunned ashore.

Gansser narrowly escaped a torpedo-boat attack as he passed through the Strait, well defended with anti-submarine nets and closely watched. In the deep channel – depths could reach 800 metres – currents could be, for a submarine, relatively strong: 3–4 knots. Gansser achieved ill-famed notoriety for his attack on the 4,796-ton *Clan Macleod*, en route to Chittagong. With a cargo of jute, she had tried to outrun him. *U.33* was spotted by the First Officer at 0745hrs on the morning of 1 December 1915. A first shot, falling short, was fired just after the hour. Thirty minutes later, around 0835hrs, the submarine's deck gun opened up again, this time the dozen or so shells landing long. The same happened fifteen minutes later. Finally, at around 0950hrs, now half a mile behind, *U.33*'s shelling found the range. Captain H.S. Southward, *Clan Macleod*'s fourth wartime master, decided to surrender but the firing continued. All the starboard boats were 'smashed to matchwood'. Southward was badly wounded, with nine sailors killed and three more fatally wounded, while preparing to board a lifeboat.[326]

Aboard was a 16-year-old apprentice, Thomas Watkinson. He'd only left Manchester's Hulme Grammar School three days before joining the ship's company. Recovering from his wounded wrist suffered in the attack, he talked with a *Daily Mail* correspondent:

> For two and a half hours we tried to escape but it was no use, and after a shell had passed through the funnel the surrender flag was hauled up and the *Clan Macleod* came to a standstill. The submarine came up at full speed, firing shrapnel shell all the time, and when she got our range, our deck was swept. Ten Lascars were killed outright, and Captain Southward, who had a portion of his bridge shot away, and Engineer Black, were wounded.[327]

As *U.33* continued to shell the wounded ship on the starboard side, damaging two lifeboats, around eighty crew members were 'scrambling' into the remaining, undamaged boats.

Southward was taken aboard the submarine, where his wounds were, as the 3rd Engineer Joseph Vize recalled, 'very kindly dressed'. He was then given more dressings for the other wounded crew members and sent back with a bottle of brandy, some wine and a 'handful of cigars'.[328] The survivors set off in two lifeboats; one, commanded by the chief officer, was rescued and her crew dropped in Malta on 4 December. After thirty-six hours in the open lifeboat, the other one with Southward was rescued by the *Lord Cromer* and reached Algiers a day later.

Foreign Secretary Grey's recounting of the loss of the *Clan Macleod* and Konrad Gansser's actions were used as an example of the 'new savagery' of the submarine war.

### SS *Persia* and the *Clan Macfarlane* Sunk by Valentiner

The submarine war of 1915 closed with another atrocity from Max Valentiner. On 30 December, not content with having just sunk one passenger ship, he attacked and sank the 7,974-ton P&O liner *Persia*. *U.38* had already sunk the even larger 10,932-ton Japanese *Yasaka Maru*, nine days earlier, on 21 December. At the time, Valentiner was flying the Austrian flag, an act which was strongly repudiated.[329] He had employed the same ruse in the previous month, on 8 November, when he opened fire on the stationary liner *Ancona* off Tunisia.

*Persia*'s master, 59-year-old William Henry Selby Hall, was an experienced officer, and signed on aboard as 'passengers' were trained gunners for the ship's deck gun. One, Lawrence Wellington, had served as a Royal Marine gunner aboard the Majestic-class battleship HMS *Jupiter*.

The ship sank fast after her boilers exploded. Valentiner's log entry for *U.38* timed at 1150hrs suggests a rather careful setup to cover his actions:

> Cruiser with course for Alexandria in sight. Dived, cleared 2nd tube for bow attack. Set depth to 3m. I can see Cruiser with two masts and two funnels of around 9,000t that I assume to be a troop transporter.[330]

Aboard the *Persia*, guests were sitting down for lunch, or 'tiffin' as they called it; the passengers had persuaded the crew to open the portholes as it was stiflingly hot. Their victory and the crew's concession would prove fatal. As the torpedo sped towards its target, blades that were mounted on its head began to spin, unscrewing the detonator clock to arm the weapon. After it struck, the whistle that had been used in the previous day's drills was silent; it had been destroyed in the explosion.

Still at speed, the water rose to wash *Persia*'s port-side main deck, making the lifeboats almost impossible to reach. The ship continued to plough forward, finally slowing only to slide, stern first, into the seabed 10,000ft below. As her funnel disappeared, the ship's 'black soul' escaped: a final cloud of sooty smoke was exhaled in the dying ship's final moments. *U.38* promptly moved off to search for another target.

## KAPITÄNLEUTNANT MAX VALENTINER (1883–1949)

A clergyman's son, Valentiner was born in Schleswig-Holstein in 1883. Aged 18, he joined the German Navy as a cadet (the class was known as 'Crew 4/02'), went on to the Kiel Naval College in 1905 and became Oberleutnant zur See in 1908. In January 1911, his first submarine, *U.3*, sank with all hands. Valentiner was able to get all thirty men out (Otto Weddigen was one) after raising the *U.3* with the hoists of SMS *Vulkan*. Not only displaying extraordinary personal courage, Valentiner was also an outstanding commander. In a training exercise in 1911, he again excelled, managing bow and stern hits on two battleships with two torpedoes apiece.

On the outbreak of war, he retook command of *U.3*. In an encounter with his Commander-in-Chief, Prince Heinrich, he complained about *U.3*'s performance: 'Your Royal Highness, my boat is like an old horse. You can give it as much sugar as you like, but it cannot gallop anymore.'[331] He called it much worse – '*dieser gottverfluchten Kaffeemühle*', 'a goddammed coffee-grinder' ('*U3*', Valentiner, p.12). Much to his surprise, he was given command of a new submarine, *U.38*.

Valentiner once nearly torpedoed Fürbringer, only stopping at the last moment when he saw the eyes that had been painted on *UB.2*'s bow: 'I was just about to push the button and then, at the last moment, I saw your gorgeous eyes! They're your lucky talisman.'[332] Painting an eye on a boat's bow wasn't unusual; it was considered good luck (when Gregor's *UB.33* was found by divers, after she'd sunk on 11 April 1918, 'like many other smallish UB boats, this one had an eye painted on the bow for good luck').[333]

NOTE: Not to be confused with Hans Valentiner, commander of *UB.16*, *UB.37*, *UC.71* and *UB.56*.

Only four of her fourteen lifeboats got free and only two of the eighteen children aboard survived. After thirty hours adrift, 158 survivors were rescued. Despite her speed (*Persia* could make 18 knots), Hall had insisted on a lifeboat drill being carried out with the passengers as soon as the ship left Valletta's Grand Harbour. Even so, the death toll was a high: 334 passengers and crew.

On the same day, a Clan Line ship, the *Clan Macfarlane*, was torpedoed by Valentiner without warning. After the torpedo struck, *U.38* surfaced and started shelling the crippled ship. At a distance of 'less than a hundred feet', she was sunk by gunfire, 'six shells striking the vessel'.[334] Five were below the water line. Despite this, her master, James Whyte Swanston, was cool-headed enough to collect the ship's confidential papers and throw them overboard.

After he'd given his ship's nationality, name, destination, cargo and tonnage, the captain and crew members abandoned ship and set off in six boats, one behind the other, following Swanston. Valentiner had apparently been in a great hurry and nervous, constantly scanning the horizon. He had dived the *U.38* and set off as soon as he was assured of the ship's fate. The crew said that he appeared 'a bundle of nerves, showing great restlessness and uneasiness'.[335] Despite very difficult circumstances ('each man's rations consisted of only half a biscuit, and half a dipper of water twice a day', while the sea was 'heavy'), the survivors' morale held. After two days, two of the boats broke free.[336] After another two, Swanston's own boat also broke loose. Two men had already died from exposure, while the survivors of the three boats which remained tied together suffered three more days at sea, during which eleven more Lascar seamen died.

On 7 January 1916, out of a crew of seventy-four, only twenty-four survivors made it to Malta. Of her European crew, James Swanston, *Clan Macfarlane*'s 3rd officer, her 3rd engineer, Steward and two other crew members had all been lost at sea. For a while, back home in Edinburgh, Swanston's wife and only child had held out hope for his safety. It had been mistakenly reported, according to the *Dundee Evening Telegraph*, that he'd survived. When the news of the three sinkings reached Jellicoe, he wrote to ship owner Sir Charles Cayzer, who had lost an experienced and loyal captain who'd given sixteen years to the Clan Line. Jellicoe's words convey a resigned tone, reflecting how he thought the war was being fought differently in the North Sea:

> I am afraid the submarines will bag some ships. But I hope it won't last and that we shall make it too hot for them. I think the minelaying is likely to be more serious than the submarine menace in the long run. The real way to stop it is for a vigorous offensive on shore with the Navy on the flank. We shall have to strike at Germany through Belgium as soon as we get more troops, but I hope in any case that we shall catch a good many of their minelayers as well as submarines.[337]

Valentiner had disobeyed the kaiser's direct orders to protect passenger vessels. His actions led to the end of the policy of sinking without warning in the Mediterranean.

After returning from China in 1901, Jellicoe had spent a lot of time at his future father-in-law's house at Ralston, just outside of Glasgow. Later, he would spend time at Gartmore, the estate Charles Cayzer next purchased 25 miles north of the city. It was Jellicoe's way to recharge after months of the incessant and deep stress that came with the job.

Sir Charles was a successful shipowner; he had started the Clan Line in 1878, ten years after the completion of the Suez Canal, with the purchase of two steamers trading primarily with India and the Far East. First established in Liverpool, the headquarters were transferred to Glasgow in 1882, the year in which he also became the MP for Burrow-in-Furness, a seat he held until 1906. At the war's outbreak, many vessels were commandeered for government service as armed merchant cruisers, troopships or hospital ships.[338] The ubiquity of Clan Line ships led to them being called the 'Scots Navy' due to their officers' sleeve rings being identical to those of the Royal Navy.

It would have been natural for he and Jellicoe to have exchanged views on how merchant shipping could be better protected, initially from surface and then increasingly from submarine attack (frustratingly, nothing could be found in the Cayzer family archives). At the start of the war, the firm operated fifty-eight vessels with a GRT of 251,482 tons.

A heavy duty was to fall on Sir Charles's shoulders; he had 'lost' three executive directors of the Clan Line and five from Cayzer Irvine. Many of his captains were being recalled, as it had been his practice to recruit RNVR officers for his ships.

Already, in 1914, two Clan Line ships – the *Clan Matheson* and *Clan Grant* – had been sunk by the German cruiser raider *Emden*. The *Clan Matheson* was the first Clan Line ship to be fired upon and the first to be sunk when she was intercepted late at night on Monday, 14 September 1914.[339] A month later, the *Emden* struck again and sank the 3,948-ton *Clan Grant* on 16 October near Colombo.

In 1915, mines, submarines and raider actions would account for five more of his ships. The family's commitment to the war effort was such that King George V even wrote to Sir Charles congratulating him on having nine members of his family in uniform.[340]

## Q-ship Tactics – The Loss of Fürbringer's *U.40*

On 23 June 1915, the British successfully tried out an early version of the Q-ship concept. Linked to the new deception was David Beatty's secretary in Rosyth, Paymaster Frank Spickernell, 'in co-operation with Lieutenant J.B. Glencross'.[341] Their idea involved a surface ship acting as 'bait', with a submarine attached which would be released once a suitable target had been lured within killing range.

'As long as submarine warfare was conducted in its restricted form', the Q-ship was effective.[342] Indeed, Jellicoe at one point thought them 'the most effective method' of defending merchant ships against submarine attack.[343] He made the comment in early 1916, but it soon became clear that their value wore off and that their tactic encouraged the replacement of the deck gun with the torpedo.

In her first action, the submarine that was in tow almost fell victim of its own trap: the 100-fathom tow-cable (which also held the telephone cable) had not properly detached from the towing trawler *Taranaki*. *C.24*'s commander, Lieutenant Frederick Henry Taylor, had to carefully manoeuvre his submarine to avoid it as he fired at the point-blank range of 500 yards into *U.40*'s beam.[344] Only Captain Werner Fürbringer's brother, Oberleutnant zur See Stobbe, and the coxswain, Bootsmann (Boatswain) Beizen, survived. Both had been on the bridge. The rest of the crew, all twenty-nine, could not escape.[345] Some of *Taranaki*'s crew heard the Germans complain 'that they had been the victims of a dirty trick'.[346] *U.40* was the first U-boat sunk by a submarine towed by a decoy trawler.

Three weeks later, the ploy was repeated and worked again. The trawler *Princess Louise* (ex-*Princess Marie José*) fooled another submarine, the *U.23*, which was snared by HMS *C.27*. Seven ratings and three officers were rescued from the doomed boat; stupidly, they were allowed to mingle with German civilians about to be sent back to Germany. From that moment, German submarine commanders were wary of any trawler on which crews could not be seen obviously working their nets; it was likely a Q-ship.

### DRIFTERS

A drifter was aptly named: it was a fishing boat designed to catch herring in drifting nets. Early in the war, the Royal Navy requisitioned them for ASW duty. Because they were designed to haul heavy loads, they could drag around 900 yards of drifting net with the aim of snarling a submarine at depths of around 120ft.

The drifter design was also used for new boats specifically tasked with ASW, so-called Admiralty Drifters. The hulls of the 9-knot boats could be made of either wood or steel, the former weighing slightly less (175 versus 199 tons), both being around 86ft long and mounting a 6pdr gun on deck. Around 100 were built in Canadian yards, recognisable as such by a numbered CD designation.

Hydrophones and depth charges were used by the Americans on 'sub-chasers' (equivalent to British MLs) and by the British on net patrol boats (drifters), patrol boats (known as P-boats, or PBs, 'frightfully bad sea boats, low in the water but capable of 24 knots'), motor launches (MLs) and CMBs (coastal motor boats).[347] Jellicoe did not have a high opinion of the PB's cost-effectiveness.

On 1 July, *U.39* successfully sunk the 4,656-ton *Caucasian*, which, for just over an hour, managed to out-run Walter's Forstmann U-boat. The German captain was so furious that, after the seventeenth shell had finally brought the British tanker to a stop, he was about to shoot the survivors in their lifeboats. The man at *Caucasian*'s wheel, Deponent, suddenly jumped overboard, trying to save his dog. Forstmann was astonished: 'You jump overboard to save a dog!' He relented, allowing the survivors to go on their way, while *U.39* sank a further 14,300 tons that same day.[348]

By this point, the costs of the submarine war – not just in tonnage – were enormous: guarding British waters alone, the Auxiliary Patrol comprised '70 yachts, 691 armed trawlers and drifters, 786 net-drifters, 270 mine-sweepers and 156 motor-boats, with 198 trawlers and drifters permanently used for boom defence, actually on station'. There were a total of 2,180 small vessels, all of which had to be manned, maintained and directed.[349]

### The *Nicosian* Incident and *Baralong*

Out in the Atlantic, the British were also working with decoy ships, but their success was double-edged.

Max Valentiner sent his cousin, Kapitänleutnant Bernd Wegener, back out on patrol after the abortive attempt to rescue Heinrich von Hennig from a British POW camp.[350] On 19 August, 70 or so miles off Kinsale, Wegener's crew spotted a British transport, the 6,369-ton ss *Nicosian*, coming from New Orleans with a cargo of ammunition and 250 mules.

*Nicosian* was caught by shellfire from *U.27* after her master, Captain Chester Manning, had attempted a zigzagging dash for safety. His radio operator sent out numerous distress calls, one after the other – at 1310hrs, 'Captured by enemy submarine. Crew ready to leave. Lat 50. 22N. Long 8. 12W.' Five minutes later, he mentioned 'two enemy submarines'. Finally, around 1430hrs, the last message was flashed: 'Help! Help! For God's sake help.' Wegener's submarine held off while a prize party of six sailors rowed over to the ship, now motionless on the water. Unbeknown to them, *Nicosian*'s messages had been picked up by a nearby Q-ship, *Baralong*, whose commander, Geoffrey Herbert, an ex-submarine commander, knew their tactics well.[351]

*Baralong* was built to take punishment to hide her real purpose: her forward and aft hold were full of empty casks to keep her afloat – 2,680 of them. As well as looking the part, she also had to be carefully equipped to do so and had to be small enough to make it not worth the cost of a torpedo, rather encouraging a U-boat to surface. Like most Q-ships, *Baralong*'s crew was a mixed bag: nineteen were regular navy, nine merchant seamen and the rest RNR and Royal Marines. They could be rowdy; in Dartmouth, after they had wrecked a pub, they failed to turn up to the court hearing as their ship weighed anchor in the still of the night.

Wegener was so focused on his prey that he took little notice of another bedraggled-looking steamer on the horizon. As Herbert closed in, his ship was flying an American flag. At around half a mile, an international flag, VICQRA, was hauled up to signify that his intent was 'To save Life only'. Wegener spotted the flag and acknowledged. His men stopped firing on *Nicosian*, and the submarine moved forward to her bow on her port side so that she could be better positioned to intercept *Baralong*.

On *Baralong*, the three 12pdrs were made ready. As she slid behind *Nicosian* on her starboard side, she momentarily dropped out of the U-boat's sight. Using the cloak provided by the *Nicosian*, Herbert ordered the Stars and Stripes lowered and replaced with the White Ensign. As soon as line of sight with the submarine was re-established, fire was opened on *U.27* with all the guns at around 600 yards. Wegener's gunners could only manage 'one retaliatory shot against the thirty-four fired that rained on and around her'.[352]

> While riflemen aboard the *Baralong* picked off the Germans on the U-boat's deck, at least 34 more shells were fired from the 12-pounders, many of them striking their target.[353]

Later, the American muleteers said that *U.27*'s deck gunners had jumped off the submarine when they saw how unevenly matched they were. Once in the water, they started swimming towards the six men who had already gone over as part of the prize crew and who were now back scrambling aboard the steamer. 'Some succeeded, despite Herbert's order to shoot them away.'[354] It was clear that the British crew had their blood up.

While trying to save themselves, eleven of Wegener's crew members were shot in cold blood. Shots killed some as they scrambled onto the ship, but four – including Wegener – still managed to get aboard. Royal Marines were then sent across, tracked down the Germans in the engine room and shot them as well. Herbert maintained his innocence and denied the actions of his men: 'six of the enemy had been found but they succumbed to the injuries received from a lyddite shell shortly afterwards and were buried at once.'[355] From some of *Nicosian*'s lifeboats, the survivors cheered. Captain Manning was heard shouting: 'If any of those bastard Huns come up, lads, hit 'em with an oar.'[356]

Later, one of the Royal Marines, Corporal Fred Collins, told a different story, saying that he remembered how specific Herbert's instructions had been: 'Don't forget, Collins – no prisoners aboard this ship. Get rid of them.' He testified that Herbert had shouted at one of the wounded German sailors as he floated past the conning tower: 'What about the *Lusitania*, you bastard.' He recalled Herbert hurling his revolver at the man's head.

It was Collins, however, who tracked down Wegener on the *Nicosian* and shot him in the head after he'd managed to jump back into the sea. At the end of his life, even Gordon Steele, his 2iC, finally spoke out and confirmed that he also heard Herbert's instructions to take no prisoners. Apparently, Herbert had already received informal, verbal instructions after the loss of the *Lusitania*, when he was told: 'This *Lusitania* business is shocking. Unofficially, we are telling you … take no prisoners from U-boats.'[357] Steele had been an 'outstanding cadet' in the Merchant Navy Training Ship *Worcester* and would later win a Victoria Cross in Russia.[358]

In his secret report to the Admiralty, Herbert admitted that the German survivors had been shot, claiming that he would have been derelict in his duty if one of them had managed to scuttle the ship. There was no denying the savagery of it: 'This shameful deed remains a blot on the fair name of the British Navy.'[359] Maybe, with knowledge of the *Arabic* sinking fresh in his mind, it might be better understood but never condoned.[360] Her distress signals had been picked up but *Nicosian* had not been able to get to her in time, despite only being around 20 miles away.

The story got out despite Admiralty attempts to keep it quiet. There were six American witnesses on the *Nicosian* who were prepared to testify. Naturally, the Germans wanted Herbert to stand trial as a war criminal. The British countered the demand by saying they would only agree if the same approach was taken for those involved in the *Arabic* sinking as well as a recent attack on a British submarine on the Dutch coast. For the Germans, trap-ship tactics were 'below the belt'. Hashagen wrote that 'both captains, Wegener and Hansen, were experienced U-Boat commanders but at that time unprepared for such elaborate trickery'.[361] He was incensed that the *Baralong* shot at 'defenceless' sailors swimming in the sea. In Hitler's Kriegsmarine, one of its flotillas, the VI U-Boot Flotille, was later renamed the Flotille Wegener in memory of the affair. When Herbert (taking Steele with him) left the *Baralong* to take command of HMS *E.22*, the ship's now infamous name was dropped and she was rechristened *Wyandra*.

As an American flag had been used in the subterfuge, word soon got back to President Wilson. He did nothing apart from commenting it was 'horrible', to which Lansing added 'shocking'.

### Q-ship Tactics – *Baralong* and *U.41*

Another September Q-ship victim was Klaus Hansen's *U.41*, *U.20*'s replacement in the Western Approaches. On 13 September, Hansen was engaged in sinking the 6,651-ton *Urbino* by gunfire and hadn't seen another ship approaching from the south. When he did, he merely thought it one more suitable target. He ordered her to stop and the ship's papers to be brought across. As his prize crew rowed over from the *U.41*, the submarine drifted closer and closer, and when the gap had closed to around 700 yards, a White Ensign was suddenly hauled up and the newcomer's guns opened fire.[362] It was *Baralong* again. Hansen couldn't escape.

*U.41* was hit at the base of the conning tower and her hull holed by a shell just as she was trying to crash dive. There were only two survivors: the helmsman, Franz Godeau, and the boat's 'Heinrich', Oberleutnant zur See Iwan Crompton.[363] *Baralong* turned towards them and the two were sucked under and nearly killed by the ship's screws. When they were finally taken aboard as prisoners, there was only one man who would treat the POWs correctly, and he dressed Crompton's head wound.[364]

In Germany, claiming that *Baralong* had not struck its false flag, there was outrage. Not content with the commercial success of one coin for the *Lusitania*, Götz now made two more coins, one commemorating the *Baralong* incident and the sinking of *U.41*, the other the *U.27*. For a second time, the dates were off. The medal, which depicts a survivor shaking their fist from the water, is dated 24 September. Around the White Ensign are the words 'ALBIONS EHREN-FLAGGE'. Only *U.27*'s medal got the date right: 'BARALONG MOERDER 19 AUG 1915 U27'.

### Q – SHIPS (TRAP or SPECIAL SERVICE SHIPS)

Quite who originated the idea of Q-ships, Mystery-ships or, as they were known by the Germans, 'Trap' ships (U-boot-Fallen), is unknown: It was either (a) Churchill after talks with the Portsmouth commander, Admiral Sir Hedworth Meux; (b) according to Marder, Captain Herbert Richmond or Captain Alfred Ellison; or (c) Beatty's secretary, Paymaster-Commander Frank Spickernell, who (along with Commander Plunkett) had the idea of a trawler working with a towed submarine. The eventual designation, 'Q-ship', might have been linked to Queenstown, where many Q-ships were based under Admiral Lewis Bayly's command. The Q-ship's job was to lure a U-boat close enough to a seemingly innocent, helpless vessel until it was too late and it could be engaged at close range by hidden guns, mounted behind a false superstructure. The first Q-ship, ss *Victoria*, was a dismal failure: she didn't even see an enemy submarine. It was the *Prince Charles*, a 373-ton converted collier armed with two 6pdr and two 3pdr guns, that scored the first success (without an escort submarine) against *U.36* as her crew were boarding a Danish ship, the *Luise*, on 24 July 1915.

A Q-ship crew's behaviour had to pass close scrutiny: crews didn't salute officers, were dressed like merchant seamen and smoked on the job. The charade was carefully choreographed: below decks, it was strictly disciplined; above, slovenly. On Stan Smith's second ship, the 2,817-ton *Pargust*, scarcely capable of more than 8 knots, one sailor even dressed as a woman hanging out the washing.[365] On the *Stock Force*, her captain insisted that one of the 'panic crew' be black. It was a 'uniquely schizoid quality of service'.[366] Ashore, they had to carry on the same charade in case there were enemy agents around: the Q-ship's commanding officer became the 'master', the engineer 'chief'. Ordinary Seaman (OS) Stan Smith recounted how his ship, *Q.12*, 'was also fitted with bell pushes around the upper decks so that if you saw a periscope you could press it with your foot sending everybody, unseen, to action stations. Then you would light a fag and stroll away casually, to your own.' (*Q.12* was eventually torpedoed 'without a shot fired in anger'.)[367] Periscopes that could be used by gun crews or the 'master' to watch the approach of a U-boat were disguised as 'small ventilators or stove-pipes'.

Because Q-ships often had to make believe that crews were abandoning ship, the number aboard was often doubled (the Admiralty had to pay 'Hard-Laying money' to compensate sailors for the increasingly cramped quarters). Q-ship captains had to have nerves of steel, knowingly accepting punishment to lure their prey. Because of the danger, crews were voluntary. Wood cargoes or empty oil cans were used to delay their own sinking. Guns crews would 'short' their fire to convince a U-boat that they had the range advantage; the risk was high but so could be the rewards. A Q-ship crew received 'double pay, abundant good food and a better leave allocation'. They could also directly benefit financially from sharing Prize money. Each crew member had to become part of the RNR or leave the ship. The ships themselves now became HMS rather than SS. Q-ship crews would be issued silver-coloured cap badges to signify that they were on war service.

The makeup of *Pargust*'s crew might have seemed comic, but her weaponry was not. She bristled: one 4in gun, four 12pdrs, two Maxim guns, two 14in torpedo tubes and, finally, stern rails for depth charges. When Gordon Campbell, the ship's commander, couldn't secure another 12pdr on *Pargust*'s stern, visibly displayed like any other armed merchant ship, he had a dummy, wooden gun built. The deck design of Q-ships impressed many German U-boat commanders. For Hashagen, Q-ships were 'a brilliantly conceived piece of camouflage'.[368]

A ship could also sail – but not fight – under a neutral flag. Hence the signal to fire was always preceded by a British flag being run up to replace the previous flag of convenience. Rather idealistically, Washington specifically demanded that their flag never be used for purposes of deception. While the British subterfuge might have been understandable, it 'completely [ignored] the fact that the use of neutral colours by British ships immediately put *all* neutrals at risk'.[369]

### Mounting Shipping Losses

The terrible losses being suffered by Britain's merchant shipping lines meant more than just ships. As losses mounted, the head of the Clan Line, Sir Charles Cayzer, sank into a deep depression. His employees were dying at sea and the fleet that he'd spent his life creating was suffering one loss after the other. Four would be sunk by one man, Hans-Joachim von Mellenthin, who torpedoed more Clan Line ships than any other U-boat commander.

Cayzer generously gave to help sailors where he could: six tennis courts were built in Invergordon for their use while ashore. John Jellicoe suggested that they be gifted in the memory of those on the *Clan MacTavish* who had lost their lives, and sent a telegram to Sir Charles when he heard the news of her sinking: 'The magnificent fight shown by the *Clan MacTavish* fills us in the Grand Fleet with admiration. We sympathize deeply with those who have lost relatives as a result of the action.'[370]

Sir Charles unburdened his own feelings to the admiral:

> Believe me, you can never hear too much of them. These men are going through trials and dangers every day and night so that they may bring to

**KAPITÄNLEUTNANT HANS JOACHIM VON MELLENTHIN (1887–1971)**

The four submarines that von Mellenthin commanded (*UB.11*, *UB.43*, *UB.49* and *U.120*) sank fifty-seven ships totalling 154,662 GRT and damaged a further seven, adding another 31,556 GRT to his record. All sinkings were in his first two commands.

Von Mellenthin entered the service as a cadet in 1906 and served until 1922. In September 1917, he narrowly escaped internment in Cadiz with *UB.49*. He was decorated with the *Pour le Mérite* and promoted to command *U.120*. At the end of the war, he served with the Marinebrigade von Loewenfeldt, one of the first Fascist Freikorps units which took part in the failed Kapp putsch (other notable members included Lothar von Arnauld de la Perière, Karl-Jesko von Putkammer and Ludwig von Schröder).

Mellenthin torpedoed four Clan Line ships, more than any other U-boat commander: the *Clan Leslie* (3,937 GRT), *Clan Farquhar* (5,858 GRT), *Clan Ferguson* (4,808 GRT) and *Clan Macdougall* (4,719 GRT).

> our shores the necessities for our existence. No words of gratitude can be too great for their service.[371]

By autumn 1916, the Clan Line was 'losing ships to enemy action at a rate of about one every two months'.[372] In one month in the spring of 1918, bad news hit the company twice: the *Clan Macpherson* and, within ten days, the *Clan Macdougall* were both torpedoed. By the end of the war, the company had lost twenty-eight ships to enemy action, representing 124,551 GRT. That represented a significant part of the U-boat fleet's total of 251,482 tons.

Initially, Cayzer 'had resisted building new ships in such uncertain times', even if he was eventually persuaded that it was better to do so.[373] The new ships included the *Clan Mackay* (launched in 1916 but sunk in 1918 after a collision) and, in 1917, a number of 5,000–6,000-ton ships, the *Clan Macbean*, *Clan Mackenzie*, *Clan Matheson* and *Clan Ronald*. It was a measure of the inflation in hull costs that Sir Charles's successor, August Cayzer, had to pay 'a vastly inflated price of £750,000 for what amounted to two vessels'.[374] He continued to replace ships, adding four 4,000–5,000-ton vessels and purchasing another nine from other lines.

Sir Charles even contemplated selling the company and, after talking with the family directors, also asked his two naval sons-in-law, Jellicoe and Charles Madden, for their thoughts. It has been suggested that this was merely a courtesy. I would like to think that he valued their opinions a little more than for mere window dressing. The three met up at Invergordon at Christmas to exchange thoughts. Both rejected Sir Charles's ideas. Jellicoe argued that since the tonnage would most likely end up in neutral hands, such an action might benefit Britain's enemies:

> I imagine financially it would be a good deal; but is there not a danger of ships going to neutrals? And from that point of view, a sale would be unpatriotic now. And I should imagine that possibly the sale of so big a business might cause a feeling of anxiety, as people might think you were doubtful about the end of the war.

A sale would hurt Britain's maritime dominance and Sir Charles, thought Madden, would probably be pilloried in the press:

> I see half a million tons have been sold to neutrals since the war commenced, which means they now run on the higher freight lines to Germany and don't feed us but our enemies.[375]

The company was not sold, but the losses continued to haunt Cayzer and his health started to decline. By April 1916, 'an average of one Clan Line ship every eight weeks had been sunk since the start of the war'.[376]

## The Pitfalls of Blockade

It should not have been surprising that relations between the Royal Navy and the Foreign Office became strained. Many times, they had different interests at stake: they 'seemed to be fighting different enemies'.[377] This was the case with blockade: 'Grey considered it part of a body of international law'; Jackie Fisher, on the other hand, 'had no intention of having the British navy abide' by any such legalistic restriction.[378]

Germany was not as susceptible to a rupture in seaborne commerce as was Britain. Britain was an island nation; Germany a central European power. It was why Grey felt that the war would be longer than others imagined. It would pull in America and, with her, other neutrals. When it came to the latter, Jellicoe was a hawk, but his arguments for bolstering the blockade against Germany in the face of neutral reaction did not win the day. In mid-December 1915, he visited the Admiralty to argue his case with the First Sea Lord and the Under Secretary for Foreign Affairs, Lord Robert Cecil. Later, in January 1916, Jellicoe wrote to Fisher complaining that he had written,

> letter after letter on the blockade questions, but the F.O. [Foreign Office] seems quite imbecile. They are afraid of their own shadows and imagine every neutral is anxious to go to war with us and can do us harm. I don't believe it and I never shall till I see the declaration of war.[379]

It is not surprising that Jellicoe started to vent his frustration with Britain's diplomatic service. His sources of intelligence were good and he 'frequently displayed an uncanny knowledge of subjects unconnected with his main responsibilities'.[380] He cited reports showing a tell-tale rise in cotton re-exports and, in August 1915, questioned why shares in the 'sixteen leading Danish shipping companies had risen on an average by 54.7 percent since the beginning of the war'.[381] In 1916, the monthly value of American exports to the Allies was worth around $300 million. Jellicoe's inquiries and observations became increasingly critical:

> I am strongly of [the] opinion that the pressure of our sea power upon Germany at present applied, cannot seriously inconvenience that country. It is in our power to cause her the greatest embarrassment, but instead we are only producing a situation of slight inconvenience. She is doing her best to stop our trade and I urge that we should let every other consideration give way to the one main issue, to crush her, both economically, and when the opportunity offers, by force of arms.[382]

Nicholas Lambert's *Planning Armageddon* quotes the writings of Captain Montagu Consett at length. At the time, he was the British Naval Attaché in Scandinavia and a critic of the British blockade's loopholes. After the war, Chatterton wrote that despite 'whatever may have been praiseworthy in the offices of Whitehall', the 'united protests of four senior officers most intimately concerned with its [the blockade's] working' stand out: Jellicoe, de Chair, Tupper and Consett.[383]

In 1923, despite the current 'tight censorship', Consett wrote that Britain had profited and 'held the economic life of the three little countries (Sweden, Norway and Denmark) in the palm of her hand' and turned a blind eye where it could from a continued trade with Germany through officially neutral countries.[384] He called the continued profits made by British banks from this trade 'the greatest untold scandal of the First World War'.

Germany was interested in maintaining the existing status of the Scandinavian countries rather than bringing them into the war: 'Sweden became Germany's workshop and Denmark her larder.'[385] Both were essential for her economy. In 1915 and 1916, Germany received around 300,000 tons of Danish food, as well as fats useful for explosives manufacture. From Sweden came iron ore, mine props, cement and brass and copper for munitions.

Jellicoe, apparently, was 'the first to suspect something might be amiss' after the Northern Patrol had intercepted 'an unusually large number of ships bound for Norway' in September 1915.[386] Another report appeared in a meeting of the Enemy Supplies Restriction Committee (ESRC), showing that suspiciously large quantities of oil had been shipped from Philadelphia to Norway.[387] Hall asked Consett for his thoughts. At first, he was very sceptical (he even said the report 'has been grossly exaggerated'), but changed his mind when he looked more closely. As intelligence started to build a picture of the weaknesses of Britain's economic war as carried out under the legal restrictions of the London Declaration, policy was considerably tightened.

It was not easy for Consett to find the statistics he needed, as the Scandinavians announced that they would no longer publish the relevant data. However, it was soon clear that US exports to Denmark had tripled in one year, and meat was now being *imported* into the Netherlands, normally a large exporter.[388] By September 1915, Jellicoe was so disgruntled with what was happening that he wrote that his country 'has become a base for the supply of Germany via the neutral countries'.[389] Much of Britain's economic intelligence was coming from the Trade Division, that until the end of 1917 was headed by Richard Webb. Its sources were wide – attaché reports, commercial sources (like Lloyd's of London), agent reports from the SSB and reports either from the Royal Navy or shipping lines.

What was happening made commercial sense: prices for strategic materials were significantly higher in Berlin than in other markets. Berlin prices for nickel were double those of the London Metals Exchange; aluminium triple;

and in November 1914, copper and antimony quadruple. Prices paid for meat in Copenhagen were also double.[390]

But the Foreign Office was also having to play a balancing act: if neutrals were starved of lucrative business opportunities, their natural reaction would be to favour profitable business with Britain's enemies. Moreover, some Scandinavian exports were much needed by the British; for example, timber for the mining industry, iron ore and certain chemicals for explosives' manufacture.

Grey's approach with the Americans was to try to shift the discussion from the questions of international legality to a concern for American public opinion. It was the 'potential of public backlash' that Grey wanted to keep at the forefront.[391]

## The Renewed U-boat Campaign

As 1915 closed, the supporters of unrestricted submarine warfare kept up the pressure. Tirpitz had become disenchanted by the High Seas Fleet's inaction and felt that a surface action was unlikely to defeat the British. He increasingly turned his attentions to the U-boat and away from the mighty ships idle in harbour. He also managed to win Holtzendorff over to his way of thinking.

Both Tirpitz and Holtzendorff talked optimistically about the speed with which the Allies could be brought to their knees: Holtzendorff's sister described her brother as 'phenomenally optimistic', but of the two, it was Tirpitz who was the more aggressive.[392] He thought it would only take a couple of months for Britain to collapse. He boasted to Matthias Erzberger of the Catholic Centre Party that 'a ruthless U-boat war would force England to its knees within six weeks'.[393] Holtzendorff was much more cautious: he was talking of four to eight months. His estimate was based on his concern for neutral reaction, that Germany's submarine forces still needed to be stronger and that preparatory diplomatic actions would be necessary to clear the way for unfettered U-boat warfare.

Bethmann-Hollweg was worried about the lack of sufficient U-boats needed for a timely victory. On 12 January, he shared his concerns with Müller. Three days later, the kaiser held another meeting with Falkenhayn, Bethmann-Hollweg, Müller and Holtzendorff. He talked of the dangers in the navy's planning and argued that 'the torpedoing of large passenger liners with women and children aboard was unprecedented barbarian cruelty, bringing only the hatred and toxic wrath of the rest of the world upon us'. Nevertheless, he asked for both Müller to prepare for a renewal of submarine war on 1 March and for Bethmann-Hollweg to clear its diplomatic path.[394]

House, the President's advisor, went to Germany at the end of January hoping to gather some first-hand impressions for Wilson. Policy, he observed, was being driven by the government's unwillingness to give in to its navy as the blockade tightened, 'consequently they are unwilling to admit to the illegality of their undersea warfare. They will yield anything but this. If you insist upon that point, I believe war will follow.'[395] House also recognised that the kaiser couldn't easily back down to the navy as long as the blockade continued. On the other hand, the kaiser didn't believe what the navy was telling him: the gap between Tirpitz and Holtzendorff's forecasts was uncomfortably large. The damage of the *Lusitania* and *Arabic* sinkings was irreversible. Wilson tried to find a compromise, demanding that the Germans apologise and admit that the earlier attacks had been illegal. It was too much for Müller, who called Wilson's demands 'impertinent'.[396] He proposed that the Germans pay compensation and that the British disarm their merchant ships.

Behind the scenes, some American initiatives backfired. On 26 January, Secretary of State Lansing told the Germans that they could go ahead with torpedoing armed Allied merchant ships. The British were furious. Grey wrote that 'the proposal of the United States is an attempt to re-adjust the balance of sea power in favour of our enemies'. The Americans increasingly tried to pressure the Allies to end the blockade, but their efforts had the opposite effect.

The new campaign, considered by Tirpitz 'the salvation of the navy', was launched on 16 February 1916. Enemy vessels, including armed auxiliaries, were to be sunk without warning; only neutrals were to be treated according to Prize Rules. Germany would start the year with considerably more submarines at her disposal than in 1914: fifty-four at the beginning of the year.

A week earlier, a shift was signalled. On 11 February, Germany announced that 'enemy merchantmen carrying guns are not to be entitled to be regarded as peaceful merchantmen'.[397] They cited nineteen examples where, it was maintained, action had been initiated by the merchantman, not a submarine. Germany now announced that *all* merchant ships would be treated as though they were armed. Importantly, early indications suggested that America would accept the campaign if adequate warning was given to her own vessels. Bethmann-Hollweg's diplomatic efforts seemed to have been successful.

British Q-ships and armed merchant ships put neutral shipping at risk. There was no longer any pretense: decoy ships now fought as part of the RN, under a White Ensign rather than the Red Duster, the merchant ensign. It ended any lingering ambiguity about their civilian status. The impact of the two actions – arming merchantmen and employing Q-ship tactics – presented any German submarine commander with a difficult choice:

> The more merciful the U-boat, the greater danger it ran, the less heed it paid to the nature of its target and the rescue of those on board, the more its safety and success were assured.[398]

**One or Two U-boat Wars?**

It was becoming clear that there was no one single submarine war, rather different wars being fought in different theatres under different commands with different means. It was only on 28 February that Scheer issued the order to the High Seas Fleet boats that 'Submarine commerce war is to begin at the west coast of England'.[399] In the Channel, the war was unrestricted; in the North Sea, restricted.

While the kaiser, Bethmann-Hollweg, the navy and the army were busy *talking* about the next steps of a submarine war, boats from the Flanders Flotilla had already started leaving Ostend, their home port, on patrol: *UB.18* on 24 February, followed by *UB.2* a day later. The latter torpedoed an unarmed British merchantman, while *UB.18* claimed an armed French freighter twenty-four hours later. According to Koerver, 'These were the first sinkings without warning in British waters since September 1915.'[400]

The navy had won the army's backing, but just why Falkenhayn had supported them poses many questions. At a year-end meeting at the Ministry of War, he agreed with Tirpitz that Bethmann-Hollweg's fear of America was misplaced. In Scheer's words, he had 'given up his previous scruples'.[401] Furthermore, Falkenhayn believed that the war could only be won on the Western Front, by defeating the British at sea by means of the submarine and the French on land by wearing down her ability to resist by a war of attrition centred on Verdun. The Chancellor's adviser, Kurt Riezler, speculated that he was keen to establish an alibi should the army's own risky Verdun strategy fail. If it did, the Chief of Staff might then be able to say that it was because the navy had failed to stem the flow of ammunition reaching the Allies on the Western Front.

In secret briefings to the Reichstag, the RMA's Capelle tried to bring some reason to the heated debate. Even if fifty-four submarines were available, with so few operational, 'it was impossible for this small number of U-boats to be able to establish an iron curtain around England's west coast and effectively cut off British supply'. He accurately predicted that German U-boat forces 'will not reach maximum strength this summer, but rather next winter or, more likely, in the spring' of 1917.[402] Eventually, Capelle's comments leaked out.

By the 4 March conference, Holtzendorff was fully on board. 'England,' he declared in a memo to Scheer, 'can only be injured by war on her trade.'[403] Falkenhayn supported him, echoing the increasing disdain for America: 'Even a state of war with America need not be shunned.'[404] On 13 March, final instructions (amending those of 11 February) were sent out:[405]

1. Enemy merchant ships, encountered in the War Zone, are to be destroyed without more ado.

2. Enemy merchant ships, encountered outside the War Zone, may only be destroyed without more ado when they are armed.
3. Enemy passenger steamers may not be attacked either inside or outside the War Zone by a submerged submarine, no matter whether they are armed or not.

The categorical 'off limits' placed on passenger liners was oddly handled by Germany, which 'never publicized their own prohibition against attacking liners, armed or not'.[406] The whole purpose of this limitation was to position Germany in the court of international public opinion as acting legally. Even with these restrictions, it was estimated that the campaign would account for around 160,000 tons a month, 'three times the tonnage that could be replaced in British yards'.[407]

Bethmann-Hollweg's prophetic opposition was a voice in the wilderness. On 29 February, he had outlined his concerns, identifying major weaknesses in the pro-submarine war argument which took little or no account of inevitable advances in Allied ASW or accelerated shipbuilding. The kaiser agreed to a phased roll-out. A restricted campaign around the British Isles under Prize Rules was announced on 15 March, with an unrestricted campaign to start on 1 April. Continuing pressure from Bethmann-Hollweg, fearing Germany's chances of ever successfully achieving a negotiated peace settlement, led to delays in implementing the second stage.

Jellicoe was kept abreast with the latest intelligence. In mid-March, Balfour wrote to him about the Admiralty's understanding of the German dilemma:

> A rumour has it that for financial and other reasons, the German Government are very much afraid of a quarrel with the U.S.A. Indeed, while their loan is still in the balance, such a quarrel would be folly. The result is (according to one informant) that Tirpitz has practically resigned.[408]

Faced with what he saw as 'procrastination in the conduct of the war', once again Tirpitz threatened resignation; this time the kaiser accepted. On 15 March 1916, Alfred von Tirpitz was replaced by Admiral von Capelle, a supporter of the more cautious Chancellor.[409] Unlike the hardliners, Capelle thought a submarine war fought with Prize Rules could work.

On 16 March, the Royal Holland Lloyd liner, the 13,911-ton ss *Tubantia*, was sunk by *UB.13*. Even if all eighty passengers and 294 crew members were rescued, it was the 'largest neutral vessel sunk during the war'. All sorts of stories were concocted by the Germans to avoid taking the blame. The first line to the press was that she had been sunk by a British mine, then it was said that a German torpedo which had been fired at a British warship ten days earlier had remained active. In 1922, Germany was ordered to pay over £800,000 in compensation. It was more than double the £300,000 previously offered – and rejected.

After the attack, Colonel House was forced to admit to Grey: 'Our relations with Germany now seem to be going steadily to the breaking point and we are making all preparations to that end.'[410]

### More Diplomatic Strains and the *Sussex*

Herbert Pustkuchen became 'best known, not for the ships he sank, but for the one he didn't'.[411] On 24 March 1916, he targeted a cross-Channel ferry, the *Sussex*, having already sunk two neutral ships. From 1,400 yards, his first torpedo hit the French ship's bow section. Eighty died, and amongst the injured were two Americans.[412] Although *UB.29*'s hit had been devastating – everything forward of the bridge was blown off – somehow the *Sussex* made it to the safety of Boulogne harbour.

Partly to blame was the inexperience of junior officers who mostly commanded the Type-*UB* submarines operating in the Channel. Pustkuchen, however, should have known better; he had been in the navy for eight years, four as a commissioned officer. He seemed blissfully 'unaware of the furor he had caused, [and] continued blithely on his way and sank the British steamer *Salybia* also without warning before returning home'.[413] Through the periscope, he'd seen groups of people on deck and, for some reason, assumed – or at least said he had – that she was a troopship. Not surprisingly, German historian Karl Spindler defended Pustkuchen, saying that he had 'mistaken' the *Sussex* for a minelayer.

By the time *Sussex* had been torpedoed, twenty other merchantmen had also been sunk, all of them without warning, twelve alone sunk by Flanders Flotilla boats. Seven had been unarmed and four neutral. Karl Bartenbach's orders had been quite specific: any steamer travelling between France and Britain was 'to be attacked by torpedo'.[414] The only exceptions were hospital ships.

The *Lusitania* and *Arabic* diplomatic rows had barely ended, and Pustkuchen's actions rekindled the fire. Wilson, true to his nature, blustered but did little. It took him almost three weeks before he addressed Congress, saying that unless Germany declared 'its abandonment of the present method of warfare', he would be 'forced to the conclusion that there is but one course it can pursue and otherwise would break off diplomatic relations'. Wilson clearly did not want to be pushed into a European conflict, saying that it was only with the 'keenest regret' that he felt obliged to make this threat.

Wilson's words sounded hollow: The attack on the *Sussex*, he said,

> must stand forth, as the sinking of the *Lusitania* did, so singularly tragical and unjustifiable as to constitute a truly terrible example of the inhumanity of submarine warfare as the commanders of German vessels for the past twelve months have been conducting it.[415]

It took almost a month, until 20 April, for the American Government to formally reply to Germany. Washington's ultimatum – the risk of a diplomatic rupture or Germany's 'abandonment of its present methods of submarine warfare against passenger and freight-carrying vessels' – was presented in Berlin. Wilson threatened to sever diplomatic relations.

Germany blinked. Four days later, much to Scheer's disappointment, she caved in: 'until further orders, submarines may only act against commerce in accordance with Prize regulations'.[416] In the face of the strong reaction, regulations were re-established and the U-boat war pulled back.[417] The very next day, submarines from both the HSF ports and Flanders were recalled. So far as the British Isles War Zone was concerned, even if minelaying continued in both the North Sea and the Mediterranean, it was the end of the submarine campaign.

Two weeks later, on 1 May, the US Ambassador, James W. Gerard, personally met with the kaiser. It was a stand-off: the 'All Highest' retorted that the United States was not acting as a true neutral and was, in fact, siding with the Allies on the restrictive operations of the blockade.

Scheer was furious. He complained that the change 'left to me until further notice to employ the U-boats in purely military enterprises'.[418] As the High Seas Fleet Commander-in-Chief, Reinhard Scheer was adamant: he would not operate his submarines under Prize Rules. Rather than allowing the *Sussex* incident to restrict him, he ordered all HSF U-boats back to port on 27 April, restricting any further activity to boarding and searching. For Michelsen, the *Sussex* sinking 'brought about the complete suspension of the submarine campaign'.[419] Due to increased Flanders-based mining and torpedoing around England, 'successes had just begun to increase' even if 'operations in the Mediterranean continued undisturbed'.[420]

In the end, however, it was Bethmann-Hollweg's line that won the day. After a diplomatic note was sent on 4 May, Germany backed down and signed the '*Sussex* Pledge' admitting the mistake and offering compensation. Germany promised to return to Prize Rules to protect passenger ships, with U-boats now required to ascertain a merchant ship's cargo before destroying it if deemed 'contraband'. Orders were even given to the Cattaro Flotilla on 9 May to avoid passenger ships, including ones which were suspected of being armed.

## The Depth Charge Makes its First Kill

There was some good news for the Allies when, on 22 March 1916, the Q-ship *Farnborough* became the first ship to successfully use a depth charge against a submarine. Her commander, Gordon Campbell, was, according to Sondhaus, 'the most successful Q-ship captain' and the first to receive a Victoria Cross. Indeed, at one point he was 'the only officer now on the active list who has a VC and a DSO'.[421] Campbell closed to around 800 yards from the submarine, had the White Ensign broken out and opened fire with a 12pdr.[422] *U.68* started going down fast by the stern.

### SUBSURFACE ATTACK – THE DEPTH CHARGE

The depth charge (DC), colloquially known as an 'ash can', born from constant experimentation and designed to destroy targets in proximity by hydraulic shock, didn't significantly develop during the First World War. In 1910, the Admiralty Submarine Attack Committee (SAC) was trying to develop a 'dropping bomb', 'launched over the stern of the attacking vessel and exploded at a pre-determined depth'.[423] Admiral Callaghan is credited with requesting its development in July 1914. Sims even credited Admiral Madden a role: his comment that 'a mine so designed that, when dropped overboard, it would have exploded when it reached the depth at which the submarine was lying', was, apparently, the 'germinal idea of the depth charge', according to Jellicoe.[424] Aside from being rolled off the stern from on-deck tracks, a DC could be catapulted from a thrower, launched by howitzer or, later, be dropped from the air. In August 1917, the British introduced a new system, throwing (rather than dropping) a charge from a ship's stern.

The explosive power had to be sufficient: even with a 300lb (135kg) charge, the damage caused to a submarine was minimal unless targeting was very accurate.[425] The larger the explosion, the more critical the throw from an attacking boat became. In July 1917, the first depth-charge throwers capable of firing the charge 40yds (35m) were delivered. The British produced three calibres of howitzer – 5in, 7.5in and 11in – which used a conventional shell which exploded on contact or at a pre-determined depth. The 7.5in howitzer could throw a 43lb charge mounted on a 100lb projectile 2,100yds, or, to a shorter distance of 300 yards, a 250lb charge mounted on a 500lb projectile. The other weapon, the bomb thrower, looked like 'a can on a stick'.[426] Four calibres – 3.5in, 6in, 7.5in and 13.5in – were produced and could be used with pre-set hydrostatic fuses set for depths of 40ft, 90ft, 140ft and 190ft. The 3.5in caliber bomb could throw a 200lb bomb 1,200 yards or a 350lb bomb 650 yards.

At the start of 1917, DCs were used sparingly: according to Jellicoe, 'we could not rely much on depth-charge attack, owing to the small stock of these depth charges'.[427] By 1918, only 377 had been delivered. Even when the DC was supplied in volume, the challenges was still very large. In *The Submarine Peril*, Jellicoe wrote that *Justicia* was sunk by *UB.64* on 19 July 1918 after seventy-nine depth charges dropped on the latter and *U.54*.[428] However, in the same engagement, *U.124* was successfully depth-charged by three escort destroyers. On 17 August 1917, however, Hersing managed to escape in *U.21* after being depth-charged for five hours. Valentiner survived one attack with 120 depth-charge explosions (Valentiner, pp.131–32).

British production capacity, however, was overstretched and help was requested from America. Lieutenant Commander A.J. Stone was given the responsibility of developing the American invention, the Y-gun. He took a Thornycroft idea and applied it to the Y-gun, which would throw two charges of a much larger 300lb some 200yds, one to starboard and one to port. Production was started on 24 November and the first deliveries, less than a month later, were made on 10 December. From then until the Armistice, 974 guns were produced.[429] Laying a spaced throw or drop to saturate the area round a submarine was the next challenge. The USN MkI system, dropping multiple charges delivered in a barrel from the stern, was developed with the help of Lieutenant Commander Isherwood RN. By the end of the war, 250 destroyers were equipped with stern mine racks, from which, by the summer of 1918, an improved version, the MkII, was able to drop five 420lb depth charges. However, experimentation on creating spaced or clustered forward throws would only be achieved much later, in 1942, when it became the basis for the Royal Navy's 'hedgehog' depth charge mortar, whose smaller charges were contact-detonated.

At first, the charges were quite unstable:

> They could be set to explode at a depth of 50 feet to 250 feet but, being a new invention, they didn't always operate as we should have liked. They would often explode on hitting the water, showering the ship with lumps of [the] cradle and causing quite a bit of damage.[430]

Two charges were dropped by *Farnborough* that forced *U.68*'s new commander, Kapitänleutnant Ludwig Güntzel, to bring his submarine back to the surface. There, she was greeted with accurate raking fire from *Farnborough*'s deck guns: 'five more shells … now struck her in the base of the conning tower', bringing the short, one-way duel to an end.[431] Her entire crew died with her; it was only her sixth day on her first mission off the coast of County Kerry in south-west Ireland.

The Allies' new weapon quickly claimed two more victims. One was *UC.7*, attacked by a British motor-boat, *Salmon*, on 7 July 1916. Not only had she been found using hydrophone, but it was the first successful attack achieved with depth charges alone. Her own mines exploded in the chutes, the Germans none the wiser of the cause.

In late July or early August 1916, *UB.44* disappeared with all nineteen crew. However, it wasn't until *U.49* – commanded by Kapitänleutnant Richard Hartmann, who was responsible for sinking almost 90,000 tons of shipping – was attacked the following September that they finally understood the danger of the new, lethal weapon: the depth charge, or what the Germans called the '*Wasserbombe*'.

## Rich Pickings in the Mediterranean

After the diplomatic chaos caused by both the *Lusitania* and *Arabic* sinkings, and now that of the *Sussex*, the kaiser wanted to shift more aggressive operations to the Mediterranean, where the danger of continued incidents with American shipping was smaller.

In many ways, the Mediterranean was an ideal theatre for submarine operations: long daylight hours, less frequent storms than in the North Sea, a fragmented Allied command, far less US commercial and passenger presence than in the Atlantic or the Channel, and transit to operational areas usually completed in only twenty-four hours. But surprisingly, unlike the Channel or the Western Approaches, German submarine attacks didn't concentrate around choke points such as the Suez Canal or the Strait of Gibraltar. The Mediterranean proved to be such a rich hunting ground that four additional submarines – *U.32*, *U.63*, *U.64* and *U-65* – were sent out.

In the summer, German submarines started arriving in the Adriatic, which was, Austrian submariner Georg von Trapp quipped, soon 'crawling with them'.[432] The young Austrian commander of the *U.V* had earned notoriety the previous year when, on 27 April 1915, from 500 metres, he attacked and sank the *Léon Gambetta*. It was the first night attack by a submarine: the French armoured cruiser sank in twenty minutes, taking with her 648 of her 820 crew.

Trapp's personal life hid a fascinating connection. His wife, Agathe, was Robert Whitehead's granddaughter and named as the heiress to his fortune. She would be mother to seven children, the famous von Trapp singers later portrayed in *A Sound of Music*.

The Germans established themselves at Pola in the northern Adriatic but would use the vast and well-protected anchorage at Cattaro (Kotor), the main base for the Austro-Hungarian Fifth Fleet, as its forward base. Originally developed by the Venetians, Cattaro was situated inside a series of bays of breathtaking beauty.

## POLA, CATTARO AND CONSTANTINOPLE

In 1915 there were eight U-boats operating from Austro-Hungarian bases in the Adriatic and a further eight from Turkish ones. At the war's outset, the boats in the western Mediterranean flew the Austro-Hungarian flag; those in the Eastern Mediterranean the Turkish flag. From October 1915, U-boats were listed as part of the Austro-Hungarian navy once past Gibraltar. With Italy's entry into the war in August 1916, the red-white-red Austro-Hungarian flag was flown but German uniforms worn. In June 1917, a new operational command was formalised for Pola and Cattaro U-boats under the FdU-Mittelmeer.

**Pola (now Pula, Croatia)**: The main base of the Austro-Hungarian Fleet was based at Pola (on what is today the Istrian coast of Croatia) 'in order to face the Italian's Venetian squadron with a superior concentration at all times' (Gould, *Adriatic*). Waldemar Kophamel, the former commander of *U.35*, became its base commander at the end of 1915. Kophamel was succeeded by Theodor Püllen and then Kurt Graßhof, who formed two separate flotillas in 1918, led by Otto Schultze (CO 1st Flotilla) at Pola and Rudolf Ackermann (CO 2nd Flotilla) at Cattaro.

**Cattaro (now Kotor, Montenegro)**: By January 1917, twenty-five U-boats were based at Cattaro, the southernmost operating base for the Austro-Hungarian navy, located in a deep and protected fjord (in fact, the southernmost fjord in Europe). Despite its naturally protected structure, a French submarine, *Cugnol*, managed to penetrate the *Bocche di Cattaro* (Bay of Cattaro) even if unable to find a target before being driven off by three Austrian torpedo boats (Gould, *Adriatic*). A cruiser flotilla and the V Ship Division used it as their base, while German submarines used it as a staging point for attacks on the Otranto Barrage and Mediterranean convoys. Its value was the fact the deep waters prevented enemy minelaying while Pola was just a refit yard. In February 1918, the sailors at Cattaro mutinied in what appeared a forerunner of the Wilhelmshaven–Kiel mutiny at the end of the year. Like the earlier German unrest, four sailors were executed (on 11 February)[433] as a show of strength; another 290 received prison sentences.

**Constantinople (now Istanbul, Turkey)**: Very early in the war, Germany sealed its alliance with Turkey after the successful escape of two German ships, SMS *Goeben* and *Breslau*.

Valentiner remembered its effect on his men:

> The Bay of Cattaro greeted us like a Nordic dream with its high, green mountains. Our hearts raced and we laughed. It was as if someone had built Norwegian fjords under a southern evening sky. Straight out of the water, the mountains rose high into the sky. A mighty natural basin opened behind the narrow sea-entrance, and where it narrows, a yet still larger harbour opens up with still higher mountains, all arranged, one after the other, as if by the hand of God, with such careful harmony it seems to be a theater backdrop.[434]

Commanders like Kurt Hartwig (aboard Edgar von Spiegel von und zu Peckelsheim's old boat, *U.32*) were reassigned to Pola, along with Robert Moraht's *U.64* and Walther's *U.52*, which sank the 12,750-ton *Suffren* as she was making her way back to Brest for repairs. She went down with all hands, almost 650 men. Another captain, Steinbrauer in *UB.47*, successfully attacked the French warship, the *Gaulois*, despite her large destroyer escort.

In the Mediterranean, seasoned German aces racked up large tonnage claims. Valentiner sank fifty-three ships (114,067 tons), Rücker's *U.34* the same number of ships with slightly less tonnage (102,616 tons), Forstmann's *U.39* sixty-eight ships (75,370 tons) and finally a relatively new commander, Lothar von Arnauld de la Perière, succeeded in sinking a record-breaking 142 ships totalling 265,649 tons.[435] In one twenty-four-day period, de la Perière managed to sink fifty-four ships: no one has ever come near that astonishing record. Valentiner gave us a powerful visual description of his own record:

> About a hundred and fifty ships, my victims, lay at the bottom of the sea. Let me give you an illustration of what this means: a railroad car can carry about ten tons. If you put together a freight train into whose cars was loaded the total tonnage of what I'd sunk, the train would stretch all the way from Hamburg to Leipzig.[436]

*Allied Mediterranean Ship Sinkings, 2nd Half 1916*

| Nationality | No. Ships | Tonnage |
|---|---|---|
| British | 96 | 415,471 |
| French | 24 | 64,829 |
| Italian | 136 | 181,831 |
| Total | 256 | 662,131 |

Source: Gould, *Adriatic*

## The Exploits of Lothar von Arnauld de la Perière

Born a Prussian aristocrat, Lother von Arnauld de la Perière's exploits as Germany's leading ace were legendary. He would be responsible for more than a quarter of a million tons of shipping sunk, including some Clan Line ships, notably the 4,835-ton *Clan Macalister* in 1915. The *Clan Macalister* had been en route to Calcutta from her home port, Liverpool, when spotted by *U.35* south of Crete. It was not surprising that no loss of life was reported;[437] she would have been boarded and sunk either with explosive charges or her seacocks opened. The behaviour of de la Perière – who in 1916 was aged just 30 – was always scrupulously correct. Hurd, however, described the sinking by praising the behaviour of the ship's company, saying that 'her crew, both British and Indian, behaved in the most admirable manner, and in the end took to their boats in perfect order'.[438]

Early in 1916 (26 February), *U.35* claimed the 13,753-ton armed transport *La Provence II*, which was hit with one torpedo at 0255hrs. She was serving as a troop transport and carrying 2,000 troops of the IIIe Régiment d'Infanterie Coloniale, a further 400 crew as well as 200 horses and mules en route to Salonika. Of those aboard, around 1,800 drowned. A cook, Lucien Monot, was lucky enough to survive. He gave his life vest to a friend who couldn't swim and jumped from the sinking ship in only his pants and a shirt:

> After nineteen hours we were fished back out by a British destroyer. Talk about a night full of anguish. I can't tell you what I was thinking about, many things. God only knows. We had no heat, there were thirty of us crammed together in a lifeboat, soaked through like chickens.[439]

It was one of the few times that de la Perière used a torpedo.[440] A few days later, on 1 March, he torpedoed the British sloop, the *Primula*, hitting her in the bow.[441] With admirable audacity, the captain put her in a fast reverse, trying to ram *U.35* with his stern. Von Arnauld's next two torpedoes missed, but he was lucky with the fourth. 'Four torpedoes for that tiny wasp,' he complained.[442] But von Arnauld did not hold grudges: 'I shall never cease admiring her skipper.'[443]

On 26 July, von Arnauld was ordered on a special mission by the kaiser: to personally take a letter to the Spanish King, Don Alfonso, thanking him for the help given to German refugees.[444] Returning to Cattaro, von Arnauld's crew sank another thirty-nine ships, totalling 56,818 tons.

In August, on *U.35*'s fourth patrol, he sank fifty-four ships, totalling more than 90,000 tons. The twenty-four-day cruise would be his most successful. *U.35* had expended 900 4.1in shells, but only used four torpedoes. He talked modestly about the extraordinary feat of arms:

> My record cruise was quite tame and humdrum. We stopped ships. The crews took to the boats. We examined the ship's papers, gave sailing instructions to the nearest land and then sank the captured prize.[445]

Von Arnauld's next patrol (13 September – 9 October 1916) reaped its usual rich harvest – twenty-one ships (70,413 tons). He was also responsible for 'one of France's greatest naval disasters',[446] sinking the 14,966-ton auxiliary cruiser *Gallia* south of Sardinia, which, like *Provence II*, was on its way to Salonika. The death-toll was as terrible: 1,852 officers and men drowned. Afterwards, he confessed: 'After what I had seen, I did not feel elated.'[447]

### *KAPITÄNLEUTNANT* LOTHAR VON ARNAULD DE LA PERIÈRE (1886–1941)

Germany's top-scoring ace only ever fired seventy-five torpedoes, with a 'record that has remained unbroken by any other submarine commander through two world wars'.[448] Arnauld started as a Torpedo Officer on SMS *Emden*, then as AdC to Alfred von Tirpitz and later in Berlin as Naval Assistant to von Pohl at the war's outbreak. He initially wanted to join the Zeppelin force, but was rejected as there were insufficient ships to command; his alternative was the Periscope School in Kiel.

He was an unusual commander in that his weapon of choice was the 88mm deck gun (torpedoes had roughly a 50 per cent hit rate and only accounted for thirty-nine of his ships, the balance from explosive charges placed inside the hulls of captured ships by his crews or the 88mm). In 1918, when in command of *U.139*, he had an even larger (5.9in) gun. It meant that his actions were rarely without warning. 'The fact that I nearly always gave warning may explain why my record ran so high.'[449] Using his deck gun rather than expending limited torpedoes meant that de la Perière's operations time was longer, plus he was able to verify the identity of his kills, not the case for most of his colleagues: 'Many officers sank more tonnage than appeared on their records because of their inability to produce names and verification,' he noted.[450] Normally, he opened fire at around 6,000yds, closed to 3,000yds and, after the crew had abandoned ship, placed well-aimed fire into a ship's bow, midships and stern.

Once, he returned to Pola with fifty-four pennants flying (26 July – 20 August 1916). He was considered a gentleman: the captain of the *Patagonia*, William Hunter, wrote on 6 May 1917 'expressing [his] gratitude for the kind and courteous treatment' he had received.[451] *U.35* had sunk her – along with the *Parkgate*, *India* and *Stromboli* – in the Atlantic.

The ship went down 'like a rocket' and the sinking remained a difficult memory:[452]

> The picture of that foundering vessel remains in my mind with an undiminished horror … there was a wild panic on the stricken vessel's crowded deck. Lifeboats were being lowered by men too much in a panic to let them down slowly and safely. Hundreds of soldiers were jumping into the water … The sea became a terrible litter of overturned … overcrowded and swamped lifeboats and struggling men.[453]

Deciding which cargoes should be sunk was not easy. Koerver talked of the difficulties faced by some U-boat captains: the definition of lumber as contraband (and therefore the validity in sinking a neutral carrying such a cargo) could depend on the wood's finished condition. Trunks were not considered contraband, but 'ready-cut pit props' were, as might have been 'boards to be used for the manufacture if the boxes were intended to store ammunition'.[454] In these situations, captains like von Arnauld would hand over a certificate of sinking that could be used before a German Prize Court (*Prisengericht*) to determine if damages were payable.

### The U-boat's New Naval Role

For much of 1916, at least in the North Sea, the U-boat war switched targets from commerce to ships of war as the unrestricted submarine war was held in check by the collective concerns of the kaiser, Bethmann-Hollweg and Müller. The kaiser, who did not agree with the 'all or nothing' approach, made his views clear:

> It is to be communicated to the Chief of the High Seas Fleet that his Majesty does not at this time grant approval for ruthless U-boat merchant warfare, although he fully understands the purely military justification. He cannot, however, agree with the High Seas [Fleet] Chief in rejecting a more moderate form of U-boat merchant war like the consistently successful one conducted in the Mediterranean.[455]

Scheer lobbied hard for the submarine to spearhead the naval war. He felt that the fate of Germany was hanging in the balance: 'If we did not succeed in overcoming England's will to destroy us, then the war of exhaustion must end in Germany's certain defeat.'[456] Some powerful voices supported him. One was Tirpitz, who would be profoundly disappointed with the outcome of the *Skagerrakschlacht*:

> Tirpitz was certain that England had to be defeated before Germany could claim to be a great power, let alone, a sea power. He did not think that this would come about through a fleet engagement rather it would be by submarine war which allowed greater freedom of action.[457]

Given the resistance, Scheer had two options: either the U-boats be unrestricted or they be used for strictly military operations against British warships. The Admiralstab 'now planned to use his submarines to whittle down the dreadnought superiority of the Grand Fleet'.[458] They planned to fight what was called a '*kleine Krieg*' ('little war') by 'numerous and repeated [submarine and torpedo boat] attacks day and night' until more 'favourable circumstances' allowed Germany's numerically weaker navy a more even-handed engagement.[459] Tirpitz 'deplored their entirely defensive plans'.[460] Scheer had already started to use submarines as an integral part of fleet operations: before Jutland, to lay traps as the British sortied from their northern bases; post-Jutland, to function as a moveable offshore picket line across which he hoped to lure Jellicoe's ships.

Scheer's decision to pull the U-boats back, however, was not popular in Germany. For many, his rationale was 'incomprehensible'.[461] Neither would Scheer now bow to the pressure to maintain the High Seas Fleet as an inactive 'fleet in being'. He pondered on how to use his submarines in combination with the surface fleet. He would now prepare them for a purely military role prior to his planned sortie into the Skagerrak.

One option was the idea that submarine operations could adopt Cruiser Rules if they were allowed to operate in conjunction with surface forces: the submarine could be the threat to stop a merchantman, while a partner surface vessel's prize crews could carry out the search, alleviating the need for the sub itself to surface. Such thinking was vetoed by Captain von Levetzow, who in 1916 became Chief of Operations of the High Seas Fleet, although the submarine's inability to keep pace with most surface ships already made the idea impractical.[462]

### 31 May 1916: Jutland

From battle reports, Jellicoe would mistakenly conclude that Scheer had used submarines as part of the action at Jutland, but Scheer's submarine strategy was still evolving. He later confirmed that 'none took part', even if fifteen submarines had been sent to lay in wait near the routes used by British warships sortieing from Scapa Flow, the Moray Firth and the Firth of Forth.[463]

On this occasion, Scheer would attempt to lure the British out into the North Sea to make a sweep, timed also to coincide with the Irish Easter Rising. Shortly before the uprising's planned start, the diplomat and Irish Nationalist,

Sir Roger Casement, was secretly smuggled into Ireland aboard *U.20*.[464] One of the ERAs (engine room artificers), Karl Wiedemann, later wrote that he had been a 'pleasant man' who 'soon became our friend'. Before leaving the U-boat, fresh shaven, he shook the hand of every crew member. Casement was caught and, on 3 August, executed by hanging in North London's Pentonville Prison. He had been planning to meet the German crew of a disguised merchantman bringing in arms for the IRA. HMS *Bluebell* intercepted the SS *Libau*, pretending to be a Norwegian steamer under the name of the *Aud*. Acting on intelligence from OB40, *Aud* was intercepted on Good Friday, 21 April, and ordered to Queenstown. Just before entering harbour, her commander (and later an official historian of the German Navy), Karl Spindler, ordered her to be scuttled by her uniformed crew. In her cargo holds, British Navy divers later found 20,000 rifles and a million rounds of ammunition.

From his earlier coastal raids, Scheer had learned that he would be 'better off moving the scouting group target just far enough north to tempt Beatty out of Rosyth, but not so far that it would make it easy for Jellicoe's forces' at Scapa Flow to bring timely help. Scheer was not planning any major naval action, rather one designed to lure out a small number of British ships hoping to safely overpower them. As part of the plan, he prepared several strategically located submarine traps.

Between 17 and 22 May, Scheer ordered ten U-boats to patrol the central North Sea (*U.24*, *U.32*, *U.43*, *U.44*, *U.47*, *U.51*, *U.52*, *U.63*, *U.66* and *U.70*) and then to take up interception positions or to start mining operations. At the start, *U.46* dropped out with engine trouble.

Two U-boats, *U.43* and Paul Wagenführ's *U.44*, were ordered to wait for Jellicoe's ships as they sortied out of the Pentland Firth, while eight would try to catch Beatty's battlecruisers in the Firth of Forth, further south. On 20 May, *UB.27* approached as far as the Isle of May. Three U-boats were to lay mines: *U.72* off the Firth of Forth, *U.74* off the Moray Firth and Kurt Beitzen's *U.75* off the Orkney Islands. All were Type-*UE* (*U.71* to *U.80*) minelayers capable of carrying thirty-eight mines apiece.[465] Erwin Weisbach's *U.74* had only sunk one ship, the *Sabbia*, before she met her end in a mine-handling accident on 27 May. Another was positioned off Peterhead, and *UB.21* and *UB.22* off the Humber, where British warships had been incorrectly reported. Three – *U.21*, *U.46* and *U.67* – were held back west of Terschelling off the Dutch coast, to guard against any possible move by Commodore Tyrwhitt's forces at Harwich, while *U.47* was diverted to patrol the Sunderland coast.

Spindler admitted that the May mission, assembling submarines close inshore near the port exit routes, 'ended … in a failure'.[466] They had been on station too long. The submarines were all in position by 23 May, a week before Jutland, but bad weather kept delaying the departure of the High Seas

Fleet; by the time Germany's fleet did finally leave harbour, the submarines had outlasted their endurance. It was at this point that Scheer changed plan: Hipper's raid on shipping in the Skagerrak would now act as bait to lure Beatty's battle-cruisers to the main German battle fleet. Repairs on SMS *Seydlitz* now further delayed the operation until 29 May. As they were close to shore, and sea conditions were extremely calm, the U-boats were forced to stay submerged, using up their batteries and consequently, for the most part, out of radio contact. However, the British were aware of their presence. Padfield maintained that the Admiralty knew that 'something was afoot for days as the great number of U-boat departures and the lack of subsequent sinkings was noted'.[467]

After engine trouble, *UB.27* managed to get as far as the north side of the Forth, near Largo Bay, by 25 May, but again ran into problems. After she damaged one of her propellers, she had to make her way back out. Four armed trawlers detected *U.74* in the Moray Firth on 27 May and sank her just south of Peterhead. *U.72* abandoned its minelaying; it had developed a tell-tale oil leak. The only sighting reports that Scheer received were from Kurt Hartwig in *U.32* off the Firth of Forth and from *U.66* off Kinnaird Head.[468] The only success, but it was considerable, was *U.75*'s minelaying off Orkney, which, in early June, would sink HMS *Hampshire*. When the Grand Fleet finally sortied on the night of 30 May, its ships passed by the waiting submarines without incident. Only a few British ships encountered the waiting picket line: HMS *Trident* was unsuccessfully attacked, as was the sloop *Gentian*.

For years, Jellicoe had been adamant that he preferred to fight a fleet action in the northern North Sea. His position was based on one major consideration: he wanted to be nearer his own northern bases, to allow any damaged ships a chance to get home while denying the same to his foe. But he also felt that the distance would force many submarines to fight at the limits of their endurance in any fleet action.

He also made it known that while 'it is evident that the Germans cannot rely with certainty upon having their full complement of submarines and minelayers present in a fleet action', he would if 'the enemy battlefleet were to turn away from an advancing Fleet'. 'I should assume that the intention was to lead us over mines and submarines and should decline to be so drawn'. This is the point on which Andrew Gordon, rather scornfully, talks of Jellicoe's 'fantasy' GFBOs (Grand Fleet Battle Orders) in which he caricatures the admiral for thinking that 'the High Seas Fleet would fight it [the "decisive" battle, ie, Jutland] as a set piece duel, by steering a parallel course and awaiting the pleasure of British gunnery officers, like coconuts in a shy'.[469]

Jellicoe went on to underline the implications of what he was suggesting:

> I desire particularly to draw the attention of their Lordships to this point, since it may be deemed a refusal of battle, and indeed, might possibly result in the failure to bring the enemy to action as is expected and hoped. Such a result would be absolutely repugnant to the feelings of all British Naval officers and men, but with new untried methods of warfare new tactics must be devised to meet them. I feel that such tactics, if not understood, may bring odium upon me, but so long as I have the confidence of their Lordships, I intend to pursue what is, in my considered opinion, the proper course to defeat and annihilate the enemy's battlefleet, without regard to unstructured opinion or criticism.[470]

For the rest of his life, Jellicoe faced just that.

Like Scheer, Jellicoe was mindful of submarines in his own planning: three were sent to cover the Horns Reef, two east of the Dogger Bank.

Returning to Germany, the High Seas Fleet sailed – unchallenged – over the three British submarines (HMS *D.1*, *E.55* and *E.26*) that had been sent to the Amrun Channel. Due to lack of communications because of the 'primitive wireless sets', their deadly power was severely curtailed.[471] The obvious lesson – that at the very minimum, integration of submarines into fleet operations required effective communication – went unheeded:

> Britain's best submarine commanders found themselves tied to the apron strings of the Commander-in-Chief, no longer lone wolves of the sea but disciplined and organized units of a great and intricate fleet.[472]

Churchill always maintained that Allied access to the Baltic had been blocked and no initiatives could be made around Heligoland. The claim is somewhat speculative: Germany's Heligoland base was closely defended, as was the Flanders coastline. Jellicoe believed that an assault on these would have been unwise: it would have been 'playing the German game, with the possible results of our losing the command of the sea and the consequent loss of the war'.[473]

Some of Jellicoe's critics believed that his failure to bring about a decisive defeat of the High Seas Fleet at Jutland was, in large part, why Britain faced such a serious submarine threat a year later:

> Had there been a decisive victory for us at Jutland, there certainly would not have been a submarine campaign in 1917, for the submarine campaign was based on the German fleet.[474]

Jutland was seen as a turning point, more discernable in retrospect for it 'led Germany to relegate the battle-squadrons to a secondary position, and to stake her whole future upon the submarine arm'. Jutland's outcome also significantly affected ongoing operations. As one Beatty biographer put it,

> The peril became acute and the evil results of the escape of the High Seas Fleet from destruction at Jutland were now apparent. For it was the existence of that Fleet which made the unrestricted campaign possible. In Beatty's words, it had become 'the bulwark behind which the submarine menace grew'.[475]

Brodie dismissed such thinking: 'not even that command which is gained by the annihilation of the enemy battle fleet' would exclude 'the likelihood that the enemy will have substantial means of inflicting damage upon one's commerce'.[476]

**The Loss of HMS *Hampshire***

The worst week of John Jellicoe's war was probably the first week of June 1916. After the disappointment of 31 May, his ships came back to port to be met with recrimination and insult. Jellicoe remained in Scapa writing up his battle reports, waiting to meet with Lord Kitchener, who was scheduled to stop over on his way to Russia. The field marshal never made it.

Three Type-*UE* minelayer submarines – *U.72*, *U.74* and *U.75* – had each been sent to lay mine traps for the Grand Fleet. Two left Wilhelmshaven on 13 and 14 May. Kapitänleutnant Kurt Beitzen's *U.75* had been assigned the Orkney Islands as a target and left Heligoland on 24 May.[477] His orders were precise:

> Mine warship route from Scapa Flow north along the west side of Orkney islands, 2 to 3 nautical miles from the coast abeam Marwick Head. If it is for mine technical reasons not possible to place the barrier perpendicular to the course, then lay it in direction NE–SW, so that it is effective against ships coming down from the north-west. Depth setting 7 metres under high water.[478]

*U.75*'s 31-year-old captain was already a decorated submariner and would go on to command two other U-boats, *U.98* and *U.102*. In a two-and-a-half-hour operation starting at 0600hrs on 29 May, he began to lay a shallow minefield of thirty-four mines, seventeen in each line, one as the sub headed south, the other as it turned north. The first eleven mines were laid on the submarine's starboard side, but then a mechanical fault made any further drops impossible: the twelfth mine stuck firm. When it was freed, seven mines were laid at a different depth setting of 8 metres. The task completed, *U.75* slipped away towards the Norwegian coast. As Beitzen moved south on 1 June, passing through what had been the area of the Battle of Jutland, the sight of one section of the stricken HMS *Invincible*'s upturned hull was still clearly visible through his periscope.

After arriving in Thurso, Kitchener transferred to HMS *Iron Duke*'s destroyer tender, the *Oak*, for the quick run to Scapa Flow. There, he was to meet for a lunch briefing with Jellicoe. By noon, a Force 7 gale was blowing from the north-east and Jellicoe suggested delaying his departure. Kitchener was in a hurry and made it clear that no delay was possible. Jellicoe then suggested that HMS *Hampshire*, the cruiser on which Kitchener was to travel, take a route that went along the Orkney Islands' western coastline. Jellicoe felt that *Hampshire* would be better protected from submarines as the destroyer escort would more likely keep pace, and that it was more probable a submarine would be spotted from Birsay at the mainland's north-west corner. Just as 'minesweeping on either side of the Orkneys had not been practicable for three or four days owing to the weather conditions', Jellicoe thought that the conditions would also make it difficult for a submarine.[479] On that he was probably right, but not against mines laid before the bad weather. At 1940hrs, one of *U.75*'s mines claimed her victim: the 10,800-ton *Hampshire*.

Only fourteen of her crew and passengers survived. Lord Kitchener's body was never found. Having missed the opportunity of a lifetime at Jutland, the heavy burden of now losing Britain's greatest soldier in the same week was almost too much.

A recent history of the *Hampshire*'s sinking strongly attacks Jellicoe. In his book *Who Killed Kitchener?*, David Laws accuses Jellicoe, saying he

> sent one of the most important members of the British Government on a sea voyage on a route chosen on the basis of outdated weather assumptions, through waters unswept for mines, on the basis of groundless hunches about the low risk of mine presence.[480]

Jellicoe was despondent, and remained so for weeks despite the many letters of support he received. 'My luck is dead out for the present,' he told First Sea Lord Admiral Henry Jackson. John Winton even suggested that he was near his breaking point:

> The first few days after the return from Jutland may have caused something of a psychological breaking-point for Jellicoe. The unceasingly hostile weather, the anxiety and shock of Kitchener's death, the growing awareness with every day that passed of just how many chances had been missed at Jutland, all produced in him an unusually depressed state of mind.[481]

### The Execution of Captain Fryatt

On 23 June, two German destroyers, the *G.101* and *G.102*, captured an English steamer, the ss *Brussels*. Her captain, Charles Fryatt, was found by his captors to have taken 'offensive operations ... in accordance with British Admiralty instruction' against the *U.33* in March 1915. Fryatt had tried to ram the submarine when it surfaced to torpedo her. As he wrote, 'he hoisted two flags for me to stop but I did not like the idea of giving up my ship to him so I decided to ram him'.[482] At the time, Fryatt erroneously reported that he had sunk *U.33*.

Earlier that same month, he had outrun another submarine on another ship, the ss *Wrexham*, steaming off at a fast 16 knots – 2 knots faster than her rated top speed – to Rotterdam. When she arrived, her funnels were visibly burned.[483] In recognition of his action, he was given a watch as a corporate gift.[484] For the second action, the attempt by the *Brussels* to ram *U.33*, the Admiralty also gave him a watch. The gift would seal his fate; on it was inscribed the details of his exploits:

> Presented by the Lords Commissioners of the Admiralty to Chas. Algernon Fryatt Master of the S.S. *Brussels* in recognition of the example set by that vessel when attacked by a German submarine on March 28th, 1915.

In captivity in Zeebrügge, he was tried on 27 July and took his last breath facing a firing squad the same evening. A notice, signed by von Schröder of Marinekorps Flandern, was posted in which his defiant act, protecting his ship by ramming a U-boat about to attack him, was labelled 'a ruthless deed' which 'has thus been avenged, belatedly but just'.[485] It was a savagely absurd sentence. Prime Minister Asquith promised Parliament that the perpetrators would not go unpunished, while international reaction fell in firmly behind him. The Swiss newspaper *Le Journal de Genève* expressed it well: 'It is monstrous to maintain that armed forces have a right to murder civilians but that civilians are guilty of a crime in defending themselves.' Then again, the British had also talked of treating all U-boat crews as war criminals.

Charles Fryatt left a wife and seven children. His family was treated considerably better than that of the boy VC, Jack Cornwell, whose mother died in poverty. The Great Eastern Railway company – owners of the *Brussels* – granted Fryatt's widow an annual pension of £250, which the government topped up with a further annual contribution of £100. In July 1919, a commemoration service was held at St Paul's Cathedral, and today there is a still a memorial dedicated to Fryatt at Liverpool Street Station.

### U-boats Come to America – the Voyages of the *Deutschland*

The blockade of Germany was starting to bite, so it wasn't unnatural – though still remarkably innovative – that the idea of transporting goods underwater should be considered viable. There were critical shortages of strategic metals – nickel for hardening steel, rubber for gas masks and tyres, and copper for electrical instrumentation and piping. So bad had the situation become that it wasn't unusual for German trucks to run on iron wheels. The *Deutschland* was the answer. The commerce submarine was ordered from Krupp in October after a Bremen businessman, Alfred Lohmann, managed to get the backing of both Deutsche Bank and Norddeutscher Lloyd.

Very occasionally, the safe passage of certain materials was made possible by agreement between the Allies and the Germans. America, for example, needed German dyes. The US textile industry, which annually purchased around 15,000 tons of German dyes, was so threatened by shortage that 400,000 jobs were at risk. A deal was worked out: bowing to American pressure, the British allowed $5 million worth of dye cargoes to be taken safely across, *Deutschland*'s outgoing cargo.[486]

When she left Heligoland on 23 June, she had 163 tons of dye as well as precious stones on board. After a 4,250-mile crossing through storm-blown seas, *U-Deutschland* finally reached US territorial waters off Maryland. Baltimore had been chosen for good reason, as it was a city with strong pro-German sentiment: in 1914, 94,000 Germans lived there. It was also America's largest wartime harbour. *Deutschland*'s arrival was greeted by an effusive editorial in *The Baltimore Sun* ('Hats off to the Deutschland') and in *The New York Times* as 'an incident which compels admiration and stirs the imagination'.[487] More 'astutely', *The New York Tribune* put its finger on the real issue: that *Deutschland*'s mission underlined 'how desperate the state of affairs in Germany must be'.[488] *Deutschland* was given a thorough inspection. When completed, Captain C.F. Hughes USN submitted his report to the Baltimore Collector of Customs, William P. Ryan:

> There is no evidence of any kind that this ship is a man-of-war, or an armed merchant ship and she could not be made a vessel of war without large structural changes, and in my opinion, she is rightly classed as a vessel of the merchant marine.[489]

Once ashore, *U-Deutschland*'s captain, Paul König, was feted by the German community. Six crew members were invited to visit Washington's Navy Yard, given a tour of The White House and even invited to meet with the Assistant Secretary of the Navy, Franklin Delano Roosevelt, who greeted them in German. The German Ambassador, Bernstorff, came to Baltimore and, together with König, was entertained by Mayor Preston at a banquet the same evening. Prominent members of Baltimore's German community included Paul Hilken and his father, Henry, who took König to the Germania Club and some of the city's best restaurants. Together, they ran A. Schumacher and Co and represented one of the German Lloyd shipping lines in America. It is now believed that Paul Hilken was also a spy and had helped set up cells on the East Coast, so was likely linked to the Black Tom Island bombing in New York Harbour on 30 July 1916, blowing up the largest munitions depot in the United States. Eventually, in an extraordinarily successful 'flip', Paul Hilken avoided prosecution by helping the US Government pursue monetary claims against Germany for that bombing.

On 2 August, König slid out of Baltimore harbour, escorted by a US destroyer, the USS *Sterrett* (DD-27). Crossing back over to Germany, she now carried '327 tons of nickel and 79 tons of tin from Krupp's American inventory, and 349 tons of rubber'.[490] She also came back with valuable quantities of zinc, copper and silver, 'a million dollars' worth' of cargo from pro-German businessmen in Baltimore.[491] Supposedly 'the entire German army could be supplied with rubber for cars and motor vehicles for four months' with what was loaded.[492] The rubber alone was enough to equip 11,000 trucks with tyres. The cargo was supposedly worth ten times the cost of her build.

The commerce submarine made it back to Bremerhaven on 23 August after an epic journey totalling more than 8,000 miles, but she ran submerged for less than 10 per cent of the time, 620 miles in total.

That October, the *Deutschland* made a second trip. She left Kiel on the second day of the month through the Kaiser Wilhelm-Kanal, but couldn't immediately continue from Wilhelmshaven on her North Atlantic cruise as one of her diving planes had been damaged by an escorting tug. It was only after a week of repairs that König was able to take her to sea on 8 October.

En route, the unarmed *Deutschland* avoided any contact with surface ships, but heavy seas lengthened the crossing to twenty-four days. As they entered New London, Connecticut, on 1 November, the crew were asked by a welcoming reception committee boat if they were the *Bremen. U.53* had not been able to make any contact with *Deutschland*'s sister ship, which was making the same voyage from Bremerhaven; the only sign of her fate was an oil-stained life-jacket that came ashore at Cape Elizabeth, Maine, in September. Koenig's engineer, Schultz, who'd come aboard as an assistant engineer from the *U.14*, had a friend from Kiel aboard her.[493] He would never see his friend again; the *Bremen* had evidently been lost at sea.

While the crew worked on maintenance and repairs, another precious cargo of rubber was loaded. Local German clubs and families entertained the visitors. It was common for *Deutschland* to be greeted with a band, and

Schultz (who also had relatives in Philadelphia whom he'd managed to visit) remembered 'Deutchland über Alles' being played as a group of sailors got off at one train station. Schultz's visit to his uncle, Josef Eichelmann, was even reported in the local German paper, and he as having arrived 'aboard as an assistant engineer from *U.14*, *Deutschland* in the capacity of engine attendant'. For them, Schultz represented 'the pride of us German-Americans'.[494]

In mid-November, *Deutschland* started its return home. However, a chance collision badly damaged her hull, making diving impossible, and the boat had to delay for repairs. It was only on 10 December that the crew finally managed to get back to Bremerhaven, where they were welcomed by 'a huge crowd with boisterous enthusiasm'.[495]

Schultz couldn't make it home in time for Christmas; he missed the arrival of the package he had sent from America, marked 'sewing machine parts'. Inside was a glorious assortment of treasure: 'twenty pounds of fine vegetable fat, ten pounds of butter, five pounds of coffee beans, five pounds of sugar, fifty bars of soap, two cans of olive oil, and lots of other bits and pieces'.[496] His Christmas gifts, in the depth of Germany's so-called turnip winter, must have been like treasure.

### *U.53*'s Provocative Mission to Newport

On 8 September, the German Admiralty staff met with the High Seas Fleet command and announced its intention of taking a normal ocean-going submarine across to the American coast. *U.53* was chosen. Her captain's orders were first to protect the *Bremen*, to then make a port and to pay respects to the commander of the Newport Naval District, Rear Admiral Austin M. Knight, after which he was to attack shipping off the American coast.

It was both an aggressive and deeply symbolic move. Ernst von Weizsäcker, at the time Admiral Scheer's flag lieutenant on SMS *Friedrich der Größe*, heard one of the Admiralty staff comment: 'That is precisely what we want. We want to finally get the ball rolling.' Ludendorff was taken aback, however, saying that the provocation 'was not boldness, it was recklessness'.[497] Some contemporary newspaper reporting was stunningly naive. The *Dundee Courier*, for example, talked of letters for Count Bernstorff, 'the delivery of which was his main purpose'.[498]

On 17 September, *U.53* left for her forty-one-day voyage with Fregattenkapitän Hans Rose, five other officers and thirty-three men. The 31-year-old captain, in Iain Ballantyne's words, successfully pulled off 'the first unsupported transatlantic oceanic projection of power by any submarine'. After being escorted inshore by an American submarine, the *D.2*, and anchoring near Goat Island, he rowed ashore to pay his respects to Knight and Rear Admiral Albert Gleaves, the destroyer flotilla commander. The 70-yard-long *U.53* was equipped with a much higher periscope than her escort and a 'particularly strong wireless set'. The *Daily Telegraph* reporter wrote that Rose, who apparently 'spoke English with a London twang', immediately asked: 'Where is the *Bremen*? I must wire her.'[499]

During the short visit, 'no stores or provisions were taken on; the visit had to leave the impression that German U-boats had the range to attack America with ease' (Rose pretended he had enough provisions for three months). Food and water supplies had both, in fact, been major concerns: additional fresh water was stored in two of the boat's torpedo tubes and extra fuel in her dive tanks.[500] The fact that no stores were boarded meant that there was no breach of American neutrality, but Rose was worried that the submarine could be quarantined if she stayed any longer when the harbour master started to raise concerns. American naval officers were invited aboard; Gleaves even brought his wife and daughter. After his three-and-a-half-hour visit, *U.53* went back out to sea at 1730hrs on 7 October.

As the sub slid back out, the crew assembled on deck, faced about and saluted the USS *Melville*. A year later, *Melville* would be in Queenstown acting as the flagship for the first American destroyers hunting U-boats off the southern Irish coast.

Back at sea, Rose immediately sank five ships, of which three were British, one Norwegian and the last Dutch. With the news that even America's coastline was no longer safe, $500 million was wiped off Wall Street in fifteen minutes of brisk trading.[501] Sixteen or seventeen American destroyers were sent to sea, 'without, however, in any way', said one newspaper report, 'concerning themselves with the military measures of the U-boat or disturbing them'.[502] One of the American destroyers picking up survivors was the USS *Jacob Jones*. In 1917, she would be sunk by Rose off the Scillies.

Sinking his targets in neutral waters, American ships watched on helplessly. One officer, Lieutenant George Fort from the USS *Fanning*, said that he'd felt 'helpless, like spectators at a dog fight'.[503] Before turning for home, *U.53* sank the Norwegian-flagged tanker *Christian Knudesen*, but only after she'd taken on fuel.

One report maintained that Rose repainted the submarine's identification number to give the impression, if spotted, that more German submarines were in the vicinity.[504] Indeed, when the *U.53* returned to Germany on 1 November, she sailed as *U.61*. Rose had used this ruse on 'four separate occasions'.[505]

The visit had demonstrated Germany's ability to bring the war not only to the United States, but also that 'the Cape Verde islands, the Canaries, Madeira and the Azores were now well within reach of the new German submarine types. In response, the Admiralty moved the 9th Cruiser Squadron to a new base in Sierra Leone on the west coast of Africa.'[506] To Rose, however, the journey had been a mistake:

> The only result of our trip was that we had made our enemies understand what they could expect from German U-boats – though this warning unquestionably turned out to be a false one. We warned them, and this warning was a mistake.[507]

### HANS ROSE (1885–1969)

Rose captained the *U.53* for fifteen of her seventeen missions, during which he sank eighty-one merchant ships of 220,892 GRT and a warship of a further 1,050 tons, as well as damaging nine ships (45,606 tons). Of the 102 inbound/outbound ships lost sailing to and from Britain in convoy, Rose was responsible for eighteen, damaging a further seven (Robinson, *Rose*, pp.171, 188). Aboard *U.53*, he covered more than 64,000 nautical miles at sea over 298 days.

Rose was well-regarded. Sims even commented favourably on his adversary: 'We acquired a certain respect for Hans, because he was a brave man who would take chances that most of his compatriots would avoid; and, above all, because he played his desperate game with a certain decency' (Robinson, *Rose*, p.17). Rose once spared a Spanish cargo ship that was carrying wine. She was called the *Anna Maria*, his wife's name. The ship's captain swore he would never sail again during the war if Rose spared his ship.[508] Rose was an officer unafraid of speaking his mind: upon his return from Newport, he told the kaiser that it was a mistake not to declare unrestricted submarine war.

The German marine artist, Claus Bergen, painted some of the best-known submarine seascapes when he was 'embedded' aboard *U.53* with Rose in the summer of 1917.

Back in Germany, Rose was invited to meet the kaiser but found himself 'disappointed by the latter's refusal to seize the strategic opportunity launching unrestricted warfare offered'. 'I felt strongly,' he wrote, 'that we should be released from all restrictions. That was the view of all the officers of the line.'[509]

## Conditions Aboard a Wartime German Submarine

Life on submarines was not for the faint-hearted. It was cramped, smelly and intimate. 'With the hatches battened down to keep out the sea, the interior stank of diesel oil, human sweat, sour cabbages and vomit.'[510] Depending on where you were, you could be either hot or cold but almost always damp.

> There is a certain discomfort from the ever-increasing warmth produced by the working of electrical machinery, and from the condensation created by the high temperature on the surface of the boat plunged in cold water, which is more noticeable in winter and colder regions.[511]

Rudolph Zentner had served with Walther Schwieger. The *U.20* was so cramped that he had to sleep beside a torpedo, stored on the same bunk: 'I got used to it, and it finally made quite a comfortable "Dutch wife".'[512] Aboard the *U.9*, Johann Spiess wrote that the bunk that the watch officer occupied was 'too small to permit one to lie on his back. One was forced to lie on one side … [one] could not sleep with [one's] feet aft as there was an electric fuse box aft in the cabin directly overhead.'[513]

Submarines mostly ran on the surface, at higher speed using their diesel engines, recharging the batteries, venting the boat and searching for targets. Working conditions on the surface were very different: the air was fresh, the crew could – with care – enjoy being on deck and, sometimes, swim and dive off the coming tower or take a sea-water shower.

Below the surface, a submariner lost any idea of time, living in a world without sunlight: 'the interior stank of petrol-vapour, bilge-water, and dampness tinged with oil'.[514] The strain was constant. As Spiegel described it to Lowell Thomas, the daring American journalist who had immortalised Lawrence of Arabia through his newsreels and articles,

> Submarine men were likely to break down with nerve strain of some kind or other and were constantly being sent away to recuperate. The ordeal of life aboard the U-boats with the constant stress of peril and terror, was too much for the human flesh to bear for long stretches. Some men went mad … All felt the grinding pressure.[515]

For a U-boat commander, it was especially hard. His every action, expression and demeanour was visible to the crew. Each time the boat dived or made contact, his presence on the bridge was required. This was so even as light broke in the mornings: this was always a moment of danger, when another boat might be discovered nearby. Nerves were essential: 'Resolution, strength, endurance and will-power are all dependent on the condition of our nerves.'[516]

Valentiner wrote about the aftermath of the sinking of the French troopship *Le Calvados* in November 1915. Despite her relatively small size (she displaced only 1,658 GRT), the death toll was heavy:

> We surfaced and watched hundreds swimming in the water … After that, they swam towards the submarine. Red fez and brown faces. We can't believe what we're hearing; they're screaming at us in German: 'Comrades, save us! We are comrades, save us!' Apparently, they are soldiers who had been on the western front and had learned some German from the Germans POWs over there. What should we do? How could our tiny submarine help so many? We dived again and saw the swimmers turning away, making for the shore six thousand metres in the distance.[517]

Valentiner, however, went to great lengths to weave his own absolution into the story, pointedly criticising the behaviour of other Frenchmen who wouldn't stop to pick up their own men:

> Two boats make a bee-line for the shore; the swimmers shout and gesticulate, but the boats don't stop, nobody pays any attention to their comrades.[518]

As a final note, he almost trivialises the drowning of 704 soldiers: 'I later heard that the majority reached the shore.'[519] It was a very different tone from Weddigen's praise for the bravery of *Cressy*'s gunners. A captain's life was clearly a lonely one. Maybe that was why companionship was so often found in pets. Von Arnauld had a monkey he named Fipps. He was quite mischievous and would steal eggs from the larder, chew his pencils and even drink from the inkwell at his desk.

Running on the surface, a sharp lookout had to be constant, even if a submarine had the advantage of a low profile, helped sometimes with an added disguise like a sail. In bad weather, 'the view from the bridge was petrifying … the duration of bridge watches had to be cut by half in these storms, for no man could stand more than two hours of battering by the seas and laceration by spray'.[520] In such storms, even though the watchmen were attached by a safety-harness cable, being washed overboard was a dangerously regular occurrence. A submarine in bad weather could feel like a death ride:

> Crystal walls tower up before us, behind us, and on every side. Great sea-mountains rise out of the deep, crash down and nearly overwhelm us, the boat creaks and groans in all her joints and rivets. Like a mad sea-monster, she leaps and wallows in the foaming flood.[521]

When they could, to avoid storms on the surface a submarine would run deep. Even so, Weddigen's *U.9* was caught in the shallows off the Dutch coast in a violent storm, his submerged boat rolled from side to side by the surface swell; being 'bumped' is how it was known to submariners.

In the confined space of a submarine, there was a level of intimacy between men and their officers that existed nowhere else. Privacy was an unheard-of luxury. You lived on top of one another, with no escape. You were completely reliant on the man standing next to you. The special nature of living and working on submarines earned the nickname 'the trade' in British submarines. Small wonder that in the November 1918 naval unrest, few U-boat commanders joined the revolutionaries. Officers and crew ate, slept and worked alongside one another, knew each other intimately and respected each other's skills. The camaraderie between boats within a flotilla was the same. When a U-boat made its maiden voyage, it would be feted and dressed for the occasion: the 'guns, periscope, and wireless masts festooned with birch bows, and huge clusters of lilacs in honour of [the] "coming-out party"'.[522]

Being away from home and family was especially difficult for U-boat crews, and radio communications were so controlled that wireless contact was unheard of. Kapitänleutnant Moraht's wife was expecting their first baby and the young captain worked out a code to let him know whether they now had a son, a daughter or twins. He finally received a cryptic message: 'Book No.14' – a boy – with a clue, the word 'periscope'.[523]

Food was better on submarines than on most ships, but on longer patrols wouldn't keep. Submariners got better rations and leave than any other: leave every six months and, until the end of 1917, the only persons in uniform receiving real coffee. Men and officers ate the same fare. Pay also was higher for submariners than ordinary seamen: '1.50 marks for each diving day and another 6 marks a month for specialist allowances', according to Schultz.[524] Maybe the most telling and difficult stowage task fell to the cooks who,

> must hunt below in every conceivable place for [his] vegetables and meats. The latter are stored in the coolest quarters, next to the munitions. The sausages are put close to the real grenades [translation note: 'shells'], the butter lies beneath one of the sailor's bunks, and the salt and spice have been known to stray into the commander's cabin.[525]

In many submarines, the 'heads' (toilets) were also used to store fresh vegetables. Fresh food soon ran out and could only be supplemented by booty taken from intercepted ships. Stopping an enemy merchant ship was often done for very basic needs: first, the galley would be plundered, which worked wonders for a crew's morale. A submariner's daily diet soon became 'unbearable': an 'interminable diet of canned stuff, with peas and bacon as the *pièce de resistance*'.[526] One ship in particular stirred great interest among *U.93*'s crew. The ship in question was coming from Egypt with a huge cargo of eggs. Ten thousand were taken: 'You can't imagine how tired a man can get of hard tack, pea soup, bacon and canned stuff … I saw one burly mechanic frying twelve eggs for breakfast one morning.'[527] Distributing the spoils, however, could sometimes cause serious unrest after extended patrols. Moraht described how his officers and crew fell out over how to distribute ham and marmalade from a Norwegian steamer, the *Tripel*. Valentiner saw how important these foraging expeditions were:

> There was wine on all the Mediterranean steamers and on French ships there were excellent preserves, vegetables, mushrooms, meat, fish. Wine, of course, was the most welcome, and we had commissioned an NCO to be responsible for the fair distribution of loot amongst the crew. Officers took nothing but what was needed in the mess, and perhaps a flag, a shell or some other souvenir.[528]

What happened on the *UC.70* was an anomaly. The minelaying submarine had six shafts, each stacked with three mines. For any U-boat cook, cooking with such limitations was an unenviable challenge. In the heat of the Mediterranean, it was even worse. Eggs and meats would go bad fast. The sailors would shave their heads to stay cool in the blistering heat. When *UC.70* was dived on by Commander Guybon Damant on 8 October 1918, a dead officer was found in the conning tower. It was Karl Dobberstein, 'a most brutal officer and very much disliked by the crew', according to one prisoner interrogation. 'He was wearing no uniform but merely two suits of underclothes marked Dobberstein and a leather suit.' Unusually, several 'heavily locked iron cases' were brought up: they contained his supply of sausages, tinned food and even potatoes.[529]

Medical care on a submarine was, at best, rudimentary. When the *U.20* grounded on the Danish coast, a medical pamphlet was found on the beach. The submarine had no doctor on board, the fifteen-page Admiralty-issued pamphlet the only source of counsel.

After a cruise, crews were filthy. The same was true for British submariners: 'The typical 1914 submariner was depicted with oil-stained hands, a mad gleam in his eye, and the appearance of a Grimsby trawlerman who had been at sea too long.'[530] Valentiner joked about how the girls would always know a submariner when they met one:

> 'Honey, how long have you been in submarines?' they asked and laughed. Everyone knew that they were with U-boats because submariners stank

to high heaven of petroleum. So that was us, unsuccessful plumbers, perfumed with petroleum.[531]

Nevertheless, 'it was practically holy writ' in the German submarine service that the commander would first go to the officer's mess to report.[532] Once, Fürbringer was surprised by his fellow officers who had not warned him that Prince Heinrich was visiting and was in the mess as he was a close friend of a fellow U-boat commander, George Gerth. Similarly, Prince Heinrich once paid a surprise visit to Moraht on *U.64*, the two enjoying drinking a fine wine together.

Submarine command could be held by relatively junior officers, and group command was usually for officers who had never actually gone to sea in a submarine. Andreas Michelsen had commanded destroyers at Jutland, while Hermann Bauer, his predecessor as Befehlshaber der U-Boote, held the rank of Korvettenkapitän at the start of the war. A novice U-boat commander might have only around nine months' training. For example, Oberleutnant Georg Gerth, nicknamed *Die Rabe* (The Raven), joined *UB.12* in June 1916 after he'd started his training the previous October.

As the war progressed, many experienced officers transferred from capital ships to the U-boat and torpedo boat services. They wanted action, not to be lying up, doing little, in harbour. This siphoning of the best officer talent added considerably to the tension on board the larger ships. Younger replacement officers were rarely well accepted.

### ARMING MERCHANT SHIPS

Even if technically illegal, an armed merchant ship would more likely escape a U-boat attack than one that was not. Jellicoe thought the likelihood of escape from a submarine was doubled when a merchantman was armed (*Submarine Peril*, p.15). An armed ship had the advantage over a surfaced U-boat, which was at its most vulnerable: a ship's gun was both higher and steadier. Forcing a submarine to dive would slow her speed, run down her batteries and, depending on how long she was down, deplete valuable oxygen. It would also force the submarine to use her limited torpedo supply instead of surfacing to use a deck gun; that meant more returns to base for rearming with torpedoes. Consequently, being submerged, 'much of the submarine's offensive power would be removed'.[533]

Progress in arming large non-military ships was initially slow; the merchant navy and commercial liners were seen as low priority for scare ordnance. In 1914, only 'thirty-nine large vessels had been so fitted (with two 4.7-inch guns) and this number was gradually added to as guns became available'. By December 1915, 766; by mid-1916, 1,100.[534] At the end of 1916, around 1,420 British ships were armed, a further 2,987 in 1917, and by 1918 it was estimated that around 90 per cent had mounted guns.[535] German U-boat commanders, such as Spiess, described the significant effects of arming merchantmen: 'Our submarine offensive was shattered by this arming of merchantmen and with the convoy system which was introduced later.'[536] Michelsen maintained that no submarines were actually sunk by an armed merchantman: 'No cases are known where submarines were sunk by gunfire from a merchantman but they were frequently prevented by such armament from searching the vessel and were at times damaged by gunfire.'[537] Valentiner added the same sentiment: 'The *Woodfield* engagement in November 1915 had already convinced me that using deck artillery against merchant ships was not easy to wage when the enemy was firing back.'[538]

The armament could be rudimentary: until armed with deck guns, individual ship owners did what they thought best. Sir Charles Cayzer, for example, sent one of his employees to a gun shop in London's Bishopsgate to buy rifles for crew members on his Clan Line ships. Thankfully, some were later equipped with 4.7in guns, and two trained naval gunners added to their crews. As a result, ships like the *Clan Macfaden* and the *Clan Lindsay* survived attack.

The Germans used arming of merchant ships as reason for their change in tactics: 'armed ships forfeited their immunity from attack', so the submarine had to violate international law to preserve itself, destroying by torpedo rather than by deck gunnery on the surface.[539]

### Scheer's August North Sea U-boat Trap

Following Jutland, Falkenhayn asked Scheer in July to block the Channel to prevent further reinforcements crossing to the continent. Scheer was unable to help 'because of the likely effect of indiscriminate sinkings on America'.[540] Scheer was simmering at the lack of support for fewer restrictions on the submarine campaign, feeling that valuable time was lost when Germany both had enough boats and the will to win.[541]

Scheer's immediate plan was bold. He had been thwarted by the kaiser and Müller. Müller had the kaiser's ear and was a 'dove', perpetually nervous, like the old Chancellor, of the consequences of Germany unleashing a new, aggressive return to unrestricted warfare. The emperor did not want to lift his own restrictions on North Sea U-boat operations. Consequently, Scheer now intended to build a large submarine trap into which he would lure not merchant ships or liners, but the Grand Fleet itself.[542] For many reasons, it did not work, but it was enough to make the British pull in the reins on the Grand Fleet and hold it back from the southern reaches of the North Sea.

Spindler talked of Scheer's boldness: 'one cannot say that the underlying principle planned in these operations was necessarily a failure ... [rather the new operations off Sunderland] gave an opportunity for a practical application of the submarine experience obtained'.[543] *U.52*'s first commander, Hans Walther, agreed:

> Experience taught us that we could not inflict significant losses on the enemy fleet using submarines alone. A new method had to be devised. The idea of operational collaboration between the fleet and submarines was obvious.[544]

OB40 observed an 'unusually large number of submarines in the North Sea' and concluded that an operation was underway. Jellicoe was not in *Iron Duke* at Scapa Flow when the Grand Fleet was ordered to sea; he was ill in bed at Sir Charles Cayzer's and had to be picked up at Dundee by a light cruiser, HMS *Royalist*. Accompanied by two destroyers, he made his way out to join the flagship. In the fading evening light, a group of ships was spotted by Dieckmann's *UB.27* but he had not been able to make out their identities. With Jellicoe still aboard, her torpedo passed just astern of *Royalist*.

> This meeting was probably the first in a series of impressions that dominated Admiral Jellicoe's thinking the following day, and of which he writes about in his memoirs, that he was in a submarine trap.[545]

At 0413hrs, SMS *Moltke* was spotted by one of three British submarines sent to patrol the area north of Terschelling, and the last ship in the line, *Westfalen*, was slightly damaged. The confirmation that the Admiralty needed came when her radio report was picked up.

*Moltke* and four capital ships would be assigned to raid Sunderland, lure Beatty out and then lead him over two lines of waiting submarines. Fifteen High Seas Fleet and nine Flanders U-boats plus eight Zeppelins were available for the operation.[546] One line of five submarines would be positioned near Flamborough Head, with a second of six further northward.[547] The morning of 19 August was 'overcast, but clear'.

Aboard *U.52*, Walther gave the order to fire a three-torpedo spread; he hit HMS *Nottingham* with two. A fourth, fired at 0626hrs, finished her off and she sank at 0710hrs.[548] Scheer, however, would not hear about the sinking until hours later when *U.52* was able to surface at 1100hrs (CET).

Jellicoe noted that 'several torpedoes were [also] fired at *Dublin*' but at this point did not know that it was a submarine that had been responsible.[549] 'This was the second U-boat attack which Admiral Jellicoe experienced in twelve hours.' He had also received some reports from merchant ships which had spotted some of the first-line submarines (['*Dies war der zweite U-Boot-Angriff, den Admiral Jellicoe im Laufe von 12 Stunden erlebte*').[550] Thinking that he was sailing the Grand Fleet right into a submarine trap, Jellicoe turned his ships back north. He only swung back south again two hours later when Admiralty signals confirmed that Scheer was close by. Despite the gap between the two fleets narrowing – at one point to only 40 miles – it was too late.

A 'force of large warships' was reported to be approaching Scheer from the south by Zeppelin *L.13*. In fact, these ships were only destroyers and light cruisers from Tyrwhitt's Harwich force. On the eastern edge of the first line, Hans Rose in *U.53* also spotted the tell-tale funnel smoke of Jellicoe's ships approaching from the north and signalled a warning to Scheer via Bauer at 1315hrs. The two reports were enough to persuade Scheer to fall back. Up until that moment, a second major fleet encounter might have taken place on the North Sea.

Shortly afterward, German submarines were again spotted by British ships. At 1323hrs, *Minotaur* made one sighting, *Boadicea* another a quarter of an hour later. Even if Jellicoe now correctly concluded that he was being pulled into a trap, he would not escape unharmed. Another sighting was made by ships of the 3rd LCS at 1520hrs and reported back to Jellicoe, who ordered a last turn away.

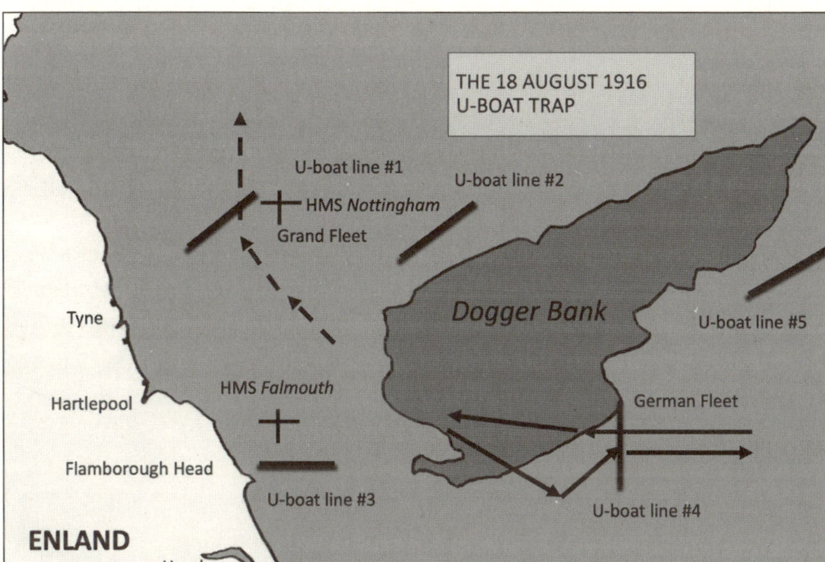


Source: Bauer, p.406

Suddenly, two torpedoes from von Bottmer's *U.66* streaked towards HMS *Falmouth*. Both of them hit. Leading Seaman Bert Stevens watched the scene unfold from his post on HMS *Chester*:

> The *Falmouth* was stopped, flames coming out of her funnel … The U-boat had hit her with two torpedoes; one in the engine room and one in the stokehold … we saw her firing at something so we went round her and we saw this periscope and dropped … depth charges.[551]

*U.49* was only driven off by aggressive depth-charging, and another submarine only narrowly missed being rammed by HMS *Pelican*. 'Their captains were both inexperienced in attacking an enemy battle fleet through a protective screen and coordinating their movements with surface units.'[552]

At only 2 knots, *Falmouth* limped home throughout the night, helped by two tugs. Off Flamborough Head, she was finally caught by another submarine, Otto Schultze's *U.63*, around midday. Despite an eight-destroyer escort, he finished her with two additional torpedoes. HMS *Inflexible* was also nearly hit; she was coming back near Farne Island when several torpedoes from *U.65* just missed her stern.

> Scheer's trap had almost succeeded and was, indeed, one of the few occasions in naval history when submarines operating in conjunction with surface ships met with success.[553]

The August submarine trap was Scheer at his best: a naval commander who knew how to integrate the three elements of the war at sea – sub, surface and air – into a lethal gauntlet against an adversary.

> This was the most perfect case of co-operation between the fleet and the submarines ever attempted. Lord Jellicoe expressed his astonishment that the submarine trap as exemplified by these operations was not made use of earlier in the war. His views were shared by Captain Bauer, commander of the submarine forces, who had expressed this wish since the beginning of the war.[554]

The torpedoing of *Nottingham* and *Falmouth* had a sobering effect on the British. Jellicoe wrote to Beatty saying that he could no longer take the same kind of risks with the Grand Fleet as he had done earlier in the war. In a letter dated 6 September, Beatty agreed: 'When you are winning, risk nothing.' It was the moment when the British ceded control of the southern North Sea to Germany. The Grand Fleet would not venture south of the line 55° 30 min

North. Jellicoe also became increasingly cautious about U-boat attacks on smaller ships in the Grand Fleet: he 'believed he could no longer deploy even light cruisers without their own screening destroyers'.[555]

The significance of what Scheer had achieved has now been lost, overshadowed by Jutland. Goldrick quotes the Naval Staff History:

> It is typical of the vagaries of naval war that while the Battle of Jutland whose name is a household word, had no immediate effect on fleet strategy, August 19, a day when not a shot was fired by either side [*sic*] marks a definite turning point in the war at sea.[556]

Both Jellicoe and Beatty pressed for the development of a submarine which would accompany the Grand Fleet. That meant a fast surface speed. Even the diesel J-class would be too slow, so the two – against Fisher's strong preference for diesel turbines rather than steam engines – pushed for the disastrous steam-powered K-class.[557] Gray felt they (and Fisher) had been looking for an answer to the wrong question:

> In fact, there was no answer to the question, for the question itself was wrong. As events proved time and time again, submarines were lone hunters. They were not, and should not be, integral parts of a large surface fleet organization.[558]

But Scheer's Sunderland operation surfaced some significant learnings: submarine operations tactically tied to the main fleet were viable and, moreover, groups of submarines working together yielded very tangible results. Of the ten submarines employed, six made enemy sightings. Surface operations – and therefore increased radio contact – were made possible by the picket lines being in open waters. 'Of the twenty torpedoes fired … eight were hits.'[559]

Submarines had forced a major shift in British fleet strategy.

### Increasing German Support for Lifting Restrictions in 1917

How to best employ the submarine continued to deeply divide Kaiser Wilhelm II's advisors:

> German deliberations leading to the U-boat decision were distorted by political polarization with the prevailing side willfully sacrificing objectivity for the sake of advocacy.[560]

As the year progressed, how best to employ the submarine increasingly turned to the question of how peace could be achieved. Which was the best approach

– military victory or negotiated settlement? 'Restricted U-boat warfare would result in a negotiated peace; unrestricted U-boat warfare seemed to promise victory but at a higher risk.'[561] The former had no popular appeal. In mid-1916, German war debt amounted to 45 billion Marks and the middle class had little stomach to shoulder the burden of increased taxes. The popular mood in Germany, however, was being shaped by being told that 'war with America is better than starvation'.[562] The more Germany felt the grip of the blockade, the more opinion hardened and support grew for a resumption of unrestricted U-boat warfare.

Whether or not Germany used unrestricted submarine warfare as the centrepiece for a wider war strategy depended on a complex constellation of supporters and detractors in the highest levels of Germany's navy and her military, and whether those vascilating in the middle ground moved to support the decision. The politicians – Chancellor Bethmann-Hollweg, Secretary of State for Foreign Affairs von Jagow and Secretary of the Treasury Dr Karl Helfferich – maintained a strong stance until the last against unrestricted warfare.[563] The kaiser, access to whom was often blocked by von Müller, circled above but, fearing international condemnation, tended to a far less aggressive approach.

Bethmann-Hollweg was unwavering in his opposition: for him, unrestricted submarine warfare was nothing more than 'an act of desperation'.[564] He believed that since U-boats could not enforce the submarine blockade at night, it was technically illegal. Helfferich talked of the planned campaign as a 'catastrophe'. Jagow was convinced that Germany would face new enemies and would end up being viewed as a 'mad dog against whom the hand of every man will be raised for the purpose of finally bringing about peace'.[565] The Chancellor's position was, as Jameson noted, 'prophetic'.[566]

Those in the middle held their ground for different reasons: Scheer, for example, because he felt that Germany should only pursue such a course if she had enough submarines available and that, once committed, it should be of the most aggressive nature possible. Falkenhayn had earlier crossed over when he saw it could be a convenient alibi should his Verdun campaign fail. Holtzendorff – like Hindenburg and Ludendorff – came aboard when he saw no alternative to the army's bloodletting on the Western Front. To Holtzendorff, only America posed a risk. The naval attaché in The Hague, Kapitän von Müller, agreed that neither the Scandinavians nor the Latin Americans would risk their profits. He thought the possibility that Holland could be brought into the war was unwarranted. Holtezndorff's support was gradually materialising as he grew increasingly concerned by the effects of the blockade. The less-than-satisfactory 'Jutland result froze in place the brutal dynamic of the war. Bloody stalemate on the Western Front and an unyielding British naval blockade.'[567] The Western Front was a meat grinder, for all belligerents. On one day alone on the Somme, 1 July 1916, the British lost 19,240 dead and a further 35,493 wounded. Day by day, Germany's position worsened. The German navy's leaders, Scheer and his Chief of Staff, Trotha, combined to push their case. Neither of them found Holtzendorff that effective. Trotha found him 'a good staff officer but not a man to ride the storm … We [Scheer and Trotha] never submitted a plan of an operation to Holtzendorff until it was too late for him to stop it. He was the class of man … who stuck closely to the book.'[568]

Behind the scenes, right-wing politicians like Wolfgang Kapp tried to persuade Paul von Hindenburg (the newly appointed Chief of the General Staff) and Erich Ludendorff on the merits of a more aggressive submarine war and for a stronger man to be Chancellor, someone like Tirpitz, seen by many as the best man to conduct an unfettered submarine war.[569]

On 2 August, Müller prepared 'A new plan to wage unrestricted submarine warfare in the English Channel'. Bethmann-Hollweg continued to be worried about American reaction; few others were. The 300-day struggle at Verdun had already been a disaster, with casualties of around 350,000, and now, with the Romanian declaration of war on Germany and Austria-Hungary on 27 August, Falkenhayn's fall from grace was complete. His departure the next day cleared the way for Hindenburg and Ludendorff to go up against the Chancellor.

On 30 August, an important conference took place at Schloß Pleß. The day after Hindenburg's appointment, Holtzendorff confidently predicted that 'England would not be able to stand' her trade being severely interdicted: 'I do not hesitate to assert that, as matters now stand, we can force England to make peace in five months by means of an unrestricted U-boat campaign.'[570] It was not as if proponents were under any illusion about the possible reaction from America: it was clear she would probably enter the fray. However, they thought her entry would be too late to reverse Germany's victory. Jellicoe later said he thought that the American threat had been minimised as the Germans had not understood her enormous manufacturing capabilities.[571] It foreshadowed Admiral Yamamoto's same fears in 1941: he had spent time in America as a student and feared the huge power of her industrial strength.

### A British Propaganda Victory – the Loss of *U.20*

On 5 November, British submarine commander Noel Laurence spotted several capital ships, including the *Moltke*. They had been sent by Scheer to help extricate the *U.20* and *U.30* after both had run aground on the Danish coast. It was especially galling for Schwieger on the *U.20*, as he had gone to the rescue of the *U.30*. She eventually managed to free herself, but Schwieger's own boat remained stuck hard: 'The tow ropes and chains broke three times. We waited for high tide at eleven o'clock. Still no use. The *U.20* refused to budge.'[572] Schwieger understood the larger issue: 'Realizing the propaganda value to the Allies if they could capture the killer of the *Lusitania* intact, Schwieger broke radio silence and sent out an urgent distress call.'[573] In the end, his crew used the explosives in *U.20*'s own torpedoes to blow her up.

Holding off at 4,000 yards, Laurence's HMS *J.1* fired a spread of four torpedoes and hit the *Kronprinz* and the *Große Kurfürst*, both of which had come to Schwieger's rescue, each with a single torpedo, the former in her engine room, the latter under her bridge. Both ships were heavily damaged and had to be dry-docked.

The kaiser was furious. Scheer defended his decision, saying that such an action had been necessary for the morale of all U-boat crews and that, had the Royal Navy captured *U.20*, it would have been a huge propaganda victory.

In the last four months of 1916, Allied shipping losses were double that of the first eight months, but less well understood was that the Mediterranean losses, with only 20 per cent of the U-boat resources employed, accounted for 40 per cent of the total.[574] Eighty per cent of ships sunk had been warned and 75 per cent sunk by deck artillery rather than torpedo. It was a testament to the success of von Arnauld's tactics. By the war's end, the Mediterranean losses accounted for around 3.6 million tons of the total Allied shipping losses.

### The German Army Comes on Board

The German Army did not immediately lend their support to the hardliners. It was felt better to wait for the situation in Romania to improve, which would mean that reserves would be able to be called upon to cover any possible switches in allegiance by either Holland or Denmark. What was 'tragic' however, wrote Gayer, was that no decision on new submarine construction was made at the same time.[575] It would turn out to be a strategy without the means. That alone restrained Hindenburg: he was in favour of the navy's plans but thought them both over-optimistic and, without the number of U-boats needed, premature: 'common sense still speaks against it', he wrote to his daughter.[576]

On 7 September, Ludendorff and Hindenburg visited the Western Front. They found the Allies' materiel supremacy sobering; Germany's land war was becoming defensive in nature and her industry lacked the most important strategic resources – rubber, copper, iron ore and nickel – to continue feeding her military machine. Convinced after their visit, Ludendorff and Hindenburg began pushing the kaiser to lift the restrictions at sea.

Hindenburg's and Ludendorff's support was critical, as 'if the army accepted, the politicians would follow'. Trotha liked Ludendorff and what he saw as his no-nonsense manner. Not only that, the partnership with Hindenburg was 'a gift from heaven'. After Ludendorff called his commander from France and – with Trotha in the room, listening in on a loudspeaker – received the news that the situation on the Western Front was 'very bad', he agreed to support the two admirals, saying that 'the unrestricted U-boat war advocated by Scheer must be implemented'.[577]

As early as 25 September, the British intercepted a telegram, sent by Bethmann-Hollweg to Bernstorff, giving them an early warning of German preparations for a new, aggressive phase in the submarine war. Jellicoe rightly assumed that a new campaign would start in February 1917, but its intensity would still take him by surprise.

The discussions at Pleß concluded that a breakthrough in the West was unlikely for either side, but that if Wilson could be persuaded to present a peace initiative under the right terms, Germany might hold back. The British weren't confident, however, that America could persuade Germany to include any of their most important needs. Therefore, a renewed submarine campaign seemed inevitable, making it likely that America would be turned against Germany.

During these months, Germany played the submarine card with caution. In October, authority was given for a renewed submarine campaign, and while there was also a clear message that 'incidents which may lead to well-founded claims by neutrals … are to be avoided', Germany was also quietly signalling its position to the United States.[578] The submarine war was being waged with a fair degree of success. In August and September 1916, the tonnage sunk rose significantly. And from October through to the declaration of unrestricted warfare the following February, Allied losses never fell below 300,000 tons a month. In September, losses rose to over 250,000 tons, due largely to the activities of the new Flanders Type-*UB.II* submarines coming on stream.

A note to Wilson, aimed at making him aware of the pressure German politicians were under from their navy, was prepared by Bethmann-Hollweg on 24 October. He was in a difficult ethical position: he couldn't easily support a submarine war while trying to open peace negotiations through Wilson. The submarine was at the core of how America viewed Germany. The theatrical arrival of the 31-year-old Kapitänleutnant Hans Rose at the doors of the United States Naval War College on 7 October had already sent Wilson's countrymen a powerful and threatening message: the large expanse of the Atlantic no longer offered America protection from the war in Europe. But while the politicians and diplomats played a careful game, the navy was – in secret orders – turning a blind eye to the continued sinking of armed merchantmen without warning.

At the end of November 1916, Foreign Minister von Jagow was replaced by the more aggressive Arthur Zimmermann. Facing unrelenting pressure, the kaiser tried to rein in the 'submariners'. He and his Chancellor had been discussing the idea of presenting their terms to Wilson for a while. The eventual proposal, however, was just as suitable for internal German consumption: the message that Germany was willing to negotiate peace, while the Allies weren't. Hindenburg thought the Chancellor's purpose was to 'paint the opponent to the world as prolonging the war and to demonstrate to his own people an honest desire for peace'.[579] In doing so, it would prepare Germans for the hardship that could come with the war's continuing. It would also build moral support for Germany declaring unrestricted warfare if needed. On 12 December, the proposals were published in Germany, and after only five days were rejected by the Allies. Wilson was caught off guard, but came back asking for proposals from each belligerent. The British, insulted at being treated as an equal amongst the belligerents, rejected Wilson's overtures two days later, saying that they wanted reparations, a guarantee against future German aggression and a restoration of the pre-war status quo. Wilson wrongly calculated that, deeply indebted as she was to American financial support, Britain would be more amenable.

There is little doubt that Lloyd George's fiery rhetoric, fanning British populist fervour, effectively worked in favour of the hardliners, but Wilson's biographer, Link, went as far as to speculate that the British position was calculated to entangle the Americans in their war. This is how Scheer saw it: 'if the enemy were now to reject, we will be utterly ruthless'.[580] OB40 intercepted both State Department as well as German diplomatic traffic between Berlin and Washington. Nigel de Grey, an America Department cryptographer, said he was 'daily decoding the messages. I knew the position between Wilson, Lansing, Bernstorff and Bethmann-Hollweg pretty well.'[581] De Grey was an Eton-educated book editor, known as 'the dormouse' as he was so quiet. In early 1917, he would be pivotal in decoding the Zimmermann telegram.[582]

The kaiser's position matched that of his Chancellor: he asked, on 26 November, 'that orders for U-boat operations be so altered that, for the foreseeable future, any entanglements with America be avoided at any cost'. As Gölitz put it, he thought that provoking a war with America would be 'stupidity'.[583] According to Koerver, his wishes were never relayed to submarine commanders and no copy was ever found amongst OB40 decrypts to suggest otherwise.[584]

Politically, the hardliners were supported by parties on the right and the centre in the Reichstag, as well as 'much of the press and by the most vocal segments of public opinion'.[585] For them, it was America that was keeping Britain's armies supplied. Not many doubted that America's interests lay with the Entente: 'the attitude of the United States in regard to the question of supply of munitions left no doubt about their one-sided conception of neutrality', complained Ludendorff.[586] Increasingly, it became Holtzendorff's point of view that a soft U-boat policy was no guarantee for keeping America out of the conflict: '[O]nly ruthless U-boat warfare will succeed in interfering with England's import of supplies from the neutrals which constitute 35% of total imports.'[587] By December, he was on board.

Six days after the fall of Bucharest (6 December), Bethmann-Hollweg spoke to the Reichstag about the possibility of peace. He increasingly felt unable to hold back the military pressure within Germany for unrestricted submarine warfare:

> Viewing the German discussions with the United States as part of a larger diplomatic and military strategy – that was to clear the way for this type of submarine warfare, meaning that the United States would remain neutral because Wilson would have assumed that Germany had made a sincere attempt at peace only to have it rejected – it became clear that the German Foreign Office was working to placate the United States as the military work[ed] to bring an end to the war on German terms.[588]

The pressure on the Chancellor did not lessen. On 22 December, Holtzendorff presented an exhaustive 200-page study, 'with statistics down to the level of the caloric content of an English breakfast'.[589] He argued that 600,000 tons a month was achievable, and that it would cripple England, promising victory 'before the harvest':[590]

> I arrive, therefore, at the conclusion that an unrestricted war, started at the proper time, will bring about peace before the harvesting period of the 1917 summer, that is, before 1 August; the break with America must be accepted; we have no choice but to do so. In spite of the danger of a breach with America, unrestricted submarine warfare, started soon, is the proper, and indeed the only way to end the war with victory.[591]

Absent from Holtzendorff's calculations was any consideration of possible developments in Allied ASW or what other initiatives might be pursued: for example, limiting imports, speeding up shipbuilding or reducing military shipping operations. Holtzendorff had been advised that the country would never, unlike Germany, introduce rationing, and this would exacerbate an already dire situation. As wheat imports from America and Canada declined, longer-routed supplies from Australia, India and Argentina would put additional tonnage strain on the British. As food supplies fell, England would face significant price increases. Since 1914, Manitoba wheat prices had already soared 258 per cent, barley and oats 250 per cent, and Argentinian meat prices had doubled and sugar tripled. Britain's coal industry was under similar strain – supporting French energy needs had helped push British coal prices up 70 per cent and Scandinavian pit timber (*Grubenholz*) 100 per cent.

Bethmann-Hollweg's initiative didn't go far, being rejected by the Allies within days. On 26 December, Wilson replied with his own plan, asking both the Allies and the Germans for an outline of their proposals. His hesitancy put him under direct attack from political Rightists:

> Right-wing opposition was aggravated by the Chancellor's refusal to take a position on the question of war objectives and by his hesitant attitude on the question of submarine warfare, which, at the insistence of the Americans, he had made it clear what limits the emperor wanted respected.[592]

It was badly received by Lloyd George, who felt that America was now meddling in European affairs, hoping to further its own interests without having to pay the price of war. Zimmermann used the occasion to underline Germany's supposed interest in ending the bloodshed, but it was more designed to make Germany look the innocent belligerent that was forced to take the decision to launch unrestricted submarine warfare. Holtzendorff concluded that a suitable start date for the most aggressive unrestricted submarine campaign would be 1 February 1917.

# 4

# Tools and Tactics of the New Submarine War

September 1916's U-boat hunting operations dramatically illustrate the ineffectiveness of early British ASW efforts. On 3 September, several submarines were detected in the Western Approaches, around Ushant, the Lizard peninsula and in the Bristol Channel. For ten days, massive resources were hurled against them – '49 destroyers, 48 torpedo boats and 468 armed auxiliaries were watching this area, and these two or three enemy submarines were actively hunted by 13 destroyers and 7 Q-boats'.[1] The three U-boats not only got away 'virtually unscathed', they succeeded in sinking thirty ships.[2] Leighton estimated that 'only one submarine was sunk in every thirty-nine attempts to destroy it'.[3]

What is anti-submarine warfare? It comprises the tools and tactics to counter and destroy both enemy submarines and the weapons they employ. In 1917 and 1918, the latter included interception, boarding and scuttling, artillery strikes, torpedo attack or sowing minefields. A range of options was developed to counter these: (a) preventing a submarine's passage by barrage or mining; (b) their detection by means of acoustic, visual or deductive intelligence; (c) destruction through mining, barrage nets, artillery, depth charge or bombing; (d) avoidance through re-routing; and (e) hindering production through blockade of relevant industrial materials. As so often the case, what works today becomes obsolete tomorrow. Submarine warfare tactics and countermeasures were, and remain, highly iterative and fast evolving.

In some respects, it was natural that the development of effective countermeasures by the Allies should take so long. All new technologies enjoy some sort of honeymoon. As war approached, few understood the submarine's potential. 'No naval brain on either side,' wrote Massie, 'had an inkling of what the submarine was going to mean.'[4] Even such an astute mind as Jackie Fisher's was far from able to grasp its magnitude and potential:

> It must be admitted that, however inhuman and barbarous it may appear, this submarine menace is a truly terrible one for British commerce and Great Britain alike, for no means can be suggested at present of meeting it except by reprisals.[5]

In 1915, author H.G. Wells complained of the slow progress in ASW methods. In a letter to *The Times* (11 June 1915), he sarcastically quipped:

> We have produced no counter stroke at all to the enemy's submarine and no efficient protection against his improved torpedo … we have not produced any novelty at all except in the field of recruiting posters.[6]

The Royal Navy's Young Turks consisted of some very able young officers, men like Dewar, Drax, Kenworthy and Richmond. Behind them, they had the support of high-profile senior officers such as Beatty, Reginald Hall, Tyrwhitt and Keyes. Dewar was pure offensive, Richmond far less so. Kenworthy (Lord Strabolgi) 'appears merely to have enjoyed unofficial links with Lloyd George'.[7] He and Jellicoe saw eye to eye on at least one key issue: 'If endeavouring to destroy the German Fleet we run risks which may prejudice our success in the greater object of the destruction of Germany, those risks are too great.'[8] They united in their openness to look beyond the Grand Fleet for the key to victory.

### A Perpetual Debate: The Lure of the Offensive

An open-minded approach was often difficult to find, given the Royal Navy's culture of the offensive; all too soon, debate became embroiled over whether to favour offensive or defensive solutions.[9] There was an obsession that no wrong can be done in 'closing with the enemy'.

Beatty complained that 'hitherto the [submarine] menace has only been met by ultra-defensive measures'. Consequently, he wanted a very special kind of officer in charge of ASW efforts and spoke the language of a fox-hunting man:

> He need not be a strategist, a theorist or a genius, but should have the ordinary qualifications of a hunter – a man who has cunning and artifice and could *hunt his force like a pack of hounds* [author's italics] and give the enemy no rest.[10]

The two approaches, however, are not mutually exclusive. ASW tactics can be both simultaneously: by bringing ships together, convoys offer submarines a temptingly large target, but by doing so lure their prey towards a mixture of fire from escorting destroyers and merchant ships, depth charges and even torpedoes.

Convoys allow for ships to be collectively managed, so not only is mass rerouting made possible, but resources used for both defensive and offensive objectives can be better applied; for example, the distribution of escort types between grouping areas, submarine-free transit zones and high-risk inshore lanes like the Western Approaches. Owen illustrates how strong the offensive lobby in the Admiralty was: in March 1918, a 30 per cent reduction in the escort destroyer force was being called for, to devote them instead to offensive patrolling.

The effectiveness of platforms and weapons evolves with context and time. Q-ships were effective under one set of conditions (restricted warfare), but their use was quickly exploited, first by German propogandists as endangering neutral shipping and then by U-boat commanders because they naturally encouraged a switch to unrestricted tactics. Initially limited in range and performance, submarine tacticians favoured inshore and defensive roles such as harbour and coastal defence. As the submarine's range and endurance increased, their role became more offensive against either military or commercial targets.

The ASW debate was perpetually dynamic as theatres changed conditions, both physical and political, and as weapons and platforms improved. Each advance would produce inevitable countermeasure and reassessment.

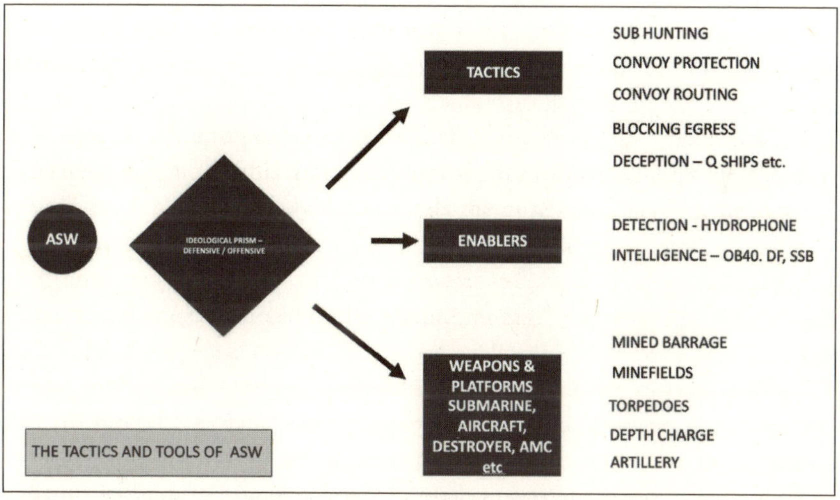


In March 1910, the Anti-Submarine Warfare Committee was set up by the Admiralty. Few useful recommendations emerged from its deliberations, with 'little progress' in developing ASW weapons, technology or tactics in the first years of the war.[11] It is often said that Germany's submarine success did not come about by the strength and superiority of her technology; rather, because of the total initial lack of British ASW response.

One of the first senior officers who seemed to have taken ASW seriously was Sir George Callaghan. In 1913, after fleet exercises, he wrote to the Admiralty that 'the performances of the submarines during manoeuvres ... show that these vessels are a far greater menace to ships than the fleet generally gave them credit for'.

> Callaghan addressed his concerns to the Admiral of Patrols and Commodore (S), posing two specific questions. The phrasing is important, as he was not afraid to talk of 'defensive' measures: '[w]hat defensive measures can ships take to minimise the risk of being attacked successfully by submarines', and '[i]n what manner can our naval bases be defended from submarines?'[12]

At the time, Commodore (S) was Roger Keyes. The combined work led to the development of the destroyer screen, designed to force submarines waiting in the path of the fleet to dive, and by July 1914 the idea was added of a second screen to tackle the threat once submerged, along with aircraft spotters. The effect of the fleet using exercises to evaluate ASW gradually introduced realism into its thinking, even if its scope was rather limited.

Supporting any open debate on new weapons platforms like the submarine was seen by some as an act of profound disloyalty, especially amongst battleship officers. Even a distinguished officer such as Sir Percy Scott, whose professional and fertile mind had revolutionised naval gunnery at the turn of the century, was attacked for his thoughtful warnings:

> Submarines and aeroplanes have entirely revolutionized naval warfare; no fleet can hide from the aeroplane's eye, and the submarine can deliver a deadly attack even in broad daylight.[13]

Scott was lampooned. He tried to draw attention to the protection of Britain's trade routes; what he'd called 'our most vulnerable point'.[14] Sounding very Fisher-like, he succinctly predicted what eventually came to pass:

> All war is, of course, barbarous, but in war the purpose of the enemy is to crush his foe; to arrive at this he will attack where his foe is most vulnerable. Our most vulnerable point is our food and oil supply. The submarine has introduced a new method of attacking these supplies. Will feelings of humanity restrain the enemy from using it?[15]

Above: HMS *A.3* (originally classed as Holland No. 6) and HMS *Victory*. The submarine had been sunk off the Isle of Wight and refloated after salvage. Below: A surfaced U-boat stopping a merchant ship on the high seas.

At the height of the submarine war in 1917, policy was dictated by three men: the British Prime Minister, the German kaiser and, increasingly, the American President, even if the most reluctant and the last to enter the European conflict.

David Lloyd George, British Prime Minister 1916–22.

President Woodrow Wilson, photographed in 1912 (in office from 1913–21).

Kaiser Wilhelm II, photographed in 1902.

The two great fleet builders, Alfred von Tirpitz (1849–1930) and Jackie Fisher (1841–1920). Fisher was one of the few visionaries who recognised the future importance of the submarine.

Colonel Edward House, President Wilson's confidante and advisor.

Theobald von Bethmann-Hollweg, German Chancellor from 1909–17. Up until the end, he was a consistent voice against unrestricted submarine warfare.

Sir Edward Grey (1862–1933) served as Britain's Foreign Secretary from 1905–16.

Johann Heinrich von Bernstorff (1862–1939), German Ambassador to the United States from 1908–17.

Admiral William Benson, USN (1855–1932), the anglophobe Chief of Naval Operations, Josephus Daniels (1862–1948), Secretary of the Navy from 1913–21, with Sir Eric Geddes (1875–1937), who took over from Sir Edward Carson as First Lord of the Admiralty in July 1917, and Alexander Duff (1862–1933), appointed by Jellicoe as Director of the Anti-Submarine Division.

Walter Page (1855–1918), American Ambassador to the Court of St James in London from 1913–18.

James W. Gerard (1867–1951), American Ambassador to Germany from 1913–17.

Above: *U.7* and *U.8* in harbour.
Below: The 8.8mm deck gun on *U.17*.

Above: The crew of SM *U.53* on deck after Hans Rose's visit to the US Naval War College in Newport, Rhode Island, on 7 October 1916. Below: Crew and officers of *U.90* in Kiel.

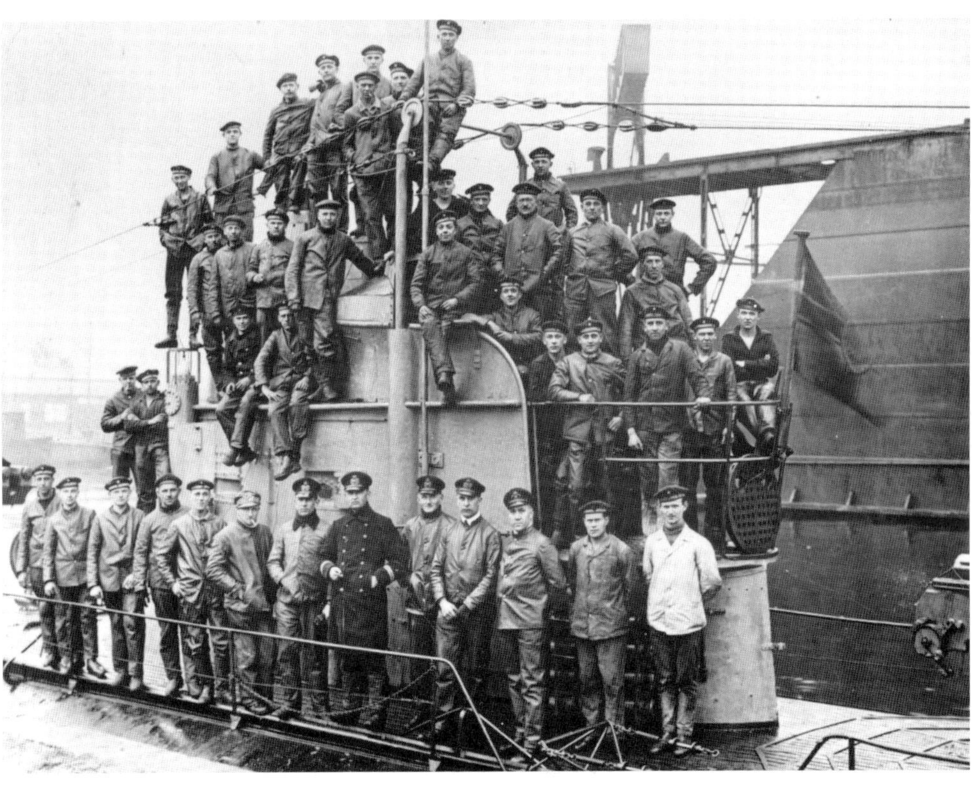

Admiral Sir John Jellicoe (1859–1935) faced the U-boat challenge when he accepted the position of First Sea Lord in December 1916. If he hesitated too long in implementing the convoy system, it was partly because the resources to make it work – destroyers – were severely lacking until America entered the war.

Effective measures against the U-boat were also hampered by mines that did not work, an under-developed depth charge, primitive sound detection and, at least in the Mediterranean, a lack of co-operation between the Allies. Even the top levels of the USN were opposed to the use of convoys. Jellicoe should at least be credited with its successful introduction.

A year before his death, Jellicoe wrote about the conduct of the war in 1917 against the U-boat. *The Submarine Peril*, written in 1934, was his response to the continued attacks over his handling of Convoy.

Sir Charles Cayzer (1843–1916), Jellicoe's father-in-law and owner of the Clan Line, gave the admiral a particularly intimate view of the human toll of merchant ship losses. The Clan Line lost twenty-eight ships to enemy action, along with sixty-one officers and 275 lascar sailors.

Vice Admiral William S. Sims (1858–1936), Commander of US Naval Forces in Europe from 1917–1918.

Henning von Holtzendorff (1853–1919), architect of the 1917 submarine campaign, optimistically aimed at breaking Britain within five months.

Admiral Reinhard Scheer (1863–1928), Jellicoe's opponent at Jutland, lobbied for the change of strategy in 1917 to switch to an aggressive unrestricted campaign against Britain.

Andreas Michelsen (1869–1932), Befehlshaber der U-Boote (C-in-C U-boats) from June 1917 to the end of the war.

SC125
S.C.325
SC349
SC252

8681

With the first successful open ocean convoy tests in May 1917, the system was rolled out in a massive operation that put the nation's merchant shipping under centralised control to bring the maximum efficiencies to the allocation of limited destroyer escorts.

OPPOSITE, CLOCKWISE: Tools of anti-submarine warfare: 1, Gordon Campbell VC, commanded the Q-ships *Farnborough*, *Pargust* and *Dunraven*; 2, hydrophones in use; 3, the American Y-mounted depth charge; 4, laying mines; 5, a Curtiss H-12 seaplane; 6, American sub-chasers at anchor at Ponta Delgada in the Azores.

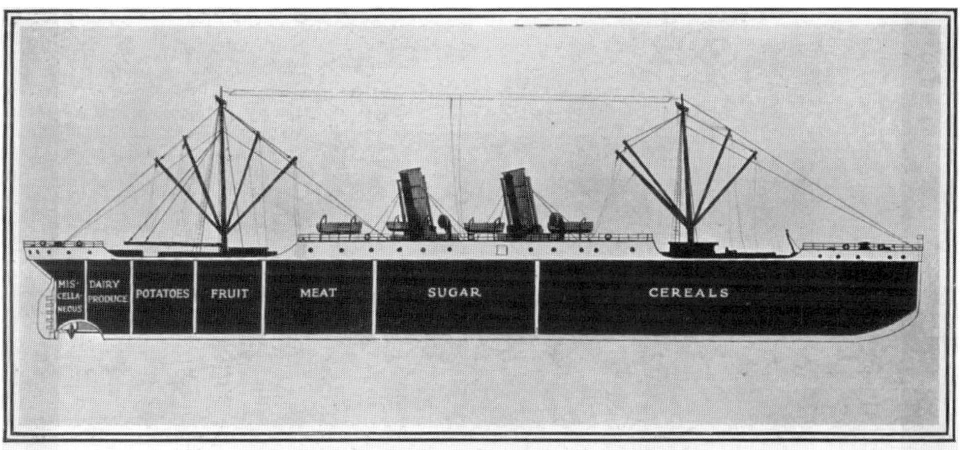


**An Imaginary Ship Showing Britain's Ship-borne Food Supply in its Various Proportions**

If we imagine one ship bringing all the foreign food which this country requires from day to day instead of many ships bringing whole cargoes of particular articles, we get a ship proportioned as above. The cereals in this symbolical vessel occupy the largest space (from the bow to the first funnel), 42·5 per cent. Then comes sugar, a goodly bulk, 18·2 per cent.; followed by meat, poultry, and eggs, 13·5 per cent. These are the three largest divisions. In the stern part of the hold we have fruit, 10·2 per cent.; followed by potatoes, which occupy 7·5 per cent. of the hold; dairy produce, 5·7 per cent.; and miscellaneous. The largest sections are towards the bow, the smaller are shown towards the stern

Illustration in *The Sphere* journal (3 March 1917) showing the approximate share of imports by category, cereals and sugar being the most important.

Sir Edward Carson MP (1854–1935) served as First Lord of the Admiralty from December 1916 to July 1917, when Lloyd George moved him into the War Cabinet to weaken Jellicoe's position.

Admiral Sir Rosslyn Wemyss (1864–1933), a friend of King George V (who knew him as 'Rosy'), took over as First Sea Lord from Jellicoe at the end of 1917.

Vice Admiral Sir Lewis Bayly (1857–1938) worked closely with USN ASW forces based out of Queenstown.

Admiral Sir Reginald Bacon (1863–1947), an early proponent of submarines and Jellicoe's biographer, commanded the Dover Patrol from 1915 until replaced by Roger Keyes of Zeebrügge fame.

SM *Deutschland*, later *U.155*, initially used as a U-Kreuzer merchant submarine, on show in London.

Below Left: A U-boat patrol in the Mediterranean.

Forgotten by history? Below left: Eldon Manisty (1876–1960), named Organising Manager for Convoys in June 1917, whom Jellicoe said was 'very largely responsible for [the] striking success' of the convoy system. Right: Reginald Henderson (1881–1935) brought his invaluable experience in organising the French coal trade.

# 1917 – THE HIGH WATER MARK OF ALLIED SHIPPING LOSSES

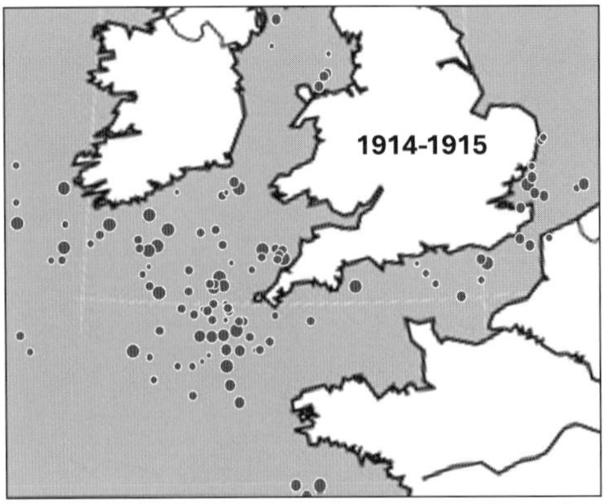


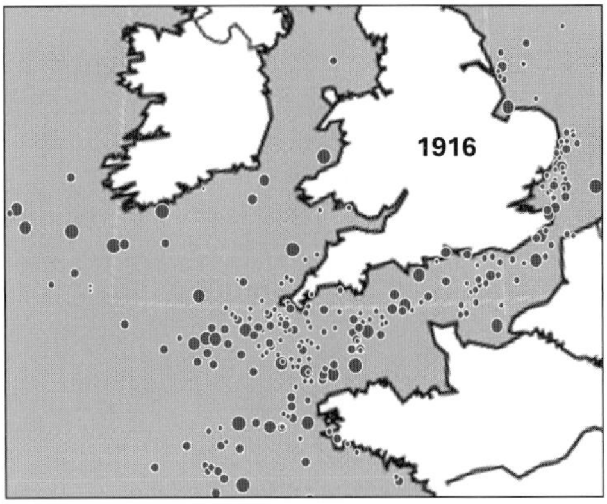


Please note that sinking locations are illustrative rather than exact. **1914:** The value of the new weapon is demonstrated by Weddigen's triple sinking in September. **1915:** The *Lusitania* sinking signals the danger to neutrals. With ambiguous orders, the U-boat war is held in check. **1916:** After Jutland, Scheer integrates the U-boat into his naval strategy and, with the arrival of *U.53* in Newport, Germany signals America that it too is vulnerable.

*U.25* with a Friedrichshafen-based FF29a seaplane at the bow.

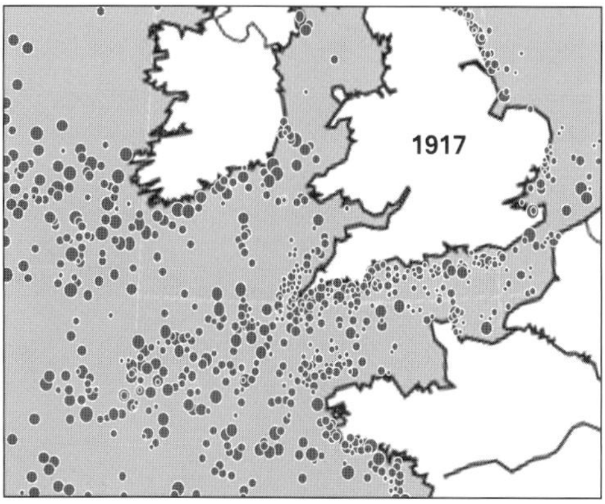


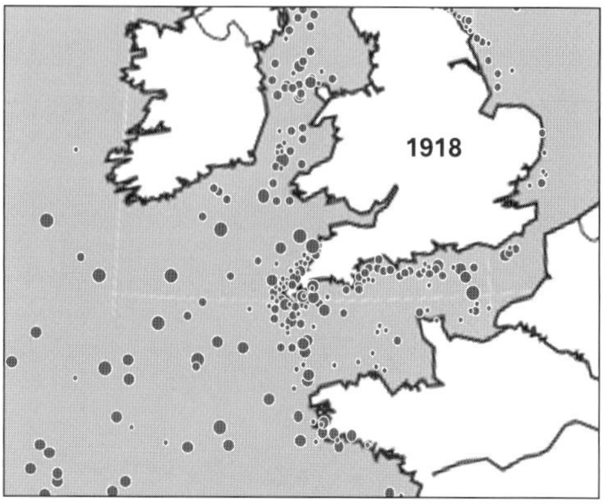


**1917:** Unrestricted submarine warfare is launched, and in April of that year 860,000 tons of Allied shipping is sunk. After the Gibraltar test in June, convoys start and are rolled out. U-boats operate off the coast of North America and down to the Azores. **1918:** The heroically commemorated but disastrous Zeebrügge raid tries to close off Channel operations. The new weapons and technologies – ASDIC, air-launched ASW – are too late to significantly impact the war; after Germany's failed Spring offensive, her Western Front gradually collapses.

*UC.97*, a Type III, one of six German U-boats given to the USN in 1919. Seen here on tour on the Great Lakes, it was eventually used as target practice by the USS *Wilmette* on Lake Michigan in 1921. She never saw active service.

The role of propaganda in war. Otto Weddigen, commander of *U.9* – which sank HMS *Aboukir*, *Hogue* and *Cressy* in September 1914 – became a national hero, while the U-boat was vilified by the Allies and U-boat commanders and their crews portrayed on the same level as pirates. Top left: actor Carl de Vogt. Top right: 1927 film poster for *U.9 Weddigen*.

United States Navy recruiting poster by William Allen Rogers (1854–1931)

## The Search for Solutions

Fisher was no sooner out of office than he was clamouring to return. To be sidelined during such a profound moment of national crisis was impossible for a man with as fertile a mind as his. Behind the scenes, he played politics fiercely. It's not surprising that even amongst former supporters, many found it hard to continue supporting him. Balfour was not at all keen on him rejoining the Admiralty Board, but came up with what could have been a novel and productive solution had Fisher not quickly tired of it. War is characterised as 'a struggle of invention', and in July 1915 the Board of Invention and Research (BIR) was established with Fisher as its chairman.[16] Not surprisingly, the BIR soon became known as Fisher's 'Board of Intrigue and Revenge'; due in large part to his 'abrasive character', there were, 'from the start, tensions between the Royal Navy and civilian science'.[17] Civilians and military men rarely see eye to eye. Between the two organisations, the BIR and the Navy, there developed an unhealthy rivalry and antagonism, and in September 1917 the BIR was disbanded. In America, Secretary of the Navy (SecNav) Daniels created an almost identical organisation, the Naval Consulting Board (NCB), a civilian body with representatives chosen from the eleven professional engineering societies, chaired by Thomas Edison. A major focus, like the BIR, was submarine detection.

Working alongside Fisher were his 'Three Magi': Sir J.J. Thompson, President of the Royal Society; Sir Charles Parsons, inventor of the revolutionary Parsons Turbine; and the chemist Sir George Beilby. Even though the work of the BIR was divided into six separate sections, that of Submarines and Wireless Telegraphy became its focal point: 14,000 out of the 37,500 suggestions that came into the BIR dealt with submarines, antisubmarine work and wireless.

It's a sad testament that, like the BIR itself, many of its ideas were ridiculed. Specific examples were pulled out to cast a damning shadow over its work:

> The first anti-submarine patrol off Portland Harbour, for instance, was carried out by picket-boats (small steamboats). Their anti-submarine armament consisted of a blacksmith's hammer and a canvas bag. The idea was that the hammer should be used to smash the periscope of the submarine, and the canvas bag to 'blind' a submarine by being tied over the top of its periscope.[18]

Throughout 1917, a number of unconventional ideas were also considered. Training seagulls to land on periscopes was one. Another, training sea lions to track German submarines, was criticised by Duff: 'Valuable time, personnel and money had, in fact, to be wasted to prove the futility and childishness of this contention.'[19] Clearly, no stone was left unturned. It's worth remembering, however, that fifty years later, the US Navy trained dolphins to locate and identify mines. That work continued through the First and Second Gulf Wars. Today, Russia's Black Sea Fleet anchorage at Sevastopol is protected by dolphins.

The Admiralty also had its own research organisations – the two most important, in this area, being the torpedo school, HMS *Vernon* in Portsmouth, and Hawkscraig, the Admiralty Experimental Station at Aberdour on Scotland's east coast.

At Hawkscraig, some of the most important work on underwater sound detection was carried out. Fisher thought they were making great progress. Already in April 1916, he rather over-optimistically wrote about the work on hydrophones to Jellicoe: 'It is so very simple and ingenious that when the sound is exactly equal on both sides, then you know you are steering directly for the enemy submarine.'[20] Because of its location, Commander Ryan, Hawkscraig's Director, constantly received visits from dignitaries and senior officers. Both Jellicoe and Beatty can be included in that long list, the latter with his wife. Beatty became a close friend and supporter of Ryan, a fellow Irishman (in fact, his wife's invitations to Ryan to stay at Aberdour House were not always welcomed by the admiral, 'causing a certain amount of strain in their marriage').[21] Even King George V, preceded the day before by Prime Minister Asquith, visited in June 1916, giving the research a strong and encouraging personal endorsement.

**HAWKSCRAIG**
**ADMIRALTY EXPERIMENTAL ESTABLISHMENT STATION, ABERDOUR**

Much of the foundation work in hydrophones was pioneered by Commander (later Captain) Cyril P. Ryan, RN, 'a fractious Irishman who didn't tolerate fools', who had retired from the Navy in 1911 and briefly worked for the Marconi company before being recalled.[22]

In autumn 1914, many from the Royal Navy's original research station at Granton were taken over by Ryan at Hawkscraig Point, ideally located on the north side of the Firth of Forth, closed at one end by an anti-submarine boom, with a seabed that sloped from 30–126 feet and a gentle tidal current that ran between ½ and 4 knots. The new post, HMS *Tarlair*, was named after the first research drifter, HMD *Tarlair*. Attached ships eventually included a submarine (HMS *B.3*), HMS *Hiedra*, *Eros*, *Venture*, *Ida Adams*, the destroyer *Dee*, the patrol boat *P.33*, trawler *Opulent* and *Nykr* (fondly translated as No Yachting Knowledge Required). By the war's end, 650 ratings and 120 officers manning thirty-one hydrophone stations spread throughout Britain and further afield were based there.

As early as October 1916, Ryan started to look at the idea of towing a hydrophone. The breakthrough for towed directional listening came with the 'Nash Fish', a 5ft-long 'torpedo-shaped device' towed at the low speed of around 6 knots at depths between 20ft and 30ft under a support vessel, inside of which two microphones were located. Each had a different purpose – a fixed one to indicate a noise presence, another, a rotating one, indicating its direction. In September 1918, Ryan's 'Porpoise' was produced, but only thirty-one units were in use by the end of the war. The 'Rubber Eel', approved in October, housed a 2in microphone listening device in an 18in x 3in rubber tube, behind which jelly was injected to dampen surrounding sounds, towed by a vessel at speeds between 3 and 8 knots; 463 units were produced by the war's end.

A good example of Hawkscraig's importance is shown by events on 25 October 1918, when a tell-tale acoustic noise was picked up by HMS *G.2* and then used to guide a sub to *U.78*, its target, and torpedo it, 'the first recorded occasion in which a British submarine's hydrophones played a major role in the sinking of another submarine'.[23] Ryan's work attracted some of the country's great scientists: one was Professor Sir Ernest Rutherford, to whom Ryan demonstrated his invention. In April 1917, he experimented with the idea of attaching 'directional plates' to either side of a submarine, and Beatty wrote enthusiastically to Jellicoe that, so equipped, the sub had been able to follow another sub 'all over the Firth of Forth and could not miss him'.[24]

In June 1918, with the need for deeper-water testing, the research group was moved from Hawkscraig to Parkeston Quay on the River Dart. At the war's end, there were a total of thirty-one shore hydrophone stations around the world. Hawkscraig itself had grown to '120 officers, 650 ratings and 12 cable-laying drifters'.[25] However, 'the listening devices generally failed to fulfill the great hopes placed in them'.[26]

(See Frost, Gary L., 'Inventing Schemes and Strategies: The Making and Selling of the Fassenden Oscillator', *Technology and Culture* (June 2001), pp.462–88)

Ryan, a retired naval officer, did not work comfortably with civilians: 'His failure to see the need for basic research in underwater acoustics resulted in bad clashes with the civilian scientists with whom he had to cooperate.'[27] It was Fisher's BIR that started this basic research. The tools were often comic and crude. Sir Thomas Paget was working on determining the predominant acoustic frequencies of submarine engines. He would listen to a passing submarine by leaning over the side of a rowing boat with an assistant using a tuning fork, tapping on his head to give him a perfect G-sharp, from which he would work up and down the scales to locate the frequency of the submarine's engine.

With America on board, her scientific community was let loose on all these challenges, the National Research Council (NRC) being the 'functional equivalent of the BIR'.[28]

## THE AMERICAN SCIENTIFIC CONTRIBUTION TO SUBMARINE DETECTION

American research into hydrophones started in the late 1880s. In 1901, A.J. Mundy, Joshua Millet and E.C. Woods founded the Submarine Signal Company (SSC), which first developed an acoustic warning signal system of underwater obstacles off the American coast that could be used by shipping. By 1912, there were 'more than a hundred bell arrays along the coastlines of North America, Europe and Asia'.[29]

A chance encounter in a Boston railway station between a Canadian professor, Reginald Aubrey Fessenden, and SSC's Harold Fay led to Fessenden being hired to develop a device to transmit Morse code underwater. His reputation as an inventor was already established: he was 'the first to successfully transmit voices using radio waves and the first to achieve a two-way transatlantic broadcast in 1906'.[30] Fessenden's device was the first 'transducer' because it 'could be used as a transmitter or as a receiver of underwater sound (pressure variations on the steel diaphragm being translated back into electrical impulses)'.[31] The 'Vibrator' was then renamed the Fessenden Oscillator. The Royal Navy were interested in Fessenden's invention and Ryan immediately went to work on reducing its weight (559kg) for it to be used on HMS *B.3*.

The main American naval laboratory was the New London Naval Experimental Station, while SSC and Western Electric established a test station at Nahant on the Massachusetts coast. In July 1917, one of Western Electric's researchers, G.H. Nash, claimed that he had found a better way to mount a towed hydrophone, inventing the 'Fish' for the Anti-Submarine Division (not the BIR, with whom he was on bad terms). In the end, however, it was Ryan's 'Eel', 18in long by 3in in diameter, that would be used on RN submarines.

The real American contribution – known as K- and C-tubes – were, in Vice Admiral Sims's words, 'measurably superior to the British devices'.[32] The K-tube was 'not actually a tube at all. Rather, it was a large, triangular frame with a microphone sealed in a waterproof rubber casing attached to each tip' that could tell an object's direction up to 20 miles away.[33] It was lowered into the water, connected by a tethering cable to the receiver, a 'compensator', which was able to determine the direction of the sound source. A compensator would exaggerate the timing difference in sounds arriving at each microphone for the operator, who would 'tune' the director until the two sounds arrived in his earphone simultaneously. That would show him the angle of detection. The C-tube had various versions; S- (for submarine), SC- (for sub-chaser) and MB-tubes. It was a T-shaped instrument built around a central pivot tube on which a cross bar housed two spaced microphones. The pivot was mounted in the hull and could be retracted when not in use. The reading would show the sound source bearing, but not its depth.

Halpern summed up the American effort as 'equally disappointing' to those of Hawkscraig.[34]

The British would not, however, find the key to detection until the last months of the war, when their focus switched from *passive* to *active* listening, sending out sound waves to bounce off targets with a tell-tale 'ping' that could then be calibrated and 'read'. Here, scientific cooperation with the French, and use of some of their research, had been essential. Rutherford had directed R.W. Boyle, the Canadian physicist, to lead a BIR initiative to look at Paul Langevin's work. The latter and Constantin Chilowsky, a Russian electrical engineer, had been looking at ultrasonic active echo-ranging since 1915. By March 1918, British scientists were able to detect a submarine at 500 yards using echoes. Just prior to the Armistice, sea trials of active echo location started on a converted trawler, *Ebro II*. However, echo-ranging would not see service until the Second World War.

### The Ineffectiveness of Early Allied ASW

For Arno Spindler, arguably Germany's leading authority on the U-boat war, the submarine had the same impact as a 'fleet in being'.[35] The mere threat of its existence could be enough to hold an enemy at bay.

Countering U-boats proved costly in men, materiel and time: 13,000 guns were mounted on merchantmen, and around 65,000 gunners manned these guns; minesweeping operations used 3,200 'English craft' with a further 25,000 personnel; around 46,000 tons of explosives were required for countermeasure torpedoes, depth charges and mines; submarine dockyards employed 112,000 men and the construction of replacement hulls another 770,000. Spindler was somewhat justified in boasting that: 'with the sacrifice of 5,087 combatants, 770,000 men were held in check'.[36]

### Dismal Results at the Admiralty

Jellicoe took over an Admiralty that seemed to be asleep at the wheel. After three years of war, an air of resignation seemed to have set in. As the submarine war intensified, the toll inexorably continued to mount, but the Allies seemed stuck. Hough wrote that 'the only major countermeasures introduced in the first two years of the war were patrols, the arming of merchantmen and the laying of minefields'.[37] Furthermore, the ASW structure which Jellicoe took over was almost totally decentralised, senior naval officers (SNO) having extensive independence of action within their assigned areas.

The war was having a devastating impact on Britain's finances; the French Army was thoroughly demoralised after the bloodletting of the Somme and Verdun; and Russia was falling into a tailspin of revolution. The decision to pursue an unrestricted strategy destroyed the chances of a negotiated peace, but 'instead, as one great power gradually collapsed another, thanks to the U-Boat campaign, entered hostilities'.[38]

At his first War Cabinet presentations in January, Jellicoe first listed the efforts being made to develop an effective ASW strategy. There was no mention of convoys.[39]

Jellicoe promised to assemble a group of ships' masters. One of several conferences took place on 22 February. Lloyd George couldn't restrain his disdain: these were passenger liner captains, he concluded, whose attitude 'was simply the arrogant sense of superiority which induces the uniformed chauffeur of a Rolls-Royce to look down on the driver of what is contemptuously stigmatised as a "tin lizzie".'[40] The 'officers of the smaller tramp were not deemed fit for so exalted a conclave'.[41] He complained that Jellicoe had acted 'without any consultation with the Ministry of Shipping', robbing Sir Joseph Maclay of an opportunity to contribute. Moreover, the Prime Minister held that 'it was highly probable that the form in which Admiral Jellicoe put the question might make the seamen fear that they could never carry out properly the station-keeping and joint manoeuvring that membership of a convoy demanded'.[42] It was a hyper-critical and biased assessment.

Nevertheless, the composition of the meeting seemed 'most strange'. Commander Henry Kenrick, RNVR, wrote a critical memo on the hurried nature of the meeting, calling out how inappropriate some of the representatives were: '[F]ive out of nine men were Masters of Coasting vessels – to whom the very idea of convoy was anathema ... two of the remaining four were Masters of ocean-going vessels – both of which had only a few days previously been torpedoed – one the *Hadley*, while under escort.'[43] It was odd that masters of coasting vessels were there. Bacon says they were *specifically* excluded: every class was to be represented, but 'masters of purely coasting or short sea trips (who were unaffected by the question) were not required and need not be bothered'.[44] Goldrick speculates that it might have been the masters' general realisation that escort destroyers themselves could actually do little to effectively carry the fight to a submarine that lay behind their opposition.[45] The conclusions of this first ships' masters meeting 'were confirmed later by other masters of merchant ships'.[46] Jellicoe acknowledged what Sims had already thought, that they under-estimated their own abilities.

Station keeping could be seriously problematic in foul weather.[47] Writing ten years after the war, an American officer made some interesting observations of his own escort experiences in 1917–18. Captain William Wheeler wrote that,

> difficulties associated with its early history cannot be overestimated. Darkening ships at night was all-essential and flashlight signaling and radio communication were necessarily reduced to cases of extreme necessity. The unfamiliarity with the system by merchant marine personnel of various nationalities, and the low speed and poor maneuvering

> qualities of the vessels, made position keeping very difficult, especially at night without lights and practically without communication. This was still more difficult in thick weather. The one signalman assigned to each freight vessel was not always proficient, so the megaphone or international code were in frequent demand … Collisions between vessels of the same convoy were not infrequent in the early stages of this duty.[48]

Wheeler was also quick to point out that 'it was remarkable how soon improvements were to be noted … especially … the difference between the first and last part of a single convoy trip'.

Days before Jellicoe's resignation, a Clan Line merchantman, *Clan Cameron*, collided with an escorting destroyer, HMS *Acasta*, in the morning darkness at 0540hrs. Later the same morning, after returning to her convoy – HL15 from Sierra Leone – she was torpedoed by Fürbringer's *U.58* at 1130hrs and sunk with a second torpedo two hours later off Portland Bill. Captain Pagan's skill as a master probably contributed to the safe return of all her crew. It was the same for a second Clan Line ship, *Clan Mackay*, in May 1918, which also collided while zigzagging in convoy south of the Scilly Isles.[49] Small wonder why convoys 'were viewed with so little favour among the small ships', especially when operating at night.[50]

**Initial Tactics**

When Jellicoe arrived at the Admiralty, the 'backbone of the British … ASW' was still defined as 'ramming, gunfire and nets':

> Depth charges were still limited to two or three per vessel and the Admiralty was just starting to issue the high-speed submarine sweep to destroyers and P-boats … More advanced devices, such as hydrophones, were in very limited use and were still being developed.[51]

Ramming a barely submerged submarine would force her to surface or to remain surfaced, where she was at her most vulnerable. Staying below risked taking on too much water if the periscope, for example, had been damaged. The earlier U-boats were easier targets because of the amount of time they needed to dive. Valentiner complained that *U.3* took more than five minutes. The tanks vented far too slowly.[52]

From 1 February 1917 until the end of the war, U-boat ramming would be used forty-two times; in half of these cases, like that of *UB.27*, ramming 'played a significant role in a U-boat's destruction'.[53] It accounted for a significant number of kills and included some of the war's 'firsts': the first submarine sunk in the war was the *U.15*, sunk after being rammed by HMS *Birmingham*. In early 1915, *U.29*, the sub that successfully torpedoed three aging British cruisers the previous September, was herself sunk after she was rammed by HMS *Dreadnought*. Ironically, sinking Otto Weddigen's submarine would be Fisher's revolutionary battleship's only contribution to the war. HMS *Halycon* was probably responsible for the sinking of the Flanders Flotilla sub, *UB.27*. After she had brought her to the surface by depth-charging, *Halycon* finished the job by ramming her. It wasn't just warships that successfully rammed U-boats: the *Dorothea Grey*'s ramming of *U.18* inside Scapa Flow in November 1914 so damaged her periscope that she had to surface and was then finished off by another ramming, this time by HMS *Garry*, after which her crew scuttled her.

Ramming wasn't always the single or even the final cause of a submarine sinking; in the case of *U.87*, the sub was first brought to the surface by depth charge and only then rammed. When her wreck was uncovered in 2017, there was a large amount of tell-tale damage to her conning tower caused by the British coastal sloop *P.56*'s ramming.

### U-BOAT WRECKS SURRENDER THEIR SECRETS

A sunken or captured submarine constituted an intelligence treasure trove. The earliest dive was on Karl Mey's *UC.2*, accidentally rammed by a coaster, *Cottingham*, near Yarmouth in July 1915. None were recorded in 1916, but in 1917, dives included *UC.44*, *UB.33* and *UC.11*. At the end of May 1917, Gregor's *UB.33* was inspected, and the following month *UC.11*. Aboard *UB.33*, divers found 'a steel chest containing signal books, ciphers, and related documents. Among them were the new call signs in effect from April 12 onwards. Nothing like this had turned up since salving *UC.44* eight months earlier.'[54] *UC.44*, sunk by mine explosion off Waterford, Ireland, on the night of 4/5 August 1917, was salvaged on 7 September and brought into Dunmore harbour two weeks later, on 23 September. Still aboard were nineteen dead seamen. Efforts to recover 'all books and documents' yielded valuable intelligence regarding the integrity of the Channel Barrage from 17 January 1917, when 'commanders were told of the re-imposition of unrestricted submarine warfare' and when the instructions were given that U-boats should pass to the west of the North Hinder light vessel using Buoy 2501 as a marker. Here they were to pass 'without being observed and without stopping', while those passing around the north of Scotland route were to 'let themselves be seen as freely as possible in order to mislead the British' into thinking that the Dover Barrage was effective in stopping egress.[55] Bacon apparently paid little attention to the evidence from both *UC.44* and Gerth's *UC.61*. Possibly the greatest benefit to the Allies was the ability to test the suitability and effectiveness of 75mm shell or mortar bombs against *UC.61*'s hull.

Although rare, sub wrecks are still being found. In spring 2017, a Type-*UB.II* submarine was discovered by Belgian marine archaeologist Tomas Termote. After failing to identify the wreck by either the usual propeller markings or an attempt to track down the periscope markings showing as the number '417', Termote finally found a small 10cm plaque showing it to be *UB.29*. She was rammed and then depth-charged by a British destroyer, *Landrail*. The twin periscopes were bent over, probably from that encounter, but Erich Platsch managed to get the sub back from what was thought to be her resting place, southwest of the Goodwin sands 6 miles off the south coast town of Deal, to within 60 miles of his home port when there was a detonation. Although lack of evidence made official Admiralty endorsement impossible, Prize was still awarded. Termote was able to see that extensive damage to the top starboard torpedo tube had occurred. It is probable that she 'hooked a mine with one of the twisted periscopes, dragging it down directly onto its hull'.[56]

In January 1919, the Anti-Submarine Division (ASD) released the list of 186 U-boats destroyed during the war on which most of the Admiralty wartime Prize payments were based (before 1916, some were made immediately).[57] Payments commenced in March 1919 and the last payment was made in 1932. Half of the wartime U-boat wrecks at sea have been found. The accuracy of the ASD list is questionable: Innes McCartney estimated that in the case of the Channel wrecks, only 48 per cent are in the locations listed in the ASD list.[58] Many of the payments were kept secret to protect the operational intelligence (although payments for U-boat destruction by merchant ships were often made immediately: little operational intelligence was risked and morale boosted). McCartney cited the example of *UC.79*: the ASD covered up facts to uphold earlier pronouncements. The wreck was found in August 1918 by Admiralty divers off Cap Gris-Nez, between Calais and Boulogne, and not off Zeebrügge, where the ASD claimed it had been sunk by HMS *E.45*. Apparently, OB40 continued to plot transmissions from *UC.79* long after the ASD claimed its sinking. Clarke noted: 'The Anti-Submarine Division ... had frequently to boost their own efforts, insisted on the success of many attacks that we in Room 40 knew to have been abortive and many officers received decorations in consequence.'[59] The number of awards was significant (see Appendix J).

Occasionally, wrecks were left alone, as was the case with *UC.42*, a minelayer that had been blown up by one of her own mines. Bayly had suggested salving her, only to be told by the Admiralty that it did 'not propose to bring her in. We have all [the] information we are likely to get and the knowledge that we had recovered her might lead to a change of codes, etc, which is most desirable to avoid.'[60]

In September 1917, *British Transport* became the first merchant ship to sink a submarine, Richard Hartmann's *U.49*, by a combination of ramming and two well-aimed shots from her 6in poop deck gun. *U.49* was first brought to the surface by ramming, where she was finished off by gunfire, the two adversaries engaging in a five-hour artillery duel. After two torpedoes fired at around 2100hrs missed, *British Transport*'s Captain A.T. Pope steered his ship over 'a luminous patch in the phosphorescent sea' that had been spotted, and in doing so mortally damaged the submarine.[61] After two 6in rounds delivered the *coup de grâce*, *U.49* sank with Hartmann and the entire crew. Pope was subsequently awarded a DSO, three officers the DSC and seven crew members the DSM.[62]

Ramming could be just as dangerous for the attacker: in May 1918, the minelayer *UC.75* was rammed so hard by an old destroyer, HMS *Fairy*, that both went down. The sub's commander, Oberleutnant zur See Walther Schmitz, had steered right in among some ships:

> Unable to believe that a German submarine was in the midst of the convoy, *Fairy*'s commander challenged twice and then rammed the submarine's stern so that the crew, if British, could escape.[63]

As some crew members were pleading for mercy, the submarine's deck gun loosed off a round. The single enemy shot unleashed forty in reply. The *Fairy* then closed at speed, ramming the submarine's hull near her deck gun. Schmitz and eleven of his men survived, but *Fairy* also sank within half an hour.

Jellicoe disliked ramming as a tactic, and in December 1914 wrote to the Admiralty 'pointing out that ramming was being resorted to for lack of a good weapon'.[64] Eventually, in the Second World War, the Admiralty discouraged ramming.

**Mine Deterrence**

A staple of British ASW was the mine, either used in large offshore minefields in areas of high submarine activity or crossing points, in smaller groups to protect harbours or anchorages, or as part of barrages. Mines were responsible for between a quarter and a third of the 178 submarines sunk in the war, despite mining's extreme inefficiency for the first few years of the conflict.

> It is possible to escape a depth-charge attack; aim is not accurate, and pursuers may perhaps be thrown off. A strong mine barrage, on the other hand, offers a submarine very little opportunity of survival. Nine out of ten times, in the World War, the striking of a mine meant death for all on board.[65]

**Anti-Submarine Barrage**

The protection of bases and strategic choke points from submarine attack required nets, often mined, whose value increased once an effective mine was developed. At the same time, mining the channels that U-boats used to sortie would, of course, mean that the High Seas Fleet had to expend considerable resources to getting the U-boats to sea, not just escorting them but clearing the channels for them as well. It was a snowball effect: the Royal Navy was, in turn, forced to use smaller ships to counter German minesweeping efforts, which was then countered by the HSF assigning capital ships to their protection.

Measures had already been taken at Scapa Flow and Rosyth, and, like the Dover Barrage, were constantly updated. New choke point barrages were initiated at the northern North Sea exit to the Atlantic (the so-called Northern Barrage) and at the heel of Italy (the Otranto Barrage).

There were a number of different types of barrage. Some were supported by net buoys; these used 'large glass balls supporting the headline of a long net of steel meshes to which a mine was attached at fifty-metre intervals at a depth of about two metres. An insulating wire from each mine was connected to a battery on the hawser at the surface.' The principle was 'fiendishly simple: as a U-boat charged through, the section of net broke away from the adjoining sections on either side and wrapped itself around the boat, entangling [in] the propellers'.[66] The first thing a commander did as he rode a submarine over the net was to cut his engines.

Talking to a Hungarian journalist in January 1916, Wenninger described what happened when his submarine, *U.55*, ran into a net hung with buoys:

> I looked through the periscope and could see a red buoy behind my boat. When, ten minutes later, I looked I saw the buoy again, still at the same distance behind us. I steered to the right and then to the left, but the buoy kept following us. I descended into the deep water but still saw the buoy floating on the surface above us. At last I discovered we had caught the chain on the buoy and that we were dragging it along with us.[67]

Wenninger felt trapped, every hidden move telegraphed to the enemy by the tell-tale buoy above on the surface. Eventually, he took *UB.55* down to 90ft and stayed there for eighteen hours, surfacing only to find his steering damaged and having to pass another stressful six hours exposed on the surface carrying out repairs. With that accomplished, he was then spotted again by a waiting destroyer and had to spend another two hours hiding from her.

Early in the war, a small minefield of around 960 mines was laid off Flamborough Head. In June 1918, with increased activity of the Flanders

Flotilla, a new, very extensive field of 9,049 mines was laid, but 'there is no evidence to suggest that any U-boats were either sunk or damaged'.[68]

**Anti-Submarine Barrage – Dover**

Protecting any cross-Channel traffic was a fundamental task for the Royal Navy:

> [W]artime traffic was huge by any standard: 24,000,000 personnel movements; 3,221,992 sick and wounded evacuated; 2,400,000 animals; 553,829 vehicles transported; 49,000,000 tons of stores (or 90,000 tons/diem in late war years) all transported without loss through what Admiral W.S. Sims of the U.S. Navy called an 'immune zone' established by the Royal Navy.[69]

At the narrowest point, the Dover Strait measure a mere 21 miles, while the deepest sections reach 180ft. Early in 1915, the decision was taken to lay net barrages across the narrowest gap between England and France, the crossing between Dover and Cap Gris-Nez. There was never one 'Dover Barrage'; it was an ever-evolving array of multiple blocking barrages in the Channel area.

The idea of the net was not just to block a submarine's path; it was to force her below surface and exhaust her batteries. 'Some 750 miles of nets were on order by 1915, each 100 yards long and 60 feet deep.'[70] Some were so-called 'indicator nets': a buoy was attached to the net and it would visibly move and ring a bell when the net was disturbed. Later, they would light up at night. The idea had first been tried in the Spithead 1904 manoeuvres.

In January 1915, around 130 drifters helped patrol the Dover Barrage. Despite all that effort, only one U-boat, Kapitänleutnant Stoss's *U.8*, was ever caught, according to German records. It has often been argued, however, that the mere presence of a barrage forced German submarines to take the longer route around the north of Scotland, even if Fürbringer wrote that there 'was a definite gap between Calais and Cap Gris-Nez' which had been discovered by Oberleutnant Haecker.[71] Another reason was the 'sagging' of the nets between the supporting buoys.[72]

For anyone on a submarine, crossing a submerged minefield was a terrifying experience. Haidt, a wireless operator in *U.54*, made it clear that there were few activities that more challenged a man's courage:

> A fight, even with a superior enemy, I find far preferable to a passage through a minefield under water. It is a very unpleasant feeling when the boat grazes against the mooring cable of a mine, and death bumps and crashes against the hull.[73]

One other submarine commander who successfully navigated the barrage was von Spiegel in *U.32*. He did say, however, that he was 'overwhelmed with the quantity of mines'. His helmsman, Lomann, added that it was a 'highly disagreeable experience': at one point they hit a mine with the periscope, but it didn't detonate.[74] The boat got caught in the barrage's net and he had to use the bow's saw-like net-cutter, moving the boat back and forward, to free himself. When *U.32* surfaced, they found themselves still wrapped in the cold embrace of steel:

> What remained of the net was still clinging to the submarine but, more seriously, the serpentine float that was used to suspend it in the water had become tangled with the débris and, resting on the surface, it had mirrored every movement of the submerged U-boat and had shown the enemy *exactly* where *U.32* was lurking![75]

The difficulties in blocking the Channel were not inconsiderable, and for much of the war it was largely ineffective, rendering the gigantic investment highly questionable. Severe Channel storms would cause even heavy 3in cabling to be torn apart.[76] The 15ft tides made it 'difficult to set mines to catch submarines on the surface'.[77] The poor quality of the British mines' contact mechanism was the barrage's Achilles heel. Admiral von Schröder, commanding the Flandern MarineKorps, found his submarines could quite easily get through, even if a lot depended on how well trained were the crews.[78] Hashagen felt it more difficult for U-boats, like his own *U.62*, because, unlike

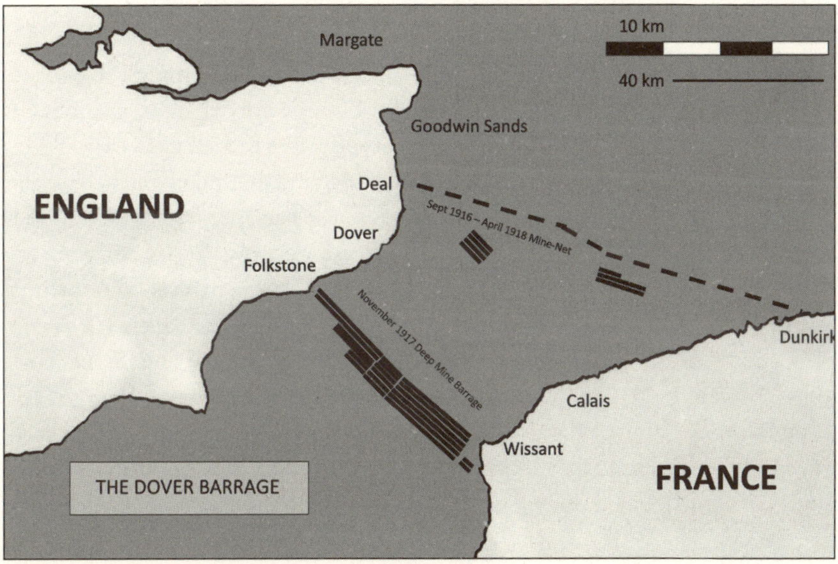

the Type-*UB* and Type-*UC* boats, they had far less experience: '[T]hey knew the position of the barrage, the individual buoys, the tactics of the patrols, and the alterations in the whole barrage-system better than we did.'[79]

The barrage line laid throughout the winter of 1916/17 was 'utterly ineffective',[80] doing little to prevent numerous submarines passing through. Between February and May 1917, intelligence estimated that the barrier was successfully passed by U-boats 122 times, and on only two occasions (both because of destroyers) were submarines lost.[81] Gibson and Prendergast cited 1917 figures to show that the barrage was crossed – on average – twenty-three times a month.[82]

In February, Bacon outlined a plan to build a 'wall' of mines across the narrower part of the straits, from the Varne Ridge to Cap Gris-Nez, to be laid at varying depths between 30 and 100ft (usually at 40, 60, 80 and 100ft). These would use new mines, their designs copied from the successful German *Herz* mine. Some 10,000 of the new 300lb-charge H2 and 150lb-charge H4 mines would be laid between 21 November and 29 December. While the new fields were laid, the old Goodwin Sands–Snouw Bank Barrage was simply left to fall apart.

By February 1918, the use of the Channel route was again forbidden to U-boats. By September, 'the straits were effectively sealed', but Bacon, its architect, had long since been removed.

> In justice and fairness, Vice-Admiral Sir Reginald Bacon must be awarded all credit and praise for originating the Folkstone–Gris Nez Barrage and the Zeebrügge–Osten blockship plans.[83]

Bacon's record might have been tarnished by his over-confidence in the barrage's effectiveness; however, once armed with the new mines, it worked: 'Judged in terms of the number of U-boats it destroyed, it was somewhat effective. Measured in terms of its deterrent effect, it was very effective.'[84]

From time to time, the Germans mounted harassing raids on the barrage. On 17 March 1917, for example, both ends of the barrage were simultaneously attacked by two destroyer flotillas. One British destroyer (HMS *Paragon*) was sunk and another (*Llewellyn*) damaged. On a subsequent raid, the fortunes were reversed. On the night of 20 April, two German destroyers (*G.42* and *G.85*) were sunk by HMS *Swift* (which torpedoed the *G.85*) and *Broke*. For a time, *Broke* and the *G.42* were locked together after the German destroyer had been rammed. Violent hand-to-hand fighting amongst the two crews ensued. It was the second time that *Broke*'s bows needed repair. Edward Evans returned home a hero, from then on known as 'Evans of the *Broke*' and promoted to captain.

The first Dover Barrage (the one laid in the winter of 1916/17) was increasingly ineffective once the Germans mastered how to slip through. Grant only attributes two U-boat losses to the barrage in 1915 (*U.8* on 4 March and possibly *U.37* in April). Results in 1916 were even worse – only one U-boat, *UB.29*, on 13 December. The truth about how she died had to wait for more than a century until her discovery by a Belgian diver.

In 1917, there was only one vessel sunk with any certainty – Valentiner's *UB.56* on 19/20 December. The submarine,

> forced to dive to escape detection, struck a mine … at 11:42 p.m. The destroyer *Gypsy*, patrolling nearby, was shaken badly by the explosion and proceeded to investigate, hearing voices calling ahead at 12:10. Two minutes later some men were seen struggling in the water ahead, but before a boat could reach them, they had all disappeared. To starboard some men were still shouting, and the searchlight made visible two of them. One of them sank before he could be reached; the other, a petty officer named Bleeck, regained consciousness on board the *Gypsy* for only a moment, and although everything possible was done to revive him, he died at 1:15 in the morning.[85]

Another sub, *UC.36*, might have been sunk on 20/21 May.[86] In 2017, David Hobbs wrote that this 'was the first time that an RNAS aircraft had sunk a submarine'.[87] A Curtiss Large America (#8663) spotted her 10 nautical miles north-east of the North Hinder lighthouse and attacked her with two bombs in the failing light.

*UB.57*'s commander, Johannes Lohs, had earlier been totally dismissive of the barrier's effectiveness. 'Go through on the surface. The patrol boats are blind. They can't see a thing [as] I go through under their very noses,' he had boasted. On 14 August 1918, he, two other officers and thirty-one crew members were killed when they hit a mine. In her short life, *UB.57* had claimed forty-six merchant ships, the 9,500-ton HMS *Moldavia* and a further ten ships damaged, a total of around 130,000 GRT sunk.

The Dover Barrage was only transformed into a 'really effective barrier' when Keyes took over on 1 January 1918 and was able to use a new mine.[88] This was the H2 mine, 'using chemical horns copied from captured German weapons'.[89] It had taken the Admiralty an inordinate amount of time to provide an effective solution. Jackson, according to Halpern, had already requested that the German mine be copied as far back as spring 1916. It took a year-and-a-half for them to do so.[90]

Sowing the new minefields started in December 1917. Two main fields were laid: one, with eight mine lines, stretched from the Colbart Bank to

Folkstone at depths between 8 and 20 metres; the other, of fourteen lines, was sown deeper at between 6 and 30 metres from the Colbart Bank to Cap Gris-Nez. Many of the older barrage nets were then abandoned – 'the buoys and nets were simply not replaced when they broke adrift'. Keyes also introduced stronger patrols and nighttime illumination, which Bacon had vociferously opposed. He had preferred shore-based searchlights coupled with uniquely designed and dedicated flat-bottomed boats and upgrades to the existing mine-net barrage. Keyes didn't want to wait. Wing Commander F.A. Brock brought his skills to set up flares. His great grandfather set up the famous fireworks company of the same name.

In January 1918, four German submarines were inexplicably lost: *U.87*, *U.84*, *U.93* and *U.95*.[91] Throughout the last two years of the war, Bauer and then Michelsen had both recommended the straits be used, even making it compulsory at one point. Soon, however, they changed their minds. By the end of January 1918 – apart from its continued use by Bartenbach's Flanders Flotilla boats – the Channel route was, 'in practice', again 'abandoned'.[92] Even if 'none of them had succumbed to mines', it was too much for Michelsen: 'in practice, the channel route was now given up'.[93]

*Estimates of Dover/Northern Route Usage (Outbound and Homeward)*

| | **Northern Route** | **Dover Strait Route** |
|---|---|---|
| December 1916 | 23 | 38 |
| January 1917 | 19 | 17 |
| February 1917 | 29 | 12 |

Source: Halpern, *Naval History*, p.408. Halpern cites 'another source' as directionally supporting the Naval Intelligence estimates but does not give a reference: December, respectively, 17 and 19; January 18 and 5; February 39 and 1.

The immediate results of the new mines and Keyes's illumination were 'marked, if not sensational'.[94] The success was probably a combination of increased patrolling and illumination forcing boats to dive into nets that were finally sewn with effective mines. Wing Commander Brock (an 'authority on pyrotechnics') was tasked with the illumination role. Between 19 January and 8 February 1918, three submarines were destroyed – one, *UB.35*, was depth-charged by HMS *Leven* on 26 January. Over her two-year life, on twenty-six missions, her three commanders had sunk forty-two ships, twenty-two of which were more than 1,000 GRT and one, SS *Mechanician*, 9,044 GRT. Another submarine, *UB.109*, failed to return. Three days after *UB.35*'s depth-charging, she had been caught in the nets. After the sinking of *UB.38* in February 1918, another nine submarines were destroyed in the remainder of the year. In July, out of seven U-boats using the Dover Strait passage, only one returned.

A variety of other net defences were tried, some quite successfully. One example was cited by Dewar: a free-floating, 20-mile section of net, pulled across a frequently traversed North Sea route. The idea came up through cooperation between Section 16, Captain Pound's Anti-Submarine Division and Captain William W. Fisher's Intelligence Division. The British 'kettled' German U-boats into the floating trap, and 'three large submarines had been destroyed'.[95] Characteristically, Dewar wrote that his ideas were not listened to: he had advocated that 'small, patrolled minefields laid across the tracks of the ongoing and incoming submarines would have been more effective than the Northern barrage'.

*UB.109* was 'the last submarine to be sunk in the straits of Dover'. It was blown up on 29 August 1918 by shore-controlled mines after tell-tale noises had been detected by a hydrophone operator at Folkstone. He passed the warning on to the minefield operator near the Shakespeare Cliff, and 'in seventeen minutes the indicator showed that she was over a line of shore-controlled mines, which blew up under the engine room'.[96] Nine crew members still managed to escape. After forty-five minutes in the water, eight were rescued by the British trawler, *D-10*. Oberleutnant zur See Ramien recalled the excruciating experience:

> I had been thrown against the periscope tube and was momentarily knocked out. After I regained my senses, I crawled into the conning tower and tried to talk to the helmsman and another sailor. Despite shouting, we could not make ourselves heard over the roar of released high-pressure air.
>
> The boat was already fully-flooded and the water was rising into the conning tower … [I] tried to open the conning tower hatch. It immediately sprang open, and I, together with the helmsman, [was] blown through the hatch. We were both jammed in the hatch opening with our upper bodies outside the boat and it took about half a minute for us to free ourselves … I surfaced just ahead of the helmsman, the sailor and a radioman. The radioman had no idea how he had gotten into the conning tower.[97]

By October 1918, a total of 9,573 mines had been laid. When it was completed, the barrage consisted of twenty parallel lines, 6 miles wide. The wartime total of barrage victims stood at twelve submarines destroyed. Seuffer's *UC.50* is a possible thirteenth.

**Anti-Submarine Barrage – Shetlands to Norway**

The more successful the efforts in the Channel became, the more the northern exit of the North Sea needed to be blocked. U-boats were using the Kattegat channel east of Denmark to avoid the southern North Sea minefields, and the Americans suggested a 'northern' Dover-like barrage. Closing the 230-mile gap between Orkney and the Norwegian coast was to be a formidable task, as the depth could reach 600ft and the distance to be barraged was ten times that of the Channel.

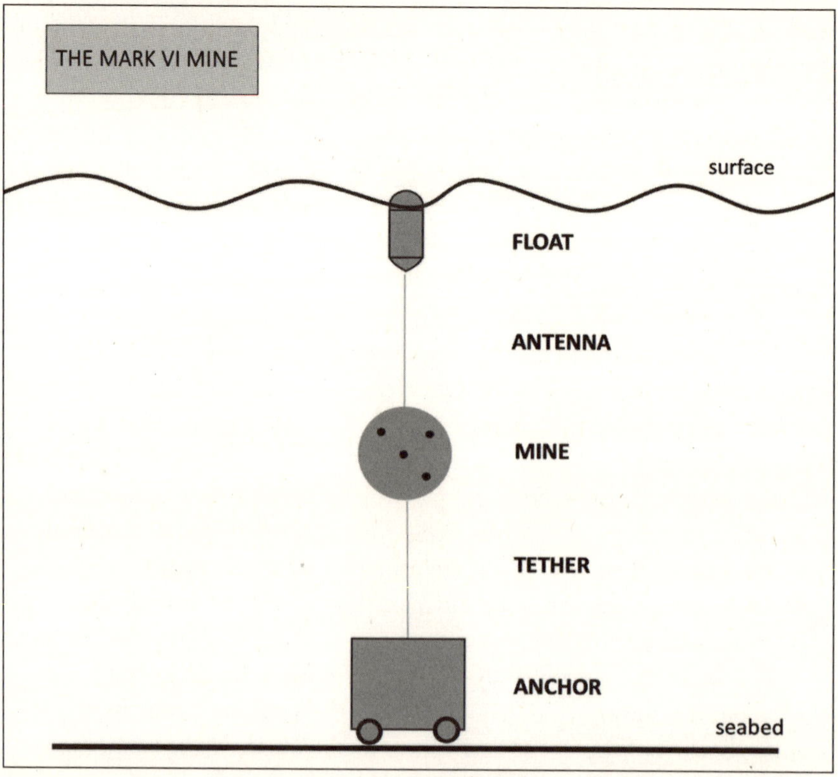


The plan called for three layers of mines: the British would lay the two outer, deep-moored ring of mines (Areas B and C), the American the central (Area A) surface ring. The deep mines would allow continued commercial traffic, so patrolling would need to supplement the programme to force U-boats to dive. The original idea was to lay nets going down to 100ft, but this was shortened to 70ft. Once built, the barrage had to be defended.

Even if Jellicoe thought the Germans would be at a disadvantage as the barrage was located some distance from their minesweeping forces, he wasn't wholly convinced. In the end, however, he concluded that if the Americans were willing to pay for it, why stop them. Part of the reason for his scepticism

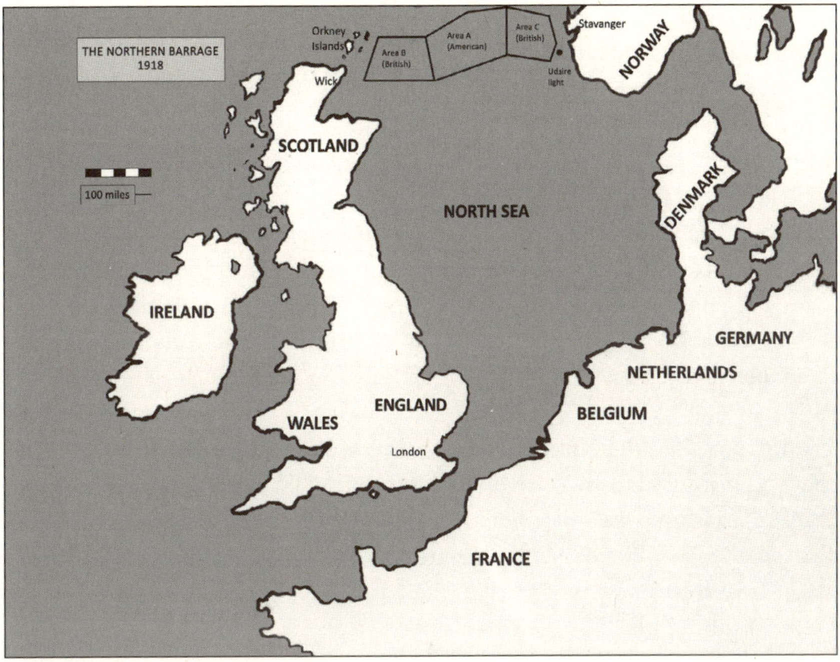


might have been that no existing mine worked in the 'great depth of water in which the mines had to be laid'.[98] Another was that the fields had 'to stop short of Norwegian territorial waters, which still provided an exit for submarines'.[99] Planners were worried that the Germans would use the gap provided by these neutral waters to skirt the barrage, just as they had done in parts of the Channel. Because it lay so close to a neutral, the Allies could use little in the way of surface vessels for patrols. American enthusiasm for the barrage might have been influenced by the depletion of their destroyer resources to defend their own coastline, and laying the barrage was seen as 'as a way of preventing U-boats from reaching the United States', or at least the Atlantic.[100]

Because of the depth, the technical design challenges were considerable. 'For a long time', Hashagen wrote, 'it was believed that the laying of mines in such great depths – in places nearly a thousand feet, was impossible'.[101] The Americans invented a mine specifically for the task.

Initially, the Germans exploited the Norwegian gap weakness. Area A was sown with shallow and deep mines to increase its efficiency. This left Area B, which Beatty wanted laid with a 10-mile corridor beside the Orkney Islands to allow passage of the Grand Fleet. It led to issues with the Americans: 'Admiral Sims holds very strong views on the subject (Beatty's marginal note: "So do I and I have to command the sea, not Admiral Sims").'[102]

Wemyss tried to calm him, as 'to lose Admiral Sims', in his opinion, 'would be a very serious matter'; his recall would be 'inevitable' if relations between the two navies worsened over the issue. Beatty thought the whole venture 'a fearful waste of time and resources'.[103] He was also highly critical of the new American mines, which, alarmingly, often detonated prematurely:

> The latest fiasco is that the Americans themselves gave up and went home after laying one line, which apparently blew up as it was laid. The mines that are remaining are of no value against enemy submarines on the surface and there is no reason for them to dive in those waters. So all we have done is waste valuable vessels, time and material, in planting the North Sea with stuff which debars us from using it and can do no harm to the enemy.[104]

Friedman praised the Northern Barrage as 'an imaginative US naval initiative' that was put forward by the Mine Section of the Navy's Bureau of Ordnance (BuOrd) within weeks of America entering the war.[105] Admiral William Benson, the US Chief of Naval Operations (CNO), later spoke enthusiastically about its effectiveness, saying that 'the barrage … practically bottled up the German submarine'.[106]

It was a huge undertaking. Starting any earlier, 'in the spring or summer of 1917 would have meant abandoning the convoy system', so great were the resources needed.[107] Hashagen said that he 'went through the middle of it, in broad daylight, in the summer of 1918', commenting that the mines were so unstable that 'it might be said that the barrage was now more of a danger to the minelayers than to the U-boats'.[108]

### THE NORTHERN BARRAGE

On 2 November 1917, the Allies decided to build a barrage across the vast northern stretch of water between Norway and the Shetland Islands. Work started immediately. From February 1918, two or more ships sailed every week from Norfolk, Virginia, packed with the mines. The cost was huge: 7,000 US sailors worked on the project and each mine cost around $300. Once in Scotland, they were assembled in two plants at Inverness and Invergordon, and then readied aboard the minelaying squadron's ships for dropping sorties.[109]

On 3 March 1918, minelaying operations started on Area B, the British sector nearest the Orkney Islands, and on 8 June, the American-run mid-section (Area A) and off the Norwegian coast (Area C) under the command of Captain Reginald R. Belknap of the Atlantic Fleet's minelaying squadron. The American Mk VI mine was used in the deep centre; the British chemical H2 horn mines at the extremities. It was dangerous work: about 4 per cent of the mines went off during the drops.

Commander Babcock, Sims's assistant, paid tribute to the work: 'Those fellows up there in Scotland are living on the edge of eternity.'[110] The Mk VI would explode even if a submarine was not in direct contact: a long copper cable – an antenna 'streamed high above and below' – was attached to the BuOrd Mk VI mine, and if this was touched by a metallic surface, it would explode. The use of antennae wires to significantly enlarge the mine's potential killing range reduced the number of mines needed but proved quite dangerous. 'This mine fired by means of galvanic action, which meant that the case itself did not have to be struck by a submarine's hull, but that the mine could also be fired by the contact of dissimilar metals in the water at some distance away, if one of these metals were connected to the mine-firing mechanism.'[111] Minelaying stopped just as abruptly as it had started; on 22 March, one of the minelayers (*Gaillardia*) blew up. While she only drew 10ft under her keel and the new American mines were set for a depth of 65ft, the sensitivity of these mines became well-known: between 8 and 15 June, one trawler reported twenty-eight 'distinct' and another thirty or so 'distant' explosions. Goldrick cited an escort recording explosions 'every two minutes over six hours', underlining that 'the statistic was not exceptional'.[112]

In thirteen so-called mining 'excursions', around 5,400 mines were laid on each trip. A minelayer could drop a mine every fifteen seconds. Escorted by twelve destroyers, mines would be laid in two parallel lines, 500 yards apart. During the summer and autumn of 1918, 56,571 and 13,546 mines were laid by the Americans and British respectively.[113] The original plan called for 200,000 mines, but less than half this number was sown, with 70,000 mines laid between March and October 1918.[114] American confidence in the new mine was unreasonably high: already by 9 August 1917, 10,000 were ordered, and the contract for the remaining 90,000 awarded was on 2 October. It was a headlong rush that Friedman, forgivingly, only calls 'a very quick design process'.[115]

Estimates of U-boats sunk vary: Grant says 'three damaged and three destroyed'[116]; Spindler has 'six confirmed sinkings'; Lowrey and Heath 'between four and eight'; while Sims lists four as 'certainly' killed. SecNav Daniels used Captain Dudley Knox's exaggeratedly high number of eight kills. Two kills that are certain, and have been dived on by Michael Lowrey and Kevin Heath, were identified in 2006 as *U.92* and *U.102*. *U.156* and *U.123* radioed in on their homeward leg shortly before crossing the barrage area and were never heard from again. Four other boats, all *UB* class, might have met their ends in the barrage – *UB.83*, *UB.104*, *UB.113* and *UB.127*. Spindler cited four as certain – the two dived on by Heath and Lowrey (*U.92* and *U.102*) and two more, *U.156* (also assumed to be included as kills by Heath and Lowrey) and *UB.127*. Tarrant cited four kills, but two of his 'certains' were different from Spindler's – *UB.104* and *UB.123* (*U.102*, a 'certain' for Spindler, was only a 'possible', while *U.92*, his other 'possible', was not even mentioned by Spindler).[117]

At the end of the day, even in sinking U-boats, the numbers are difficult to confirm. This is why Meacham concluded that there was 'no indication that this barrier ever served as more than an irritant'.[118] In fact, the costs of laying the barrage were not inconsequential: 'ironically, more allied minelaying ships … were sunk or damaged due to the tendency of the mines to explode prematurely'.[119]

**Anti-Submarine Barrage – Otranto**

The 45-mile gap between the Italian and Albanian coasts seemed to provide the Allies with a natural choke point at which to control German and Austrian submarine access from the Adriatic to the Mediterranean, restricting naval efforts from the Austro-Hungarian bases at Pola and Cattaro. At the very start, the Otranto Strait were patrolled by twenty armed British drifters (two divisions), with a third based at Brindisi. The drifters would tow steel Indicator nets behind them to snag an enemy submarine. In May 1915, when Italy joined the war, a barrage finally became possible and Brindisi was available as a forward Allied naval base. According to Marder, the decision to build one was 'probably' proposed at the April–May 1917 Inter-Allied Conference in Corfu. It was only when America also entered the war that substantial additional forces were added.

ASW air patrols were initiated from Malta at the end of 1916, and the island was also used as a kite balloon base. In 1917, flying boats were added. A Drifter Flotilla (with general overall Italian command and under direct operational command of Captain A.W. Henege) was based at Taranto with thirty MLs and 120 net drifters. Other elements, for example American sub-chasers, were based, from 1918, at the French Fleet HQ on Corfu.[120]

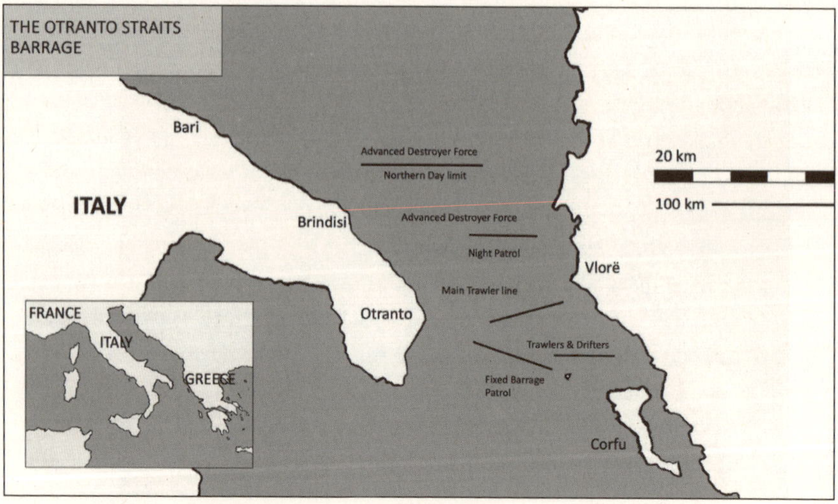

Initial British attempts to control the straits with armed drifters were not effective. It was 'a large sieve through which U-boats could pass with impunity'.[121] Work on a fixed barrage was started in April 1918. Most probably, Sims exaggerated when he wrote that anxiety among Austrian U-boat crews at Otranto caused them to become markedly less keen to cross the barrage after the Americans started to operate from Corfu.

### THE OTRANTO BARRAGE

Work on a fixed barrage started in April 1918 but was only completed in September, five weeks before the war ended. It consisted of nets down to a depth of 150ft, to which numerous mines were attached.

Like the Northern Barrage, the resources it required were enormous: a sub hunt in April 1918 involved '35 destroyers, 4 torpedo boats, 6 sloops, 52 trawlers, 74 drifters, 31 motor launches, 36 U.S. submarine chasers, 8 submarines, excluding French and Italian, 3 squadrons of bombers, 2 of fighters and various seaplanes. In addition, there were some 200 large and small craft in the British Adriatic Force.'[122]

The problem was that the Otranto Barrage pulled the most effective escort resources away from Mediterranean convoy duty. Only 35 per cent of Mediterranean convoys were escorted, and even then, the defenders never appeared to use their boats to attack, only to keep submarines away. This lack of escorts in itself encouraged more independent traffic: in March 1918, around 650 ships a month.

For most observers, the Otranto Barrage was an 'out-and-out failure'.[123] German U-boats made 121 passages through the barrage, with only one casualty: Sprenger's *UB.53* was forced to surface after damage from two mine explosions and scuttled by her crew on 3 August 1918. During the war, the only submarine that was snared was the Austro-Hungarian *U.VI,* commanded by Linieschiffsleutnant Hugo von Falkhausen, on 13 May 1916. Later the same year, on 30 July, *UB.44* was sunk by depth charges. Tarrant contended that Mediterranean convoys accounted for far more sinkings (nine U-boats) than the barrage.

One of the 'most spectacular' operations of the sub-chasers was the attack on the Albanian harbour of Durazzo (now known as Durres) on 2 October 1918, where eleven US sub-chasers (squadrons B, D, G and H) joined five British and three Italian light cruisers with the dreadnought *Dante* and three Regia Marina armoured cruisers. The sub-chasers' role was to protect the cruisers from submarine attack while they bombarded the port, the nearest one to the actual barrage. Two submarines were spotted and were set upon by the chasers. *SC.128*'s commander, Ensign Hilary Chambers, claimed a kill by *SC.215* after she opened up with her 3in guns and hit the sub's periscope, leaving a trail which *SC.215* and *SC.128* followed. The sub-chasers dropped fourteen depth-charges, 'with the result that up came pieces of the underwater craft', although they 'did not stop to pick up evidence'. After the war, *SC.80*'s captain, Ensign Blumenthal (who was not at Durazzo), met with Admiral Catinelli, who gave a clue about the likelihood of a sub having been sunk by the sub-chasers at Durazzo: 'I had under my command at that time three destroyers in the harbor and two submarines ... One of these U-boats ... torpedoed a small English cruiser (type *Glasgow*) ... Now a German U-boat was missing at the end of October and I therefore assume that this might possibly be the one sunk by you.'[124] In reality, no U-boat was lost or damaged.

### Q-ships: Wolves in Sheep's Clothing

Merchant ships were used by the Royal Navy to lure unsuspecting U-boats to close in for a kill and be surprised, at the last moment, to find that the innocent prey was armed to the teeth. Initially, Q-ships were successful in luring U-boats to their death, but as news spread, their mere existence became a salutary warning to U-boats to approach any merchantmen with more caution. That caution then became the reason why U-boats started to approach their targets hidden underwater and to use their expensive and limited supply of torpedoes to sink their target. In his book *Crisis of the Naval War*, Jellicoe commented that it wasn't until March 1917 that torpedoes came into 'general use'.

The change of U-boat tactics played to the English exploiting the danger for neutral ships; neither they nor their cargoes could be identified before destruction. In part, this meant that once the Q-ships ruse was uncovered, its military value was gone. Sixty-four Q-ships were sunk during the war; and for that, all they could account for was eleven kills. Nevertheless, the Q-ships' now limited military value was replaced by an arguably far more powerful weapon in Britain's arsenal – propaganda.

### The Armed Merchantman

It was inevitable that unarmed civilian merchantmen be armed to defend themselves. Their arming arguably changed belligerent status.

Around 13,000 guns – guns which were much needed on land – were mounted on merchant ships during the war. Not only the dock time involved but the additional personnel needs – trained gunners were required – added to the 'cost' of arming merchant ships. Some 4in guns were even stripped from the Grand Fleet's older ships.

During 1917, the number of guns mounted increased significantly.

*Armament Mounted on Merchantmen 1916–1917*

| Period | Number mounted | % increase |
|---|---|---|
| Sept 1916 | 1,749 | |
| Feb 1917 (end) | 2,899 | 66 |
| May 1917 (15th) | 3,253 | 12 |
| Dec 1917 (end) | 3,636 | 12 |

Source: Bacon, *Jellicoe*, p.353.

### The Destroyer

The destroyer was a platform that was fast and relatively cheap, the name describing its first role as a 'destroyer' of torpedo boats. Their role expanded as torpedoes started to be used more frequently by attacking submarines. Destroyers had the added advantage because of their relatively shallow draft, which would often protect them from any deep-running torpedoes. There were differences in how British and American destroyers were built. According to Sims, while American craft were capable of longer sea duty, British destroyers were capable of higher speed. British destroyers' short seagoing endurance (of around three days) severely limited the length of time the Grand Fleet could be at sea, which normally would have been doubled. Sims's command of the Atlantic Destroyer Flotilla for three years (July 1913–1916) gave him an excellent education in the virtues of the small escort ships that would dominate the convoy debate.

It may have been, as Hashagen later wrote, that 'at the beginning of the war [destroyers] were harmless as long as one took precautions not to be rammed ... later they dogged us in the North Sea'.[125]

Particularly in the early days, submarines normally preferred, if they could, to use a deck gun or to board with explosives to destroy a merchant ship rather than use an expensive torpedo, only a small supply of which were carried on board. This was more frequently the practice in the Mediterranean, where ASW operations were often severely hampered by the poor level of inter-Allied cooperation.

Today, much of the discussion over the use of convoys exaggerates the effectiveness of destroyers in the First World War. Twenty years on, Second World War destroyer tactics were greatly aided by both better detection and effective depth charges. Before, a destroyer could not easily find an enemy submarine to kill it. What it could do was to estimate the submarine's approximate position, usually based on any remaining torpedo track, and then keep the submarine submerged until the convoy it protected had passed out of effective range or was at a distance that could not be closed by any submarine running at depth under reduced speed.

Beatty described the value of a destroyer for convoy duty:

> One or two destroyers are an essential feature of an escort for a convoy; these vessels are fast, they force submarines down, they can steam around a convoy keeping it closed up and they have efficient W/T communication. The latter is most important.[126]

At the start of 1917, Britain possessed 320 destroyers – 'all but thirty-seven in home waters, i.e. around 283 available'.[127] It sounded like a large number, but in fact, the shortage was dire. Commander Cunningham commented on the shooting accuracy of his new command in 1918: 'Dover destroyers were so desperately hard worked that they had no time for firing practices or exercises.'[128] At a London Naval Conference, Beatty worried about the impact of German submarine operations on the Grand Fleet's ability to defend its capital ships when at sea. So long as a surface threat to the Grand Fleet was thought to exist, its destroyer screens could not be released for any ASW role. This is where Germany's 'fleet in being' had a very real impact.

> By keeping its dreadnought fleet intact, always refusing to give battle and yet always threatening an engagement, the Germans thus were penning up 100 British destroyers in the Orkneys.[129]

It led to Beatty's announcement that he would no longer seek a fleet action even if one was presented to him. It was crucial for British naval strategy in the First World War as it dovetailed German naval aims: 'It was not the way of weakening the Grand Fleet that the Germans had envisaged, but it was highly effective, nevertheless.'[130]

Sims was an early supporter, saying that 'the destroyer has shown itself to be by far the most efficient enemy of submarines operating against commerce'.[131] Nevertheless, dropping a pattern of depth charges without the aid of adequate sound detection could only be done in the most methodical way, something rarely possible in combat conditions. The first available escort destroyer would rush to the point from where the submarine most probably fired its torpedo.

> [S]he would commence to drop depth charges in a circle having a radius in proportion to the time consumed in describing it. Thus, if a destroyer started to describe a circle towards the right, as she continued the circle, the rudder would be eased and the radius would be increased until it over-lapped at the point from which it started.[132]

If two destroyers were attacking, the second started the same manoeuvre but would make a turn to the left, more likely trapping an escaping U-boat by starting from the opposite direction. At 7 knots submerged, the submarine could cover 233 yards (1 knot equals 33 yards per minute), giving the attackers an idea of the possible distance covered.

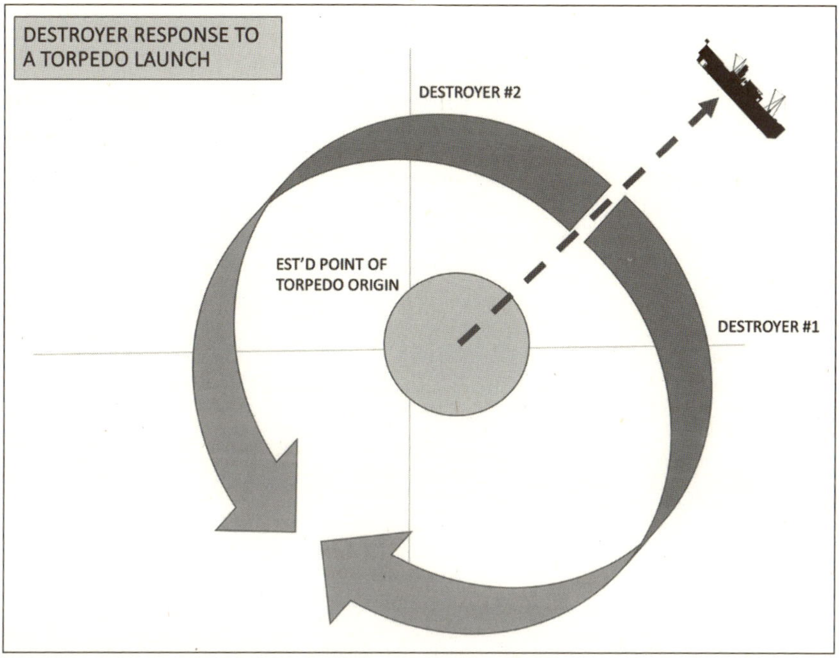


The destroyer would play a vital role in protecting capital ships and later the submarine. Despite its great effectiveness, for the Americans it 'had become a kind of ugly duck of the Navy'.[133] It was never given sufficient funding to produce the quantities needed for their own planned dreadnought-building programme.

The vulnerability of the U-boat was that while it could dictate the terms of battle, once its cloak of invisibility was shorn, either by surfacing or being located under water, its protection was minimal and it could not take punishment. The initial problem was that it was hard to spot on the surface. Under similar conditions, a surfaced U-boat could be seen from around 4 miles, while a U-boat could spot a destroyer from 15 miles.[134] Even though a submarine lay low in the water, additional height could be found: 'We erect our big masts, make a tackle fast to the masthead, and hoist the bos'n's chair aloft. From there one gets a wider view.'[135]

Even if destroyer escorts were placed as screens around convoys, an attacking U-boat 'would occasionally dive under the screen and destroy a ship; but most such attacks were unsuccessful'.[136]

At this point, the destroyer worked best when U-boats were lured in to close with a convoy rather than as an offensive sub-chaser. Active submarine-hunting patrols did not seem to work: U-boats would simply leave the area. It was best to keep the destroyers close to the ships they were protecting as convoy screens. As Sims put it, 'we should compel any submarine which was planning to torpedo a convoyed ship to do so only in waters that were infested with destroyers'.[137]

It became clear to the attacker that now 'every target met has an attendant defender'.[138] Vice Admiral C.H. Dare (based at Milford Haven) stated the case very succinctly: convoying meant that 'a submarine would be compelled to attack within reach of a vessel capable of active retaliation'.[139]

Once on the high seas, a destroyer would hand over its assigned ships to a larger warship, normally either a battleship or cruiser, more suited to a surface protection role:

> Its mission was not, as most people mistakenly believed, to protect the convoy from submarines, but to protect it from any surface German raider that might have escaped into the high seas.[140]

### SUB-CHASERS

The sub-chaser (SC) was an American craft specifically designed for ASW. The 550 80ft boats the Admiralty had in 1915 were not seaworthy, so a larger 110ft version was designed by yacht architect Mr A. Loring Swasey and ordered in March 1917. The longer version was 'much more effective' (Michelsen, p.90) than the shorter British and French versions (85ft) and better able to cross the Atlantic. More than 400 of the 70-ton vessels were built during the war.

The first American flotillas, consisting of thirty-six boats, arrived in Plymouth on 30 June 1917. Orders for 350 boats had been made in March that year; the first was launched on 7 May and gun trials held two days later. That was fifty days from order to completion.[141] The first fifty boats were given to the French, who had the most urgent need – they moved to Brest and the Scilly Isles, while other units would later be based in Corfu (Bay of Gavino), guarding the Otranto Barrage, and in Queenstown.[142] The French found the performance so good that another fifty were ordered for La Marine Francaise in January 1918, and in March 1918 another forty-two for the USN.

Under the overall command of Captain Lyman A. Cotton USN, the force was able to establish 'the historical fact [...] that not a single merchant ship was sunk between Lizard Head and Start Point as long as subchasers were assisting in the operations'.[143] SCs worked British inshore waters – the west coast in the North Channel, the Irish Sea, and in the St George's and English Channels – where ships no longer had the protection of convoy escorts. Manned by two officers and a small crew, SC boats worked in threes, a mile apart, and triangulated their readings with propellers idling for five minutes while quietly drifting and listening in one centre 'flagship' boat's plotting room.

The boats used two types of hydraphone: K-tubes could be lowered over the sides and trailed, or a faxed system, the MB- or SC-tube, could be lowered through the chaser's solid hull. Once a submarine 'fix' was made, they would speed to that spot and launch depth charges from a stern-mounted Y-gun.

| | |
|---|---|
| Overall Length | 110ft |
| Beam | 14ft 8in |
| Displacement (full load) | 85 tons |
| Max. Speed | 17–18 kts |
| Crew | 30 |
| Armarment | 1 x 3in 23-cal gun |
| | 2 x machine guns |
| | 1 x Y-gun |

Only two submarines were sunk by the Corfu-based SCs: one on 18 June and another at Durazzo (proving the effectiveness of the 3in gun) on 18 October. For Woofenden, that wasn't the most appropriate metric: '[T]he over-arching objective, after all, was to defeat the enemy, not to sink submarines.'[144] Leighton agreed. In May 1918, before the SCs arrived, sub sightings near Plymouth totalled sixty-five; in July there were forty-five. Some commanders, like Hashagen, felt the same: 'It paid now to chase a submarine at a distance. Before, that had been pointless: now they could fasten on our tracks. Underwater, they could feel for us, listen, grope, and hunt. Underwater, they could kill us too.'[145]

In January 1918, the Ford Motor Company was asked to build a 200ft steel version, the EAGLE boat. By the time it was delivered, the war was practically at an end. Sub-chasers continued to be employed for much of the early post-war years in North Sea mine clearance, described by Todd Woofenden as involving 'months of breath-takingly dangerous work'.[146]

An interesting dissenting voice is that of Fletcher Pratt, writing in 1935. For ASW work, his vote comes down clearly in favour of a smaller, cheaper, politically more acceptable solution – the sub-chaser:

> As a convoy ship the destroyer's wartime duties may be divided into two parts –convoy against submarines and convoy against surface vessels. For the first purpose, although the task was well performed, the destroyer

> was wasteful again; her high speed was of very little use, her gun power superabundant and her torpedoes of no use at all. Besides she lacked the endurance necessary for over-sea, long-distance convoy work. As a protection against surface raids the destroyer was a flat failure; the history of the two German raids against the Norway convoy, in which the protecting destroyers were slaughtered without even being able to radio news of their plight, shows that.[147]

**The Hunter-Killer Submarine**

Hull-for-hull, Sims claimed the submarine's hunter-killer role 'proved more successful than any kind of surface ship'.[148] In four years, a total of seventeen U-boats were sunk by other submarines (Sims claimed Allied submarines sank around twenty enemy boats).[149] Some 10 per cent of German submarine casualties in the First World War were by way of an enemy submarine attack (the German record against British submarines constitutes the same percentage).

**HUNTER-KILLER SUBMARINES**

Also known as attack submarines, the hunter-killer was an effective, but minimally recognised, ASW solution in the First World War. It exemplified how badly the vessel had been under-estimated. Even Fisher thought 'the submarine was no answer to the submarine' as 'its blindness prevented it from acting against an enemy submarine except under very peculiar circumstances'.[150] The relative success of the hunter-killer role persuaded the Admiralty to develop a specific class, the six-torpedo R-class boat with a fast, submerged speed of 15 knots, sustainable for thirty minutes. The speed was possible because of two electric motors. The new submarine also received the first of the RD hydrophones (RD for Revolving Directional), which could be used while underway.

One of the first enemy submarines to be sunk by a British equivalent was Wegener's sinking of HMS *E.3* on 18 October 1914; another was Walther's *U.52*'s torpedoing of HMS *C.34* after spotting her conning tower above water near the Shetlands on 17 July 1917. Although the plan nearly went horribly wrong, in June 1915, a submarine was first used with a trawler to act as bait in sinking *U.40*. Given that history, it's surprising to hear a commentary like that of Owen – 'another of Sims's ideas had been to use submarines to catch submarines'.[151]

As they improved, 'the primary mission' for British submarines in the last two years of the war became ASW.[152] In 1917 and 1918 there were between 364 and 390 sightings of German submarines by British counterparts, and 103 German sightings of British counterparts. German records estimate seventy torpedo attacks launched from Allied submarines, in which thirteen were sunk. The number would have been higher: eight torpedoes failed to explode on contact.[153]

While the number of submarines sunk by other submarines was relatively small – seven in 1917, six in 1918 – the fact is that the submarine was an equally lethal platform against its own kind.

### Submarine Detection

Many of the platforms used in and the weapons developed for ASW were useless until the position of a hidden submarine was known. Before 1917, all hydrophones could really do was to alert an operator to its presence in the vicinity. It wasn't possible to tell its bearing, distance or depth. Even then, the noise could not always identify the source as coming from a submarine.

It could even be argued that hydrophones were more usefully employed by submarines themselves, especially German U-boats, as their use did not require the vessel to stop since a submarine's quiet, electric motors would be in use. Being rigged to a static net barrage had the same advantages.

> More could have been accomplished, maybe, if the wasteful dualism of approach between BIR and Hawkscraig had been put aside. Captain Ryan, for example, was constantly arguing with the scientists in BIR's Section II at Parkston Quay in Harwich over the continued use of HMS *B.3*.[154]

### The Depth Charge

In the First World War, the depth charge owed its success to quantity. What really hindered depth-charging was that without effective detection, area saturation was the only reliable approach, and that was only possible if enough depth charges were available.

> A total of 38 submarines were sunk by this means, giving an average expenditure of over 1,000 depth charges for each submarine sunk.[155]

Some suggest that the number should be doubled.[156] (Of the 166 submarines destroyed 'because of enemy anti-submarine measures', Spindler attributed thirty-three to depth charges.[157]) In 1916, three submarines were successfully sunk with depth charges; in 1917, eleven; in 1918, twenty-four. It would take more reliable detection and a radical rethinking of the launching concept and explosive pattern before the Allies had an effective weapon in the Second World War. The forward-firing, multiple-warhead Hedgehog, combined with asdic/sonar, was the result.

Since US destroyers were 'considerably larger than nearly all their British counterparts', more depth charges could be carried, 'typically about 30'.[158] The increase in output encouraged use: monthly use increased from 200–300 to 2,000 by the end of 1917.[159] In her role as a Gibraltar escort cutter, USS *Seneca*, for example, dropped more than 100 300lb charges.[160]

## Anti-Submarine Warfare from the Air

Like the submarine, the development of aircraft technology and a supporting air force structure during the war was rapid. Many would argue, however, that the results were disappointing. In the entire war, only nine submarines were destroyed by aerial attack; of these, six were German. The choice of metric, however, considerably alters one's conclusion. Air cover clearly helped more convoys get through without attack, while the constant threat from the air – both from attack and surveillance – undoubtedly also led to an increasing level of fatigue and strain on U-boat crews.[161]

The Royal Naval Air Services (RNAS) was established on 1 July 1914. Jellicoe's appointment as First Sea Lord, as far as ASW is concerned, acted as a stimulus. Vice Admiral Vaugh-Lee was replaced as head of its Air Department by a young Commodore Godfrey Paine, 'ideally suited' to expanding the RNAS's role in ASW. On 10 January 1917, Paine was added to the Admiralty Board as the Fifth Sea Lord, tasked with expanding ASW air patrols, taking the attack to the submarine pens and increasing convoy air coverage. Reversing Balfour and Jackson's decentralisation of ASW, Paine was instructed to centralise east- and west-coast airship and aircraft patrols in March.

The early development of aircraft and seaplanes was plagued with failure and only maintained through the sheer courage and persistence of their pilots. The new technology often came at a very high price: '21 October 1918. One of our pilots went off in search of F S L Budd, but he had not gone far when his engine stopped and he had to land on a tremendous high sea, and of course, sent the unfailing pigeons for help.' Seaplanes were sent to look for the missing Short – five seaplanes and three MLs – in the process of which 'two more machines were lost and three pilots almost done in'.[162] From his HQ in Queenstown, Bayly was 'decidedly lukewarm on aircraft' as he hated his ships spending time looking for downed aircrews rather than hunting submarines.[163]

Before 1917, aircraft played 'a relatively small role' in ASW.[164] They were both unreliable and lacked the lifting power needed to carry the necessary weaponry or ordinance. When an aircraft spotted a submarine, it communicated that information, either by signal lamp or wirelesss.

The use of aircraft for anti-submarine patrolling did not start well. The first large airplane used was the Blackburn Kangaroo, which was able to carry a 920lb bomb load. With the introduction of the American Curtiss H12.S, the Allies significantly increased the effectiveness of aircraft as a means of sighting and, sometimes, tracking submarines. The Curtiss H12 flying boat had a six-hour endurance and soon began flying ASW patrols out of Felixstowe and then Yarmouth.[165]

Where air cover would help was in providing coverage over the weak points of ocean convoy: the vulnerability of escort cover evaporating the closer a ship came to shore suited the airplane's limited endurance. The vulnerability of unescorted coastal shipping also drew the U-boats inshore.

The air threat pushed a submarine below the surface, increasing her transit time to the open waters of the Atlantic. On 13 April 1917, a new aerial surveillance tactic was introduced for air patrols: the 'Spider's Web', an octagonal search grid centred on the North Hinder light vessel east of Felixstowe. U-boats were known to pass it on their route to the North Sea. The 60-mile diameter ring was divided into eight search quadrants, 10, 20 and 30 miles out from its central point. A surfaced submarine would take around ten hours at speed to pass through the patrol area, the time taken for a plane to cover half of the same area. Using the Hinder light vessel as the focus of the circle, the patrol planes flew an ever-increasing circle around the central spot from their bases. The structured search approach finally gave the Allies an edge:

> Under average conditions, a flying boat could search two sectors, a quarter of the whole 'web', in five hours or less.[166]

Immediate results were impressive: eight U-boats were sighted in the first twenty-seven missions and three of them attacked.[167] The first attack, on 20 May, took place when a U-boat (probably *U.36*) was sighted from a patrol 10 miles east of North Hinder:

> Two bombs were released, which hit the submarine directly in front of the conning tower, the periscope being then still above the water. A large patch of oil was noticed for some time after the explosion of the bombs but owing to the failing light nothing else was seen.[168]

By August 1917, the British had added kite balloons, towed by destroyers. *U.69*'s destruction in July had been aided by the submarine's visual sighting from a kite balloon towed by HMS *Patriot.* Like aircraft, the balloons gave their spotters a much better chance of sighting enemy submarines over longer distances, allowing either for a convoy's accompanying destroyers to peel off and attack at a safe distance, or for the convoy to alter its track around the submarine's assumed path.[169] Convoys departing Liverpool for Canada or the Americas would often stop off in Lough Swilly, County Donegal, where the leading ship would be fitted with the suitable towing apparatus for a kite balloon, for which an observation basket was attached. Some critics, however, argued that the presence of a kite balloon brought its own danger: it provided a U-boat with a clue to a group of ships being near.

In the early stages, the only real deterrence value of aircraft would be one of intelligence; they could help bring other resources to bear. This happened frequently in 1917: *UB.32*'s fourth commander, Oberleutnant zur See Benno von Ditfurth, blamed the lack of success of his June Scilly Isles trip to the fear of being spotted;[170] Kapitänleutnant Walter Remy said that he had to constantly dive *U.90* to avoid the twenty or so bombs that were dropped on him (17 November); and Oberleutnant zur See Wecker in *UB.22* said the same as von Ditfurth for two of his voyages (20 June and 9 August).[171]

The 'effective' role of aircraft was more often that of spotting rather than bombing. Bill Argent was an observer/wireless operator flying H.12s (the American Curtiss known as the 'Large America', the smaller H.4 the 'Small America') and F.2As out of Calshot:[172]

> My first attack on a U-boat was on 21 June 1917. We dived as quickly as possible but the U-boat submerged rapidly, so we dropped four 100-lb bombs with two-second delayed-fuses which sink some way before they explode. Nothing happened, and no oil appeared on the surface, so we dropped calcium flares to indicate its probable whereabouts, so that ships could drop depth charges. On our next occasion, 26 June, we caught a U-boat on the surface. The captain obviously panicked because he gave the order to 'down hatch' and abandoned some of the crew on the deck.[173]

On 28 August 1918, Karl Dobberstein's *UC.70* was attacked from the air after she'd been spotted in shallow waters off the Yorkshire coast. While No 246 Squadron's Blackburn Kangeroo did little (or no) damage, the sub was later successfully depth-charged by HMS *Ouse* and sunk, taking with her the entire crew as she plummeted into the depths.

Even in 1917, an air attack could be dangerous: Christian Mildenstein's *UC.1* on 24 July and Hermann Glimpf's *UB.20* a few days later were both claimed by pilots as having been hit and damaged.[174] Mildenstein's boat (which over its life had claimed forty-one ships) was attacked by six seaplanes, each in succession dropping their bombs, which reportedly 'took effect'.[175] The first two 1,000lb bombs were dropped by a Curtiss Large America (#8689) around 50ft ahead of the sub's periscope as she was diving. Two aircraft spotted Hermann Glimpf's U-boat near the North Hinder and attacked. They reported that she had been badly damaged and sank, claiming twenty-four crew members.[176] Another Curtiss Large America (#8687) spotted the submarine passing 10 miles north of the North Hinder light and dropped two 230lb and two 1,000lb bombs that hit the stern. Another Curtiss (#8662) dropped two more bombs, which hit just forward of the conning tower, finally sinking *UB.20*.[177] Reportedly, Oberleutnant Glimpf, known as the 'Playboy of the Flanders Flotilla', had taken some officers and their lady friends aboard for an outing.[178] *UC.16* was caught by surprise off North Hinder by two aircraft on 29 July.[179] Some of the crew had been ill and the watch under-staffed. 'The explosions sprang the torpedo doors, flooded the torpedo room, popped rivets and damaged the batteries.'[180] A week later, the captain's body drifted ashore on Jutland's west coast.

Blimps were very effective for ASW – 'by 1918, twelve-hour patrols were routine'.[181] 'Between 18 March 1915 and 11 November 1918, only two ships were sunk while under convoy with blimps.'[182] Marder stressed the value added to convoy escort by the extra visibility they gave: '[O]f the 17,082 ships convoyed on the Atlantic routes from May 1917 to the end of the war, only 167 were lost … only 5 ships were sunk when both air and surface escort were provided.'[183]

Blimps (and Zeppelins), however, were very susceptible to the weather. Indeed, 'airship work from Scapa was frequently affected by the high winds'.[184] When an airship got out of control on the ground – in an action called 'ripping' – a panel at the top could be opened to release air and collapse the airship envelope. A hidden benefit of this increased susceptibility to the winds was that, 'especially in their early raids, [Zeppelin crews] were apt to be loquacious'. It meant that D/F (direction finding) stations could track them more easily, and if in their chatter a message saying 'Only H.V.B. on board' was intercepted, it probably meant that a raid was coming as the crew was confirming that the more important codebooks were not being carried in case they were shot down.[185]

Factors that weighed heavily in the use of aircraft and lighter-than-air craft in ASW operations included operational endurance, communications and physical conditions (visibility from the air and the opaqueness and state of the sea).

American support in aircraft was essential. Starting with the first bases in 1917, by the end of the war, planes had increased to 'over 500, with 2,500 officers and 22,000 men'.[186] By November 1918, the Americans operated six air stations, three airship fields and three captive balloon stations, as well as the Northern Bombing group, chiefly employed against Brügge.[187] Their activities 'certainly seriously hampered submarine activities'.[188]

There were many exaggerated but few confirmed aircraft kills. Four are known in 1918: *U.49*, for example, was spotted and bombed by a DH-6 but finished off by surface ship depth-charging. But judging the value of aircraft in ASW just on the number of 'kills' missed the point; a parallel benefit was their role as a deterrent, keeping enemy submarines below the surface and, therefore, less able to position themselves for attack. It is worth noting that 'down to the end of 1917 there was only one instance of a ship being lost from a convoy receiving air support'.[189] The presence of air cover was enough to act as a deterrent: in 1918, only six U-boat attacks were made on convoys thus protected (in which two were successful, sinking three ships). Only two more ships were sunk from air-protected convoys during the war. But why were so few submarines sunk? Partly, it was because the technology was so new, but maybe just as important was the minimal interest in, and in some cases active opposition to, using aircraft for this task:

> The representatives of the so-called offensive strategy in the Air Force were even of the opinion that anti-submarine patrol flights and aircraft escorts for the convoys were a waste of resources that should have been used more effectively against the German submarine bases.[190]

By the war's end, aircraft had shown their value in protecting shipping, 'providing escort cover on 4,869 occasions, with only two ships attacked in those convoys'.[191]

The air power question is an interesting illustration of the potential effectiveness of inter-dependent weapons systems. The use of a mine barrage, for example, might be examined more holistically: it 'should not be seen in isolation, but rather as a part of a broader system of war'.[192] A Plans Division memo outlined the thinking:

> The stopping power of the mine barrage should not be overrated. It is the patrol craft armed with various anti-submarine devices on which we must rely actually to kill the submarines.[193]

# 5

# Strategic Command, Part 1: Jellicoe as First Sea Lord

## Jellicoe Takes Over as First Sea Lord

In the closing months of 1916, Jellicoe watched on as merchant shipping losses by U-boat attacks mounted. He was particularly concerned that the Admiralty neither seemed to understand its gravity nor have any coherent plan of action. Henry Jackson, the incumbent First Sea Lord, 'recognized his limitations and was willing to step aside'.[1] Prime Minister Asquith wanted Jellicoe to bring new thinking to the Admiralty.

Jellicoe's frustration at the Admiralty was evident: his 'one and only terror is the German submarine menace'. He also worried that 'Admiralty apathy has [been] so prodigious as to be almost beyond cure!'[2] On 24 November 1916, Balfour challenged Jellicoe, as the new First Sea Lord, with the task of defeating the German submarine threat. Four days later, Jellicoe made his farewells to the officers and men of the Grand Fleet from the deck of his beloved flagship, *Iron Duke*. He would not take up his post in London, however, for another week, having come down with a bad case of flu.

In accepting the position, Jellicoe 'was under no illusion about leaping from the frying pan into the fire'. The previous incumbent had not felt himself up to the challenge.[3] Andrew Gordon summed up Jackson's contributions as 'lacklustre'. He had come in for a large amount of criticism, unusually even from Jellicoe.[4] At the start of 1917, he wrote to Beatty complaining: 'Everything has been left on the wait and see principle. The late government is much to blame.'[5] The First Lord of the Admiralty was also relatively new, Sir Edward Carson having only just taken up his post in June. Jellicoe would work closely with the Ulster Unionist Member of Parliament, who had joked, upon his appointment, 'I am here, gentlemen, because I know nothing at all about the job. My only great qualification for being put at the head of the Navy is that I am very much at sea'.[6] In reality, the new First Lord had 'a keen mind and a powerful personality'.[7] He 'struck up a firm and cordial understanding' with Jellicoe and 'the two liked and trusted each other'.[8]

Jellicoe's position on some of key elements of ASW is not easy to unravel. Before his appointment, he had written to Balfour on 29 October, stressing that the 'lack of shipping could lose the war without a single major engagement at sea', yet his focus seemed to stay stuck to killing submarines rather than protecting the ships they attacked. He had earlier concluded that 'there were only three ways of dealing with the submarine menace'. 'The first, naturally, was to prevent the vessels from putting to sea; the second was to sink them after they were at sea; and the third was to protect the merchant ships from their attack.'[9]

He decided to focus on the second method. Was this the Navy's preference for the offensive spirit talking? Within two months, Jellicoe's health was already visibly suffering, despite the consistent regime of exercise he followed, running at least a mile a day.[10] In late January, Admiral Sir John Fisher came to see him when he was in bed with an attack of 'neuritis'. 'Mother Gwen', as his wife was affectionately known by her children and grandchildren, announced that the great man could only stay ten minutes. Fisher 'overstayed' his visit by an hour.

In trying to understand what Jellicoe believed, it is always wise to separate institution from the individual. The institution he now headed was like an old man, set in his ways, unwilling to accept new thinking or have his rulings challenged. It was beset with bureaucratic inertia.

On some matters, like that of convoys, the Admiralty's position was all too well known. The War Staff published a small pamphlet on commerce protection, in which convoy was singled out:

> The system of several ships sailing in company, as in a convoy, is not recommended in any area where submarine attack is a possibility. It is evident that *the larger the number of ships forming the convoy, the greater the chance of a submarine being enabled to attack successfully* [author's italics], and the greater the difficulty of the escort in preventing such an attack.[11]

Did Jellicoe support that fundamental conclusion? The booklet would, in all likelihood, have already been in printing before Jellicoe took up office. According to Neal, the new First Sea Lord was at pains to distance himself. Jellicoe later said that it had been 'in the course of preparation prior to my arrival at the Admiralty', adding that he 'did not think the paper came before [him] personally'. He should not be judged guilty by association – 'the truth of the matter was that naval thought was focused too exclusively on battle and too little on the protection of shipping'.[12]

Certainly, in the 2 November meeting with Jackson and Oliver, Jellicoe voiced the concern that larger concentrations of ships would be more dangerous, but he later said that the position 'had been written before unrestricted submarine warfare was in operation'.[13] I don't know if that alone lets him off the hook.

## The New First Sea Lord's Increasing Concerns

Jellicoe knew his new job would be thankless. He had, said Goldrick, 'no illusions as to the workload or the infighting to come'.[14] When Asquith was replaced by David Lloyd George as PM, Jellicoe faced a whole new ball game: he and the new Prime Minister had clashed in 1909 over the fight for increased naval funding, eventually only won at the expense of the new PM's plans for social welfare. The fiery Welshman never forgave Jellicoe.

Lloyd George was the country's choice for a war leader. He was nothing if not the inspirational figure to take Britain through the dark year of 1917. Like Churchill a quarter of a century later, Lloyd George was a leader whose charisma, drive and conviction was central to leading a nation through the darkness of war, but whose tendency to override his military and naval leaders could, on occasion, be extremely damaging. Jellicoe's demeanour could not have made for a worse combination: he was a realist whose manner amongst his civilian colleagues in the War Cabinet often came across as defeatism.

Sims maintained that Lloyd George 'always refused to acknowledge that it [the submarine war] was grave'. Rather, he would say that 'we shall get the best of the submarines – never fear!'[15] Maybe that was the attitude that was needed, but in some ways it exacerbated Jellicoe's reaction:

> It was necessary to be very outspoken in the War Cabinet on the subject of the submarine danger even at the risk of being accused of pessimistic views, for it was very difficult during the first half of 1917 to get the magnitude of the danger realised.[16]

Jellicoe hated political intrigue, the 'cut and thrust' of Westminster, and felt his time was wasted in endless meetings. His concerns led to a meeting with Balfour on 1 November and the suggestion that Jellicoe take up the post of First Sea Lord. He had been working on a memo outlining his thinking for a while. He had been so busy that he wasn't able to leave the Home Fleet in mid-October when his mother, Henrietta, died.[17] He sent something close to his heart: *Iron Duke*'s Union Jack.[18]

Jellicoe arrived at the Admiralty at almost the same time as the new government took office. In the thirteen-page memo, he addressed the submarine threat. Jellicoe talked of the increasing destructive power of the German U-boat, whose sinkings had reached 'very serious proportions'.[19] He was now very concerned by the economic war being waged on Britain: '[T]he enemy's attack on trade is by far the most pressing question at the present time.'[20] Between May and October 1916, monthly tonnage sunk had almost trebled, from 122,793 tons to 352,902 tons.[21] Jellicoe warned of the 'serious effect' that he anticipated 'by early summer 1917'.[22]

While the word 'convoy' never appeared, Winton felt that Jellicoe came close, even if routing ships into 'safe areas' echoed the approach of protected sea-lanes. What Jellicoe had said was that

> the destroyer, although very effective in confined waters and when present in large numbers, is ineffective for offence in open waters … but … is, of course, very efficient defensively *as a screen to individual ships, or to a large number of ships* [author's italics].[23]

He suggested that a battle squadron should be held back so that its assigned destroyer flotilla could contribute to the numbers needed for these protective screens. Balfour was 'profoundly impressed' and invited Jellicoe to present ideas to the Cabinet the next day. In addition to Oliver, Henry Jackson, Walter Runciman (President of the Board of Trade) and Bonar Law (Chancellor of the Exchequer), Lloyd George also attended, there to confront, in his words, the 'blind obstinacy' of the Admiralty.

At the meeting, Jellicoe painted an ominous picture: mounting Mediterranean losses, the decline in available neutral shipping and the overall loss of shipping stock. Despite the agreement between Jellicoe and Cabinet Secretary Sir Maurice Hankey's figures, 'Hankey was complacent, even complimenting the Admiralty on its defensive measures'.[24] Given Hankey's later championing the cause of convoy, this is surprising. The figures showed that despite the average number of U-boats at sea being half those employed in the 1915 unrestricted campaign, the amount of tonnage sunk was 80 per cent higher.

Lloyd George questioned Jellicoe. At this point, according to Sir Henry Newbolt, Jellicoe 'did not approve of convoys, as they offered too big a target'. The new Prime Minister suggested a dozen or so ships being convoyed rather than groups of one, two or three. Again, Jellicoe demurred, saying he doubted if it would be possible. He said they needed to 'be able to keep merchant ships sufficiently together to enable a few destroyers to screen them' and that there 'was no advantage in speed' as a convoy would only move as fast as the slowest ships.[25]

Boyd's assessment of Jellicoe's performance is critical: 'poor presentation … weakened his case', 'his recommendations looked mundane and muddled' and, in the end, all the meeting did was to 'demonstrate [the admiral's] support for two entrenched Admiralty policies ... opposition to convoy and a fixation of arming as many merchant ships as possible'.[26] Critical as the commentary has been about Jellicoe's performance, what he said persuaded Asquith to conclude that 'the protection of shipping and maintenance of our tonnage is one of the gravest questions at present confronting the Allies'.[27] He had understood Jellicoe's message. Twenty years later, Churchill would speak of the new U-boat war in much the same way, saying 'the only thing that ever really frightened [him] during the war was the U-boat peril'.

Newbolt commented that 'it is probable that the view put forward by Sir John Jellicoe on this occasion was more the Admiralty's than his own', as Jellicoe had been careful to point out that he had no intention of presenting any plans at this point.[28] Lloyd George, on the other hand, even if he did not really grasp all the requirements of convoy, was full of invective, referring to the written output of the meeting as a 'paralytic document penned by a trembling hand'.[29] Clearly, his and Jellicoe's was not going to be an easy relationship.

Before Jellicoe joined the Admiralty, the War Council had received a despairing – but, at the time, realistic – assessment from the Admiralty on the submarine threat. It was clearly not the kind of sentiment that Lloyd George wished to hear. It sounded very similar to Jellicoe's first meeting with Vice Admiral Sims in the coming April:

> No conclusive answer had yet been found on this type of warfare. Perhaps no conclusive answer will ever be found. We must, for the present, be content with palliation.[30]

On 4 November, Germany relaunched unrestricted submarine warfare in the Channel – 'ships on a course between England and France may be sunk without warning between Beachy Head & the St Albans Head – Cap de la Hague'.[31]

The creation of the War Cabinet was one of the very first moves made by the new PM. Chaired by Lloyd George, it was composed of selected Cabinet members, with senior military commanders invited to attend. BEF Commander-in-Chief Douglas Haig, Sir William Robertson (Chief of the Imperial General Staff, CIGS) and Jellicoe usually attended, even if not, technically, War Cabinet members. Jellicoe found himself allied with Haig and Robertson in their efforts to focus more on the Western Front. Lloyd George's inclusion of multiple fronts – from Salonika to Egypt – was putting a huge strain on naval resources, wearing an already thinly spread Navy even thinner. The support given to French and Italian needs only exacerbated an already difficult challenge. Jellicoe argued that every effort should be made to limit the number of 'sideshows', 'so that more adequate protection be given to ships bringing supplies to our country and to our allies'.[32] Victory, he believed, would only be achieved on the Western Front.

On 5 December, Sir John Jellicoe officially took up his new position as First Sea Lord to face 'the gravest peril' the country ever faced. He was shocked by what he found:

> The shipping situation is by far the most serious question of the day. I almost fear it is nearly too late to retrieve it. Drastic measures should have been taken months ago to stop unnecessary imports, ration the country and build ships. All is being started now, but it is nearly, if not quite, too late.[33]

Some, like Fisher, in his earlier days Jellicoe's greatest mentor and supporter, didn't like Jellicoe's move to the Admiralty, feeling that his strengths were those of a battle commander, unsuited to the often more administrative role. Fisher may have been right. His views, however, were very volatile. In January 1917, he wrote to Jellicoe complaining that he did not agree with the new First Sea Lord that 'the submarine menace is more important than the Grand Fleet'. Jellicoe had to defend his decision with Fisher:

> It is *because* I agreed with you that the great danger now threatening us is the submarine menace that I have now left the Fleet to come to the Admiralty. I could do nothing with the Fleet to cope with that menace … I may not succeed, but I am here to try. I know, of course, that all the criticism hitherto aimed at Jackson will now fall on me.[34]

The first day, he told Rear Admiral Sir Douglas Brownrigg, Britain's wartime Chief Naval Censor, that he didn't expect to last long, predicting his own demise with uncanny accuracy. He said much the same when he left *Iron Duke* on 28 November: addressing his officers and men, he 'said that they must expect to see me the object of the same attacks as those to which my distinguished predecessor, Sir Henry Jackson, had been exposed'.[35]

Jellicoe brought his 'centralizing tendency' to bear two weeks after moving to the Admiralty, merging the Operations Intelligence Division and the Anti-Submarine Committee to create the Anti-Submarine Division (ASD). On 13 December 1916, Rear Admiral Alexander Duff was named its first head.[36] The ASD 'relieved the Operations Division of control of all vessels and aircraft which were engaged in anti-submarine offensive and defensive work, and also took control of minesweeping operations'.[37] Jellicoe leaned heavily on old connections, bringing some of the best brains of the Grand Fleet with him to help breathe new life into a moribund Admiralty, and personnel from the former Submarine Committee to staff it. Jellicoe surrounded himself with officers whose skills and outlook were 'tried and tested': Lionel Halsey (Fourth Sea Lord) and Cecil Burney (Second Sea Lord) – both of whom had been at Jutland – Alexander Duff (Director of the Anti-Submarine Division), who had been second-in-command of the 4th Battle Squadron, and Frederick Dreyer, his old Jutland Flag Captain (Assistant Director of the Anti-Submarine Division). Jellicoe and Dreyer would maintain a regular, almost weekly, correspondence until Jellicoe's death. Unsurprisingly, this favouritism led to criticism. Kenneth Dewar said of Jellicoe:

> [L]ike Fisher, [he] instinctively mistrusted mental independence in his subordinates. Like Fisher, he had a partiality for 'yes men' and preferred to surround himself with officers and friends who would acquiesce easily to his views. Helpful to those who did not ask awkward questions, he displayed a spirit of hostile incomprehension to those who did.[38]

Jellicoe also combined the responsibilities of First Sea Lord and the Chief of Naval Staff (CNS) The previous practice of decentralised SNOs being responsible for trade protection ended.

A staff was added to the new ASD, comprising four commanders, three lieutenant commanders and two engineering officers, all from the Grand Fleet. Jellicoe brought with him Sir Henry Oliver (up until that point the Chief of the War Staff), serving as his Deputy Chief of Naval Staff (DCNS) with responsibility for operations, while Duff later became Assistant Chief of Naval Staff (ACNS) with the added responsibilities for the minesweeping, trade and convoy sections.

Churchill had first set in motion the move to create an efficient Naval Staff when he became First Lord in 1911. It was a difficult challenge: there was little favour from the Sea Lords, who 'regarded staff work with distrust, not to say contempt'.[39] Few liked the idea of a lower ranked officer like a captain or commander having delegated responsibility for major areas of specialisation within the Admiralty. Nevertheless, it was 'an important step towards decentralization, marred only by the characters of Jellicoe and Oliver, both men who tended to regard delegation as dereliction of duty, both accustomed to accept enormous and unremitting workloads'.[40]

On 1 March, Dreyer took over as the new Director of Naval Ordnance (DNO) and Rear Admiral Fitzherbert was appointed responsibility for torpedoes and mines. Jellicoe noted that he had 'for some time' felt that the area needed 'a larger and more independent organization' because a very extensive mining policy was planned.[41] Lloyd George suggested that some of this work be 'transferred to a civilian'. Such a transfer would not only cover mercantile needs but also those of the Navy. Jellicoe agreed to the principle; lessening unwarranted competition for materials between the two 'appealed' to him. Jellicoe similarly agreed to support Sir Eric Geddes's new work as Admiralty Controller in charge of munitions production. Although 'the admirals did not take kindly to a civilian Controller', since it was 'the first time the incumbent [of the office] was a civilian', Jellicoe 'accepted the situation with grace and even with optimism', confident that he could smoothe ruffled feathers within the Admiralty.[42]

In the May reorganisation, Captain William Fisher was brought in to head the ASD. Jellicoe thought highly of the former captain of HMS *St Vincent*, calling him 'an exceptional officer'. Jackie Fisher also wrote to him, saying that he was 'absolutely the right man in the right place'[43] – good reason why Sir Henry Newbolt dedicated his Official History of the War to one William Wordsworth Fisher.

*Admiralty Organisation, May 1917*

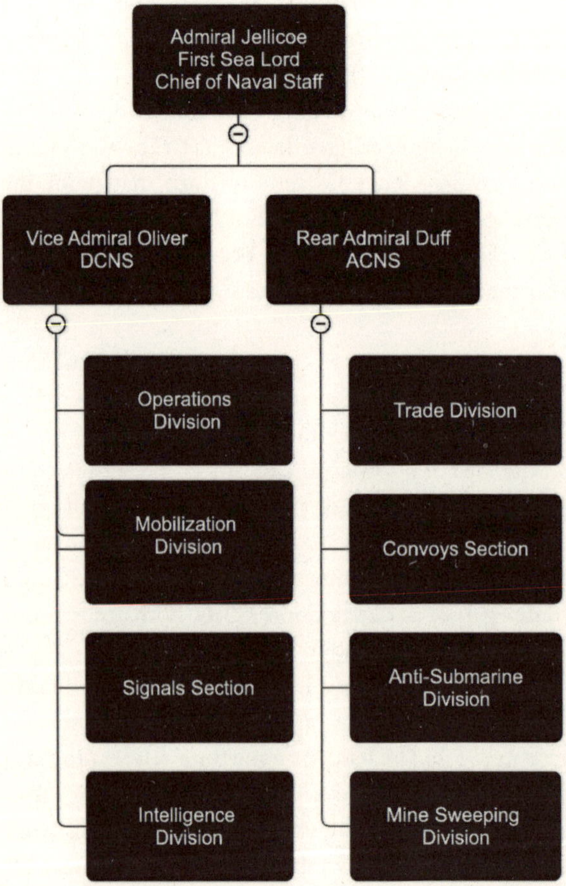

Geddes argued that his work on the Army's munitions would be a transferable skill. Jellicoe accepted the proposal, even though he did not find the amalgamation of functions of 'design, inspection and production under one head' – as Geddes was proposing – logical. The new organisation was 'so great' that extra office space was needed; it also 'threw a vast volume of extra work on [Jellicoe's] shoulders' and 'was much disliked by the Admiralty departments'.[44] Jellicoe admitted that the plan was an experimental one, for which '[he] bore a large share of responsibility', one that was carried out at the worst possible moment, right in the middle of the submarine war. He hoped, however, that it would result in 'greatly increased production' of desperately needed ships.

**The New Admiralty Focus under Jellicoe**

Stepping into the new position, Jellicoe immediately acted to provide structure to the challenge at hand. With the new Anti-Submarine Division being created, Grand Fleet officers who had earned Jellicoe's trust and confidence – like Dreyer and Duff – were needed to take it forward.

Jellicoe approached the challenge in his usual way; his hallmark was a combination of structured method and conservatism. He had been strongly shaped by Victorian naval culture. The preference for the offensive over the defensive meant that he would put ASW before commerce protection. Jellicoe's approach was informal but businesslike. William Clarke commented on the admiral's presence around the Admiralty:

> During the same period there were five 1st Sea Lords, Prince Louis, Lord Fisher, Sir Henry Jackson, Lord Jellicoe and Lord Wester Wemyss. Of these again I only saw one at any time, in our room. This was Lord Jellicoe. I shall never forget his visits to us; in mess undress, he would come in, not only when there was more than the usual activity, but two or three times a week, ask to see our log, read it, ask pertinent questions which showed he [author's note: assumed 'had' as text missing] the situation well in mind and then say, 'Good night and thank you all'.[45]

The problem was fivefold: how to stop U-boats before they could even leave their home harbours; how to prevent them from getting to their operating areas; how they could be found once at sea; how they could be destroyed once detected; and how merchant ships could protect themselves (and later be protected).

Jellicoe felt there was no silver bullet, no single solution. Weapons, platforms, strategy and tactics were thoroughly interdependent and best worked in combination: nets, for example, were ineffective without reliable mines. The question of destruction was academic if submarines could not be detected, and there was little value in detection if the means of destruction wasn't reliable.

Lloyd George did not feel that Jellicoe's reforms or restructuring had gone far enough. Under pressure from younger officers of the Young Turks, he pushed for a permanent offensive plans section to be created. To the PM, Jellicoe's attitude smacked a little of both defensiveness and arrogance.

Where the First Sea Lord was most criticised was on the bundling of many of these individual options into a delivery system around which they could be consolidated. The establishment of the convoy system would become an approach where the whole would be greater than the sum of the parts. Historically, while Jellicoe's name is more closely associated with mines, barrage, arming merchant ships, deploying Q-ships and the depth charge, his broad approach – keeping the portfolio of options as his goal – was not incorrect. It just fell short of the final hurdle – convoy. Sims credited him with laying the foundations for the later success of Allied ASW, but said the best strategy would fail without the right weapons and tactics. Four days after Jellicoe had been forced out of office, Sims wrote to him, apologising for being late as he'd been ill with lumbago:

> [O]therwise I would have written sooner to say how much I was distressed to learn of your leaving the Admiralty, particularly [when] the effects of your anti-submarine measures are showing such promise of complete success. I assume, of course, that the government's action is based on the supposed political necessity of responding to the pressure of the ignorant criticisms of 'the man on the street'.[46]

The most effective weapon in destroying submarines was the mine, but until 1917, British mines were 'largely ineffective because of design flaws; both in the mooring system and the firing device'.[47]

Early on, Jellicoe had consistently pushed for heavy mining of the Heligoland Bight. In January 1917, Beatty recommended the same. Efforts, however, were hampered by 'the insufficiency of mines and the poor quality of those in use'.[48] Roskill concluded that Jellicoe 'was right to pour cold water on this scheme'.[49]

It was not just the mines; it was how they were laid and, most importantly, how they were patrolled. A deep minefield was almost useless unless surface ships could force submarines under the surface: 'The efficiency of these deep minefields entirely depends on the ability of our patrol vessels to force enemy submarines to make a deep dive.'[50] But in Bacon's view, patrols often betrayed the position of the fields.

As late as January 1917, Jellicoe maintained that the Allies 'did not possess a mine that was satisfactory against submarines', and that of 20,000 mines, only 1,500 were 'fit for laying' in April.[51] Immediately upon his arrival at the Admiralty, Jellicoe started trials on British mines.

He found 'only about *one mine in three* could be depended upon'.[52] The firing mechanisms on the spherical mine – either the British service mine or the converted Italian Elia mine – were defective. The result was an unacceptably high rate of failure: 'Our deficiency was clearly showed in trials which I ordered, when one of our submarines was run against a number of our mines with the result that only 33 per cent of the mines (fitted, of course, only with small charges) exploded.'[53] Additionally, more than 18,500 mines were 'kept back from use because their mooring systems were found to be faulty'.[54] Vice Admiral Sims added an interesting side comment on British mines, saying that 'oysters and other sea growths, attaching themselves to their prongs, made many of them harmless'.[55]

Both sides strongly supported their own minelaying operations. In September 1917 the Germans, as part of renewed efforts to recover their faltering timetable; the British, now that they finally possessed an effective mine. The Germans started sowing new minefields where they thought the British would themselves choose to block their Flanders-based submarines getting out to sea and moving north through neutral Dutch and Danish waters. German minesweeping was quite effective, and British mining off Zeebrügge and Ostend 'accomplished little, for the Germans swept them up almost as fast as they were planted'.[56]

Beatty, however, wasn't happy. He told Jellicoe that he should push for fast and effective research and development, adding that 'we must think of it on the largest scale possible or we shall be done in, and it will be the lack of foresight of the Navy that has caused our defeat'.[57] In his support, Jellicoe had considerably increased the number of ships available for minelaying. In March, *UC.55*, having laid eighteen mines off the Orkney Islands, reported 'the astounding promptness of the [British] countermeasures; within an hour and a half to two hours, twelve destroyers, a submarine chaser and two sweepers were on the spot'.[58] Such alacrity hadn't, however, prevented the tragedy of Kitchener's death a year earlier.

It was not just minelaying that consumed resources; minesweeping was the same. In 1917 alone, 536 groups of mines were located and 3,989 mines swept.[59] The work was fraught with danger and the strain on minesweeper crews constant. With new types using a delayed fuse, an area could be declared mine-free one day, only to be infested the following day.[60] On the east coast, the British swept the 'War Channel' daily as it was the Grand Fleet's route south. The minesweeper strength was huge. It grew to '726 vessels, consisting of 110 fast minesweepers in twenty flotillas, 52 paddle sweepers, 10 *Dance*-class sweepers and 412 trawlers'.[61] Just off Harwich, 500 mines were swept between January and September 1917 at a cost of three trawlers, one paddler and one drifter, but 'without injury' to a single merchant ship.[62]

The other impact of British minefields, of course, was to increase the enemy's need for logistical support for each submarine sortie: with increasing frequency, destroyers and minesweepers escorted German submarines to and from their bases. Indeed, it was 'impossible for a submarine to enter or leave without being escorted'.[63]

## January 1917: Restrictions Lifted, the Pleß Conference

Another war conference took place at Schloß Pleß in early January 1917. However, before the formal meeting started, the kaiser decided to meet with representatives of the navy alone to decide for or against a new, very aggressive submarine war.

Of the roughly 10.7 million tons of shipping to which Britain had access, '6.75 million tons of this shipping was British, a little under a million belonged to other Entente powers and the remaining three million tons was owned by neutral countries'.[64] Holtzendorff, chief of the Admiralstab, argued that part of the submarine campaign's effort should be aimed at scaring the neutrals, forcing them to withdraw their tonnage. It would severely reduce British carrying capacity; he estimated by around 39 per cent. Only the ruthless execution of an unrestricted campaign could achieve the level of fear that he felt necessary.

His logic 'accepted some risks and ignored others'.[65] Holtzendorff had wrongly assumed that Britain would never introduce rationing and that her response would be 'slow and evolutionary', the improvement of existing weapons and tactics rather than a fundamental reorientation such as was brought by the convoy system.[66] He also had not included the half-a-million tons of German shipping interned in American ports, which would now be of potential benefit to the Allies. Crucially, what was totally missing in the planning was increased U-boat resources: according to Goldrick, only forty-five Type-*UB* boats and six larger U-boats were ordered in this period.

In the background, the heads of the Supreme Army Command (3.OHL), Ludendorff and Hindenburg, had grown impatient with Chancellor Bethmann-Hollweg's opposition. They now 'bypassed him and [went] directly to the kaiser [whom, normally, they scarcely troubled to consult] with the veiled threat that if unrestricted submarine warfare was not begun before February 1, they could no longer be responsible for the outcome of the war'.[67] Müller wrote that the kaiser 'has suddenly come round to the idea that unrestricted submarine warfare is now called for and is definitely in favour even if the Chancellor is opposed'. It was a crucial moment.[68] The circumstances now favoured Holtzendorff, even if he found working with Trotha and Scheer difficult. The enfeebled Chancellor had been outmanoeuvred and now had little choice but to fall into line, saying that 'if the military authorities consider that the U-boat war is essential, [he was] not in a position to contradict them'.[69] It sounded like Pontius Pilate 'passing the buck'. Bethmann-Hollweg threw in the towel but didn't resign, because, as he put it, he wanted to show an outward sign of unity.

Once the decision was taken, a campaign was 'shaped skillfully to appeal to the Socialist working classes ... it was stressed that the campaign was a means for ending hostilities quickly'.[70] The messaging was heavily supported by poster advertising that helped the sixth War Loan drive, doubling subscriber numbers to nearly seven million individuals. The Admiralty's Department B-1 produced a vast array of materials to support their case for an unrestricted campaign.

On 31 January, a brief W/T signal was transmitted to U-boat commanders:

> Beginning on February 1st, U-boats that left base before January 20th are to attack all ships, including armed passenger ships, without warning. For U-boats that left base after January 20th, the sealed orders given them remain in effect.[71]

Jellicoe had already been informed by OB40's 'Blinker' Hall that, according to 'very secret information', Germany was about to begin the new campaign.[72] On 25 January, Beatty was also 'read in'.

Three days later, another signal pushed the start back to 10 February. Until that date, neutral merchant ships and unarmed passenger ships were to be treated according to Prize Rules. After that, they would be fair game. Hospital ships were excluded, but only if they were out of the zone Ushant–Lands End and Flamborough Head–Terschelling. Other vessels, such as Belgian relief ships or unarmed passenger ships, would be given some extra time to clear the area, but would then be treated like other enemy shipping.

To keep the number of operational craft on patrol to a maximum, the Germans had already improved their repair logistics, moving submarine flotillas to achieve this: in March, the 1st U-Flotilla was moved from Heligoland to a new facility at Brunbüttel, then in July, the 3rd U-Flotilla transferred from Emden to Wilhelmshaven.

*Distribution of U-Boat Forces, 1 February 1917*

| Command | Brèzet | Howlett |
|---|---|---|
| High Seas Fleet | 46 | 49 |
| Flanders Flotilla | 23 | 33 |
| Pola | 23 | 24 |
| Courland (Baltic) | 10 | 3 |
| Constantinople | 3 | 2 |
| Total | 105 | 111 |

Sources: (i) Brézet, *La Guerre Sous-Marine Allemande 1914–1945*, p.166 ; (ii) Howlett, online post, 5 July 2019.

**Unrestricted Submarine Warfare (USW) Resumed**

Unsurprisingly, the announcement was met with almost universal approval from U-boat officers. Many had been champing at the bit, frustrated by the seemingly endless political to-and-fro of the discussions at the Supreme Command. German submariners felt a certain amount of pride. Unlike the visible inactivity of the main surface fleet, they were being asked to break the deadlock in which the nation found herself. Hans Rose recalled the reactions amongst Bauer's commanders:

> Everyone was impressed by the gravity of the situation and while champagne was served, one of the older commanders offered three 'hurrahs' for the decision. The same evening the commander of *U.53* returned to Heligoland with his friend Werner of the sister ship *U.55*. While on the destroyer [the meeting with FdU Bauer was held on the SMS *Hamburg*], they wondered whether the decision had not come too late.[73]

The reaction of Austrian submariner Georg von Trapp was typical: 'Thank God, they have finally understood. But it is rather late! … For a whole year we are supposed to do absolutely nothing, and now everything is supposed to go fast, fast.'[74] At the same time, even if there clearly were some submariners still uncomfortable with the idea of torpedoing merchant ships without warning, Michelsen later wrote (in May 1917) that any warnings would 'delude steamer crews about the seriousness of the U-Boat war'.[75]

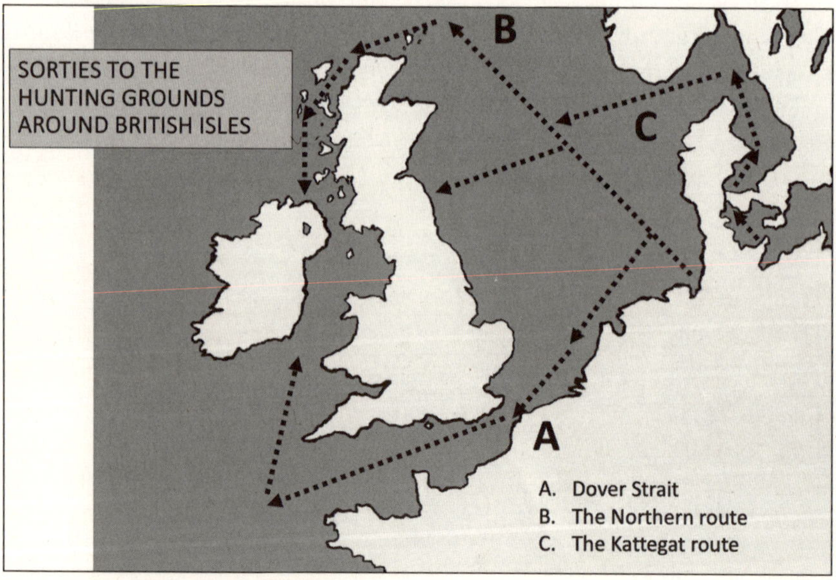

Everything was geared towards an immediate acceleration in tonnage sunk. The northern route around Scotland was abandoned for the riskier, but faster, Channel route, gaining around six days of patrolling. Submarine servicing and maintenance time was reduced to a minimum, tours were limited to fourteen days and torpedo expenditure encouraged.

With caution thrown to the wind, American-flagged vessels now started to figure prominently on the lists of the vessels sunk. On 3 February 1917, the first, the 3,143-ton freighter *Housatonic* (in her previous life she had, in fact, been the German freighter *Georgia*), was stopped by Rose near the Scilly Isles. She had been carrying wheat to England. Her crew was set adrift off the Cornish coast. As was his practice, spotting some British craft, Rose sent up a flare to let them know the position of the lifeboats.

On 11 February, a Norwegian vessel, the *Dalmata*, was torpedoed and sunk. In her case, despite the bad weather, the submarine commander ordered the crew, including the captain's pregnant wife, put into four lifeboats and set adrift. The captain's wife was later interviewed by the *Afterposten* newspaper: 'The sea was extremely heavy, it was piercingly cold, and my two coats and blanket were soaked as a result of sea washing over the boats.' After three days, they were rescued and taken to Queenstown. She survived, but one man died of exposure.

The most important loss was the 18,099-ton Cunard liner *Laconia* on 25 February, 1,160 miles west by north-west of the Fastnet Rock. A relatively small number were killed – six crew and six guests – but among these were two Americans. While the number of Americans might have been – relatively speaking – small, each death at sea was a constant reminder to Americans of Germany's assault on her neutrality and, for Wilson, the terrible inevitability of war.

Over the next days, victims were picked up and brought into Queenstown. One was a young journalist from the *Chicago Tribune*, Floyd Gibbons. In a 4,400-word report, he told the harrowing story of how two American women, 59-year-old Mary Hoy and her 34-year-old daughter, Elizabeth, had died at sea of exposure, lack of food and dehydration. Mary Hoy had died in her daughter's arms.

Two weeks after the *Laconia* sinking, another freighter, the *Vigilancia*, was sunk on 16 March. Fifteen of her forty-five-strong crew were killed; a dozen were American. In the weeks that followed, more ships went to the bottom – ten merchant ships with the loss of sixty-four lives, twenty-four of whom were US citizens. In February and March, the US lost eight merchantmen to German submarines.

Stories like these were steadily but surely pulling an unwilling country closer to war. *The New York Times* wrote that 'it was unofficially admitted here [in Washington, DC] tonight that virtually a state of war exists between the United States and Germany'.[76]

### The High Seas Fleet's New, Supporting Role

With the new campaign, the role of the High Seas Fleet fundamentally changed. Its operations were redesigned to support the submarine, not the other way around – 'The German battleship was the power behind the submarine campaign'.[77] Heavy capital ships took on the 'primary duty' of protecting minesweepers.[78]

That was why Beatty later insisted on significant armistice measures for Germany's HSF. As he put it, 'the submarine menace would completely collapse' without their surface support.[79] What did this mean? First, that the ongoing threat from the HSF meant that the British had to maintain the Grand Fleet's screening vessels, principally its destroyers, in effect holding back resources from convoy or anti-submarine duty. 'As long as the German fleet remained intact', the British could not free up the very type of surface ship that could most effectively contribute to Allied ASW efforts: fast destroyers. So fundamental was this issue that Michelsen concluded 'one cannot conduct a submarine campaign without a battle fleet, which is able to bind [a better word might be 'tie up'] the auxiliary forces of the enemy fleet'.[80]

Secondly, it meant keeping open the channels through which German submarines could sortie out into the North Sea. And that meant the British also had to deploy smaller vessels to prevent these minefields being cleared. Dewar argued that it was the presence of German capital ships that kept the Heligoland Bight and the Kattegat open: 'it was their support which countered our mining policy in the Bight' as increasingly German capital ships started to support sweeping operations.[81] After one German minesweeper, *Kedingen*, was captured and the enemy's light cruiser protection pushed back, the Germans were able to regain some semblance of control by dispatching the SMS *Kaiser* and *Kaiserin*, supported by four light cruisers and several destroyers, as heavy protection.[82] Two more German battlecruisers, SMS *Hindenburg* and *Moltke*, then successfully pushed the British back. Thereafter, the High Seas Fleet maintained a group of supporting capital ships at the Amrun Bank.

The German 'fleet in being' certainly denied the British access to the Baltic, but it was probably the threat of submarines and mines in the Baltic's enclosed confines that made any deep foray far too risky. In turn, that made it difficult for the British to supply Russia. Some, among them Andrew Boyd, think this might have accelerated Russia's collapse.

### The Sinking of the *Alnwick Castle*

One of the largest ships to go down in March was the 5,893-ton *Alnwick Castle*, sunk without warning on 19 March some 310 miles west of Bishop's Rock.[83] The Union-Castle ship had left Plymouth headed for Cape Town two days earlier with a cargo of silver. Aside from the 100 crew, there were another fourteen passengers.

On her first day at sea, the day before she was torpedoed, she had picked up twenty-five crew members from the steamship *Trevose*, earlier torpedoed by *U.81*. In what almost appeared to be a petty act of vindictiveness, Oberleutnant zur See Raimund Weisbach went after his first victim's rescuer. At around 0610hrs, one of her lookouts spotted a torpedo racing towards the ship off her port bow. The First Officer ordered full astern and a turn hard to starboard, but it was too late. The *Alnwick Castle* sank within ten minutes, though her captain, a Southampton man, Benjamin Chave, managed to get her passengers, including a mother and a 4-month-old baby, and crew into her six lifeboats.

They watched as *U.81* headed off, following her for about 4 miles. After she'd disappeared from sight, a muffled explosion indicated that Weisbach had found another victim. Over the next few days, in stormy weather, many of the survivors died. As the weather worsened, contact having already been lost between some of the boats, two were never seen again. The First Officer was in one, along with thirty-one other survivors, including two women, a stewardess and the mother with her baby.[84] For the rest of the day, the group sailed to the north-east, strung out in a line, one boat following the other. That night, however, they became separated and by the following morning, a Tuesday, the First Officer's boat was nowhere to be seen. With the wind getting up, they pulled in their sail and rowed for the rest of the day. During the night, however, they lost their sea anchor; in its place they lashed some oars together. As the hours ticked by, on Wednesday morning, the wind died off and they were able to sail again. During the day, however, the Italian chef and one of the galley staff, Richard Phillips, would also be counted among the dead. Water started to be rationed and the next day, Thursday, the storekeeper died. In the night, as he became increasingly delirious, he had to be lashed down. Later the same day, another passenger passed away. By Friday, all were suffering severe dehydration and another able-seaman died. Saturday brought two more deaths, a fireman and a third-class pantry-boy, the Londoner William Godwin. On Sunday, one of the men killed himself by jumping overboard. On his fourth attempt, the sea finally claimed him. At 1500hrs on Monday, even though they spotted land, they couldn't make it any further and it wasn't until the next day, 28 March, that two fishing boats came out from the harbour at Carino near Cape Ortegal in northern Spain. They were in such bad shape that two men had to be carried from the boat. Six days later, one of the babies that had survived the ordeal also died in the Ferrol hospital. Two weeks later, another survivor died of gangrene in the same hospital. Out of the original thirty-one survivors, eleven had died.

On another boat, only five of twenty-five survived. Chave's boat was adrift for five days but was spotted by a French Fabre liner 200 miles south of where the *Alnwick Castle* had sunk. The survivors were taken aboard the *Venezia* and dropped off in New York. Two of the six boats that left the sinking *Alnwick Castle* were never seen again.

In total, forty of her 139 passengers and crew – including three from *Trevose* – died. The names of those who died are engraved on the memorial to the Fallen of the Merchant Navy at London's Tower Hill.

### A New Ferocity to the Submarine War

U-boat commanders now felt that they 'had been unchained'.[85] One commander whose name stood alone in ignominy was Leutnant Wilhelm Werner. His behaviour was completely at odds with men like Hans Rose. After torpedoing the 5,597-ton *Torrington* on 8 April, Werner deliberately submerged, leaving twenty British crewmen on the deck. His actions were premeditated: the men had been stripped of their lifejackets.[86] Only the master survived, after he'd been separated and held prisoner inside the submarine. Four days later, Werner did the same to the crew of the *Toro*. Another commander, Paul Wagenführ, followed his example in July, submerging his submarine and leaving crew members of the *Belgian Prince* on deck. In April 1917 alone, a total of twenty-four ship's masters were taken prisoner, 'a practice intended to daunt the spirit of British merchant [navy] officers'.[87]

### U.83 Sunk by the Q-ship *Farnborough*

On 17 February, the Q-ship *Farnborough* managed to sink the *U.83*. It was a triumph for Commander Gordon Campbell, who had literally used his ship as live bait: 'I came to the conclusion that the only way for us to ensure decoying the enemy to the surface was deliberately to get torpedoed and trust to still being in a position to fight with our guns afterwards.'[88]

That morning, around 0945hrs, after a tell-tale torpedo track was spotted, Campbell altered course so that it would hit with the least loss of life, just abaft of the engine room. In the explosion, the bulkhead collapsed and two-thirds of the ship flooded. A carefully orchestrated charade of panic came to life aboard *Farnborough* as the crew pushed off in lifeboats and the U-boat circled her prey. They had to at least *appear* panicked. Other crew members waited on board, ready for Campbell's order to open fire. From below deck, a one-word signal went out at 1005hrs: 'Torpedoed'.

Satisfied that the merchantman was ready to be finished off with his deck gun, Bruno Hoppe surfaced and stopped 300–400yds off the port bow, then drifted in closer to around 100yds. At that moment, 'the wheel-house collapsed, the ship's sides fell away' and 6pdr fire opened up.[89] As soon as

Hoppe emerged from the conning tower, a barrage of forty-five shells started to rain down at point-blank range into the hopelessly vulnerable submarine.

The 'water was thick with oil and blood, and air bubbles were very conspicuous'.[90] The first shot decapitated Hoppe.[91] Campbell later admitted:

> It seemed almost brutal to fire at such range … [*U.83*] finally sank with the conning-tower shattered and open, the crew pouring out as hard as they could. About eight men were seen in the water which was bitterly cold and thick with oil. I ordered the boats to their assistance, and they were just in time to rescue one officer and one man.[92]

*Farnborough*, meanwhile, was also on the verge of sinking. Campbell nonchalantly signalled: 'Q.5 slowly sinking, respectfully wishes you goodbye.' The sloop *Buttercup* and a destroyer, HMS *Narwhal*, were immediately sent to pick up her crew.

Under tow by *Buttercup*, *Farnborough* stayed afloat. Campbell stayed on board until finally, at around 0200hrs the next day, water extinguished the ship's donkey boiler and the ship started to roll dangerously. *Buttercup* stayed with her until the end: it wasn't until an unexploded depth charge went off that she slipped her towline. Her captain thought she been hit by another torpedo. Taking *Farnborough* back under tow, the Q-ship was finally beached at Mill Cove at 2130hrs. A signal arrived from Bayly in his usual, clipped style: 'Very good piece of work. Well done.'

**THE DECREASING EFFECTIVENESS OF Q-SHIPS**

The high point of the Q-ship was 1917. That year, sixty-three duels were fought between Q-ships and submarines: 'Of the 54 U-boats lost to all causes in 1917, six were destroyed by Q-ships, 7 by British submarines, nine rammed by surface craft and nineteen lost by detonation of mines.'[93] The Q-ships' growing success forced U-boat commanders to more closely look for tell-tale clues on their targets. Unrestricted submarine warfare allowed U-boat captains the luxury of not having to identify either a ship's origin or its cargo. Now the Q-ships' success bred increased caution and less U-boat action on the surface, even if it was also certainly true that 'the mere fact that a number of Q-ships were at sea, even if they did not succeed in sinking many submarines, forced the Germans to make a radical change in their submarine tactics'.[94] During the periods of restricted submarine warfare, the submarine was obliged to 'approach on the surface and take a chance with a craft that might be an armoury of concealed guns'.[95] The advent of the convoy system 'put the decoy vessels out of a job', as lone merchantmen were looked upon with increasing suspicion.[96] A seeming convoy straggler was often a Q-ship in disguise, and U-boat commanders became very wary when they spotted single ships trailing a convoy.

By November 1918, more than 180 Q-ships were in service, but with only eleven confirmed kills their overall effectiveness was questionable, especially since their kills came at a staggering cost of sixty-one British and three French Q-ships. Most successes were registered early in the war. Up to March 1917, Q-ships had 'sunk seven submarines at a cost of four of their number, thereafter they sunk only four more, with a totally disproportionate loss of 27 Q-ships'. After *U.88*'s sinking on 17 September 1917, they only had one kill: on 9 November 1918, the Q-ship *Privet* helped sink *U.34*.[97] As the Germans grew increasingly wary, Q-ships were sunk in increasing numbers by the enemy: twenty-four in 1917 (six sloops and eighteen other 'special service' vessels).

Prize money of £1,000 was shared out amongst the crew and decorations awarded. Included was Lieutenant Ronald Stuart. Despite having been ordered off the sinking ship, Stuart had gone back to search for his captain, Campbell, who had nearly been killed by an exploding mine. For reasons of secrecy, it was normal that the awards be hushed up. All that was known was that a VC had been awarded, so the press now referred to it as 'the mystery VC'.[98]

**Despite Few U-boats, a Rising Allied Toll**

Scheer was dissatisfied with how the preparations for the new campaign had been handled, talking about 'how many opportunities for sinking shipping in the blockaded areas were lost'.[99]

Not only too late, perhaps also badly planned: 'just 105 U-boats of various types were available for frontline use', but, because of other operational commitments, 'only ninety-two boats were available for anti-shipping operations'.[100] The most U-boats operating in 1917 was in June, when there were 129: 'for the remainder of the year it did not fall below 120, ending the year at 125'.[101]

The pace of new U-boat production was hampered by

> the hesitant attitude of the RMA towards the intensification of U-boat construction at the expense of other shipbuilding programmes, especially capital ships.[102]

Despite the shortcomings, Germany's new campaign quickly reduced neutral traffic arriving at British ports. It wasn't just the sinkings that were hurting; it was also that the tactics of terror were effective. Neutral entrances and clearances fell from 471 and 832 respectively in January to 299 and 660 in February and March combined.[103] In sum, 'neutral entrances and clearances from British ports during the two months were little more than 25 per cent of the previous year's total'.[104]

Holtzendorff, however, would only be partially correct. By March, neutral traffic picked up again and '*à la fin du printemps, le traffic était redenvenu presque normal*' ('at the end of spring, traffic was almost normal again'), leading Holtzendorf, on 4 May, to complain that the Foreign Office wasn't applying enough pressure to the neutrals.[105] When he visited Ludendorff's headquarters, he was told, in no uncertain terms, that putting a schedule on England's downfall had been '*Unsinn*' ('nonsense').

By April 1917, submarine tactics and the weapons used bore little resemblance to the earlier phase of the war at sea: 64 per cent of sinkings were now without warning, while from 1915–16 they had only increased from 21 per cent to 29 per cent. The figure soared because 'as anti-submarine defences improved, the U-boats had no choice but to sink or be sunk'.[106]

*German Submarines Active in Primary Theatres, 1917*

| Group | Feb | March | April | May | June | July | Nov |
|---|---|---|---|---|---|---|---|
| HSF | 46 | 52 | 54 | 56 | 59 | 59 | n/a |
| Pola | 23 | 24 | 25 | 26 | n/a | n/a | 31 |
| Flanders | 23 | 31 | 33 | 34 | n/a | n/a | 29 |
| Total | 92 | 107 | 112 | 116 | n/a | n/a | n/a |

Source: Karau, *Naval Flank of the Western Front, The German MarineKorps Flandern 1914–1918*, p.115.[107]

Even before the full scale of April's losses was known, Douglas Haig wrote to the Minister of War, Lord Derby, lamenting that 'we have lost command of the sea'.[108] April would be the worst month on record – 155 ships lost to submarines and a further fourteen to mines, with a loss of 1,155 souls. On one day alone, 19 April, submarines claimed eleven ships, a further two sunk by mines. A third of the total worldwide loss of 870,359 tons took place in the Mediterranean.[109] On top of that, another 127,587 tons of shipping was out of commission because of damage. A total of 227,447 tons of neutral shipping was sunk. Holtzendorff had emphasised the importance of scaring off the neutrals, and the attack on neutrals was indeed significantly impacting Britain's overall cargo-carrying capacity. The burden on British shipping thus became even heavier.

Some writers attributed the success to the number of submarines at sea, not the tactics:

> In the campaign's first five, most successful months this rate [the average daily rate of sinkings] rose by a measly average of 54 tons per day. In the Mediterranean, the average sinkings per U-boat actually dropped.[110]

After April, tonnage losses started to decline, sinkings falling off as U-boats returned to base for resupply. In May, 106 vessels – amounting to 320,572 tons – were torpedoed, and a further 28,114 tons mined. What was gratifying – if one could call it that – was that the number of British deaths, 580, was halved.

Ship damage had almost the same impact as a sinking. The amount of tonnage in the repair yards was simply staggering:

> In one particular week there were actually under repair the colossal figure of 2,120,301 tons – more than one ninth of British mercantile tonnage in 1914. To give a more graphic idea, those two million odd tons represented an average of 600 ships, of 3,500 tons each, out of cargo carrying service.[111]

The impact of the submarine war at sea could also be measured in other ways. The ratio of submarines lost to the merchant tonnage was telling: nine German submarines from February to the end of April, at a cost of 1,104 ships. Newbolt calculated the heavy – and seemingly ineffective – cost of British ASW: 'every German submarine was diverting some twenty-seven craft and their crews from other duties'.[112]

Of course, there was an impact on Britain's imports too. Additionally, low worldwide wheat harvest yields 'gave the Germans another opportunity'.[113] With Argentina in the same position, Britain was forced to import from India and Australia, the increased distances using another 720,000 tons of cargo space which had not been anticipated. With Britain's grain supply reportedly down to six weeks' supply, President Wilson implored the US Congress to declare war. This was now a war of attrition at sea: 'The end of the war could be fixed with arithmetical precision at no very distant date.'[114]

### The Zimmermann Telegram – America's Final Rush to War

There was widespread agreement in Washington that Germany had been duplicitous, knowing that unrestricted submarine warfare was about to be launched while at the same time giving the appearance of negotiating peace terms. It was what Bethmann-Hollweg had feared. As late as 4 January 1917, Wilson, along with his most trusted advisor, House, continued to insist that the country 'does not intend to become involved in this war'.[115] On 22

January, Wilson appealed to the Senate, saying that Europe should make 'a peace without victory'. He totally misunderstood that both belligerents were more determined than ever to see the war carried through to victory. Too much had already been lost to walk away. Bethmann-Hollweg's note of 28 January, hoping for peace, was delivered within days of unrestricted submarine warfare being announced. Secretary of State Lansing wanted an immediate declaration of war. Even Colonel House, not one to consciously take sides, commented that it was better to deal with the British, as 'they may be stubborn and may be stupid, but at least they are reliable'.[116] On 26 February, Wilson asked Congress that American merchant ships be armed with naval guns and crews. The request died in the Senate, so the President went ahead by Executive order.

Behind the scenes, an extraordinary catalyst now unravelled. One of the channels through which Germany's Foreign Office messages passed was the US State Department's own telegraph line. In one message, Germany's new Foreign Minister, Arthur Zimmermann, had proposed an alliance with Mexico if war broke out between Germany and the United States.

When Wilson was informed of the telegram's content, he reacted by cutting diplomatic relations with Germany, recalling his own ambassador and obliging the German embassy staff in Washington to leave. The Zimmermann telegram had decisively 'accelerated [the] confrontation' between Germany and America.[117] What had been designed as a possible means of tying America up with a war in her own backyard, and therefore an incentive to continued neutrality, completely backfired.

> As the United States and Germany were still at peace, this proposal to arrange conditionally for stabbing in the back the Power whose good offices as a peacemaker the Germans were still seeking, was made even more remarkable by the method of its transmission.[118]

On 1 March, the startling news of the telegram's content was unveiled in the American press. Germany's meddling increased the pressure on Wilson's already limited room for manoeuvre. Even in Germany, the public's reaction was immensely hostile. The *Berliner Tageblatt* labelled Zimmermann's communication 'boundlessly naïve', and in mid-April, the German capital saw its first political strike.[119]

Ambassador Gerard had been remarkably accurate about German intentions. His earlier predictions that, under public pressure, Germany would return to a more aggressive unrestricted form of war, if not by the autumn of 1916 then certainly by February or March 1917, turned out to be spot-on. It was now clear that Germany's *Arabic* Pledge had been worthless.

**America Enters the War**

Lloyd George had been anxiously awaiting news: 'I wonder if America will come in this week? It will be the best piece of luck we have had for some time.'[120] On 4 April, the vote was taken in the House and passed by 373 to fifty; two days later, the Senate also came on board in a vote of eighty-two to six in support of war. Of the 125 who spoke, only twenty-five opposed the motion.[121] Wilson, however, still insisted on entering the fray with qualification: the United States would only come to Europe as an 'associated power', not as a full ally of the Entente. It meant that the Mediterranean naval war against the Austro-Hungarian navy would not be supported by the Americans (destroyers coming from the Philippines only patrolled the Strait of Gibraltar without joining the war in the Adriatic).

Things had moved fast in the last two weeks of March. The sinking of three ships on 18 March might have been the trigger. Six days later, Wilson asked SecNav Daniels to work out possible avenues for naval cooperation before Congress acted. By 29 March, the Admiralty passed a message to Admiral Sir Montague E. Browning, Commander-in-Chief North America and the West Indies, that facilities would be provided in Ireland for American anti-submarine operations.[122] Days earlier, on 23 March, Daniels ordered 87,000 men called up.[123] Two weeks before that, on 9 March, Wilson ordered the arming of American merchantmen, moving the US posture to one of armed neutrality. Lansing was pushing, arguing that 'continued neutrality would mean a loss of future influence in world affairs'.[124]

William Sims was dispatched to London on 29 March, only six days after Ambassador Page had suggested the need to send a senior American naval officer. He had not been the first choice. He was 'the most junior flag officer in the ranks, standing 31st among 31 admirals'.[125] Former President Theodore Roosevelt and his cousin, the Assistant Navy Secretary, Franklin Roosevelt, supported him over the choice of Daniels and Benson, the captain of the USS *Pennsylvania*, Captain Henry Wilson. FDR knew Sims and admired his professionalism.[126] Admiral Henry Mayo, commander of the US Atlantic Fleet, was supposedly also among the initial choices. A week before leaving, Sims was promoted a two-star rear admiral.

Sims and his aide, Commander John Vincent Babcock, travelled together, trying to be incognito, on the *New York*, Sims introducing himself as V.J. Richardson (Babcock went by the name of S.W. Davidson). Few were fooled; their monogrammed shirts suggested otherwise.

Sims 'faced an unclear mission complicated by insufficient authority to establish clear organizational ties between the Admiralty and the Navy Department'. He was to find out 'all possible information as to what the British were doing, and what plans they had for more effective warfare against

[German] submarines'.[127] The day of his arrival was sobering. Sims faced the same threat to his life that Allied seamen had been facing for three years. It was the very reason he had come.

> Admiral Sims, while on his way to England as a passenger in a US merchant ship, got some firsthand experience when a U-boat torpedoed [author's note: this is wrong; the ship hit a mine as it neared Liverpool] the ship he was on, and he became a survivor. Admiral Sims … had been strongly opposed to convoys. After his personal experience, he became a strong proponent of convoys.[128]

Burke's assumption that it was this close encounter with peril which converted Sims to support the convoy system borders on the absurd. Nevertheless, as they came ashore, Sims and Babcock were met by Captain George Hope, Jackson's assistant at the Operations Division at the Admiralty. He was carrying a letter of introduction from Jellicoe.[129] Sims was confident.

> The situation is far from easy, solely on account of the submarine warfare, but difficulties are there to be overcome, and they will be overcome, I am convinced; although I fully expect our losses to be very heavy before all is over.[130]

However, when he and Jellicoe met in person at the Admiralty on 10 April, Sims was handed a summary of the losses and the grim reality of Britain's plight became clear. Britain's merchant fleet was being decimated.[131] Jellicoe's conclusion is now well known, but his task was less straightforward:

> It was his business to paint the canvas in the darkest shades and to show its position in the darkest light, so as to bring home to the American Navy Board the critical nature of our commerce, and the need for immediate action on their part.[132]

Jellicoe is reported to have said, after being asked if there were any solutions: 'Absolutely none that we can see now.'[133] In *The Grand Fleet*, published in 1919, however, Jellicoe added an important qualification: 'I knew that no fresh measures, involving the production of fresh material, *could become effective* [author's italics] for a period of at least six to twelve months.'[134] In 1934, in *The Submarine Peril*, he repeated his position: 'What I did say was that the counter measures being devised could not be immediately successful as time was required for their production.'[135] He refuted some of the misleading narrative that had emerged for this first meeting:

> We were certainly not in a state of panic … but we did want those engaged in the war on the Allied side to understand the situation in order that they might realize the value that early naval assistance would bring.[136]

Some estimated that Britain could be defeated as early as the following November unless a solution to the submarine threat was found:

> The limit of endurance would be reached by November 1 1917; in other words, unless some method of successfully fighting submarines could be discovered almost immediately, Great Britain would have to lay down her arms before a victorious Germany.[137]

At a Cabinet meeting on 11 April, Jellicoe reported the previous day's conversation with Sims. Jellicoe painted a dark picture. His message was that time was critical: 'It is impossible to go on with war if losses like this continue … the situation is very serious and we shall need all the assistance we can get.'[138]

Sims hadn't appreciated the severity of the submarine menace: 'I was fairly astounded; for I had never imagined anything so terrible.'[139] As he was leaving the meeting, Sims confessed that he had thought they had the submarine-menace in hand: 'to us it appeared that Allies were holding their own', he would later write. Until that conversation, Jellicoe maintained that neither Sims 'nor anyone else in the United States had realized that the situation was so serious'.[140] The situation was indeed extremely bad. In the twenty-three months prior to February 1917, average tonnage lost per sub was 8,909 tons; in the six months before the convoy system was instituted, it had increased dramatically, to 12,708 tons.[141] So long as this view prevailed in America, Admiral Sims considered that the United States could not do much to help Britain in anti-submarine warfare. Sims immediately started to feed the dismaying news back to Daniels:

> The submarine issue is very much more serious than people realize in America. The recent success of operations and the rapidity of construction constitute the real crisis of the war.[142]

While Jellicoe and Sims were meeting in London, French and British battleships were sailing into the Hampton Roads on the north-east coast of the US under the command of Admiral Sir Montague E. Browning and Admiral R.A. Gasset. Two weeks later, on 24 April, the Balfour Naval Mission arrived in Washington.[143] Earlier in the month, the Foreign Secretary, Arthur Balfour, had written to the

American Ambassador in London, Walter Page, saying: 'Without a doubt the most pressing need of the Allies at this moment is shipping.'[144] Page had long been an advocate of American intervention. The Foreign Secretary was well-placed to talk about naval matters; he'd been First Lord of the Admiralty in the Asquith Coalition from 1915–16 and, as such, Jellicoe's political counterpart. Over the next few weeks, the mission's members would meet Woodrow Wilson and his advisor, Colonel House, as well as address the two houses of Congress. Its purpose was to clarify Britain's treaty position with its allies and what the country needed in munitions and exports.

Page's friendship with Wilson 'had been severely eroded if not destroyed by the countless letters and cables … [in which he] bemoaned the lack of US participation in the war'.[145] Eventually, the mission would ask the Americans for fifty-five escort destroyers, forty-one convoy cruisers, four battleships, 100 aircraft, 100,000 mines and 250 small minelaying craft.[146] In the end, the US Government agreed to cover the British overdraft.

In some quarters, however, the British delegation was met with considerable ill-will, particularly from the strongly represented Irish–American community. Ambassador Page even blamed the strength of the Irish lobby for the 'failure to establish a permanent embassy in London':[147]

> The President wishes that, when you next meet the Prime Minister, you would explain to him that only one circumstance now appears to stand in the way of perfect cooperation with Great Britain. All Americans who are not immediately connected with Germany by blood ties find their one difficulty in the failure of Great Britain so far to establish a satisfactory form of self-government in Ireland. In the recent debates in Congress on the War Resolution, this sentiment was especially manifest. It came out in the speeches of those enemies of the Declaration who were not Irish themselves nor representatives of sections in which Irish voters possessed great influence – notably members from the Southern States.[148]

The immediate effect of the US declaration of war was the provision of destroyers, desperately needed for inshore anti-submarine work. It was not the hulls alone that made the difference; it was how they were offered. Sims was adamant that

> our forces should be considered chiefly in the light of reinforcements to the Allied navies, and that, ignoring all questions of national pride and even what at first might superficially seem to be national interest, we should exert such offensive power as we possessed in the way that would best assist the Allies in defeating the submarine.[149]

For his fellow naval officers, the position Sims took was controversial, as it meant that American naval forces would operate *under*, not just in cooperation *with*, the British. Because of Sims's influence and channels, Jellicoe kept him very closely in the loop. By the end of 1917, he would be sent the *Daily Submarine Return* put together by the Intelligence Division.[150] This was a summary of all the U-boats known to be at sea, how long they'd been on patrol, known routes and their signals. The same spirit in sharing intelligence did not apply to the French, who in any case had their own sources.

**Jellicoe and Sims: Friendship and Partnership**

William Sowden Sims's seniority, expertise and background made him the perfect candidate to meet with Jellicoe. The two knew each other from their days in China during the Boxer uprising. He had come to know Jellicoe well. Jellicoe, then a 40-year-old captain, had been the Chief of Staff to Admiral Seymour, the Commander-in-Chief of Allied forces in the ill-fated first international relief expedition to Peking.[151] Sims's open Anglophilia very nearly blocked what was to be the defining moment in his naval career. Daniels, the US SecNav, said his selection was 'not because of your Guildhall speech, but in spite of it'.[152] It was clear that Sims was not well-regarded by Daniels or, even though to a lesser extent, by Benson. With Daniels, Sims disagreed on a fundamental point of strategy:

> Sims felt that the US Navy's principal role was the protection of trade and the maintenance of the supply lines to Britain, while Daniels wanted to concentrate on protecting the transit of the army to France.[153]

Without FDR's support, Sims would probably not have been selected.

Like the British admiral, Sims's reputation was that of an expert, 'a gunnery officer of the very first rank', according to Jellicoe.[154] Jellicoe took considerable risk in putting so much faith and support behind the American. He admired Sims because of his 'habit of speaking his mind with absolutely fearless disregard for the consequences'.[155]

Sims's approach was anything but conservative: he 'resisted the urge to micromanage. He had a reputation for not holding back when seeking innovative reform. He decided the "what" to be done, permitting subordinate officers to decide the "how".'[156] 'Officer rank was left at the door.' He was a very different kind of officer to Jellicoe.

The working relationship between the two, however, became a model for the effective Allied partnership. Jellicoe encouraged Sims to run against the prevailing philosophy of the Wilson administration. He followed the general philosophy that the word 'cooperation' ought to be struck out from the war dictionary and have 'consolidation' written in its place; 'the preservation of its individual identity by one force or another is all wrong'.[157] Sims reasoned that 'unified methods of signal and radio procedure ... ensure[ed] efficiency in joint operations with the British'.[158]

The existing relationship between Sims and Jellicoe was fundamental to the astonishingly fast integration of a new naval partner: 'Perhaps Sims' greatest success was encouraging the USN into a partly subordinate posture rather than the early ideas of a fully independent role.'[159] It would be the first time American naval officers and ships would be directly under the command of the Royal Navy.

The US Navy honoured Sims's singular accomplishments by naming two ships after him, one launched in 1939 and another, after the sinking of the first in the Coral Sea, in 1943.

### The First American Naval Units Arrive

The first American ships to arrive in Europe were six destroyers of Division 8 of the US Atlantic Fleet's Destroyer Force. Led by Commander Joseph Knefler Taussig, the six destroyers had left Boston on the evening of 24 April and crossed the Atlantic to arrive outside Queenstown in the early morning of 4 May.[160] Taussig had received minimal warning and not actually been given a deadline for the ten days it took to get his boats and crews ready for 'long and distant service'.[161] More than that, they didn't know. It wasn't until the day before sailing that he received some clues as to his destination. When 50 miles offshore of Cape Cod, he found out that his small flotilla would be the first American aid Britain would receive.[162] He was to head to the southern Irish coast and signal Vice Admiral Queenstown, Lewis Bayly, with the call-sign 'GCK'.

Two British ships went out to meet the Americans: the first, the destroyer HMS *Parthian*, wasn't sighted. When the second, the *Mary Rose*, was spotted, a short signal was immediately hoisted, reading: 'Welcome to the American Colours'. Taussig answered: 'Thank you. I am glad of your company.' Off Roche's Point, British officers boarded the American destroyers to help pilot them into Queenstown's protected waters, fittingly known as the Chicago Knoll. The 36-year-old Edward Evans (soon to be Captain Evans DSO) was one of the RN officers who came aboard. Popularly known as 'Evans of the *Broke*', the name of his destroyer at Jutland and in the Dover Strait battle earlier that year, he had joined Scott's Antarctic expedition as second-in-command. Sims's aide, Babcock, Paymaster E.C. Tobey and the American Vice-Consul, Sherman, all boarded the *Wadsworth* as they headed to Queenstown. Sims himself couldn't join, as he'd been urgently called to Paris.

Once docked, Taussig was met by the American Consul, Wesley Frost. Taussig was handed an envelope by Evans. It was dated 1 May and was from Jellicoe:

> My dear Taussig, I retain very pleasant and vivid recollections of our association in China, and I am indeed delighted that you have been selected for the command of the first force which is coming to fight for freedom, humanity and civilization. We shall have our work cut out to subdue piracy. My experience in China makes me perfectly convinced that the two nations will work in the closest co-operation, and I won't flatter you by saying too much about the value of your help. I must say this, however. There is no navy in the world that can possibly give us more valuable assistance, and there is no personnel in any navy that will fight better than yours.[163]

Jellicoe and Taussig had a somewhat special relationship, despite the difference in ranks; both had also served in China in 1900, and both had been wounded … on the same day. Taussig had been recovering from his leg wound at Wei Hai Wei with Jellicoe before being transferred to Japan. From his China days, Jellicoe also knew Captain Bowman McCalla,[164] Seymour's 2iC, but he wasn't present on this historic day. The mutually shared experience would give Taussig privileged access to Jellicoe and his family. Taussig would sometimes bring scarce foods, such as sugar, as gifts to Lady Jellicoe and would be invited to lunch with the family at 'The Mall', the admiral's London quarters, today known as Admiralty Arch. The American had the impression that, despite the quarters being 'sumptuous', they 'lived very simply'. Once, Taussig gave the youngest of the four daughters, Prudie, a cap tally from the *Wadsworth*, but the 4-year-old 'refused to wear it when I told her it made her a little American girl'.[165]

That night, the Americans were invited to dine with Lewis Bayly, arriving at Admiralty House at 1945hrs.[166] Asked when he would be ready to take his boats back to sea, Taussig's answer impressed all:

> We are ready now, sir, that is, as soon as we finish refueling. Of course, you know how destroyers are – always wanting something done to them. But this is war and we are ready to make the best of things and get to sea immediately.[167]

Bayly was an 'autocrat who acquired the reputation of a martinet'. Descriptions of his looks and demeamour conjure up all manner of images: Admiral Robert Carney described him as 'a very crusty old bird' who had 'an almost cynical indifference to popular opinion'.[168] His face was weather-beaten, with a very prominent, beaked nose, 'through which he blew or spoke "with almost equal resonance"'.[169]

Nevertheless, Taussig's response was all Bayly needed to hear. Despite his no-nonsense reputation, Bayly's welcome was warm, greeting the Americans by saying: 'Gentlemen, the Admiralty are afraid I shall be rude to you. I shan't if you do your work; I shall if you don't.'[170] Jellicoe had warned Sims about Bayly's reputation. Sims did initially find Bayly's behaviour 'rude', but he later wrote more diplomatically 'there was nothing about his manner that was effusive, there were no unnecessary words, yet there was a real cordiality that put our men at ease'.[171] Reputedly, Jellicoe had even offered to remove Bayly should Sims find that he couldn't work with him. Sims decided to make a go of it instead. The two would forge one of the most special inter-Allied working relationships of the war. Joseph Taussig was equally complimentary about Bayly:

> [M]ost of us … consider him a most efficient officer. Although his manner is brusque at times, he has always treated me with the utmost courtesy and consideration … There has not been the slightest sign of friction. Our relations have always been cordial. The cooperation between the two navies has been intimate and successful.[172]

Bayly would regularly entertain the Americans at his HQ, where his niece, Miss Voysey, would add a much-needed woman's touch. Taussig found her 'a charming young woman'.[173] She would often prepare meals, after which Bayly and Sims would both help with the drying-up in the kitchen. Bayly had little interest in social activities and had few interests other than gardening. It was his niece who acted as his social ambassador and secretary.

It seemed that the Germans were aware of the impending arrival of the newcomers. The day before, a substantial minefield was laid and the news of the arrival was carried in the German press before that of the British.

The US boats were immediately equipped with depth-charge racks and their masts were cut back to lower their profile. Each was equipped with four 21in torpedo tubes and four 4in/50cal machine guns. The commanders were warned neither to stop to pick up survivors nor to ram periscopes, but to shoot at them first: the Germans had, apparently, used a decoy with the appearance of a periscope attached to a mine. They were also advised to keep signals short, never to repeat the name of another ship and to watch out for fishing vessels, as they could often be submarines in disguise. On 8 May, only four days after arriving, the US destroyers were ready for operations, re-equipped and re-weaponed.

Following Taussig's arrival, a second wave of US Navy destroyers assembled off Newfoundland and sailed to European waters without immediate support from refuelling warships. On 7 May, six additional destroyers sailed with Lieutenant Commander Charles E. Courtney, assuming the role of first among equal ranked officers.[174] Four days later, Commander Henry B. Price sailed at high speed to Queenstown directly in the destroyer tender USS *Melville* (AD-2).[175] Assigned to act as Sims's flagship, she arrived on 22 May. Soon afterwards, on 15 and 25 May, sixteen additional destroyers departed from American ports in two separate waves.[176] Commander Joel R.P. Pringle subsequently sailed in *Dixie* (AD-1) on 31 May, with seven further destroyers sailing to Queenstown between 14 and 17 June.

By June, a total of thirty-five American destroyers were operating in European waters, and by the war's end, of America's ninety-three operational destroyers, seventy were in European waters.[177] Jellicoe had previously calculated that roughly seventy-five would be needed, although they 'could divert only forty-three' at first.[178] Sims's immediate contribution partially filled the gap, and larger numbers for operations based out of France's Atlantic west coast, at Brest, were supplied in 1918. Queenstown was run with extraordinary efficiency, given the almost constant pressure for the ships to be at sea. Admiral William Halsey recalled that the standard of maintenance operations

> was one of the best I have ever encountered … [O]n return from a trip, no matter the hour of day or night, the repair officer of the mother ship would come on board and request a list of necessary repairs.[179]

America's contributions significantly drew down her reserves, and while the pressure was on for American yards to continue the battleship building programme envisaged by Wilson's 1916 Navy Act, the British managed to persuade them to focus their enormous industrial strength on building smaller vessels. In total, 266 destroyers were built, as well as over 400 wooden-hulled sub-chasers. These small, 70-ton craft were equipped with depth charges, a deck gun and hydrophone. Both were vital to the ongoing ASW efforts.

Some of the early American contribution even appeared as yachts, as the sailboats and 'gin palaces' of the rich and famous were converted for naval duty. Two groups, under the overall command of Rear Admiral W.B. Fletcher, started to arrive in France in July and August. The names of their illustrious owners read like a page from *The Social Register*: leading businessman Vincent Astor (*Noma*), philanthropist Mrs E.H. Harriman (*Sultana*), prominent railroad director Frederick W. Vanderbilt (*Vedette*), financier and philanthropist George

F. Baker Jnr (*Harvard*), explorer John Borden (*Kanawah II*) and successful businessman Irving T. Bush (*Christabel*). All arrived on Independence Day, 4 July. The second group of a further six yachts assembled at St John's, Newfoundland, on 5 August, ready for the Atlantic crossing.

How these yachts were prepared illustrates the sudden arrival of war in the United States. One, the 196ft *Emeline*, had become part of the US Patrol Squadron of the United States Navy's Atlantic Fleet a month earlier, on 14 July. After she had been stripped out, a bulkhead replaced, a ½kW Marconi radio installed, storage areas increased for ammunition and weapons mounted (two 3in 50cal and two 30cal guns), the newly named USS *Emeline* was entirely repainted with a camouflage coat. Her crew was 'fairly intercollegiate with eleven colleges represented: Amherst, Brown, Cornell, Harvard, Lafayette, Lehigh, New York University, Trinity, University of Missouri, Union and Yale'.[180] Only Princeton, Dartmouth and Pennsylvania were missing.

## The Ambiguity of American Support

On 31 April, Sims cabled the background to the pivotal decision that the Admiralty had 'decided to give trial to convoy system described in my last dispatch', adding that 'it will strain British resources of personnel and ships and we must assist by taking one route at least, if the plan is to be carried out'. Sims ended with a plea: 'I very urgently recommend favourable action.'

Sims kept up a relentless blitz of requests and recommendations by telegram and letter. Promoted to the three-star rank of vice admiral on 25 May, his European assignment was given a more concrete purpose: he was to assume command of United States destroyers operating from British bases. At the same time, he was appointed Commander, United States Forces Operating in European Waters. Three weeks later, on 13 June, he outlined the mechanics of the convoy system and cabled again the next day, and the next and on 17 June. Despite sinkings starting to rise again in June after declining in May, no glimmer of a reply came from Washington until 20 June, when Daniels wrote back again totally refuting the employment of convoys: 'In regard to convoy, I consider that American vessels having armed guards are safer when sailing independently.'

The partial rejection of the convoy system implied in the cable about vessels with armed guards, coupled with the suggestion that some anti-submarine craft could not be spared from American waters, made it clear to Sims that he had failed to establish his case after two months of exposition.[181] Daniels later tried to deny his hand in the authorship of the cable, saying it had been written by Benson.

It was not the case that the USN was a 'powerful advocate of convoy' during these critical months, as Eric Grove suggested. Indeed, nothing was forthcoming from Secretary Daniels or Benson, the CNO.[182] Small wonder that Sims later would be highly critical of the civilian politicians, calling Daniels the 'dictatorial head' of the US Navy and concluding in his rebuttal that 'Mr Daniels' handling of the Navy during the first very critical months after our declaration of war, was so ignorantly contrary to the established principles of warfare as to result in great losses of time, property and life'.[183]

It was extraordinary, given the fundamental change of direction in policy at the Admiralty. Sims immediately cabled back (21 June) that the Admiralty 'has now adopted the convoy system and will put it into effect as fast as ships can be obtained for high sea convoy against raiders and destroyers for escort duty in the submarine zone'. Although the Navy Department replied on 24 June, saying that they recognised the need to send all anti-submarine craft 'which can be spared from home waters', the note added that 'the question of supplying adequate guns and trained gun crews to merchant ships … coupled with a rigid system of inspection … is believed to constitute one of the most effective defensive submarine measures'.[184] Sims kept up his plea for convoys, saying that arming ships was not by itself the answer, and that it actually exacerbated the danger for merchant shipping by forcing the submarines below water, where the use of torpedoes was the only means of attack. 'The mission of the Allies must be to force submarines to give battle.'

Yet it clearly made little difference now, as German submarine commanders had long since decided surface attack was too dangerous. This was the great truth in what Sims was writing about the use of convoys: they forced German submarines to engage in circumstances where they would be brought to the destroyer rather than destroyers having to find them. His position was echoed by Beatty, or he may have just echoed what Beatty was picking up.

Even if Marder felt Sims was 'an ardent advocate of convoy', Sims nevertheless had 'reservations', writing that 'he felt very strongly that the only promising effective solution of the submarine problem lies in the field of listening devices'.[185] He kept on circling around to the basic fact that killing submarines is impossible without knowing where they were. Without advanced hydrophones, effective ASW was impossible: 'Hydrophones, although not a weapon, laid the foundation for a major technological innovation in ASW – sonar.'[186] Unless lying on the seabed, a sub is always mechanically 'swimming', producing even the minutest of noise:

> A submarine cannot stop under water; it can only come to a full rest on the bottom. But if there is no bottom within seventy meters at the most, then the submarine has to keep going because it has no chance of staying still in the water.[187]

### SUBMARINE DETECTION – HYDROPHONE

Accurate detection was critical to effective ASW, but it was only in 1916 that the first submarine located by hydrophone was destroyed. The whereabouts of a submarine could be pinpointed with both passive or active acoustics: the former picked up sounds like engine, pump and propellor noise; the latter used the reflection of a sound wave, like a 'ping', after it hit a solid object. The scientific challenges – detection, differentiation and identification of sound – were daunting.

It was useless developing weapons to destroy submarines if they couldn't be found. Underwater sound detection had advantages over surface acoustic detection: 'It was discovered that acoustic signals were badly affected by wind velocity gradients and by temperature. Underwater sound did not suffer from these defects and had the added advantage that its velocity was four times faster than in the air.'[188]

Earliest efforts weren't impressive. A non-directional listening device would be hung over a stationary ship's side; a moving ship had to stop engines, lower equipment, take a reading and then reverse the whole process in a never-ending and time-consuming sequence, 'a repetitious move, stop and listen procedure'.[189] These models were bi-directional in that they only gave the operator the angle on which a sound was detected but not its direction. The actual position could be wrong by 180 degrees. An operator, no matter how skilled, couldn't tell the direction from which the sound was coming. 'Prior to 1917 all that these instruments showed was that there was a submarine somewhere in the vicinity.'[190] An experienced operator would rotate the listening dial until the strength of sound was equal in both ears, which would then give him the bearing. From propellor sounds, an operator could distinguish the 'smaller ships such as trawlers with reciprocating engines [which] had a characteristic beat due to engines, while destroyers and larger ships fitted with turbines emitted a continuous rushing sound'.[191]

The use of hydrophones at sea only started in April 1915: fifty sets were supplied to drifters and another 2,000 were ordered in August.[192] By the end of the war, after a surge of technological inventiveness, 'no fewer than eleven types of non-Directional (2) and Directional (9) hydrophones were perfected and produced'.[193] The hydrophone most produced by the British was the non-directional 'Portable General Service' Hydrophone (PGS), or Drifter. Some 3,430 were produced by the war's end (844 of the Mk.I and 2,586 of the Mk.II).[194]

Even if the Allies hadn't yet found the answer by the end of the war, German submariners became increasingly fearful of underwater detection. *U.62*'s captain, Ernst Hashagen, voiced the concern: 'The last year of the War is the worst. For three long years we have allowed our enemies time to study the nature of the submarine, to pry into its most intimate secrets. They pursue and fight us on the surface, through fog and storm, from the air and in the depths of the sea, on the coasts and in the open ... They listen-in for us, to hear the distant beat of our screws; and feel for us with electric fingers along the seabed.'[195]

The U-boat war would only come to US shores a year later. If the Germans had brought the U-boat war across the Atlantic earlier, Jellicoe later confessed, the American aid which proved so vital in 1917 would not have been forthcoming.

**Decreasing Support for Submarine War in Germany**

In April 1917, at the very moment U-boats were wreaking havoc, splits amongst the Central Powers began to appear. On 14 April, the new Austrian Emperor, Karl, sent a warning letter to Kaiser Wilhelm, showing his deep concern for the political impact of the British blockade:

> We are now fighting against a new and more dangerous enemy than the Entente: social revolution. It is an enemy which finds the strongest possible ally in hunger.[196]

The German Army also started to voice concerns that Holtzendorff's submarine war was not going to be won within his optimistic time framework. Hindenburg wrote to Bethmann-Hollweg in mid-July saying that he saw 'a grave danger in hopes which are ... linked with a particular date'. He wanted, therefore, to 'control these hopes and inform the Press of the true position'.[197] In the Reichstag, Matthias Erzberger was ruffling feathers with his enquiries. He'd heard that the army was actively preparing for another winter campaign: a colonel on Ludendorff's staff had confirmed that planning was underway. Erzberger had also heard that the army was placing large munitions orders, which cast doubts on all the assurances he was getting from the RMA.

Against this background, Erzberger sought allies to support his Catholic Centre Party's push for peace. The military pushed back. Ludendorff demanded that the kaiser get rid of Bethmann-Hollweg, threatening to resign. Although the kaiser very nearly called his bluff, Bethmann-Hollweg's view prevailed. Sacking a popular general would have had grave consequences for the nation's morale; getting rid of a Chancellor, very little. On 14 July, Bethmann-Hollweg formally resigned.

Despite enormous difficulties, Erzberger's resolution was passed on 19 July. The Reichstag declared that Germany's war was and should have remained a war of defence. It was declared: 'Forced annexation of provinces, and political, economic and financial oppression are incompatible with a peace of the kind.' The declaration sent the Allies a clear signal that political pressure in Germany for peace was mounting.

### Continued Successes in the Mediterranean

By mid-1917, the presence of German and Austro-Hungarian submarines in the Mediterranean was firmly established (the Austro-Hungarian KUK boats were limited to the Ionian Sea, as generally they were too small). Twenty-seven German U-boats, supported by another thirteen Austrian submarines, operated in the theatre.[198]

From the start, the toll on Allied shipping was high: on 15 February, the unescorted Italian troopship, the 2,854-ton *Minas*, was torpedoed by Forstmann's *U.39* with the loss of 870 lives. Two days later, the 12,698-ton French troopship *Athos* met a similar fate south of Malta. She sank in less than a quarter of an hour after being torpedoed by *U.65*. Out of a crew and complement of 1,950 people, 754 died, including her captain. West of Sardinia, two torpedoes from *U.64* sank the 18,400-ton French battleship *Danton*. The kill was easy, but the submarine nearly met a similar fate when she rocketed to the surface out of control near one of the escorting destroyers, *Massue*. After all but 296 of *Danton*'s 1,100-man crew had been picked up, *U.64*'s skipper, Moraht, surfaced. The only visible witness to the catastrophic events of the day was a box, quietly bobbing on the water, full of letters.

By the autumn, the fragmented nature of Allied control in the Mediterranean was making the implementation of convoys especially difficult. It had already been evident in the 'apparent unwillingness to assist with an effective patrol system' by both the French and the Italian navies to protect the Otranto Barrage.[199] The July 1917 Inter-Allied Naval Conference eventually placed the participating naval forces officially under a single, unified command, an English admiral based in Malta, but it never really worked as 'both France and Britain wanted the supreme control of the new organization'.[200]

Already in January 1917, fixed patrol routes were abandoned and in May, Malta-based Admiral Ballard introduced the convoy system, 'it seems on his own initiative'.[201] With Vice Admiral Sir Somerset Gough-Calthorpe's appointment in August, even the small amount of progress made was lost. The new vice admiral was no supporter of convoys, which he regarded as entirely too defensive.

### Targeting Oilers, Colliers and Hospital Ships

One of the worst characteristics of the 1917 spring submarine offensive was the indiscriminate attack on hospital ships. At midnight on 20 March, off Devon, the 12,002-ton *Asturias* was hit by a torpedo from Herbert Pustkuchen's *U.66*. She was clearly marked as a hospital ship, with two green bands interspersed with three large red crosses. As she settled, what started as an orderly evacuation of the wounded quickly turned chaotic. A Cardiff doctor, William Dobson, recalled that as his boat was being lowered, three of the twenty-six survivors fell out and were crushed against the hull. Astonishingly, after an hour in the freezing water, one was rescued by a man who had been one of his patients before the war.

While most of the ship's wounded were successfully taken off, the final count of the dead included twenty crew members and eleven military personnel, with another dozen unaccounted for. The *Asturias* was beached off Salcombe in Devon and later refloated. Two years before, she had narrowly missed a torpedo when it 'passed close under our stern'.[202] On an earlier voyage, a young officer from the 11th Lancashire Fusiliers was aboard, sent home to convalesce with a severe case of trench foot. His name was J.R.R. Tolkein, the celebrated author of the *Ring* trilogy. Over the next weeks, a spate of other attacks was made.[203]

As a result of the attacks, hospital ships in the Channel ceased to be marked with the regulation red cross. Instead, they 'sailed under escort with the new designation of hospital transports, camouflaged and armed like ordinary transports'.[204] Allied reprisals and countermeasures might only have added fuel to a burning fire. On the Atlantic, the designated hospital ship markings were removed; in the Mediterranean and other routes they remained.

But oilers and colliers were also targeted. From March to September, a total of sixteen oilers were sunk. For the year, 115 colliers met the same fate. 'One consequence of this heavy tanker loss was the reduction of the usual six to eight months' reserve of oil fuel to *eight weeks' supply*.'[205]

### U-BOAT CREW INTERROGATION

Valuable information was pieced together from captured U-boat crews: those of 'at least a quarter of the 150 U-boats sunk in 1916–1918' were interrogated and 'composite' reports produced.[206] Fürbringer was impressed: '[T]he man spoke as though he had been among us in the mess, listening to our chatter.' He concluded that 'the British espionage system in Brügge must be far more efficient than any of us had suspected'.[207] He even said that his captors knew more than he did after being told that he could rejoin two fellow prisoners, Lafranz and Wenninger ('Lala' Lafranz went missing in November 1917 and Sepp Wenninger hadn't returned after leaving Zeebrügge in April).

*UC.61* provides a useful illustration of how the smallest details could be of value. Reginald Hall's August 1916 report lifted information directly from Georg Gerth's own notebook. Supposedly, it 'read like a check list for readying a U-boat for war'. Additionally, twenty-nine specific findings were deduced from close inspection of the sub.[208] For example, the peculiarity of the design of the double jumping wires which worked together with the submarine 'scissors', the immediately recognisable wire net-cutter mounted on a sub's bow, the placement of rudders behind each of the propellers by which 'maximum steerage can be obtained' or the siting of the dual bow hydrophones on rubber mountings to reduce engine- and machinery-related noise.[209] One that particularly interested me was the deck well, designed to hold the sub's folding boat, the Klepper-designed Folboat used by the submarine's crew while at sea. The design was 'still being used by the British Special Boat Service in the 1970s and 1980s'.[210] Gerth's notes also alerted the NID and Bacon that their codes might have been compromised.

Bacon obstinately defended the Dover Barrage, but problematic evidence was later found in his own safe.[211] During Gerth's interrogation, Captain William Fisher concluded that it was a 'delusion that submarines operating in the Channel proceed thither north about' and that – from January to August – twenty-seven boats were 'certain to have passed through the straits, thirty nine were probably and thirteen possible'.[212] One was von Spiegel's *U.32*. From the crews of Erich Sittenfeld's *U.45* and Horst Rühle von Lilienstern's *UC.55* (both of which were sunk in September 1917), 'Blinker' Hall was able to detect a growing dissent in the U-boat forces.

## The Exploits of the *Prize*

At the end of April, *U.93* was sunk by a Q-ship. It was her very first voyage along with her new commander, Graf Spiegel von und zu Peckelsheim. Displacing 1,000 tons, the new 235ft-long submarine was armed with six torpedo tubes and two 10.5cm deck guns, and on the surface could run at 16 knots. *U.93*, a formidable addition to the German submarine fleet, slid out into the North Sea on 13 April, a Friday. Within days, *U.93* sank eleven ships, taking five masters and twelve gunners from armed merchant ships prisoner.

One ship, the *Horsa*, was sunk on 30 April. From one of the overturned lifeboats, the sound of knocking was heard. Unhesitating, a German sailor tied a line around his waist and dove in, intent on rescue. Spiegel talked about the way his men treated prisoners once aboard:

> We were hardened by war. Incessant danger and the sight of death had dulled our sensibility to horror. And yet my men were naturally kind-hearted. The sight of those poor fellows battered and broken on our deck touched them sharply. They held a veritable competition of doing things for them … Some gave up their bunks to our injured prisoners.[213]

On the same day, Hersing met up at sea with Spiegel. He had spotted a three-master sailing at a leisurely 2 knots. He was on the conning tower sharing a quiet moment, enjoying a smoke with a British master, A.B. Burroughs. His prisoner was the captain of a ship he had just sunk, the ss *Ikbal*. Despite the late hour, the conditions were perfect: a light wind, calm sea and good visibility. Approaching the schooner from her stern at 2045hrs, *U.93* fired warning shots from 4,000yds. Spiegel closed to 150yds and landed direct hits from one of his two 10.5cm deck guns. Aboard the Q-ship *Prize* (*Q.21*), a 'panic party' was lowered while the rest of the crew, lying in wait, continued to hide, nerves fraying as the shelling continued.

There was not a little irony to this particular duel: *Prize* was a converted German ship, the *Else*, and had 'earned a place in naval history as the first enemy vessel to be seized in the war'.[214] Originally renamed *First Prize*, after twenty minutes of steady fire from Spiegel's sub, she was ablaze and her engine room wrecked. Spiegel assumed no one could have survived the bombardment and came in closer to identify his victim. Much as Saltzwedel's *UC.71* had done with Campbell's *Dunraven*, *U.93* came up on *Prize*'s stern, where the ship's deck gun could not register 'owing to the position of the wheel'.

Finally, at 2105hrs, their young New Zealand commander, Lieutenant William Edward Sanders RNR, raised the White Ensign, the signal to fire. Almost immediately, *U.93*'s conning tower and deck gun were badly damaged by *Prize*'s superb gunnery. 'Willie' Sanders's parents were both British and so had answered the call early. In fact, at 34, he was 'one of the youngest officers in charge of a Q-ship'.[215] It was only a year before, in April 1916, that he'd been commissioned a sub-lieutenant. Because he'd been recognised early on as having potential, he'd been promoted full lieutenant and given command of the *Prize* in February 1917.

The submarine had also kept her guns well-trained and, despite having taken heavy casualties, had simultaneously scored hits on *Prize*, badly injuring her Lewis gunner.

The sub's first officer, Oberleutnant zur See Wilhelm Ziegner, who had been up above with Leutnant Usedom, took shelter behind the conning tower while the Chief Engineer quickly climbed down into the control room. A duel started and Spiegel, temporarily blinded, was nearly killed when another shell hit the aft deck gun. He'd been lucky. A petty officer hadn't; he'd been decapitated, while two others 'had their legs all but blown off'.[216] On the bridge crouched Burroughs, not daring to jump; he couldn't swim.

*U.93* took on a sharp list to starboard. The deck was holed in at least eight places – 'five diving tanks were blown open and three oil bunkers were leaking like sieves'.[217] Spiegel and his helmsman, Knappe, were both blown overboard when a shell exploded on the conning tower. A German gunner had been blown apart and his body had hit Spiegel, knocking him off. After 500yds, the sub slowed to a standstill, then sank below the waves. As she went, 'a white vapour was emitted from the hull', which Spiegel thought must have been the saltwater hitting her batteries.[218]

The captain, in the water with two crew members – Maschinenmaat Dieppe (probably spelt Deppe[219]) and the helmsman – were rescued by *Prize* and Knappe administered first aid to some of the enemy wounded, and Dieppe got the ship's diesel engines going. He was a good mechanic and 'knew diesel engines as a parson knows his bible'.[220] *Prize* was holed so badly that Sanders decided to sail her back on a port tack. Everything was done to weigh the boat's starboard side down – coal and stores were shifted, even the lifeboats swung out on their davits and filled with water. Two days later, *Q.21* arrived back at Queenstown. From there, she departed the same evening, 4 May, under tow to Milford Haven.

Ashore in Milford Haven, Spiegel was confronted by a British officer, who asked who sank the *Horsa*. When his questioner found out it was the man standing in front of him, the Englishman took his hand, saying: 'I have wanted to meet the man who rescued and took care of a crew as you and your men did.'[221] The story goes that, as he said goodbye to Sanders, Spiegel invited the young New Zealander to come and visit him on his estate after the war. Spiegel did not withhold his admiration: 'I marvelled at the bravery of these Britishers who in their hiding place could take a shelling like that and then run their gun platform out and start to fight.'[222]

### GRAF KARL GEORG EDGAR VON SPIEGEL VON UND ZU PECKELSHEIM

Spiegel was a superstitious commander but, like Weddigen, also a 'gentleman' submariner.

In March 1915, he sank one merchantman and then gave the survivors three bottles of wine, one for each of the three lifeboats in tow. Such was the attitude amongst his crews ('my men were naturally kind-hearted') that when *U.93* sank the *Horsa*, one of his crew dived into the sea to right an overturned lifeboat under which some survivors were found (eventually, the captured crew members were transferred to a Swedish ship).

After *U.32*, Spiegel took command of *U.93* but spent much of the war as a POW at Donnington Hall. After the war, he became successful in the shipping business and then had to restart in the automotive business.

Spiegel spent the rest of the war as a POW in Donnington Hall near Derby, where, after the scuttling of the German High Seas Fleet at Scapa Flow on 21 June 1919, many of von Reuter's officers would also end up.

Writing during the war, Spiegel maintained that he had himself seen hospital ships laden with troops, but after his capture, 'Blinker' Hall personally interrogated him. Spiegel then confirmed that he had never personally witnessed such a thing – his 'eye-witness' account was based on hearsay only. By contrast, however, Spiegel emphasised the fact that his own boat had been diligent, presumably in the early days of the war, in allowing neutral shipping safe passage:

> Seven times in three days we had experienced the same disappointment. Seven times we met neutral ships with no contraband on board, and which we were obliged therefore to allow to proceed on their way.[223]

Three weeks after he arrived as a POW at Donnington Hall, Spiegel found out that *U.93* hadn't actually sunk.[224] Ziegner had taken over her command and, somehow, was able to get back, via Sylt, to port at Wilhelmshaven on 11 May. Aboard were five badly wounded sailors: a bosun's mate, 'cut to pieces by the same shell splinters that had miraculously missed' Ziegner, two petty officers and two other seamen.[225] However, one of the petty officers called Bay died on the first night. In vain, Usedom had tried to keep the rest alive, but all died of their wounds.

Ziegner had taken the U-boat far north to the Arctic and selected a route east of Iceland to escape in 'a nine-day voyage that deserves to be ranked as one of the great epics in submarine history'.[226] They had very little water on board; the water tanks had been damaged and sea water had been mixed in. They had such little fuel that they had to cover 'two thousand miles at a snail's pace'.[227] When they finally got back to Wilhelmshaven, *U.93* was welcomed back by the whole fleet, including Reinhard Scheer, who decorated Ziegner on the submarine's deck. Ziegner would eventually get his own command, a Type-*UC*, and when the war ended he took her to internment in Sweden. In December 1919, he died of diptheria in a military hospital in Wilhelmshaven. *Prize* just managed to get back to Kinsale and then went on to Milford Haven. En route, she nearly fell victim to one of her own, *U.62*.

### The Fate of the *Tulip*

On 30 April 1917, Hashagen's *U.62* spotted *Tulip* 200 miles or so off the Irish coast. He shadowed her, noting the Q-ship's zigzag. It didn't take long for them to conclude that the ship was consistently altering course by 15 degrees every ten minutes.

A torpedo was fired; after twenty seconds it detonated, and two seconds later came a second detonation. It was, apparently, the ship's boiler exploding. When *U.62*'s periscope broke the surface, the Q-ship's guns opened fire, so Hashagen took his submarine out further and at a safer distance resurfaced, his own guns opening rapid fire. It wasn't long before *Tulip* was in her death throes. Her hull was split at the stern and she went down.

In the floating debris, a waterlogged addressed postcard was found: 'To Able Seaman Jackson, HMS *Tulip* (*Q.12*)'. In a POW camp in Freiburg, *Tulip*'s captain, Commander Norman Lewis, eventually heard that his men had been picked up the same day of the attack. Twelve years later, on 20 November 1929, sitting on deck on a steamer in Southampton harbour about to return to Germany after giving a lecture in Reading, Hashagen had a fortuitous encounter with a survivor from *Tulip*, who told him: 'I was the Chief Engineer of *Q.12*, the ship Commander Lewis was in charge of in the war … I saw you twelve years ago looking down from your conning tower at our little band in the life-boats. I have come down here to see you again and to shake hands with you.' Lewis had died before being able to meet Hashagen in person, but he had written to the commander of *U.62*, saying that he was 'always most grateful for the treatment that I received from the Captain and officers'.[228]

### Exploits of the Q-ship *Pargust*

Another Q-ship victim was *UC.29*. Gordon Campbell, who had earlier commanded the Q-ship *Farnborough*, was now sailing another ship, the *Pargust*, in familiar waters: he'd been there before aboard the Q.5.

In the early morning of 2 June, at 0800hrs, a torpedo streaked across lightly choppy waters and hit his ship in the engine room. Campbell acted out the now well-rehearsed charade, the 'panic party' leaving the ship to lure his prey into closer range. The 'actors' even included one sailor with a stuffed parrot. Still leery, *UC.29* held off until the lifeboats were seen rowing back to the ship. The lifeboats, however, blocked the U-boat's view of Campbell's guns.

Finally out of the way, *Pargust* opened fire at 0836hrs, her first shot hitting the conning tower and blowing off both periscopes. Under continued accurate and heavy fire (thirty-eight rounds were fired, along with one torpedo, which missed), *UC.29* rolled over and sank along with her commander, Kapitänleutnant Ernst Rosenow, and twenty-two of her crew. In seven patrols, she'd been responsible for sinking eighteen ships. One officer and one crewman survived and were brought on deck. When *Pargust* arrived back in Queenstown on 8 June, Bayly sent his congratulations. He arrived alongside in his admiral's barge with some fresh eggs, a very typical personal touch of Bayly's.

The *Pargust*'s crew was awarded £1,000 and Campbell was decorated. He became 'the first and only naval officer to receive a bar to the Victoria Cross',[229] an extraordinary achievement. *Pargust* was finally sunk on Christmas Eve 1917, having itself claimed two U-boats and nearly a third.

### The Sinking of the *Clan Davidson*

After dropping off her deadly cargo, the minelayer *UC.17* engaged and sunk a couple of small ships. Then the silhouette of a large merchantman, the 5,058-ton *Clan Davidson*, 'a nice fat tub, very broad in the beam and deeply laden', was spotted by her lookouts.[230] *Clan Davidson* also had lookouts on her bridge, and it wasn't certain whether *UC.17* had also been identified.

Fürbringer had been given command of *UC.17* at the last minute when her captain was taken ill. He'd taken his previous boat, *UC.70*, into Ostend for maintenance and repairs but, while moored, the harbour had been bombarded by a British monitor and a 38cm shell had exploded nearby. *UC.70* slowly sank.

The Clan Line merchantman altered course from heading directly towards Fürbringer to one that was slightly off; he could tell as her two mastheads became individually visible. It meant that *UC.17*, which was now submerged, would be ideally lined up for an attack. Or so he thought, for as he brought the U-boat up for another look, what greeted him was the sight of the *Clan Davidson* bearing down on him at full speed. The engines were immediately reversed at full power: 'the motors were hammering so furiously that the whole boat trembled ... the din was appalling'.[231] Fürbringer took a snap shot and hit the merchantman midships. It was 24 June, 130 miles south by south-west of the Scillies.

Fürbringer could see the immediate panic on deck and grimly concluded that it was the inexperience of the Lascar crew that was the reason – 'their attempts to get the lifeboats lowered [were] almost hilarious'. The sea was calm and the submarine surfaced amongst the lifeboats which had gathered at the ship's stern. The master was taken aboard by Fürbringer, who asked about her cargo and the routes she had travelled while a prize crew went over to set explosive charges in her holds. The ship was briefly searched to see if there were any additional hidden documents. The merchantman had been carrying 3,000 tons of butter; it was the reason she was sinking slowly, as the fat 'gave her a lot of buoyancy'.

The prize crew was rowing back and had just reached the submarine when three very large explosions were heard. The engine rooms were now flooding fast, the additional water speeding the *Clan Davidson*'s descent to the ocean floor, 3,000 metres below. After the last howling roar from air being expelled had subsided, loud pops were heard as half a dozen or so barrels came 'rocketing' up to the surface, followed by a single sheep:

> Mouths agape we watched the animal get under way as if it were the most natural thing in the world to start paddling for home after having been ejected to the surface by ten atmospheres of pressure.[232]

After a while, a rope was thrown over and the sheep taken aboard, where it was slaughtered. The lifeboats had drifted off and were now way to the east under lugsail.[233] Another steamer was spotted altering course, evidently looking for survivors. Although he wrote that he had some misgivings – as he put it, he 'reflected on the morality of the impending situation' – Fürbringer decided to attack the rescuer when she was picking up the last, the fifth, of *Clan Davidson*'s lifeboats. At 900 metres, *UC.17*'s single torpedo hit home.[234] After waiting for fifteen minutes, *UC.17* surfaced and finished her off with fire from the 8.8cm deck gun. After five hours in their lifeboats, her master, Captain Cowrie, and his crew were picked up by the *Crown of Aragon*. That's where their luck ended; she was then also torpedoed. The unlucky crew was picked up again by the destroyer HMS *Lyra* and taken to Plymouth. More than a dozen of her crew had perished.

An American destroyer was seen bearing down fast 'with a westward heading'. She headed to the spot where *UC.17* had sunk the second ship and dropped a single depth charge. Although 'it exploded very close with a great blast', no more were dropped. *UC.17* escaped and later that same night would claim a four-master, the *Monarque*. *UC.17* survived the war with an impressive record of ninety-six ships sunk – by mine or torpedo (as a Type-*UC II* she had both) – in twenty-one patrols.

**Kapitänleutnant Werner Fürbringer (1888–1982)**

In his time, Fürbringer, better known as Fipps to his friends, commanded six separate U-boats: the *UB.2*, *UB.39*, *UC.70*, *UC.17*, *UB.58* and *UB.110*. From April 1915 until July 1918, he was based at Brügge with a unit which, by the war's end, had suffered an 83 per cent loss rate. Luckily, he'd been in hospital when *UB.58* was sunk.

*UB.110* was bombed by an American plane piloted by Ensign J.J. Schieffelin. The attack only damaged her rudders, but three hours later she was successfully depth-charged and brought to the surface, where the destroyer *Garry* successfully rammed her. Thirteen of her crew were picked up: 'Some of *Garry*'s stokers came on deck with large lumps of coal, throwing them at the men in the water.' Fürbringer said that 'stokers fired revolvers at them'.[235] Twenty-three crew members died. *Garry*'s commander, Lightholler, was awarded a DSC, despite the behaviour of his men. In his memoirs, he wrote that 'it was simply amazing that they should have had the infernal audacity to offer surrender, in view of their ferocious and pitiless attacks on our merchant ships'.[236]

Fürbringer rejoined the navy after the war, entering the Kriegsmarine in 1933. As a Korvettenkapitän, he was sent to the Kiel-Wik, as the senior instructor. Since Germany was not technically allowed submarines, the school was officially called the Anti-Submarine School. On the outbreak of the Second World War, he became the Senior Planning Officer for U-Boats at the OKM (Oberkommando der Marine) and was Assistant to Admiral Erich Raeder's Chief of Staff, Admiral Schniewind.

Konteradmiral (Rear Admiral) Fürbringer retired in 1943, aged 55.

Death at sea came in many forms: aboard ship, by drowning, starvation, dehydration or worse. One appalling episode was documented on 15 July 1917 when the 2,908-ton steamer *Mariston* was torpedoed and sunk by *U.45* 82 miles west of the Fastnet Rock. Eighteen men managed to get off the ship and struggled in the water. 'One by one', however, sharks caught and dragged their victims under the waves, and 'even the submarine commander was so appalled that he dived to escape the sight'.[237] The sinking was reported in *The Times* under the headline 'Torpedoed Crew Devoured by Sharks', stating this was 'another instance of the barbarity of German submarine commanders'. Only one man survived.

### *UC-71* and *Dunraven*: The Duel

Gordon Campbell now had command of the *Dunraven*, a slightly larger Q-ship than *Pargust*. This vessel was equipped with an armoured bridge and even carried the old dummy 12pdr salvaged from *Pargust*. Many of his old crew came with him, although Ronald Stuart had taken command of his own Q-ship.

*Dunraven* was a formidably armed ship: she had six deck guns and two torpedo tubes. Perforated pipes ran along the deck to give the impression, when steam was pumped through them, that the ship was badly damaged. A washing line camouflaged one of the guns, and on deck, four collapsible railway trucks – the type commonly used in the Middle East – completed her disguise.

Once under fire, the Q-ship often did what it could to confuse enemy firing. On *Pargust*, for example, there were

> containers scattered around the ship which were electrically operated from the control tower. These would be activated to cause a miniature

> explosion, showering fire, sparks and smoke all over the show. If the submarine sent a shell over the ship, its crew would be confused into thinking they had scored a hit. Being low in the water, they wouldn't be able to spot an 'over' if it was in line with the ship.[238]

Many times, Q-ships were specially adapted to withstand heavy fire. *Q.7, Penshurst,* was a case in point; 'her three holds were fitted with wood and caulked so that they could float if torpedoed and she had a deep gun-whale which concealed the movements of her crew'. In another unrelated incident, a ship carrying rice from India 'floated for hours after being hit by a torpedo' as the rice, once wet, expanded and plugged the leaks.[239] Never were more than three crew members allowed on deck at the same time 'in daylight hours'.[240]

On 8 August 1917, *UC.71* was spotted in the Bay of Biscay, 130 miles west of Ushant. Campbell had been alerted to her whereabouts and given some very good intelligence that the U-boat's commander, Leutnant Reinhold Saltzwedel – the 'fair-haired boy of the Flanders base' – preferred to sink his targets with long-range gunnery fire.[241] *UC.71* had barely been in service a year. Her first commander, Hans Valentiner, had launched her the previous November, as was the tradition, 'with three cheers for the kaiser and the Reich'.[242]

As predicted, *UC.71* opened fire at 5,000 yards. Still flying a 'red duster', Campbell concentrated on drawing his victim closer, deliberately 'shorting' his fire and pretending that his ship had engine trouble. Tempting decoy signals were sent out '*en clair*' by Campbell ('Submarine chasing and shelling me', followed by 'Submarine overtaking me, help, come quickly', finally sending position coordinates and saying that he was abandoning ship). The ship stopped, blowing off steam through a specially installed vent, making it look like the boilers had been put out of action. Campbell then lowered the 'panic party'. While her gun crews anxiously waited, *Dunraven* continued to take a heavy amount of punishment.

At the precise moment Campbell was going to order 'Open fire!', the U-boat 'drifted into the cloud of smoke wafted off to leeward from [*Dunraven*'s] burning deck'.[243] Further shelling detonated one of *Dunraven*'s magazines, seriously injuring some of the hidden gunners. By now, Saltzwedel had guessed *Dunraven*'s identity, submerged and fired a torpedo as he dived. Just after 1320hrs, there was an explosion abaft the engine room.

Even as boats were being lowered, Campbell's 'core' fighting crew remained at their posts. *Dunraven* now launched her own torpedoes; both missed, even if the Germans 'were oblivious to their narrow escape'.[244] For the most part, the sub's shooting was bad, so bad in fact that Campbell had to simulate hits by letting off steam. Finally, however, the German gunners got the range. One after the other, three shots hit the poop deck, detonating one of the depth charges and badly injuring two seamen and a 32-year-old lieutenant, Charles Bonner RNR. He later reported to Campbell on the bridge, in a classic apologetic understatement: 'I am sorry, sir, for leaving my gun without orders. I think I must have been blown up.'[245]

One of the boats which picked up *Dunraven*'s signals (around 1145hrs) was Vincent Astor's yacht, the *Noma*. She approached the sub from behind her periscope and got close enough to roll two Sperry mines over the side. They didn't explode, but they did give away the U-boat's position. Two other Royal Navy ships now joined in: HMS *Attack* and *Christopher*. Around 1800hrs, *Dunraven*'s wounded were brought aboard *Noma*: one was a gunner, Alexander Morrison, who wasn't expected to live.

Despite all the attention, *UC.71* got away. *Dunraven* was put under tow, but went down on 10 August after her crew were taken off by HMS *Christopher*. Her captain, Frederick Peters, went on to win a Victoria Cross in the Second World War.[246] Forty-one of *Dunraven*'s crew members were awarded decorations, many posthumously, and fourteen were 'MID' (Mentioned in Despatches). Sims wrote Campbell a glowing commendation: 'I know nothing finer in naval history than the conduct of the after-gun crew.'[247] As was the practice, Lieutenant Bonner was elected by the crew for a VC and was surprised when he was summoned. No official announcement had been gazetted. That night, he was taken to dine with the King at York Cottage, Sandringham. Campbell dedicated his 1938 book, *Abandon Ship*, 'to my old friend and shipmate, Captain Charles George Bonner, VC, the bravest man I ever met'.[248]

Saltzwedel would be killed later that year, in December, when his new submarine, *UB.81*, hit a mine while attempting to pass through the Channel barrage. Hector Bywater, the Anglo-American journalist, described the loss of a large Flanders submarine, possibly *UB.81*:

> [T]his submarine was off her course and about to cross a newly laid German mine field when in the darkness she mistook the mine layer's warning signal for the challenge of a patrol and dived into the field. The explosions which followed were observed by patrols, and the mines were swept up … The submarine's ballast tanks aft had been destroyed by the mine, and water began to pour in through the stern. The electric motors continued to function, but the after tanks could not, of course, be blown, and her stern sank to the bottom in 15 fathoms. The after bulkhead began to leak, and the engine-room soon filled with water. The gauges showed the bows to be out of water to a height of about 12 feet, with the boat lying at an angle of 60 degrees. One torpedo was then lowered from its tube and the sea cap opened; seven men climbed out, but the cold was so bitter and the strain of hanging on so great that

> after sending up distress rockets five of them went back down and joined those below who were breathing oxygen from the flasks in order [not] to lose consciousness … two survivors were picked up.[249]

**The Death of William Sanders**

On 13 August, William Sanders, the man who had thought he'd sunk *U.93* the previous May, was off the Irish coast again with a hidden D-class submarine in tow. He had turned down the command of a different ship in favour of remaining with *Prize*, now repaired and seaworthy again. *UB.48*, en route to the Mediterranean, came across her and is thought to have recognised the *Prize* for what she was. Warnings had probably been sent out from *U.93*'s surviving crew. *Prize* had been in an earlier encounter in June which suggested that her identity was known. In that fight, Sanders was wounded and remained conscious only long enough to give the order to fire on the attacking submarine. That submarine escaped.

On patrol on 13 August, *UB.48* was spotted by *Prize* as she slipped below the surface. A number of shots were exchanged and damage was sustained by both vessels. *UB.48*'s commander, Oberleutnant zur See Wolfgang Steinbauer, resurfaced after dark and then, in a fluke, spotted *Prize* again. It was 0300hrs. At a distance of 1,000 yards, he tried a shot. Not surprisingly, he missed. He correctly concluded that *Prize* wasn't under sail but was using her engine. A new firing solution was calculated and when Steinbauer's second torpedo hit her magazine, the U-boat 'utterly expunged the three-masted schooner from the face of the waters', leaving no survivors.[250]

Sanders never saw the gazetting which announced his Victoria Cross on 14 September. The first man to hold the newly named position of Governor-General of New Zealand, the Earl of Liverpool, presented his son's VC to his father, Ted, in June 1918. Before his successor, John Jellicoe, took over the Governor-Generalship, he conducted a tour of the Empire on HMS *New Zealand*. When his ship arrived in Auckland, he asked the mayor to arrange a meeting with Ted Sanders and was taken to see him at his boot shop. His visit 'gladdened the old man's heart with his glowing admiration of his son's bravery'. Jellicoe gave Ted some watercolours of *Prize* and later unveiled a memorial in Takapuna, where Sanders had grown up.

While there, my grandmother, Gwen, announced that she had lost her gold net purse. It was found that evening by the son of a local grocer, and Jellicoe was informed. His wife was rather 'shocked to hear that the boy wanted a favour for finding the purse'. When Jellicoe found out that what the boy really wanted was to come aboard his battle-cruiser, the admiral's cutter was sent to Takapuna's Bayswater Quay to collect him. After being met as he boarded the ship and being taken around by the admiral, he was given a small 'many bladed' pocketknife as a memento. Today, there is a sailing cup named by Jellicoe in Sanders's honour (the admiral competed in a small boat which he called *Iron Duke*), as well as streets named for Sanders and Jellicoe in Takapuna. I hope the story behind the names has not faded from today's memory.

### Changes in the Submarine War Strategy

In September 1917, the Germans again changed strategy. With little sign of a British capitulation, Holtzendorff's famous prediction that they would not last more than six months was starting to look hollow. In fact, quite the opposite: so far as the submarine war was concerned, a steady, although undramatic drop had been taking place in the tonnage war. German losses, on the other hand, were mounting:

> The morale of the crews was beginning to show signs of deterioration – leave was overstayed, and sickness feigned. Faults arising from inexperience had to be overlooked … Shorter and shorter became the periods of refit and overhaul.[251]

In his new role as the BdU (Befehlshaber der U-boote), Andreas Michelsen took the decision to allow the larger U-boats to risk running the Dover Barrage. His orders were designed to get higher results in a shorter time, to devote more time to combat rather than towards transit.

The German strategists 'proved adept at locating chinks in the Allies' new armour'.[252] Thwarted by the new protection afforded inbound convoys, they switched their targeting with more success to the unescorted returning, outbound convoys.

Another change of tactics saw increased submarine attacks closer to shore. In the second half of 1917, the number of ships attacked 'within 10 nautical miles of the shore' tripled to 58 per cent of cases, whereas in July it had only been 20 per cent.[253] Operating inshore, however, increased the chance of being spotted from the air. In shallower waters, they were more visible too. Submarines operating from the Bight had a recognition marking ('a white ring, about 12inches broad and about 4 feet in diameter') fitted forward on the deck. The decks of most North Sea and Atlantic submarines were black; the Mediterranean submarines sometimes dark blue.[254]

### The Theatre of U-boat Operations Widens

It was evident that oceans were being cleared of targets: between October and December 1917, 'just 39 of the 219 Atlantic convoys that sailed were even sighted by submarines'.[255] As a consequence, the decision was taken to explore the Bay of Biscay, the eastern Channel and further into the North Sea.

The Germans wrongly equated lack of sightings to the absence of ships. John Terraine noted that 'they [the Germans] did not understand' the true situation:

> So far from being emptied, the zones to the west and south-west of the Scillies and to the south-west of the Fastnet were more crowded with traffic than they had been in the days when [the U-boats'] devastations were most easily executed … What was to tell them that through the very zone they were abandoning as no longer fruitful, the indispensable British merchant fleet with all its vital cargoes was passing unobserved and in increasing numbers?[256]

Although Hans Rose's *U.53* reached American waters the previous summer, the converted U-kreuzer *Deutschland*, now renamed *U.155*,[257] returned to Germany on 2 September after a long, 10,220-mile voyage, during which 'only one hostile enemy war vessel' was seen by Karl Meusel and his crew.[258] She had gone north to Norway, rounded Scotland, headed down to the Azores and shelled Ponta Delgada on 4 July 1917.

The day after her return, one of her sister submarines, *U.151*, left for an equally extended cruise which would cover 12,000 miles down through the Azores, during which she destroyed thirteen vessels, totalling 30,000 tons. One of her officers, Leutnant Körner, summed up the feeling of pride amongst the crew at the significance of what they were doing:

> We had shown a skeptical world that even the wide expanse of the Atlantic was not enough to keep us from a super-raid to the coast of far-off America. Surely this is a warning of what later wars may bring … America's isolation is now a thing of the past.[259]

One of the ships *U.151* commander Waldemar Kophamel sunk was the 5,040-ton Italian freighter *Caprera*, which turned out to have been carrying 1,000 tons of explosives. Her crew put up a 'spirited defence' and only abandoned their ship when the ammunition cargo was hit.[260] *U.151*'s commander was thankful that he hadn't been too close:

> A shell hit the steamer squarely amidships [and] I thought the end of the world had come. Where the steamer had been was now a vast billowing cloud of smoke. The sky darkened and the air became thick and grey … the ship had been blown to atoms.[261]

When *U.28* destroyed British ammunition ship *Olive Branch* on 2 September, the outcome was very different; she exploded with such force that Schmidt's boat was sunk. A truck was sent hurtling skyward and came crashing down on to the sub's deck, mortally wounding her. None of the crew were pulled aboard the lifeboats by the surviving merchant seamen. Although they had only suffered one death in the sinking, the German sailors were left to die of exposure in the freezing seas.

The day after *U.155* arrived back in Germany on 4 September, Waldemar Kophamel took *U.151* out through the Baltic to the Kattegat and then into the Atlantic, using the northern route. He was joined by Karl Meusel, now commanding *U.155*, and Gansser in *U.156*. On 3 December, the three shelled Madeira's Funchal harbour.[262] *U.151* returned to base after sinking several more ships, including two from Brazil, as did Meusel after sinking 40,000 tons. After Konrad Gansser had cut the five telegraph cables off the Azores, *U.156* sank a British merchantman, *Britannia*, and a Portuguese vessel, *Briziela*.

Salgado points out that the statistics for the Atlantic convoy system as a whole look good for the British. Looking at the years 1917 and 1918, of the convoyed ships sailing to Britain across the Atlantic from South America (1,644 ships in 155 convoys) and from Mediterranean ports (2,076 ships in 142 convoys), only 0.7 per cent and 1.1 per cent of ships, respectively, were sunk while in convoy. However, on the Portuguese Atlantic routes, where the combined escorted and unescorted sinkings reached 5 per cent, the U-boat was a new menace.

A concerted effort was made in minelaying, although the results only yielded eight merchantmen in September. Seven U-boats were sunk in October, less than the September high but still a significant number.[263]

### The Q-ship *Stonecrop*

On 17 September, another Q-ship, *Stonecrop*, was attacked by a submarine which shelled her from 10,000 yards.[264] Schwieger on *U.88* used the same tactics that Saltzwedel had used with *UC.71* against the *Dunraven*. As soon as *U.88*'s 4.1in guns opened fire, *Stonecrop*'s commander, Maurice Blackwood, organised as much visible chaos as he could. Crew members ran up and down her decks, while from the radio room a message was sent out in clear: 'I am being shelled by a submarine. Hurry up, or I shall have to abandon ship.'[265] Two of the 'panic party' that took to the boats were dressed in naval uniforms, as they were part of her gun crew. It looked as if no professional naval crew remained.

Even though *U.88*'s gunners had not scored any hits, smoke canisters were lit to give the impression that the ship was in trouble. The submarine was lured in, closer and closer. Around 300 yards off her port beam, Blackwood hesitated, as 'it was too close for the torpedo to pick up its depth'.[266] He waited a little longer.

> I lit the smoke apparatus, the effect of which was particularly good: the phosphorous leaked out of the container and caught fire outside [of] it on the deck. The port side of the after-deck house was a mass of flame and being before the wind, the whole ship was enveloped in smoke.[267]

Finally, he ordered 'Open fire!'. At 600 yards abaft her starboard beam, the Q-ship gunners quickly zeroed in:

> The fourth shot hit the base of the conning tower, causing a large explosion and splitting [it] in two. The fifth shot got her just above the waterline under the foremost gun, the sixth struck between that gun and the conning-tower, the seventh thirty feet from the end of the hull, the eighth got her just at the angle of the conning-tower and the deck, the ninth and tenth shells came whizzing onto the waterline between the after gun and the conning-tower, whilst the eleventh hit the deck just abaft the conning-tower and [tore] it up.[268]

After the last hit, *U.88* looked done for; her stern sank at 45 degrees, but then rose again. It was no good, however. Nobody could get out as the conning-tower's hatch was jammed closed.

*Stonecrop*'s victory, however, was short-lived, as the very next day she was sunk by torpedo. Three officers and twenty-eight men were killed in the explosions; more would die at sea. Blackwood's lifeboat was spotted two days later, but the other boat, with Lieutenant Smiles, two other officers and twenty men, had drifted apart during the night. Six days after *Stonecrop* went down, thirteen crew had died. The youngest was a 16-year-old, John Watson, from Belfast.

September finally gave the British some good news, with a drop in the average tonnage of the ships torpedoed, from 3,500 to 2,500. While only three U-boats were sunk during August, eleven – some sources say as many as thirteen – were sunk in September. Indeed, September 1917 was the month in which the highest number of U-boats were sunk in the entire war.[269]

### The Surface Threat to Convoys

Jellicoe and Sims shared a common fear. Sims, with a 'foresight [that] was both remarkable and timely', raised the prospect of a surface threat to convoys from capital ships.[270] A decision to take specific offensive action was taken.

The Admiralty had planned to ambush U-boats with a large force of twenty-four trawlers, forty-two drifters, twenty-one destroyers, a flotilla leader and four submarines. Operations commenced on 1 October 1917. It was known that submarines were operating there, as the destroyer HMS *Tancred* was attacked on 9 October and sightings were made by some other destroyers. Contemporary German sources suggested that three U-boats – *U.50, U.66* and *U.106* – were all present, but later discoveries cast doubt on that.[271] Three times, however, bad weather drove the destroyers back, while crashing sounds in the windswept ocean made effective hydrophone use almost impossible. The ambush ended in abject failure.

Admiralty operations supporting the Scandinavian convoys cast an even deeper shadow.[272] After intelligence from U-boats reported a Bergen coal convoy leaving for Lerwick, Scheer chose two fast cruisers, SMS *Bremse* and *Brummer*, to make the 500-mile crossing to head north of Bergen. Both were 3,800-ton, 34-knot ships. Intelligence had also reached OB40 that something was being planned, and Beatty sent out a substantial force of forty-two ships in anticipation: three cruisers, twenty-seven light cruisers and twelve destroyers. Because Scheer had chosen fast minelayers, 'nobody connected them with any possible sortie'. Beatty, however, wasn't informed.[273]

On 15 October, an eastbound convoy of twelve merchant ships, carrying coal, left Lerwick, escorted by two destroyers, HMS *Mary Rose* and *Strongbow*, along with two armed trawlers, the *P. Fannon* and *Elise*.[274] Once at sea, Lieutenant Commander Edward Brooke took *Strongbow* up ahead to RV with the homeward-bound convoy assembling off Bergen.

Two days later, on 17 October, the two German cruisers were sighted by *Strongbow* at 0600hrs but weren't recognised for what they were. The mast configuration made them look like British C-class cruisers. *Strongbow* made three signal challenges, the last of which the Germans answered in broken Morse – then with shellfire. *Bremse* and *Brummer* opened up at 3,000yds. After suffering several hits, Brooke ordered 'Abandon ship!' and *Strongbow* sank around 0930hrs. Forty-four of her crew were rescued, but she lost half her ship's complement, including four officers.[275] She had not even been able to transmit a warning signal.

The distant engagement could be heard from the *Mary Rose.* The second escort was also badly hit in her engine room although some, notably her torpedo crew, fought on. Lieutenant Commander Charles Leonard Fox, Sub-Lieutenant Marsh RNVR and around seventy crew were killed. Only one of the escorting armed trawlers, *Elise*, bravely joined the fray, returning what fire she could with her meagre armament. The two German cruisers now picked off nine ships, one by one, with more than 250 lives lost. After the action, *Bremse* and *Brummer* returned home unhindered.[276]

The next attack on a Scandinavian convoy took place on 11 and 12 December, when the Germans employed a full flotilla of new destroyers, half of which were sent to harry the convoy assembly point, the other half up to Bergen to wait. The Allies received no prior knowledge: 'the Germans were learning the value of radio silence'.[277] When they pounced, two British destroyers (HMS *Pellow* and *Partridge*) were escorting six ships, only one of which was British-flagged. As the convoy approached the Norwegian coast, the two destroyers went ahead in heavy seas gusting Force 6–7. Ships were spotted to the north and, after some delay, a challenge issued. The wrong reply came back. *Partridge*, put out of action with early hits on her engine room, was then torpedoed twice and sank half an hour later. *Pellow* ran for home (or, as Winton more forgivingly described it, escaped as the Germans 'turned away').[278] It was, all in all, an inglorious episode. All six merchantmen and four trawlers were sunk. Ships from the 3rd LCS sent by Beatty from Scapa Flow failed to intercept the Germans, who took the Baltic route home via the Skagerrak.

### The USN Draws its First Blood ...

On 17 November, a US-bound convoy from Queenstown left for the States, escorted by six destroyers, a Q-ship and a sloop. At 1615hrs, lookouts from the USS *Fanning* spotted a periscope close to the 5,730-ton liner *Welshman*. A depth charge was dropped, then the *Nicholson* rushed forward and dropped another.

For several minutes nothing happened, then suddenly the *U.58*'s stern broke the surface, whereupon she was immediately struck by 4in gunfire. *Nicholson* came over to help pick up German survivors, but was unable to stop them scuttling their boat. The entire crew had come up on deck, but then two went back in to open the sea cocks. It later emerged that her electric motors had been damaged and her helm wasn't responsive. *U.58* sunk in 278ft of water and her commander, Kapitänleutnant Gustav Amsberger, felt he had no choice other than surrendering with the thirty-eight remaining crew. Proudly, an ensign off the *Nicholson* concluded:

> To the *Fanning* went the credit and distinction of being the first American ship ... to get a submarine and take any prisoners at all.[279]

While the sinking of the *U.58* was 'the only submarine sunk by United States naval forces unaided', US forces 'contributed indirectly to the sinking of three others'.[280] The boarding of *U.58* would be a forerunner of *U.505*'s capture in the next war.[281]

### ... and Suffers its First Casualties

The same day that the Scandinavian convoy described above left Lerwick, the first American ship, USS *Cassin*, was damaged. She had sighted Victor Dieckmann's surfaced *U.61* and had closed to engage. As *Cassin* overran the position of sighting, a torpedo was spotted at 1330hrs. As luck would have it, the torpedo 'porpoised' twice, finally shooting out of the water to strike the destroyer 'abaft the propellor struts and above the waterline'.[282] Too late, Gunner's Mate FC Osmond Ingram tried to release the ship's depth charges. He was killed and five others injured in the explosion. *U.61* was eventually driven off by fire from *Cassin*'s 4in guns, but the ship was trapped in an endless circle with her propellor gone and would be out of service until July 1918. She had lost 20ft of her stern section.

The very next day, sixty-seven US servicemen were killed when the troop transport *Antilles* was torpedoed west of the Bay of Biscay; 'had [she] been sailing east loaded with troops', the consequences would have been catastrophic.[283]

With November came a gradual reduction in losses on all the key metrics – ships, tonnage and loss of life. Nine U-boats were sunk, just one short of September's total.[284] And 'by November, the [ship] sinkings amounted to only 30% of their total in April', which was the single highest month for the entire war.[285]

## The First American Destroyer U-boat Victim

On 6 December 1917, the USS *Jacob Jones* (DD-61) was successfully torpedoed by *U.53*. The ship, the fifth of the Tucker class, an improved version of the Cassin class, had already experienced a chequered start, having failed her sea trials and nearly being sent back to the yards for a rebuild. But once Division 7 arrived in Queenstown, she had shown her worth: she 'rescued more stranded sailors than any other American warship', rescuing 305 survivors of the 19,777-ton British liner RMS *Orama* as well as survivors from some of Rose's sinkings off Nantucket.[286] The *Jacob Jones* had left Queenstown a week before, on 29 November, to bring back two convoys.

Off Brest on her return journey, she had been zigzagging but was spotted by Rose in *U.53* from 3 miles at 1530hrs. *U.53* quickly closed to around 1,000 metres and fired a torpedo. It hit her starboard side, 3ft below the water line, and left her drifting with no engine and ruptured fuel lines. Her mainmast, radio antenna and starboard side torpedo tube were all destroyed, and electrical power was lost.

As the *Jacob Jones* started going down, stern first, one of the officers, Lieutenant Richards, went aft to disarm her depth charges.[287] However, he couldn't reach the switches, which were blocked and already submerged. Shots were fired off, hoping to attract attention from other boats. Eight minutes after being hit, the *Jacob Jones* went down. Two officers and sixty men were lost in the original explosion, the follow-up explosion from the primed depth charges and from hypothermia in the cold winter waters. The fact that forty-six survived of her 110-man complement was due to the extraordinary heroism shown by all. In the cold water, men struggled for their lives, helped by a young lieutenant, Stanton Kalk, who died of exposure later that night after he'd given up his place on one dangerously overloaded boat. The USN named a Benson-class destroyer, DD-611, in his memory.[288]

Two badly injured sailors, Seaman Second Class Albert De Mello and Ship's Cook Second Class Petty Officer John Francis Murphy, were taken aboard *U.53* when she surfaced. They would remain prisoners until the Armistice. When they left his custody, Rose was touched by their words:

> I was deeply moved myself. I liked these Americans, the earnest, honest Murphy and the grateful, sprightly Albert, and hated to see them led away to the terrible monotony of their prison. I was glad, as a last service, to be able to send a letter to de Mello's mother.[289]

Rose had been the first German submarine commander to sink shipping off America's coastline and was now, a year later, the first submariner to sink a US destroyer. Both prisoners heard his call for help that he transmitted giving his position. However, no Allied warships came. The first six *Jacob Jones* crew members rescued were brought aboard a British merchantman, the SS *Catalina*. It was only at daybreak the following morning that the main group of survivors was spotted by another British ship, the sloop *Camellia*. The group with David Worth Bagley, the captain of the *Jacob Jones*, had started rowing towards the Scilly Isles. Bagley, his Navigation Officer, Lieutenant Scott, and six 'of the strongest men' weren't picked up until almost twenty hours after going into the freezing water. In an extraordinary twist, Captain Bagley was not only the brother-in-law of Josephus Daniels, the US Secretary of State for the Navy, but he had also personally met Rose the year before in Newport. He'd been lucky enough to have been invited aboard *U.53*.

# 6

# Strategic Command, Part 2: The Convoy Controversy

The intimate connection between England's fortunes and the sea have been recognised for centuries. Sir Walter Raleigh even commented: 'There are two ways in which England may be afflicted. The one by invasion … the other by impeachment of our Trades.' Trade was, and remains, Britain's lifeblood. For protection, the British turn to their Navy. Centuries after Raleigh, the naval thinker and strategist, Sir Julian Corbett, echoed his sentiments, saying that 'trade protection and security from invasion were dependent on sea power'.

## Convoy in British Maritime History

For centuries, the convoy offered protection to large groups of ships transporting goods across the world's seas. It was used by the Spanish transporting gold and silver from the Americas and by the British to export their most important national product – wool – and to import wine. The returning Bordeaux wine convoys would generally sail in January and February and consist of between 200 and 300 ships. Large, mostly seasonal, wool convoys were regularly organised. Their ships would sail under the command of the Wafter of the Wool, a forerunner of a convoy commodore.

The British also convoyed troops across the Channel to fight the French. In 1346, Edward III took 32,000 troops in 1,600 ships; in 1413, before Agincourt, Henry V took the same number over from Southampton to Le Havre, and two years later even more over to Harfleur in preparation for his march on Paris. The first use of a convoy in the First World War would be to transport troops from Britain's far-flung Empire.

The Spanish originally brought silver and gold back to Europe over what they had imagined to be safe routes, ones on which Spanish men o'war roamed. From 1526, sailing alone was forbidden and twenty years later there existed a well-established system of convoy known as the *Flota*, the treasure fleets. They 'usually sailed twice a year and consisted of some thirty or forty merchant ships with a dozen or so escorting warships'.[1]

'Many of the most famous naval engagements ... were convoy actions'[2]: the Spanish Armada in 1588, in September 1652 against the Dutch in the Battle of the Kentish Knock, and the 'Glorious First of June' in 1794. The Armada was a massive affair, whose role was to protect the sizeable army that Philip II wanted to land: 55,000 infantry, 1,200 cavalry and 4,000 sappers. Admiral Howe might have been lauded by the British as the victor of the 'Glorious First of June', but it should be remembered that the French rear admiral, Villaret de Joyeuse, still managed to get the Chesapeake grain convoy safely back to France: 'That was what mattered most.'[3] The 1793 harvest had failed and France was facing starvation. Despite losing seven ships of the line, the French 'achieved a major victory'.[4]

Admirals and sailors of this period understood the importance of the merchantman. In the eyes of the great naval leaders – Howe, St Vincent, Nelson – the 'protection of Britain's overseas trade was an integral part of the naval offensive against France and her allies and satellites'.[5] Indeed, Nelson wrote: 'I consider the protection of trade the essential service that can be performed.'

So important was the convoy that by the eighteenth century, the insurance industry established different rates based on whether goods were convoyed or not. Lower insurance rates reflected the increased likelihood of goods arriving safely at their intended destination. Sometimes, ships would try to benefit from lower convoy rates and then 'run' ahead, leaving others behind to be the first to land their goods. Offenders would face stiff penalties.

The word 'convoy' is now used without any real understanding of what it represented at the time, with the surface threat being dealt with at distance. In the eighteenth century, a group of ships being convoyed would be left while its protecting escorts would sprint off to hunt an enemy often lurking on, or just over, the horizon.

Britain continued to actively support regular convoys to the far-flung reaches of its empire and maintained such operations with Hong Kong until 1815. Almost fifty years later, troops used in the Crimea campaign were taken by escorted convoy.

## The Context of Convoy in 1917

Why, when war finally came in 1914, did the British not confidently fall back on what had worked so well in the past? Something seen by many as a 'tried and tested' system? Had the nature of the war at sea so fundamentally changed that only an almost unrecognisably new response was valid? Was conveying troops on liners so different to protecting cargoes in merchant ships?

Throughout history, so-called 'tried and tested' methods have often failed. When pitted against entirely new, mostly unseen weapons, naval tactics like convoy had to evolve. It had, in fact, been proposed several times before Jellicoe moved over to the Admiralty. He himself had done so while still the Grand Fleet's Commander-in-Chief, 'but it was pointed out to [him] that the number of cruisers available for escort work was entirely insufficient'.[6] Coming to the Admiralty in December 1916, he knew that cruisers would not be the only issue: small, fast, shallow-draught vessels were also needed. He knew the launch of unrestricted submarine warfare was imminent. The attacks would be unseen – by torpedo rather than by shelling from a deck-mounted gun.

What was under discussion in 1917 'differed materially' from the earlier age of sail: convoys in the age of sail were almost unrecognisable to convoys in 1917 or what they became in the Second World War. The early convoys had not been required to sail in a particular formation, nor did they have to manoeuvre in such a confined sea space.[7] The timing and routes taken by major convoys were strongly dictated by the weather and the trade winds. Ships would be amassed for convoy to take advantage of the optimum sailing conditions. Moving at a desultory 3–5 knots, time wasn't *that* important for these early convoys. Sims concluded that 'these circumstances make the modern Convoy quite a different affair from the happy-go-lucky procedures of the Napoleonic era'.[8]

Running in convoy already demanded disciplined station-keeping; convoys in 1917 needed to occupy as small an ocean footprint as possible to lessen the strain on escort requirements and to allow escorting destroyers to react speedily to torpedo attack.

Merchantmen always sought the shortest routes: points of concentration, so-called 'choke points', were a natural outcome. These were essentially heavily trafficked sea lanes or routes. Steam gave a ship's captain more flexibility on the choice of route and, therefore, timing. Perhaps it was because this involved the transition from following the winds to plotting the shortest distance that the Royal Navy 'lost sight of the vital truth that it was not the sea-lanes which needed to be guarded but the *ships* which used them'.[9]

The great strength of convoys was not always in evading submarines or holding them off. Indeed, the irony of the 'defensive' convoy was that it was more effective in *finding* submarines; it acted in the same way a magnet does. Like a siren, the richness of a convoy target lured a submarine to it rather than relying on 'offensive' anti-submarine patrols to find the needle in the haystack. In the past, the convoy escort would give chase to enemy ships seen in the distance. Now, their best chance lay in enticing those enemy ships to close with their prey.

As the twentieth century dawned, most naval thinking – and much misunderstanding – revolved around Mahan's concept of the decisive battle. The attack on – and therefore the protection of – trade was seen as secondary, a distraction that would drain resources from the main battle fleet, whose purpose had less to do with commerce protection than annihilation of an adversary fleet. However, 'the problem in real life was that opposing fleets seldom were equal in size, or eagerness to seek out the enemy'.[10]

If there was a threat to commerce, the British thought that it would most likely be a surface threat from enemy cruisers. This was important both at the end of the war against the Scandinavian trade and at the start as part of the initial German naval strategy of emptying the North Sea of British capital ships. The surface threat in the Atlantic and further afield was short-lived; the real threat was the unseen one against which no sure defence had yet been found:

> Convoy sailing for the protection of merchant ships against torpedo attack by submarine was quite a different matter from such a system as a preventative against attack by surface vessels and involved far greater difficulties.[11]

As a result, the legal framework for commerce protection, embodied in the 1909 Declaration of London, took little account of the submarine. It was assumed that the rules that applied to surface attack should be equally applicable. Few understood the logic of Jackie Fisher's brutal warnings.

**Key Issues in the Convoy Debate**

When Jellicoe took over at the Admiralty, he stepped into a hornet's nest. The frustrations of many front-line naval officers at the Admiralty's handling of the naval war was running high, and the increasing loss of shipping by German submarine attack was fanning the flames.

The convoy debate became a beacon for the disaffected, a point of division between the new and old guard, between the civilian political leadership and service 'experts'. Many claimed that solutions, like the use of convoys, were obvious, but the new type of trade protection was anything but 'tried and tested'. Few had foreseen a commerce war; fewer still a submarine-led commerce war.

Matthew Seligmann gently, but I feel appropriately, reminded an online conference audience in 2021 that the convoy system 'looks, with hindsight, and from the outside, a very obvious solution', but that 'it wasn't necessarily that straightforward in 1917'.[12] Marder was critical but more forgiving: all he said was that Jellicoe 'had been dangerously slow to appreciate the value of the general Convoy system'.[13] Even if Norman Leslie, from his perspective at the Ministry of Shipping, thought that 'had the Convoy system then been put into force immediately on all routes, as we strongly urged ... there is every ground for saying ... that the losses of the next two months would only have been a fraction of the ships which were sunk before the system was started on a grand scale'.[14]

The convoy system involved a massive streamlining and coordination of resources, not only at sea but also on land. Inevitably, feathers would be ruffled in many quarters, for the convoy 'is a subjugation of private enterprise to state control on a scale that the most enthusiastic and visionary socialist would hardly dare to advocate'.[15] Bacon's description highlighted the scale of the convoy system's technical challenges but fell far short of its enormity:

> [N]o successful convoy system could have been inaugurated unless those in control had *dictatorial powers* [author's italics] over the times of sailing, the cargoes carried, and the constitution of the convoys.[16]

Indeed, attempts to institute convoys in the late nineteenth century, when sail was gradually giving way to steam, were usually opposed by the same shipowners who would most directly benefit from their protection. They hated the idea of the state taking away any advantage such as speed. In grouping ships together, it was 'kowtowing' to the lowest common denominator. According to Lord Sydenham, opposition to the 1879 Royal Commission's findings on convoys was largely due to 'the great steamship owners who resented the slowing down entailed'.[17]

What were the key issues? First and foremost, we have already talked about the tension coming from those naval thinkers still obsessed with the pursuit of a decisive surface engagement, *à la* Mahan. For them, the defence of commerce was a strategic distraction and a potentially dangerous reason for drawing down resources. The perpetual drive for the offensive over the defensive always lurked close behind. In the context of the submarine war, the ideological line was drawn between those who saw value in escorting merchant vessels and those who preferred to use destroyers, smaller craft and sub-chasers to actively hunt out the submarine aggressor.

Secondly, convoys increasingly occupy an ambiguous space between the defensive protection of trade and offensive tactics aimed at bringing the attacker to its prey. Convoys should be as much about reducing shipping losses as their offensive use in escorting warships. 'Naval thought,' wrote Marder, 'was focused too exclusively on battle and too little on the protection of shipping.'[18] Since Trafalgar, Britain's Royal Navy has lived in the shadow of Nelson, maybe because we all too often see him only as a 'fighting admiral'. At Jutland, the call to 'close with the enemy' was equated with a quintessentially Nelsonian spirit, whether or not it made sense with faster ships and longer-ranged guns. In the convoy debate, that spirit was embodied by those who wanted to take the battle to the enemy with sub-hunting patrols. Both Jellicoe and Beatty leaned towards this school of thought. Defending convoys was likened to surrendering the initiative.

Thirdly, once the principle of the escorted convoy was accepted, the resources needed to realise that objective had to be found – at the opportune moment, in adequate quantities, of the most applicable design and in the right place. Before all else, it was critical to be able to understand how many escorts were needed: how many sailings needed to be protected, what the appropriate ratio of escort to convoyed ships was and where to find these resources. In sum, convoys opened a Pandora's Box; dependencies multiplied endlessly.

Fourthly, how would a convoy's organisation affect the neutrals? Belligerents were normally allowed to assemble convoys in neutral harbours, but the privilege could be denied if, as a result, a neutral understood it to increase the danger of enemy forces in their waters. What made this issue so germane was that the arming of merchantmen redefined their legal status. America's changed belligerent status after 6 April 1917 seems to have been a factor for Jellicoe and Duff in the immediate run-up to the adoption of the wider convoy system as it changed how British armed merchantmen would be treated.

Finally, debate continued between those who supported protecting the sea lanes used by merchant ships and others who preferred to protect the ships using those lanes. Oliver and Duff, claimed Roskill, were 'wedded to the system of patrolled lanes'.[19]

Swirling around all these issues lay a veritable swamp of tactical and technical considerations.

## Timing is Everything

Jellicoe was categorical about *his* Admiralty keeping an open mind on convoys. 'This matter [convoy],' Jellicoe wrote, 'was receiving constant consideration at the Admiralty in the early part of 1917, but the objections to it were, *until a later date* [my italics], far too strong to admit of its adoption.'[20] Three pages later, he emphasised that,

> had the system been instituted earlier than was the case [author's note: before the tests and initial implementation had shown it to work], I have no hesitation in stating that the results might well have been disastrous.[21]

Sims agreed: 'I do not see how otherwise it could have been established in any complete or systematic way at such an early date.'[22]

It took time to persuade what would, arguably, become one of Britain's most important naval allies in the war. Initially, the US Navy was strongly against convoys, even if SecNav Daniels and Chief of Naval Operations Benson later tried to appear as early supporters. Although Colonel House reported differently, Jellicoe, while diplomatic, privately wrote to Beatty that he did not hold Benson in high regard:

> You will find Benson very willing to help, but very ignorant of sea warfare. He has never had his flag up afloat and had odd ideas.[23]

Jellicoe was even strongly opposed to any idea of a partial convoy system being implemented, pointing to the heavy losses in the outward-bound trade 'owing to the withdrawal of vessels from patrol duty for convoy work'.[24] It looks like, at this point, Jellicoe's preference remained firmly with hunting patrols.

Why did Jellicoe think he was right? He raised several issues where timing was crucial: as long as America remained neutral, destroyers for effective escort would be scarce; depth charges were in short supply; little or no organisational structure could be based on the American side of the Atlantic; and station-keeping practice prior to an ocean crossing was almost impossible.

Here, Jellicoe's character was completely at odds with that of Beatty, who 'could not tolerate half-measures or delay, and whenever he felt convinced of the right course of action, would ignore official procedure and hammer away at the responsible authority until it was adopted'.[25] Rather indiscreetly, Beatty wrote to his lover, Eugénie Godyfrey-Fausett, the wife of one of his captains, about his relationship with Jellicoe, saying that 'J.J. was always a half-hearted man'.[26] His point of view, expressed forcefully by Beatty in a 'private and personal' letter to Carson, the First Lord of the Admiralty, would have been very close to Lloyd George's. He deplored what he called 'the fetish that exists that an officer with four stripes on his arm must be a better man than he with three'.[27]

### Calculating the Resources Needed

Calculating convoy escort requirements was, Jellicoe concluded, 'not easy to decide', but behind the principal of bringing ships together was the assurance that the distribution of escorting vessels would be optimised. The number depended on many factors, the most important of which was undoubtedly the volume of traffic to be escorted, but also, for any given grouping of ships, the ratio of escorts to escorted ships.

It would depend on how many submarines were assessed to be operating in each area, a convoy's station-keeping proficiency as well as its routing. The latter would determine, amongst other things, the amount of vulnerable time at sea, the hours of daylight and the speed of the escorted ships.

Despite the submarine war being characterised as a 'tonnage war' or a 'war of numbers', the glaring lack of reliable statistics used by, or available to, key decision-makers at the Admiralty and subsequently the War Cabinet was almost criminal. Here, two of Kenneth Dewar's colleagues in the Trade Division, Commander Reginald Henderson and Fleet Paymaster-Commander H.W. Eldon Manisty, are central to the story of the convoys.

Eldon Manisty became the Organising Manager of Convoys on 25 June 1917 when the Convoy Section of the Naval Staff was established. The manager title belied Manisty's pivotal role in convoys while he was in the post (only until 10 September). These were the critical months in which the backbone of the oceanic convoy system was established. Working with the Ministry of Shipping and the Intelligence Division (ID), Manisty was responsible for all convoy routes, schedules and composition, with the help of the ACNS, Duff. Later, in September, the Admiralty became directly responsible for the movements of all British shipping, naval or merchant, the latter under the control of Captain Frederic A. Whitehead of the Mercantile Movements Division. Control of a convoy's movements was taken over by the local area naval commands at Queenstown, Devonport, Portsmouth and Dover once the convoy closed to an effective operating range from shore-based A/S assets.

Reginal Henderson's contribution was also vital. Working with Norman Leslie at the Ministry of Shipping to look at customs tabulations, it was Henderson who reputedly helped solve one of the significant obstacles to the convoys: the lack of available escorts.

His experience with the French coal trade and its success possibly 'set him thinking, … not least about the light it threw upon the question of [convoy] vulnerability'.[28] Sims's American biographer, Elting E. Morison (also his son-in-law), suggested that Henderson came to his conclusions after completing a study that Jellicoe had ordered 'at Sims's insistence'.[29] Sims certainly might have suggested such a study, but 'insistence' sounds exaggeratedly self-important considering he had only just arrived in London. In a footnote, Marder concluded that Morison 'gives the Admiral more credit than he would seem to deserve'.[30] Sims himself never made any post-war statement to specifically support or negate these claims. Marder quotes a letter dated 3 July 1917 in which Sims said that he had been 'devoted to this Convoy system ever since the first week I got here in London', but said that he could find nothing 'to bear this out' in his April correspondence and that 'neither Sims nor the Navy department was thinking beyond the needs of the patrol system'.[31] For his part, Jellicoe said that Sims never brought up the subject of convoys and seems to have been irked by how Sims's role in the convoy debate was documented.

It turned out that the number of weekly sailings compiled by the Customs authorities were grossly misleading: they made multiple counts of the same hull as coastal ships went from port to port, as well as including ships that were used for Channel traffic. What was reported by Customs as 1,800 sailings in a week for cross-Channel traffic was, in fact, only 200 ships. The average daily number of *ocean-going* arrivals totalled twenty ships, and therefore the same number of departures.

Norman Leslie was struck by Henderson's passion: 'When I found out what this extraordinary young man had in mind, I caught fire with enthusiasm at once and worked out my side of it eagerly.'[32] It might be that it was through General Jan Smuts at the War Cabinet that Henderson was introduced to Lloyd George, as Leslie knew him.

Generously, Newbolt put forward the notion that this mistake with the figures had arisen for avoidable, but innocent, reasons:

> *With a view to discouraging the enemy* [author's italics], the figures showing the number of arrivals and departures of ships in the weekly statement published by the Admiralty had been made to include the repeated calls of all coasters and short sea traders of 300 tons and upwards; and by this method the figures had been swollen to about 2,500 sailings a week each way. … the average number of voyages made weekly by British ocean-going ships (1,600 tons gross and upwards) had in time of peace been under 200 each way.[33]

Aiming to confuse the enemy, the Admiralty might thus have ended up confusing itself. This conclusion is disputed by Nicholas Black. He agreed that the figures were 'deliberately misleading' since, by 1916, 'it cannot be true to say that the Admiralty was unaware of the exact numbers of ships crossing the Atlantic'.[34] Black then quotes a study made by Captain Bertram Smith which showed that in early January 1917, the volume of British traffic en route to Europe from American ports was 128, with a further 122 vessels in port. The average monthly sailing was around 304 ships. It was wrong, Black concluded, to 'ascribe the "startling discovery" … to the work of Commander Reginald Henderson, as has often been the case'.[35]

Sadly, neither Henderson nor Manisty received their due. Jellicoe wrote in the introduction to *The Submarine Peril* of the need to make sure that the historical record highlighted their contributions. Of Henderson, he wrote that he 'was in constant conference with shipowners and members of the shipping world and was a valuable asset in working out the Convoy system'.[36] He added that Manisty was 'very largely responsible for striking success achieved by the Convoy system'.[37] His work showed 'quite exceptional skill', which was 'rare praise indeed from one who failed to appreciate at the time the value of the Convoy system', noted one recent review.[38]

Working in the Admiralty Operations Division was Kenneth Dewar, who had been asked to give a weekly appreciation of the submarine war that would be circulated among the War Cabinet. Trying to find a reliable source, he was advised to speak to the Ministry of Shipping.

Dewar's research might have taken place at the same time as, or shortly after, Lloyd George's famous visit to the Admiralty, as he wrote that he 'was able to make a start with statistics in [his] *second* appreciation *at the end* of May' (author's italics).[39]

Dewar's recollection of events smacks of paranoia. He felt persecuted: '[I]t seemed to me that I was being banished as a reprisal for not conforming.'[40] He wrote that the excuse used to shut him down was because he did not respect the rules of the bureaucracy – 'a docket should have been started'.[41] He claimed that his discovery of the real numbers was being deliberately hampered; the mix-up over numbers 'had been started as propaganda for the public'. It was purposefully misleading: '[N]o responsible naval officer can have imagined that the weekly return of the Customs was any criterion of escort requirements … the authorities did not want figures which might prove the possibility of convoying in general.'[42] Dewar's defence bore the distinct whiff of a man with a chip on his shoulder.

Jellicoe apparently ordered Dewar's immediate reassignment to a derelict cruiser lying in Colombo harbour, but Dewar succeeded in changing the sentence. He wrote to a friend of his wife's, Herbert Lewis, who also happened to be a friend of Lloyd George.[43] Dewar's assessment was predictable:

> The forgoing incident helps to explain why no one at the Admiralty dared question the idea that convoy was impracticable. So long as officers are liable to disciplinary reprisals for daring to disagree with their superiors, little reliance can be placed on naval opinion in such cases.[44]

If Dewar's story is true, Jellicoe's name does not come out well. Maybe he just disliked junior officers taking information directly – without his knowledge – to politicians. If so, I would think his position perfectly reasonable. According to Roskill, Cabinet Secretary Hankey got his ideas on convoys from Dewar. Jellicoe protested: 'Personally, I had never heard of their proposals … it was strange that they did not ask to see me nor some other officer in authority.'[45] Jan Breemer echoed Jellicoe's sentiments about Henderson, but not Dewar, when he wrote that the convoy system was merely the result of 'two forgotten Royal Navy Officers'.[46] Whatever the case, the idea that this episode 'ended Jellicoe's "honeymoon" with Lloyd George' is rather far-fetched: Jellicoe had long been at loggerheads with the Prime Minister.[47] Lloyd George's characterisation of the people surrounding the introduction of convoys sometimes borders on the infantile. He constantly talked of the 'high admirals' and alleged that 'these disappointing successes simply irritated the Admiralty into sullen recalcitrance'.[48] He frequently seemed to stand against the 'experts' and their 'blank wall of assertion'.

Whatever the real story was, Lloyd George made the Admiralty look incompetent. It seemed they had little idea about the number of ships they were trying to protect or escort, that they had massively overestimated the need and had possibly done this deliberately.

The infrastructure of the convoy system was enormous; it simply could not be implemented overnight. It rested on top of the enormous bedrock of ASW, which included improved weapons, better intelligence and close cooperation with new allies. Michelsen, for example, cited the size of Gibraltar, whose operation was

> assigned for this service under an American admiral, 314 officers and 4,660 men (American personnel), while the vessels assigned to this base (small cruisers, gunboats, yachts, destroyers etc.) are reported as having escorted more than 562 convoys in one year.[49]

American forces in Gibraltar were under the command of Vice Admiral Albert 'Nibs' Niblack, 'one of only two officers [in] the service who called Sims "Billy"'.[50]

Writing at the start of 1918, Wemyss was certain that 'Convoy has so far proved eminently successful', and in a paper for the Imperial War Cabinet said that 'the principal factor in reducing losses from enemy submarine attack has undoubtedly been the introduction of the Convoy system'.[51]

**Convoy at the Stroke of a Pen?**

Jellicoe was adamant that convoys could not be fully implemented overnight: 'They seemed to think that such a system could be put into operation by giving a simple order, or by a mere stroke of a pen.'[52] It was both a matter of the physical resources needed and how they could be used.

For good reason, Jellicoe argued with Lloyd George about the number of fronts the Royal Navy was being asked to protect. Writing to Carson, Jellicoe complained that it was 'a continual fight to prevent more side-shows being started. He [Lloyd George] is at present mad on one in Palestine, fed from the sea.'[53] Jellicoe then directly challenged the Prime Minister's war strategy, saying that 'reducing our commitments for the supply of various expeditions in Salonika, Egypt, East Africa and Mesopotamia' was the only practicable way to free up the ships needed for convoys.[54] He estimated that 'over 1.5 million tons', some 333 merchant steamers, were allocated to these theatres. Dropping the sideshows, Jellicoe concluded, would 'assist in providing protection for convoys bringing … essentials in the way of food and munitions'.[55] It wasn't only Lloyd George whom he held responsible: he also included 'our allies' mistakes in the past' for this 'much too extended naval front'.[56]

It is important to understand why Jellicoe resisted an accelerated introduction of the convoy system. I think Brayton Harris is only half-right when he writes that 'Jellicoe understood the situation, but not the solution'.[57] Jellicoe's job was to prioritise and best allocate the Navy's limited resources. The most obvious physical resource needed was escort destroyers. However, while Jellicoe argued that Britain did not possess enough, others like Dewar felt that the problem actually was the *allocation* of existing hulls: [I]t was not so much lack of escorts as the more efficient use of those we had.'[58]

So far as Sims was concerned, there seemed to be some contradiction as to where he stood. Morison wrote that he had pushed Jellicoe for a convoy trial, but such a sentiment is misleading. Sims talked of the lack of destroyers as the 'one really serious impediment' to adopting the convoy system, saying that 'the number of destroyers available was insufficient'.[59] Would Jellicoe have succeeded in getting immediate US naval resources had he downplayed either the destroyer shortage or the possibility of Britain's defeat? It is doubtful. Particularly after Rose's *U.53*'s Newport visit, there was strong opposition in some US naval circles to denuding their own defences by sending American destroyers over the Atlantic to help the Europeans.

Jellicoe was succinct in *The Crisis of Naval War*: 'Any system of Convoy was at this time out of the question, as neither the cruisers to marshal the convoy to the submarine area, nor destroyers to screen it when there, were available.'[60] Even Beatty admitted that, despite their obvious value, 'the difficulty is to find destroyers'.[61]

Of the roughly 280 destroyers in home waters at the start of 1917, many were outdated, and even the newer models were badly worn after three years of constant service. The other important factor was the suitability of those destroyers which were available:

> At the Nore, Portsmouth and Devonport there were about sixty destroyers in all. More than half of these were too old and small for escort service in the outer approach routes … between twenty and thirty older destroyers of the 'River' class *might* be used for escorting Channel convoys.[62]

The best 100 destroyers were assigned to the Grand Fleet, and no one wished to send the dreadnoughts into battle without their protective screen.[63] Jellicoe had been equally adamant not to draw down these protective screens.[64] When unrestricted submarine warfare opened, Beatty released eight destroyers. Neither he nor Jellicoe felt this problematic for ongoing operations: Jellicoe had already expressed the opinion in late 1916 that he thought the High Seas Fleet 'would not be risked again in a Fleet action'.[65] Additionally, he argued that the HSF itself lacked sufficient escort destroyers to sortie with confidence.

*Destroyers available start 1917*

| Location | Hulls |
|---|---|
| Scapa Flow | 80 |
| Rosyth | 30 |
| Refitting, detached | (20) |
| **Sub-total** | 90 |
| Harwich | 55 |

Source: Newbolt, *Naval Operations*, vol.V, p.6.

At this point, there was insufficient experience to really know how many destroyers would be needed. One truth could only be learned with experience at sea:

> Larger convoys did require more escorts, but proportionately fewer than small convoys. That is so because the number of ships needed for a screen is determined by the size of the convoy's perimeter, not the number of ships per se. It has been learned, in fact – though only after analysis many years after the war – that the larger the convoy the safer the ships.[66]

Looking for efficiency in ratios primarily defined by the number of ships needed to be qualified, as larger convoys are more complex to manage.

**Did Concentration Offer U-boats More Opportunities?**

One of the main reasons why the Admiralty opposed grouping ships together in convoys was the thinking that, in doing so, a larger number of targets would be presented to U-boats in a shorter amount of time. It was, as it turned out, not only a very simplistic conclusion, but also the wrong one.

In January 1917, the Admiralty released its infamous report, *Remarks on Submarine War*. Although it was a report that Jellicoe said he had not actually endorsed, let alone seen ('I don't think this paper came before me personally'), he was guilty by association.[67] It may not be surprising, but it's certainly interesting to note that the architect of Germany's campaign of unrestricted submarine warfare thought the same. Holltzendorff said that British convoys, what he would have called a *Geleitszugsystem*, 'would be a most welcome sight'.[68]

While the Admiralty report might have been categorical, the reality couldn't have been more different. Grouping ships together cleared the ocean of targets by reducing the probability of a sighting by a patrolling U-boat. Convoys 'gathered the prey of the raiders into a single area which was after all swallowed up like a mere speck in the ocean's vastness'.[69]

'In mathematical terms, there's more probability of spotting one out of 40 ships sailing independently than a single convoy made up of 40 ships.'[70] Creating the two scenarios on which forty ships might be distributed, one ship evenly distributed amongst 400 grid references illustrates the point. A restricted distribution under grouped convoy conditions might offer thirty-two possibilities for a submarine to be in an adjacent grid, while the distribution of ships under independent sailings increases the possibilities to 160. In effect, the chances of a ship being spotted by a submarine in an adjacent grid increases by five times. Conversely, under convoy rules, a 40 per cent chance of a ship being spotted from a submarine in an adjacent grid could be reduced to just 8 per cent.

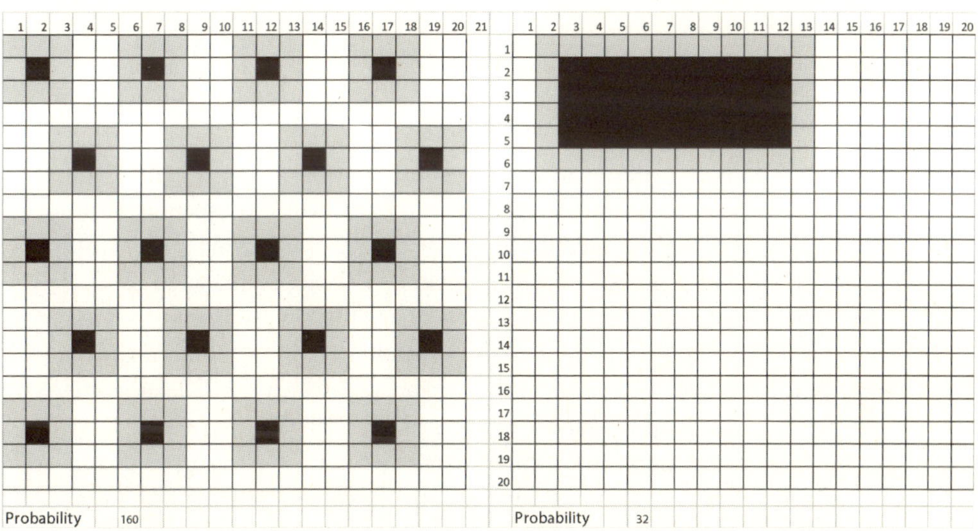


If a single ship could be spotted by a U-boat more than 10 miles distant, a broad front of convoyed ships centred around the same spot as an individual ship would only marginally increase the range of visibility to a submarine. It's ironic that here Bacon dismissed the logic of probability that he used so convincingly in defence of Jellicoe's 'turn away' at Jutland: '[A]t sea, mathematical odds do not always give the anticipated result. The danger to a convoy lay rather in the intrepidity of a submarine commander', like Weddigen or the captains of *UB.64* and *U.54*.[71]

Karl Dönitz, at the time a young submarine commander in the Mediterranean, said the results of convoying were stark: '[T]he oceans at once became bare and empty.'[72] Dönitz would survive when his submarine, *U.68*, was sunk in the war's last days.[73] Later, he became an Admiral of the Fleet (GroßAdmiral) and was named by Hitler as his successor.

For Howe, this aspect of utilising convoys was key: 'Although this system had been employed in earlier times, its principal utility now lay not in the strength of the escort, but in depriving the U-boat of target contact.'[74] Submarine commanders found themselves with

> not many *individual ships* to attack but of only a *few convoys* [author's italics]. That in turn meant that if a submarine missed a convoy not only would it have missed many ships, but it would be some time before it got another chance to attack.[75]

Missing a convoy, 'the [U-boat] commander would have to wait around for days for the next one to present itself'.[76] Even if the convoy had been spotted and an attack launched, '[i]n very few convoys was more than one ship sunk'.[77]

If a large concentration of ships was found, there were advantages in numbers. The larger the convoy, the more the 'shoal factor', as Jeremy Black calls it, comes into effect – 'when they found one [a convoy], [they] only had time to sink a limited number of ships' before becoming the target itself.[78] The more concentrated a convoy was, the more advantageous its position versus an attacking U-boat; 'the increase in the number of ships convoyed', wrote Grove, 'resulted in an increase in the number of U-boats destroyed'.[79]

It soon became apparent that once a U-boat had fired its available torpedoes, the surface escorting ships were alerted and would peel off to the approximate point of the torpedo's origin (or to the area around which the U-boat might have dived) to keep the submarine submerged. By doing so, they would force a submarine to run at a slower speed, consume more electrical power and increasingly prevent it from catching up with a convoy moving at a faster surface speed.

But it certainly was not always the case that an attacking submarine would find itself 'being aggressively counter attacked by escorts with depth charges', as some commentators would have it.[80] Allied ships, at this point, had only a limited number of depth charges on board, and even if they had more, detection was so poor that accuracy was unlikely.

While concentration reduced targets for the U-boats, however, Jellicoe felt that the possibility of large groupings of ships running into minefields could prove catastrophic. In hindsight, his fear was unfounded: according to Marder, only 'a total of five ships appeared to have been mined in convoy during the whole war'.[81]

### If Convoy at Sea Worked, Would Land-based Logistics Keep Pace?

Many of Britain's ship owners opposed the use of convoys because they felt it would mean a slowdown in port turnaround time.[82] Marder suspected they were simply against anything that could 'threaten their swollen profits', although maybe this was too harsh a conclusion.[83] Michelsen, however, agreed, saying that 'on average, the total time loss to shipping as a result of the Convoy system amounted to about thirty percent'.[84] Longer unloading times resulted from the sharply increased labour shortages in British and allied ports as men were increasingly called to the front to fight.

One would have assumed that Britain's railways might have better supported the introduction of convoys, given that the system should have introduced more planned reliability into port arrivals.[85]

### What Contemporary Sources of Learning About Convoys Existed?

It is one thing to talk about the obvious success of the convoy system in Britain's maritime past, but another to look at where and how wartime convoys were being used up to 1917. It's not accurate to say that it had 'simply been dropped from the programme of naval measures by an oversight'.[86] It is true, however, to say that the Royal Navy had never thoroughly tested the convoy system or evaluated it with anything close to scientific rigour. In fact, Goldrick felt that the 'intellectual exercise' of thinking through 'the fundamental advantages of the system' was not, arguably, 'formally undertaken until after World War II'.[87]

In 1906, some convoy tactics were war-gamed by Admiral Wilson, Commander-in-Chief of the newly created Channel Fleet, but the conclusions seem merely to have reflected the deeply ingrained ideological biases existing in the Royal Navy.[88] Wilson's idea was that merchant ships, while crossing the Atlantic, should be as widely dispersed as possible, while naval forces would be appropriately positioned to tackle enemy raiders as they sortied. Despite the results of the exercise showing that this would have been catastrophic (fifty-two of ninety-four merchantmen were 'sunk'), the umpire declared that 'the third week of the war would have seen all commerce-destroying ships either captured or blocked in their defended ports'. Astonishingly, the Admiralty upheld this wishful thinking, saying that 'the defeat of the aggressor could not long be delayed'.[89] The exercise hardly constituted a real test!

As the start of the war, convoys were used under very limited circumstances, mostly with transports from Canada, New Zealand, Australia and South Africa. The experience of one such convoy is interesting. In October 1914, a thirty-three-ship Canadian convoy left home waters. The perceived threat was not submarine attack; it was from either elements of the High Seas Fleet or armed German liners. Close escort was provided by four cruisers under the command of a future Sea Lord, Sir Roslyn Wemyss, and deep field cover by two battleships, HMS *Glory* and *Majestic*. Without prior warning, the force was joined by the battle-cruiser HMS *Princess Royal*. After the convoy successfully docked, experiencing only one U-boat scare off the Isle of Wight, Wemyss echoed the Navy's established opinions on 'sea lanes':

> It would have been a better plan to sail each transport separately, causing her to pass through a stated rendezvous with ships guarding the route.

Before February 1917, convoys had been used for troop carrying, but no system of general convoy existed for merchant ships.[90] Three additional examples are often quoted: the French coal trade, the Scandinavian convoys and the Dutch trade.

Duff gained practical experience from the 'protected sailings' of coal to France and talked of 'the unexpected immunity from successful U-boat attack'.[91] Many French coal mines had been destroyed or were now under enemy control, so the country had to rely on imported coal. It was soon realised that France was effectively under a 40 per cent blockade, as each new sinking of a French ship led to others being held back in harbour any time U-boats were sighted.

In the last three months of 1916, with the waters heavily patrolled by Flanders-based Type-*UB* and Type-*UC* boats, deliveries of coal had dropped 39 per cent.[92] French factories, using around 1½ million tons of coal a month, were clamouring for support from the British to at least introduce 'protected sailings' for the 800 or so colliers that crossed the Channel each month.[93] Because of these losses, 'controlled' or 'protected' sailings as they were called (the Admiralty did not want to call them 'convoys') were finally approved on 22 January 1917.

The first sailing took place on 10 February.[94] Even if the protection might have been more apparent than real, the proximity of significant British naval assets at least gave the outward appearance of a credible threat. Messimer cited encouraging results: from March ('when the coal trade of France had been brought under convoy') to August 1917, the British only lost fourteen ships out of 8,825 coal sailings.[95] By the end of the war, only fifty-three of the 39,352 ships convoyed had been lost. What the coal trade protection did was provide a useful learning curve. According to Commandant Vandier,[96] 'You, yourself [the British] will be forced to form convoys and to escort them to continue to trade. We forced you to do it twice in the past, with our pirates.

You will be forced to do it once more. The organisation of the French coal trade that I am requesting will be a trial for you.'[97]

The success of the French coal trade convoys can be misleading. It prompted Harris to ask why the lessons gained from them could not have been directly translated to the Atlantic, even labelling this failure as 'bizarre'. However, comparisons between a short Channel crossing, accompanied by trawler escorts and within close reach of further shore-based A/S assets, and the barren wastes of an Atlantic crossing were unrealistic. Bacon was highly critical of the coal trade's applicability:

> [A] protection was afforded which was adequate for ships which traversed only *protected* waters, that is, waters which already were patrolled and in which submarines found it well-nigh impossible to make systematic attacks; but the protection against submarines that was required in *unprotected* waters was in quite a different category … under these conditions a closed up formation was unnecessary; in fact, taking collision into account, it was safer to let the ships straggle rather than to keep the convoy in fairly close formation – a condition that was entirely reversed in open sea convoy.[98]

Besides, the first large Gibraltar convoy test was only two months after the coal trade was first convoyed. There is good reason why Black contends that employment of convoys wasn't a case of a sudden change of mind at the Admiralty; it was 'a gradual erosion' of the case against them and the increasing demands from the French.[99]

The supply route between Britain and the Hook of Holland was dubbed 'the beef trip' by Commodore Tyrwhitt, from whose Harwich forces twelve destroyers were assigned. The route on which, in 1915, one movement of ships occurred every four days was divided into eight sections, each of which was patrolled by a fast destroyer zigzagging at 15 knots. At the end of the year, in November, the method of directly escorting a group of ships was reinstated.

The word 'convoy' is purposefully not used, as these were very loose arrangements. From July 1916 until the end of the war, there were 1,861 'individual ship passages (with a brief interlude of "patrolled routes" for one month in November 1916)'[100] and up to June 1917, only six merchantmen were lost although quite a number of escorts were sunk or damaged.[101] For the whole war, Thompson estimated 37,927 ships were convoyed for the loss of only fifty-three (or 0.13 per cent).[102] Later in the war, flying boats based out of Felixstowe added air cover.

For the Scandinavian trade, convoys would have been introduced sooner, but Norwegian demands for escorted convoys in September 1916 were initially turned down as they would not accept the routes selected by the Admiralty. Norwegian losses were so heavy by the end of the year (over 160,000 GRT in the last quarter alone) that for almost three weeks no ships sailed, their merchant seamen simply refusing to take the risk.

From December 1916, they operated under a system of 'protected sailings', individual ships passing through 'protected' routes. With continued losses, Vice Admiral Frederick Brock (SO, Orkney and Shetland) started to push for 'group' sailings, the first being on 24 February.[103] A month later, Brock let it be known that he had switched some of the destroyers in his area from patrol to escort duty, 'a step on dangerous ground' as 'aggressive anti-submarine patrolling was part of the canon of beliefs held by Beatty, Jellicoe and much of the Admiralty'.[104]

Given better escort support, however, in the first full month of operation, 'the loss rate fell 120-fold, to 0.24 per cent.' And, just as important, the neutrals were appeased. *Kapitänleutnant* Hans Walther spoke of the increasing difficulties facing the attackers:

> Steamer traffic is only found in strongly escorted convoys that travel regularly, daily to and from Norway. British submarines are found everywhere along the steamer track. Airships, each with a destroyer under it, are very bothersome. As a result, it is rarely possible to overtake a convoy and make a second attack on it.[105]

Brock was adamant: 'a system of escorts would be more efficacious than a patrol system.'[106]

*Scandinavian Shipping sunk, 1916–1917*

| | **Norwegian** | **Danish** | **Swedish** | **Total** |
|---|---|---|---|---|
| | | | | |
| September | | | | 13 |
| October | | | | 29 |
| November | | | | 56 |
| December | 10 | | | |
| January | | | | |
| February | | | | |
| March | 27 | | | |
| April | 27 | 6 | 2 | 35 |
| May | 13 | 5 | 3 | 21 |

Source: Dunn, *Southern Thunder*, pp.92–95, 115–127

Not everything went smoothly. The convoys were 'always very scattered' and because they were, in Jellicoe's words, 'composed largely of neutral vessels… (they) presented exceptional difficulties in the matter of organization'.[107] Convoys, Admiral Sims pointed out, were made up of 'perhaps thirty entirely strange vessels of different sizes, shapes, speeds, nationalities and manoeuvring qualities.'[108] Norwegian vessels would not always make the required rendezvous.

It was the continued losses on the Scandinavian trade that led Jellicoe to ask Beatty and Brock for their recommendations and Brock, at Beatty's initiative, to organise the Longhope Conference. Worried about the increasing loss of Norwegian confidence in British ability to protect their trade, the Foreign Office was also pushing for a change. On 3 April, under Brock's chairmanship, the conference convened. Its task was to decide the relative merits between protecting and patrolling the coast or protecting traffic along the coast.

Their final collective recommendations (sent to Duff on 5 April) were that a minimum convoy size of nine ships was recommended escorted by two destroyers, a submarine and four to six trawlers. Lloyd George's conclusion that 'the naval officers at that conference were unanimously of the opinion that instead of the loose and defective system of protected sailings hitherto adopted for these ships, they ought to be placed in regular convoy' doesn't tell the whole story.[109]

Although unable to provide an answer to how, the conference came out in favour of convoy escort:

> Escorts have, however, proved an effectual protection, and a system of escorts does, to a large extent, fulfil the conditions of a patrol, the escorting vessels being placed in the best position for meeting and attacking hostile submarines.[110]

It is clear that Beatty's support for convoy helped swing the final vote behind convoy, but Jellicoe pointed out that – at this point – he was only concerned with the Scandinavian trade:[111]

> I have seen statements to the effect that Sir David Beatty expressed himself in favour of a general convoy system on this occasion. This is quite incorrect. All reference was to the Scandinavian convoy alone.[112]

I don't think one can be that definitive: Beatty's position was not that fixed. Writing to Carson on 29 April, Beatty said that he thought that the only option for the 'western trade and the approaches to the British Isles' lay in 'some form of convoy' and that 'a system which permits of 9 vessels being sunk in a small area in the course of 6 days cannot be a good one.'[113] It sounded like a more general statement of support but later, when convoy needs threatened taking escorts from the Grand Fleet, Beatty balked.

According to Dreyer, 'The conference unanimously agreed that a system of Convoy should be tried, but the representatives were unable to state whether the necessary vessels could be spared from their respective areas.'[114] All the area command admirals – Nicholson, Pears and Commodore Startin (SO, Granton) – resisted the idea of handing over any of their destroyers. They all added their thoughts. Rear Admiral Stuart Nicholson (SO, East Coast, based at Grimsby) disagreed with escort for any but the larger ships, each of which should be individually escorted 'by a single trawler'.[115] Rear Admiral Edmund Pears (SO, based at Invergordon) recommended convoys be more limited in size: 'four or five merchant ships should be escorted at a time'. Most interesting was the warning that came from Nicholson and Rear Admiral Sir Frederick Hamilton (SO, Rosyth), who both felt that 'sooner or later, the Germans would raid convoy in strength'.[116] For the Scandinavian route, they were right. It seems no use was made of the valuable intelligence starting to be accumulated.

Following the conference, Duff received the discussion papers on 11 April. He immediately agreed to respect the findings supporting escort for the Scandinavian trade where long daylight hours and the uniformity of the ships' speed facilitated the task. Jellicoe concurred, adding that he wanted fortnightly progress reports.

Beatty's position might have shifted in favour of adopting convoy for the Scandinavian trade, but his support came with important qualifications: he 'later attacked the use of Convoy when it threatened the number of destroyers attached to the Grand Fleet'.[117]

There were those in the Admiralty who continued to be hostile. Rear Admiral Thomas Jackson (Director, Operations Division) came out strongly against the use of convoy, saying that they 'invite torpedo attack and the available escorts are too few for the number of ships proposed in the convoy'.[118] Henry Oliver's opposition was also prominent but the most influential might have been the Director of the Trade Division, Captain Richard Webb, a strong supporter of 'protected sailings'.

On 21 April, however, Jellicoe finally agreed to a trial, approving the recommendations from Oliver and Duff after Beatty had complained (with the Prime Minister's support) saying that the 'convoy system has not yet had a fair trial'.[119] Three days later, Duff announced that old River-class vessels must be released by the reluctant area commands. It fell short of what was needed but, as Jellicoe later explained, 'urgent requests [for destroyers] were being received at the Admiralty from every command and it was impossible to comply with them since the vessels were not in existence'.[120]

Lloyd George continued to be highly critical. In his memoirs, he later wrote that no valuable experience was garnered from either the French coal trade or the Scandinavian trade practices: '[T]he fact that the experiment was not a systematic convoy, was imperfectly organized and was therefore not given a fair chance, was not considered [by the admirals]. It was not a success and the admirals "had told us so".'[121]

## The Political Battle for Convoys

The tone of the Admiralty's February 1917 pamphlet embodied the ridicule expressed by the naval writer, F.T. Jane: convoys were 'a splendid prize already prepared for the enemy'.[122] Jellicoe would later distance himself, saying that the paper had been in preparation 'for some time prior to [his] arrival at the Admiralty'. It was not an altogether unreasonable position to take.[123] In his memoirs, however, Lloyd George was categorical that Jellicoe was anti-convoy:

> The Director of the Trade Division, Sir Richard Webb, was against convoys. The Director of the Operations Division, Sir Thomas Jackson, was inconclusive.[124] Admiral Duff, the Director of the Anti-Submarine Division, was definitely opposed. Sir John Jellicoe agreed with the latter and so did the rest of the Board of the Admiralty.[125]

Not surprisingly, the Admiralty's pamphlet came in for strong criticism. John Winton wrote:

> It would be difficult to find, even in the long record of Admiralty bureaucracy, a more stupid document and one which more pigheadedly ignored all the lessons of past naval history.[126]

On 13 February, Carson, Jellicoe and Duff attended a breakfast meeting with Lloyd George at Downing Street, where Sir Maurice Hankey, the Cabinet Secretary, presented his case for the use of the convoy system. Hankey's paper, which he'd talked over with the Prime Minister two days before, covered existing A/S weapons but none of the wider national logistics implications or intelligence contributions.

> It involves the substitution of a system of scientifically organized convoys, and the concentration on this service of the whole of the anti-submarine craft allotted to the protection of our trade routes, excepting only those vessels devoted to the anti-submarine service of our main fleets. It further involves the concentration on to the convoy system of every means of

> anti-submarine warfare – the gun, the submarine, the net, the depth charge, the mortar, the hydrophone, and wireless telegraphy.[127]

Apparently, Hankey talked to the two admirals as though they had never thought about the subject.

Hankey's 'brainwave', as he called it, was formulated well before Henderson and Leslie made the all-important shipping statistics discovery that helped undermine the escort insufficiency issue. His main point was that 'the attack on trade routes was a "soft thing" for the submarine, with a constant stream of isolated merchant ships almost devoid of offensive power, to choose from'.[128] Even Hankey supposedly harboured the niggling suspicion that the resulting concentration of ships could increase their chances of being found by an enemy submarine. Hankey's conclusions made a strong impression on Carson. He promised to convene a meeting of ship's masters and to look at the results of the French convoys. According to Marder, Carson was 'almost from the start … in favour of giving the system a trial, but in line with his announced policy of backing his naval advisers, and giving them a free hand, he would not press his case'.[129]

A few days before, Lloyd George, complaining bitterly about the 'apathy and incompetence of the naval authorities', had lunched with the Military Affairs correspondent of *The Times*, Colonel Repington.[130]

When asked, Jellicoe told Carson that he could not yet give a 'useful assessment of the U-boat campaign', an admission Andrew Boyd – again with the benefit of hindsight – calls 'a disgrace'.[131] He assumes that because of the admission, Jellicoe wasn't using intelligence effectively. However, Jellicoe, of all people, understood the value of intelligence. He had even wanted to have his own more immediate access to decrypts and operational intelligence on *Iron Duke*.

Jellicoe's pessimism had a hugely damaging effect on his own standing. It wasn't just Lloyd George who was increasingly frustrated. Lord Curzon also complained that his fellow members of the War Cabinet did not have an up-to-date grasp of the situation, proposing that this be remedied on a weekly basis by a small committee.

On 23 April, in two meetings, the War Cabinet was briefed by Jellicoe, in part a response to Curzon's complaint. The second session, at the end of the day, was to discuss a memorandum that Jellicoe had put to the War Cabinet titled 'The Submarine Menace and Food Supply'. In it, Jellicoe briefed his colleagues on the huge losses sustained up to five days before: 419,261 tons, 97 per cent of which was caused by submarines. Another 27,074 tons was sunk in the preceding twenty-four hours. Lamely, he noted that 'the situation calls for immediate action and the adoption of such measures as are possible'. The only immediate solution was 'to keep them submerged and so "cramp" their activities'. Measures which had been successful against surface attack (Q-ships, arming merchantmen, smokescreens) 'have all diminished very much in value'. Mining channels of egress was not as effective, as 'our present pattern of mine is not satisfactory'. The new mines wouldn't be ready before July. To supplement shipping stock, Jellicoe suggested building 'a very large number of small merchant ships' which would offer less fruitful targets, and, conversely, building the 'largest ships that can be designed … [to be] practically unsinkable'.[132] There was no mention of rethinking patrolled areas; no mention of convoys being under active consideration.

All in all, Jellicoe gave the impression that his strategic thinking had not significantly evolved.

Jellicoe noted that the French and Scandinavian trials had not been 'altogether successful', pointing out that 'two vessels in separate convoys had already been torpedoed and sunk'.[133] At this point, he had a full fifteen weeks of data from the French tests, but only two weeks' worth from the Scandinavian routes. Any conclusions from the Scandinavian test were premature.[134]

The reason for Jellicoe's seeming lack of vision can only be the issue of escorts. Foremost in his mind was the lack of destroyers. This single fact is what was making him hesitate: 'There are no destroyers at all to carry it out on Western approaches, *but someday I may be able to carry it out, and the arrangements for doing are being prepared* [author's italics].'[135]

The convoy issue was again raised by Lloyd George, who now cited support from Beatty and the newly arrived Sims.[136] Jellicoe's reply was non-committal, saying that convoys were under review and that the destroyer shortage was still a defining issue. As the meeting's minutes stated,

> one of the chief obstacles to adopting such a scheme [was] the shortage of torpedo-boat-destroyers. He stated that there was some prospect of American destroyers being sent to assist us, and that six had already been ordered to leave for this country. A much larger number would, however, be necessary before any scheme of convoy could be introduced.

That Jellicoe expressed 'the gravest doubts', as Hough puts it, appears exaggerated.[137] Jellicoe later said that the convoy issue was 'very nearly' put forward, 'as it was obviously close to settlement'.[138] Might it not have made sense for Jellicoe to have at least mentioned the imminence of Duff's recommendations, even if not yet seen or approved? All Jellicoe agreed to was to 'make a further report on the matter to the War Cabinet'.

At the 25 April War Cabinet, Jellicoe was busy writing letters, showing a remarkable lack of political acumen on his part. Jellicoe was frequently critical of such meetings, writing to Beatty almost as soon as he took up his new position at the Admiralty that 'War councils waste half my time'. Two weeks later, again to Beatty, he said that the council had 'decided nothing' after a day of deliberations.[139] In April, he would complain that the constant meetings of the Imperial War Cabinet and the 'ordinary' War Cabinet left him 'little time for the work of war'.[140] Lloyd George was equally frustrated, concluding that 'it was clear that the Admiralty did not intend to take any effective steps in the direction of convoying'.[141] Other than his own bias, the Prime Minister had few grounds on which to make such a statement. Theatrically, he announced his intended visit to the Admiralty to deal with the 'High Admirals'. It was a myth in the making.

Back at the Admiralty, on 26 April, Duff presented his long-awaited recommendations, now influenced by the American declaration of war and by Henderson and Manisty's findings on escort needs. With America on board, 'the three main difficulties to convoy were to a great extent wiped out', Bacon concluded. After the war, Jellicoe, with Duff and in conversation with Newbolt, underlined 'that the shortage of escorts was the principal difficulty and that [the] situation in that respect was changed by the entry of the USA'.[142] America's formerly neutral harbours were now Allied ports, so could be used for convoy assembly and offshore for station-keeping practice. The change in status also meant that agents could be posted to the assembly ports to take charge of 'bunkering, discharge and taking-in of cargo and arrangements of the constitution of the convoys'.[143]

On 29 April, Sims visited the Admiralty and was shown Duff's findings, 'a well-digested, formal study' which revealed that the system was 'entirely practicable'.[144] It was 'detailed, and contained so many considered points and tabulated conclusions, that it suggested that Duff, or somebody, must have been working on it for some time beforehand'.[145]

Duff's report got right to the point:

> It seems evident to me that the time has arrived when we must be ready to introduce a comprehensive scheme of convoy at any moment … The sudden and large increases in our daily losses of Merchant Ships, together with the experience we have gained of the unexpected immunity from successful submarine attack in the case of the French Coal trade,[146] afford sufficient reason.[147]

He added:

> [T]he United States having come into the war eliminates some of the apparently insuperable difficulties to a comprehensive scheme of convoy.[148]

By this, he was referring to the critical thirty-five or so destroyers that the United States was able to provide almost immediately.

Duff denied that he changed his mind because of Lloyd George's planned visit, as did Jellicoe: 'There is no foundation for the belief that his visit was in any way the cause of my suggestion that the time had arrived for starting Convoy.'[149] He felt that he had always wanted to keep an open mind on the subject.[150] He talked with Newbolt about Lloyd George's claim, shortly to appear in his memoirs, that he was againt the convoy system. Jellicoe contradicted him, saying 'it was the heavy daily losses at that time that led to the change' and that he had remembered Duff coming to see him, saying the same.

Some of Duff's writings make the depth of his conversion questionable. In June, for example, he talked of how 'the slow speed of the convoy lays it particularly open to attack, and even one S/m getting into close quarters may result in the loss of two or three ships'. He was extremely cautious about how overenthusiastic, in his mind, the War Council Cabinet had become, saying that 'a recent visit … showed me very clearly that they took on convoy as the only salvation to a very critical position'.[151] Marder wrote that this looked like Duff was 'not completely sold on a regular system of ocean convoy'.

It's understandable, therefore, that even Winton commented that 'it is difficult to believe that Duff was the sole author of the memorandum, the views expressed in it are so at variance to his previous statements'. But who else could it have been? Jellicoe would never have overridden Duff.

With America's entry, all manner of help would finally be available, not only in hardware like destroyers, but also in economic, financial and diplomatic support. Convoys became a practicable strategy, something realistically executable even if there was still a mountain of logistic issues that needed to be addressed. Duff's short memo walked through the considerations in what had clearly been a much larger and well-thought-out plan.

It has been said that Duff 'shared his [Jellicoe's] scepticism'.[152] It would certainly fit Lloyd George's caricature of his senior admirals. But I don't think Jellicoe was being overly sceptical. Given the stakes, he had to be extremely cautious, even if he did not appear at the outset to have been very keen. The implementation of the convoy system was a gargantuan task. Lloyd George even said he understood Jellicoe's position.

> He [Lloyd George] had worked – so he told his biographers – in complete harmony with Sir John Jellicoe and the other Sea Lords; he had understood the reason for their cautions and delays in the matter of convoy; they were due entirely, in his opinion, to practical difficulties which had to be overcome.[153]

Political expediency needs scapegoats. The very next day, 27 April, Jellicoe agreed with Duff's recommendation for a convoy test with one word: 'Approve'. There are no grounds for Van der Vat to conclude that Jellicoe gave his endorsement 'without enthusiasm'.[154]

Jellicoe then attended the War Cabinet, where he delivered the second memorandum on Admiralty recommendations. The atmosphere was tense, and Jellicoe's opening remarks could only have added to the sense of gloom when he said, 'the Admiralty can no longer accept responsibility for conducting the war on its present basis', in part blaming his colleagues for the situation: '[T]he War Cabinet entirely fails to realise the position, despite the repeated efforts I have made to explain its gravity. It may be that I have not spoken or written with sufficient emphasis to explain its gravity.'[155] Jellicoe knew that the adoption of convoys would not only be extremely complex, but would also take time before the benefits would be felt.

Why, having just approved Duff's recommendations, did he not hold out some measure of optimism to his colleagues? The convoy recommendations had been fleshed out by Duff, so why was there no mention of findings that were about to be presented?

It was possibly because he was not convinced that the convoys were the 'silver bullet'; he saw the wider picture, which had to include rationalisation of trade, rationing and the geographic shrinking of operational theatres. He wanted those recommendations to also be considered; a premature announcement on the convoy system might have killed them off. Instead, Jellicoe stressed the fundamental importance of securing Britain's maritime lines of communication: 'History has shown from time to time the fatal results of basing naval and military strategy on an insecure line of communications.' He feared that 'disaster is certain to follow' if the 'present policy' was not dramatically changed.[156] Jellicoe felt that it came down to a lack of understanding that Britain's traditional pillar of prosperity and strength, its sea power, was now fundamentally in question:

> [W]e are carrying on this war … as if we had the absolute command of the sea. We have not … It is quite true, of course, that we are absolute masters of the situation as far as surface ships are concerned, but it must be realized … all this is quite useless if the enemy's submarines paralyse, as they do now, our lines of communication.[157]

Immediate action to reduce the number of fronts would not only free up escort shipping, but also increase overall cargo-carrying capacity at a time when the yards weren't able to replace ships fast enough. He had for a while been warning the War Cabinet that monthly losses 'may be substantially exceeded' (above January's 425,000 tons) in the months that followed as more German submarines became operational and as neutral shipping returned to the seas.

What Jellicoe was getting at was the need for the country to ruthlessly adopt a siege mentality. The handling of any non-essential cargo should cease immediately. Britain's economy was hemorrhaging; by April 1917, the country's grain was reportedly down to six weeks' supply and there was only enough sugar in reserve for four days' normal consumption. To cap it off, the nation's 'account' with J.P. Morgan now stood at £400 million in the red.

Jellicoe was not the defeatist Lloyd George made him out to be, but he needed to make sure those around him understood the profound gravity of the situation:

> When with this help supplies have been received and the country is in a position to withstand a siege, then we can reconsider the whole position. Without some such relief as I have indicated – and that given immediately – the Navy will fail in its responsibilities to the country and the country itself will suffer starvation.[158]

Certainly, Hankey understood. At the 23 March War Cabinet, he had already called for a reallocation of priorities to what was carried by the ships supplying Britain and had proposed 'the most urgent measures', for example, to 'switch shipping from moving ammunition to bringing wheat from the United States and Canada'.[159] He was also frustrated by Lloyd George, complaining at one point that '[I] cannot get at Ll. George in regard to it, as he is so full of politics'.[160]

Jellicoe had similar ideas and had been justifiably critical of the failure to curb Britain's unnecessary imports or to introduce wartime rationing earlier. He had argued, along with Sir William Robertson, who was 'inclined to agree', for the introduction of rationing in May 1917. On 31 March, the War Cabinet decided 'to extend rationing to the trenches', calling for 'one potato-less day and fewer on the other six days'.[161] In Britain, there were already two meat-less and two potato-less days in public establishments.[162] A Ministry of Food was created to manage the nation's dwindling food stocks, with limited rationing introduced and more land put under plough.[163]

To prevent the loss of access to neutral shipping, Britain applied pressure and threats; her dominant position in the supply of coal gave her all the leverage she needed to cajole compliance. Withholding supplies from its bunker network would mean that if an ocean-going concern did not tow the British line, their operations would be seriously curtailed. Coal provided the British with critical leverage: up to 1917, she had shipped almost 22 million tons of coal to Scandinavia. Sometimes the British would even hold up Dutch and Scandinavian neutral shipping in their ports, only allowing their departure once another ship arrived with new cargo.

The impact of the Royal Navy's constant requisitioning of small vessels suitable for patrol-work significantly impacted Britain's fishing industry. 'The supply of one of the staple foods of the working class' was threatened by this drain: at the start of 1917, 1,400 of Britain's 1,900 trawlers had been requisitioned for A/S and minesweeping work.[164]

On 30 April, Jellicoe wrote to Sims saying that, while 'the Admiralty had not definitely decided that the Convoy system should be adopted, there was every intention of giving it a fair trial'. Significantly, orders had already been dispatched two days previously to Gibraltar requiring the first convoy test to be readied to leave in ten days.

At this critical turning point in the submarine war, recollections of what happened at the 30 April Admiralty meeting do not agree. Lord Beaverbook, a close press friend of Lloyd George, portrayed a picture of the Prime Minister taking control. Lloyd George, he said,

> descended upon the Admiralty and seated himself in the First Lord's chair … for one afternoon the Prime Minister took over the full reins of Government from the head of a major department of state.[165]

This reflected how Lloyd George would have liked others to have seen him: '[W]hen I arrived at the Admiralty, I found the Board in a chastened mood.' Nevertheless, Lloyd George 'distinctly left on record that it was anti-submarine work and not convoy that was discussed and that the interview in no way affected the introduction of the convoy system'.[166]

The lines were clearly drawn. Carson labelled Lloyd George a 'little popinjay' whose recall of events amounted to 'the biggest lie ever told'.[167] Duff, maybe understandably, denied the connection – 'there is no foundation for the belief that his visit was in any way the cause of my suggestion that the time had arrived for starting Convoy'.[168] Unsurprisingly, Dewar was sceptical of the Admiralty's policy change and noted that the evidence supporting Lloyd George's assertion was 'strongly supported by documentary evidence, written at the time', while the opinions of the 'naval authorities' were 'only expressed when the war was over'. The myth that Lloyd George created has survived for many years. Sir Henry Newbolt completely discounted Lloyd George's visit, while Marder thought it 'a long way' from having 'forced the hands of the Admiralty'.[169] Lloyd George was probably relieved that, finally, the Admiralty seemed to have come around to his thinking. Since he was at the meeting, Hankey's opinion is important, even if Terraine called him 'a deeply interested party'. His description of the atmosphere paints a picture that is more in line with how Jellicoe and Duff remembered events:

> This morning Lloyd George and I went to the Admiralty and spent the whole day there very pleasantly, lunching with Lord Jellicoe and his wife and four little girls – Lloyd George having a great flirtation with a little girl of three.[170]

The little girl in question was my aunt, Prudie Loudon. Like Terraine, Hankey considered Lloyd George's account 'good stuff for the port and brandy or the gossip columns'.[171]

That Lloyd George's intervention alone created 'clarity' is debatable, but the confrontation did lead to useful decisions. One outcome was the evolution of the Naval Staff. Others included the diversion of shipping from the east to the west coast, the introduction of Japanese destroyers in the Mediterranean, the introduction of a weekly Admiralty Appreciation of the War from the Director of Operations for the First Sea Lord and a longer-term planning section. With the convoy system now in hand, the Prime Minister also turned his attention to replacement of lost tonnage. The creation of a Ministry of Shipping in December 1916 had not managed to address the issue. Naval construction was still the purview of the Admiralty. On 11 May, he 'took a grip on the Admiralty' by making Sir Eric Geddes Third Sea Lord and Controller.

It didn't take long for the Prime Minister's disdain for Jellicoe's Admiralty to again come to the boil. After the decision to launch a test for the extension of the convoy system, Lloyd George switched the axis of attack: it now became not the principle of convoy but that, in his view, it was being implemented too slowly. His immediate note to the War Cabinet framed his issue, writing that he had

> much regret that some time must elapse before convoy can be in full working order and I consider that the Admiralty ought to press on with the matter as rapidly as possible.[172]

## The Strains of the Anglo-American Partnership

Leading up to and during the early years of the First World War, Britain's relationship with America was often strained. President Wilson was not Anglophile: 'To him, "British navalism" was just as deserving of censure as was "German militarism".'[173] America, however, had been benefitting economically from the war with sales of food and munitions to the Allies, only complicated by necessary compliance with the British blockade of Germany. When Wilson tried to intervene to oblige Britain, France, Germany, Italy and

Austro-Hungary to define the terms under which a peace might be negotiated, nothing was forthcoming.

The new German state was quick to recognise the United States, and from its founding to 1914, 1.5 million Germans emigrated to the New World. During the Civil War, while Britain refused to underwrite Union bonds, the Northern German states led by Prussia had been ready to offer financial support. It was only when competition for new colonies started that the first friction between the two nations surfaced. 'Conflict between the two was bound to occur': Germany and America argued over Samoa, for example, in 1877 as both young nations were looking for their 'place in the sun'.[174]

A large factor to the success of the convoy system was undoubtedly the American contribution, not only the immediate supply of desperately needed escort destroyers but, as the war continued, access to American industry, its financial muscle, technological innovation, labour force and industrial capacity.[175] Indeed, 'without the participation of the Americans, probably there would have been no Allied victory'.[176] In the purely naval sphere, it was the friendship between two men, William Sims and John Jellicoe, that helped establish the right footing for a successful partnership.

**The Americans and Convoy: Sims Versus Washington**

Supposedly, when Sims met with Jellicoe and asked about the convoy system, Jellicoe's response was that, *even if he did not yet personally endorse it*, the Admiralty supported dispersion rather than convoy. This was in line with its thinking dating back to 1912, even after the 1906 Wilson exercises. Jellicoe advised Sims that 'after trying various methods of controlling shipping, the Admiralty now believes the best policy to be one of dispersion'.[177]

Jeffrey Harley, President of the US Naval War College from 2016–19, believes that Sims, 'despite the Admiralty's and *Jellicoe's resistance*' [author's italics], became one of the principal voices supporting convoys.[178] He argues that 'the Royal Navy was finally *compelled* [author's italics] to adopt the system that would turn the tide against merchant shipping losses'.[179] While the Admiralty had officially published its position, Jellicoe's tenure as the First Sea Lord was barely four months old. He needed more convincing, not necessarily on the merits or demerits of convoys, but on whether they could be implemented.

Jellicoe did not argue against convoys on strategic or tactical grounds, rather he focused on the lack of available escorts, the enabling factor. The surface fleet, the Grand Fleet, was always key, but it robbed his thinking of flexibility, to be able to think in any other terms than a fleet engagement:

> The presence of the powerful High Seas fleet, which could choose its moment to attack, acted as a containing force for a large share of the

> Royal Navy … The entire British naval strategy, and therefore [Britain's] entire strategy, was underpinned by the Grand Fleet's ability to counter German sorties.[180]

Jellicoe was worried about the 'risk of sacrificing surface control in the quest of sub-surface control'. As Commander-in-Chief, like Beatty, he had worried about the threat of the Grand Fleet being stripped of its supporting destroyer flotillas.[181]

At the 11 April Cabinet meeting, Jellicoe reported a conversation the previous day with Admiral Sims. It was at this point that the War Cabinet 'authorised' Jellicoe 'to communicate freely and frankly with Admiral Sims in regard to the submarine menace'.[182] It was hardly necessary; Jellicoe had already been shockingly open with Sims. His task was to convince Sims of the gravity of the situation.

> Admiral Sims had been convinced, in the course of the conversation, that the position was very serious, and proposed, after further consultation with Sir John Jellicoe, to send a telegram to that effect to his Government, which he thought would result in every effort being made by the Americans to assist us in every possible way to combat the submarine menace, more especially as the Government of the United States of America held very strong views relative to the 'Freedom of the Seas'.

On 14 April, Sims cabled Daniels at the Navy Department, stressing that 'control of the sea is actually imperilled' by the German submarine threat and urging the 'maximum number of destroyers to be sent, accompanied by small anti-submarine craft [with] the utmost dispatch'.[183] On 19 April, he wrote to Daniels 'amplifying [his] cable of April 14th as follows':

> One of the principal demands is for convoy of merchant shipping and more definite and real protection within the war zone … The answer, which is manifestly not publicly known, is simply that the necessary vessels are not available, and further that those which are available are suffering from the effects of three years of arduous service.

Clearly, Jellicoe succeeded in communicating the gravity of the moment. He may even have gone 'overboard'. He could hardly paint a rosy picture, but from these and other conversations came the strongly negative impressions about his gloomy outlook and an attitude that many found defeatist. Around the same time, Balfour was in Washington talking about the pressing need of shipping for the Allies.

Was Jellicoe really *opposed* to the convoy system, as Harley, Andrew Gordon or Hough have written? The latter even suggested: 'No voice condemning the Convoy was more authoritative than Jellicoe's.'[184] The fact is that he never *condemned* the use of convoys. He just was not ready to approve it without having done his homework or before having the resources he needed to make it work. Had he really approved Duff's memo 'although his heart was not in it'?[185] Was he just wary of introducing a scheme without the proper understanding or preparation? His analysis made a clear distinction between the mercantile and naval difficulties. One person who was close to Jellicoe was Manisty:

> I am not certain now, but I believe my feeling at the time was that J.R.J. [Jellicoe] did not seem confident as to the success of the system, but he believed it to be the only chance, and that he was prepared to take the responsibility of the decision, and to support the scheme to the full, as he did.[186]

Morison maintained that Sims had 'suggested that merchant ships would have to be convoyed eventually in fleets', but that the idea 'was not received with approval' by Jellicoe.[187] This must have been, at the most, two weeks before, as Duff was working on his final recommendations to extend the convoy system to the Atlantic. In his own book, *The Crisis of the Naval War*, Jellicoe makes a rather obvious snipe:

> It is interesting to note the number of persons who claim to have been the first to urge the Admiralty to adopt convoys as a method of protecting merchant ships against submarine attack.[188]

Jellicoe ended by saying that 'the claimants to this distinction *are not confined to Great Britain*' [author's italics]. In my mind, he could only have been referring to Sims. Daniels and Benson were strongly opposed to convoys, no matter what they might have written later. Daniels's scepticism continued at least until CNO Benson visited Europe in the autumn. Daniels shared Benson's distrust of the British but believed that Sims 'accepted the plans of the British Admiralty as sacrosanct'.[189]

Marder said that Jellicoe was 'disturbed mightily' when he heard Lloyd George quoting Beatty and Sims's position on convoys. Sims, because he'd only been in the country two weeks; Beatty, as the views he expressed at Longhope seemed more to apply to Scandinavian convoys rather than Atlantic convoys. Jellicoe was dismissive of the idea, saying that 'it seems to me to be in the highest degree absurd to quote the views of Admiral Sims as if they could possibly at that period have been of value'.[190] The 'western trade' comment by Beatty came after the principle had been accepted by the First Sea Lord. As the saying goes, success has many mothers; failure is an orphan. Sims, according to Lloyd George, 'definitely favoured convoys' and 'expressed his dissent from the Admiralty view that convoy was impracticable'.[191]

Jellicoe bristled at the idea of Sims championing convoy: 'Sims had not at that time [April 1917] suggested convoy to me, and I saw him daily.' Even Marder said that Sims's point that merchantmen would be able to steam in formation in his 19 April communiqué 'was, by itself, hardly an endorsement of a convoy system', even if he clearly addressed one of Jellicoe's concerns.[192]

It is highly doubtful that Sims was regarded as an expert on convoys at this stage. Lloyd George was more likely fishing for *anyone* who would support Hankey's proposals. Morison likely overstated Sims's influence and role on convoys. What he wrote sounds, today, like pure conjecture:

> Admiral Sims, through his messages to the State Department, had proved the determining factor in finally bolstering up the courage of the Admiralty Board to accept responsibility of adopting the convoy system. Admiral Sims's messages were so vehement and telling in force of argument that the Admiralty officials, who saw them all, did not dare risk post-war analysis of their régime in the face of such documents which would, of course, eventually receive publicity.[193]

It is not clear on what evidence Morison comes to this conclusion. Later, Sims's own position cooled. Escorts, he held, only provided 'temporary effectiveness in protecting shipping'.[194] The value of the destroyer escort in protecting convoys only kicked in after the handover of a convoy from its larger (and less numerous) open ocean escorts, normally old battleships. As such, American destroyers were needed in European waters. Both Sims and Jellicoe appeared to retain a fear of an open ocean, surface threat to convoys.

The American journalist Lowell Thomas, in *Raiders of the Deep*, concurred, saying it was Sims 'who advocated instituting escorted merchant convoys', which 'prompted the Royal Navy' to take decisive action.[195] He went as far as saying that Sims should be 'credited' with the 'lion's share' for the convoy system's adoption.[196] It seems likely that Sims's name became associated with convoys from a very early stage because of the efforts of his biographer – and of course his son-in-law – Elting Morison. Lloyd George, according to Morison, argued for the convoy system's adoption in Cabinet, using 'the arguments of Sims and Beatty to support his own views'.[197] The views of David Beatty carried weight; he was well known. Sims, by contrast, was a newcomer whose own navy did not even support convoys.

In Sims's defence, it is abundantly clear that he understood the complex interrelationships of ASW. He also seems to have understood the escort destroyer role better than either Beatty or Jellicoe, even if he later put more importance behind the problem of locating submarines. Destruction was impossible without detection. Sims would refocus the conversation on detection, the hydrophone. It's interesting to note that Sims is also credited with the birth of the hunter-killer submarine: Owen wrote that the use of submarines to catch other submarines was 'another of Sims's ideas'.[198] However, there are enough examples of successful attacks before Sims arrived on the scene.

Morison, like Holloway Frost, judged events with the certainty of hindsight: he talks of the British 'using the patrol system to combat the submarine despite its *obvious* [author's italics] inadequacy'. His account ignores some of the key players and is, consequently, rather imbalanced: Hankey, for instance, is not even mentioned; neither is Norman Leslie, with whom Sims worked closely. It was, after all, Leslie, whom Marder said 'deserve[d] equal praise' as was given to his collaborator, Reginald Henderson. Henderson, of whom Marder said 'it is not too much to call him the chief architect of the convoy system', is mentioned four times.[199] It was Henderson who had worked 'behind the back of his Chief, Rear Admiral Alexander Duff', in urging the adoption of convoys on Lloyd George.[200]

Sims had supposedly learned from Jellicoe that 'no systematic study had been made of the [convoy] problem'. In writing to his wife, Anne, Sims maintained that 'After some discussion he convinced the Englishman that it was imperative that such a study be undertaken.'[201] In Morison's view, the study that Leslie and Henderson completed was eventually done at Sims's 'insistence'. Sims himself never made any statement after the war to clarify this aspect of his role. Marder quotes a letter dated 3 July in which Sims said that he was 'devoted to this convoy system ever since the first week I got here in London', but said that he could find nothing 'to bear this out' in his April correspondence and that 'neither Sims nor the Navy department was thinking beyond the needs of the patrol system'. And, as noted, Jellicoe said that Sims never brought up the subject of convoy and was clearly irked by how Sims's role in the convoy debate had been documented.

In both *The Submarine Peril* and *The Crisis of Naval War*, Jellicoe emphasised that 'we were certainly not in the state of panic which has been ascribed to us in certain quarters'.[202] He said the same in *The Morning Post*.[203] To which 'quarters' he was referring is not clear, but Jellicoe went to great pains to defend what he had said during his first meeting with Sims. As President Wilson had been extremely critical of Allied anti-submarine efforts, he might be to whom Jellicoe had been referring. It was 'incorrect', he said, to infer that 'the Admiralty [or Jellicoe himself?] held the view at this time there was no solution to the problem created by the enemy's submarine campaign'. He referred to his 26 April communiqué to Admiral de Chair, which ended with the words, 'Our methods will not be effective until July and the critical period is *April to July* [author's italics].'[204]

**Testing the Convoys**

Jellicoe wrote to Sims confirming the decision to test the convoy system: 'The Admiralty had not definitely decided that the Convoy system should be adopted but that there was every intention of giving it a thorough and fair trial.'[205] On 28 April, SO Gibraltar was signalled orders to prepare a test convoy: around twenty ships with speeds equal to, or lower than, 11 knots were assembled. Each ship was to be fitted with a telegraph connecting the bridge with the ship's engine room. On 2 May, Captain H.C. Lockyer left Devonport with the special service ships *Mavis* (acting Commander A. St. V. Keyes) and *Rule* (Lieutenant R. Langton-Jones). The seventeen-ship group finally left Gibraltar on 10 May with Captain Lockyer on the bridge of the convoy's leader, the 3,589-ton *Clan Gordon*. Ten days later they docked in Plymouth.[206]

The slow (6½ knot)[207] convoy was escorted by 'three armed yachts, and two Q-ships as ocean escorts'.[208] As soon as the convoy reached coastal waters, around 200 miles from Devonport, it was met by eight Devonport-based destroyers, while a Scillies-based flying boat covered its approach from above. It was clearly much more heavily covered – both in transit and at arrival – than Duff had recommended. 'Despite fog and heavy weather, station keeping had been excellent.'[209] It was no surprise that 'the chief opponents of the convoy now became its most enthusiastic advocates'.[210]

Two weeks later, on 24 May, a similar convoy test took place on the other side of the Atlantic, from the Hampton Roads, despite the US Navy's 'deep misgivings'.[211] Only one ship, the 10,000-ton armoured cruiser HMS *Roxburgh*, was available as escort to twelve ships. When they arrived at the danger zone, eight destroyers met them. The results were excellent; *Roxburgh*'s Captain Whitehead was reported to have said that 'station keeping was excellent and that he was prepared to take charge of thirty ships instead of twelve' on the next convoy.[212]

On 21 May, the Admiralty agreed to the wholescale introduction of convoys. During May and June, another five Atlantic convoys left Hampton Roads and 'out of a total of seventy-three ships in these convoys only one, a straggler, was torpedoed and sunk'.[213] Once decided, the convoy system was slowly introduced to the main theatres – the South Atlantic routes in September, the Mediterranean in November and British inner coastal convoys in December.

With the entry of the United States into the war, the escort issue was partly addressed. From fifty-one available craft, seven of the USN's best destroyers were immediately supplied. *DD-8*'s arrival in Queenstown on 6 May 1917 sent a highly visible message to the British public. By 15 July, there were thirty-four in Allied waters.[214] By the year's end, massive air ASW support was also added – 'nearly 100 airships, 291 seaplanes and twenty-three aeroplanes, over 400 aircraft'.[215] U-boats not only had to scan the horizons for a hunter, but now also the skies.

**Convoy Organisation, Training and Tactics**

At the Admiralty, a detailed plan for the extension and operation of convoys was presented on 6 June. It called for eight homeward and eight outbound convoys to operate to and from Britain every eight days.[216] The choice of routes had to balance commercial importance and ease of implementation against potential threat. The Mediterranean, for example, offered German submarines longer daylight, calmer seas and warmer weather; by contrast, securing tight Allied cooperation and coordination was a real challenge. Very early on, it was suggested that convoys would be slowed to the speed of their slowest ship.[217] That was largely overcome by careful groupings of similar-speed ships. Ships that could be convoyed were to sail at between 12 and 8¼ knots; those that could travel at higher speeds were advised to sail independently. Ships that sailed at speeds less than 8¼ knots were seen to be a danger to other faster ships (although an exception was made for the Gibraltar convoy route). The planning assumption was that six destroyers would be needed for twenty merchantmen, the average convoy size. With escort flotillas of six destroyers each, organised from Gibraltar (two flotillas), Lough Swilly, Portland, Queenstown and Plymouth (three flotillas each), a total of 84 destroyers were needed, in addition to fifty-two cruisers or AMCs. The recommendations were formally approved by Jellicoe on 14 June. The first open-ocean convoy left New York on 14 August. Sixteen days later, a second convoy left.

In the final worldwide network, seven ports were to be used: Sydney (Cape Breton, Nova Scotia), Halifax (Nova Scotia), New York, Hampton Roads, Gibraltar, Sierra Leone and Dakar. Only Gibraltar was not 'remote' from German submarine bases.[218] Few German submarines in 1917 were of large enough tonnage to operate at the ranges needed to molest the assembly points. Indeed, few would represent a threat for much of the Atlantic crossing: U-boats 'rarely operated beyond three hundred to four hundred miles from land'.[219]

In the assembly port, one ship's captain was usually designated convoy commodore, while the escort commander remained responsible for the defence of the convoy. Since convoy commanders tended to be 'vastly senior', this division of responsibility could cause friction.

As the system started to form, assembly in neutral waters was used for training new crews, used to sailing independently, how to work as a group.

Ships' masters felt a lack of confidence from junior officers; they had lost their best deck officers to the navy. Practice was devoted to zigzagging, closing to offer overlapping fire zones and reporting intelligence. Signals, chains of command and the latest intelligence were reviewed before sailing.

Jellicoe, however, had overstated the need for perfection. He had written that 'the ships composing the convoy should be handled in a manner that approached the handling of battleships in a squadron'.[220] Leighton's statement that 'Sims and a few British officers stepped into the breach of opinion thus formed, and declared that the Merchant captain had underrated his abilities', does not seem to be supported.[221] The absence of 'suitable engine room telegraphs' compounded the danger for Jellicoe. In his defence, Jellicoe quoted a February 1918 circular relating the experience of Atlantic and Scandinavian officers:

> [A]n unduly large number of British vessels in Convoy, on the main and Scandinavian routes, are adversely reported on by Senior officers of Escort, principally with regard to their station-keeping … great improvement … is urgently called for.[222]

A tight formation was not only needed for safe zigzagging, but would also mean that the impact of any preceding minesweeping force would be more effective. Crossing the Atlantic, the lines between the ships would be around four cable lengths, or 800 yards (a nautical mile is made up of 100 cable lengths, or 6,076ft), apart, with two cables between each ship in the line. If the weather was bad, the ships would close the gap on the ship in front to just one cable's length, with an object towed behind to keep the distance.

Early on, Jellicoe wrote to Sir Charles Cayzer, saying that 'the only safety from submarines is to keep right away from all headlands and to go full-speed and zigzag'.[223] These manoeuvres added considerable distance to a voyage – 'sometimes by as much as twenty percent'.[224]

As the success of convoys was increasingly understood, submarines were forced to adopt new tactics:

> *L'application du système des convois obligea les U-boote à recourir à des tactiques nouvelles, dont la principale fut l'attaque du nuit en surface* ['The application of the convoy system forced the U-boats to resort to new tactics, the main one of which was the night attack on the surface'].[225]

Especially at night, a destroyer would be placed at the rear of the convoy to catch any submarine that was chasing the merchantmen on the surface. According to Kemp, in the last nine months of the war, 37 per cent of the

Atlantic and 67 per cent of the Mediterranean submarine attacks were executed at night and on the surface.[226]

Gradually, the tactics within convoys were improved. One important consideration was to reduce the amount of time a U-boat could sit on the flanks of a passing convoy by increasing its breadth over its length: 'thus a convoy of twenty-four vessels, or six groups of four, would have a width of about three miles and a depth of one'.[227] In mid-ocean, the threat is not from submarines so much as potentially from longer-range surface ships, while protection cannot be easily afforded by ships without the necessary range or air cover provided by shore-based aviation assets. In these waters, larger battleships or cruisers provided escort.

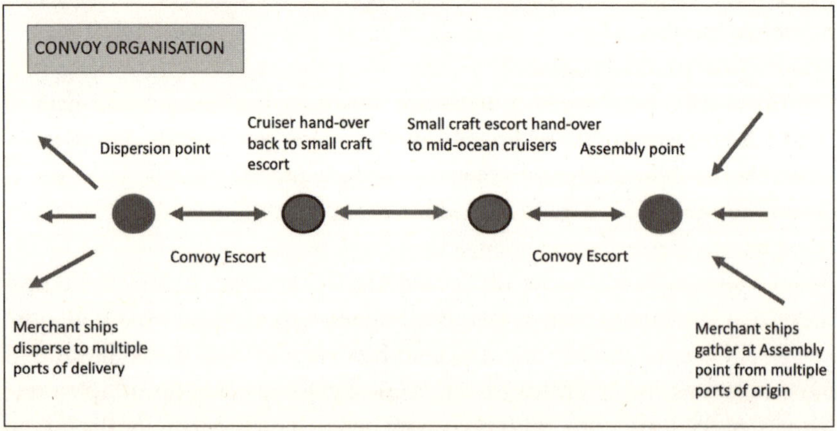


The 'weak link in the convoy armour', however, lay in the routes to and from the convoy assembly and dispersal points.[228] Closer to land, fast destroyers took over, being able to race at speed to a U-boat once spotted, the idea being to create a 'moving anti-submarine zone' in areas of expected U-boat concentration in the Western Approaches.[229] It wasn't just destroyers; the arriving convoy would also be met 'by armed yachts, PQ vessels, trawlers etc'.[230]

Three major corridors, known as 'cones', brought the traffic through to Liverpool, Bristol and Southampton. A fourth, Approach D, brought traffic around the north of Scotland through the Shetlands gap. Whether these 'cones' made sense is open to challenge: 'Far from offering protection … the patrolled approach cones became magnets for U-boats and a death zone for merchant vessels.'[231] However, there seemed to be no logical alternative; the only suggestion was that ships travelling from the point of concentration to the shallower coastal waters should do so under the cover of darkness.

Kommodore Bauer, the FdU, submitted proposals to change U-boat tactics, only to have them rejected by von Holtzendorff. In April 1917, he proposed that *U.155* (formerly *U.Deutschland*) act as on 'offshore radio command post' to vector U-boat assets on to an intercept point with incoming convoys as they were spotted. The idea was that *U.155* would become a '*Milchkuh*' ('dairy cow'), acting as a floating supply-ship with extra supplies, fuel and torpedoes. By June, however, it seemed clear that the convoys were an Allied tactic that needed a tailored response. U-boat commanders recognised that under the new system, 'Gun attacks are almost impossible and submerged attacks are much more difficult'.[232] Special training convoys were sent out from Kiel so that submarine officers could find how best to deal with a formation of zigzagging merchant ships.[233]

**The North Atlantic Convoys**

The 'first regular' convoy from Hampton Roads (HH6) left on 2 July 1917.[234] HH7, which included vessels from the West Coast of the USA, left five days later. During July, 162 ships sailed in eight convoys; in August, 158 ships in another eight convoys.

Ships from ports north of Philadelphia gathered at New York and sailed every eight days. HN1 sailed on 14 July. During July, thirty-seven ships sailed in two convoys; in August, a further sixty-seven ships in four convoys.

Sydney, Cape Breton, was used as the assembly point for ships from Canadian ports. HS1 left on 10 July, escorted by HMS *Highflyer*. During July, forty-five ships sailed in three convoys, losing one of the two ships lost on these routes in July, SS *Whitehall*, which had strayed. In August, sixty-seven ships ships sailed in eight convoys.

The first convoy from Halifax (HX1) sailed on 22 August.

Escorts for the North American routes were provided by seven cruisers: HMS *Berwick*, *Roxburgh*, *Antrim*, *Drake*, *Cumberland*, *Iris* and *Highflyer*. They were supported by another four AMCs, normal merchant ships that were armed and took on additional naval gunnery ratings and officers (the *Virginian*, *Almanzara*, *Kildon* and *Victorian*) and five commissioned escort ships (*Carrigan Head*, *Cambrian III* – aka *Bostonian* – *Knight Templar*, *Sachem* and *Discovery*). At the eastern end of the route, thirty-seven American destroyers were based out of Queenstown under Admiral Bayly.

Curiously, Bayly and Sims had similar experiences on their separate career paths. Both had been plucked from naval academia, where they had been put out to graze. After the loss of the pre-dreadnought HMS *Formidable*, Bayly had been 'shunted to the presidency of the Royal Naval College'. One writer suggested that 'it was as if his active career had ended'.[235] Sims would become

President of the United States Naval War College in Newport after the war, reverting to his former rank of rear admiral.

When Sims and Bayly first met each other at the Admiralty, the atmosphere bristled – 'he [Bayly] was as rude to me as one man could well be to another. He was apparently deeply incensed at having been sent for … When he had gone, Admiral Jellicoe apologized to me and said that he would remove the admiral if I thought it was necessary.'[236] Jellicoe made sure that Bayly understood the importance of getting on with Sims, telling him as much in front of Sir Edward Carson. Sims warned Taussig that despite being 'a peculiarly difficult man', he should step carefully as Bayly was 'very able and valuable'. Sims, for his part, purposefully submitted a draft of his operational orders to Bayly to appeal to his ego. Bayly finally appeared to ease up. His niece, Miss Violet Voysey (to whom Bayly dedicated his memoirs, *Pull Together*, 'To V.V. who made me write it', with the book's foreword written by no less a man than Franklin D. Roosevelt), eventually told Sims that 'he had walked around' him for three days and eventually concluded 'that man is on the square'.

In Queenstown, Jellicoe and Bayly perfected Anglo-American joint naval command. The sharing of command was carried right through to the courts martial. Each court revolved between two Americans and one British or two British and one American. Bayly had to leave Queenstown shortly after the arrival of the first Americans destroyers. In June, he asked Sims if he'd like to 'run the show from here in my absence?'. It would be 'the first time an American admiral had commanded Royal Navy ships'.[237] Bayly insisted that Sims raise his flag. It was completely unprecedented, and Sims hesitated before agreeing. The idea had been planted cleverly by Sims, but to Bayly it seemed to be his idea: 'I have a suggestion. If I go on leave from June 18th to 22nd, would you like to run the show from here in my absence? I should like it (and you are the only man of whom I could truly say that), your fellows would like it and it would have a good effect all round.'[238] Bayly's own conclusion was a moving one: 'We met as strangers; we worked as allies; we part as friends.'[239]

In 2017, I visited the very same flagpole with Sims's grandson, Dr Nat Sims.

As rumours started to go around about Lloyd George's run-ins with Jellicoe, Bayly wrote that he felt that 'you [Jellicoe] and Admiral Sims will defeat intrigues; I only wish I could help you'.[240]

### The Atlantic Convoys – Gibraltar, Dakar and Sierra Leone

The first homeward-bound (HG) convoy sailed from Gibraltar on 26 July, followed by seven convoys in August with 119 ships. The first convoy from

Sierra Leone (HL) sailed on 11 August with eleven ships. The first of two August convoys sailed from Dakar (HD) on 22 August, with thirty ships.

On 25 June, as part of the Trade Division, a new section was formed to manage the convoys, headed by Manisty. It is sad testament that Manisty's name, along with that of Henderson, 'have become footnotes at best in most histories of the U-boat campaign'.[241] Manisty's official title – Organising Manager of Convoys – and his small staff of initially ten, and later fifteen, did not match the importance of his role.

By October 1917, six American cutters were 'assigned duty as Gibraltar Danger Zone escorts, protecting freight convoys bound from or approaching' the port.[242] They would only act as a last escort in or out before handing over to ocean escorts. By that point, using longer, safer routes, the trip would take between seven and twelve days, depending on speeds and weather. Before each convoy, a conference attended by the masters and COs of both the escorted ships and escorts would take place. Written instructions were distributed with details such as the 'names and positions of all vessels, and the height of mast of each, for the better keeping of positions by means of sextant angles'.[243]

The convoy section would be responsible for managing convoys worldwide. A large chart (6ft by 9ft) showed each convoy's position at sea, its track shown by a red silk thread. Flags – colour-coded red for today, blue for yesterday and grey for the preceding day – showed any known submarine positions. Strategically placed minefields 'began to force U-boat commanders to give away very much more information about their positions and movements'.[244]

The Ministry of Shipping – where Norman Leslie worked – was responsible for 'the domestic aspects of convoyed ships – their destinations, employment, which cargoes they should carry, the bunkering of all ships requiring escort'.[245]

## Convoys in the Mediterranean

ASW in the Mediterranean was more difficult to achieve than in any other zone. Allied response in the Mediterranean was hampered by the fragmented command from a 'hotch-potch of nationalities': operating within the Allied camp were ships from Britain, France, Italy, Greece, Portugal, the United States and even Japan.[246]

With America's entry to the war in 1917, her vessels were added, and on top of that there were Japanese naval elements operating. Without complete agreement on who did what and under whose ultimate command operations fell, the area was bound to fall short.

American and neutral shipping was far less visible than on the Atlantic or in the North Sea. For Austro-Hungarian and German boats, it meant that less care needed to be taken to avoid severe diplomatic incidents.

*The state of ocean-going convoys, 1 September 1917*

| Assembly Harbour | Destination/s | Frequency (days) | Speed limits (knots) | 6 day running av'g no. Ships in convoy | Direction | Sub. zone Escorts | Composition Sub. Zone Escort | Ocean Escorts | Composition Ocean Escort |
|---|---|---|---|---|---|---|---|---|---|
| Sydney, CB | Canada | 1/8 | 8.5 to 12.5 | 18 | alt. E and W | 1 | 6 destroyers | 5 | British cruisers |
| | | | | | | | 5 sloops | | |
| New York | Portland M | 1/8 | 8.5 to 12.5 | 18 | alt. E and W | 1 | 6 destroyers | 6 | U.S. cruisers |
| | Boston | | | | | | 5 sloops | | |
| | New York | | | | | | | | |
| | Philadelphia | | | | | | | | |
| Halifax | N America | 1/8 | min. 12.5 | 12 | W only | 1 | 11 destroyers | 5 | armed aux. Cruisers |
| Hampton Roads | Ports S. of Colon incl. Gulf and W Indies | 1/4 | 8.5 to 12.5 | 44 | alt. E and W | 2 | 22 destroyers | 12 | 4 British cruisers |
| | | | | | | | | | 8 armed merchant escort ships |
| Dakar | Brazil | 1/8 | 8.5 to 11.5 | 16 | mix. E and W | 1 | 11 destroyers | 6 | British mercantile auxilliary |
| | Argentina | | | | | | | | |
| | Eastern ports | | | | | | | | |
| Sierra Leone | Brazil | 1/8 | min. 11.5 | 10 | mix. E and W | 1 | 11 destroyers | 5 | British mercantile auxilliary |
| | Argentina | | | | | | | | |
| | Eastern ports | | | | | | | | |
| Gibraltar | Mediterranean | 1/4 | min. 7 | 34 | alt. E and W | 2 | 4 destroyers | 10 | 6 special service vessels |
| | Huelva | | | | | | 48 trawlers | | 3 armed boarding steamers |
| | | | | | | | | | 1 sloop |

Source: Bacon, *Jellicoe*, p.364.

Then there were the opinions of British naval officers 'on the ground'. The attitude of Mediterranean naval command was certainly part of the problem: Admiral Gough-Calthorpe was

> personally antipathetic to the convoy system, regarding it not as a scientific system of A/S warfare, for fighting the enemy in the most effective way, but as a purely defensive palliative involving the misemployment of naval forces.[247]

It was at the Inter-Allied Naval Conference in September 1917 that the ball was set in motion for a theatre-wide introduction in the Mediterranean.

## British Coastal Convoys

Convoys, of course, had a weakness, which the U-boats quickly exploited: while ships under escort to and from assembly or dispersion points might be protected, when sailing individually without escort from a loading port or to a final delivery port they were again vulnerable.

At the start of 1918, the major east coast ports linking with the Humber and the Tyne were put under escort.[248] While the average convoy size was around fifty ships, UT18, the 'largest oceanic or coastal convoy during the war', numbered seventy-three ships and eighteen escorts.[249] The east coast convoys' record was impressive: according to Halpern, of the 23,000 ships escorted during the war, only seventy-one (or 0.4 per cent) were lost. Vice Admiral H.C. Dare (SO Milford) recommended a similar programme for the Irish Sea, and by June 1918 it was running on a regular basis.

## How Successful was the Convoy System?

The hurdles the convoy system would have to overcome in 1917 were daunting. In the spring, one in four ships departing British ports didn't come back.[250]

Convoys cleared the oceans of targets. Admiral Karl Doenitz, who later became commander-in-chief of Hitler's Kriegsmarine, saw it as the final straw that 'the German submarine campaign was wrecked by the introduction of the convoy system'.[251] Because of the escorts, U-boats could no longer close on their targets on the surface. A U-boat was forced to accept slower submerged speeds than that of its targets, and in doing so found it increasingly difficult to find firing solutions. At each step, convoys delivered benefits. First, the system forced the elusive hunter, the submarine, to concentrate on the convoys when they spotted them. It meant that the convoy's escorts did not have to leave the ships unprotected while 'sub-hunting' further afield. Second, once brought to the convoy, the submarine would likely only have one chance of a firing solution. Third, the offensive nature of convoy, that of counter-attacking submarines, which emerged with the development of suitable technologies (sound detection, depth charges, aerial surveillance and destruction etc). In short, convoys 'removed the initiative, for the first time, from the U-boat commanders'.[252]

Success is always, however, fleeting. Strategies change, countermeasures are developed and intelligence uncovers previously hidden solutions. The submarine war and the Allied response was, if nothing else, combat in perpetual flux. One side's fortunes rose and fell as if in a game of Snakes and Ladders. Lautenschlager points out that 'as the newer boats went to sea with 8 to 12 torpedoes, the monthly rate of sinkings total went above 200,000 tons for the first time'.[253] It wasn't anything the Allies were or were not doing; it was changes in German submarine design.

Convoys did not work all the time, nor did they work everywhere. The high level of cooperation required between different units, navies and players did not come about in the Mediterranean. Diplomatic pressure would shift submarine force allocation from one theatre to another. Seasons, weather and sea conditions could either be supportive of, or work against, U-boat activities. As cohesive convoy tactics developed, attackers would find a new chink in the armour. As countermeasures took root in one area, attacking forces would be moved to exploit their absence in another. Fighting the submarine war thus had no 'fronts'; it was constantly shifting.

### The Continuing Appeal of Sub-Hunting Flotillas

Despite the convoy system's success, it was always questioned. The composition of supporters and detractors was fluid. Beatty strongly supported convoys at Longhope, but just as vehemently opposed his Grand Fleet destroyers being taken to meet convoy escort needs. When Richmond took command of HMS *Conquerer* at Scapa, Beatty sought him out for advice, 'but had to avoid mentioning [his] name if it was connected with any proposal sent to the Admiralty while Jellicoe was First Sea Lord'. It's quite ironic, as Daniel Baugh points out:

> He thought the use of destroyers in a defensive mode for the Grand Fleet was a mistake, that destroyers should be used to give the enemy problems – to worry them – not to sit there and try to counter the enemy's torpedo boats [or submarines].

Why the portfolio concept of ASW is important is that it helps one understand the value of different weapons systems and platforms at different stages of ASW. At the early stages of development, airborne assets were useful to find submarines, but less, once found, in any attack role. Trawlers too might be ineffective in destroying a submarine, but their presence could keep a submarine under the waves, using up valuable battery reserves long enough to force it to surface and face a surface threat from torpedoes, guns or even ramming. Marder succinctly addresses this: 'The convoy system alone could not possibly have defeated the submarines had it not been accompanied by an ever-increasing expenditure of depth-charges by the escort vessels.'[254] Messimer's view is a little wider and cited both the convoys and America's entry into the war, but added that the increased availability of destroyers and the introduction of the depth charge were the 'two other factors that worked to ensure the success of the convoy system'.[255] Importantly, he adds that despite their weak surface escorts, 'it is evident that convoys ... were only possible because of British surface command'. It was the combination of 'the

*Non-convoy escort submarine sinkings 1917–18*

| Sub (Patrol) | Escort (Patrol) | Escort (Convoy) |
|---|---|---|
| UC.32 | UC.39 | U.58 |
| UC.68 | UC.46 | UB.69 |
| U.45 | UC.26 | UC.66 |
| UC.62 | UC.66 | U.89 |
| UC.63 | U.99 (SS *Valeria*) | UB.17 |
| UC.65 | U.69 | UB.70 |
| UB.16 | UB.27 | U.32 |
| U.154 | U.44 | UC.35 |
| UB.72 | U.49 (*British Transport*) | UC.56 |
| UB.52 | U.33 | UC.75 |
| UB.90 | UC.55 | UC.64 |
| U.78 | UC.51 (*Firedrake*) | UB.124 |
| | UC.47 | UB.110 |
| | U.48 | UB.30 |
| | UC.38 | UB.68 |
| | U.84 | |
| | U.109 | |
| | UB.35 | |
| | UB.63 | |
| | UC.50 | |
| | U.110 | |
| | UB.82 | |
| | UB.71 | |
| | U.104 | |
| | UB.85 | |
| | UC.78 | |
| | UB.78 (*Queen Alexandria*) | |
| | U.103 (*Olympic*) | |
| | UB.74 (*Lorna*) | |
| | UC.77 | |
| | UB.107 | |
| | UC.49 | |
| | UB.83 (*Ophelia*) | |
| | UB.103 | |
| | UB.115 | |
| | U.34 | |
| 12 | 36 | 15 |

Source: Annotations to Gibson and Prendergast, Appendix III, Table L, German Submarine Losses.

full historic system of battlefleet command and convoy' which proved to be the winning solution. Maybe, then, 'The battleship was still the backbone of sea power'.[256]

Valuable work was accomplished by Fleet Paymaster Ernest Thring (ID Section 25b, previously known as the Enemy Submarine Section) in October 1917. He argued that sub-hunting could only be successful if A/S assets were held ready in concentrated areas for known U-boat traffic, for example the north coast of Scotland or the Channel.[257] Thring argued that convoys had been effective in stabilizing merchant shipping losses but not in reducing the submarine threat. The horrific toll of April 1917 was an aberration, but it took from January 1917 to January 1918 for the sinking tonnage to fall back to around the same level that existed before the unrestricted campaign. Convoys were not the *immediate silver bullet* so many made them out to be. First, because convoys protected ships; they did not sink submarines. Second, looking at sinkings under convoy is misleading. Many ships continued to be sunk close inshore in waters nearing their final ports, after they had left the protection of convoy.

It seems clear that Jellicoe also maintained an open mind on the value of sub-hunting – either by armed trawlers, escorts or hunter-killer submarines – for sinking submarines. He annotated his copy of Gibson and Prendergast, noting that, of the 178 submarines sunk, thirty-six were due to non-convoy escort, half that number to escorts attached to convoy from 1917 to the war's end.

It seemed that 'finding the submarine was in fact the least of the British Navy's problems'.[258] This was being increasingly accomplished through air patrols, kite balloons and better dispersion of improved W/T equipment to larger aircraft.

Surface patrols did not work in isolation; as an example, the Northern Barrage was 'part of a coordinated strategy' in which different elements, working together in a combined operations approach, used different

*British and worldwide submarine-related shipping losses 1914–18*

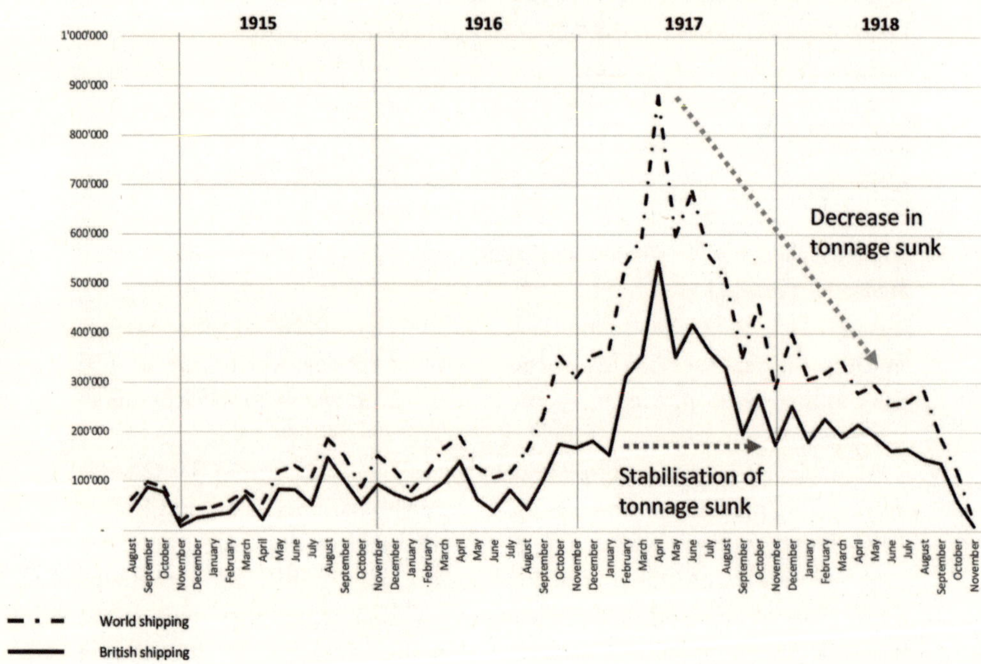


Source: Jellicoe, *CONW*, pp.12–13.

technologies, weapons and platforms for different tasks in the sequence of A/S operations. This meant assigning operations areas (patrol areas) to be worked by a destroyer, a kite balloon and several trawlers connected to centralised intelligence on the mainland by W/T.

This shows the importance of timing in tactics. The same approach was made in June 1917 by Grand Fleet destroyers off the northern Scottish coast. Although sixty-one submarines were sighted and twelve attacked, not a single one was sunk or damaged. The supporting technology in aircraft, W/T and depth charges was lacking. The operation, however, resulted in an ASD officer, in July 1917, making the suggestion of creating two 'Chase Flotillas', anticipating Thring's thinking on concentration.[259] Lewis placed rather too much faith in the development of the hydrophone, but his idea was that the submarine, once it dived to avoid continued air surveillance, would be tracked by hydrophone-equipped trawlers to exhaust its batteries and force it to the surface, where it could be finished off.

Amid frantic efforts to counter the submarine, the surface threat to convoys was overlooked. Both Jellicoe and Sims shared the same opinion, and their concerns became only too apparent with the brutally successful German anti-Scandinavian convoy operations. The use of the fast minelayers *Bremse* and *Brummer* was well-planned; it disguised their real purpose.

# 7

# After Supreme Command: From the Hot Seat to a Cold Shoulder

## Preparations to Remove Jellicoe

Shipping was becoming increasingly scarce, as 'the world's ports were ransacked for tonnage. The hope was to answer the immediate objective of over-riding unnecessary and costly competition for the nation's ship-building resources. Decrepit steamers fetched fabulous prices.'[1] Midway through 1917, on 2 May, plans to reorganize the Admiralty's War Staff were passed by the War Cabinet. The old title of Controller, which had previously come under the responsibility of the Third Sea Lord, was, for the first time, given to a civilian whose extensive experience in managing rail systems in America, India and Great Britain had made him a brilliant logistics aid to Douglas Haig. Eric Geddes had served Haig as the Director-General of Transportation, British Armies in France, from 1916–17 and would now control all shipping construction – *both* naval and mercantile.

Geddes was a dynamo. Sims described him as 'big, athletic, energetic, with a genius for reaching the kernel of a question and of getting things done', and Jellicoe had also spoken highly of him. Jellicoe understood the Edinburgh-born businessman's value as a direct conduit to the Prime Minister: 'Geddes is a superman, an excellent fellow and has the complete whip hand of L.G. [Lloyd George] so we shall get all the steel we want.'[2] Initially, Geddes worked well with Jellicoe, the admiral trying hard to accept him despite his previous close working relationship with Carson. For his part, Geddes said he was 'on the best of terms with Jellicoe'.[3] Nevertheless, it wasn't long before the two clashed. A few weeks before he was dismissed, Jellicoe wrote that Geddes 'had occasion to take exception to the methods' of the new First Lord.[4] But he added that 'no serious disagreement occurred'.

Supposedly, Geddes had not wanted the job and had only accepted it when he was assured of Jellicoe's support and because of Lloyd George's persuasiveness. Jellicoe, according to the Prime Minister, had insisted on the post not being held by a civilian.[5] So Geddes was given the honorary rank of vice admiral, prompting Lord Esher to quip: 'Geddes – a general to-day, and an admiral tomorrow.' When he was working for Haig, he had been equally insistent on being given the rank and allowed to wear the uniform of a major general.

With Geddes now being carefully manoeuvred into place by Lloyd George, the Prime Minister started to intervene more actively in naval policy.[6] The PM was right in backing his case for better statistics, and in May 1917, Lieutenant Colonel George Beharrell was appointed to head up a relevant section in the Admiralty. DCNS Oliver's staff cooperated minimally: they used 'to make up data mixed with weather conditions and the phases of the moon' so that they 'could keep the statisticians out of their way'.[7] If true, it was short-sighted, childish and hugely irresponsible. After all, the submarine war was essentially a numbers game.

There seemed to be little let-up. At the end of June, in a letter to his wife, Ethel, Beatty complained about the ongoing U-boat threat:

> The submarine menace is no more in hand to-day than it was three months ago!!! They might flood the Admiralty with civilians and soldiers, but it will serve no purpose unless the heads change their views and adopt the strongest measures.[8]

Marder wrote that what Beatty meant by his words 'the strongest measures' was the full adoption of convoys on the Atlantic routes, but it should be added that Beatty also supported aggressive sub-hunting. Lloyd George was frustrated too. Having, in his mind, achieved the Admiralty's consent to test the convoy system, he now felt that they were dragging their heels. After the success of the 10 May Gibraltar convoy, it seemed to take an age, until 26 July, for the next convoy to be dispatched.

Despite glowing reports from the Shipping Department stating that the success had been 'phenomenal', American opposition was hard to overcome. In retrospect, it's difficult to believe that, after fourteen convoys had come through without a single vessel being lost (only a tanker, the *Wabasha*, was hit by a speculative long-range 'browning' shot on the fourth convoy), the official American naval line remained negative. Commodore Guy Gaunt, the British Naval Attaché in Washington, reported:

> The Navy Department does not consider it advisable to attempt the character of convoy outlined. In large groups of ships under convoy, fog,

> gales, inexperience of personnel, and general tension on merchant vessels make the hazards of the attempt great and the probability of a scattering of the convoy very strong.[9]

In July, the Jellicoe–Haig–Robertson War Cabinet triumvirate was finally given the go-ahead for the Flanders campaign, supporting Jellicoe's aim of sealing off the Flanders Flotilla's bases of Ostend and Zeebrügge. Jellicoe thought that,

> So long as the Belgian coast ports remained in German possession, the Naval force that could be based there constituted a very serious menace to the cross-Channel traffic.[10]

Behind the scenes, Jellicoe was anxious and wrote to Beatty about his concerns: 'I fancy there is a scheme on foot to get rid of me … I expect it will be done by first discrediting me in the Press. That is the usual political move and I have seen signs of it already.'[11] He was right. Beatty's response was described by Massie not only as 'ambivalent', but also, given his own attacks on Jellicoe's handling of the fleet at Jutland, 'hypocritical'.[12] Beatty urged Jellicoe to hang on – 'you must stick at all costs to your intention to not volunteering to go; that would be fatal. Do not be goaded into any step of the kind no matter what the press or anybody else says.'[13]

That December, Beatty and Jellicoe needlessly fell out after the Scandinavian convoy fiasco. Only one escort destroyer, HMS *Pellow*, got away after her convoy had been attacked on 12 December. Geddes infuriated Beatty by suggesting language from Jellicoe (which Jellicoe had never actually used) in a request for a Naval Court of Enquiry. Jellicoe was also concerned by Geddes's suggestion of bringing Fisher into the enquiry, a move that he felt would only 'cause great ill feeling in the fleet and would, moreover, produce no good result'.[14] Relations between the two never recovered after Fisher's disappointment with Jutland's outcome.[15] The result of the inquiry was the recommendation that the responsibility for convoy routing and diversion be taken over directly by the Admiralty. But it was the decision to set aside a battle squadron from the Grand Fleet that should be seen as 'the most significant indication of the importance convoys had assumed'.[16]

Jellicoe's strong opposition to a naval bombardment of Zeebrügge and Brüges rather than a combined naval and land operation, and his pessimism over food supplies, was riling the Prime Minister. Like Jellicoe, Beatty felt that there were too many 'hare-brained schemes' and that it was essential that 'there be no question of any difference of opinion between us'.[17] Jellicoe might have done well to take some of the advice of Beatty, who was far more politically astute.

Jellicoe's presentations to the War Cabinet were *purposefully* negative. 'It was necessary,' he later said,

> to be very outspoken to the War Cabinet on the subject of the submarine danger even at the risk of being accused of pessimistic views, for it was very difficult during the first half of 1917 to get the magnitude of the danger realized.[18]

Jellicoe had become increasingly disenchanted and briefly considered resigning, but that would have gone against his sense of duty. Lloyd George's dislike of Jellicoe wasn't that remarkable or unique; he was rude with anyone with whom he disagreed, including senior commanders.[19] The PM's leadership style – much needed in a public figure in times like these – was of eternal optimism. Jellicoe, however, saw it another way. Writing to Beatty, he complained: 'He is a hopeless optimist … He gets figures from any source and believes them if they suit his views. It is a continual fight to prevent more side-shows being started.'[20] Sims, who said that he had 'frequent' meetings with the Prime Minister, remembered him admitting: 'Oh yes, things are bad, but we shall have the best of the submarine – never fear!'[21]

Lloyd George liked to listen to younger officers, the Royal Navy's Young Turks – men like Dewar, Henderson and Kenworthy, as well as the 'indefatigable if petulant' Captain Richmond. He felt that he had 'more converse with fighting officers and men, untabbed with scarlet, straight from the trenches, than any member of the Staff either at general Headquarters or at the War Office'.[22] He supported their idea of establishing a group to continually develop aggressive offensive planning. It was something the CIGS, Sir William Robertson, supported but that Jellicoe strongly opposed. The section was formally put in place on 16 July, with Captain Dudley Pound (who as Admiral of the Fleet served as the First Sea Lord from 1939–43) at its head. Its duties, however, were scaled back: it was to *plan* not to *initiate* planning. Even if Geddes was not satisfied – he had wanted to create a separate division – it brought more manpower into the Naval Staff. Nicholas Black wrote that it was 'in many ways … the single most important change to the staff in 1917 … It was numbers, rather than structures, which were more significant.'[23]

One of the officers who joined the section was Commander Joseph Kenworthy.[24] He wasn't happy, feeling that he was amongst 'mediocre minds'. Like many of his fellow officers, he was very outspoken: 'We [the Young Turks] were in mental revolt against the policy of the Admiralty.'[25] What they most wanted was offensive action; convoy and blockade were seen as the antithesis, an entirely defensive policy. A raid like Zeebrügge was the kind of action they wanted.

Lloyd George's desire to get rid of Jellicoe was growing. After talking with the Prime Minister, Hankey confirmed on 3 July that he was 'hot for getting rid of Jellicoe', but Lloyd George was being warned off making any aggressive moves because of Jellicoe's reputation and following in the Navy and the country at large. Lloyd George's plan was first to remove Carson. He and Jellicoe worked well; Carson had given him his total support when he knew the situation was difficult, even confirming that 'the First Sea Lord came to see me several times and pressed me to accept his resignation'.[26] Carson liked Jellicoe and held him in high esteem, saying that he was the 'best man at his job that I met with in the whole course of the War – for knowledge, calmness, straightness and the confidence he inspired in his officers'.[27] Even Beatty had agreed he was 'the best possible man to be First Sea Lord'.[28]

Field Marshal Douglas Haig led the attacks on Carson, and then Jellicoe. The admiral, he said, 'does not impress me. Indeed, he strikes me as being an old woman!' When Jellicoe opposed a purely naval attack on Zeebrügge and Ostend on 16 June, and then, two days later, talked of the possibility of defeat, Haig was able to turn the War Cabinet against him. 'There is no good,' Jellicoe had said, 'in discussing plans for next Spring – we cannot go on' because of the lack of shipping.[29] Three weeks later, the War Cabinet approved plans for the disastrous Flanders offensive, later to be pulled back on 23 September. Haig made a special note of the meeting in his diary:

> A most serious and startling situation was disclosed today. At today's conference, Admiral Jellicoe, as First Sea Lord, stated that owing to the great shortage of shipping due to German submarines, it would be impossible for Great Britain to continue the war in 1918. This was a bombshell for the cabinet and all present … No one present shared Jellicoe's view, and all seemed satisfied that the food reserves in Great Britain are adequate. Jellicoe's words were, 'There is no good discussing plans for next spring – we cannot go on.'[30]

Lloyd George considered replacing Carson with Robertson. The general, thankfully, persuaded the Prime Minister against the move. Viscount Milner came up with the plan that Lloyd George eventually adopted: with the support of Bonar Law, Curzon and Maclay, Lloyd George invited Carson to join the War Cabinet.[31] He then filled the vacancy with his own man, Geddes, after another idea – that of Hankey taking the position – had been rejected. At first, Carson did not respond positively; he had to be pressured by the fear of the discussions becoming public: 'I did not want it. Even at that stage I had seen the political side of ministerial posts, which I have increasingly disliked.'[32] When the announcement was finally made, both the Navy and the Conservative press reacted badly. Typically, Lloyd George gives his readers a misleading impression of his motives: 'I was convinced that Sir Edward Carson's great gifts would be better employed by giving him a seat in the War Cabinet.' Carson had, in his mind, been 'unsuited' for the position of First Lord.[33]

## The London Naval Conference

By September, Jellicoe was starting to feel some of the extreme pressure dissipate. At least ten German submarines had been sunk in the month and shipping losses were falling.

When the First Lord, Geddes, had to return to the War Cabinet, Jellicoe hosted the 4 September London Naval Conference. Initially, he pushed for a concerted effort to block German harbours. One idea was to use older battleships, as there were simply too few merchant vessels available. It was a massive scheme: it was proposed that eighty-three ships would be sunk in the Heligoland Bight.[34]

The Japanese, however, spoke of their own experience in failing to keep the Russian navy blockaded. Admiral Funakoshi recounted Japan's unsuccessful efforts: '[W]e blocked the entrance to Port Arthur but on the following day the Russian fleet came out … We then laid a new barrier … all our efforts were unavailing.'[35] Jellicoe backed away from the proposal, saying it was 'most attractive in theory' and that it 'appealed with force to that considerable section which feels vaguely, *and rightly* [my italics], that offensive action is needed'.[36]

The alternative was mining on a massive scale, coupled with a barrage at the northern exit of the North Sea. That was the step eventually taken, even if neither the French nor the Japanese were in favour. Funakoshi's reasoned opposition was seconded by Admiral de Bon, the Chief of Staff of the French Navy.

## The Dismissal of Sir John Jellicoe

Jellicoe was feeling that the political tide was turning against him, even if September's anti-submarine figures looked promising. There were disagreements between Jellicoe and Geddes: one was about Duff, for whom Jellicoe had recommended an honour. The problem was that Geddes disliked Duff's 'manner'. In Winton's words, very much echoing Lloyd George's own, it was the way that Duff 'thought of the difficulties in the way of introducing convoy rather than of the possible benefits of introducing it'.[37] Jellicoe defended Duff, saying that the honour was for his services, not his demeanour.

In the end, Lloyd George's discontent polarized around a completely different issue. Admiral Wemyss, Jellicoe's deputy, wanted to replace Vice Admiral Bacon, the architect of the Dover Barrage.[38] Marder believed that this was the *immediate* cause, 'the catalyst that prompted [his] dismissal', even if the break had been brewing for months. Others, such as Temple Patterson, thought it more the accumulated strain of twenty-eight months of command at sea and eleven months at the Admiralty.

From intelligence newly recovered from the sunken wreck of *UC.44*, it emerged that enemy submarines were having little difficulty passing through the barrage.[39] In February, Bacon had asked the Admiralty to strengthen the original September 1916 barrage, but none of the newly redesigned mines were supplied until towards the end of 1917, in November. Upon taking command at Dover, Bacon's copy of the *UC.44* file was supposedly found by Keyes in his safe and used as proof positive that the Dover Barrage was ineffective. Geddes agreed to the firing of Bacon – Jellicoe did not.

Under Bacon, submarine sinkings had been minimal – only two had been accounted for by barrage mines in two years. But the conclusion is certainly clouded by the fact that increased patrolling, illumination and, finally, effective mines all came together around the same time. Passing through the straits became too dangerous, and 'in practice, the Channel route was now given up'. German U-boat commanders were authorized by Michelsen to decide which route to take for themselves. It was a significant moment: having to take the still-navigable northern route meant adding almost ten days to a U-boat's journey, cutting down the patrol time within its assigned area.

In 1932, Bacon published his account of the Dover Patrol. He gave a signed copy to Jellicoe with a very personal note:

> The writing of the book brought back to me many memories but none more vivid than the unfailing support you gave me during the latter end of 1917 when forces at the admiralty were strongly arrayed against me – that support enabled me to continue the work begun and prepare for the results which were reaped the following year. I also know that *your stand on my behalf increased the difficulty of your position at the admiralty* [author's italics]. These are matters which could not be touched on in the book – but their memory remains.

I wish Bacon *had* written about those matters, as so much still remains murky.[40]

On Monday, 24 December 1917, Jellicoe was fired. He had been in his Admiralty office around 1800hrs.[41] As he was about to leave to join his family for Christmas, a messenger arrived with a letter from Geddes:

> My dear Sir John Jellicoe,
> After very careful consideration, I have come to the conclusion that a change is desirable in the post of the First Sea Lord. I have not, I can

> assure you, arrived at this view hastily or without personal regret and reluctance. I have consulted the Prime Minister and with his concurrence, I am asking to see the King to make this recommendation to him.[42]

Jellicoe replied immediately: he would be glad to be relieved as soon as possible. The strain of the last few years, and particularly the amount of time devoted to Cabinet, was enormous. A letter from Lloyd George (which he, rather sarcastically, characterised as 'courteous'), awarding Jellicoe a title, arrived on Christmas morning. It was one sentence long: 'Dear Sir, I have the honour to inform you that His Majesty has been pleased to approve of my recommendation, that the dignity of a peerage of the United Kingdom be conferred upon you. Yours faithfully, D Lloyd George.'[43] Jellicoe's first inclination was to refuse the peerage, but, after talking with Gwen (and others, including Lord Beresford), he decided that, for posterity's sake, it would be better to accept.

The manner of Jellicoe's sacking was 'a strange curtain-line for the most brilliant officer of his time'.[44] It had been well-timed, avoiding any effective outcry; Parliament had adjourned for Christmas, and over the holidays there were no newspapers. Although the Prime Minister denied it, the sacking had been carefully coordinated with Lloyd George to minimize political fallout or the appearance of primary responsibility falling at his feet. He even intimated that it was only after the King had assented that Jellicoe was removed, saying that he resigned on 26 December. Geddes denied that the decision was Lloyd George's, rather 'a result of my own uninfluenced judgement'.[45] Geddes's own brother, Sir Auckland Geddes, however, made it plain that he saw David Lloyd George as the puppeteer who pulled his brother's strings, the instrument through which he could rid himself of Jellicoe.[46]

The reaction after Christmas was ferocious. Prince Louis of Battenberg, who had been First Sea Lord at the outbreak of war, was livid: 'I cannot find the words to express my disgust and indignation.'[47] Admiral William Goodenough agreed: 'Never a man stood higher in the estimation of his friends, his brother officers and every man and boy in the Service.'[48] Former PM Asquith said what Lloyd George should have: 'No one knows better – perhaps no one as well as I do – what the State and the Allied cause owes you.'[49] Messages from the Grand Fleet demanding his return poured in, but of course, he could not go back.

There is no doubt that Jellicoe had been under a huge strain for over three years, both as the Grand Fleet's Commander-in-Chief and as First Sea Lord. Despite what he did to maintain his fitness, it must have taken a toll. Many historians highlight this physical aspect. Some of the criticism was politically motivated, much of it reasonable; Ballantyne, for example, cautioned that 'his fragile constitution and unbending dedication to doing his duty by his nation … threatened paralysis'.[50]

## Changes at the Top – Britain

The first day of 1918 started with what looked to be a major crisis at the highest echelons of the Royal Navy. The Sea Lords threatened resignation *en masse* if they did not get a satisfactory explanation from Geddes for Jellicoe's removal. Some notable names, however, were missing: neither Wemyss, Duff nor Oliver had attended the meeting.[51] Wemyss one would understand, and also maybe Oliver. But Duff's reaction was surprising.

The dissenters, Jellicoe's supporters, issued a statement expressing 'full confidence in Sir John Jellicoe's ability and fitness to perform his responsible duties … [and that] they were most gravely concerned and disturbed by this sudden removal of a most able and distinguished officer'.[52] They only backed down when asked to do so by Jellicoe; it wasn't in his character to show any dissent in public.[53] 'I advised Halsey that the Sea Lords should not resign as it would do no good and be bad for the country.'[54]

Geddes claimed that others had been in favour of the dismissal, Carson in particular, whom he said also had doubts as to Jellicoe being 'the best man for the position'.[55] Carson flatly denied this, maintaining that when Geddes raised the issue in October, asking what he should do, Sir Edward's reply was crystal clear: 'Do? Why stand beside him and think no more about it.'[56] Carson and Jellicoe had been close; indeed, the First Lord later made it clear when he spoke to the House of Commons that Jellicoe had been targeted by Lloyd George for months.

Angrily, Jellicoe wrote to Beatty on Christmas Day, saying that his dismissal had nothing to do with being 'war weary' or that he was 'lacking in offensive spirit'. It was more that he did not agree to the Royal Navy 'being run by an autocrat like a railway'.[57] In a more respectful tone, he wrote to the King, concluding that if the King did not feel that he had failed, then he (Jellicoe) was 'indifferent' to what had happened.[58] The King had been told that Jellicoe had lost the confidence of the Cabinet.

Rosslyn Wemyss, known as 'Rosie' to friends, amongst whom he included the King, was named the new First Sea Lord. The King was conscious of Wemyss's intellectual shortcomings but was also very confident of his friend's suitability, knowing that he was good with people as well as being practical.

Beatty found working with Wemyss easy at the start but later came to disagree with him on policy, particularly on how Britain's limited destroyer resources should be used. Wemyss found the Admiralty far too defensive, saying that 'to counter the submarine menace Defence only had been used. To me it appeared absolutely necessary that the tables must be turned and that we must hunt the enemy submarines instead of them hunting us.'[59] His ideas for submarine-hunting groups never came to fruition, however, as 'senior members of the Staff chose not to reduce the readiness of the Grand Fleet in the face of opposition from Beatty'.[60] Others, like Madden, Jellicoe's brother-in-law, weren't happy. He wrote that he was 'full of fear for the future; the Grand Fleet is all right as Beatty is strong enough to refuse to throw it away on wild cat schemes, but the wider field of operations is not in such able hands'.[61]

### And Changes at Dover

Once the new British mines were laid, the minefields off the Belgian coast proved more effective. In the last six months of 1916, six U-boats were sunk in the Zeebrügge approaches.[62]

Days after Jellicoe was forced from office, Bacon was removed from the Dover command. He had obstinately defended the questionably effective Dover Strait Barrage. Many, like Churchill, admired his phenomenal work habits.[63]

Rear Admiral Keyes, Director of the Plans Division, was appointed as Chairman of the Channel Barrage Committee, set up by Sir Eric Geddes, on 17 November. He proved to be Bacon's nemesis. Leading up to his demise, Geddes acted with little tact. Despite his huge experience, Bacon was appointed to the same committee.

Some of the committee's recommendations included illuminating the minefield at night and increasing the number of patrols around possible submarine dive areas to dissuade them from riding through the barrage on the surface. Bacon strenuously objected, saying that he did not have the resources. Besides, he argued, such actions would have made sitting targets for the guardships. According to Churchill, 'The area was as bright as Piccadilly Circus in peacetime and its occupants scarcely better armed.'[64] Bacon's preference was for the lighthouses, at the 'gates' at each end of the barrage, to use their powerful beams to illuminate the area rather than the million candle-watt flares Keyes was suggesting. He also wanted to keep the supporting surface ships to the west so that they could clearly see any illuminated targets in silhouette. Even though Bacon's timing was off – *UB.56* was almost immediately caught and sunk – he 'saw in these orders the probability of a massacre (and he was not wrong)'.[65]

Bacon used a conference on 18 December to defend himself. He followed up with Geddes in writing. Neither man was known for diplomatic skills, so the situation did not bode well:

> The above statement put, as politely as I possibly could, the obvious fact that it was better to leave the defence of the Strait to the Admiral who

> had local knowledge, experience, and the whole responsibility entailed by the command at Dover, than to allow dabbling by a committee who had no local knowledge, experience or responsibility.[66]

Jellicoe had defended his fellow admiral: 'I am not able to accept the sweeping indictment of the work of the VA [Vice Admiral] Dover, as stated by the Director of Plans. The VA's dispositions are based on experience, not only of submarine action but of destroyer attacks, and he is naturally reluctant to ignore the latter in the attempt to deal with the former.'[67]

Jellicoe, however, also supported Roger Keyes's recommendations to increase both patrolling and illumination. On 14 December, he gave Bacon written orders to this effect. The effectiveness of illumination, however, was questionable: *UB.35* passed through on the night of 1 January 1918, staying close to the English coastline. Her captain, Oberleutnant zur See Karl Stöter, said 'the boat was frequently illuminated which made things very uncomfortable when passing a patrol. However, we remained unobserved.'[68]

Jellicoe noted that the Admiralty had information that showed that the volume of U-boat traffic going through the Dover Strait was large.[69] Despite the fact that during Bacon's command only seventy-three of the 125,100 merchant ships that passed through were sunk, his removal was a diplomatic censure, also letting it be known that there was a preferred way to handle these disagreements. Geddes, Jellicoe felt, had been too impatient.[70] The year before, the Germans had very successfully attacked British destroyers in the Channel. On the night of 26/27 October, they raided the Channel, sinking some drifters and a destroyer, so severely damaging two other ships (HMS *Zulu* and *Nubian*) that a new vessel, HMS *Zubian*, was born after the two hulls were joined together in subsequent dockyard repairs.

The captain of *UB.57*, Oberleutnant zur See Lohs, noted that 'since the raids, the patrols are much reduced', even if this was only temporary.[71] The timing coincided with the sinking of Max Valentiner's *UB.56* during the night of 19/20 December. She had been caught in the bright illumination and forced to dive to her death in the minefield between Le Colbert and Cap Gris-Nez. Only one dead German was found.

A week after Jellicoe's 'resignation', on 29 December, Bacon was also dismissed. It is interesting to note that while *The Crisis of the Naval War* features the Barrage Committee, neither Jellicoe nor Bacon (in his biography of Jellicoe) mention Roger Keyes. Keyes was, after all, complimentary about Bacon's achievements, even if both thought him an upstart: 'The activities of the Dover Patrol were immense and Admiral Bacon had built up an enormous organization, which carried out its daily duties with great regularity and efficiency.'[72] Beatty, too, said that he 'did well but [that] he was too theoretical'.[73] That sounded even-handed, but Beatty never liked Bacon. In corresponding with his friend Horace Hood (a former commander of the Dover Patrol, who was killed at Jutland), Beatty would, for some reason, 'contemptuously' refer to Bacon as 'the Colonel'.[74]

Bacon was removed over Jellicoe's strong opposition. Between 8 January and 8 February 1918, another four U-boats were sunk in the Dover Strait, three by mines. Keyes seemed vindicated, until the German destroyer attack on 14 February. What Bacon had feared, happened: seven drifters and trawlers were sunk, with another five drifters, one trawler and a minesweeper severely damaged, while eighty-nine officers were killed or wounded. Keyes's victory had been short-lived, and consequently his 'reputation hung on a thread'.[75] His reputation was saved – indeed he was lionized – by the courageous action in the attack on Zeebrügge the next year.

Things had not gone well at the end of 1917: seventy-six ships were torpedoed in December and a further eight mined, the largest casualty being the 7,046-ton *Vinovia*, sunk on 19 December 8 miles south of Cornwall's Wolf Rock Lighthouse. A series of losses was inccurred on 22 December by destroyers in the Harwich force protecting the Dutch 'butter convoys' and the 'beef trip'. The convoy had mistakenly entered a minefield and three escort destroyers – *Surprise*, *Tornado* and *Torrent* – foundered. Luckily, 193 survivors were pulled from the waters.

An attack on Christmas Day 1917 met with poetic justice of sorts. The 4,821-ton *Agberi* was sunk by *U.87* 18 miles north-west of Bardsey Island on the north-western coast of Wales. A patrol boat, the *PC.56*, then attacked the submerged submarine, which had been inadvertently hit by a sloop, *Buttercup*. It had been circling the sinking ship. *U.87* was brought to the surface with a depth charge and successfully rammed. Count von Speth-Schülzburg and all his crew were killed.

Meanwhile, Holtzendorff's promise that Britain would be finished off before America could make a difference proved naïve. Six months after America's declaration of war, US troops started to enter the trenches along the Western Front. General John Pershing, commanding US forces in North-West Europe, didn't waste any time: as soon as a batch of troops were ready, they were sent to the front. Two million would be in France 'by the time of the 1918 armistice, a year before Ludendorff claimed that the first of them would arrive'.[76]

### 1918: The Continued U-boat Menace

The key question following John Jellicoe's dismissal was whether the new team – Wemyss as First Sea Lord and Sir Eric Geddes as First Lord of the Admiralty – made significant improvements.

Britain's position remained critical. Merchant shipping losses topped 6 million tons and merchant shipping output had fallen: it was 30 per cent below the total for each of the last three years of peace, 1.1 million tons.[77] It was also estimated that the *efficiency* of the system had declined to the same degree – roughly 30 per cent – due to 'not having enough labourers to load and unload ships, the inevitable back-up of heavily laden ships waiting to discharge or take aboard their cargoes and bureaucratic delays in issuing sailing orders'.[78] While nothing like the scale in Germany, 'police in London counted up to 550,000 people standing in food queues'.[79]

In 1918, however, the war at sea kicked off with a string of immediate successes – 'marked, if not sensational' was how Marder described it – against U-boats trying to get through the Dover Strait. From 19 January to 8 February, three were sunk.[80] One of them, *U.109*, on 26 January, and another, *UB.38*, on 8 February. Both U-boats had been lost like Valentiner's the previous December. With the appointment of Roger Keyes on 1 January, it appeared that the Dover headquarters had been imbued with a new life, even if he had only served as a rear admiral for nine months.

Britain's shipyards had also been overwhelmed with repair work. As the year opened, 1.5 million tons was under repair: 'With such losses, the programme of new construction was utterly unable to cope.'[81] However, the lack of repair facilities similarly plagued the Germans: in the Mediterranean, for example, only five of a total of thirty-three submarines were at sea in January 1918, the remaining twenty-eight being under repair. Such was the overload that those with more severe repair needs were sent all the way back to German yards.[82] Finally, mutiny broke out, first at the Pola base in January and then, on 1 February, at Cattaro. Although abortive, they added to the ongoing difficulties of submarine operations.

News of atrocities at sea continued. On 4 January 1918, a 7,308-ton hospital ship, the *Rewa*, was torpedoed by Wilhelm Werner's *U.55*. She had been transporting 279 patients. This was the same Werner who had torpedoed the *Torrington* the year before, in April, and had tried to do the same to another ship, the *Guildford Castle*, on 10 March. The latter, a Clan Line ship, had been carrying 438 sick and wounded.[83] Dockworkers later found that the way in which the hull had been dented and scraped showed that she had a very lucky escape: a torpedo must have glanced off her hull and failed to explode.

### *U.155*'s Opening Cruises

Long-range U-boat operations also continued. Under the new command of Korvettenkapitän Erich Eckelmann, *U.155*, a militarised ex-freighter, left Germany in early January, and by mid-February had made it as far as Lisbon after taking a circuitous route through British minefields. After she parted with her two escort torpedo boats, she had to run south at a depth of 40 metres to avoid the strong surface swell. Even at 35 metres, those on board 'didn't feel much relief'.[84] Once in position, her task was to cut enemy telegraph cables, and to do so she stealthily crept closer inshore. There, shears were lowered and dragged along the seabed until they hooked a cable. Three were successfully severed before the equipment fouled.[85]

The task completed, *U.155* then attacked shipping. On 10 March, she stopped a Danish cargoman, the 4,271-ton *Wegadesk*, her holds full of precious metals. Some 45 tons of brass was transferred off the ship.[86] A week later, a huge cargo of flour was taken off a Norwegian ship, the 3,570-ton *Reidar*. At first, the *Reidar* escaped under the cover of darkness, but when she was again spotted the next morning, there was 'not a soul on the ship'. She had been abandoned in the night. 'We were only left with one beautiful dog.'[87] Then, in April, *U.155* stopped a Portuguese freighter, *Lusitano*, carrying cotton and steel goods. For survivors, there was little chance as the weather was so bad. Some had even tried to cling to the side of the U-boat, only to be pushed off by crew members:

> As difficult as it was to use violence against the poor men, we had no choice. They too, were our enemies; they too provided enemy armies with war material which had to be destroyed. We were not allowed and could not be merciful. For a long time we saw the unfortunates floating on the waves in their tiny boats. We had no doubts about their inevitable fate in this sea.[88]

From a crew of twenty-seven, there was not a single survivor from the *Lusitano*. At the end of the week – Sunday, 7 April – *U.155* got into a ferocious, if initially one-sided, duel with an Italian tanker (which Eckelmann's engineer, Schultz, identified as an 'auxiliary cruiser'), the 9,500-ton *Sterope*. Early on in the exchange of fire, shell shrapnel pierced one of the U-boat's dive tanks before her own deck gun was able to land multiple hits on the tanker's superstructure and bridge. Despite a white flag being run up, she then 'disappeared completely with a direct hit'. Schultz was jubilant: they had come out on top against a ship armed with four 76mm guns and a 'revolving cannon'.[89] *Sterope* had taken a lot of casualties: three officers, including the captain, had been killed. After helping the wounded and being provisioned, the survivors were set adrift, but out of the 113-strong crew only six survived.

On 4 May, having first rendezvoused with the guard ship *Hannover*, *U.155* entered Kiel harbour. However, it wasn't a happy moment: despite their successes, they already felt Germany had lost the war.[90] Schultz jumped ashore with a 'cloth sack full of groceries', heading directly to his family and then to his parents in the Rhineland. They were 'suffering terribly from the lack of food'.[91]

### Death in the Strait of Dover

Keyes, who himself even admitted that he was 'very conscious of being thick headed', like Bacon, correctly anticipated the German response to the illumination and small vessels being installed around the nets – a strong surface attack on the British patrols.[92]

On the night of 14/15 February, a strong destroyer attack was launched by the HSF's 2nd Destroyer Flotilla. The encounter may have only lasted an hour (from 0030hrs to around 0130hrs), but heavy damage was inflicted on the British: seven drifters and a trawler were sunk, with a further five drifters, one trawler and a minelayer all 'severely damaged'.[93]

Incredibly, even knowing something was afoot, not one of the four British destroyers close by counter-attacked. From HMS *Amazon*, Lieutenant Adam Fergusson later said that he had challenged suspicious ships three times with a hand-held lamp and that they had passed 'within two cables astern'.[94] Under Standing Orders, without a reply, he should have opened fire. Feebly, he said he was 'certain' that they had been British. Fergusson was very lucky: the German commander, Kolbe, reported that one of his own destroyers had been having condenser problems so he wasn't looking for a fight. Fergusson and his CO, Bernard, were both relieved, and Keyes tightened up the Standing Orders, cutting to the chase: 'Suspicious vessels are to be regarded as enemy, unnecessary challenges are to be avoided.'[95]

### Hospital Ship Attacks: the *Glenart Castle* & *Llandovery Castle*

In February 1918, the *Glenart Castle*, originally named the SS *Galician*, met her end. One year earlier, she had survived *UC.45*'s mine. On the night of 26 February, the 6,576-ton converted hospital ship left Newport, heading to the port of Brest on France's Atlantic coast. She was clearly lit, identifying her mission of mercy, 'painted white with large green stripes and three Red Crosses on each side full[y] illuminated'.[96] John Hill, aboard a small fishing smack, the *Swansea Castle*, watched her closely:

> I saw the hospital ship with green lights all around her – around the saloon. She had her red side lights showing and the mast-head light, and also another light which I suppose was the Red Cross light

Around 0400hrs, a single torpedo hit near the No. 3 hold, destroying many of her lifeboats. In just over five minutes she went down near Lundy Island. Only thirty-eight out of 208 on board survived, a number of the dead being found in lifeboats with wounds that 'could only have been inflicted by firearms'.[97] A merchant marine officer was found, dead in the water, with two bullet wounds. The dead included her captain, Bernard Burt, eight nurses from the Queen Alexandra's Imperial Military Nursing Service, seven RAMC medical officers and forty-seven orderlies. There were 'no patients on board' at the time.[98] Among the dead was *Glenart Castle*'s 50-year-old matron, Kate 'Kit' Beaufoy, who had served in the Boer War and was a highly decorated nurse whose story was later told in *Matron at War*. During her career, Beaufoy was reputed to have had 30,000 patients under her care. Ironcially, one of the nurses who died, Charlotte Henry, was of German descent: her family had changed their name by deed poll from Heinrich to Henry. A submarine surfaced and came to within 50yds of some of the boats, two German officers clearly visible on the conning tower.[99] Most of the survivors were picked up by a French schooner, *Faon*, and an American destroyer, USS *Parker* (DD-48), picked up a further nine. Two of her crew jumped into the sea to swim the 50yds to rescue *Glenart*'s navigating officer.[100] More than eighty years after her sinking, a small memorial stone was unveiled at Hartland Point; Katy Beaufoy's ancestors return there each year, on 26 February, to remember her, holding a small service overlooking the sea.

After his submarine had been interned, *UC.56*'s captain, Kapitänleutnant Wilhelm Kiesewetter, was briefly held by the British in the Tower of London and charged with war crimes. *UC.56* had been successfully depth-charged by one of the American yachts, *Christabel*, on 21 May 1918 off the Spanish coast. Kiesewetter had tried to torpedo a ship that had fallen behind her convoy. After dropping three charges,[101] *Christabel* was able to sufficiently damage the U-boat to force her to put into Santander a few days later, where she remained interned until the end of the war.[102] On his way back to Germany after the war, Kiesewetter's ship made a call at Falmouth. Here, he was taken off and briefly held for two weeks, released on the grounds that he could not be held during the Armistice. In November 1940, aged 62, Kiesewetter became the oldest-serving U-boat officer in Hitler's Kriesgmarine.

Attacks on hospital ships continued: on the night of 27 June, the 10,639-ton *Llandovery Castle* was hit by *U.86*. Aboard were 258 passengers, including ninety-four medical officers and nursing sisters of the Canadian Medical Staff. Kapitänleutnant Patzig launched a single torpedo that cut open the ship's portside No.4 hold. After ten minutes, she slid below the waves, so fast that several lifeboats were still being lowered and were dragged under. The ship was relentlessly pushed forward by her engines, which couldn't be reversed. No distress signal was sent out; there was no power after the explosion. When *U.86* surfaced, Patzig went after the survivors, claiming that eight Canadian doctors were, in fact, American pilots. Swinging his sub away from Captain Sylvester's lifeboat, he savagely hunted down survivors:

> [He] took his U-boat on a smashing up cruise among the survivors and by hurling it hither and thither he succeeded in ramming and sinking all the boats and rafts except one [the master's boat] which escaped. The survivors in this boat heard the sound of gunfire behind them for some time [and] it can only be conjectured that the murderers were finishing their work with shrapnel.[103]

Patzig opened fire and after more than a dozen shells had been fired, 234 people are thought to have died in their boats. Fourteen of them were nurses.[104] After the war ended, Patzig (whose full name was Brümmer-Patzig) was never convicted. He, along with two of his lieutenants, Ludwig Dithmar and Johann Boldt, were briefly held, but he managed to escape to Danzig. Both hospital ships had belonged to the Union-Castle line.

**The Zeebrügge Raid**

If convoys were one approach to tackling the submarine threat, bombarding, occupying or blocking the port entrances was another.

As early as autumn 1914, Vice Admiral Lewis Bayly, then commanding the Grand Fleet's 1st Battle Squadron, outlined a plan to attack Zeebrügge. Tyrwhitt developed another approach using a ship to block the lock, and presented it to Jellicoe, Oliver and Bacon. The plan was rejected, mostly after Bacon's criticisms. Tyrwhitt wrote scathingly to his sister that Bacon had 'referred to it as a scheme for the self-glorification of aspiring young naval officers'.[105] With the failure of Haig's offensive – and with it the idea of cutting off the Flanders bases with an enclosing pincer by land – the idea of occupying them was also binned. Beatty's thoughts of using a blockship to close off the harbour was more in line with the eventual attack, but his idea of its progress being 'directed by wireless from aircraft' was far ahead of its time.

When asked to give his thoughts on bombardment from the sea, Jellicoe expressed strong misgivings. It would be, he wrote, 'an operation which I am sure no responsible naval officer would recommend, and it is, indeed, hardly practicable'.[106] In a speech given on the deck of the USS *Pennsylvania* in August 1917, Wilson, however, complained that in the submarine war 'we are hunting hornets all over the farm and letting the nest alone'.[107] Fisher felt the same way: 'When you have a plague of wasps, you don't send little boys with butterfly nets to catch individual wasps. You take the wasp's nest.'[108] The separate approaches were strongly Mahanian: 'Intercept the enemy at the Point of arrival or departure.'[109] Nevertheless,

> The problem with bottling up the submersibles is enourmously difficult, because it necessitates operations in the enemy's territory.[110]

Wemyss asked Keyes, whom Alfred Dewar described as 'a very limited man absolutely obsessed with the idea of doing something striking and brilliant',[111] to take over from Bacon:

> Well, Roger, you have talked a hell of a lot about what ought to be done in the Dover area, and now you must go and do it.[112]

The core of the attacking force was the 500-strong 4th Marine Battalion, after Keyes had insisted on Marines being present for the Navy to have some more 'time in the sun'. They would be supported by a further 200 sailors who would be landed from the specially adapted armoured cruiser, HMS *Vindictive*, supported by a couple of ferries, the *Daffodil* and the *Iris*. Behind the attack was a force of ships larger than the Grand Fleet at Jutland – 156 in total. The reasoning was clear:

> The inability of the Royal Navy to attack and destroy the High Seas Fleet meant that any operation aimed at capturing or destroying the U-boat bases themselves, or attempts to mine the U-boat areas of operations, could potentially prompt a fleet action in the enemy's thoroughly mined waters: raising the prospect of catastrophic losses for the Royal Navy.[113]

The German Flanders bases of Oostend and Zeebrügge were both connected to the inland city of Brüges by major canals, allowing U-boats better protection from attack by being moved inland.

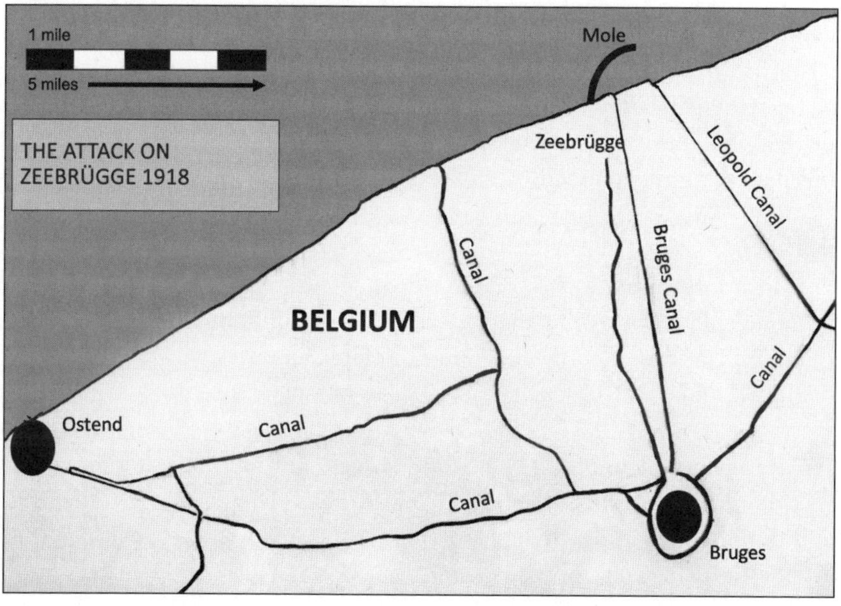

At Zeebrügge, the canals were protected by a heavily defended mole on which was massed impressive firepower. The entrances would be blocked by some old Apollo-class cruisers – at Oostend, HMS *Brilliant* and *Sirius*; at Zeebrügge, HMS *Thetis*, *Intrepid* and *Iphigenia*. Two submarines, HMS *C.1* and *C.3*, loaded with explosives, were to be taken through the gap behind the mole to blow up a bridge.

After a false start on 11 April, the force set off again on the 22nd, the eve of St George's Day. *Vindictive*'s captain, Alfred Carpenter, signalled: 'May we give the dragon's tail a damned good twist.'[114]

*Vindictive* didn't manage to tie up properly at the mole, but was held in position with *Daffodil*'s help. Meanwhile, Lieutenant Richard Sandford guided *C.3.*, loaded with 5 tons of Amatol, through to the rail viaduct, where a time-delay fuse would do the job. Even though he was temporarily caught in the beam of a searchlight, he decided to stay on board to light the fuses himself. He wasn't fired upon; the Germans had assumed his was a returning U-boat. With the viaduct destroyed, the badly wounded Sandford was picked up.

For a public craving good news, Zeebrügge was served up as a brilliant feat of British arms and courage. Lloyd George showered praise on Keyes, calling the raid 'one of the most gallant and spectacular achievements of the war'.[115] However, the raid did not achieve its stated goals. As an anti-submarine effort, it was 'fruitless'.[116] Bacon's account wrote of the laughable inability to close both exits: 'In order to keep dogs in a house, and out of the street, it is well to close both the front door and the back door.'[117] By itself, the raid could not do this; the canal system was connected to Ostend, where a concurrent attack had been 'an out-and-out fisasco'.[118] A plethora of VCs was awarded, with Churchill talking of the attack – which Carpenter had summed up as 'merely a glorified trench raid' – as 'the finest feat of arms during the Great War'.[119]

Losses were heavy: 176 British killed, 412 wounded and forty-nine missing; by contrast, German manpower loss was minimal, with just eight killed and sixteen wounded.[120] Holloway Frost wrote of the raid's symbolism, claiming that,

> British losses were a cheap price to pay for its immense moral effects. Exploited by world-wide propaganda, the heroism of British seamen and marines in those gloomy days created a tremendous impression in Allied and neutral countries, perhaps even in Germany.[121]

His sentiments are mirrored by Richard Hough, bowing to the importance of tradition in the culture of the Royal Navy: the raid, he said, was 'a courageous and thrilling exploit deserving its place in history, not for its tangible results … but for its inspiration'.[122]

A number of historians have criticised Jellicoe for his support of the attack. Nick Lloyd quotes the number of submarines based at Ostend and Zeebrügge as 'about twelve', saying that it was not this that concerned Jellicoe; what he was worried about was their impact on communications.[123] That the Passchendaele campaign turned into such an unmitigated disaster, with the loss of a quarter-of-a-million British soldiers, shouldn't be attributed to Jellicoe's desire to neutralise the Flanders U-boat pens, rather to the execution of the plan on the ground. Macdonald is critical of Jellicoe's support for a land offensive aimed at Flanders, saying his arguments were 'unfounded' and grossly misinformed, as 'submarines were mainly operating from German ports'. She maintained there were 'few submarine bases on the Belgian coast'. She may have been correct as for the number of bases, but in terms of the impact of the Flanders Flotilla submarines in the Channel theatre, she was wrong. While shipping losses were certainly 'showing signs of diminishing', 'thanks to Convoy', this is, again, a global metric rather than one that takes account of the peculiarities of each local theatre.[124]

The Germans were more reserved in their judgement. Scheer commented that 'the connection between the harbour at Zeebrügge and the shipyard at Brüges was never interrupted even for a day'.[125] No one doubted, however, the bravery:

> [A]ll the great daring that was displayed was in vain and the aim not achieved. Furthermore, if one of the two harbours had been completely blocked, this would not have meant the immobilization of Flanders. The operation would have achieved its object only if both harbours, Zeebrügge and Ostend, had been simultaneously and completely blocked.[126]

The day after the raid, four torpedo boats left Zeebrügge for minelaying operations. Each had a draught of 7½ft. A day later, another five left, these ones with less draught but, at 375 tons, higher displacement. The same day, *UB.16*, with an additional 3ft, managed to get out without any problem. On 14 May, the channel had been dredged to a low tide depth of 11½ft, sufficient for any vessel in the Flanders Flotilla.

Keyes 'remained supremely confident that his exploit had done the job'.[127] Even if the NID realised that the raids had achieved little from a purely naval point of view, his biographer claimed that the raids had made the Zeebrügge canal 'useless to the enemy for many critical weeks'.[128] This is still largely the perception today. As Marder wrote in 1970, 'the fiction … has so far not been overtaken by the truth'.[129]

## The High Seas Fleet's Last Sortie

Concurrent with the Zeebrügge raid was what became 'the very last sortie of the High Seas Fleet in the war'.[130] Scheer decided to use his forces for a major surface attack on a British convoy, thirty-four ships that had departed Norway with an escort of two destroyers, after a rendezvous at sea. But when the *Moltke* developed engine problems, radio silence was broken and the British alerted. Little surprise could then be achieved. A very large British force went to sea – thirty-one battleships, four battle-cruisers, two cruisers, twenty-four light cruisers and eighty-five destroyers.

Hipper was ordered back. It was on the return on 25 April that HMS *E.42* successfully torpedoed *Moltke*, which, though damaged, still made it home.

## Continued Long-range Submarine Operations

Off the West African coast, the momentum was turning to the Allies' favour. The Azores and Cape Verde had earlier claimed large shipping losses, and it was only in May 1918 that 'there was [...] a real decrease in ships sunk'.[131]

April also saw another U-boat, *U.154*, reach far south, down the West African coast to Liberia, where she shelled the radio station at Monrovia. Hermann Gercke was joined by Goetting's *U.153* and the two spotted the Q-ship, *Willow Branch*, off Cape Blanco on 25 April. The disguised merchantman was no match and, after a struggle lasting three hours, was abandoned. Some of her survivors drifted for nine days aboard a lifeboat. Eleven 'went mad after drinking seawater', and by the time they made landfall on the Senegal River, twelve more had died. Of her total crew of fifty-three, only three survived. *U.154* wouldn't escape revenge: going back north, she was spotted on 11 May by HMS *E.35*, which hit her second and third torpedoes, each exploding under one of her two deck guns. Her three survivors could not be picked up.

## The Black Months – April and May 1918

May 1918 was 'a black month for the U-Boat office with sixteen submarines destroyed'.[132] April had hardly been any better: 'between 11 April and 3 May', five submarines were destroyed in the Dover Strait.[133] On 8 May, *UB.70* was depth-charged by convoy escorts and Kurt Albrecht's *U.32* mortally damaged by fire from the sloop *Wallflower*, and then sunk by depth-charging, while attacking a convoy from Alexandria.[134] She sank with all hands.[135] The French destroyed *UC.35* by shellfire on 25 May, while *UC.39* ended up being towed into internment at Cartagena, Spain, having been irreparably damaged by seaplane attack. Another, Launburg's *UB.52*, was attacked by a British submarine, the *H.4*, which sunk her with two torpedoes, leaving no survivors.

The effect on morale within the U-boat service must have been significant, although Gibson and Prendergast dispute this, contrasting the lack of revolutionary fervour among the battleship and battle-cruiser crews with that amongst submariners: 'Contrary to the generally-accepted opinion, the discipline of the German submarine crews was never broken.'[136] They put this down to work conditions rather than combat factors – the everyday lot of a sailor on board one of the kaiser's submarines: 'The crews of the U-boats were provided with better food, received longer leave, and were allowed other privileges; they were also granted special rewards.' This is not to say that their nerves weren't shattered, Spiess (*U.135*) citing examples of this, saying that a good deal of sloppiness began to be noticed onboard.

Not all went well for the British, with whom the obsession with the 'offensive' use of escorts still flourished. At one point, escort destroyers were pulled off convoy duty and formed into hunting groups to kill submarines that were using the northern Scotland passage: not one submarine was sunk. According to Eric Grove, they 'made no contribution to the defence of shipping'.[137]

**The Voyage of the U.151**

Under her second commander, Korvettenkapitän Heinrich von Nostitz und Jänkendorff, *U.151* (formerly *U-Oldenburg*) left Kiel on 14 April, heavily provisioned for a five-month cruise with sixty-five men under eight officers aboard. On 2 May, Sims cabled his superiors, saying that the large vessel could be expected off American waters around 24 May. Although forbidden from attacking shipping en route (to keep their presence from being discovered), a British steamer, the 4,997-ton *Huntress*, had a near escape on 15 May when one of *U.151*'s torpedoes missed. At 1254hrs on 19 May, an SOS was intercepted by Atlantic City Radio of a ship (the 9,213-ton *Nyanza*) being shelled by a submarine. A subsequent series of messages indicated she was moving west.

Arriving at Cape Hatteras on 21 May, Nostitz started mine-laying operations. On 28 May, he cut the underwater cables to Europe and South America off New York. After these initial operations, which saw insurance rates immediately rise, *U.151* sank seven ships in one day, 2 June.

The sinking of one particular ship, however, made headlines. The 5,093-ton liner ss *Carolina* was carrying 217 passengers and crewed by another 113 men. The only loss of life occurred when one of her lifeboats capsized in a storm, drowning thirteen of its occupants (nineteen others were rescued by the British freighter, *Appleby*). The arrival of one of the lifeboats on the shore in Atlantic City caused a sensation. A parade of the Knights of the Mystic Shrine was in progress and, seeing the bedraggled condition of the exhausted survivors, some of the Shriners surrendered their colourful Masonic cloaks to warm them.

One of the survivors, a 12-year-old girl, was photographed blowing kisses to the crowded onlookers as the band struck up *The Star-Spangled Banner*.

Continuing her journey, *U.151* loaded 2,000 tons of desperately needed copper after she'd stopped a Norwegian steamer, *Vindeggen*. 'It took two days of the hardest kind of work before we had our plunder stowed away,' Nostitz said.[138] Among her passengers, however, was a small child, Eva Ugland. She was quickly adopted by the crew, and soon she could do no wrong by the hardened submariners. Precious copper ingots were dumped to allow her on board, and the cook laid on 'cakes, candies, and dishes of canned fruits with whipped cream'.[139] As the steamer went down, the Norwegian flag fluttered, having been specially hauled back up at the request of her captain. After sinking another Norwegian steamer, the *Henrik Lund*, her captain, Kaltenborn, gave his attackers beer, champagne and some recent newspapers. Nostitz then placed all his prisoners in lifeboats, including little Eva.[140] Before they were cast off, the cook handed over more cakes he had specially baked for her: she had 'become the ship's darling'.[141] It was a propaganda victory: one newspaper article carried the headline 'Human Huns'.

Another trawler had more luck: she had come up from Mississippi and 'was owned by several poverty-stricken families' who were looking to do some whaling, helping to supplement their income. Nostitz took pity on the group of obviously hard-at-heel fishermen in the ancient tub. On deck, the German sailors 'wondered how a German whaling boat would have fared similarly in the hands of its enemies'.[142] Nostitz said he simply could not bring himself to destroy their only source of livelihood. The crew's behaviour was the same just before sinking the *Carolina*, when another freighter, *Texel*, with a cargo of sugar from Peurto Rico, was stopped. After the crew had transferred, one of the seamen, Paddy Barnnan, remembered that the ship's mascot cat, Mickey, was still aboard. She was somewhat special: she'd been born aboard and had seven little claws on each of her front paws. A German officer allowed him to go back for her.

*U.151*'s attack on the former German liner *Kronprinz Wilhelm* nearly ended in disaster. The torpedo missed, but made the submarine's presence known, subjecting her to a withering series of depth charges. Initially taken down to 180ft, the boat continued its descent to the depths and did not slow until it reached 278ft. When they were finally able to surface, nothing remained: just an empty sea.

At 0930hrs on 20 July 1918, *U.151* finally slid back into Kiel, being met with great fanfare. The kaiser's son, Prince Adalbert, came out to greet the returning crew members. Having been at sea for ninety-four days, she had claimed twenty-three ships sunk (61,000 tons) in an epic 10,915-mile voyage. Some of her mines were also attributed with the sinking of two more ships, increasing her tonnage claim by 10,000–12,000.[143]

### The Continued U-boat Assault on America

On 8 August, Kapitänleutnant Otto Dröscher arrived off the American coastline aboard the *U.117*, eventually adding another thirteen ships sunk. Within two days, he had claimed nine fishing vessels, and on 13 August he accounted for 7,127-ton tanker *Frederick R. Kelllog*, heading for Boston with a cargo of 7,500 barrels of oil. On 29 September, long after *U.117*'s mid-August mining operations, one of her mines severely damaged the USS *Minnesota*, which would be laid up in dock until March 1919.

*U.155* set off again in mid-August with a new commander, Studt. Once past Skagen, the sub headed out into the North Sea where, after a few days, a curious event took place. In the distance, it looked like another submarine engaging a ship, with huge columns of water spotted shooting up into the air. When they went to investigate, they discovered that what they'd seen were spouts from a whale pod.

Cold reality returned when, on the last day of the month, a Portuguese steamer, the *Gamo*, was stopped. Despite her master's entreaties to take his 18-year-old son on board so that his family would not be left without a breadwinner, Studt cast them all off. 'He had to be tough,' Schultz explained.[144] In the end, all but five of the thirty-nine crew made it back. Schultz left his readers wondering if the boy was one of the lucky ones.

Entering Halifax harbour, *U.155* had a narrow escape. Resting on the surface to lay mines, a nightwatchman appeared on the deck of a nearby steamer and suspiciously scanned the night sea, but somehow they weren't spotted.

### Changes in Germany's Naval Command

In late summer 1918, persuaded by Scheer's Chief of Staff, Rear Admiral von Trotha, the kaiser agreed to significant changes at the most senior levels of naval command. In a move that further reduced the kaiser's influence, the new Seekriegsleitung (SKL) was restructured on 11 August, closely resembling the OHL. Holtzendorff (Admiralstab) and Capelle (RMA) stepped aside, with Scheer himself replacing the former and Behnke the latter. Müller promised to resign as head of the Imperial Marine Kabinett, and until he did von Trotha maintained control through his position as Chief of Staff. Inside the RMA, the U-Boat Office had already come under the command of Rear Admiral Ernst von Mann in December 1917, one of Scheer's protégés. By August 1918,

> Scheer had accomplished what von Tirpitz had always coveted in vain. Complete control over strategy, operations and construction.[145]

Scheer immediately met with Hindenburg and Ludendorff, and with their support was optimistic about getting the resources he wanted, primarily workers to realise his ambitious submarine construction programme. A month later, he outlined his thinking to the kaiser in Spa. It was already too late: on 29 September, the Army High Command admitted to the kaiser that the war was lost and that negotiations needed to be reopened with President Wilson. A week later, the new Chancellor, Max von Baden, did just that.

Scheer's estimates for increased labour were initially put at between 20,000 and 25,000, but Behnke, now von Capelle's deputy at the RMA, correctly assumed more would be needed. Not only was the labour impossible to find – the companies had signed on poached workers from other competitors and from the Imperial yards – but the critical shortage was skilled engineers. No amount of cost-cutting, construction simplification or streamlining of submarine types produced made any significant difference.

Unilaterally, Wilson responded to overtures from the new German Chancellor, and on 19 October, to remove possible obstacles, the decision was taken to curtail unrestricted submarine warfare: passenger liners would no longer be targeted. For Scheer, it was the end of *any* kind of submarine war; he knew that the orders would be impossible to execute. Hipper, the new Commander-in-Chief of the Hochseeflotte, would now use his submarine forces as Scheer had – in conjunction with surface elements, for a final attack.

On 30 October, the foundations of the Central Powers Alliance started to crumble as the Ottoman Empire surrendered; the next day, Hungary announced her separation from Austria.

**The Final Days – Unrest and Recall**

On 22 October, the U-boats were recalled. A month earlier, on 29 September, orders had already been given for the dismantling of the Flanders bases. Four Flanders Flotilla submarines were scuttled rather than withdrawn. While ten subs in the Mediterranean – the smaller Type-*UC* and Type-*UB* boats, incapable of making the long sea voyage home – were scuttled on 28 October, the remaining fifteen started back.[146] They left Pola on 28 October and Cattaro on 1 November.

Naval command in Gibraltar received intelligence that between seventeen and twenty-one U-boats would try to break through the strait in the following days. A first line of defence was set up on the Otranto barrage, with a second at Gibraltar. There, a 2.5–4-knot incoming current worked against outgoing traffic, and the necessity of a long-submerged run would mean that the enemy submarines would have very little margin for manoeuvre.

At the same moment, eighteen newly crewed and trained sub-chasers were on their way from the States with the support vessel, USS *Parker*. When they arrived at Leixoes in Portugal, however, they found they only had enough fuel for six to proceed to Gibraltar independently and for a further three to be towed. By 6 November, they were ready to form a picket line and await the expected oncoming submarines.

Chasing down one submarine sighting after another, they were foiled at each turn, one when 'a neutral merchantman stood in through the Strait and all trace of the suspicious sound was lost owing to the much louder noise from the merchantman's propellers'. The sub-chaser's dismal performance demonstrated how difficult a task they had using their hydrophones:

> The hydrophones were very good fair-weather devices but those developed up to that times were not much good even in moderately rough water, or through interference. The ship itself caused 'water noises' when it rolled, the sound of the waves was also picked up and both interfered seriously with the detection of faint sounds. But the worst interference was caused by other vessels.[147]

On her last patrol, two days before the signing of the Armistice in Compiègne, *UB.50* attacked and sank the 16,350-ton battleship HMS *Britannia* just off Cape Trafalgar. She was the 'last British warship sunk by submarine attack during the war', but did not go down without a fight.[148] For two hours, her crew stayed aboard and, when a periscope was eventually spotted, kept firing until she went down. Leutnant Kukat's torpedo was the very last one fired in the war. The Americans in the sub-chasers could only watch helplessly as 'some 200 of her crew were burned to death or asphyxiated while their comrades in their own and near-by ships were helpless to aid them'.[149]

That same night, 8/9 November, *U.34* was spotted and brought back to the surface by depth-charging from two MLs. She was then peppered by gunfire from the Q-ship *Privet*, whose accurate 12pdr firing and depth-charging sent her back down with eleven direct hits. Johannes Klasing, her captain, didn't make it home.

The boats were still aggressively patrolling on the morning of 11 November, a day that 'dawned bright and clear with a spanking easterly breeze kicking up the whitecaps. A fine day.' Their disappointment at not making a kill was heightened when the Armistice message was received, ordering that they 'should take no hostile action against any submarines proceeding on the surface'.[150] The Armistice had just been signed.

Four submarines based at Constantinople surrendered, but Püllen ordered others that could make their way back to Germany, or head to Spain to ask for internment, to do so. Kurt Hartwig took his *U.63* into the Atlantic after surviving a heavy depth-charging, only escaping as the counter-attack was so fast that the U-boat didn't have time to descend to the depth he normally would have chosen and where the detonations were set. *U.35* chose internment in Barcelona.

Meanwhile, a message went out from the Admiralty Staff in Berlin and was received in *U.152*: 'Commence Return cruise immediately. Because of current negotiations. All manner of merchant warfare forbidden. U-boats already returning. Attack warships only by day.'[151] News of unrest amongst the Fleet crews in Kiel and Wilhelmshaven also started to spread.

On 4 November, Adolf Franz on *U.152* received new instructions: 'To all U-boats: fire without warning on ships with red flag. All of Kiel hostile: occupy opening of Kiel Bay … let no ship dock or depart.'[152] *U.155* returned from the Americas. Stopping again to make a report on the *Hannover*, Studt then told his crew that an armistice had been signed and at Sassnitz, on the island of Rügen, a Soldier's Committee would be awaiting their arrival: they ordered the captain to lower the boat's battle flag. It was the end.

**Plan Z: Hipper's Abortive November Sortie**

As the submarines were being withdrawn from Flanders and the Adriatic, Franz Hipper planned a last sortie, Operationsbefehl 19, for the High Seas Fleet for 29 October. Not surprisingly, even after Scheer's recall, rumours spread like wildfire. The Navy had been chosen as the instrument of Germany's final blow against Britain, an eleventh-hour attempt to improve its bargaining positioning in any upcoming peace negotiations.

Thirty submarines were allocated their assignments. It was a laughable plan, seen by many as a one-way ticket.

*U.78* was sunk by a British sub while en route to the Scottish coast, having been sent there to lay mines. On 28 October, *UB.116* was sunk in Scapa Flow. Oberleutnant Hans Joachim Emsmann's submarine became the 'first, last and only submarine destroyed by shore-detonated mines in the First World War'.[153] At around 2330hrs, hydrophones picked up the sounds of her twin screws. Her periscope was spotted, and when she passed over a galvanometer cable (three indicator loop cables), mines were activated and then triggered from the shore. After additional depth charging, she finally sank near the Hoxa boom. Admiralty divers, collectively known as 'the Tin Openers', were immediately ordered to dive on the wreck. Commander George Wheeler had just finished raising the *UB.110* off Whitby and was ordered to join Commander Damant in Scapa in the hope of raising the wreck of *UB.116*.[154] Wheeler, however, recommended against the raising, as he feared that the bow section in which there were still torpedoes could break off and explode. The DNI did not insist.[155]

For one reason or another, seven other submarines were unable to carry out Hipper's orders. Only one had any success: *UB.67* (Dömming) was able to torpedo the British minesweeper *Ascot*.

Inside the Jade Basin near Wilhelmshaven, two battleships, SMS *Helgoland* and *Thüringen*, threatened open mutiny. Spiess, aboard the *U.135*, had been singled out by Hipper for a difficult task: to sink one of his own navy's battleships if the mutineers didn't back down. Hipper asked if he was 'absolutely sure of his crew', but refused to give him written orders for the odious mission.

> First one, then another of the 15cm casemate guns were trained on the *U.135*. Soon all the guns were trained on us. Very unpleasant. The distance was about 550 yards. One hit would have sufficed to finish us.[156]

Spiess placed *U.135* between the two ships. Bow and stern torpedo tubes were loaded and ready to fire.[157] A company of marines under the command of a suitably named officer, Grimm, went aboard the *Helgoland*, with bayonets fixed. It had been a close call. Spiess had already been given the orders to fire. He was furious when they quickly surrendered: he complained that 'they should have been fired upon at once'.[158]

On 14 November, de la Perière arrived back in Kiel with *U.139*. The most celebrated U-boat commander handed the boat over to his 2iC and went ashore quietly, dressed as a civilian.

### Beatty's Plan ZZ: The Final Surrender

The popular mythology of the First World War portrays the High Seas Fleet as *surrendering* to Admiral Sir David Beatty's impressive forces gathered at Rosyth in November 1918. His meticulous planning of the last naval act of the war, Plan ZZ, belies the reality. The day was very carefully stage-managed to create the sense of victory that the Royal Navy had been unable to attain through battle at sea. The only German naval forces that were obliged to surrender by the terms of the Armistice were the submarines.

On 20 November, the first twenty-four U-boats arrived off Harwich, where they were met by Admiral Tyrwhitt. They were escorted across by SMS *Helgoland*, one of the two ships Spiess had threatened just days before. Another sixty-two were found by the Control Commission in German ports, plus 149 in construction in German docks. The final handover was accomplished the following year, on 24 April 1919, also at Harwich, when 176 submarines were turned over. An almost equal number, 178 submarines, had been destroyed, sunk or lost over the preceding five years of war.

Neither Jellicoe, Fisher nor Battenberg were invited to attend Beatty's event in Rosyth or the actual surrender of U-boats at Harwich. Amongst the first group of U-boats was a leading seaman named Wehner, who tearfully recounted the terrible feeling of defeat and surrender: 'When the English flag was hoisted, we turned our backs on it, and looked towards our own land.'[159]

# 8

# Measuring Success and Learning Lessons

## A Strategy Without Metrics

Hans Joachim Koerver defined the submarine war as one that was quintessentially 'calculated in numbers', what Admiral Doenitz, twenty years later, would label as a 'tonnage war'.[1] In waging the submarine war, the difficult and prolonged search for strategy, however, clearly illustrated the paucity of data on which it was built. Passionate discussion on key strategic issues was almost always without any recourse to empirical data.

The Royal Navy might have come to accept the responsibility for trade protection, but it made little effort to understand the details of the challenge or to define the metrics that could be used to measure its effectiveness. The war started, and finished, without the strategic choices of anti-submarine warfare being carefully considered or evaluated.

It's vital to understand on which metrics any evaluation of the submarine war should focus. Like Jutland, the purely quantitative approach of comparing ships sunk or men injured provides only a very partial view on the strategic impact of the battle on Germany's naval strategy. Even Jellicoe seemed to have been guilty: reflecting perhaps the ideological obsession with the 'offensive', he talked about his objectives in the same way. However, I am not sure that it goes as far as saying that his views were very traditional and showed a limited understanding of what exactly 'defeating the U-boat' meant:

> Our object was to destroy submarines at a greater rate than the output of the German shipyards. This was the surest way of counteracting their activities. It was mainly for the purpose of attack on the submarines that I formed the Anti-submarine Division of the Naval Staff.[2]

The submarine fought its war in a unique way. The physical destruction of Allied shipping and crews was supplemented by the deliberate use of submarines against neutral shipping, hospital ships and civilian passenger liners. Reducing the effective carrying capacity of neutral shipping by targeted terror tactics was initially very effective. As a weapon of war, the submarine's value was sometimes as effective psychologically as it was physically. Hans Rose's visit to Newport, ostensibly to pay his respects, sent a powerful diplomatic threat.

The impact of the submarine was felt far and wide. Not only did it challenge Britain with food shortages, its consequences forced Britain to implement national economic measures that reached deep into the fibre of the nation and were politically abhorrent. The capacity and quality of the nation's shipbuilding industry, its distribution system, docks and the skills of its labour force were all stretched to their limits. It is the sheer breadth of issues that underlines the difficulty in finding the most appropriate metrics. The field of choice is wide: shipping tonnage sunk, input cost inflation, U-boats sunk, merchant tonnage losses, transportation and insurance costs, tonnage replacement rates etc.

What about the volume of Allied and neutral ships being able to deliver their cargoes safely? As Thompson put it: '*The safe arrival of merchant ships* with their precious cargoes, not sinking enemy submarines, was what ultimately counted in the U-boat war and was the *aim* of the game.'[3] Merely translating the Germans' own metric of tonnage into submarines sunk maybe misses the point. It meant that the focus of ASW strategy was sinking submarines, not protecting trade.

Answering Q&As after a 2022 presentation on the rivalry between Sims and Gleave, Sal Mercogliano made a passing but very illustrative comment about Germany's submarine blockade of Britain: post-war, the US Naval Academy trained a generation of officers by war-gaming the big fleet confrontations, the likes of Jutland. They still do. But they say nothing of the submarine war. Mahan is thus victorious! The Admiralty did, however, produce several technical histories after the war. Of those produced from 1919–21, convoys and mercantile protection 'featured most prominently appearing in eleven'.[4] However, they were mainly concerned with topics like the creation of the ASD, the Naval Staff and the Hydrographic Office.[5] The doctrinal emphasis on Fleet action ill-prepared Britain for the Second World War.

Exercises involving mercantile protection were held, but without actual merchant shipping involved. The Royal Navy also tested alternatives to the convoy system, one being evasive routing. What was not carried forward in learning was the construction of escort carriers, while

> the responsibility for Coastal Command rested with a service committed to having a general-purpose force able to meet most operational taskings, but wary of developing specialist units.[6]

**Submarine Sinkings**

Confirming the exact fate of a submarine is far more difficult than one might imagine. One hundred years after the conflict, historians still don't have a complete picture. It is still a matter of debate. Submarines had many ways of giving the impression of being heavily damaged by merely applying standard procedures. Cold sea water rushing into the hot exhaust pipe of a boat's engine would produce clouds of steam, and since steam in the exhaust pipe would be blown out with great force, to a gunner it often looked like a hit. Sub commanders would try to fool attackers by blowing out oil or ejecting tell-tale evidence of a kill that might even include a way to assign an identity to a boat, things like clothing with something in a pocket, cap tallies or a life vest.

The number of kills gradually grew each year: three in 1914, nineteen in 1915, twenty-two in 1916, a jump to sixty-three in 1917 and sixty-nine in the final year of the war.

There is a great truth in what Marder wrote when talking about the single-minded focus on recording a submarine kill:

> Sinking submarines is a bonus not a necessity … what matters is that the ships deliver cargoes regularly and adequately … Indeed, one can safely go a step further; it really did not matter how many U-boats the Germans had, if they were forced to keep out of the way and the British and their Allies got their ships with their literally vital cargoes through and without being delayed by fear of attack.[7]

**German Submarine Production**

Even if Germany manufactured large numbers of submarines, she was never able to organise production of them in the quantities or in the time needed. Michelsen complained that shipyard capacity was never optimally organised – 'at times they complained of lack of work and at other times they were overcrowded and delayed'.[8] Herwig also spoke of the significant delays:

> Throughout the war, only 12 vessels were delivered on time; 50 arrived at the front more than 6 months and 114 more than nine months behind schedule.[9]

A serious delay in ordering new submarines occurred right at the outset. From September 1915 to May 1916, neither the larger types nor *UB*-type boats were contracted. Even with the order of fifty-eight boats in May 1916, 'many of the boats never saw active service and quite a few were not even delivered'.[10]

There were not enough suppliers. MAN (Machinenfabrik Augsberg Nürnberg), for example, had an outright monopoly on submarine diesel engines, while both Elbing's Schichau and the Hamburg Reihersteig Works were unsuccessful in their bids to produce submarines.

Requests for new submarines were being held up, not because of manufacturing capabilities, but because of lack of crews and deteriorating training. In December 1917, to focus on this production problem, a special U-boat office was created, under the command of Vice Admiral Ernst von Mann Edler von Tiechler.[11] He immediately placed orders for 120 submarines, followed by another for 200 within six months.[12] Nevertheless, it was too late. Only eighty-eight boats were added in 1918 – forty-seven *UB* craft, sixteen *UC* class and twenty-five *U* class. The workforce in submarine yards, meanwhile, increased from around 2,500 to 7,000, and monthly torpedo delivery from twenty-five to 375.

Tackling repairs became increasingly difficult. In September 1918, the head of the Mediterranean Flotilla, Pullen, reported that two of his submarines had been out of service for a year, while five more needed such long repair times that they were effectively mothballed.

Scheer was concerned, not only about the U-boat's declining success against Allied shipping but also the significantly weakened forces at his disposal: new submarine construction was not keeping pace with sinkings. Realising that the war was lost, Scheer's principal objective was to gain the best peace terms possible. He wrote to the kaiser on 21 September 1918, promoting a new submarine campaign and his projections for a production rate of sixteen boats a month in the last quarter needed to build an adequate force for the task. His aim was ambitious: to reach a monthly average of thirty-six boats by December 1919.

> The U-boat weapon is now the only offensive weapon at our disposal. With defence alone, we will not obtain a satisfactory peace. It is therefore absolutely necessary that we build up our offensive weapons with all the resources that Germany has at her disposal so that we may attain our goal – a satisfactory peace.[13]

Scheer's reasoning is interesting. It is not certain that he believed he could produce these targets. Behnke doubted whether the German Army would release the skilled labour, and there were shortages of key materials. On 1 October, the most important yards were estimating that the real number of workers needed was close to 69,000.[14] Four days later, Max von Baden was sending President Wilson peace overtures. Various reasons have been put forward for Scheer's plans for a fresh submarine campaign: that it would be a morale booster; that it could give Germany more bargaining power; certainly, the promise of huge profits was alluring. It was also a way that the German

Navy could signal its commitment to the kaiser's war, its 'determination to continue the struggle against the Entente'.[15]

**Rate of Ship Sinkings and Damage**

In the spring of 1917, on average, German submarines sank a ship every two days on patrol. However, by the summer of 1918, an average of fourteen days on patrol was needed to achieve a sinking.[16] The great lesson learned, wrote Prof Grove, was that ship sinkings was directly linked to the submarine force strength, not necessarily to improved Allied ASW or changes in German tactics:

> Actually, the rise in ships sunk in and after February 1917 was almost entirely caused by the correspondingly great increase in the number of operational U-boats, and not by the fact that warfare was unrestricted.[17]

The impact of damage was as important, but gets less attention than actual sinkings. 'For every five ships sunk, a sixth was damaged', amounting, during the first six months of 1917, to 700,000 tons of immobilised cargo-carrying capacity. Of that, 50 per cent were unrepairable, so equivalent to a ship sunk. The other 50 per cent required, Geddes reported, an average of four months' repair time before they could be brought back into service.[18] The drain on the capacity of British shipyards and loss of vital carrying capacity snowballed.

**Cargo Capacity**

Much of what was learned from the submarine war was purposefully obfuscated. One reason, maybe, was because the originally proposed official text made for overly 'gloomy reading' and as such could 'encourage potential enemies'.[19] Churchill's own writings are an example of the drive for a positive recounting of the history: he proudly proclaimed, 'the seafaring resources of Great Britain were, in fact and in the circumstances, always superior to the U-boat attack'.[20] It would only be with the publication of Newbolt's *Official History* that some 'lost' chapters of this war of numbers were reinserted.

In early 1917, Jellicoe strongly argued the case for a reduction in the number of Allied theatres of war. It was massively straining resources. In March, for example, it was calculated that 631 ships with a capacity of over 2 million tons was tied up in shipping troops and supplies to the various fronts, from France to others as distant as Mesopotamia and Salonika. Indeed, 150 ships or 600,000 tons were tied up in the latter alone. Jellicoe felt his pleas had fallen on deaf ears:

> I have urged time after time the absolute necessity that exists for reducing the number of lines of communication which the Navy is called

> upon to safeguard and for increasing the protection of those lines of communication which remain. So far the only result of my efforts has been increased calls upon the Navy without any sort of reduction of liabilities and with no appreciable increase of our resources.[21]

The entry of the United States into the war added hugely to the availability of tonnage: according to Watson, an immediate 2.7 million tons in April 1917, an amount which rose to 9.5 million tons by September 1918.[22]

On a completely different level, it must be said, however, that the severe shortage of carrying capacity led to benefits: more efficiencies in cargo consolidation and ship-loading as well as cuts in imports of non-essential items, mainly foodstuffs and non-military materials.

**Merchant Ship Replacement and Build Costs**

In the first year of the war, Britain's merchant fleet increased. Britain was able to commandeer over 700 ships of the Central Powers, with, in many cases, their cargoes. The result was no pressure to build new hulls. These were the wasted years that Jellicoe would later decry:

> Self-satisfied, the Admiralty cut back on the construction of new merchant ships in favour of new warships and delayed endlessly the repair of existing merchant ships in favour of repairs to warships.[23]

Part of the issue was the time taken to replace sunk or damaged tonnage. British shipyards were unable to handle the hugely increased demands of war losses and repairs. In parallel, American yards were overwhelmed with smaller-vessel construction. When war broke out, 'the shipbuilding industry was almost stagnant'.[24] And despite increased demand and rising prices, British shipbuilding output initially even declined. It 'decreased dramatically' from a 1914 monthly new tonnage level of 142,000 tons to a 1916 average of 53,000 tons.[25] Only then did it increase, from 53,000 tons in 1916 to around 102,000 tons in 1917.

In 1916 and 1917, the amount of time taken to build a destroyer in a British yard was eighteen months, at best fifteen, while Germany was able to produce smaller ship types like destroyers in only twelve months.[26] Furthermore, in Germany, submarines took a mere 25 per cent of the construction time needed in British yards – six versus twenty-four months.[27] Later, however, skilled labour could not be found for German yards.

The critical state of British shipbuilding called for strong leadership, and in December 1916, Joseph Maclay was appointed Minister of Shipping. Up until that point there had been no formal governmental control of merchant shipping. Even then, Maclay's new department wasn't ready for operations until April the following year. He started tackling the problems with a wide array of initiatives:

1. Streamlining the number of ship types that could be produced, initially reducing the choices to four 'standard' designs in February, expanded to twelve by the year's end. By 1918, 76 per cent of all shipbuilding used one of these 'standard' designs.
2. Increasing skilled shipbuilding's supply of labour. Maclay's target of 1.8 million tons required another 35,000 skilled labourers, so in January 1917, certain shipbuilding-related skills were exempted from military service.
3. Reducing naval ship construction. Of the new battlecruisers in planning, the decision was taken in the February Cabinet meeting to only proceed with HMS *Hood.* At the same time, work on five light cruisers was also halted.
4. Increasing steel supply.

In Marder's words, however, the results were 'dismal'.[28] The actual production level of 1.1 million tons was not even close to the 1.8 million tons target. In the second half of 1917, it increased by 59 per cent, but even with additional Japanese-produced tonnage, was 340,000 tons short of the million tons Lloyd George had promised Parliament on 16 August 1917.

At the start of 1917, 131,000 tons of British shipping (for ships of 1,600-plus GRT) was under repair. By April, that figure had increased to 262,000 tons and by June it had surged to 454,000 tons.[29] The burden on yards was enormous; the diversion to laying down new ships was catastrophic.

*Merchant shipbuilding*

| | **UK Production (million tons)** | **US Production (million tons)** |
|---|---|---|
| **1913** | 1.93 | 0.23 |
| **1914** | 1.68 | 0.16 |
| **1915** | 0.65 | 0.16 |
| **1916** | 0.60 | 0.38 |
| **1917** | 1.16 | 0.82 |
| **1918** | 1.31 | 2.60 |

Source: Michelsen, p.111.

Production in 1918 only increased by 47 per cent, leaving Geddes's over-optimistic forecast of 2 million tons some 415,000 tons short. The gains sought from optimised steel allocation and improved labour supply had not materialised. America's contribution to the Allied cause totalled 2.6 million tons, 48 per cent of the total produced of 5.4 million tons.[30]

Repairs, however, improved and helped balance the overall availability: 382 ships were repaired in August (1,188,000 GRT), but in November this number rose to 542 (1,509,000 GRT).

Forecast and delivery of some naval vessel types weren't aligned. While Jellicoe said that 'we were never satisfied' with deliveries, either under Geddes or the previous regimes, the deviation of deliveries from forecast was more troubling. This made planning very difficult. Jellicoe highlighted the shortfall for the June–December 1917 period: actual submarine delivery was only 55 per cent of forecasts, minesweepers 41 per cent, trawlers 29 per cent and sloops 26 per cent. The only categories near forecast were destroyers and P-boats, both still off by more than 15 per cent.

**Insurance Rates**

Insurance rates – for ships and their cargoes – reflected the severity and success of U-boat operations. The introduction of the War Risk Insurance programme has been criticised by many because the subsidising of shipping losses by the taxpayer might have discouraged collecting hard statistics of the causes and circumstances of losses. The scheme compounded the Royal Navy's ignorance: the programme made no distinction between ships sailing independently from those in convoy, and in maintaining a flat rate rather than a rate calculated on risk it 'relieved the insurance market of keeping an actuarial check upon the system of shipping defence'.[31]

Marder added that the Admiralty was only 'concerned with the protection of shipping routes, and not of merchant ships'.[32] The final indignity was the Admiralty's failure to master 'the first elements of the problem': the number of sailings that needed escort. He attributed this largely to the absence of a proper Naval Staff.[33] No single individual was responsible for these vital statistics, upon which Allied ASW strategy was built.

During the war, rates fluctuated wildly. Before the war, a charge of 0.25 per cent of the value of a ship and its cargo was common. As the war opened with intense cruiser warfare, rates ballooned to 21 per cent. They then fell back to 4.5 per cent and then 3 per cent around December 1916. With the introduction of unrestricted submarine warfare in February 1917, they jumped back to 8 per cent, but by February 1918 were back down to 4.5 per cent.[34]

**Food stocks – Victory Through Starvation**

Food replacement and rationing measures were introduced in Germany far ahead of Britain: by October 1914, *Kriegsbrot* (or *K-brot*), made up of a mix of 55 per cent rye, 25 per cent wheat and 20 per cent potato meal, quickly became a staple. It was, more accurately, *Kartoffelbrot*, flour mixed with potato. It could equally be 'ground maize, lentils, peas, chestnuts, soya beans, clover and bran'. Substitute products (*ersatz*) blossomed – there were thirty-three substitutes, for example, for eggs, 837 for sausage.[35]

In February 1915, Berlin citizens were issued bread ration cards; by the end of 1915, most foodstuffs had been added but the cards 'offered no guarantee that one would get the indicated amounts … [they] merely indicated that under no circumstances could one get more'.[36] In Hamburg, one observer wrote that she regularly witnessed 'how queues of 600 or 800 people formed outside shops whenever consignments of butter were delivered'.[37] Long queues became routine, the pastime being christened '*la Polonaise*' as the hungry citizens snaked forward. In 1916, meat in Germany was rationed to 600g a week; in May, potatoes was restricted to 2.5kg per week and sugar to half a kilo a month. It did not help that the summer was bad, with the fields 'drowning in rainwater'.[38] By July 1918, meat rations for most Germans amounted to a mere 12 per cent of pre-war consumption.[39]

In April 1917, a Wiesbaden medical official noted that the loss of 60lbs in body weight for a healthy adult since the war started was 'no rarity', while a Munich study found that the difference in pre-war weights and heights in children and those in 1916–17 was 2.35kg and 2.3cm.[40] By 1916, wrote one observer, Berliners already 'look more like Mongolians. Their cheekbones stick out and with the loss of fat their skin has become wrinkled.'[41] Princess Blücher, the English wife of a Prussian aristocrat, echoed the observation: 'we are all growing thinner every day, and the rounded contours of the German nation have become a legend of the past.'[42] Already by December, she worried that 'it isn't going to be possible to get through the winter'. Even in Bachmann's diaries, one finds references to the acuteness of food shortages. His entry for 15 June 1918 talks of food riots in Kiel; two days later of shortages in potatoes and on 27 June in coffee and tea.[43] In Austria, the situation was even worse. In Vienna, a quarter-of-a-million people would queue up for food daily.[44] The average daily calorific intake fell from around 3,000 to 1,000 by 1917, but had a slight uptick in 1918 due to better harvests.[45] By contrast, 'at its lowest point in 1917, the calorific value of the average British diet was only 4% lower than in 1913', much being achieved by substitution – bacon for meat, brown for white bread and margarine for butter.[46]

Shortages of metals did not only affect construction: Bachmann's diaries note the withdrawal of canned vegetables from the civilian population and their use being 'only permitted for submarines, torpedo boats and airships'.[47]

**Germany Initiates Rationing**

In Germany, the effects of the British blockade were felt almost immediately; it soon became known as the 'starvation blockade', part of Britain's policy of starving her enemy into submission ('*Aushungerungspolitik*'). Even before the formal declaration of war and the imposition of the blockade, Berlin experienced a bank run.

The wartime role of the Royal Navy was to cut Germany off from overseas resources by imposing a blockade from afar, a so-called 'distant blockade'. It was the submarine that heralded, in Massie's words, 'the beginning of the end of the classic British naval strategy of close blockade of enemy's ports'.[48] Goods that had previously been widely and easily accessible now grew scarce, including Chilean saltpeter, useful both in agriculture as a fertiliser but also for explosives production.

**Decreased Reliance on Imports**

Britain started the war massively dependent on agricultural imports. A sustained effort was made to reduce that dependency: by rationing, prohibition, substitution and increased domestic production. Britain's efforts to reduce food imports paid off handsomely: in 1913, 18.1 million tons of food was imported; in 1918, 11.4 million tons, a reduction of 6.7 million tons.[49]

Even if by the terms of the 1914 Defence of the Realm Act, land could be appropriated by the government for farming, implementation only started in 1917. Some 2.5 million acres were repurposed. There was substantial room for change: domestic acreage assigned to wheat production was lower in Britain (43 acres per 1,000 population) than in Germany (308 acres) or France (468 acres). Over the next two years, around 7.5 million acres of pastureland was turned over to arable. The effect was a substantial increase in potato and cereal production (Watson estimated a 40 per cent increase over the average annual production between 1904 and 1913), even if this only had a 'limited impact on overall calories'.[50] Over the war years, cereal production increased dramatically – wheat by 1 million tons, oats by 1.4 million tons and potatoes by 2.6 million tons. Production of rye also grew substantially, with an estimated increase from 47.4 million bushels in 1916 to 62.7 million in 1917 and 91 million in 1918.[51]

Paradoxically, Britain had fewer acres under cultivation in 1915 than 1913. Arable land was increasingly cultivated for crops – annually, around 1 million acres were added each year from 1917–19. While this reduced meat production, 'net food output increased by 2.3 million tons'.

It is often said that in 1917, Britain's grain reserves had fallen to six weeks' supply, but some have disputed this. One such person was Prof Eric Grove. Boyd quotes him as saying that during the terrible months following the massive April 1917 shipping losses, 'Britain increased imports of wheat and flour to a wartime maximum of 1.8 million tons'.[52] At one point, after the spate of tanker sinkings (in 1917, 115 were sunk), Britain's oil fuel stocks were down to two months' supply.

### The War's Continuing Impact

Like almost any war, the economic impact was felt for many years after the guns had fallen silent. Starvation and privation did not end with peace. While they negotiated the terms of settlement in Versailles, the Allies kept the blockade in place. It added pressure on Germany to accept the terms on offer. Additionally, Germany's ability to feed her people or to revive her industries was severely hindered. Herring fishing in the Baltic, for example, was banned. Nor would the French allow Germany to use her gold reserves to pay for additional food imports from the United States. Indeed, the French were even responsible – as the Germans had been in the 1870s – for flooding German mines 'to make the production of coal impossible for the next five to six years'.[53]

The harsh treatment would provide ample succour for German nationalism to rise again, phoenix-like, from the ashes of defeat.

### Alternative Source of Supply – The Black Market

For those who could, the only way to survive was to head out of the cities on 'hoarding journeys' into the countryside armed with empty rucksacks to engage in 'hamstering' (*hamstern*). Women would pretend to be pregnant – all sorts of foods strapped to their tummies. For the rich, with money, most luxuries could still be easily found; for the poor, it was almost impossible. Petty crime, for example the theft of coal to use as barter, shot up, as did prostitution. Social divisions between the 'haves' and 'have-nots' and increased criticism of the government's inability to manage an equitable distribution of goods were exacerbated. Some have argued that it even deepened the 'long-standing antagonisms between Bavaria and Prussia'.[54]

By the last year of the war, 'an estimated one third of Germany's food supplies was being sold on the black market'.[55] 'The black market has become the norm for the exchange of goods.'[56] By 1918, Watson estimated, 20 per cent of agricultural products in Germany were *Schleichhandel* (black market). Food prices fluctuated wildly. In 1917, white flour in western Galicia was selling at six times the official market price. With the dramatic rise in food prices, the government instituted local soup kitchens in towns with more than 10,000 inhabitants. In October 1916, 1,438 kitchens operated in 3,357 towns; four months later, another 769 were added in a further 114 towns. By April 1917, a daily average of 200,000 meals were served by Hamburg soup kitchens.

Britain approached rationing very differently to Germany. Initially, an appeal was made to the population's sense of civic duty. When the Food Ministry was created with Lord Devonport as its head, civilians were asked to voluntarily ration their intake of staples and skip meat on certain days. The weekly ration target was 4lbs (1.8kg) of bread, 2½lbs (1.1kg) of meat and 12oz (340g) of sugar per person.

When Devonport was replaced by Lord Rhondda in 1917, the approach was tightened. Like in Germany, 'war bread' was introduced. Despite its nutritional value, it was, again like in Germany, very unpopular. At the start of 1918, an even more stringent approach to rationing was adopted. From January, sugar was rationed, followed in February by meat and in April by butter, cheese and margarine. Bread was never rationed. The irony of all this was that, by some measures, the strict control of diet meant that the nation's health *improved*: Herwig notes that the female death rate (attributable to cardiovascular and diarrheal disease, plus complications linked to pregnancy) was lower in 1917 than from 1912–14. Surprisingly, by 1918, 'per capita caloric intake amongst civilians was probably higher than it had been in 1914'.[57]

*Britain's weekly food allowance, 1918*

| | | |
|---|---|---|
| Butter or margarine | 4oz | 113g |
| Tea | 1½oz | 40g |
| Sugar | 8oz | 226g |
| Meat | 15oz | 425g |
| Bacon | 5oz | 142g |

Source: Ball and Hudson, pp.8–9.

This was not the case for the Central Powers. As the blockade tightened, health declined. The German Board of Public Health estimated that the war cost the lives of 762,796 civilians as a result of starvation, which was heavily skewed to cities.[58] From 1913–18, while the general increase in civilian deaths registered at 65 per cent, in rural Bavaria it was 43 per cent. It was the cities that drove the incidence upwards: for example, 81 per cent in Oldenburg, 93 per cent in the Ruhr, 76 per cent in Hamburg and 71 per cent in Berlin. It was so bad that 'German insurance companies reported that the death rate of the civil population was beginning to compete with the death rate on the battlefield'.[59] Boak estimates that tuberculosis deaths in towns of more than 15,000 inhabitants rose by 91 per cent between 1913 and 1917, while dysentery in one city, Dusseldorf, rose from just eight cases in 1914 to 351.[60] By December 1918, more than 40 per cent of German school children suffered from rickets, caused by vitamin D deficiency.[61]

Like many other submariners, Valentiner recounted the shock of seeing how emaciated his father had become when he visited Sonderburg: 'My parents also complained about the lack of food and had become so thin that I hardly recognized them. My father had lost over forty pounds in weight.'[62]

Even the Crown Prince looked the worse for wear. After seeing his parents, Valentiner visited his commanding officer in Kiel and noticed how thin Prince Heinrich had become – 'his temples had caved-in and his hands had become even thinner'.[63]

## The Lost Lessons of the First Submarine War

During the inter-war years, many lessons from the submarine war were forgotten, sometimes even *deliberately* discarded, as new priorities and challenges emerged. Writing about the stunning successes of a weapon his namesake had developed for the US Navy, Rear Admiral William Holland writes:

> Even the success of the German Navy's submarines in World War I did little to change the opinion of the U.S. Navy's leadership. During and after that Great War, submarines were viewed as commerce raiders – immoral in their methods and tactics – and robbers of funds from battleships and cruisers.[64]

Just as Germany had started the war in 1914 with little understanding of the weapon that very nearly won the war, and failed to ramp up new U-boat production before launching unrestricted submarine warfare in February 1917, the outbreak of war again in 1939 did not give Raeder the time he needed to rebuild the Kriegsmarine. There were no plans for a resumption of commerce war, and consequently, few U-boat assets. However , with access to new bases on France's west coast from the summer of 1940, the threat to Allied Atlantic convoys would be more dangerous.

The Allies came out of the Great War without a serious, analytical evaluation of their ASW efforts. The idea that ASW is often a combined weapons exercise also seemed to go astray. Huge strides had been made in aerial detection, a capability catapulted forward from merely the enhanced visual role of aircraft into magnetic anomaly electronic detection. Too much of the literature is about how many (or few, as was the case) sub sinkings were achieved by aircraft rather than their role in the chain of appropriate response: aircraft were extremely efficient at spotting, smaller surface vessels at driving submarines below the surface, and destroyers at dispatching them once they resurfaced.

For a while, the convoy system seemed to be the answer, but gradually, as the Germans searched for a counter, its efficacy was challenged. It seemed that while ships under convoy were protected, the moment they left the convoy groupings they were vulnerable again. But for the more daring U-boat commanders, the answer was to surface within the convoy lanes, the merchant ships themselves now offering screening against the escorting destroyers on the outside. The key was to understand that convoy effectiveness, like any other tactic, could only be evolutionary. It was a path of response, not a single static answer. It would suffer setbacks as enemy countermeasures developed. Some of it was tactical, some technology-driven.

In closing, Frank Uhlig summarised many of the counter-intuitive learnings that we somehow lost:

> For now the most important ideas revealed by these long-ago experiences are that in war – and before war – we should be clear strategically, operationally and tactically, about what we need to protect and what we need to attack; we should understand that sometimes the best defense is a good defense; we should observe that when a dominant instrument is displaced by another, instead of losing all value the old system may merely step down to a supporting role; and we should bear in mind that our next dominant instrument of war, or our enemy's, may prove to be something already in hand. So might its antidote.[65]

### Anti-Submarine Wars 1917–1942

All periods of conflict test established doctrine. So many of the 'obvious' lessons of the submarine war in the First World War had to be relearned in the Second World War. The great strength of destroyers as escorts meant that Britain ended the Great War with over 400 of them, yet in 1930 she had only 180. At the start of the Second World War, 'British Antisubmarine craft carried no radar, no long-range aircraft were assigned to anti-submarine patrols, and the short-range aircraft carried 100-pound bombs quite unsuited to their task'.[66]

The tools and tactics of ASW constantly evolve. Just as the Royal Navy's approach radically evolved during the First World War, it is noteworthy that not only were so many of the lessons of the Great War unlearned, even the effectiveness of convoys was never seen as a 'given'. It depended on circumstance; on personalities just as much as technology. Royal Navy tactics were, 'in the early stages of the war, miserably ineffective. The British ships had no radar, and only a few were equipped with ASDIC'.[67] It was as if the lessons of the 1914–18 war had been entirely forgotten. Without 'eyes', a destroyer is next to useless as an ASW platform. In the first half of 1941, the British could only claim the sinking of twelve enemy submarines, with none in January, February or July. Against this, the losses for the year topped 1,200 ships. Pre-war levels of imports had been cut by two-thirds.

Some early convoys were catastrophic. Jonathan Dimbleby cited the horrific losses of two October 1940 Atlantic convoys, SC7 and HX79. Working with their wolfpacks, Otto Kretschmer and Günther Prien succeeded in sinking seventeen of SC7's thirty-five ships and 25 per cent of HX79's. No wonder he darkly concluded:

> It was clear beyond reasonable doubt that naval escorts could not prevail by numbers alone: they needed to be well led, highly trained, closely coordinated, and equipped with a coherent plan of action. All these ingredients were notable by their absence.[68]

Britain had all but forgotten the lessons of 1917–18. Donald Macintyre complained about the uselessness of tactics at the outset of the Second World War:

> They were exasperating, futile days when the ships so badly needed to escort convoys were being battered by fruitless hunts in storm-swept seas, without any hope of reaching the enemy before he had slipped away into the vast blank spaces of the ocean.[69]

Within twenty years of the end of the Great War, the Royal Navy was back to hunting patrols and there were even independent sailings of high-value cargo ships, particularly oil tankers off the North American coast. The first convoys were not organised until March 1942, after losses had already climbed to 500,000 tons. Even so, there were no convoys south of Boston, and June sinkings rose to 700,000 tons. It prompted a bitter commentary from the USN's Commander-in-Chief, Admiral Ernest King:

> I might say in this connection that escort is not just *one* way of handling the submarine menace, it is the *only* [emphasis in original] way that gives any promise of success. The so-called patrol and hunting operations have time and again proved futile.[70]

Despite the obvious successes of the U-boat in the First World War, Doenitz was only able to start offensive action with forty-six boats. He had been unable to convince his predecessor, Grand Admiral Raeder, of the value of the U-boat. Raeder returned to surface raiding and built Germany's new pocket battleships to accomplish the task. A wargame played at the Royal Naval College at Greenwich in January 1938 had 'correctly estimated the time of war's outbreak but assumed that the threat to convoy ships would not come from U-boats, but from German raiders disguised as merchant vessels'.[71] Again, the lessons of the early success – and failure – of German surface raiders in 1914 had not been taken on board.

Even on both sides of the so-called *Todesloch*, the mid-Atlantic Death Hole, convoy air cover was sparce. After Germany was able to use the western French bases of Lorient, Brest and La Pallice, the U-boat's operating range was dramatically extended and its time on target similarly increased because return to bases in Germany was no longer necessary. Despite persistent requests for bomber cover, Churchill bought into Sir Arthur Harris's obsession with the value of strategic bombing.[72] Sir Charles Portal, Chief of the Air Staff, brushed aside Sir Dudley Pound, saying that 'to divert [the RAF's bombers] to an uneconomical defensive role would be unsound at any time.[73] It would be doubly so now when we are about to launch a bombing offensive.'[74] As late as January 1943, only twelve RAF bombers were specifically tasked to support the convoys. On the other side of the fence, Otto Kretschmer had directly lobbied for increased German air cooperation, with the U-boat forces to act as spotters for the packs.

# 9

# Was Jellicoe the Right Man for the Job?

John Jellicoe remains a controversial admiral, criticised and praised in equal measure. All too often, he's seen as a vestige of a bygone age; an officer molded by a Victorian age. His name is now mostly associated only with Jutland, the first, biggest and last clash of dreadnought navies in the twentieth century. A hundred years later, little has lessened the intensity of debate and controversy surrounding the battle.

Jutland has consumed rivers of ink; far less the unrestricted submarine war it unleashed. The debate around Jutland remains emotionally and personality driven. Jellicoe's time as First Sea Lord is, I think, remembered for one thing, and one thing alone: the long-delayed implementation of the convoy system, which some say was because he *opposed* convoys. What saved Britain, his critics have it, was the 'silver bullet' of the convoy. I wanted to challenge the so-called self-evident truths of the submarine war. Jutland left the Royal Navy badly divided for almost a century; the convoy debate provided a less obvious context but was built around much of the same ideological bias. Both provide valuable lessons.

The actual implementation of the convoy system was far more complex than is now understood. The submarine threat was so new that it made the principle of convoy defence a very different consideration from its obvious historical context. Around the debate swirled the Young Turks' generational grievances against institutions at the very core of the Royal Navy and the ideological impasse between Mahanian battle fleet officers and those wanting to focus on the protection of trade. It involved new concepts, strategies and tactics whose efficacy and viability evolved with time and with their integrated use. Like so much of what we see today in the age of fake news, ideological confrontation and political radicalism, the telling of the story of the naval war has suffered from all these influences.

Had John Jellicoe been the right man for the job? Would others have done, or did others do, better? Jellicoe took on his final, challenging position at the Admiralty with some serious enemies, not the least of whom was Lloyd George. As Jellicoe himself recognised at the outset, without the requisite political skills, his days were numbered. He said as much to Brownrigg on his first day in the job. His prediction of not lasting a year was spot-on, almost to the day. Would Beatty, for example, have done better? Marder seemed to think so: he was 'much younger … had a more flexible mind, was more receptive to new ideas, and exploited to the full the brains of his staff'. Most important, 'he was better endowed with the non-naval talents needed for success as professional head of the Royal Navy'.[1] However, he also 'in many ways … represented a backward step'.[2] His position on convoys, for example, evolved from the support he voiced at Longhope (for Scandinavian convoys) to a protectionist defence of the Grand Fleet's destroyer flotillas. Beatty felt that they were 'wasted' on convoy protection. His impetuousness might have led to convoys too early; possibly as dangerous as Jellicoe's tardiness.

Few would dispute that John Jellicoe was loved by his officers and men. But having the confidence and loyalty of the Fleet is seldom the best measure of a commander or leader; his legacy should be judged on what was achieved, both as the Grand Fleet's Commander-in-Chief as well as First Sea Lord. The qualities and characteristics needed for one were not necessarily the same as those required for the other.

In *The Rules of the Game*, Andrew Gordon concludes that Jellicoe 'failed … to get to grips with the submarine menace' when he was at the Admiralty.[3] Andrew Boyd was similarly critical, saying that, for the first half of 1917, Jellicoe was incapable of focusing beyond 'reducing maritime supply to overseas theatres' (what Jellicoe called the 'sideshows') and a land offensive to capture the Flanders bases.[4] Others, like Admiral Sims, felt differently. Through the creation of the Anti-Submarine Division, he maintained that Jellicoe had laid solid foundations for the future success of the submarine war: 'I am distressed to hear of your leaving the Admiralty when the effects of all your anti-submarine measures are showing such great success.'[5] The comment is a little incongruous with Sims's later position on convoys as well as Jellicoe's own rather tardy support.

Jellicoe's valid reasons for careful timing are often brushed aside with anecdote, ridicule or extreme judgement. The contributions of the Young Turks, along with Sims and Beatty's positions, are often exaggerated. Jellicoe's implementation of a convoy system that had a gargantuan impact on not only operations at sea but also on land has been minimised. In general media messaging and leverage in political battles, complexity loses out every time. Soundbites and anecdote win the day.

However, it was probably in 1917 – during Jellicoe's tenure as First Sea Lord – that the submarine war turned. Lloyd George, never one of Jellicoe's greatest admirers, wrote that 'the greatest allied triumph' and the 'real decision of the war' was meeting and *defeating* the U-boat threat in 1917.[6] To be fair, between the lines of what Lloyd George wrote is his self-congratulatory assessment of his own decisive role in initiating convoy. Jameson addresses this fairly:

> [Jellicoe] may have been slow to decide (when there was no evidence to help him) that convoy would thwart the U-boat, and stubborn in concentrating on the so-called 'offensive' methods. But it was he who had given 'teeth' to the anti-submarine organization without which convoys could not have enjoyed their present success.[7]

Some felt that by November 1917, the submarine threat had been defeated. Leighton wrote that the submarine war 'assumed the aspect of a thorn in the side of the Allied Naval position rather than as a cause for defeat'.[8] Clearly, this wildly overstated the success of Allied ASW.

### The Nature of the Man

Modesty and professionalism were traits typical of Admiral Jellicoe. He was 'intellectually brilliant, modest and warm-hearted'.[9] 'He was one of the most simple and modest men I ever came across,' remarked one member of the War Cabinet, General Smuts.[10] Jellicoe would win men over by his own easy manner and sense of humour.

Jellicoe, whose intellect could grasp a wide range of complex issues, would be tested to the extreme:

> His voluminous writings point to a thoughtful and literate mind and an almost encyclopedic grasp of the principles and details of his various professional positions.[11]

Maybe because of the experience of being at sea when his 5-year-old daughter, Betty Agnes, died, or Jutland's terrible toll of death, dismemberment and destruction, much of Jellicoe's attention and concerns focused on his men's welfare. He was a deeply religious family man. In his later years, lying sick in bed at home, he would sing his favourite hymns. He was close to his brother, the Reverend Frederick, and in later years, after Frederick died, to his cousin, Father Basil Jellicoe, whose great social works in the London slums near King's Cross he very visibly supported. Gwendoline, his wife, while a strong-willed woman who rarely took 'No' for an answer, still recognised the importance of her duties and responsibilities as the wife of the Commander-in-Chief. She would regularly visit injured sailors in hospital and sometimes worked as a nurse. 'Mother Gwen' died in 1964, two years short of the fiftieth anniversary of Jutland.

**A Sailor at Heart**

Jellicoe had the sea in his blood. His father, John Henry, had gone to sea aged 12, and within ten years commanded his first ship. When he ended his career, he had risen to become commodore as well as a board member of the Royal Mail Steam Packet company in Southampton. On his mother's side, his great-great-grandfather, Admiral Philip Patton, had fought at La Hogue in 1692, one of the key battles in the Nine Years' War against France. Philip's son, also named Philip, rose to flag rank and served as Second Naval Lord at the Admiralty in the years around Nelson's victory and death at Trafalgar.

Jellicoe's appointment in 1884 to the Whale Island Gunnery School, HMS *Excellent*, was arguably one of the most important in his career. It was there that he came to the attention of Captain 'Jackie' Fisher, who no doubt helped engineer his next posting to HMS *Colossus*, which, armed with breech-loading 12in guns, was considered the most modern ship afloat. When Fisher became Director of Naval Ordnance (DNO) in 1889, Jellicoe was invited to become his assistant. Here, with responsibility for the development of the Royal Navy's weaponry, he developed an intimate knowledge of his ships which became a hallmark of the man.

After several postings in the Mediterranean, Jellicoe accepted Vice Admiral Sir Edward Seymour's request to join the China station. Here, he made important professional contacts in both the German and American navies: Guido von Usedom, Prince Heinrich, Holtzendorff, McCalla, Taussig and Sims. Invalided back from China, with a growing reputation and public profile, Jellicoe was asked by Admiral Sir William May, Third Naval Lord and Controller, to act as his assistant in November 1901, taking responsibility for the design, construction and repair of all the Navy's ships. In October 1904, he was brought into the small, select team assigned to the design of Fisher's revolutionary battleship, HMS *Dreadnought*, where he would work alongside Jackson and Bacon. He could vouch for them, as he had 'tested each of them for many years'. The move was a very visible tribute to Jellicoe's reputation.

Four years later, promoted to rear admiral, he took on a command in the Atlantic Fleet, joining the pre-dreadnought HMS *Albemarle* in August. While in Quebec, the First Lord, Reginald McKenna, offered him the post of Third Sea Lord and Controller. Jellicoe hesitated; he knew that with the job would come political controversy – the great question of the day was whether the

Exchequer would fund the government's ambitious social welfare programme or build dreadnoughts. In December 1910, John Jellicoe took his first fleet command, raising his flag in the pre-dreadnought *Prince of Wales*, the flagship of the Atlantic Fleet.

It's not surprising that Fisher and others concluded, as the country readied for war in 1914, that few naval officers had the breadth or depth of experience that Jellicoe possessed. But the real question was whether he was able to survive in the different, more political world of supreme command at the head of the Admiralty.

Jellicoe was widely respected. He would always have the support and loyalty of officers such as Dreyer, Duff, Harper and Reginald Bacon, his official biographer. It was the same among some key United States Navy officers and, ironically, even those of the Kaiserliche Marine. Given the antipathy of both the American Admiral Benson, CNO, and Josephus Daniels, SecNav, Jellicoe's connections and quiet, diplomatic approach would prove particularly vital for the smooth integration of American forces under British naval command in 1917. Most well-known, perhaps, is Jellicoe's relationship with Admiral William S. Sims. Sims was a strong supporter of Jellicoe, but also claimed a very significant, and immediate, authorship in the development of the convoy system even though he'd only recently arrived in London.

Of course, Jellicoe also had his detractors: while it was an unfortunate characteristic of the times that the Royal Navy was (and would remain) hopelessly divided between the Jellicoe and Beatty camps following Jutland, Beatty might have been privately supportive but, not unexpectedly, could be equally silver-tongued when needed. Among the Young Turks, Jellicoe had few supporters. Many felt he had ridden rough-shod over the likes of Richmond, Henderson, Kenworthy, Kenneth Dewar and his brother, Alfred. Gordon feels these men were the real heroes, not the older school: '[I]t illustrates how Britain was saved from defeat in 1917 by a handful of quite junior mavericks of the sort which Jellicoe cordially disliked, and which armed forces usually try to suppress.'[12]

Jellicoe was also eventually attacked by his peers in the War Cabinet. While he had supported Haig and Robertson in their constant struggle for increased focus on the Western Front, neither felt they could support him. In his diaries, Haig ridiculed Jellicoe, calling him 'an old woman'.[13] Lloyd George didn't make life easy for any of his top commanders: he would undercut them in Cabinet, citing his own anecdotal evidence. Basil Liddell Hart, the historian and military theorist who shared much of the spirit of the Young Turks, even commented that 'the advocacy of younger officers was decisively influenced [by Lloyd George's] intervention'.[14]

### A Fighting Admiral

Today, the weathered busts of Beatty and Jellicoe might rest only yards apart on Trafalgar Square, their gaze perpetually focused on the fountains dedicated to their historic encounter, but the two were 'a study in contrasts':

> While Jellicoe was calm, deliberate and realistic in assessing his own forces and those of his enemy, Beatty was highly strung, impatient for action, and supremely confident of his superiority over his enemy.[15]

Under fire, Jellicoe was tough and self-controlled, physically and mentally. He had a justifiable reputation for remaining absolutely calm under fire, for taking difficult decisions under pressure without showing it. One such moment was what Julian Corbett called 'the supreme moment in naval war', the decision to deploy to port when the battle fleets confronted each other at Jutland.[16] It fostered a high degree of confidence from his men. Beatty was undeniably courageous under fire, but arguably lacked the emotional distance that Jellicoe displayed.

Beatty hero-worshipped Nelson, and much of how he commanded, issued orders or renamed Jellicoe's Grand Fleet Battle Orders (GFBO) as 'Instructions' was shaped through that lens. While Jellicoe might not have had 'the Nelson touch', he 'showed something far greater, he showed self-abnegation'.[17]

A constant and widely felt weakness many saw in Jellicoe was his seeming inability to delegate. In part, this reflected a lack of confidence in some officers at Jutland; on the day, battle conditions necessitated a firm controlling hand to maintain the cohesion of the Grand Fleet as a fighting unit. But it was also Jellicoe's way of working, micromanaging and taking on too much detail. At Jutland, he was roundly criticised for not allowing independent tactics, not delegating enough operational command. It was a tendency that *might* have been valid on the North Sea in the confusion of battle, but it did not serve him well later. This failure overwhelmed him with unnecessary detail and characterised his tenure as First Sea Lord, possibly less about grand strategy and innovative policy development and more about administration and form.

Jackie Fisher felt that Jellicoe's great strengths were wasted at the Admiralty: he thought of Jellicoe as a commander of men and ships at sea, a fighting admiral, not a desk-bound administrator. Neither did Jellicoe play the political game in Whitehall.

### The Test of Supreme Command

What exactly was the job that Jellicoe agreed to at the end of 1916? It may sound slightly academic, but as the ferocity of unrestricted submarine warfare took hold in early 1917, a furious debate was unleashed on to how to deal with the menace.

Mahanian to the core, the only thing that seemed to matter to many RN officers was the actual *annihilation* of the High Seas Fleet. For them, that alone held the key to Britain's supremacy at sea.

The role of the HSF evolved under Scheer's command, particularly after 31 May 1916. U-boats were only able to operate because they were protected and supported by the larger ships of the HSF – directly, by clearing Allied minefields; indirectly, by establishing a constant threat to the Royal Navy and a drain on Allied resources as a 'fleet in being'. It was largely because of their fundamental belief in the Grand Fleet's pre-eminent role in the war that both Jellicoe and Beatty were loathe to surrender destroyers, either initially to hunt submarines or later to supplement convoy escort.

The predilection of the Royal Navy was to take the attack to the enemy, in this case, to destroy his submarines. This was always presented as the Nelson way: no admiral could do wrong if he ordered, 'Close with the enemy'. The old argument that the best form of defence is offence kept coming back, hence the background rationale to both Jellicoe and Beatty's support for submarine hunting groups.

The alternative was for the Navy to address Germany's ultimate objective in waging the submarine war in the first place. It was the destruction of British trade, the starvation of the country, depriving her population in the same way that Germany had been pushed by the British blockade into the 1916/17 'Turnip Winter', that most mattered.[18] The protection of trade, providing foodstuffs and the raw materials needed to wage war in an industrial age, was key.

However, the metrics of success weren't clear. What was more important: the volume of cargo getting through to British and Allied ports, or the rate of submarine destruction? One was protectionist and defensive in nature, the other offensive and aggressive. Ultimately, with the convoy system, the offensive and defensive schools shared common ground in the realisation that by luring the U-boats to it, if a submarine was lucky enough to spot a convoy, the chances of successful offensive action were exponentially increased by the concentration of ships and their own weaponry, along with that of escorting destroyers and other smaller ASW craft. The submarine's invisibility, the difficulty this posed to the British in finding a needle in a haystack, became redundant, but few at the time recognised this as clearly as William Sims later explained in *Victory at Sea*.

One of the institutional challenges any leader must face is the balance between a strong culture – be it a work or fighting culture – and the requirements for speedier innovation. It's a seeming contradiction: one encourages a more permanent buying into of common goals, the other constantly challenges the status quo. It has pushed the envelope beyond the comfort zone of many officers.

Where Jellicoe has come in for criticism is in his apparent inability to deal with open doctrinal disagreement and debate, both of which are essential ingredients for innovation. This was Sims's great strength; the recognition that sponsoring healthy *constructive* debate is a requirement of leadership and vital for an officer's education. It implied great confidence in not only being challenged but also in fostering intellectual competition. Hough wrote that Jellicoe's 'conscientiousness combined with a distrust of others to work to one's own high standards' was a path to 'deterioration of performance'.[19]

Jellicoe was never *inflexible*. One can quote enough occasions where he aired his frustration at the inability to learn lessons, but his approach was often driven by the etiquette of committee inquiry rather than encouraging younger officers to air controversial ideas. His post-Jutland appointment of multiple committees to examine the battle's mistakes and lessons is more typical of his way of working: a careful guiding hand. Once a decision or doctrinal position was taken, Jellicoe clearly felt that to voice opposition further was counterproductive. That is not to say that he did not want to *learn* from mistakes. Goldrick commented:

> Jellicoe's determination to learn and apply the lessons of the battle [Jutland], even if some ran contrary to existing policies, must stand as an important contribution to the Royal Navy.[20]

Jellicoe's name will never, however, be associated with great policy shifts. He did not share David Beatty's penchant for breaking the rules, probably a prerequisite for true 'out of the box' innovation. Jameson concluded that Jellicoe

> was a man of great ability and strength of character, but he was a developer, not an innovator. Discipline and loyalty were outstanding facets of his character. He did not close his mind (as is proved by an early minute to the staff on the subject) to the fact that convoys might eventually be necessary, but he did not think, and supported his reasoning with what seemed to him to be solid arguments, that such drastic re-thinking of the whole basis of the Navy's approach to the protection of trade was called for.[21]

It was not that Jellicoe lacked political acumen – he was usually aware of the machinations being played out behind his back – it was more that he was not a political animal. He neither felt comfortable not did he enjoy having to play the political game; he would rather tell it as it was than 'spin' a story.

Bacon wrote that Jellicoe 'had a great objection to publicity and dealings with the Press'.[22] Beatty, by contrast, was extremely adept: he would openly nurture and invite journalists on to his battlecruisers, frequently embedding journalists in his flagship, HMS *Lion*, while Jellicoe was extremely wary. Jellicoe had not understood the value of well-managed press relations. In the end, it worked against him. When he became the object of press attacks in Lord Northcliffe's *The Times* and *Daily Mail*, he lacked wider public support.

On his first day at the Admiralty, Douglas Brownrigg offered to help Jellicoe with his public profile, which the former considered under attack; the new First Sea Lord curtly replied that he wouldn't be needing his services as 'he did not expect to last twelve months and had no time to read the newspapers'.[23] It was a disturbingly accurate prediction. The same day – 4 December 1916 – Herbert Asquith's government fell and David Lloyd George was asked to form a new administration. It was not a good omen: both Lloyd George and his Cabinet Secretary, Sir Maurice Hankey, felt that Jellicoe should never have been appointed to the supreme position of First Sea Lord. Jellicoe had also locked horns with the new Prime Minister eight years before over the Royal Navy's dreadnought construction budgets.[24] The Prime Minister's war memoirs endlessly refer to his disdain for the 'high admirals', as he collectively called the Admiralty – to the point of childishness. Jellicoe knew he had to tread carefully. From Jellicoe's first War Cabinet presentation, Lloyd George was disdainful and talked of the admiral's 'trembling hand'.

In Cabinet, Jellicoe's performance was described by some as lacklustre. He complained about the amount of time he was forced to devote to meetings – both in the War Cabinet and the Imperial Defence Committee – and would use the time to write letters. This wasn't advisable. Even if he felt that his time was being wasted, he could not pull himself away for fear of something of which he didn't approve sneaking through. Neither was he a strong or impassioned orator: he sounded patrician. His voice was clipped and could sound decidedly condescending. Not only Lloyd George, but many of his War Cabinet colleagues, mistook his realism for pessimism, and some – even worse – for defeatism. In short, Jellicoe helped dig his own political grave.

## Jellicoe's Contribution to ASW and Trade Protection

Before dealing with the central issue of convoys, it is important to understand how Jellicoe brought focus to the anti-submarine war, first by choosing the right people and giving them the right structure within which to work, then by pushing the Admiralty to advance an effective ASW portfolio of weapons and weapon platforms.[25] Without these two, the convoy system would never have succeeded. Convoys were never just about the assembly of ships in an escorted group; there was also the provision of intelligence, effective detection, defence and deterrence, seaborne and land-based logistical organisation, and, above all, escorts that contributed to the effective protection of trade. Jellicoe always believed that eventual solutions would be found in a range of weapons, weapon platforms and systems. Arguably, the success of the convoys would not have been possible without Jellicoe's work.

Getting the right people and the right structure behind the organisation of the Admiralty was of paramount importance. As Jellicoe said, 'war is largely a matter of efficient and adequate organization'.[26] As the Commandant of the US Marine Corps put it: 'Amateurs talk about tactics, but professionals study logistics.'[27] Black writes that this was one of Jellicoe's principal achievements: before the arrival of Geddes, he 'laid the foundations for the successful development of the [Naval] Staff in late 1917 and 1918'.[28]

Contrary to his close, centralised control of the Grand Fleet, many of Jellicoe's structural reforms were devolutionary: for example, giving senior officers area responsibility and control on ASW operations, or, in the case of mining, devolving planning down to an Operations Staff Officer who presented the plans up to Herbert Hope and Oliver (until December 1916, Oliver had drafted mining plans himself).

Structural reforms inside OB40 (now called ID25), the D/F Section and the Convoy and Tracking Sections led to improvements in the work: 'reports published regularly from mid-1917, formed the foundation of the first truly scientific attempt to get to grips with the U-boat menace'.[29]

Jellicoe's agreement to redefine the role of the Third Sea Lord, handing over large areas of responsibility and power to the new civilian controller, Sir Eric Geddes – a decision in which he admitted shared responsibility – contributed to some of the shortcomings of British A/S efforts. Geddes's new organisation under-delivered in some critical production areas, some classes of naval vessels and the replacement of lost mercantile tonnage.

Another significant aspect of the reorganisation was the creation of the Director of Air Services (DAS) to the Admiralty Board as the Fifth Sea Lord, 'responsible for all naval air matters, both within the Service and as a member of the Air Board'.[30]

### Developing an Effective ASW Portfolio

For the sake of clarity, I would like to look at Jellicoe's impact on the weapons and weapon platforms as well as the enabling factors before looking at the question of the convoy system itself.

Jellicoe always stressed the importance of a diverse portfolio of solutions working together to then effectively address the German submarine threat.

Open-ocean convoys would not only be impossible without adequate escort resources, weapons and tactics, they would be equally dangerous if prematurely implemented.

> No single countermeasure defeated the German submarine campaign in 1917, although reintroduction of the ancient convoy system is often cited. The combination of Allied shipping control, the availability of neutral shipping, the merchant convoy, special anti-submarine weapons, thousands of mines laid in the approaches to German submarine bases, and a vigorous construction program to replace shipping losses *all contributed in significant ways* [author's emphasis].[31]

So, for what was Jellicoe either directly or indirectly responsible? As Jellicoe wrote to Asquith in the autumn of 1916, he fully expected a dangerous phase of the submarine war would be unleashed 'by early summer 1917'. While Allied ASW had little to show for itself outside of ramming, anti-submarine nets, mines and surface gunfire, new weapons and facilitators started slowly to come online, particularly the hydrophone and the depth charge, but the long-drawn-out development of the former held back effectiveness of the latter.

Jellicoe pointed to the positive changes he made in the main 'portfolio': an almost 200 per cent increase in mine production between July and November 1917, almost 300 per cent for depth charges and 37 per cent from the third and fourth quarters for guns of all calibres. He admitted, however, that 'it was not until 1918 that the full fruits of the orders placed in 1917 became apparent'.[32]

Jellicoe quietly approached the task in his typically methodical manner – he examined what he had at hand, identified what seemed to work, what did not and what was in the development pipeline. He did not harbour untested assumptions.

Regarding existing defences, Jellicoe supported the Dover and Otranto Strait Barrages, the former achieving a reasonable and increasing success, the latter having little impact. The Dover Barrage eventually achieved the desired end: driving more submarines north, resulting in their extended transit time and a consequent decrease in actual war patrols. Jellicoe did not support the Northern Barrage (neither, apparently, did Sims according to Halpern), but finally agreed to the USN taking the key role. America would not only provide the financing but also the manufacturing volume, as well as playing a major role in the laying. It was in US interests to prevent German boats egressing into the Atlantic once Hans Rose and Paul König demonstrated America's vulnerability. But the Northern Barrage came with a huge price tag and showed little for the investment. Beatty was highly critical – 'a fearful waste of time and resources' – but maintained a diplomatic silence despite the ironic fact that more Allied minelaying ships were sunk in minelaying accidents than German submarines were lost to mines.

Given the eventual importance of mines in the ASW arsenal, it was extraordinary that as late as 1917, British mines could not be relied on.[33] In April 1917, more than 92 per cent of the existing mine stock was considered unusable. Jellicoe had been scathing about their unreliability. Therefore, one of the most critical basic improvements in the submarine war came in the form of new mines. The approach was down-to-earth: the fastest and easiest route was to copy the German mine. Despite best efforts, it was only in September 1917 that the first new 650lb H2 mines were delivered, and then only 1,500 of them. Some 12,000 of them were laid before the end of the year, 'resulting at once in nine or ten losses'.[34] The new mines also meant that they could be employed on the Dover Barrage – the first section was laid on 21 November 1917; on 19 December, *UB.56* was sunk.

The British laid huge minefields in the German Bight and around Heligoland, intent on making egress as dangerous, costly and difficult as possible for the U-boats. To give an idea of the scale, 22,000 mines were laid in the German Bight in 1917, another 15,000 in 1918. Naturally, increased British efforts to mine were countered by increased German minesweeping. And in 1917, almost 4,000 German mines were swept by the British from over 500 locations.

Next, we will examine the platforms. By July 1917, seventy-eight Q-ships were in operation.[35] Jellicoe was a proponent, but held on to a belief in their effectiveness beyond their useful life. He never forgot their contribution. When, as Governor-General of New Zealand, he went to pay his respects for the courage shown by the commander of the Q-ship *Prize*, he visited Ted Sanders, skipper William Sanders's father. Like the Q-ship, arming merchant ships had the double-edged effect of driving the U-boat below the surface. It certainly gave ships that were confronted with the rarity of a surfaced U-boat a fighting chance, but the practice also trod a fine legal line on how such vessels should be treated under Prize Rules. With around 65,000 trained ratings manning these guns, the ships were no longer solely crewed by civilians. The level of arming increased rapidly from the end of 1916. In the end, it was very often a combination of ramming and surface gunfire that worked. Such was the case for the ss *British Transport*'s sinking of *U.49*. In 1917, Taussig attributed some of the early recovery in shipping losses to this initiative:

> The average [rate of sinkings] increased until the end of April. This was probably due to a gradual improvement in the weather. During this period the sinkings of ships was an easy matter as they were not armed and all that a sub had to do was come to the surface and use her

> guns. During April the British began arming their merchant ships and establishing more effective patrols. The effect of these measures began to be felt by the end of April and from that time the average sinkings began to decrease.[36]

As for secondary ship armament, Jellicoe placed a high value on escort destroyers, a key ingredient for convoys, but his views were developed with the Grand Fleet in mind, not the convoy system. For him, the Grand Fleet was the key to winning the war, not the defence of trade *per se*. He characterised the destroyer as 'very efficient defensively as a screen' but held that it was 'ineffective for offense in open waters'.[37] Intuitively, Sims had a much clearer idea of how an escorted convoy could act as a magnet to lure submarines to it, turning the tables on any would-be attacker. However, in terms of actual numbers sunk, the escort destroyers' performance while on convoy duty was not that impressive – from May 1917 until the end of the war, '11 submarines were sunk by the convoy escorts', but what the bare statistic does not do is put a value to the deterrence effect of their presence.[38] Aside from escort destroyers, one of the great American contributions to Allied ASW in 1917 was the mass-produced, low-cost wooden sub-chaser, which was used extensively in the Mediterranean to man the Otranto Barrage. More than 450 of the 70-ton wooden boats were produced. Jellicoe was generally favourable to the construction of smaller ASW vessels because of their speedier manufacturing time, lower cost and wider visibility. Jellicoe's position on the hunter-killer submarine is not clear from his writing, but given the paucity of naval targets and no active anti-commerce role, hunting other submarines effectively became the only role available to the Royal Navy in the last two years of the war. Air support was put into place in 1917, significantly extending the 'eyes' of the Allies, and in February aircraft supplemented sub-hunting patrols. During 1917, in roughly 1.5 million flying hours, 169 submarines were spotted. By 1918, while flying hours increased dramatically to 4.8 million, there was no commensurate increase in sightings: these only rose to 192.[39] One of Jellicoe's learnings from the 19 August U-boat trap was how effective spotting U-boats from the air could be: the airship '*SS41* reported that she could see the submarines at periscope depth from a height of eight hundred feet'.[40]

Between Beatty and Jellicoe, the former comes out as the stronger and more visible proponent of airpower in ASW. Jellicoe's Admiralty can be held responsible for not putting more weight behind the development of naval aviation, particularly deck-launched, fixed-wing operations. James Goldrick even speculated whether a torpedo attack on German anchorages might have been possible in 1918 had more support been given. The idea of long-range bombing of Kiel and Wilhelmshaven was eventually shelved. The Large

America seaplanes weren't available in sufficient quantity until summer 1918, but the plans were dropped when the number of pilots required couldn't be found.

Jellicoe had always been interested in the depth charge and is assigned a major role in its creation by at least one researcher, Fraser McKee. He wrote that Jellicoe was responsible for the development of the 1,150lb Service Mark II Cruiser mine: 'At Jellicoe's request, the SAC asked the torpedo school for an antisubmarine "droppable mine".'[41] McKee concluded that 'Although it was not appreciated at the time, *Vernon* had in fact invented the depth charge, complete with the most satisfactory type of firing mechanism', a hydrostatic pistol.[42]

Under Jellicoe, depth-charge production increased rapidly: in July 1917, weekly production levels were at around 140; by the end of the year it was 800. At the start of 1917, escort destroyers on average carried only four depth charges; low production levels, coupled with the need for high volume availability for saturation attacks, limited the overall kill rate.

Finally, regarding the enabling factors or technologies, the issue of detection always lurked in the background. Sufficient progress was not made to impact the anti-submarine war and Sims eventually declared this his overriding concern. Commander Cyril Ryan, the director of the Hawkscraig Research Station, was a regular visitor to Aberdour House – some even suggested that Lady Beatty might have had an affair with him – but Ryan's proximity probably kept Beatty more attuned to hydrophone development than Jellicoe.

Having coordinated operations at sea with intelligence from the safety of the Admiralty in London, Jellicoe fully understood the revolutionary role of wireless communications and intelligence.[43] At Jutland, he had been frustrated by its lack (although not as angry as he later became when the full scale of the failure became clear). Merely by his frequent visits – he would stop by most evenings – OB40 started to command a wider respect in 1917.

HUMINT (Jellicoe had always listened to his own 'on the ground' contacts) and SIGINT were not the only sources. There was also wreck intelligence, POW interrogations and the combination of D/F and decrypts. With OB40 also coming under the supervision of the DNI, 'the door was now opened wide enough to permit intercepts and directionals [to be] plotted on the convoy chart', and consequently, the possibility of redirecting convoys away from potential submarine contact.[44]

Naturally, the organisation of previously independent ships into convoys accelerated the flow of operational intelligence, bringing information from the Intelligence Division directly to a convoy leader by W/T. However, as the theatre of submarine operations widened, so did the need for a geographic expansion of the D/F and W/T network, adding strain to the system's resources.[45]

Few secrets were kept from the Americans: Sims was entrusted by Jellicoe with the most sensitive sources of OB40.[46] Small wonder, he concluded, that the 'organization of the British Admiralty includes a highly efficient Intelligence Division'.[47] Sims would later meet daily with Jellicoe, either at the Admiralty or his London home at The Mall. He had, in his words, been 'given entire freedom of the Admiralty and access to all Government officials'.[48]

As a civilian volunteer, Tracy Barrett Kittredge helped acclimatise Sims to the close-knit and often informally organised circle of trusted friends within the intelligence community of London.[49] The sheer diversity of the assembled talent made an impression on Sims, who described it to Captain Roger Welles, Director of Naval Intelligence:

> [A]t the British Admiralty, they have a corps of grey-haired Oxford Professors, Egyptologists, Cuneiform Inscription Readers etc., who break ciphers with great facility, and, I may add, have broken practically every cipher that they have been put up against.[50]

The Mediterranean, however, proved more difficult, with better application of operational intelligence being hindered by personalities. Both the French and Italians in Malta refused to pool their intelligence or partner naval resources. In a similar vein, despite the enormous need, it took the Signals Section until September 1917 to get the convoy signal codes organised and distributed to 30,000 ships.

### Jellicoe and Convoy

'Contrary to folklore, Jellicoe was in no way ignorant of convoy, nor was he personally averse to its introduction; he was, however, the recipient of some extremely poor advice.'[51] Bernard Ireland's forgiving assessment is somewhat misleading. The source of much bad decision-making wasn't 'poor advice', rather the lack of analytical discipline in dealing with the information at hand (the port entries, for example) and the overall lack of statistical research. The background to all this, of course, was the Navy's predilection for the offensive and the overwhelmingly biased atmosphere this created among senior officers.

Jellicoe's methodical approach was as much to blame for the delayed introduction of convoys; what James Goldrick called his 'critical, perhaps even an egregious, failure'.[52] How many months could have been saved? If we accept that the tests were worthwhile exercises for such a monumental strategy change, I would say less than two months. What Jellicoe did was to maintain a certain distance. He wanted to avoid seeing the convoy system as the only answer. He was half-right: convoys would not have succeeded without significant advances in and increased availability of weapons, changes in escort tactics and convoy management, full cooperation of the USN and full access to American ports. Convoys could not be implemented at the stroke of a pen.

The success of any strategy depends on implementation, which needs leadership, mission clarity, task assignment, delegation, resources, metrics, monitoring and review: in sum, systems, people and equipment.[53] This included having the right type of escort ships available, in the right quantities and in the right places. It also needed the setting-up of effective logistics and for the available weapons and technologies to be used in an increasingly integrated tactical manner. It was the combination of the tools of A/S and trade protection – weapons, tactics, weapon platforms, intelligence, logistics etc – that ultimately rendered positive results.

It must be said that once Jellicoe saw the possibility of convoys being effectively implemented, he added the weight of his Admiralty behind it. 'I am convinced convoy system is a necessity and only method left to us,' he cabled the Americans on 29 June.[54] It was 'effective in greatly reducing losses'.[55]

To make convoys work across the Atlantic, Jellicoe needed the wholehearted support of the Americans, which initially he didn't receive. Sims spent much of June selling the idea to his colleagues and countrymen. Some wanted to try 'bolder actions such as attacking well-defended submarine bases'. Sims even tried to directly address the ideological issues. In his 16 June cable to Daniels, he stated: 'This convoy system is looked upon as an offensive measure.' That clearly wasn't the case. Benson and Daniels 'still viewed arming merchant vessels as a viable solution to the submarine'.[56] Despite Sims and Jellicoe's united call, Commodore Guy Gaunt reported back from Washington with bad news: 'Just discussed your and Sims' cable of the last three days with Admiral Benson. He is still opposed to convoys and strongly in favour of armed merchant vessels.'[57] Expressing his frustration, Jellicoe went on to say that they were

> pressing the United States to strengthen our escorting forces as far as possible in order to extend the convoy system, when a telegram arrived from Washington to the effect that it was considered that ships which were armed were safer when sailing singly than when in convoy.[58]

The considerations that employing the convoy system entailed were gargantuan. It was a situation where the wise were made to look stupid and the foolish, wise. Convoys were not 'just putting ships together' or 'finding escorts'; they were also about the huge infrastructure of distribution, a precursor of what 'Just-in-time' (JIT) manufacturing now means: precise coordination all the way through the value chain. Crucially, convoys were just as much about the bureaucracy that was going to run the system. Jellicoe's approach was probably ideal for those needs, but he failed to provide the impassioned leadership that accompanies significant change, and it certainly didn't help that the USN initially opposed the system, making the implementation of the all-important Atlantic convoys considerably more difficult.

## Did the Allies Actually *Defeat* the U-Boat?

Convoys and improvements in ASW may have won the trade protection war, but was the U-boat defeated? As late as 27 September 1918, Geddes wrote to Beatty expressing his concern that not only were Allied A/S methods ineffective, but the U-boat threat was still growing:

> I am getting very concerned, as are we all, at the reduction in killing power of our anti-submarine methods. We are not getting them as we should, and although we know, to a great extent, the reasons, there is no doubt that the submarine fleet is *growing* [author's emphasis] on us.[59]

Geddes's conclusion was that Germany was preparing for another U-boat offensive, estimating that she would possess around 180 boats by the year's end. As late as September 1918, Duff and Geddes, for example, went to meet with SecNav Daniels in Washington. There was a real need to keep American funding and supplies coming, but Geddes's own notes reveal his deep concerns about the continued U-boat danger, estimated in late October to still number 181 submarines:

> Up to May of this year submarines were being successfully dealt with. Since May, mainly on account of the diversion of the British hunting forces to American escort work, the submarine situation has steadily become more formidable, and we are faced with a tremendous submarine effort, on the enemy's part, whilst our hunting forces are inadequate … In fact, it is doubtful whether the Allies can continue this policy of escort without incurring the grave risk of the submarines again becoming a serious menace.[60]

Exactly one year earlier, in September 1917, Allied ASW efforts claimed eleven U-boats sunk, and a few months later, on 9 November, 'the highest number of U-boats … sunk in the entire war'.[61] Jellicoe's efforts were not for naught. More important, maybe, was that shipping sinkings were down to only 30 per cent of April's disastrous total.

What he said highlighted a declining kill rate, which he attributed to the diversion of resources *from sub hunting to escort duty*, a point of view that smacks of both Beatty's and Jellicoe's predilection for the offensive. At the same time, he was also requesting more destroyers be delivered.

Post-war, professional U-boat officers such as Spindler maintained that the U-boat threat remained very real until the end: 'The English version that the submarine menace was overcome at the conclusion of the war is not in agreement with the facts of the case.'[62] Spindler's treatment of the facts was, however, often questionable.

Marder had a very different view. By 1918, he wrote, 'the worst was definitely over by June, and the U-boat campaign as good as defeated'.[63] Even comments by some U-boat captains would support this. Writing in July 1918, Werner Fürbringer, for example, mirrored Sims's point of view:

> In the last twelve months, the British had made unbelievable strides towards improving their anti-submarine defences. The convoy system had proved itself beyond all expectations. Their depth charges were packed with more explosive. They had perfected a mine copied from the German model. They had put into service much improved underwater listening devices … In May 1918, the Entente succeeded for the first time in launching more tonnage than U-boats destroyed.[64]

The average U-boat commander, Marder continued, had previously been sinking 700 tons per day; by the summer of 1918, that plummeted to around 275 tons. Conversely, the Allies were more successful in killing U-boats in 1918 than at anytime during the war: a monthly average of 6.8 submarines were being destroyed.[65]

At the same time that Germany increased submarine production, the high losses of personnel meant that the quality of the manning crews declined. There wasn't enough time for training, repairs, refits and maintenance. Experienced officers were also increasingly difficult to find.[66] Max Valentiner said what many of his fellow captains felt:

> Around me, everything slowly changed. As the war wore on, we were torn apart. The fact was that every single man among my trained and experienced crew was worth almost more than an entire newly trained U-boat crew. My old comrades were taken, one by one, to be placed in new U-boats to give new crews a backbone.[67]

A total of 343 German U-boats served during the war, with around 13,000 men ('including the highly trained replacement crews').[68] With war, the submarine service's ranks had expanded to 11,917, but half of that number – 5,924 men – were lost, along with 178 boats.[69] Among officers lost, the composition was 'about one-half of the lieutenant commanders and one-third of the lieutenants and junior lieutenants', leading to the characterisation of the

U-boat war in Germany as 'the war of lieutenants'.[70] They had been responsible for the sinking of 4,837 merchantmen ('*Transportschiffe*') of around 11 million GRT, with 15,313 merchant seamen losing their lives.[71] The Cayzer family's Clan Line alone had lost twenty-nine ships (twenty-eight to enemy action), sixty-one officers and about 275 lascar sailors.[72] The Allies threw everything they could against the U-boat threat, with 1.1 million sea mines, 4,000 armed merchantmen, their 13,000 guns and the 65,000 men manning those guns.

> If one adds up the assets used in anti-submarine warfare and for clearing submarine minefields, one arrives at an almost unimaginable figure of 9,000 ships of varied classes and almost 3,000 airplanes and dirigibles that acted to protect British sea communications which were still not able to solve the problem of anti-submarine warfare.[73]

As a military weapon, the submarine was effective, but nothing approaching the spectacular success it had against commerce. Around ninety-four naval vessels were sunk, 'including ten battleships, 18 cruisers, 21 destroyers, and 13 submarines'.[74] The thirteen submarine victims included four of their own boats.

### Jellicoe's Legacy

John Jellicoe was a widely respected, highly credible professional naval officer: intelligent, astute and decisive, but also a quiet, modest man of integrity. However, he had his flaws. He wasn't the dashing, charismatic public hero which the media or public craved, or even an outspoken 'out-of-the-box' thinker. He was the exceptional product of a Royal Navy steeped in tradition.

Jellicoe never opposed the use of convoys. His actions certainly cannot be labelled a disgrace. The simple fact is that Jellicoe wasn't confident enough that, even if properly resourced, convoys alone could be the answer. He understood the interdependence of weapons systems and tactics. Once he did finally start to appreciate the potential of the convoy system, he still had to tackle the very severe resourcing issue that he'd been left with, and not just at sea: the system was all-encompassing, the dependencies and facilitators also covering Britain's wider distribution and transportation infrastructure. The introduction and support of a trade protection system *either side of the Atlantic* needed American support too. Instead, until well into the summer of 1917, the highest leadership of the USN stood in its way. By the Armistice, American naval support amounted to a massive '54 bases, stations and other shore facilities in Europe'.[75] Jellicoe's responsibility had been enourmous; if he got it wrong, Britain was doomed. Others, excepting the Prime Minister, did not have that cross to bear.

Success is mostly based on collective rather than individual thinking. Jellicoe brought professionalism and method (some would say 'plodding'), diplomacy to win over allies, technical understanding and quiet leadership, but was unable to delegate, did not play the vastly different political game at War Cabinet well and was not an innovator. It took the combined wits of many – men with widely differing skills, innovators, administrators, diplomats and politicians – to bring the submarine beast to heel. That is not to downplay the charismatic political leadership of Lloyd George, the contributions of officers like Henderson and Sims, or even civilians such as Manisty. But just over twenty years later, the submarine menace again nearly brought the country to its knees. With all the lessons of 1914–18, Britain still had to relearn much that had been lost or overlooked.

Jellicoe was no Young Turk. The chain of command was fundamental, blocking him from embracing 'out of the box' thinking even though much of the Board of Invention and Research's work was ridiculed for having tried to deliver that spirit. Nevertheless, it is difficult to understand why the infamous harbour statistics were not sooner understood or that the statistical support for cloaking convoys with oceanic invisibility was not explored. But there were huge improvements: in mines, detection (both hydrophonic and aerial), intelligence exploitation, depth charges etc.

By June 1917, Jellicoe was firmly on board with the extension of convoys to the Atlantic routes, despite ongoing resistance from the top ranks of the US Navy, from both Daniels and Benson, both of whom later made out that they were always supporters. In this, Jellicoe was strongly aided by Sims, an earlier passionate convert, a man who intuitively understood the effective role of the escort destroyer but by no means the author of the convoy system.

Lloyd George wrote of the successful progress that had been made in 1917 in ASW in an ambiguous acknowledgement – for it could easily be also interpreted as Lloyd George congratulating his own role – of Jellicoe's achievements before he had to leave the Admiralty on Christmas Eve:

> That is why I regard the steps taken to counter the submarine attack as the most important contributions made to victory during the year 1917.[76]

# Appendices

# Appendix A

# German Submarine Types, Tactics and Performance

**German Submarine Types**

**U-class:** Initial German submarine models used a Körting kerosene engine severely restricting range and operability; from *U.19* onwards, diesel engines were used. Attrition rates in these early submarine models was high. Spiess noted that by July 1915, 'of the fourteen older boats that we had at the beginning of the war, the class of which *U.9* was one, seven had been lost'.[1]

**Ocean-going U-class:** All the ocean-going Type-*U.31* vessels were double-hulled and all – except *U.35* – were equipped with an 8.8cm deck gun. *U.35* had started the war with a smaller-calibre 7.5cm variety which was, in 1916, upgraded to a 10.5cm gun. All were fitted with four 50cm (20in) torpedo tubes, with two astern and two in the bow. The boats carried a further six torpedoes on board.

Of the *U.31* class, the last class built before the opening shots of the First World War (of which *U.35* was), only *U.33*, *U.35* and *U.38* surrendered, the rest being sunk in operation. The class had a lower mortality rate than the heavier and larger UC-class: 128 out of the 256 built were lost.

Three of Germany's top aces were associated with the class: Lothar von Arnauld de la Perière (*U.35*), Max Valentiner (*U.38*) and Walther Forstmann (*U.39*). Between them, they claimed an astonishing 1.2 million GRT sunk.

Initially, Valentiner's *U.38* was equipped with an 8.8cm gun behind the conning tower. Valentiner was very critical about the set-up, although he did attribute 75,000 GRT sunk to the gun:

> The first gun mounted on *U 38* was a very short 8.8cm gun, positioned behind the conning tower. This setup was unfavorable: Come up on the target, shoot and then turn away every time because the conning tower was in the way. Nevertheless, while on patrol in the Irish Sea, I managed to sink seventy-five thousand tons in three days with this gun.[2]

The table below shows the most important specifications by class. While length and beam remain constant, as do – broadly speaking – the number and placement of tubes as well as deck artillery, there is a gradual increase in displacement, speed and crew size. The *U.51* class exceptionally falls back on some key measures.

| | | Class numbers | Length | Beam | Displaceme nt (Tons) | | Speed (knots) | | Tubes | Tubes | Torpedo | Reserve | Deck Gun | Machine gun | Officers | Crew | Notes |
|---|---|---|---|---|---|---|---|---|---|---|---|---|---|---|---|---|---|
| | | | Mtrs | Mtrs | Surface | Submerged | Surface | Sub'gd | Bow | Stern | cm | | cm | mm | | | |
| U | 5 | | 57.3 | 5.6 | 505 | 636 | 13.4 | 10.2 | 2 | 2 | 45 | 6 | 3.7 | | 4 | 24 | Hotchkiss |
| | 16 | | 57.8 | 6 | 489 | 627 | 15.6 | 10.7 | 2 | 2 | 45 | 6 | 5 | | 4 | 25 | |
| | 19 | | 64.2 | 6.1 | 650 | 837 | 15.4 | 9.5 | 2 | 2 | 50 | | 8.8 | | 4 | 25 | SK L/30. from 1916 two |
| | 27 | | 64.7 | 6.3 | 675 | 878 | 16.7 | 9.8 | 2 | 2 | 50 | | 8.8 | | 4 | 31 | |
| | 31 | | 64.7 | 6.3 | 685 | 878 | 16.4 | 9.7 | 2 | 2 | 50 | 6 | 8.8 | | 4 | 31 | |
| | 43 | | 65 | 6.2 | 725 | 940 | 15.2 | 9.7 | 2 | 2 | 50 | 6 | 8.8 | | | 36 | complement |
| | 51 | | 65.2 | 6.4 | 715 | 902 | 17.1 | 9.1 | 2 | 2 | 50 | 7 | 8.8 | | | | Two SK L/30. |
| | 57 | | 67 | 6.3 | 766 | 956 | 14.7 | 8.4 | 2 | 2 | 50 | 7 | 8.8 | | | 36 | complement |
| | 63 | | 68.3 | 6.3 | 810 | 927 | 16.5 | 9 | 2 | 2 | 50 | 8 | 8.8 | | | 36 | complement |
| | 66 | | 69.5 | 6.3 | 791 | 933 | 16.8 | 10.3 | 4 | 1 | 45 | 12 | 8.8 | | 4 | 32 | Later SK L/45 10.5cm |
| | 81 | | 70.6 | 6.3 | 808 | 946 | 16.8 | 9.1 | 2 | 2 | 50 | 12-16 | 11 | | 4 | 31 | U.84 also 8.8cm and 12 torpedoes |

Source: multiple sources, including uboat.net.

**Coastal *UB* class:** Specifically designed for shallow coastal water operations, the smaller Type-*UB*-class vessels were initially single-hulled and displaced 127 tons, measured 92ft and had a 10ft beam and draft. For Terraine, the fighting power of the early models, 'feeble instruments of war', was 'almost laughable'.[3] They were derisively nicknamed 'Tadpoles'. The sub had a mere 1 knot difference between their surface (6.5kts) and submerged (5.5kts) speeds. Twenty Type-*UB.1* submarines were built; nine survived the war and four were converted into minelayers.

The *UB.1* design class (*UB.1* to *UB.8*) were all prefabricated in Germany, transported in sections and assembled in Belgium. Only Werner Fürbringer's *UB.2* was treated differently: she was 'the first boat of the Flotilla to come down to Flanders from Germany by the sea route'.[4] All the others in her class had been shipped by rail to Antwerp and assembled there. The *UB* was 'only one fourth the size of the newer U-boats, [but] they could be built in about one-seventh the time: seventy-two days in construction for the major sections, fourteen days for final assembly, compared with eighteen months'.[5]

The small, fourteen-man crewed boats (one officer and thirteen men) were so simple that they were derisively called 'sewing machines' by their crews. The earliest boats could only travel 45 nautical miles dived at 4kts before needing to surface and recharge their batteries. There were only two bow torpedo tubes and a deck-mounted machine gun. They only had two torpedoes on board, with no reloads. The Type-*UB* could be operational for around two weeks before having to return for resupply.

When Ernst Hashagen compared his first boat, *UB.21*, to a U-boat, he used the word '*zwerg*' (dwarf), even if he complemented her diving speed, describing it as happening 'astonishingly quickly'.[6]

But their contribution shouldn't be dismissed: the *UB-1* class submarines were operational in the Baltic, Constantinople and Flanders Flotillas. In July 1915, *UB.14* (under an Austro-Hungarian flag as *U.XXVI*) claimed the 10,118-ton armoured cruiser *Amalfi*, 'Italy's finest armoured cruiser'.[7]

A common problem for the Type-*UB.1* was the inability to maintain trim after firing a torpedo. *UB.14*'s first commander, Heino von Heimburg, described his first torpedo firing:

> I was knocked sprawling as the boat made a wild leap. It took me bewildered moments to figure what had happened. I had never fired a torpedo from a sewing machine before and had not anticipated what would happen. The boat was so small that when relieved of the weight of the torpedo at the bow she popped up like a jack-in-the-box.[8]

The *UB-II* class, introduced in 1915, were larger (270 tons), cost between 1.1 and 1.3 million DM and were fitted with two 50cm bow tubes, initially firing four and later six torpedoes. The design corrected many of the problems of the Type-*UB.I*: overall weight was increased to accommodate twin shafts, larger batteries and two torpedo tubes, stacked at the bow. As a result of these improvements, they were capable of longer-duration missions, making them available for Southern Irish coastal use or even the Bay of Biscay.

| | | Class numbers | Length | Beam | Displacement (Tons) | | Speed (knots) | | Tubes | Tubes | Torpedo | Reserve | Deck Gun | Machine gun | Officers | Crew | Notes |
|---|---|---|---|---|---|---|---|---|---|---|---|---|---|---|---|---|---|
| | | | Mtrs | Mtrs | Surface | Submerged | Surface | Sub'gd | Bow | Stern | cm | | cm | mm | | | |
| UB | I | 1-17 | 28.1 | 3.2 | 127 | 421 | 6.5 | 5.5 | 2 | | 45 | | | 8 | 1 | 13 | |
| | II | 18-47 | 36.9 | 4.4 | 274 | 303 | 9 | 5.7 | 2 | | 50 | 4 | 8.8 | | 2 | 21 | Later 6 torpedoes |
| | III | 48 | 53.3 | 5.8 | 516 | 651 | 13.6 | 8 | 4 | 1 | 50 | 10 | 8.8 | | 3 | 31 | 107 boats in the series from 48-155 |

In the autumn of 1917, the first of the new medium-sized Type-*UB.III* series boats, *UB.48*, built 'especially for the Mediterranean', appeared.[9] It was the first of thirty Type-*UB.III* boats ordered for the German Navy. 'It was not until *UB.48*, the precursor of the Type-*VII* of later fame, that a powerful, long-range, and stable submarine came into production.'[10] Wolfgang Steinbauer's boat, a very successful Mediterranean U-boat with forty-two ships sunk to her name, was typical of the series. At 510 tons, they were closer to the North Sea boats, the *Mittel U-boote*. Each carried four bow tubes and one stern tube, with a total of ten torpedoes. The *UB.III*s were able to travel at almost 14kts surfaced and 8kts submerged.

Altogether, 157 Type-*UB* boats were produced for the German Navy (twenty Type-*UB.1*, thirty Type-*UB.II* and 107 Type-*UB.III*).

**The Minelayer *UC* class:** The Type-*UC.I* submarine was the first minelayer submarine. The fifteen boats of the Type-*UC.I* series had a surface displacement of around 170 tons and a fourteen-man complement. This initial series were solely armed with mines, although *UC.11* had a hull-mounted tube added in 1916. Like the Type-*UB.I*, they were also extremely slow.

They were built by AG Vulcan (Hamburg) and AG Weser (Bremen) and launched between April and August 1915 (the keel of the German-built Russian *Krab* was laid down earlier, but the German *UC.1* was the first *operational* boat). The 'first cruise of a minelayer from Flanders was made by *UC.11*, one of her mines hitting a British destroyer at the southern entrance to the Downs on 1 June 1915'.[11]

| | | Class numbers | Length | Beam | Displacement (Tons) | | Speed (knots) | | Mines | Mines | | Tubes | Tubes | Torpedo | Torpedo | Deck Gun | Machine gun | Officers | Crew | Notes |
|---|---|---|---|---|---|---|---|---|---|---|---|---|---|---|---|---|---|---|---|---|
| | | | Mtrs | Mtrs | Surface | Submerged | Surface | Sub'gd | 100 cm | UC 120 | UC 200 | Bow | Stern | No | cm | cm | mm | | | |
| UC | I | 1-15 | 34 | 3.2 | 168 | 183 | 6.2 | 5.2 | 6 | 12 | | | | | | | 8 | | 14 | complement. UC.II was fitted with an external torpedo tube in 1916 |
| | II | 16-79 | 49.4 | 5.2 | 400 | 480 | 11.6 | 6.7 | 6 | | 18 | 2 | 1 | | 50 | 8.8 | | | 26 | complement |
| | III | 80-105 | 56 | 5.5 | 474 | 560 | 11.5 | 6.6 | | | 14 | 2 | 1 | 7 | | 8.8 | | | 32 | complement |

Source: For specifics on Type-*UC.III*, see Uboat.net

Mining operations were extremely precarious and Admiralty dive operations to discover the boat's secrets and weaknesses were extensive. *UC.12* blew up on 16 March 1916 outside of Taranto, where, with a German crew, she served under the Austro-Hungarian flag. Her wreck was later found at a depth of 31 metres, where it was seen that from her cargo of twelve mines, she had dropped eight, two others were still in her chutes but two had exploded. One of these, it was surmised, had floated up after it had been dropped and blown up the sub. The mechanism which would normally hold the mine for about fifteen minutes before releasing it from its cradle had failed.

Eleven of the first series were sunk, mostly by mines. Small wonder, then, they were nicknamed the 'sisters of sorrow'; very few survived.[12] Overall, Type-*UC* boats had a high mortality rate: fifty out of the seventy-nine built were lost, achieving what Sondhaus called 'the dubious distinction of being Germany's first expendable U-boats'. In 1916, a Flanders boat was four times more likely to be sunk than a Mediterranean-based vessel; a year later, almost twenty times more likely.[13]

Type-*UC.II* series boats (*UCs.16–79*), introduced in 1915, were larger 410–420-ton minelayers that were also equipped with two bow and one stern tubes, capable of launching seven 50cm torpedoes. Each had an 8.8cm deck gun (later upgraded to 10.5cm) and was built with six mine shafts carrying up to eighteen mines.

The *UC.III* class (*UCs.80–105*) were 470-ton, three-tube boats capable of firing seven torpedoes, a deck gun and the same six mine shafts, though limited to fourteen mines.

Nearly half of the 149 U-boats in construction at the end of 1916 were Type-*UC*, the characteristic appearance of which was a 'gun in the dip between [the raised forecastle] and the conning-tower'.[14] Sixty-four of the Type-*UC.IIs*, 'one of the war's largest classes of U-boats', were completed, but forty-six of them were sunk. Forty-one other Type-*UC.I* and *UC.III* boats were built. Type-*UC.II* boats were built by AG Vulcan and Blohm und Voss (Hamburg), AG Weser (Bremen) and Germania (Kiel), and at least one writer has called it 'the most successful design in submarine history', citing the sinking of at least 1,800 vessels by *UC.II* submarines alone.[15] From 18 September to the end of 1915, just six *UC* boats managed to sink fifty-one merchant vessels (71,386 tons) in the North Sea, as well as a British submarine and destroyer.[16]

**Ocean-going Minelayers Type-*UE* class:** Displacing 477 tons and crewed by four officers and twenty-eight men, the Type-*UE* class were equipped with only four torpedoes, a 3.45in deck gun (8.8cm) and could carry thirty-four mines. An improved feature was that they could stern-drop the mines (from two tubes), which made them considerably safer than some of the previous hull-dropped minelayers.

| | | Class numbers | Length | Beam | Displacement (Tons) | | Speed (knots) | | Tubes | Tubes | Torpedo | Reserve | Deck Gun | Mines | Mines | Machine gun | Officers | Crew | Notes |
|---|---|---|---|---|---|---|---|---|---|---|---|---|---|---|---|---|---|---|---|
| | | | Mtrs | Mtrs | Surface | Submerged | Surface | Sub'gd | Bow | Stern | cm | | cm | | | mm | | | |
| UE | 71 | 71-80 | 56.8 | 5.9 | 755 | 832 | 9.9 | 7.9 | 1 | 1 | 50 | 4 | 8.8 | 38 | | | 4 | 28 | 2 mine tubes |

Source: multiple sources, including uboat.net.

***U-kreuzer* class:** These converted merchant U-boats (*U.151–157*) displaced 1,870 tons submerged and could carry eighteen torpedoes. They normally had two 5.9in guns, sometimes also (according to Gibson and Prendergast, p.218) two 3.4in weapons.

Of the nine built, seven were converted from commerce carriers and only two were purpose-built from the keel up.[17] Five Deutschland-class submarines survived the war.[18] These displaced 2,500 tons submerged, were 311ft long, carried two 5.9in deck guns and mounted six torpedo tubes. The *U-kreuzer* had 'considerably more beam' than ordinary U-boats.

| | | Class numbers | Length | Beam | Displacement (Tons) | | Speed (knots) | | Tubes | Tubes | Torpedo | Reserve | Deck Gun | Machine gun | Officers | Crew | Notes |
|---|---|---|---|---|---|---|---|---|---|---|---|---|---|---|---|---|---|
| | | | Mtrs | Mtrs | Surface | Submerged | Surface | Sub'gd | Bow | Stern | cm | | cm | mm | | | |
| U | 151-157 | | 65 | 8.9 | 1'512 | 1'875 | 12.4 | 5.2 | 6 | | 50 | | 18 | | 6 | 50 | Built as U-Kreuzer and converted |

Source: multiple sources, including uboat.net.

The U-boat's extended range meant that it could now operate as far south as the north-west coast of Africa.

## Operation

A submarine's outer hull, 'shaped like that of a sleek destroyer', sheathed a 'tubular internal pressure hull', made of nickel steel, protecting most of the regulating equipment and the crew.[19]

The outer hull was where the ballast tanks were located. The regulating tanks were used to cause the boat to sink or rise, while trim tanks, forward and aft, corrected any misalignment of the boat in the water. With the tanks empty, the boat gained buoyancy and rose to the surface; as buoyancy was lost, the boat sank. Shifting weight almost always needed a crew's full cooperation. As Valentiner put it, 'thirty-six men make up my human ballast'.[20]

Buoyancy and trim control on a submarine is a precise and exacting art, fundamental to the existence and functioning of the craft. It required 'an extremely delicate balance between the weight of the submarine and that of the water which it displaces'.[21]

A submarine's trim needs constant adjustment by regulating its ballast tanks: to account for the consumption of fuel, the variability of salinity, depth, heat and the submarine's load (including crew food consumption etc). More water pumped into their boat's tanks give it negative buoyancy, a tendency to sink; less water in the tanks give positive buoyancy, a tendency to rise. Hydroplanes at the bow and stern help the engines power the submarine upward and downward.

A difficulty faced by many German submariners was adjusting buoyancy for the different salinity levels. The high-brine North Sea water weighs more than that of the Baltic, particularly the western basin, 'composed of practically fresh water'.[22] When transiting through the Kiel Canal between the Baltic and North Sea in October 1917, Johannes Spieß, *U.52*'s second commander, nearly paid with his life for one faulty adjustment. His sub took on a heavy negative buoyancy and sank fast by her stern. This difference means that the very same submarine needs to take on more water in the North Sea to stay in trim than when it is in the Baltic. Especially tricky conditions present themselves to a submariner going close to shore and passing an estuary, where high salinity is replaced by fresh water in an instant.

The relationship of the submarine to the water it displaces needs to be kept constant to maintain a constant depth. In combat conditions, adjustments and settings need to be made with a combination of speed and precision. For example, diving a submarine to avoid detection can be dangerous if the sub takes too steep and too rapid a descent, although Forstner said that German submarines were equipped with a 'hydrostatic safety system which automatically causes the discharge of water from the ballast-tank when dangerous pressures are reached'.[23] The time taken to dive was improved from around one minute to thirty seconds, 'while the fastest surface unit could only cover a thousand yards in the same time'.[24] It meant that a submarine would be close to invulnerable if it could submerge fast enough, do so fully and maintain correct trim.

Diving a boat required setting trim, buoyancy and closing all hatches (including the diesel motor vents). Emergency dives could end with a crew member being left on the outside or a hatch improperly closed if not relentlessly practiced. For some submarines, for example Russian subs operating in the Baltic, it could be a lot worse:

> when on the surface one man was constantly responsible for chipping ice from the conning tower hatch so that emergency diving was possible.

> The doors of the torpedo tubes froze up, the periscope could not be raised.[25]

When von Arnauld de la Perière got his first command in the Adriatic aboard *U.35* in December 1915, he had an early encounter with decoy ships. After attacking the *Baron Napier*, the radio operator called for help. The Dutch Q-ship *Margit* responded and soon came over the horizon. When the decoy ship's commander, Lt Cdr G.L. Hodson, ordered fire to be opened, *U.35* dived so fast that her watch officer, Oberleutnant Lauenberg, was left on deck. Without hesitating, von Arnauld surfaced his boat, pulled the bedraggled man aboard and submerged his boat again so fast 'that she reached 180 feet before the dive could be checked and the vessel trimmed onto an even keel'.[26]

**Propulsion**

A submarine's propulsion system depended on whether it was on the surface, where combustion gases coud be expelled, or below the surface, where air was a precious commodity for both breathing and buoyancy. On the surface, the options were steam, gasoline or diesel; below, there was only electricity.

Gradually, kerosine engines were completely replaced by diesel for operating on the surface. Strangely, despite being a German invention, diesel was only adopted by the German Navy in 1911, 'seven years after the French' and 'four years after Britain'.[27] The Royal Navy's first diesel tests were a failure; until 1914, engines were licenced from FIAT.[28] MAN engines were installed on French submarines in 1904, and on the British D-class boats in 1907. Diesel would be 'a form of propulsion which endured in all navies until the advent of nuclear power'.[29] Post-war, British and American evaluation suggested that

> any German submarine design advantage derived largely from the efficiency of their diesels which generated three times the horsepower with much greater reliability than British models. German submariners regarded the British E-class diesels as a 'cheap blacksmith's job'.[30]

The diesel engine, which had been in production since 1893, was invented by a German engineer, Rudolf Diesel. In 1913, MAN (Maschinen-Fabrik Augsberg-Nürnberg) installed one of their engines in *U.19*. Until that point, the Körting kerosene engines produced clouds of black smoke, prompting *U.9*'s Johannes Spieß to joke, 'we went off sailing like the children of Israel, attended by a pillar of smoke'.[31] Diesels emitted no tell-tale smoke.

Running below the surface, where speed and range were dramatically reduced, the submarine's electric motors were run for as long as the batteries lasted; they were recharged off the main diesel engines while surfaced. Oil was supplied from tanks outside of the pressure hull, and vents were opened to allow the engines to 'breathe'.

For those working in the engine rooms, conditions were brutal. Paul Schultz had been on *U.14* and made no bones about it: 'I literally gasped for air, could hardly keep my eyes open and the acrid gases caused tears to roll down my cheeks.'[32] The heat was intense, like a blanket of fire. The noise was simply staggering: one ERA, Nicklaus Jaud, said that 'it drowned any attempt at speech, and communication was only possible by signs'.[33] The diesels also needed constant overhaul. Work started the moment a sub docked, sometimes even at sea, and often in very difficult conditions:

> While one engine remained in operation, the other was completely taken apart. Every free space was occupied with dismantled machine parts. The work was made even more difficult by rough seas which threw the boat back and forth, up and down, causing the machine parts to repeatedly tumble over and over.[34]

**Operational Endurance**

Time at sea gradually increased from an average of five days before the war to eleven (*U.20*, October 1914), eighteen (*U.21*, May 1915) and twenty-five days (*U.35*, July 1915). Finally, *U.53*'s voyage to and from the United States took forty-two days. Longer range was needed because of the gradual closing-down of the shorter Channel route to the Western Approaches and, later, the extension of the submarine war down to the Azores and across to American waters.

**Air Quality**

Clean, oxygenated air is vital in a submarine. When surfaced, air would be vented out by strong pumps and fresh air sucked in. Below the surface, air grew foul. German submariners would use potash cartridges 'to absorb the poisonous carbon monoxide content of rebreathed air'.[35] If there was an emergency, a sailor could hold a cartridge to his face and breathe through it directly. It wasn't comfortable, as the potash would gradually heat up. They found 'the best remedy was to wrap it in a handkerchief soaked in seawater'.[36] For those obliged to work with both hands, it was impossible.

Endurance was significantly impacted by activity. Forstner estimated that a sleeping man 'required hourly only fifteen litres of air', while 'a man working hard' needed 85 litres.[37] Something as simple as raising, lowering and swiveling a boat's periscope took a surprisingly high level of strength: it was tightly screwed in to counter water pressure.

Temperatures aboard fluctuated wildly. Diving in cold water produced dripping condensation within the boat, where 30 degrees Centigrade was normal; in engine rooms it could soar to 40. The stench of body odour was overpowering in a regime where a sailor could only wash (very superficially) once a week. Body sores caused by high levels of diesel in the boat's atmosphere were common. In good weather, being on deck could be absolute paradise, with fresh warm sea breezes and sunshine.

Chlorine gas poisoning was a constant danger. On Bruno Hoppe's *U.22*, a crash dive went horribly wrong: the boat would not respond and kept sinking. At 200ft, water was forcing its way into the boat and getting into the batteries. As the batteries' sulphuric acid combined with the seawater, deadly chlorine gas was given off. Ernst Hashagen, his 2nd Officer, described the horror:

> Everything else lost its importance … I caught the acrid smell of chlorine gas and everyone was coughing, spluttering and choking … I don't think there is anything that will strike such fear in a submarine man as the thought of being trapped inside the iron hull while choking gas seeps from the batteries bit by bit. No death could be more agonizing … Better to be shot to pieces and drown in a quiet way than death by choking torment.[38]

## Tactics

Estimating a convoy's direction and speed was essential for a submarine to position itself for a torpedo attack. Convoy zigzagging tactics made the task considerably more challenging:

> Because of the escorts he had to avoid closing on the surface. Compared to most merchantmen a submarine's speed on the surface was high; submerged, its speed was low. Therefore, unless from the first moment the U-boat was ahead of the convoy, it was not likely ever to get into a firing position.[39]

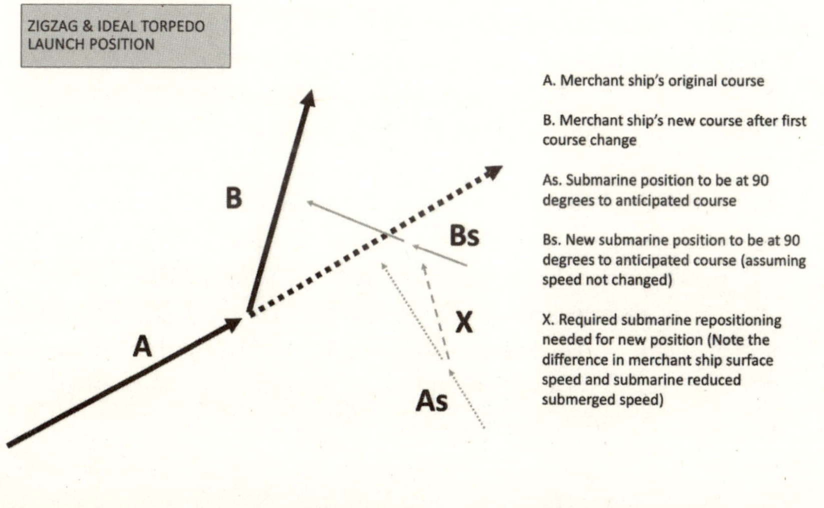

Germany 'had toyed with the idea of hunting convoys with packs of submarines' for some years.[40] It would be a forerunner to Doenitz's Rudeltaktik, or Wolfpacks. FdU Bauer had thought about operating groups of submarines supported by a U-kreuzer in the Western Approaches, but had been turned down by Holtzendorff. Throughout 1917 and 1918, Holtzendorff continued to oppose the idea 'as widely as possible'. Michelsen tried to get permission to try the tactic in November and December 1917, and again in April, May and July 1918, but Holtzendorff continued his opposition.[41] He had suggested converting one of the *U.151* class into a command boat to coordinate multiple U-boat attacks on convoy.[42] Even the kaiser is said to have supported a tactical trial.[43]

In the early hours of 28 May 1918, in what Gray called 'wolf pack assaults', three boats attacked the 9,737-ton Union-Castle vessel *Leasowe Castle*, which was sunk with the loss of thirteen officers and seventy men. Some Allied naval officers had anticipated this development:

> Bayly … forecast the adoption by the Germans of wolf-pack tactics, but Sims believed correctly that the U-boats would find co-ordinated tactics difficult and would be a danger to themselves.[44]

In early 1917, Taussig mentioned that 'submarines often work in pairs'. This was more the exception than the rule, because of inadequate communications between craft.[45] Admiral Ernest J. King deserves a mention here. In the Fleet Problem 1 exercise in 1923, he worked with sixteen submarines in group tactics, coordinated by radio.

**Communications**

As the war progressed, submarines developed increasingly sophisticated communications capabilities to send and receive information back to their bases and between other U-boats. Tactics, particularly those coordinated amongst several boats, heavily relied on the reliability and strength of signals.

A ship's wireless operator was one of the most valued, highly skilled jobs on board a submarine. *U.53*'s operator was able to imitate his British counterpart on a British merchantman, *Durango*. In a successful ruse, radio operator Zummack ordered the British crew to abandon ship: 'OGZ to *Durango*: Leave the ship before the lifeboats are damaged.' When a British destroyer sent a message asking for her position so that she could close, *U.53* answered: 'Too late, *Durango* awaits you at the bottom of the ocean. Signed UUU.'[46]

U-boat messages were kept as short as possible to thwart D/F triangulation. To shorten them, W/T operators used a structure. An April 1918 message from Rose's *U.53* serves as an example. The message was '1-2-9-068*a*-U53', meaning 'he had sunk one ship of 2,000 tons, still had nine torpedoes, and was in quadrant 068 alpha at the western end of the English Channel'.[47] Of course, once identified, messages became the source of a torrent of information. After the war, Sims underlined the importance of tracking using this information, saying that 'more shipping was saved through us keeping track of submarines and routing ships clear of them than by any other single measure'.[48]

Keeping a watchful eye on the swept channels used by submarines to sortie was essential. They were colour-coded, 'notably, Weg Gelb [away yellow], Weg Grün [green], and the coastal Weg Schwarz [black] near the Frisian Islands in the south; Weg Blau [blue] and Weg Rot [red], the northerly routes west of Horns Reef; and the centrally located Weg Braun [brown]'.[49] The tracking would start right at the point a submarine was leaving or returning to German waters: 'they *had* to give a position where they could be met by minesweepers, so we always knew whenever a submarine had sailed and when she was returning'.[50]

## Submarine Escape

Submariners knew their chances of surviving the war were slim. That's why it was a voluntary branch of the service and a major reason why U-boat crews were granted so many special privileges.

In January 1911, Max Valentiner displayed extraordinary courage under very difficult circumstances when his sub, *U.3*, started sinking. The opening of the 25ft-long torpedo tube remained above water and Valentiner was able to crawl through the tube. Two other crew members got out, hauled through by ropes; a third stuck and Valentiner had to push him back in with a stick. Valentiner went back into the boat and, with the help of others, managed to get thirty crew members out this way. During the night, *U.3*'s cable slipped and she sank to her grave at 13 metres along with the remaining three crew who couldn't get out. During the night, after two divers gave up from exhaustion, Valentiner himself went down, but by the time the boat was surfaced the three crewmen were gone; still warm, but dead.

Being in or near the conning tower was a sailor's best chance of survival if the boat was hit. Those in the engine rooms stood no chance, but those forward or aft near torpedo tubes sometimes managed to get through the tubes and be 'fired' out by the build-up of compressed air behind them as the sub sank.

A particularly gruesome story highlighting the chances of escape involved *U.51*. On 14 July 1916, a British submarine, HMS *H.5*, successfully torpedoed the *U.51* in the Weser estuary.[51] Hit below the conning tower, the German submarine quickly took on water and plunged to the bottom, 20 metres below. Her eighteen-man crew crowded into a forward compartment, but with only twelve emergency escape breathing apparatus (the Dräger Tauchretter, Modell

1912) available, the captain did not want to have to choose who would have to die. After two hours in which the air turned foul, two men tried to escape to the surface without the kit; both died. After fifty hours, three men who were in the boat's stern compartment did manage to get out with escape kits; only two survived. The wreck was salvaged in 1968 and twenty-one skeletons were later buried in Bremen. Two of the skulls had bullet holes.

Leading Seaman Schlichting described the terrible death of a group of submarine cadets. When the sub failed to make harbour, her absence was reported and an aerial search organised from the air station at Hottenau. The sub was quickly found, lying motionless underwater. Two salvage vessels, *Vulkan* and *Meteor*, were immediately sent. Initially, they looked set to rescue some of the survivors, who were quickly contacted by knocking on the hull. However, despite heroic efforts, the cables kept on snapping and, when a storm hit, the work had to be called off as *Vulkan* (which had stayed longer on the scene than had *Meteor*) was starting to sustain damage. When the sub was eventually brought ashore, fellow submariners had the grim task of bringing the bodies out. The evidence of the terrible last hours was there to see:

> The scratches on the steel walls, the corpses' torn fingernails, the blood stains on their clothes and on the walls, bore all too dreadful witness. Carefully, as though they were still alive, they were lifted, put into hammocks, and carried ashore.[52]

**Weapons Systems**

The submarine could limit trade either by physical destruction of a ship's cargo or by scaring off cargo carriers (belligerent or neutral) with the threat alone.

The weapon most associated with submarines is the torpedo, but at the start of the war, before the Allies started to arm merchant ships or covertly employ Q-ships, boarding and scuttling a ship was common practice. That was replaced with deck artillery when the risk of exposure was too high. The torpedo was necessitated by the submarine's need to remain concealed, but they were expensive, difficult to use and in limited supply. The last weapon in their armoury – initially used uniquely on submarines without torpedoes – was the mine.

When stopping to search a merchantman, flags were normally first used, and when nearer, the submarine 'broke out two code letters – "A.B." (stop immediately)'.[53] If those went unheeded, a warning shot was fired and, ultimately, general fire opened. If the instructions were understood and to be complied with, the ship's master would run up a white and red striped pennant.

Then, either the submarine's prize crew went across to the ship or, more likely, the ship would be asked to send a party across with her papers. These would include the ship's nationality, the ports from which it had sailed and to which it was sailing, the bill of lading (showing the details of her cargo), crew list and (if a passenger steamer) passenger list. While boarding a ship, the sub would often be tied up:

> When a steamer is stopped, it usually turns at a right angle to the wind. If you want to approach the steamer, you must approach it from the windward side, that is, from where the waves are coming. You approach the steamer perpendicularly and bring out a line from the bow of the submarine, roughly to the middle of the steamer. Because the steamer always protrudes higher out of the water than the submarine, it's more open to the wind. She drifts away in front of the submarine which she pulls after her.[54]

The rules were applied with a wide degree of variance, depending on the U-boat commander, the operating theatre and the period in the submarine war. Generally speaking, if the cargo was defined as contraband, it was confiscated and destroyed, 'but if it exceed[ed] half of the total cargo, then the ship [was] also condemned'.[55]

**Deck Artillery**

Most German submarines were not equipped with a deck gun at the outbreak of war – they either had nothing or a small machine gun. *U.20*'s 8.8cm gun was the first to be mounted on a submarine's deck. Intercepting and stopping a merchant ship could not be done before that with a 'shot across the bows'; it was done instead by flag or flares.

Jellicoe made the comment that 'the torpedo did not come into general use until March 1917' as Cruiser Rules had dictated the submarine's tactics so deeply.[56] That changed with the advent of unrestricted submarine warfare.

Some captains – for example Germany's top ace, von Arnauld – prided themselves on employing a submarine's deck gun to sink an enemy ship rather than use up an expensive and very finite weapon, the torpedo. It was somewhat surprising – and not that believable – to read Spiess's account of sinking a fishing vessel with a torpedo:

> I took revenge for our fright and fired in the fishing vessel with one of our bronze torpedoes. The ship literally broke in two.[57]

Spiess continued, saying that 'as a last resort [he] decided to make use of the gun'.

The size of these guns was impressive. Several examples (one from von Firck's *U.59*) of the 10.5cm SK/L45 can be seen in Denmark's Sea War Museum. This was the deck artillery used on *U.35* after she had been upgraded from her older 7.5cm gun. With the barrel lying horizontal, the sailors are hardly high enough to see each other over the gun's breech mechanism. From breech to muzzle, the gun measures almost 5 metres. In a 1917 propaganda film made aboard *U.35*, her deck gun is seen being fired in action and it is possible to appreciate the finely adjusted gearing and the speed with which the gun-layer can raise and lower the gun's heavy barrel.

**Mines**

Type-*UC* submarines were designed to lay mines, with specially developed chutes into which the mines were loaded and from which they could be dropped. Laying mines was an inherently dangerous business. If a commander wasn't careful, he could blow up his own boat:

> It was a complex operation having to take into account best tidal conditions which did not always allow the minelayer the best light conditions. With a two-metre diameter, a submarine would have to always allow at least three metres under the keel. To allow for 5 metres above the boat, this would mean a 'tideway depth' of at least 13 metres.

**Torpedoes**

Even if the torpedo was a precious weapon that was a high-cost way of killing ships, Jackie Fisher was an early staunch supporter of the potential of its killing power.[58] Indeed, in 1876 he wrote that 'the issue of the next naval war … will chiefly depend upon the use that is made of the torpedo, not only in naval warfare, but for the purposes of blockade'.[59] By 'torpedo', 'what is normally referred to is the automobile torpedo, which was gyro-stabilized and perfected by the Bolton engineer Robert Whitehead in the last quarter of the nineteenth century'.[60] With the invention in 1869 of the gyroscope by an Austrian naval officer, Ludwig Obry, the torpedo's range was significantly increased. According to Sondhaus, it was 'doubled'.[61]

With the advent of the submarine, the torpedo was given a more dangerous platform from which to be launched. However, the submarine's attack was always constrained by its slow underwater speed and its limited range of operations. It had little time to set up an attack position or reload. In the *U.35* film, one can see the tubes being loaded with an 'eel', four or five men straining to push the heavy weapon in. While four men push, a fifth 'helps' by booting a fellow sailor's backside!

Talking of his experience as a U-boat commander, Forstner wrote:

> He is so placed that his range of vision is extremely limited and, on account of the low speed of his boat while submerged, he can operate over only a very limited area of water.[62]

When it was within 4,000 yards, speed would be dramatically reduced, to around 2kts, to minimise tell-tale periscope waves. The submarine-launched torpedo was different to the one launched from the deck of a destroyer:

> It was seldom effective if fired at more than 2,000 yards, and beyond that distance its chances of hitting become very slight.[63]

In November 1917, Lothar von Arnauld de la Perière watched as a torpedo came straight towards his boat, only to be saved at the last moment: 'When a dozen yards away it rose from the water like a flying fish … This one had been set for too shallow a run.'[64] At the time, on deck were Oberleutnant Lauenberg and Prince Heinrich's son, Sigismund.[65] It's ironic that Germany's greatest ace was thus almost killed by a torpedo. At the end of her career, his *U.35* claimed 223 sinkings with a GRT of 535,700. It only sank thirty-nine by torpedo.

# Appendix B

# Methods of Destruction

| | 1914 | | 1915 | | 1916 | | 1917 | | 1918 | | 14-18 | |
|---|---|---|---|---|---|---|---|---|---|---|---|---|
| | Total | | Total | | Total | | Total | | Total | | Total | |
| Mine | 2 | 40.0% | 5 | 25.0% | 9 | 39.1% | 26 | 40.0% | 19 | 21.1% | 61 | 30.0% |
| Nets | 0 | 0.0% | 1 | 5.0% | 0 | 0.0% | 0 | 0.0% | 0 | 0.0% | 1 | 0.5% |
| Artillery | 0 | 0.0% | 5 | 25.0% | 5 | 21.7% | 6 | 9.2% | 6 | 6.7% | 22 | 10.8% |
| Depth charge | 0 | 0.0% | 0 | 0.0% | 3 | 13.0% | 5 | 7.7% | 18 | 20.0% | 26 | 12.8% |
| Explosive Sweep | 0 | 0.0% | 0 | 0.0% | 0 | 0.0% | 0 | 0.0% | 1 | 1.1% | 1 | 0.5% |
| Ramming | 2 | 40.0% | 2 | 10.0% | 0 | 0.0% | 11 | 16.9% | 6 | 6.7% | 21 | 10.3% |
| Torpedo | 0 | 0.0% | 4 | 20.0% | 3 | 13.0% | 7 | 10.8% | 6 | 6.7% | 20 | 9.9% |
| Stranded | 0 | 0.0% | 2 | 10.0% | 2 | 8.7% | 4 | 6.2% | 0 | 0.0% | 8 | 3.9% |
| Aircraft | 0 | 0.0% | 0 | 0.0% | 0 | 0.0% | 4 | 6.2% | 0 | 0.0% | 4 | 2.0% |
| Accident | 0 | 0.0% | 0 | 0.0% | 0 | 0.0% | 1 | 1.5% | 0 | 0.0% | 1 | 0.5% |
| Interned | 0 | 0.0% | 0 | 0.0% | 0 | 0.0% | 0 | 0.0% | 4 | 4.4% | 4 | 2.0% |
| Scuttled | 0 | 0.0% | 0 | 0.0% | 0 | 0.0% | 0 | 0.0% | 14 | 15.6% | 14 | 6.9% |
| Unknown | 1 | 20.0% | 1 | 5.0% | 1 | 4.3% | 1 | 1.5% | 16 | 17.8% | 20 | 9.9% |
| TOTAL MONTH | 5 | 100.0% | 20 | 100.0% | 23 | 100.0% | 65 | 100.0% | 90 | 100.0% | 203 | 100.0% |

Sources: There are usually some discrepencies on submarine peformance data, but the primary source used for all technical performance charts was U-boat.net. Additional information and comments were also gathered from some of the following:

Dunn, *Bayly's War*, Appendix 6
Grant, *U-Boats Destroyed*
Herwig, *Luxury Fleet*, Table 28
Lowery, *Fates List*, 2024
Michelsen, *Submarine Warfare*, pp.188–91
Gibson and Prendergast, *The German Submarine War*
Messimer, *Verschollen*
Schröder, *Die U-Boote des Kaisers*

The data on submarine losses should not be taken as completely reliable. Rather, its value and use should be seen as directional.

It is not always possible to link a submarine sinking with one cause alone. A successful sinking often involved different ASW weapons and tactics – ramming, depth charge and artillery were very often in unison. The attempt has been made, where possible, to establish primacy of one.

Where wrecks have been dived on, positive identification can be made and, very often, the exact causes of a sinking ascertained. Otherwise, information from other sources (POW interrogation, eyewitness accounts, official histories etc) can be accessed, but as Dr Innes McCartney's research has shown, 'official' records can be highly inaccurate and misleading.

## Situation of German submarines sunk, 1 June 1918

| | Total | | Not | | | | | | |
|---|---|---|---|---|---|---|---|---|---|
| Class. | Built | Identified | identified | Total | Not yet operating | Total in actual commission | School subs. | Total actively operating | Total remaining in commission |
| Cruiser | 19 | 1 | -- | 1 | 12 | 6 | -- | 6 | 18 |
| U | 121 | 56 | 4 | 60 | 5 | 61 | 11 | 45 | 61 |
| UB | 122 | 37 | 5 | 42 | 6 | 80 | 8 | 66 | 80 |
| UC | 79 | 51 | 2 | 53 | -- | 26 | 3 | 23 | 26 |
| Total | 341 | 145 | 11 | 156 | 23 | 163 | 22 | 140 | 185 |

Source. *Anti-submarine Tactics,* O.N.I. Publication No.4, 1918

# Appendix C

# The German Navy, 1900–1918

| | Battleships | Cruisers | Destroyers | U Boats | Total | BRT (000) | Crews |
|---|---|---|---|---|---|---|---|
| **1900** | 10 | 36 | 80 | - | 126 | 256 | 16,747 |
| **1905** | 17 | 32 | 99 | - | 148 | 379 | 23,984 |
| **1910** | 26 | 37 | 134 | 5 | 202 | 604 | 36,841 |
| **1915** | 41 | 26 | 141 | 34 | 242 | 1,067 | 56,203 |
| **1916** | 33 | 23 | 203 | 68 | 327 | 1,021 | 54,166 |
| **1917** | 27 | 21 | 258 | 124 | 430 | 1,024 | 54,362 |
| **1918** | 23 | 19 | 295 | 117 | 454 | 1,008 | 54,345 |

Source: Koerver, *Eyes*, p.xii (pamphlet)

# Appendix D

## Submarine Attacks, 1 Jan 1916–25 Jan 1917

| | Attacked | Escaped | Sunk by torpedo | Sunk by gun |
|---|---|---|---|---|
| Armed ships | 310 | 326 | 62 | 12 |
| Percentage | | 76.1% | 20.0% | 3.9% |
| Unarmed ships | 302 | 67 | 30 | 205 |
| Percentage | | 22.2% | 9.9% | 67.9% |

Source: Jellicoe, *The Submarine Peril*, p.15

# Appendix E

## Increases in Naval Munitions Production, 1917

| Area | Period 1 | Amount | Period 2 | Amount | % Change |
|---|---|---|---|---|---|
| Guns (all calibres) | Q3 1917 | 1,101 | Q4 1917 | 1,515 | 37.6% |
| Mines | July 1917 | 625 | Nov 1917 | 1,835 | 193.6% |
| Depth Charges | July 1917 | 542 | Nov 1917 | 2,078 | 283.4% |

Source: Jellicoe, *CONW*, p.246

# Appendix F

## Mercantile Shipping Production, 1917–1918 (GRT)

| | | | | | | | |
|---|---|---|---|---|---|---|---|
| **1917** | **January** | 46,929 | **July** | 81,188 | | | |
| | **February** | 78,436 | **August** | 100,900 | | | |
| | **March** | 115,654 | **September** | 60,685 | | | |
| | **April** | 67,536 | **October** | 145,844 | | | |
| | **May** | 68,038 | **November** | 158,826 | | | |
| | **June** | 108,897 | **December** | 112,486 | | | |
| | | | | | | | |
| | **1st Half** | 485,490 | **2nd Half** | 659,929.0 | Annual | 1,145,419 | 57.6% increase |
| | | | | | | | |
| | | | | | | | |
| **1918** | **January** | 58,568 | **July** | 141,948 | | | |
| | **February** | 100,038 | **August** | 124,675 | | | |
| | **March** | 161,674 | **September** | 144,772 | | | |
| | **April** | 111,533 | **October** | 136,000 | | | |
| | **May** | 197,274 | **November** | 105,093 | | | |
| | **June** | 184,159 | **December** | 118,276 | | | |
| | | | | | | | |
| | **1st Half** | 813,246 | **2nd Half** | 770,764 | Annual | 1,584,010 | 48.7% increase |
| | | | | | | | |
| | **Difference** | 327,756 | | 110,835 | | 438,591 | |
| | | | | | | | |
| | Change % | 40.3% | | 14.4% | | 27.7% | |

Source: Jellicoe, *CONW*, p.243

# Appendix G

## Naval Shipping Forecast and Delivery, Jul–Nov 1917

| Vessel Type | Delivered | Forecast | Difference | Change % | Shortfall % |
|---|---|---|---|---|---|
| Submarines | 9 | 20 | 11 | 45.0% | 55.0% |
| Minesweepers | 10 | 17 | 7 | 58.8% | 41.2% |
| Trawlers | 97 | 138 | 41 | 70.3% | 29.7% |
| Flotilla Leaders, TBDs | 26 | 31 | 5 | 83.9% | 16.1% |
| Patrol Boats (P-boats) | 16 | 19 | 3 | 84.2% | 15.8% |
| Sloops | 14 | 19 | 5 | 73.7% | 26.3% |

Source: Jellicoe, *CONW*, p23

# Appendix H

## Naval Shipping (Pre-Dreadnoughts and Armoured Cruisers) Sunk by Submarines

| Target | Date | Attacker | Range (metres) | Tgt Speed |
|---|---|---|---|---|
| *Aboukir* | 22.09.14 | *U.9* | 500 | 10kts |
| *Hogue* | 22.09.14 | *U.9* | 350 | slowing |
| *Cressy* | 22.09.14 | *U.9* | 350 | dead slow |
| *Pallada* | 11.10.14 | *U.26* | 500? | |
| *Messudieh* | 13.12.14 | *B.11* | 800 yds | at anchor |
| *Formidable* | 01.01.15 | *U.24* | 1,000 yds | 10kts |
| *Léon Gambetta* | 27.04.15 | *U.5* (AH) | 500 | 6–7kts |
| *Triumph* | 25.05.15 | *U.21* | 300 | dead slow |
| *Majestic* | 27.05.15 | *U.21* | 600–700 | at anchor |
| *Prinz Adalbert (i)* | 02.07.15 | *E.9* | 400 yds | 18kts |
| *Amalfi* | 07.07.15 | *UB.15* | | 17kts |
| *Prinz Adalbert (ii)* | 23.10.15 | *E.8* | 1,300 yds | 15kts |
| *Suffren* | 26.10.16 | *U.52* | 350 mts | 10–12kts |
| *Drake* | 02.10.17 | *U.79?* | | 19kts |
| *Britannia* | 09.11.18 | *UB.50* or *U-50?* | | 11kts |

Source: Steve McLaughlin

# Appendix I

# Naval Shipping (Smaller Ships) Sunk by Submarines

| Target | Date | Attacker | Range | Target Speed |
|---|---|---|---|---|
| *Pathfinder* | 05.09.14 | *U.21* | 1,200m? | |
| *Hela* | 13.09.14 | *E.9* | 9,600 yds? | |
| *S.116* | 06.10.14 | *E.9* | 500 yds? | |
| *Jean Bart* | 21.12.14 | *U.12* (AH) | 600–800m | 9 knots |
| *Udine (Undine)* | 07.11.15 | *E.19* | 1,100 yds? | |
| *Grosse Kurfürst* | Nov.16 | *J.1* | 2,500 yds? | |
| *Kronprinz* | Nov.16 | *J.1* | 4,000 yds? | |

Source: Steve McLaughlin

# Appendix J

## The Admiralty Prize Fund

| | |
|---|---|
| Number of U-boats listed | 186 |
| Prize Money paid | 93 |
| Prize Money rejected | 37 |
| Prize Money awarded after decision changed | 3 |
| U-Boat not considered 'destroyed' | 21 |
| No ASD record | 13 |

Source: McCartney, *Paying the Prize*, p.45

# Notes

**Citations:** At the time of editing (Nov–Dec, 2023), the British Library had closed all access to online Cabinet materials due to a cyberattack. Many of the CAB and ADM citations have, therefore, not been rechecked at the time of publication.

### Foreword

**1** Alfred Von Tirpitz, *My Memoirs* (Vol. I) (Dodd, Mead and Company, New York, 1919), p. v. **2** Tirpitz (Vol. II), p.134. **3** Tirpitz (Vol. II), p.170. **4** https://usnwc.edu/News-and-Events/News/Sea-control-foreign-policy-focus-of-Naval-War-College-conference. **5** While at the college, the younger Sims donated several items from his family collection to the archives at the NWC. **6** https://usnwc.edu/News-and-Events/News/Sea-control-foreign-policy-focus-of-Naval-War-College-conference.

### Introduction

**1** The American, Alfred Thayer Mayan (1840–1914) was arguably the most important influence on naval strategy in the nineteenth and early twentieth centuries. **2** Vice Admiral Philip Howard Colomb (1831–99) and his younger brother, Sir John Colomb (1838–1909), were both British naval strategists. In *Naval Intelligence and Protection of Commerce in War*, Captain John Colomb defended the idea of protecting the sea lanes or, as he called them, 'the imperial sea roads'. He was strongly against convoys, saying 'it is a human impossibility to put that commerce without paralyzing it into a position applicable to the conditions of Convoy.' Four years later, following a war scare with Russia, a Foreign Intelligence Committee pulled even further away by recommending that trade could be protected by blockading the Russian Fleet in harbour. In 1887, Philip Colomb wrote a far-sighted paper entitled 'Convoys: are they no longer possible', where he set out many of the considerations that would be revisited thirty years later: the regularisation of convoys under government appointed mastery, equipped with sailing instructions, sailing formation and the legal requirements to join and follow the convoy for the whole route. Convoys were, moreover, only seen as a solution for the slowest-moving ships. **3** Sir Julian Corbett (1854–1922) was a British naval strategist of the nineteenth and twentieth centuries whose most famous work, 'Some Principles of Maritime Strategy', is regarded as a classic of geostrategic thinking. He has been widely written about – James Goldrick and John Hattendorf, for example. See *Mahan is not Enough: The Proceedings of a Conference on the Works of Sir Julian Corbett and Admiral Sir Herbert Richmond* (1993) or Andrew Lambert's 'Writing the Battle: Jutland in Sir Julian Corbett's Naval Operations' in *The Mariner's Mirror* (103, #2, 2017, pp.175–95). **4** 'the foundation of…', May, p.95. **5** 'courtier', Gerard, 13 July 1915. Foreign Relations Papers, File No. 763.72119/83. **6** *ibid.* **7** Harley (p.64) quotes article 50 of the 1909 London Declaration, which the United States was keen on supporting: 'Before the vessel (as a neutral prize) is destroyed, all persons on board must be placed in safety, and all the ships' papers and documents which the parties interested consider relevant for the purpose of deciding on the validity of the capture must be taken on board the warship.' Even though the signatories included the USA, Germany, Austria-Hungary, France, Italy, the Netherlands, Spain, Russia, Japan and England, the latter never fully ratified the treaty. **8** Source: Downembs, Alexander B., *Targeting Civilians in War*. **9** The loss of those two warships…', correspondence, Enrico Cernuschi, 22 August 2023. **10** Admiral Gustav Bachmann (1860–1943) became Chief of Staff of the Admiralstab on 2 February 1915. **11** 'attacks intended for hostile ships…', Hoffman, p.284. **12** Sims would later launch a withering attack on the state of preparedness of the USN: 'only 10 percent of its ships (were) fully manned and only one-third were ready for service.' Of the seventy-four available destroyers, only fifty-four were 'actually modern and capable of anti-submarine activities' (Naumes, *Anglo-American ASW*, p.121). **13** 'the submarine had a greater impact…', Middleton, p.36. **14** Source: Jellicoe, *CONW*, p.38. **15** Schröder (p.325) quotes a lower amount: 841,118 tons, 458 merchant ships. **16** Source: Brézet, p.199. Of course, numbers differ: Jameson, *Formidable*, p.251, puts the number at 515 officers and 4,894 ratings having 'been killed in action'. Spindler, regarded as one of the key German writers on the submarine war, puts the total at '5,087 combatants' (Spindler, *The Value of the Submarine*).

### 1 War in an Industrial Age

**1** 'it's not invasion that…', Dunn, *Bayly*, p.27. **2** Peter Hore's figure is 48 per cent with a GRT of 11,540,000 (*Dreadnought*, p.53). **3** 'almost 60 per cent of the food…', Heal, p.262, citing Offer, *Working Classes*, pp.204–05. Redford (p.99) offers some further detail: 60 per cent 'of the calorific value of food consumed in Britain, about 40 per cent in crude weight and around 50 per cent in value was from overseas'. **4** Source: *Forgotten Wrecks, Black and Asian Seamen*, p.8. **5** 'based her strength and foreign policy…', Olmstead, p.53. **6** 'expected to win the war…', Stokesbury, p.303. **7** 'If only we had realized…', quoted in Chamberlin, *German Naval Strategy*. **8** Source: Ball and Hudson, p.3. **9** 'felt that it was clear…', Armstrong, B.F., *Twenty First Century Mahan: Sound Military Conclusions for the Modern Era* (Naval Institute Press, 2012). **10** 'wage economic war…', May, p.4. **11** 'was developing more and more into a passive…', Schoultz, p.205. **12** 'their plans traditionally…', Halpern, *Naval History*, p.22. **13** 'quite wrong in assuming…', Roskill, *Naval Hero*, p.212, Jellicoe to Beatty, 4 Feb 1917. **14** 'Commerce warfare was for centuries…', Peifer, *Commerce Warfare*, p.85. **15** 'Legally Britain had to decide…', Boyd, p.185. **16** Source: Koerver, *Assault*, p.36. **17** 'Protection of British trade…', Liddle, p.89. **18** 'the submarine is the coming type…', Temple Patterson, *Jellicoe*, p.54. **19** 'cannot capture the merchant ship…', wrongly quoted in Terraine, *Business*, p.5, as being June 1913. Fisher's memo was written in January 1914 (Temple Patterson, *JP1*, pp.31–36, MSS.48993). **20** 'It is suicidal to forego our advantageous position…', Harris, p.169. Harris only quotes the first part and suggests it was written by Jellicoe after the sinking of HMS *Hawke* by *U.9*. **21** 'it is difficult to avoid…', Temple Patterson, *Jellicoe*, p.55. **22** See ADM 137/995, pp.14–24. **23** 'estimated that attacks on British Commerce…', Breemer, *Defeating the U-Boat*, 36, p.10. **24** 'the destruction of the enemy's…', Dewar, Cdr KCB, 1912. **25** 'a waste of naval force…', Winton, *Convoy*, p.24. Quoted from *Brassey's Annual*, 1904. **26** 'History is the record…', Fisher to Selbourne, 20 Oct 1904, *Fisher Papers*.

### 2 Fisher's Apprentice

**1** Murray Fraser Sueter (later Sir Murray Fraser Sueter) joined the DNO in 1909 and, despite the early failed development of HMA No 1, the *Mayfly* (consequently caricatured as the '*Won't Fly*'), was promoted and ended up commanding the Royal Navy's Air Department in 1912. **2** 'there can be little…', Sueter, *Evolution*, p.174. **3** Conan Doyle wrote an imaginative piece for *The Strand Magazine* in 1914 talking of Britain's defeat by a sustained unrestricted commerce war waged by submarines. **4** 'Victory has never so…', Hannay, David, 'The Fire Ship', *Blackwood's Magazine*, vol. CXCV (1914), pp.781–91. **5** 'I need hardly say …', *The New York Times*, 19 February 1915. **6** Weir, p.148. **7** 'more as an adjunct…', Stokesbury, p.316. **8** 'panic the British into ceasing…', Theodore Ropp, *Development of a Modern Navy*, p.170. **9** 'The use of the phrase…', Redford, *Submarine*, p.71. **10** 'eventually a weapon…', Gray, *Un-English Weapon*, p.12. **11** 'be useful to us in many places…', Lambert, *Naval Revolution*, p.46. **12** The *Gymnote* was named after 'gymnotid', the family of fish that includes the electric eel. After the death of her original designer, Henri Dupuy de Lôme, the work continued under Gustave Zedé and Arthur Krebs. Krebs finally completed de Lôme's work. Krebs was, maybe, the most important: he was responsible for the designs of the periscope, the naval electric engine and the gyroscope. **13** In Trieste, Ludwig Obry successfully tested a gyroscope on a torpedo, 'removing one of the chief uncertainties in the performance of the submarine's irresistible weapon' (Padfield, *Battleship Era*, p.154). The Austrian engineer applied Foucault's 1851 invention to the torpedo and sold the patent to Robert Whitehead. **14** Source: Breemer, *Defeating*, p.6; Heal, p.264. **15** 'combine offense and defence…', Padfield, *Battleship Era*, p.111. **16** 'took after a pencil, sharpened at both ends', Lake, p.17. **17** Holland, Rear Admiral William J. Jr, USN (Ret.), '100 Years of Submarines', *Proceedings* Vol. 126/1/1,163 (January 2000). Even Tirpitz felt this way: (Greig, SAMHS) 'The early war successes of the U-boats surprised him.' **18** 'When a common sense…', Lambert, *Naval Revolution*, p.44. **19** 'well after every other major navy…', Gray, *U-Boat War*, p.24. **20** Captain Persius joined the navy in 1883 but never served on a U-boat. In 1908, his articles in the *Jahrbücher für die Deutsche Armee und Marine*, critical of Tirpitz's Fleet policy and specifically supporting the submarine cause, led to his dismissal from active service. In 1912, in *Submarines to the Front!*, he presented a dramatic story of submarines attacking the German Fleet. He had previously written under the pseudonym 'Rahtol'. **21** 'Ach! My dear Forstner…', Forstner, *Journal*. **22** '*Hatte Tirpitz recht…*', Valentiner, p.12. **23** 'far less dangerous animal', Gray, *U-Boat War*, p.32. **24** 'refused to throw money away…', Botting, p.17. **25** 'for experiments connected with submarines', Hough, *GWAS*, p.170. **26** Source: Michelsen, p.3. **27** 'U-boats were designed and their crews trained…', O'Hara, Dickson and Worth, p.106. **28** The idea of the submarine commerce war was suggested by Kapitanleutnant Rust in 1904, Karl Galster and Vice Admiral von Schleinitz in 1908 and Kapitanleutnant Blum in June 1914. Source: Dash, Michael Wynford, 'British Submarine Policy 1853–1918', thesis, King's College Dept of War Studies (1990). The original *U.1*, a converted *Karp* design, is now on display in Munich, in the Deutsches Museum. **29** Source: Schröder, p.32. **30** Karl Galster, *Is our Coastal Defense Enough?* (Wilhelmshaven, 1907). **31** 'The practice and manoeuvres of the U-boats…', Gray, *U-Boat War*, p.36. **32** 'severe violation…', Herwig, *Luxury*, p.218. **33** *U.5, U.7, U.8, U.9, U.13, U.14, U.15, U.16, U.17, U.18*. **34** 'The thought of cutting…', Hough, *GWAS*, p.173, quoting Hermann Bauer, *Führer der U-boote* (1956), pp.17–18. '*Der Gedanke, England durch U-boote von seiner Seeversorgung abzusperren, hatte dabei noch in keine Weise mitgesprochen, da ein solcher Krieg der U-boote gegen den englischen Seehandel mit der Londoner decklaration nicht vereinbar gewesen wäre. Erst als die englische regierung diese Vorschriften, soweit sie ihr hinderlich waren, durch ihre orders in Council planmäßig beseitigte und Deutschland durch seine Blockierung vom Weltmeer absperrte, da war auch fur Deutschland der Zwang zur gegenwehr und zur Vergeltung gegeben.*' Rough translation: 'The idea of using U-boats to cut off England from its sea supplies had not been taken into account in any way, since such a war by U-boats against English sea trade would not have been compatible with the London Declaration. Only when the English government systematically eliminated these regulations, insofar as they hindered it, through its Orders in Council and blocked Germany from the world ocean by Blockade, did Germany also feel compelled to defend itself and retaliate.' **35** 'Most senior naval officers viewed…', Hough, *First Sea Lord*, pp.167–68. **36** 'The submarine was Lord Fisher's…', Massie, *Dreadnought*, p.452. **37** 'didn't blame [him] for the submarine business', Fisher, *Memories*, p.31. **38** Admiral Prince Louis Battenberg (1854–1921) worked closely with Jellicoe when he became First Sea Lord in 1912. Facing rising anti-German feeling in the country, he was persuaded to resign by Churchill in October 1914. He contributed nothing further to the war effort and a resumed post-war engagement was turned down by Lloyd George. **39** 'Drop a battleship out of the programme…', Gough, *Titans*, p.79. **40** Bacon's 1929 two-volume biography of Fisher is disappointing: there is very little written about the crucial support that he gave the weapon's development programme. **41** He worked with five Holland boats (licensed to Vickers) and a new Type-A boat. **42** 'an ardent supporter', Bacon, *Fisher*, vol. 1, p.218. **43** 'brilliant, if somewhat difficult, officer', Halpern, *Naval History*, p.406. **44** 'Between 1901 and August 1914…', Preston, p.38. **45** 'If we build as quickly as we ought…', Fisher to Selbourne, 19 Dec 1900, Marder, *Fear God*, vol. I, p.174. **46** 'too small to operate…', Lambert, *Naval Revolution*, p.51. **47** Source: Lambert, *Naval Revolution*, p.54, Memo Lord Selbourne, 10 October 1902. **48** 'turned serious attention to…', Massie, *Dreadnought*, p.451. **49** 'The *Whitehead* torpedo can be…', Hough, *First Sea Lord*, p.168. **50** The prince's visit was a great success, although Fisher thought he had lost his cook; the prince took a fancy to her cooking and she was whisked away to the Palace to witness how a great state dinner was managed. **51** 'the King knew a great deal…', Hough, *First Sea Lord*, p.170. **52** 'I shall be very disappointed…', Massie, *Dreadnought*, p.455. **53** 'suspected battery explosion', Wren, p.25. **54** 'beloved submarines are going…', Heal, p.264. **55** 'It is astonishing to me, perfectly astounding…', Harris, p.151, quoting Fisher, 20 April 1904. **56** Christopher Cradock used the same expression when talking to his friend (Dunn, *Blockade*, p.19). **57** 'the submarine has the smallest value…', Dunn, *Bayly*, p.29. **58** 'unless the ordinarily accepted…', Hore, *Dreadnought*, p.97. **59** Despite an early promising career (commanding HMS *Dreadnought*, torpedo schools and founding *The Naval Review*), Richmond was pushed aside to work as a liaison officer with the Italian navy. It was only after Jutland, when he was picked by Beatty to command HMS *Conquerer* and then *Erin*, that his career recovered. **60** 'Satan disguised as an angel of Light…', Gough, *Titans*, p.78. **61** 'the reason is obvious…', Hore, *Dreadnought*, p.97. **62** 'While remarkable for anticipating…', Hore, *Dreadnought*, p.97. **63** 'they'll never be any use in war…', Preston, p.34. **64** 'recognized the potentialities…', Jameson, *The Fleet*, p.295. **65** 'The really serious danger…', Temple Patterson, *JP1*, p.35, 19 November 1910. **66** 'If he is right, and his argument appears…', Hough, *First Sea Lord*, p.169. **67** 'to have written Fisher out…', Captain Peter Hore, Churchill College online conference, 'A Veritable Volcano: The Life and Legacy of Admiral Lord Jacky Fisher', 4 November 2020. **68** 'a young sea-going captain of forceful character', Gough, *Titans*, p.81. **69** While Fisher was First Sea Lord, Keyes was blacklisted. Evidently, Fisher had mixed up Roger Keyes with another officer (spelt 'Keys') who worked as Beresford's secretary. **70** 'There never was such a mistake…', Jameson, *The Fleet*, p.299. **71** 'thought it fantastic…', McKillip, p.21. **72** 'not believe this (commerce raiding) would ever be done…', Ballantyne, p.103. Redford, p.57, quoting Churchill, *World Crisis*, vol. II, p.721. **73** 'No other class of vessel yet designed…', Gray, *U-Boat War*, p.35. **74** 'For the first time…', Uhlig, *Revolution*, p.139. **75** 'Each design has been carefully…', Lake, p.16. **76** 'could be taken to mean…', Redford, p.26. **77** Admiral Sir Richard Webb (1870–1950) was appointed Director of the Admiralty's Trade Division in 1914 and in this position liaised with the Merchant Navy on the operations of the blockade. His next position was as commander of the battlecruiser, HMS *New Zealand*. **78** 'Anything, therefore, which we…', Redford, p.96, quoting 'Some Principles of Maritime Strategy' (1911), p.99. **79** 'had enough submarines truly to menace the North Sea', Breemer, *Defeating the U-Boat*, 36, p.11. **80** 'The situation is a difficult one…', Wragg, p.224. There is no date attributed to the quote. **81** 'looking at me very sourly asked me why we had not…', Jameson, *The Fleet*, p.296. **82** 'we all discarded', Winton, *Convoy*, p.5. **83** From 1906 until war's declaration, Fisher had allocated 5 per cent of the naval budget for submarine development (source: Harris, p.154). The exact number of craft differ: Epkenhans, for example, quotes the initial number as sixty-eight; Harris, seventy-four. **84** 'did not have the numbers…', Black, *Naval Warfare*, p.65. Weir cites twenty-eight afloat and nineteen in construction. Prof Dr Frank Jacob (*Submarine Warfare and the First World War*) cites Germany twenty-seven, Britain seventy-six, France seventy, USA twenty-nine. **85** Source: Preston, p.36. **86** 'unless the whole engineering and shipbuilding…', Fisher, *Memories*, p.88. **87** 'a dozen more were actually…', Fisher, *Memories*, p.89. **88** 'we know from experience that it is…', Fisher, *Memories*, p.89. **89** 'the five best brains…', Winton, *Jellicoe*, p.101. **90** 'intelligent, extremely energetic…', Hone, *War on the Rocks*. **91** The 'Fishpond' was a group of officers selected by 'Jackie' Fisher to help spearhead innovation and naval reform. It included John Jellicoe, Reginald Bacon, Sir Percy Scott, Charles Madden, Herbert Richmond, Battenberg and Sir Charles Ottley. Bacon was selected for his knowledge of TBDs and submarines; Scott and Jellicoe because of their gunnery expertise; Madden was a torpedo expert; Bacon, Madden and Richmond had worked as Fisher's assistants. **92** 'splendid pushing', Gough, *Titans*, p.188. **93** 'become vulnerable once…', Lautenschlager, p.95. **94** 'either to employ divisional…', Lambert, *Naval Revolution*, p.216. **95** 'lack of speed, which prevented…', Rayner, p.3, quoting Jon Sumida, 'A Matter of Timing: The Royal Navy and the Tactics of Decisive Battle, 1912–1916', *The Journal of Military History*, vol. 67, n.1 (2003), pp.85–136 (132–33), p.92. **96** 'it will be necessary…', Winton, *Jellicoe*, p.108. **97** Admiral Sir Francis Bridgeman (1848–1929) served under Churchill as First Sea Lord from 1911 until his resignation in 1912. A specialist, like Jellicoe, in gunnery, as C-in-C Home Fleet in 1907 he hoisted his flag on HMS *Majestic* and *Dreadnought*. He said that Churchill fired him because of, again like Jellicoe, his technical diagreements: 'I was forced out without warning, but it was not because I was too weak, but because I was too strong' (Marder, *FTDTSF*, vol. I., p.259). **98** Today's technology uses explosive armour to protect tanks. **99** 'but not until late 1912…', Lambert, *Naval Revolution*, p.218. **100** 'with the centre engine-room…', Bacon, *Jellicoe*, p.163. **101** Held annually in Kiel the last week of June, *Kieler Woche* (Kiel Week) started as a ship and yacht racing regatta, gaining prominence when Kaiser Wilhelm II attended in 1889. **102** 'The almost fabulous success…', Hopman, Diary entry 23 September 1914. **103** 'It is now exaggerated as a result of the success of *U.9*', Sondhaus, Kindle Location 221. **104** 'we never dreamed that they would…', Forstner, *Journal*. **105** 'depend for their sustenance…', Forstner, *Journal*. **106** 'a very serious and ever-increasing…', Jellicoe, *Submarine Peril*, p.2. **107** 'For each U-boat lost…', Keegan, *Admiralty*, p.220. Simpson, p.113, uses a slightly different total: 5,408 ships totalling 11,189,000 tons.

**3 Operational Command**

**1** 'perilously close to impertinence', Winton, *Jellicoe*, p.143. **2** 'the most powerful fleet…', Temple Patterson, *Jellicoe*, p.59. **3** De Chair was succeeded by Rear Admiral Sir Reginald Tupper. **4** 1,059 were held in neutral ports, 245 in Allied ports and a further 221 ships blocked in Germany's own ports (Osborne, p.61). **5** German cables from Monrovia to Brazil and from the Azores to New York were cut later the following year (Boyd, p.103). **6** 'In all, 80 million messages…', South, *Room 40*. **7** 'The object of diplomacy…', Olmstead, p.39, quoting Grey, *Twenty-Five Years*. **8** 'any project of twisting the tail of the British…', Temple Patterson, *JP2*, p.134. **9** 'fancied himself in the role…', Otte, p.573. **10** 'found himself in a world…', Olmstead, p.69. **11** 'second personality', Olmstead, p.57. **12** He preyed on House's ego…', Olmstead, p.57. **13** 'spoke of England, Germany and…',Olmstead, p.50. **14** 'frequently informed Grey that he did not support…', Olmstead, p.81. **15** 'destined for the enemy…', Götter, p.62. **16** The rules had to be relaxed. In November, 'a deal was struck with a private organization, the Netherlands Overseas Trust, allowing them to trade in contraband, if there would be no trade with Germany. Similar agreements were signed for other countries like Switzerland' (Götter, p.68). **17** 'sold at full value…', Olmstead, pp.77–78. **18** The first submarine attack occurred during the American Civil War (17 February 1864). The eight-man-crewed, hand-cranked submarine *H.L. Hunley* (Gray, *Captains*, p.30) sank the Union corvette, USS *Housatonic*, using a spar torpedo off the coast of Charleston, South Carolina. **19** By 9 October, a draft existed outlining twenty-one articles to be reconsidered as 'Absolute' and a further fifteen added to the 'Conditional' category. **20** 'considered their use…', Jameson, *Formidable*, p.135. **21** 'every merchant ship met in this war zone…', Ballantyne, p.105. **22** 'for all practical purposes…', Götter, p.67. **23** 'at slow speed west in the day', Liddle, p.90. **24** 'One might in truth say…', Chatterton, *Blockade*, pp.13–14. **25** Source: Marder, *FTDTSF*, vol. II, p.373. **26** 'we see nothing but sea and sky', Liddle, p.92. **27** 'We used to find that if…', 'Voices of the First World War', IWM. **28** 'failure to hold so many of the…', Liddle, p.91. **29** 'The fate of the detained ship…', Chatterton, *Blockade*, p.26. **30** 'only three or four could be maintained…', Terraine, *Business*, p.9, quoting Hermann Bauer, who maintained that of only twenty-seven boats, just three or four were ready for operations (*fahrfertige U-boote*). **31** 'buoyant sentry boxes', Gibson and Prendergast, p.1. **32** '*In ersten KriegsJahr herrscht Unsicherheit…*', Pemsel, p.500. **33** 'they provided the means…', Winton, *Convoy*, p.9. **34** '*Damit war der erste Schritt getan, dem U-Boot seine Unsichtbarkeit zu nehmen*' (Krause, p.23). **35** Ranft, vol. I, p.115. **36** Considerable work was needed on the protection of the Moray Firth range at Cromarty, which was only effective in late 1915. **37** Winton (*Convoy*, p.2) states the number of dead as 171. Presumably the mismatch were the twenty German prisoners from the minelayer *Königen Louise*, which was witnessed 'throwing things overboard' (i.e. mines) off the East Anglian coast (Hawkins, p.13). The mines were laid in open waters, rather than in the approaches to British harbours, which made them a peril to neutral shipping. **38** '23 per cent of the 78 battleships…', Herwig, *Luxury*, p.207. See author's amalgamated figures for submarine destruction by mine in Appendix B ('Means of U-Boat Destruction'), which gives a total of 30 per cent for sixty-one sinkings. **39** 'responsible for a minimum of…', Grant, *U-Boats Destroyed*, p.17. **40** 'four merchant ships…', Jellicoe, *Submarine Peril*, p.61. **41** 'for fear of catching their own capital ships', Ballantyne, p.92. **42** 'systematically', Marder, *FTDTSF*, vol. II, p.368. **43** 'Our mines were designed for use against ships', Messimer, p.25. **44** 'caviar on toast', Hashagen, p.112. **45** 'virtually every instance the cable parted', Messimer, p.26. **46** The Germans developed the Type-*UC* as the principal submarine minelayers. Seventeen were destroyed in 1917. **47** 'the most effective use for these nets…', Marder, *FTDTSF*, vol. II, p.352. **48** 'nut for nut and bolt for bolt', Herwig, *Luxury*, p.206. **49** Source: Jellicoe, *Submarine Peril*, p.60. **50** Jellicoe to Sims, reply to Sims's letter (of 21 July 1919). **51** See Jellicoe, *CONW*, p.92. **52** 'changed the contempt of…', Gibson and Prendergast, p.207. **53** 'rose dramatically from two…', Boyd, p.207. See Appendix B ('Means of U-Boat Destruction') for an amalgamation of sources which show the same directionality but higher numbers. **54** 'They fully realized for the first time…', Barnes, *German Submarine Action*. **55** Grant lists her as probably sunk by mine or by accident off the Heligoland Bight ('Known Sunk'). **56** *Monarch*'s captain (Captain E. Hyde Smith) suggested that it was *U.13* that had fired the torpedo. This might not have been the case – it would have put *U.13*'s position 60 miles west of her defined patrol route. At this early point of the war, no mines had yet been laid off the German coast (source: Michael Lowrey). **57** 'the first torpedo ever…', Hawkins, p.17. **58** 'either on the surface or breaking…', Gray, *U-Boat War*, p.43. **59** The wreck of the *U.15* was found in one of Gert Normann Andersen's archaeological surveys. **60** 'she turned quickly and rammed…', Naval Staff Monograph, vol. X, CB 917H, Home

Waters, Pt. 1, p.43. **61** Two further submarine missions penetrated the Flow during the First World War. The first was that of the *U.18*, on her third sortie, on 23 November (at the time, two other boats, Claus Hansen's *U.16* and Bruno Hoppe's *U.22*, were also known to be operating close to the Orkney Islands). No ships were spotted. Her periscope was seen by the Examination steamer, *Tokio*, and, on the way out, minesweeper *D96* (the Aberdeen trawler, *Dorothy Grey*) rammed her, badly damaging the sub's scope and hydroplanes. *U.18* got away but was so badly damaged that she was scuttled; by the time two destroyers, HMS *Garry* and *Erne* arrived, she was sinking. Twenty-six crew were picked up. Her wreck still lies in around 70 metres just off Hoxa (a visual of the remaining archaeology can be seen on Simon Brown's *UB.116*). The second submarine, *UB.116*, wasn't so lucky. On 28 October 1918, she was caught and destroyed in a shore-based detonation of the minefield into which she'd gone. The Germans also had a version, called the Schiffmeldepost (SMP), which was used to defend the coast from the Frisian Islands to Heligoland) *UB.116* had only received orders to attack the Flow on 23 October, weeks before the Armistice. All of her thirty-six hands were killed, along with her captain, Hans-Joachim Emsmann. **62** '*untergegangen mit Mann...*', Valentiner, p.12. **63** 'Eight weeks earlier...', Lake, p.50. **64** 'All three incidents occurred...', Chalmers, pp.138–39. **65** 'protection against submarine attack...', Jellicoe, *GF*, p.89. **66** 'naval form of the shell game...', Goldrick, *Before Jutland*, p.153. **67** 'The fact that the great battleship...', Gray, *Un-English Weapon*, p.62. **68** Source: Everitt, p.13. **69** As Jellicoe described these movements, he mentioned two incidents that should have raised serious concern with the maintenance of the Fleet – first, that one of *Hibernia*'s 12in guns cracked, 'the fifth since the war broke out', and that *Iron Duke*'s condenser tubes needed re-tubing, 'although the ship was quite new' (Jellicoe, *Grand Fleet*, pp.96, 104). **70** 'it was not until...', Temple Patterson, *Jellicoe*, p.65. **71** 'it is, I regret to say...', Temple Patterson, *JP1*, pp.89–90. **72** 'the inner line of anti-submarine...', Temple Patterson, *JP1*, pp.128–29. Churchill to Jellicoe, 26 January 1915. **73** 'There is no doubt that strategically...', Jellicoe, quoted in Lavery, p.231. **74** 'the two possible places...', Lavery, p.231. **75** Ballantyne, pp.85–86. 'The torpedo had hit below the waterline, under HMS *Pathfinder*'s bridge, and detonated ammunition in the forward magazine.' Winton (p.2) qualifies: it was 'the first time in naval history that a warship had been struck by a self-propelled torpedo fired from a genuine submarine in the open sea'. The first battleship sunk by a submarine was the *Messoudieh*, sunk on 13 December 1914 by Lieutenant Norman Holbrook's *B.11* off Chanak (source: Jameson, *Formidable*, p.141). **76** 'a ray of light', Ballantyne, p.87. **77** 'the report that the *Pathfinder* was sunk...', Scrimegeour, p.54, 12 September 1914. **78** Better known as SONAR in American naval circles before being picked up, according to Marder, by the British in 1943. **79** 'returned empty handed', Fürbringer, p.5. **80** 'As long as he could keep...', Chalmers, p.139. **81** 'three of which were considered...', Lavery, p.211. **82** A lookout on HMS *Falmouth*, anchored west of Holm Sound, signalled that a periscope had been spotted 50 yards away. Both she and HMS *Vanguard* opened fire. Half an hour later, HMS *Drake* repeated the warning, unleashing renewed fire. Lough Swilly is located in County Donegal on the Northern Irish coastline, a little west of Londonderry. **83** The 2nd Battle Squadron was sent to Loch na Keal on 17 October by Jellicoe, while the main battle fleet was sent to Lough Swilly. See Temple Patterson, *JP1*, p.45. **84** 'we have no place to lay our heads...', Lavery, p.210. **85** 'Here was a pretty kettle of fish', Gray, *U-Boat War*, p.63. **86** Vice Admiral Paul Behnke of the HSF 3rd BS was quoted by Marder (*FTDTSF*, vol. II, p. 66) as saying that there wasn't as large a threat as Jellicoe imagined, as German naval planners 'gave the English credit of supposing they had protected their bases the same as we had'. **87** Source: Footnotes, Temple Patterson, *JP1*, p.104. **88** 'steaming in formation...', Barnes, *German Submarine Action*. **89** 'The discipline of the watch...', Neureuther and Bergen, p.111. **90** 'Her bow was high...', Thomas, *Raiders*, p.21. **91** 'The periscope revealed a fearful picture...', Botting, p.21. **92** 'Her men stayed at their guns...', Gray, *Captains*, p.36. **93** 'the minimizing effect...', Thomas, *Raiders*, p.27. **94** 'two-thirds more than the number...', Preston, p.41. **95** 'It would be idle to deny...', Parrish, p.61. **96** '*der "Weddigen-Moment" der k.u.k...*', Kern, p.13. **97** German subs also zigzagged to avoid an equally dangerous surface contact with an Allied submarine (see Neureuther and Berger, p.71). **98** 'They continually altered course...', Gibson and Prendergast, p.12. **99** 'Before it became clear...', Goldrick, Anderson Medal Lecture, 2017 Awards, National Maritime Museum. **100** 'I gazed at the little picture...', *Ballymena and the Great War*. **101** 'It is pure murder...', Scrimgeour, pp.81–82. **102** 'dismissal from the...', Scrimgeour, pp.81–82. **103** 'I was on the bridge...', 'Local Lives Lost', *Belfast Telegraph*, 14 October 2014. **104** 'Those on deck for an instant...', 'Local Lives Lost', *Belfast Telegraph*, 14 September 2014. **105** 'Manoeuvred for a shot...', *Ballymena and the Great War*. **106** 'We were struck right amidships...', Western Front

Association, quoting Sparrow, *The Sinking of HMS Hawke*, p.14. HMS *Hawke*'s wreck was discovered by divers of the 'Lost in Waters Deep' group in July and August 2024, 70 miles east of Fraserburgh, in 'remarkable' condition. One of the divers, Steve Mortimer, said that 'She clearly was taken completely by surprise because lots of the portholes are still open.' Ben Philip, *BBC Scotland News*. **107** 'an attempt to man the…', 'Local Lives Lost', *The Belfast Telegraph*, 14 October 2014. **108** 'A second more and we would have…', Gray, *U-Boat War*, p.62. **109** Source: *Portsmouth Evening News*, Tuesday, 27 July 1915. **110** Source: Götter, p.67. **111** 'I *long* for a submarine defence…', Jellicoe to Churchill, 30 September 1914, quoted in Marder, *FTDTSF*, vol. II, p.67. **112** 'was only Divine Providence that…', quoted in Marder, *FTDTSF*, vol. II, p.69. **113** 'the German mind could…', Temple Patterson. **114** Source: *Manchester Courier and Lancashire General Advertiser*, 22 October 1914. **115** Source: Schröder, p.92. **116** 'he might get a court martial…', Gray, *U-Boat War*, p.65. **117** 'breathed easier…', Spiess, p.49. **118** 'not yet justified…', Jameson, *Formidable*, p.135. **119** 'has the greater experience', Temple Patterson, *JP1*, p.157. **120** 'looks as if he had lost…', Jellicoe to Beatty, 26 April 1915. **121** 'a model demonstration of compliance…', Hoffman, p.283. **122** There were also, in fact, some wounded soldiers aboard. **123** Source: *The Times*, 28 October 1914 ('struck a floating mine'). **124** The presence of any military personnel could jeopardise an entire ship. On 26 October 1916, the cross-Channel steamer, *The Queen*, was stopped by German destroyers. She carried troops across to Boulogne but would normally return empty at night to Folkstone. On this occasion, a British Army Staff officer, 'a not undistinguished one', G.R. Roupell VC, was aboard. Knowing the predicament in which his presence could put the ship, Roupell disguised himself and 'obediently jettisoned overboard his cap, Sam Browne and service jacket and donned over his riding breeches, puttees and army boots, a khaki shirt, a blue mackintosh and a sailor's cap'. **125** 'One woman, carrying a small…', Lorraine Sencicle, *The Dover Historian*, 2 October 2016. **126** Captain Carey later commanded *Maid of Orleans*, which brought back survivors from Dunkirk in 1940; reportedly, 'blood was running down her sides'. **127** 'an average savings of two…', Michelsen, p.54. **128** 'such aggressive ideas…', Scheer, p.224. **129** 'Why not? England wants to starve us', Granier, pp.50–51, *Interview des Staatssekretärs des Reichsmarineamtes mit dem amerikanischen Journalisten von Wiegand*, Berlin, 21 December 1914. Tirpitz had been requested by the Centrist Member of Parliament, Matthias Erzberger, to grant the interview. The interview appeared in *The Times* on 24 December. **130** 'extremely unfortunate…', Koever, *Assault*, p.38. **131** 'Is it wrong to make…', Granier, p.53, *Kriegstagebuch des Staatssekretärs des Reichmarineamtes*, Charleville, 22 December 1914. **132** 'the chancellor allowed…', Olmstead, p.104. **133** 'blunderingly failed', May, p.117. **134** 'Publicly, the enemies…', Koever, *Assault*, p.39. **135** 'it was courting disaster', Jellicoe, *GF*, p.107. **136** 'express[ed] his astonishment…', Gayer, *Submarine Operations*. **137** 'will endeavour to make full use…', Temple Patterson, *Jellicoe*, p.70. **138** 'It is suicidal to forego…', Temple Patterson, *JP1*, pp.71–72. Jellicoe to Churchill, 30 September 1914, MSS. 49012. **139** 'holding an unswervingly straight…', Gray, *U-Boat War*, p.72. **140** See Neureuther and Bergen, p.68. **141** Jameson, *Formidable*, p.145, states a different toll, saying that 547 of her 780-strong crew did not survive. **142** 'approximately half the merchant…', Jellicoe, *CONW*, p.1. **143** 'The kaiser acted as the sole conduit…', Olmstead, p.96. **144** 'to be his own Commander-in-chief…', Olmstead, p.101. **145** 'eventually turned him…', Jellicoe, *Jutland*, p.5. **146** See Karau, pp.41–42. Tirpitz had already announced that 'he intended to create a new submarine flotilla in Flanders as soon as four boats each of the UB and UC-classes were in service' (25 February 1915). **147** 'the man most associated with…', Sondhaus, Kindle Location 762. **148** 'continuously on patrol', Jameson, *Formidable*, p.146. **149** 'our own Prize courts…', Koever, *Assault*, p.38. Admiral Staff memo to von Ingenohl, 26 January 1915. **150** In the first phase of the U-boat war (starting in February 1915), Falkenhayn sided with Bethmann-Hollweg, who, along with the kaiser, blocked Tirpitz. Falkenhayn changed sides in the second phase (January–May 1916), saying that unrestricted submarine warfare was critical to success at Verdun. The kaiser 'shelved the debate' (Vecchio, p.13) by not declaring his position. By January 1917, Falkenhayn's attrition strategy had failed and the British blockade was working. Bethmann-Hollweg caved in to Ludendorff's support for the final aggressive campaign, as did the kaiser. **151** 'the first half-hearted attempts…', Hough, *GWAS*, p.301. **152** 'Early U-boat successes…', Weir, *Building*, p.142. **153** 'brought a new threat to the primacy…', Weir, *Building*, p.142. **154** 'partly because he agreed to…', Kelly, p.401. **155** 'Believe me gentlemen…', Kelly, p.403. **156** 'questioned the value of…', Weir, *Building*, p.170. **157** 'The opinions of the state secretary…', Weir, *Building*, p.144. **158** Boyd's estimate is 'only 16 officers and 9 clerks in 1914', if one excludes SSB (Boyd, p.95). **159** 'several thousand', Boyd, p.101. See p.119 for decrypt volume growth. **160** 'We could be perfectly certain…', Grant, *Hunters*, p.12. See also Waldeyer-Hartz, pp.236–38. **161** 'In many ways, the newly formed…', Bird and Hines, p.116. **162** Oliver held the position of DID from December 1913–October 1914. He was preceded by Captain Thomas Jackson (January 1912–December 1913) and succeeded by Sir William Reginald 'Blinker' Hall (October 1914–January 1919). Initially, Jackson was assisted by an Assistant Director, fourteen naval and marine officers and a further thirteen civilians. Jackson was described as 'a boorish, self-opinionated man' (Beesely, p.9; see also Marder, *FTDTSF*, pp.41–42). Jackson's choice was controversial. He was 'an officer steeped in the traditions of the Royal Navy and deeply suspicious of new-fangled developments' (Downing, p.118). William Clarke, a newly hired codebreaker, a 34-year-old barrister in 1915, commented that Jackson had only ever visited OB40 a couple of times, one of which was to complain about cutting his finger on one of the red decrypt boxes. Hope's successor, James, saw Clarke's writings later and commented that Clarke 'seemed to dislike a lot of people' (Gannon, p.147). **163** Vice Admiral Sir Henry Oliver (1865–1965). Before becoming Director of the Admiralty's Intelligence Division (ID), Oliver commanded HMS *Thunderer* and the armoured cruiser, *Achilles*. **164** 'extreme taciturnity', Beesley, p.8. **165** Ewing was succeeded by William James when Hall became DNI and James acted as DDNI. **166** 'to take charge of a department to unravel…', South, *Room 40*. **167** 'the chance of success…', Ewing, p.174. **168** 'in the first few days I visited Lloyd's…', bibliography, pp.10–11. **169** The German equivalent was known as E-Dienst (Entzifferungsdienst), based on Neumünster, with day-to-day operations divided between the stations at Tondern, Brügge and Libau. The main naval station was at Nauen, near Berlin. Transmitting on 800 meters, 'it could be received in the Mediterranean and the Adriatic' (Terraine, *Business*, p.32). **170** One Osborne recruit was the headmaster, Charles Godfrey, whose brother headed NI in the Second World War. **171** 'the most significant', Boyd, p.105. **172** 'In a conflict from which the Admiralty…', Grant, *Hunters*, p.28, quoting Roskill, Hankey, *Man of Secrets*, 1.159. **173** 'flash like a Navy signal lamp', South, *Room 40*. **174** 'lay not only in organizing the admirable…', Hoy, p.9. **175** 'shrewd penetrating glance…', Hoy, p.52. **176** 'got rid of him, rather abruptly…', Clarke, *OB40*, Ch.3, p.2. **177** 'the Russians found the body…', Ewing, p.179. **178** The SB contained 34,300 instructions grouped into separate three-letter codes. **179** 'the current key, a copy of the German…', Grant, *Hunters*, p.34. **180** There was a considerable and unnecessary delay when the materials on board *Theseus* had to wait until 'six trunks of clothes belonging to the wife of the First Sea Lord, Prince Louis of Battenberg', were taken on board. **181** 'superenciphered: once encoded…', Downing, p.108. **182** 'died in the years…', Clarke, *OB40*, Ch.4, p.3. **183** The HVB was first issued in 1913 to warships and then to eighteen German steamship companies. As the codes were also issued to submarines that would be out of contact before receiving new codes, the repetition of the old codes made possible 'immediate, valuable and a comparative pair of sources' (South, *Room 40*). **184** 'bizarrely it remained unchanged till 1916', *Room 40*. **185** 'the miraculous draught of fishes'; source: Beesly, p.7. **186** 'tuned into German naval signals…', Downing, p.105. **187** Beesly, pp.13–14. **188** 'more limited', Boyd, p.109. **189** 'the immense value of the work', Ewing, p.208. **190** 'the point at which…', Bywater and Ferraby, p.200. **191** 'the top interrogator of U-boat prisoners', Heal, p.361. **192** 'The busiest month of all was June 1917…', Bywater and Ferraby, p.203. **193** 'wireless intercepts and direction-finding…', Bruton and Coleman, p.254. **194** 'Macro-level data interpretation proved useful…', Sondhaus, Kindle Location 1806. **195** 'it remained oblivious…', Goldrick, *After Jutland*, p.43. **196** 'wireless instructions to merchant vessels…', Ballantyne, p.179. **197** 'SIGINT would be managed…', Boyd, p.112. **198** 'would [have been] compelled…', Oliver to Balfour, 8 November 1916, Boyd, p.116. **199** 'acute fear of compromising…', Boyd, p.121. **200** 'its most important source', Boyd, p.146. **201** 'described by Hall…', Boyd, p.178. **202** '[he] personally observed…', Temple Patterson, *JP1*, p.135. **203** 'the navy was waging its own…', Koever, *Assault*, p.44. **204** 'He is fed up with his lies…', Koever, *Assault*, p.55. **205** 'convinced that Great Britain will end the blockade…', Gray, *U-Boat War*, p.84. **206** 'mere threat of submarine warfare…', Olmstead, p.105. **207** 'as a reply to the British starvation blockade', Schoultz, p.207. **208** *Imperial German Gazette* (*Deutsche Reichsanzeiger*), 4 February 1915. **209** 'The first consideration is the safety…', Scheer, p.227. **210** 'For urgent political reasons…', Scheer, p.230. **211** 'so long as no hostile act was committed…', Gray, *U-Boat War*, p.82. **212** 'Of course, many neutrals…', Forstner, *Journal*. **213** 'The Germans were understandably…', Jameson, *Formidable*, p.149. **214** 'neutral flags, preferably American…', Gray, *U-Boat War*, p.97. **215** 'he had been greatly alarmed…', Preston, p.66. **216** 'favourable for any discussion…', Otte, p.578. **217** 'an indefensible violation…', Olmstead, p.114. **218** 'The real difference between blockade…', Olmstead, p.116, quoting John Coogan, *The End of Neutrality*. **219** 'sent a subtle message…', Olmstead, p.116. **220** 'a gift from heaven…', Koever, *Assault*, p.44. **221** Source: Hoffman, p.284. **222** 'the brightly painted buoys…', Gray, *U-Boat War*, p.91. **223** The Dover Patrol hunting group consisted of HMS *Cossack, Falcon, Fawn, Gurkha, Kangaroo, Leven, Maori, Mohawk, Nubian, Syre, Ure* and *Viking*. Two destroyers – *Gurkha* and *Maori* – were actively involved in *U.8*'s destruction, both shelling her conning tower. **224** 'The flagrant illegality of the German…', Fayle, vol. II, p.6. **225** In contrast to Weddigen's respect for Prize Rules, another commander, Kapitänleutnant Freiherr von Forstner on *U.28*, fundamentally changed the image of the submarine war. After sinking the merchantman *Aguila* on 27 March, he fired on crew and passengers. The next day he sank a 5,000-ton liner, *Falaba*. Among the 104 lost was an American. The accusation, whether propagandist or not, that the baron and his crew jeered at the survivors, burnt a deep scar into the American public conscience. **226** 'She passed aft, slowly becoming…', Liddle, p.96. **227** 'much oil and bubbles on the surface', Gray, *U-Boat War*, p.96. **228** 'No U-boat in the First…', Koerver, *Assault*, p.51. **229** 'It must be very disconcerting…', Larson, p.384, reference note no. 146. **230** 'complained strongly', Temple Patterson, *Jellicoe*, pp.83–84. **231** 'defensive patrols in the Heligoland Bight', Gray, *U-Boat War*, p.97. **232** 'the *average* number of submarines…', Jameson, *Formidable*, p.162. **233** 'the kaiser entrusted the Belgian…', Frost, *Zeebrügge*. **234** 'twenty-three per cent of…', Frost, *Zeebrügge*. **235** 'ultimately bear the brunt of Germany's aspirations', Fürbringer, p.68. **236** 'the Jesuits had built the place…', Thomas, *Raiders*, p.226. **237** 'This unit of the German navy…', *Paying the Prize*, p.50. **238** 'ideal vessels for the shoals and narrows…', Gray, *U-Boat War*, p.101. **239** 'little or no denunciation…', Heal, p.350. **240** 'the submarines seem to have…', Temple Patterson, *JP1*, p.157. **241** In 1905, Germany built a powerful radio station at Norddeich with two Telefunken transmitters. In 1907, the station started transmitting to naval ships. With the declaration of war, the Navy took over operations. **242** Source: Schröder, p.128; among other things, *Lusitania* was carrying materials from arms supplier Bethlehem Steel, including 4.2 million Remington cartridges in 4,926 boxes. **243** 'The reference to *Lusitania*…', Larson, pp.149–50. **244** 'repeated the boat's position…', Larson, p.88. **245** *Lusitania*'s previous Captain, Daniel Dow, asked to be relieved the previous March. **246** 'wanted to arrive at Liverpool bar…', Gray, *U-Boat War*, p.16. **247** 'He had the lifeboats swung out…' Dunn, *Bayly*, p.43. **248** *U.20*'s conning tower, periscope and 8.8cm deck gun can today be seen at the Danish Sea War Museum. After she had run aground at Vrist, just south of Thyborøn, these artifacts were taken off. The deck gun was the earliest example on any German submarine. **249** 'four funnels and masts…', Thomas, *Raiders*, p.95. **250** 'exactly into the U.20's path', Botting, p.28. **251** 'suddenly stopped dead in her dive…', Botting, p.31. **252** 'The suction of the liner…', 'Voices of the First World War', IWM. **253** As with almost all sinkings, reported losses vary. Brady (pp.22–23) notes 1,201 for the *Lusitania*, forty for *Arabic* and thirty-two for *Hesperian*. **254** *Lusitania* was carrying 'more than 1,000 cases of 3-inch shells, nearly 5,000 boxes of small arms ammunition and ten tons of explosive powder' (Ballantyne, p.107). Terraine (*Business*, p.10) clarifies the type of explosive: '18 boxes of percussion fuses containing fulminate of mercury, a highly explosive substance.' **255** The decks of the *Lusitania* had been strengthened to take the weight of naval guns and her owners received an annual payment from the Government to make the ship available if needed. *U.20* carried copies of *Jane's Fighting Ships* and *The Naval Annual*, both of which described *Lusitania* as an 'armed merchant cruiser'. **256** The purpose of the zigzag manoeuvre was to make it difficult calculating the best position a submarine should aim when firing its torpedo. That required a very careful set-up, with calculations of the target's speed and course. Specific variations were designed before and put into the convoy briefing document to avoid setting up patterns that a submarine commander could deduce: Zigzag A might mean, for example, 'turn 35 degrees starboard'. **257** If this, indeed, was the case, others, like Grey, were strongly against the idea of bringing the United States into the conflict too early: 'it would be folly … endeavouring to persuade the United States to take part in the war. Should they do so it must be entirely … as a result of their own spontaneous action' (Otte, p.580). To this effect, Grey was strongly against the over-zealous use of anti-German propaganda, as it could take the control of events out of the politicians' hands. **258** House had been in London on 7 May with Grey and had said that if a passenger liner with Americans were to be sunk, 'a flame of indignation would sweep across America, which would, in itself, probably carry us into the war' (Koerver, *Assault*, p.64). Even the King, apparently, had speculated on *Lusitania* being sunk. **259** 'through acts of omission…', Preston, p.401. **260** 'As our main interest…', Preston, p.401. **261** 'if the United States wanted…', Olmstead, p.124. **262** 'largest individual triumph…', Olmstead, p.126. **263** 'unusual Teutonic subtlety', Gray, *U-Boat War*, p.83. **264** 'It is in the military interest…', Koever, *Assault*, p.45. Bachmann to Pohl, 12 February 1915. **265** 'In the interest of the state…', Koever, *Assault*, p.66. At the time, of course, there was no proof of the ship carrying ammunition and this could have been established by a 'stop and search'. **266** 'let the crew disembark…', Koever, *Assault*, p.63. **267** Jellicoe had been invited to the annual reunion of the China comrades during the now-famous 1914 Kielerwoche (Von Trotha, 13 July 1914, *JP1*, p.37). **268** 'hostile merchant ships are to be destroyed', Jameson, *Formidable*, p.156. **269** 'had sown the seed…', Jameson, *Formidable*, p.164. **270** 'instruction to merchant ships…', Hillman and Huck, p.716. **271** 'would be deeply regrettable…', Franken, *Bachmann*, p.717. **272** Franken, *Bachmann*, p.715. **273** 'would be particularly unpleasant…', Franken, *Bachmann*, p.715. **274** 'He doesn't even demand…', Franken, *Bachmann*, p.718. **275** 'the release of enemy passenger steamers…', Franken, *Bachmann*, p.720. **276** 'was not allowed to be…', Koever, *Assault*, p.69. **277** 'Since such a restriction…', Franken, *Bachmann*, p.720. **278** 'The Kaiser regrets that the issue…', Franken, *Bachmann*, p.722. **279** 'Through such an order, Germany loses…', Franken, *Bachmann*, p.723. **280** 'KptzS [Kapitän zur See] von Levetzow advised me…', Fürbringer, p.9, quoting from Hipper's diaries from *Die schweren Kreuzer der Admiral Hipper-Klasse* (Koop & Schmolke Bernard & Gräfe Verlag, Bonn, 1992). **281** 'was as good as to renounce it', Hashagen, p.59. **282** Hashagen prided himself on his treatment of survivors. In *U Boats Westward!*, he talked about taking survivors from the *Harald* aboard the *UB.21*, his first command. After a warming pea soup, the Swedish crew was transferred to a Norwegian steamship. After *UB.21*, he commanded the *U.22*. In November 1916, he took his final command, *U.62*. Crewed by forty, she was a 1,000-ton submarine with 2,000hp diesel engines that could give her a 16-knot speed on the surface. **283** 'having been elected…', Temple Patterson, *JP2*, p.134, quoting Beatty MSS. **284** 'I am greatly disturbed…', Temple Patterson, *JP1*, pp.161–62. Beatty to Jellicoe, 25 May 1916. **285** 'moderately useful', Marder, *FTDTSF*, vol. II, p.357. **286** 'It was extremely rare for patrols…', Marder, *FTDTSF*, vol. II, p.358, quoting Lt Cdr D.W. Waters. **287** 'fundamentally unsound', Marder, *FTDTSF*, vol. II, p.367. **288** Source: Marder, *FTDTSF*, vol. V, p.102. **289** 'never looked at it in the military…', Marder, *FTDTSF*, vol. V, p.101. **290** Source: Marder, *FTDTSF*, vol. V, p.105. **291** 'anti-convoy lobby…', Owen, p.42. **292** 'our system of hunting him…', Temple Patterson, *JP1*, p.164. **293** Roskill (*Naval Hero*, p.129) attributed the recommendation of Bayly and the establishment of hunting forces to Beatty, not Jellicoe. **294** In 1914, Fisher referred to Bayly in a letter as 'the busy Bayly', whom he contrasted with 'the dismal Burney' (see Temple Patterson, TJP, vol. 1, p.117). **295** 'not very successful…', Temple Patterson, *Jellicoe*, p.84. **296** Figures for the death toll vary. Liddle (p.99) puts it at thirty-nine lives lost out of 429 passengers and crew (this is also the figure used by Alan Wren, p.41). Koerver (p.74) quotes forty-four. **297** 'I know that you do not wish…', *The New York Times* Current History. **298** 'she was recognized…', *The New York Times* Current History. **299** 'many life boats', Koerver, *Assault*, p.74. **300** 'the people of this country count…', Koerver, *Assault*, p.75. **301** 'Until that fateful afternoon…', Gray, *U-Boat War*, p.100. **302** 'Remember the limitations…', Koerver, *Assault*, p.75. **303** 'almost impracticable…', Winton, *Convoy*, p.8. **304** 'possibly in anticipation…', Jellicoe, *CONW*, p.39. **305** 'fighting mood', Koerver, *Assault*, p.77, quoting two diary extracts, 4 and 13 September. **306** Hansen was famous for torpedoing four ships in a single convoy. See Pearl story (Thomas, *Raiders*). Valentiner and Hansen shared a house in Kiel and even jointly owned an old Ford (Valentiner, p.11). At the start of the war, when Valentiner took command of *U.3*, Hansen took *U.16*. **307** 'full of wounded vanity', Koerver, *Assault*, p.77. **308** Robert Lansing (1864–1928), an American diplomat and lawyer who became Wilson's Secretary of State from 1915–20. **309** 'at last felt able to court the wrath of the US South…', Padfield, *Maritime Dominion*, p.149. **310** 'internecine conflict', Hough, *GWAS*, p.176. **311** 'liners will not be sunk by our submarines…', *The New York Times* Current History. **312** 'big dim shadow', Koerver, *Assault*, p.78. **313** 'much more likely the boat…', *The New York Times* Current History, p.9. **314** 'So, I am very sorry…', Korever, *Assault*, p.90. **315** 'the respite in diplomatic tensions…', Sondhaus, Kindle Location 1216. **316** 'Much to my surprise…', Koerver, *Assault*, p.80. **317** 'petering out from lack of numbers', Jameson, *Formidable*, p.173. **318** 'west of Britain and in the English Channel', O'Hara, Dickson and Worth, p.121. **319** 'mining operations were seen…', O'Hara, Dickson and Worth, p.108. **320** 'partially equipped with mines…', Michelsen, p.63. **321** 'there were few passenger steamers…', Michelsen, p.63. **322** '*Keins der vier Boote hat auf der Reise auch nur den geringsten Erfolg gehabt*', Valentiner, p.79. **323** 'sink 50,000 tons…', Wren, p.46. **324** '*Ich hätte damals, 1915, nicht ins Mittelmeer fahren sollen, ich war damals, 1915, der gefürchtetste*

*U-Boot-Kommandant der Nordsee*', Valentiner, p.269. **325** 'the humanitarian skipper…', Gray, *U-Boat War*, p.131. **326** 'smashed to matchwood', Hurd, *Clan Line*, p.25. **327** 'For two and a half hours…', *The Daily Express*, 28 December 1915. **328** 'very kindly dressed', *The New Ross Standard*, 31 December 1915. **329** Italy was at war with Austria-Hungary but not yet with Germany. In November, Valentiner sunk several Italian merchant ships, including *Ionia* (4 November), *Elisa Francesca* and *Ticino* (6 November), *Ancona* (8 November) and *Firenze* (9 November). **330** 'Cruiser with course…', Wren, p.96. **331** 'Your Royal Highness, my boat…', Wren, p.34 (*Königliche Hoheit … U.3 ist ein altes Pferd. Einem alten Gaul kann man noch so viel Zucker geben. Königliche Hoheit. Ein alter Gaul macht keinen Galopp mehr!*). **332** 'I was just about to push the button…', Fürbringer, p.32. **333** 'like many other smallish *UB* boats…', Grant, *Hunters*, p.67. **334** 'less than a hundred feet…', Hurd, *Clan Line*, p.27. **335** 'a bundle of nerves…', *The Dundee Courier*, 15 January 1916. **336** 'each man's rations…', *Montrose, Arbroath* and *Brechin Review*, 21 January 1916. **337** 'I am afraid the submarines will bag…', Muir and Davies, pp.279–80. **338** The Cayzer company would continue the tradition of service in the Second World War. One of its ships, HMS *Bonaventure*, would be called on to serve as a depot ship for midget submarines north of Ullapool. Jimmy Benson, the co-author of *Above us the Waves* (with C.E.T. Warren), served there as they trained for the successful September 1943 attack on KMS *Tirpitz*. The Clan Line lost more ships (thirty) in the Second World War than in the Great War, with 70 per cent of their crews going down with them. The company recovered slowly after the war, and by 1950 owned ninety-nine ships, 'the largest fleet under the British flag' (SAMHS, newsletter, May 1997). **339** Based on the testimony of the ship's master and reported in *The Englishman's Overland Mail*, 24 September 1914. **340** Sir Charles himself was honorary Colonel of the Lowland Brigade RFA. **341** 'in co-operation with…', Chalmers, p.204. **342** 'As long as submarine warfare…', Michelsen, p.88. **343** 'the most effective method…', NA, CAB 23/1, 11 January 1917 meeting minutes, p.3. **344** A fathom is equal to 6ft. *C.27* had unsuccessfully tried the same tactics two weeks earlier against *U.19*, which escaped. **345** The wreck of *U.40* was discovered in March 2009, 40 miles from the Berwickshire coast, far from the site of its reported sinking. **346** 'that they had been the victims of a dirty trick', Gray, *U-Boat War*, p.103, quoting William Guy Carr, *By Guess and By God* (Hutchinson, 1930), p.152. **347** 'frightfully bad sea boats…', Arthur, p.84, quoting Sub-Lt Bill Fell, *P.11*, Dover Patrol. **348** Also sunk on 1 July by *U.39* were the ships *Craigard*, *Gadsby*, *Inglemoor* and *Richmond*. **349** '70 yachts, 691 armed trawlers…', Fayle, vol. II, p.104 Footnotes. **350** In mid-August, the Germans attempted a daring escape of one of their captured commanders whose submarine had been sunk the previous November near Scapa Flow. The sinking of *U.18* protected the secret that Scapa Flow's defences were minimal. Max Valentiner's *U.38* was sent to lie off the North Wales coast to pick up Heinrich von Hennig. For three nights, *U.38* waited. To no avail. Unbeknownst, Henning had been invisible to his rescuers, waiting in an adjacent bay. On 13 August, Valentiner rendezvoused with Bernd Wegener's *U.27* in preparation. Henning, a fellow April 1902 crew intake, was languishing with Herman Tholens and Korvettenkapitän Hans von Heldorf (2iC on the SMS *Mainz*, sunk on 28 August 1914 in the Battle of the Heligoland Bight). Valentiner turned up and waited off Orme for the prearranged signal; it never came. Rather, the would-be escapees were recaptured. Returning to Germany on 23 August, Valentiner made up for the failed rescue attempt by finishing his patrol with '22 steamers, 3 sailing vessels and 5 fishing boats' to his credit (Gray, *U Boat War*, p.110). **351** Herbert used the *nom de guerre* William McBride (Michelsen, p.62). He was an early submarine commander, being 2iC of HMS *A.4*. With his captain, Eric Nasmith, he and the crew survived her sinking in 90ft during her sea trials in October 1904. He constantly bothered the First Sea Lord with ideas for improving the performance of early Q-ships. Eventually, he was tasked with carrying out his ideas on the SS *Baralong*, pendant Y9.5. Bayly asked Herbert to join his staff. Jellicoe's substitute, Commander Kettlewell, did not last and Bayly eventually succeeded in getting Herbert on board. **352** 'one retaliatory shot…', Wren, p.39. **353** 'While riflemen aboard the *Baralong*…', Botting, p.41. **354** 'Some succeeded, despite…', Wren, p.39. **355** 'six of the enemy had been…', Wren, p.39, quoting Compton-Hall, Richard, *Submarines and the War at Sea 1914–1918* (Macmillan, 1991), p.204. **356** 'If any of those bastard…'; the source is mistakenly assigned by Military-History-Fandom as Messimer. The story got out, both from British and American crew members, and was presented in a 'Memorandum of the German government in regard to Incidents alleged to have attended the destruction of a German submarine and its crew by his Majesty's Auxiliary Cruiser "Baralong" on August 19, 1915, and Reply of his Majesty's Government thereto' (presented to Parliament in January 1916). **357** 'This *Lusitania* business…', source unknown. **358** 'outstanding cadet', Lake, p.72. **359** 'This shameful deed remains a blot…', Michelsen, p.63. **360** Liddle (p.100): it was 'not unlikely that revenge was a strongly motivating factor'. After arriving too late at the scene of the *Lusitania* sinking, the memory haunted many. According to Lieutenant Gordon Steele, the sight 'rouse[d] the deepest hatred in the *Baralong*'s crew', who had agreed 'to show no mercy to any U-boat man who fell into their hands' (Wren, p.29). Herbert's biographer (Chatterton, E. Keeble, *Amazing Adventure – A Thrilling Naval Biography*) wrote that the crew was 'wild with desire to destroy an unchivalrous enemy'. According to one account (Coles, Alan, *Slaughter at Sea? The Truth behind a Naval War Crime*, 1986, p.50), Herbert was summoned to the Admiralty by Herbert Richmond and told in no uncertain terms: 'The *Lusitania* is a shocking business, and our unofficial answer is – take no prisoners from U-boats.' **361** 'both captains, Wegener and Hansen…', Hashagen, p.77. **362** The hauling down of the Stars and Stripes before fire was opened was disputed. **363** Iwan Compton later wrote about the incident, *U-41*, in *Der zweite Baralong-Fall*. **364** The man is often cited as Collins. Corporal Fred Collins was the man who shot Wegener in the head while in the water. **365** After Campbell lost *Farnborough* (Q-5), he next commanded *Pargust*, previously named *Snail* and the ss *Vittoria*. **366** 'uniquely schizoid quality of service', Botting, p.48. **367** 'was also fitted with bell pushes…', Arthur, p.75. **368** 'a brilliantly conceived price of camouflage', Hashagen, p.74. **369** 'completely (ignored) the fact that…', Gray, *U-boat War*, p.82. **370** 'The magnificent fight…', *Beverley and East Riding Recorder*, 12 February 1916. **371** 'Believe me, you can never hear…', *Maritime History* (online), 'Nick Messinger's Old P&O'. **372** 'losing ships to enemy action…', Sinclair, p.50. **373** 'had resisted building new ships…', Sinclair, p.59. **374** 'a vastly inflated price of £750,000…', Sinclair, p.59. **375** 'I imagine financially it would be a good deal…', Muir and Davies, p.290. **376** 'an average of one Clan Line ship…', Muir and Davies, p.293. **377** 'seemed to be fighting different enemies', Gray, *U-Boat War*, p.59, quoting Admiral Sir Dudley de Chair. **378** 'Grey considered it part of a body of international law', Sondhaus, Kindle Location 442. **379** 'letter after letter on the blockade…', Marder, *FTDTSF*, vol. II, p.375. **380** 'frequently displayed…', Lambert, *Armageddon*, p.478. **381** 'sixteen leading Danish…', Lambert, *Armageddon*, p.478. **382** 'I am strongly of (the)…', Lambert, *Armageddon*, p.479, quoting Jellicoe, 1 September 1915, ADM 137/1915. **383** 'united protests of four senior…', Chatterton, *Blockade*, p.274. **384** 'held the economic life of…', Gade, p.333. **385** 'Sweden became Germany's…', Gade, p.334. **386** 'the first to suspect something…', Lambert, *Armageddon*, p.273. **387** Source: ESRC 12th Report, 1 October 1914, ADM 137/2988. **388** The Scandinavians unanimously decided to cease publishing trade statistics at the Malmö meeting. This should have shown 'which way the wind was blowing' (Jade, p.334). **389** 'has become a base…', Koerver, *Assault*, p.83. **390** Source: Lambert, *Armageddon*, p.276. **391** 'potential of public backlash', Olmstead, p.65. **392** 'phenomenally optimistic', Jameson, *Formidable*, p.186. **393** 'a ruthless U-boat war…', Korever, *Assault*, p.92 (10 January 1916). **394** 'the torpedoing of large passenger liners…', Korever, *Assault*, p.93. **395** 'consequently they are unwilling…', *Assault*, p.95, quoting Link, *Wilson*, p.92. **396** 'impertinent', Korever, *Assault*, p.94 (31 January 1916). **397** 'enemy merchantmen carrying guns…', Marder, *FTDTSF*, vol. II, p.347. **398** 'The more merciful the U-boat…', Liddell Hart, *History of the World War*, p.284. **399** 'Submarine commerce war…', Koerver, *Assault*, p.107. **400** 'These were the first…', Koerver, *Assault*, p.106. **401** 'given up his previous scruples', Scheer, p.105. **402** 'will not reach…', Koerver, *Assault*, p.109. **403** 'England can only be injured by war on her trade', Gray, *U-Boat War*, p.137. **404** 'Even a state of war with America…', Jameson, *Formidable*, p.186. **405** 'Enemy merchant ships, encountered…', Marder, *FTDTSF*, vol. II, p.347. **406** 'had never publicized…', Breemer, *Defeating the U-Boat*, p.36. **407** 'three times the tonnage…', Padfield, *Maritime Dominion*, p.150. **408** 'A rumour has it that for financial…', *JP1*, p.230. Balfour to Jellicoe, 13 March 1916, ADM MSS.48992. **409** 'procrastination in the conduct of the war', Gray, *U-Boat War*, p.138. **410** 'Our relations with Germany…', Koerver, *Assault*, p.111. **411** 'best known not for the ships…', Levine, *UB.29* (May 2018). **412** According to Koerver, four Americans. **413** 'unaware of the furore he had caused…', Gray, *U-Boat War*, p.145. **414** 'are to be attacked by torpedo', Koerver, *Assault*, p.106. **415** 'must stand forth, as the sinking…', Terraine, *Business*, p.11. **416** 'until further orders, submarines…', Marder, *FTDTSF*, vol. II, p.348. **417** *UB.29*'s 27-year-old commander, Oberleutnant Herbert Pustkucken, maintained that he had seen people wearing uniforms on her decks. **418** 'left to me until further notice…', Scheer, p.130. **419** Michelsen, p.59. Michelsen states 'April 24'. I think he meant 24 March, the date on which *Sussex* was sunk. **420** 'operations in the Mediterranean…', Michelsen, p.65. **421** 'the only officer now…', Taussig, p.45. **422** 'the most successful Q-ship captain', Sondhaus, Kindle Location 1874. **423** 'launched over the stern…', MacFarlane, p.58. **424** 'a mine so designed that, when dropped overboard…', Sims, *Victory*, p.85. **425** Jellicoe (*CONW*, p.61) provided information on the expected damage to a submarine from a charge given varied distances: 'It is necessary to explode within 14 feet of a submarine to ensure destruction; at distances of up to 28 feet from the hull the depth charge might be expected to disable a submarine to the extent of forcing her to surface, when she could be sunk by gun-fire or rammed, and at distance of up to 60 feet the moral effect on the crew would be considerable and might force the submarine to surface.' **426** 'a can on a stick', Messimer, p.158. **427** 'we could not rely much…', Jellicoe, *CONW*, p.33. **428** *U.54*'s W/T operator, Haidt, described the ferocity of the depth charging: 'Two depth charge explosions underneath us forced – nay, flung – us to the surface' (p.169). And later, 'four times we tried to come up, but the enemy forced us below again. At our fourth appearance, the air pressure shot our commander like a ball through the conning tower hatch' (see Neureuther and Berger, p.170). *UB.64* had fired a torpedo at *Justicia*, which was returning for repairs, when *U.54* was able to finish the job (see Neureuther and Berger, p.171). **429** Michelsen (p.84): the Y-gun was introduced in July 1917, and by 1 December 1917, 238 were in service. **430** 'They could be set to explode…', Arthur, p.90, quoting OC Stan Smith, HMS *Montbretia*. **431** 'five more shells from…', Botting, p.51. **432** 'crawling with them', Trapp, p.60. **433** Jerko Sizgoric, Frantiske Ras, Anton Grabar and Mato Brnicevic. Two had served on the flagship, the *Sankt Georg*. **434** '*Die Bucht von Cattaro…*', Valentiner, p.126. **435** In total, *U.34* would sink 119 ships (257,652 GRT) over eleven patrols. One of her later commanders would be Wilhelm Canaris, the future head of Hitler's Kriegsmarine. Her fate is unknown; she went missing in mid-October 1918 (according to Marder, sunk by the Q-ship, *Privet*). **436** '*Etwa hundertfünfzig Schiffe…*', Valentiner, p.268. **437** Source: *The Irish Independent*, 11 November 1915. **438** 'her crew, both British and Indian…', Hurd, p.23. **439** 'After nineteen hours we were fished… [Nous avons était repêchés…]', Europeana.com, *Le torpeillage en 1916 du bateau La Provence II vu par un cuisinier du bord*. **440** Of the four torpedoes he fired, only one missed. All his sinkings were done with a deck gun. **441** Mistakenly noted by Thomas, *Raiders*, p.151, as HMS *Primolo*. **442** 'Four torpedoes for that tiny wasp', Gray, *U Boat War*, p.209. **443** 'I shall never cease admiring…', Thomas, *Raiders*, p.151. **444** Spain was constantly lobbied by the belligerents. The British put enough pressure on Spain in February 1917 that German consular wireless traffic from the Canaries was restricted and in early 1918, plans were made to cut the cables themselves. **445** 'My record cruise was quite tame…', Botting, p.36. **446** 'one of France's greatest naval disasters', Gray, *Captains*, p.88. **447** 'After what I had seen…', Gray, *Captains*, p.89. **448** 'record that has remained unbroken…', Gray, *Captains*, p.82. **449** 'The fact that I nearly always…', Thomas, *Raiders*, p.147. **450** 'Many officers sank more tonnage…', Gray, *Captains*, p.86. **451** 'expressing [his] gratitude for the…', Gray, *Captains*, p.89. **452** 'like a rocket', Thomas, *Raiders*, p.153. **453** 'The picture of that foundering…', Gray, *U Boat War*, p.211. **454** 'ready-cut pit props', Koerver, *Assault*, p.135. **455** 'It is to be communicated…', Koerver, *Assault*, p.162. **456** 'If we did not succeed…', Marder, *FTDTSF*, vol. IV, p.49. **457** 'Tirpitz était convaincu…', Brézet, p.153. **458** 'now planned to use the U-boats…', Padfield, *Maritime Dominion*, p.150. **459** 'numerous and repeated [submarine and]…', Padfield, *Maritime Dominion*, p.131, quoting Kennedy, *German Naval Operations Plans*, p.69. **460** 'deplored their entirely defensive…', Padfield, *Maritime Dominion*, p.131. **461** 'incomprehensible', Jameson, *Formidable*, p.190. **462** Magnus von Levetzow (1871–1939) commanded SMS *Moltke* in the first two years of the war, took part in both the battles of Dogger Bank and Jutland, and, after an Operations Planning role in Operation *Albion*, became Chief of Staff of Scheer's new Seekriegsleitung in 1918. **463** 'none took part in the battle', Sondhaus, Location 2126. Nine boats (*U.24, U.32, U.43, U.44, UC.47, U.51, U.63, U.66* and *U.70*) were sent out between 17 and 22 May. Additionally, *U.72* was sent out on 23 May, *UB.27* on 20 May, *U.47* (replacing *U.46*) and *U.75* on 24 May. *UB.21* and *UB.22* were sent to the Humber, while three submarines – *U.22, U.46* and *U.67* – were sent north of Terschilling. **464** Originally, *U.19* was assigned the task, but she developed engine problems before the *Aud* departed and the crews were switched to *U.20*. **465** Source: Uboat.net. **466** 'in a failure', Spindler, *Value*. **467** 'something was afoot for days…', Padfield, *Battleship Era*, p.220. **468** *U.32* was nearly 'run down' by HMS *Galatea* and fired two torpedoes at her sister ship, *Phaeton*, although Spiegel wasn't spotted; *U.66* spotted Vice Admiral Martyn Jerram's 2nd Battle Squadron to the north, but neither Bottmer's nor Spiegel's reports made any significant impact on Scheer's planning. (Gordon, p.66) **469** 'the High Seas Fleet would fight…', Gordon p.465. **470** 'I should assume that the intention…', Temple Patterson, *JP1*, p.76 (30 October 1914). **471** 'primitive wireless sets', Gray, *Un-English Weapon*, p.199. **472** 'Britain's best submarine commanders…', Gray, *Un-English Weapon*, p.199. **473** 'playing the German game…', Jellicoe, *Submarine Peril*, p.24. **474** 'Had there been a decisive victory for us…', Breemer, *Defeating the U-Boats*, pp.36, 37, quoting Major A.C.B. Alexander, *Jutland. A Plea for a General Naval Staff* (London, Hugh Rees, 1923). **475** 'The peril became acute…', Rawson, p.197. **476** 'not even that command which is gained…', Brodie, p.116. **477** *U.75* would be sunk by a mine in the North Sea a year later, in December 1917. **478** 'Mine warship route…', Laws, p.134. **479** 'minesweeping on either side…', Laws, pp.176–77. Laws states that 'This was, in fact, untrue', and that 'these particular waters, to the west of Orkney, had not been swept for mines' (p.177). Laws also states that it was also 'simply not true' that the wind was blowing from the north-east 'by late afternoon'. By 5.00 pm, 'exactly when Kitchener was leaving Scapa Flow, they were blowing from the north-north-west' (p.178). Jellicoe (*GF*, pp.420–22) states that the *Hampshire* sailed at 5.30 pm. He assumed, however, that it would be a ship laying mines, not a submarine. **480** 'Jellicoe sent one of the most…', Laws, p.266. **481** 'The first few days after…', Winton, *Jellicoe*, p.221. **482** Fryatt's report of the encounter with a German submarine (catalogue reference FO 383/195). **483** Michelsen (p.62): 'Although the arming of merchantmen for defensive purposes might have been a generally recognized measure [which it was not], we could not condone such offensive operations against our warships.' Considering that the SS *Brussels* had tried to ram *U.33*, Michelsen is way off base. **484** Inscribed on the watch: 'Presented to Captain C.A. Fryatt by the chairman and Directors of the G.E. Railway Company as a mark of their appreciation of his courage and skillful seamanship on March 2nd, 1915.' **485** Quoted in *Great Eastern Railway Magazine* (2003), pp.189–90. **486** When she unloaded in Baltimore, 3,042 500lb cases of dyes were off-loaded (Messimer, *Deutschland*, p.62). **487** 'an incident which compels…', Messimer, *Deutschland*, p.58. **488** 'how desperate the state…', Messimer, *Deutschland*, p.58. **489** 'There is no evidence…', Duncan, *Deutschland*. **490** '327 tons of nickel…', Koerver, *Assault*, p.155. **491** 'a million dollars', Bottting, p.37. Messimer, *Deutschland*, p.63, noted that there was also 'half a ton of jute'. **492** 'the entire German army…', Schultz, p.57. **493** *U-Bremen* had left Germany on 15 August. **494** 'on the pride of us German-Americans…', Schultz, p.61. **495** 'a huge crowd with boisterous…', Schultz, p.65. **496** 'twenty pounds of fine vegetable fat…', Schultz, p.65. **497** 'That is precisely what we…', Koerver, *Assault*, p.173. **498** *Dundee Courier*, 9 October 1916. The Reuters story line was picked up by multiple newspapers, for example *The Western Times* (same date), *The Aberdeen Press and Journal* (same date) and the *Newcastle Journal* (same date). **499** 'spoke English…', *Western Times*, 10 October 1916. **500** See *NDGSA*, p.19. (Navy Department, Office of Naval Records and Library. German Submarine Activities on the Atlantic Coast of the United States and Canada (NDSA), Government Printing Office, 1920). **501** Source: Ballantyne, p.158, quoting Justus D. Doenecke, *Nothing Less than War*. **502** 'without, however, in any way…', *Nottingham Evening Post*, 10 November 1916. **503** 'helpless, like spectators at a dog fight', Ballantyne, p.158, quoting A.A. Hoeling, *The Great War at Sea*, p.169. **504** Evidently, this was quite normal: an ERA on *U.19*, Karl Wiedemann, reported that his commander, Kolbe, 'told me to paint out the large white figures on the side of the hull, so that the enemy might not discover the boat's number' (Neureuther and Bergen, p.61). **505** Source: *NDSA*, p.23. **506** 'Cape Verde islands…', Ponce, *Commerce Warfare*, p.339, quoting Newbolt, *Operations*, Vol. IV, pp.177–78. **507** 'The only result of our trip…', Robinson, *Rose*, p.136. **508** The episode is wonderfully charming. Rose obtained a written pledge from the cargo ship captain that he would cease operations: 'I the undersigned Al Villemartin boatswain pledge to Monsieur the German commander of *U.53* to abstain during the present war to navigate myself and my comrades in recognition of the good will to generously give us our liberty' (see Robinson, *Rose*, p.142). **509** 'I felt strongly that we should be released…', Robinson, *Rose*, p.135. **510** 'With the hatches battened down…', Gray, *Captains*, p.53. **511** 'There is a certain discomfort…', Forstner, *Journal*. **512** 'I got used to it…', Thomas, *Raiders*, p.89. **513** 'too small to permit…', Spiess, p.3. **514** 'the interior stank…', Gray, *Un-English Weapon*, p.16. **515** 'Submarine men were likely…', Gray, *U Boat War*, p.180. **516** 'Resolution, strength…', Spiegel, p.27. **517** '*Wir tauchen auf…*', Valentiner, p.113. **518** '*Zwei Boote rüdern…*', Valentiner, pp.113–14. **519** Valentiner, p.114. **520** 'the view from the bridge…', Botting, p.17. **521** 'Crystal walls tower up before us…', Neureuther and Bergen, p.97. **522** 'guns, periscope, and wireless masts festooned…', Thomas, *Raiders*, p.257. **523** Source: Thomas, *Raiders*, p.268. **524** '1.50 marks for each…', Schultz, p.2. **525** 'must hunt below in every…', Watson, p.428. **526** 'interminable diet of canned stuff…', Thomas, *Raiders*, p.263. **527** 'You can't imagine…', Thomas, *Raiders*, p.178. **528** '*Auf allen Dampfern…*', Valentiner, p.108. **529** 'a most brutal officer and very much disliked…', Grant, *Hunters*, p.83. **530** 'The typical 1914 submariner…', Hough, *GWAS*, p.178. **531** '*Schatz, seit wann…*',

Valentiner, p.13. **532** 'it was practically holy writ', Fürbringer, p.101. **533** 'much of the submarine's…', Marder, *FTDTSF*, vol. II, p.354. **534** 'thirty-nine large vessels had…', Marder, *FTDTSF*, vol. II, p.354. **535** Source: Michelsen, p.97. Brézet (p.175) puts the total number of ships armed in May 1917 at 3,253. **536** 'Our submarine offensive…', Spiess, p.91. **537** 'No cases are known where…', Michelsen, p.97. **538** 'The Woodfield engagement...', Valentiner, p.107. **539** 'armed ships forfeited their immunity from attack', Marder, *FTDTSF*, vol. II, p.343. **540** 'because of the likely effect…', Jameseon, p.192. **541** See Scheer, p.246. **542** Goldrick (*After Jutland*, p.55): Scheer's military use of the submarine was as much 'from recognition that achieving consensus on unrestricted submarine warfare would take time, given the objections of the chancellor and significant elements in the political leadership and civil service'. **543** 'one cannot say that the underlying principle…', Spindler, *Value*. **544** 'Experience taught us that…', Robinson, *Rose*, p.130. **545** Bauer, p.407. **546** Four Zeppelins would move ahead of the HSF; the other four would patrol the northern end of the North Sea. **547** Spindler: four across from the mouth of Humber; six at the latitude of Sunderland. **548** Bauer (p.408) noted that HMS *Nottingham* was sunk at 7.24 am (Berlin time) by *U.52*'s third torpedo. **549** 'several torpedoes….', Jellicoe, *GF*, p.436. **550** 'This was the second U-boat attack…', Bauer, p.408. **551** 'The *Falmouth* was stopped…', 'Voices of the First World War', IWM. **552** 'Their captains were both inexperienced…', Ballantyne, p.153. **553** 'Scheer's trap had almost…', Gray, *U Boat War*, p.159. **554** 'This was the most perfect case…', Gayer, *Summary*. **555** 'believed he could no longer…', Goldrick, *After Jutland*, p.80. **556** 'It is typical of the vagaries…', Goldrick, *After Jutland*, p.79. **557** The K-class submarine used a diesel generator for charging batteries while running on the surface. **558** 'In fact, there was no answer…', Gray, *Un-English Weapon*, p.181. **559** 'Of the twenty torpedoes fired … eight were hits', Spindler, *Value*. **560** 'German deliberations…', Gompert, *Germany's Decision*, pp.63–64. **561** 'Restricted U-boat warfare…', Koerver, *Assault*, p.122. **562** 'war with America…', Koerver, *Assault*, p.108. **563** Karl Theodor Helfferich (1872–1924), Secretary of the Treasury 1916–17. As such, he found the necessary means to finance the kaiser's war. See CB 01381, *German Views on Unrestricted Submarine Warfare*, November 1917. He was considered 'the greatest expert in Germany on international finance and commerce' (p.3). **564** 'an act of desperation', Terraine, *Business*, p.12. **565** 'mad dog against whom…', Conference Notes, Pless, 31 August 1916. **566** 'prophetic', Jameson, *Formidable*, p.186. **567** 'Jutland result froze in place the…', Ballantyne, p.151. **568** 'a good staff officer but not a man…', Hough, *GWAS*, p.302. In May 1939, von Trotha visited England. This quote was noted by F.C. Sillas after a conversation with the German admiral. It was also included, Hough noted, in a letter to Marder dated 4 October 1966. **569** Wolfgang Kapp (1858–1922), an American-born German nationalist politician, the organiser of the failed 1920 putsch in Berlin, after which he fled to Sweden. **570** 'I do not hesitate to assert…', Greig, SAMHS. **571** See Jellicoe, *CONW*, p.154. **572** 'The tow ropes and chains…', Thomas, *Raiders*, p.107. **573** 'Realizing the propaganda value…', Gray, *U Boat War*, p.167. **574** Boyd (p.210) demonstrates the extrapolation: 428,000 tons achieved with 20 per cent would have yielded a total estimate of 2.8 million tons. **575** Only two 800-ton boats, sixteen 400-ton boats and nine submarine cruisers were ordered (Gayer, *Summary*). **576** 'common sense still speaks…', Koerver, *Assault*, p.199. **577** 'if the army accepted, the politicians would follow', Hough, *GWAS*, p.302. **578** 'incidents which may lead…', Gray, *U Boat War*, p.164. **579** 'paint the opponent to the world…', Koerver, *Assault*, p.207, quoting Pytha, *Hindenburg*, p.238. **580** 'if the enemy were now to reject…', Koerver, *Assault*, pp.207–08. **581** 'daily decoding the…', Koerver, *Assault*, p.210. **582** In the Second World War, de Grey was instrumental in uncovering references to the extermination role of German Police battalions in 1941. **583** 'stupidity', Gölitz, Walter, *The Kaiser and His Court: the Diaries, Notebooks and Letters of Admiral George Alexander von Müller, Chief of the Naval Cabinet 1914–1918* (New York, 1959), pp.141–42, quoted in Olmstead. **584** 'that orders for U-boat…', Koerver, *Assault*, p.203. **585** 'much of the press…', Gompert, *Germany's Decision*, p.64. **586** 'the attitude of the United States…', Watson, pp.423–24. **587** 'only ruthless U-boat warfare…', Koerver, *Assault*, p.205. **588** 'Viewing the German discussions…', Olmstead, p.196. **589** 'with statistics down…', Gompert, *Germany's Decision*, p.65. **590** Holtzendorff used the following assumptions: (a) the destruction of 600,000 tons per month for four months and 500,000 thereafter given the decreased amount of target traffic; (b) that neutral shipping could be reduced by around 40 per cent (1.2 million tons) by demonstrating the harshness of unrestricted submarine warfare so scaring off masters and crews; and (c) that 1.4 million tons of interned shipping could be rendered inoperable by their crews. British merchant shipping tonnage had been severely depleted – starting the war with around 21 million tons, 8.5 million had been requisitioned for military purposes, 1 million was under repair, 2 million being used by allies, leaving around 8 million tons on paper. **591** 'I arrive, therefore, at the conclusion…', Newbolt, vol. IV, pp.345–46. **592** '*Cette opposition de droite…*', Brézet, p.152.

**4 Tools and Tactics of the New Submarine War**

**1** '49 destroyers and 48 torpedo boats…', Gibson and Prendergast, p.149. **2** 'virtually unscathed', Heal, p.270. **3** 'only one submarine was sunk…', Leighton, p.124. **4** 'No naval brain on either side', Heal, p.265, citing Devlin, *Too Proud,* p.190. **5** 'It must be admitted that…', Heal, p.165. **6** 'We have produced no counter…', Manstan, p.23, Kindle Location 588. **7** 'appears merely to have enjoyed…', Gordon, p.532. **8** 'If endeavouring to destroy…', Richmond to Captain Plunkett-Ernle-Erle-Drax and Lieutenant W.S. Chalmers, 29 August 1916 (*Portrait of an Admiral,* p.209). **9** For example, Dunley, Richard, *Anti-Submarine Warfare in the Pre-First World War Royal Navy: A Cultural Failure?* (UNSW, 2019). **10** 'He need not be a strategist…', quoted in Dunley, p.641. Churchill Archives Centre, DRAX 1/12, 'Action required to deal effectively with the submarine menace from an offensive point of view', 4 December 1914. **11** 'little progress', Marder, *FTDTSF,* vol. II, p.349. **12** 'the performances of the submarines…', Dunley, p.636. **13** 'Submarines and aeroplanes have entirely revolutionized naval warfare…', Harris, p.163. Scott wrote to *The Times,* 6 July 1914, expressing his views. **14** 'our most vulnerable point', Gray, *The U Boat War,* p.55. **15** 'All war is, of course, barbarous…', Botting, p.19. **16** 'a struggle of invention', Wilson, *Avian ASW,* p.8, quoting H.G. Wells. **17** 'abrasive character', Wilson, *Avian ASW,* p.5. **18** 'The first anti-submarine patrol…', Marder, *FTDTSF,* vol. II, p.349, quoting Commander Kenneth Edwards. **19** 'Valuable time, personnel…', Marder, *FTDTSF,* vol. IV, pp.77–78. **20** 'It is so very simple and ingenious…', Gough, *Titans,* p.421. **21** 'causing a certain amount…', Lavery, p.252. **22** 'a fractious Irishman…', Maxwell, *Listening Beneath the Waves,* 25 June 2014. **23** 'the first recorded occasion…', Maxwell, pp.33–34. **24** 'all over the Firth of Forth…', Roskill, *Naval Hero,* p.143. **25** '120 officers, 650 ratings and…', Bruton and Coleman, p.257. **26** 'the listening devices generally failed…', Halpern, *Naval History,* p.334. **27** 'His failure to see…', Hackmann, *Sonar research,* p.93. **28** 'functional equivalent of the BIR', Hackmann, *Sonar Research,* p.94. **29** 'more than a hundred bell…', Dinneen. **30** 'the first to successfully transmit…', Dinneen. **31** 'could be used as a transmitter…', Hackmann, p.91. **32** 'measurably superior to the British devices', Michelsen, p.86. **33** 'not actually a tube at all…', Woofenden, p.39. **34** 'equally disappointing', Halpern, *Naval History,* p.344. **35** Arno Spindler (1880–1967), considered Germany's foremost submarine war historian. Having served as Chief of the 1st Submarine Flotilla in 1913 and as Head of the Submarine Affairs Department in the RMA, he published the authoritative four-volume history of Germany's submarines in the First World War, *Der Handelskrieg mit U-Booten.* **36** 'with the sacrifice of 5,087 combatants…', Spindler, *Value.* **37** 'the only countermeasures introduced…', Hough, *GWAS,* p.303. **38** 'instead, as one great power gradually…', Watson, p.417. **39** Jellicoe's report, ADM 1/8480, 21 January 1917, listed twelve ASW activities, including smokescreen, air patrols, Q-ships, submarine-escorted shipping, hydrophones, increased merchant ship arming, development of the bomb howitzer (i.e., depth charge), mines, protected shipping lanes (see Temple Patterson, *JP2,* pp.148–49). **40** 'was simply the arrogant sense…', Winton, *Convoy,* p.52. **41** 'officers of the smaller tramp…', Lloyd George, *Memoirs,* p.689. **42** 'it was highly probable…', Lloyd George, *Memoirs,* p.689. **43** 'five out of nine men…', Black, p.178. **44** 'masters of purely coasting…', Bacon, *Jellicoe,* p.356. **45** See Goldrick, *After Jutland,* p.134. **46** 'were confirmed later by other…', Jellicoe, *CONW,* p.106. **47** James Goldrick (*After Jutland,* p.36) cited the Harwich flotillas: 'In 1916, there were twenty-two collisions, six groundings and six berthing incidents compared with twenty-one collisions, seven groundings and eleven berthing incidents in 1917.' **48** 'difficulties associated with its early history…', Wheeler, *Reminiscences.* **49** The *Clan Mackay*'s crew were rescued by the USS *Birmingham,* with no loss of life. **50** 'In 1916, there were twenty-two…', Goldrick, *After Jutland,* p.36. Goldrick also cited the experience of one destroyer captain, Lionel Dawson: four collisions and two groundings. Three other incidents were never officially reported. **51** 'the backbone of the British…', Messimer, p.101. **52** '*Unsere U-Boote tauchten zu langsam. U.3 brauchte für das Tauchmanöver mehr als fünf Minuten … Es braucht für sein Tauchmanöver so lange Zeit, wie ein Mann braucht, um eine Zigarette zu rauchen.*' ('Our submarines dived too slowly. *U.3* needed more than five minutes for the diving maneuver … It takes as long to dive as it takes a man to smoke a cigarette.') Source: Valentiner, p.30. **53** 'played a significant role…', Messimer, p.102. **54** 'a steel chest containing signal books…', Grant, *Hunters,* p.67. **55** 'without being observed and without stopping', Heal, p.372. **56** Source: Smithsonian, *The Hunt for the Notorious U-Boat UB.29* (May 2018). I met Tomas Termote in 2018 at the commemoration ceremony held aboard the FGS *Brandenburg*, along with Reinhard Scheer-Hennings and Randolph Churchill, as guests of the Governor of West Flanders, Carl Decaluwé. **57** See ADM 239/26, Reported Destruction of Submarines Aug 1914 to Jan 1919. **58** 'the 1919 Admiralty tally…', McCartney, *Paying the Prize*, p.40. **59** 'The Anti-Submarine Division … had frequently…', Clarke, *OB.40*, quoted in McCartney, *Paying the Prize*, p.41. **60** 'I do not propose to bring…', Grant, *Hunters*, p.59. **61** 'a luminous patch in the…', Gibson and Prendergast, p.207. **62** Another occasion was 20 June 1917, when the 5,865-ton Cunard cargo ship, *Valeria*, struck something off the coast of Ireland en route from New York. It was the periscope of the *U.99*. With three shots, the *Valeria*'s gun crews finished her off when she surfaced. **63** 'Unable to believe…', Grant, *U-Boats Destroyed*, p.123. **64** 'pointing out that ramming…', Henry, *Depth Charge*, Kindle Location 281. **65** 'It is possible to escape…', Grant, *The Use of Mines*. **66** 'large glass balls supporting the headline…', Fürbringer, p.100. **67** 'I looked through the periscope…', Gray, *U Boat War*, pp.142–43. **68** 'there is no evidence to suggest…', Tarrant, *U-Boat Offensive*, p.63. **69** 'wartime traffic was huge…', McKillip, pp.25–26. **70** 'Some 750 miles of nets were on…', Terraine, *Business*, p.108. **71** 'was a definite gap between Calais and Cap Gris-Nez', Fürbringer, p.15. **72** Gibson and Prendergast, p.222: from January–November 1917, German submarines made 253 crossings. **73** 'A fight, even with a superior enemy…', Neureuther and Berger, p.166. **74** 'overwhelmed with the quantity…', Gray, *Captains*, p.57. **75** 'What remained of the net…', Gray, *Captains*, p.59. **76** For a quick discussion on the barrage's construction, see Admiral Sir Reginald Bacon, *The Concise Story of the Dover Patrol* (Hutchinson, 1932), pp151–55. **77** 'difficult to set mines to catch submarines…', Gibson and Prendergast, p.144. **78** The Flandern Marine Korps was set up as an integrated military command with air, land and sea assets on the coast of Belgium, using the 'triangle' ports of Ostend, Zeebrügge and Brügge as harbour facilities for the destroyers and pens for the submarines. It was under the command of Admiral Ludwig von Schröder. **79** 'they knew the position…', Hashagen, p.147. **80** 'utterly ineffective', Tarrant, *U-Boat Offensive*, p.61. **81** Karau, p.118, quoting Tarrant, *U-Boat Offensive*, p.61. **82** Tarrant, *U-Boat Offensive*, p.61, uses a higher figure: 'at least thirty U-boats (of all types) were passing through the straits every month.' **83** 'In justice and fairness…', Gibson and Prendergast, p.223. **84** 'Judged in terms of the number…..', Messimer, p.169. **85** 'forced to dive to escape…', Grant, *The Use of Mines*. **86** Gibson and Prendergast, p.180, date the aerial attack on *UC.36* as 20 May, carried out by seaplane (a Curtiss Large America #8663) in the North Sea, 10 nautical miles ENE of the North Hinder Light Vessel (source: Hobbs, p.243). Other research now suggests that *UC.36* was, in fact, successfully rammed by a French steamer, *Molière*, on 21 May, sometime after her periscope was spotted at 6.55 am. *UC.36* was on patrol in the English Channel, not the North Sea, at the time. Reports identified that submarine as *UC.21*, however *UC.21*'s Kriegstagesbuch (KTB, 'War Diary') made no mention of that attack. Later sources identified *UB.36* as the attacking submarine (see Lowery, *Re-assessing UB.36 and UC.36*). **87** 'was the first time that an RNAS…', Hobbs, p.243. **88** 'really effective barrier', Sims, *Victory*, p.30. **89** 'using chemical horns copied…', Meacham, p.87. **90** Source: Halpern, *Naval History*, p.345. **91** *U.84* (Roehr) had earlier gone through the Channel and operated off the Penmarch area, and was returning via the northern route when rammed by a patrol boat, *PC.62* (Grant, *U-Boats Destroyed*, p.109). Divers working on the site in 2021 had not yet formed a conclusive picture of what happened to *U.95*, only a working hypothesis. One of the team, Lieutenant Colonel Dom Robinson, gave his opinion: 'We did find open hatches in the conning tower and engine room … we think this confirms that it was sunk by ramming which destroyed the submarine's buoyancy system while concurrently pushing it under' ('Devonport Divers help solve WW1 U-Boat mystery', *Navy News*, 21 June 2021). **92** 'in practice', again 'abandoned', Tarrant, *U-Boat Offensive*, p.62. **93** 'in practice, the channel route…', Marder, *FTDTSF*, vol. V, p.42. 'None of them…', Meacham, p.88. **94** 'marked, if not sensational', Marder, *FTDTSF*, vol. V, p.41. **95** 'three large submarines had been destroyed', Newbolt, vol. V, p.149. **96** 'the last submarine to be sunk…', Grant, *Hunters*, p.80. **97** 'I had been thrown against…' Messimer, pp.168–69. **98** 'great depth of water…', Jellicoe, *Submarine Peril*, p.61. **99** 'to stop short of Norwegian territorial…', Jellicoe, *Submarine Peril*, p.62. **100** 'as a way of preventing…', Friedman, *Great Mine Barrage*. **101** 'For a long time…', Hashagen, p.115. **102** 'Admiral Sims holds very strong views…', Marder, *FTDTSF*, vol. V, p.67. **103** 'a fearful waste of time and resources', Terraine, *Business*, p.115. **104** 'The latest fiasco is that the Americans…', Marder, *FTDTSF*, vol. V, p.68. **105** 'an imaginative U.S. naval initiative', IOGRAPHYL, *Great Mine Barrage*. **106** 'the barrage to which we…', Jackson, *Benson*, p.41. **107** 'in the spring or summer of 1917…', Sims, *Victory*, p.240. **108** 'went through the middle of it…', Hashagen, p.115. **109** The minelayers included *Canonicus, Shawmut, Quinnebaug, Housatonic, Saranac, Roanoke, Aroostock* and *Canandaigua*. All were renamed to emphasise their American heritage. Two US cruiser minelayers – the USS *Baltimore* and *San Francisco* – accompanied the minelayers. **110** 'Those fellows up there…', Leighton, p.74. **111** 'This mine fired by means…', Meacham, p.89. **112** 'every two minutes…', Goldrick, *Antiaccess*, p.24. **113** Friedman's numbers (in *The Great Mine Barrage*) are only slightly different: 56,611 (US) and 13,652 (British). **114** 56,033 mines were laid in Area 'A' and 15,093 in Areas 'B' and 'C' (Marder, *FTDTSF*, vol. V, p.66). **115** 'a very quick design process', Friedman, *Great Mine Barrage*. **116** See Grant, *Known Sunk – German Submarine Losses, 1914–1918*, for details of the Northern Barrage losses. **117** Source: Tarrant, *U-Boat Offensive*, p.63. **118** 'no indication that this barrier…', Meacham, p.90. **119** 'Ironically, more allied minelaying ships…', Breemer, *Defeating the U-Boat*, No. 36, p.64. **120** See Gould, *Adriatic*. **121** 'a large sieve through which U-boats could pass…', Wilmott, H.P., *The First World War* (Dorling Kindersley, 2003), pp.186–87. **122** '35 destroyers, 4 torpedo boats…', Terraine, *Business*, pp.115–16, quoting Barley and Waters, pp.11–12. **123** 'out-and-out failure', Tarrant, *U-Boat Offensive*, p.63. **124** 'I had under my command…', Woofenden, p.105, quoting from a letter dated 5 March 1921. **125** 'at the beginning of the war…', Hashagen, p.206. **126** 'One or two destroyers are an essential…', Jellicoe, *Submarine Peril*, p.105. **127** 'all but thirty-seven in home waters', Terraine, *Business*, p.25. **128** 'Dover destroyers were so desperately…', Goldrick, *After Jutland*, p.38. **129** 'By keeping its dreadnought fleet intact…', Sims, *Victory*, p.38. **130** 'It was not the way…', Terraine, *Business*, p.118. **131** 'the destroyer has shown itself to be…', cable, Sims to Daniels, 18 April 1917. **132** 'she would commence to drop…', Leighton, pp.130–31. **133** 'had become a kind of ugly duck of the Navy', Sims, *Victory*, p.81. **134** The distances are quoted from Sims, *Victory*, p.87. **135** 'We erect our big masts…', Hashagen, p.227. Hashagen's CPO on *U.62*, Paulsen, jealously guarded the privilege of being the one to act as lookout. He had 'the eye of an eagle'. **136** 'would occasionally dive under…', Sims, *Victory*, p.91. **137** 'we should compel any submarines…', Sims, *Victory*, p.97. **138** 'every target met…', Watson, p.439. **139** 'a submarine would be compelled…', Terraine, *Business*, p.100. **140** 'Its mission was not, as most people…', Sims, *Victory*, p.115. **141** Source: Furer. **142** The British were astonished the sub-chasers had crossed the open Atlantic. Captain Cotton was told, 'Those boys can't bring a ship across the ocean', to which he is said to have replied, 'Perhaps they can't, but they have' (Sims, *Victory*, p.175). **143** 'the historical fact is that…', Sims, *Victory*, p.179. **144** 'the over-arching objective…', Woofenden, p.174. **145** 'It paid now to chase a submarine…', Woofenden, p.177, quoting Hashagen. **146** 'months of breath-takingly…', Woofenden, *Taking Aim*, p.43. **147** 'As a convoy ship…', Pratt, 'The Destroyer Grows Up'. **148** 'proved more successful…', Sims, *Victory*, p.217. **149** Source: Terraine, *Business*, p.34. **150** 'the submarine was no answer…', *Fisher*, vol. 1, p.218. **151** 'another of Sims's ideas…', Owen, p.34. **152** 'the primary mission', Messimer, p.140. **153** Source: Messimer, p.141. **154** Source: Black, *British Naval Staff*, p.212. **155** 'A total of 38 submarines…', Doughty, *Effect of Depth Charges*. **156** See McKee, *An Explosive Story*, p.51. **157** Source: Spindler, *Value*. **158** 'considerably larger than nearly…', Friedman, *Armaments and Innovation*. **159** Source: Bacon, *Jellicoe*, pp.352–53. **160** During her service as an escort cutter, *Seneca* had been involved in twenty-one submarine alarms – one was a dead whale – but used a depth-charge attack in eight instances (source: Wheeler, *Reminiscences*). **161** '*Die Allgegenwärtigkeit der Flugzeuge und Luftschiffe, die in vielen Fällen von den U-Booten nicht oder zu spät ausgemacht wurden, zwang die Besatzungen zu äußerster Wachsamkeit und belastete die Männer physisch und psychisch?*' (Krause, p.76). **162** '21 October 1918. One of our pilots…', Liddle, p.179. **163** 'decidedly lukewarm…', Winton, *Convoy*, p.107. **164** 'a relatively small role', Messimer, p.130. **165** The Short Type 184, the aircraft type flown by Rutland at the Battle of Jutland, became the RNAS's principal aircraft – 'a mainstay of anti-submarine patrol' – and around 650 were built, but the endurance was only around two-and-a-half hours compared to the H.12's six (Terraine, *Business*, p.37). It crawled along at just less than 90 miles an hour. **166** 'Under average conditions…', Hobbs, p.242. **167** Source: Terraine, *Business*, p.74. **168** German sources indicated the U-boat was the *U.36*. This boat had already been sunk on 17/18 May (Terraine, *Business*, p.76). **169** Because there was concern that a balloon over a convoy would attract the attention of a U-boat, Beatty experimented with an independent submarine-hunting group of balloon-equipped destroyers. It achieved its first success on 19 July 1917 when a balloon tethered to the destroyer *Patriot* (with an observer, F/L O.A. Butcher) spotted *U.69* from 28 miles, which *Patriot* then successfully sank. **170** The wreck of *UB.32* was found in the late 1980s, but only positively identified in

2021 when one of her two propellors (already identifying her as a Type-*UB.II*) was found, stamped '*B&V, 1150mm, 660, Projiz Flache 8416, Mangan Bronze, STB Schiffschr. 6, UB.32*'. The main damage was on her deck, which suggested that, rather than a mine, she had been hit either by artillery or from above by a bomb. The pilot of a Wright seaplane based in Cherbourg dropped two 1,000lb bombs, the first of which was credited with having sunk the submarine (Hobbs, p.261). Owen states that it was a British flying boat which 'sank the surfaced German submarine *UB.32* in the Eastern approaches to the Channel … with two heavy 230-pound anti-submarine bombs' (Owen, p.41). **171** Source: Messimer, p.131. **172** The F.2A was based on the Curtis H.12 design. It became 'one of the most successful warplanes of the First World War' (Winton, *Convoy*, p.106). **173** 'My first attack on a U-boat…', Arthur, p.96, quoting Bill Argent. **174** *UC.1* was reported missing on 18 July. **175** 'took effect', Gibson and Prendergast, p.192. **176** *UB.20* was a Type-*UB.II* – heavier and longer than the Type-*UB.I*: 263 tons surface displacement (vs. 127) and 118ft long (vs. 92ft). **177** Source: Hobbs, p.246. **178** Grey, *U-boat War*, p.200. **179** Lowell Thomas recalled the rather improbable story (*Raiders of the Deep*, p.235). **180** Messimer, *Find and Destroy*, p.131. **181** 'by 1918, twelve-hour patrols were routine', Messimer, p.133. **182** 'Between 18 March 1915…', Messimer, p.133. **183** 'of the 17,082 ships…', Howlett, *Royal Naval Air Service*, p.42. **184** 'airship work from Scapa…', Liddle, p.175. **185** 'especially in their early raids…', Ewing, p.190. **186** 'over 500, with 2,500 officers…', Michelsen, p.87. **187** The group consisted of 112 planes, 305 officers and 2,000 men. Another 20,000 men were based at Pauillac Repair and Maintenance Works. **188** 'certainly seriously hampered…', Michelsen, p.88. **189** 'down to the end of 1917…', Terraine, *Business*, p.90. **190** 'The representatives of the…', Krause, p.77. **191** 'providing escort cover…', Liddle, p.177. **192** 'should not be seen in isolation…', Black, *Naval Staff*, p.207. **193** 'The stopping power…', Black, p.205, quoting PD memo, 7 January 1918, 'History of the Northern Barrage', ADM 137/2711.

**5 Strategic Command, Part 1**

**1** 'recognized his limitations…', Goldrick, *After Jutland*, p.123. **2** 'Admiralty apathy has made so prodigious…', Ballantyne, p.161. **3** 'was under no illusion about leaping…', Ballantyne, p.161. **4** 'lacklustre', Gordon, p.519. **5** 'Everything has been left on the wait…', letter, Jellicoe to Beatty, 25 January 1917, Temple Patterson, *JP2*, p.140. **6** 'I am here, gentlemen, because I know nothing…', Colvin, p.217. **7** 'a keen mind and…', Marder, *FTDTSF*, vol. IV, p.55. **8** 'firm and cordial…', Colvin, p.219. **9** 'there were only three ways of dealing…', Marder, *FTDTSF*, vol. IV, p.70. **10** Jellicoe was a keen sportsman all his life: he sailed, was an avid cricketer and tennis player, a keen shot and an accomplished ice skater. In Scapa, he would play golf and run between the shots. Therefore, he was the only golfer on the Britain's northernmost golf course on Flotta who was allowed to 'run through'. David Beatty made a point of arranging for him to use his tennis court. **11** 'The system of several ships sailing in company…', Admiralty pamphlet, *Remarks on Submarine War*, January 1917. **12** 'The truth of the matter was that naval thought…', Greig, SAMHS. **13** 'in the course of preparation prior to my arrival…', Jellicoe, *Submarine Peril*, pp. 103–04 **14** 'no illusions as to the workload…', Goldrick, *After Jutland*, p.123. **15** 'always refused to acknowledge…', Sims, *Victory*, pp.22–23. **16** 'It was necessary to be very outspoken…', Jellicoe, *Submarine Peril*, p.118. **17** Henrietta Jellicoe (née Keele) died in Ryde, 17 October 1916. **18** The flag returned to Ryde on the Isle of Wight, where it remained for many years before, fittingly, in 2022, it found a home at the new Scapa Flow Visitor Centre in Lyness. **19** Memo, 29 October 1916. Newbolt commented, 'which with notable prescience, he anticipated would increase in the following spring' (vol. V, p.3). This was a common pattern: submarine operations increased with calmer weather and longer days. **20** 'the enemy's attack on trade…', Winton, *Convoy*, p.41. **21** 'very serious proportions', Jellicoe, *CONW*, p.4. **22** 'serious effect', Colvin, p.224. **23** 'The destroyer although very effective…', Winton, *Convoy*, p.42. **24** 'Hankey was complacent…', Boyd, p.204. **25** Surface speed was eventually used as one of the critieria of convoy organisation, slower ships being grouped together. **26** 'poor presentation…', Boyd, p.204. **27** 'the protection of shipping…', Cabinet Minutes, 20 November 1916, CAB 24-2 (Combined Strategy in Connection with Submarines). **28** 'did not approve of convoys…', Newbolt, vol V, pp.3–4. **29** 'paralytic document penned…', Winton, *Convoy*, p.44. **30** 'No conclusive answer…', Gray, *U-Boat War*, p.170. This was curiously close to what Balfour had written in a Cabinet paper the previous October (1916): 'No conclusive answer has yet been discovered to this mode of warfare; perhaps no conclusive answer ever will be found. We must for the present be content with palliation. Nevertheless, we are not wholly helpless; and I will endeavour to describe what has been and is being done to diminish an evil which unfortunately we cannot wholly cure.' **31** 'ships on a course between England…', Koerver, *Assault*, p.201. **32** 'so that more adequate protection…', War Cabinet Papers, 21 February 1917, CAB 24-3, BL ADM 1/8480. **33** 'The shipping situation is by far…', Massie, *Castles*, p.717. **34** 'It is because I agreed with you…', Jellicoe to Fisher, 1 December 1916, Lennoxlove papers, quoted in Hough, *GWAS*, p.305. Fisher's position was stated in a letter of 26 January 1917. **35** 'said that they must expect…', Jellicoe, *GF*, p.325. **36** Rear Admiral Duff was 2iC, 4th Battle Squadron, at Jutland. According to Grigg, p.50, when Jellicoe became First Sea Lord, 'he brought with him as Anti-Submarine chief an officer who shared his skepticism. Admiral Alexander Duff.' As far as I know, there is little evidence to support this assertion that suggested that Jellicoe himself was sceptical of the convoy system in itself; he was concerned about the *effective implemention* of convoys. Geddes did not like Duff and objected to Jellicoe's request for a KCB for Duff, 'as he did not like his manner on the wording of some minutes' (Temple Patterson, *Jellicoe*, p.201). Jellicoe replied that 'he was being recommended for his services, not his manner'. **37** 'relieved the Operations…', Dreyer, p.214. **38** 'like Fisher, instinctively…', Dewar, p.242. **39** 'regarded staff work with distrust, not to say contempt', Beesley, p.8. **40** 'an important step towards decentralization…', Terraine, *Business*, p.67. **41** 'for some time', Jellicoe, *CONW*, p.228. **42** Marder, *FTDTSF*, pp.174–75. **43** 'an exceptional officer', James, pp.72–73. **44** 'threw a vast volume of extra work…', Jellicoe, *CONW*, p.235. **45** 'During the same period…', Clarke, Ch. 3, p.1. **46** 'otherwise I would have…', letter, Sims to Jellicoe, 29 December 1917 (dated 1918 in error). **47** 'largely ineffective due to design flaws…', Messimer, p.25. **48** 'the insufficiency of mines and…', Marder, *FTDTSF*, vol. II, p.369. **49** 'was right to pour cold…', Roskill, *Naval Hero*, p.218. **50** 'The efficiency of these deep…', Black, *British Naval Staff*, p.190, quoting Captain Arthur May. **51** 'did not possess a mine…', Jellicoe, *CONW*, p.50. **52** 'only about one mine in three…', Jellicoe, *Submarine Peril*, p.60. **53** 'Our deficiency was clearly showed in trials…', Jellicoe, *CONW*, p.50. **54** Source: Macfarlane, p.62. **55** 'oysters and other sea growths…', *The World's Work*, p.502. **56** 'accomplished little, for the Germans…', Sims, *Victory*, p.36. **57** 'we must think of it…', Colvin, p.225. **58** 'the astounding promptness of the counter-measures…', Gibson and Prendergast, p.188. **59** Source: Gibson and Prendergast, p.153. **60** These German mines would be untethered and rise to the surface at pre-determined intervals. **61** '726 vessels, consisting of…', Gibson and Prendergast, p.155. **62** Source: Gibson and Prendergast, p.188. **63** 'impossible for a submarine…', Spiess, p.92. **64** '6.75 million tons…', Watson, p.418. **65** 'accepted some risks…', Goldrick, *After Jutland*, p.129. **66** 'slow and evolutionary', Breemer, *Defeating the U-Boat*, p.41. **67** 'bypassed him and gone directly…', Watt, p.136. **68** 'has suddenly come round…', Koerver, *Assault*, p.216. **69** 'if the military authorities…', U-Boat Conference, 9 January 1917. **70** 'shaped skillfully to appeal…', Watson, p.444. **71** 'Beginning on February 1st…', Koerver, *Assault*, p.222. **72** 'very secret information', Boyd, p.219. **73** 'Everyone was impressed by the gravity of the situation…', Robinson, *Rose*, p.138. **74** 'Thank God, they have finally…', Trapp, p.89. **75** 'delude steamer crews…', Michelsen, quoted in Watson, p.431. Source: BA-MA-Freiburg RM86/226. **76** 'it was unofficially admitted…', Ballantyne, p.168. **77** 'The German battleship was the power…', Dewar, *The Navy From Within*, p.235. **78** 'primary duty', Goldrick, *Antiaccess*, p.24. **79** 'the submarine menace…', Boyd, p.184, quoting Beatty to Hankey, 23 October 1918. **80** 'As long as the German fleet remained intact', Michelsen, p.90. **81** 'it was their support which countered…', Dewar, *The Navy From Within*, p.235. **82** The German light cruisers included SMS *Königsberg*, *Pillau*, *Frankfurt* and *Nürnberg*. **83** *Daily Mail*, 12 May 1917. **84** Source: Wrecksite.eu. **85** 'had been unchained', Fürbringer, p.66. **86** The *Torrington*'s master presented his case against Werner at Bow Street on 31 August 1921. The same fate was meted out to the crew of the 3,066-ton *Toro* on 12 April 1917, 200 miles WNW of Ushant. Werner would later sink the British liner, the 13,603-ton RMS *Carpathia*, the following year on 17 July. She had gone to the rescue of the RMS *Titanic* in 1912. **87** 'a practice intended to daunt…', Gibson and Prendergast, p.169. **88** 'I came to the conclusion…', Snelling, p.143. **89** 'the wheel-house collapsed…', Snelling, p.145. **90** 'The water was thick…', Snelling, p.145. **91** Spiegel (*U.32*) was extremely superstitious. He'd left Wilhelmshaven on Friday 13 January 1915. With him were Bruno Hoppe (*U.22*) and Siegfried Wachendorff (*U.31*), leaving for a patrol in the North Sea. Hoppe came back to harbour to report that he'd torpedoed another German submarine, *U.7*, thinking she'd been an enemy submarine. Twenty-four crewmembers were killed: one survived. *U.31* was never seen again; neither of her two radio operators, Karl Meyer and Fritz Zöllner, made any reports. She had been sunk by a mine with all hands. Her wreck was found in September 2012 and identified three years later when her hull number was found on the Manoeuvring Settings Table

(*Fahrt Tabelle*). She was lying 30 metres deep, 91km from Caistor-on-Sea, Norfolk. Scottish Wind Farms' planned wind turbine was moved to preserve the area as a war grave. **92** 'It seemed almost brutal…', Gray, *U Boat War*, p.178. One was sent to England as a POW (Messimer, p.109). **93** 'Of the 54 U-boats lost to all causes…', Liddle, p.181. **94** 'the mere fact that a number of Q-ships…', Sims, *Victory*, p.147. **95** 'approach on the surface and take a chance…', Sondhaus, Kindle Location 1904. **96** 'put the decoy vessels out of a job', Messimer, p.106. **97** 'sunk seven submarines…', Marder, *FTDTSF*, vol. II, p.356. Marder noted that thereafter, the last U-boat sunk by a Q-ship acting as such was *U.88* on 17 September 1917. *Privet*, which helped in the sinking of *U.34* on 9 November 1918, was not, strictly speaking, working as a Q-ship. **98** Snelling, p.124. **99** 'how many opportunities for sinking…', Robinson, *Rose*, p.138. **100** 'just 105 U-boats of various types…', O'Hara, Dickson and Worth, p.122. Terraine, *Business*, p.17, put the number at 111, comparing this to what Hermann Bauer had said was a necessary number to defeat Britain, concluding that it was 'precisely half the number' Bauer had recommended. **101** 'for the remainder of the year…', Halpern, *Naval History*, p.338. **102** 'the hesitant attitude of the RMA…', O'Hara, Dickson and Worth, p.122. **103** Source: Breemer, *Defeating the U-Boat*, p.41. **104** 'neutral entrances…', Terraine, *Business*, p.40, quoting Crutwell, *A History of the Great War 1914–1919*. **105** '*à la fin du printemps*…', Brézet, p.170. **106** 'as anti-submarine defences…', Gray, *U Boat War*, p.176. Figures quoted are from the same. **107** Gibson and Prendergast, p.142: Michelsen cited as a reliable source for the U-boat strength at the campaign start: forty-nine North Sea, thirty-three Flanders, twenty-four Adriatic, three Constantinople, two Baltic (111 in total). Of the forty-nine in the North Sea, twenty-three were on active service in February; four more in March. **108** 'we have lost command of the sea', letter, Field Marshal Haig to Lord Derby, 18 April 1917, Terraine, p.47. **109** Sources for monthly losses, Jellicoe, *CONW*, p.51. **110** 'In the campaign's first five…', Watson, p.427. **111** 'In one particular week there…', Gibson and Prendergast, p.162. **112** 'every German submarine…', Newbolt, quoted in Breemer, *Defeating the U-Boat*, p.47. **113** 'gave the Germans another opportunity', Halpern, *Naval History*, p.337. **114** 'The end of the war could…', Breemer, *Defeating the U-Boat*, p.48, quoting Leslie, *Convoy System in 1917–1918*, p.148. **115** 'does not intend to become involved in this war', Koerver, *Assault*, p.219. **116** 'they may be stubborn…', Koerver, *Assault*, p.225. **117** 'accelerated this confrontation', Boyd, p.202. **118** 'As the United States and Germany…', Ewing, p.204. **119** 'boundlessly naïve', Theodore Wollf in the *Berliner Tageblatt*. **120** 'I wonder if America will come in…', Koerver, *Assault*, p.255. **121** Source: Brézet, p.163. **122** Source: Naumes, *Anglo-American ASW*, p.119. **123** A crewman from Daniel's yacht, *Dolphin*, Boatswain John T. Eopolucci, would become 'the first American serviceman killed in action against Germany' when his merchantman, *Aztec*, was attacked on 31 March. **124** 'continued neutrality would…', Naumes, *Anglo-American ASW*, p.120. **125** 'the most junior flag officer…', Kohnen, *Centurion*, p.16. **126** Trask (p.162) reports a story that it was FDR's physician, Dr Cary Grayson, who urged the President to appoint Sims. Sims was 'much disturbed by this episode, realizing that to act on such information (that "he would receive support from the highest authority") was to fish in extremely troubled waters. He determined ultimately to report the whole matter confidentially to Admiral Benson.' **127** 'faced an unclear mission…', Kohnen, *Centurion*, p.16. **128** 'Admiral Sims, while…', Burke, p.67. **129** Jellicoe, *CONW*, Organisation chart Admiralty, April 1917, p.271. **130** 'The situation is far from easy…', Morison, *Admiral Sims*, p.341. **131** I think that Morison wrote about the meeting (*Admiral Sims*, p.342) with a fair amount of hindsight on Sims's part: the losses in April accelerated in the last two weeks. It is interesting to note that in early March, Beatty wrote to his wife playing down the effect of the German submarine campaign while still criticising the Admiralty: 'I do not think their SM campaign has yielded the result they quite expected but it has been a terrific and indeed a big pill for us to swallow. I think we can say we know the worst and that as time passes we shall be able to minimize it some but not very much unless we take the very strongest measures, which even now the authorities seem to be incapable of doing' (Ranft, *Beatty Papers*, vol. I. pp.410–11, Beatty to Lady Beatty, 14 March 1917). **132** 'It was his business to paint…', Bacon, *Jellicoe*, p.361. **133** 'Absolutely none that we can see now', Morison, *Admiral Sims*, p.342. **134** 'I knew that no fresh measures…', Jellicoe, *GF*, p.324. **135** 'What I did say was that…', Jellicoe, *Submarine Peril*, p.71. **136** 'We were certainly not in a state of panic…', Bacon, *Jellicoe*, p.362. **137** 'The limit of endurance would be reached…', Ballantyne, p.174. **138** 'It is impossible to go on with war…', Sims, *Broadside*, p.476. **139** 'I was fairly astounded…', Lloyd George, *Memoirs*, p.690. **140** 'nor anyone else in the United States…', Jellicoe, *CONW*, p.158. **141** Source: Robinson, *Rose*, pp.168–69. **142** 'The submarine issue is very much more serious…', cable, Sims to Daniels, 14

April 1917. **143** The Balfour Mission left England on 11 April, made land at Halifax just over a week later and arrived in Washington on 22 April. **144** 'Without a doubt the most pressing need…', memorandum from A. Balfour to W. Page, forwarded to Lansing on 6 April 1917. **145** 'had been severely eroded…', Harley, p.71, quoting Liam Nolan and John E. Nolan, *Secret Victory. Ireland and the War at Sea, 1914–1918* (Mercier Press, 2009). **146** Source: Botting, p.58. **147** 'failure to establish…', Naumes, *Anglo-American ASW*, p.108. **148** 'The President wishes that, when you next…', Walter Page. **149** 'our forces should be considered…', Sims, *Victory*, p.44. **150** Copies can be found in the National Archives in Washington, DC. Sims was so concerned about conflicting reports coming from London that he managed to succeed in getting the US naval attaché, Captain McDougall, removed so that the reporting went through him alone. Sims was also appointed as an honorary member of the Board of Admiralty. Sims was in a difficult position and on 17 September Jellicoe and Robertson 'both complained of American inaction at a meeting of the War Cabinet'. Admiral Mayo did not seem to be empowered to take decisions. Much of this led to the eventual European visit by Admiral Benson with Colonel House in November 1917. Three days after his arrival, Sims's recommendations to release USN coal-burning dreadnoughts to join the Grand Fleet was approved on 10 November. The grounds for distrust were real: 'each country suspected that the other was developing wartime shipping policy with an eye to international trade in peacetime' (Trask, p.170). **151** The force was formed to rescue foreigners trapped inside the legations. Jellicoe also got to know Captain McCalla USN and, from the German side, Guido von Usedom, who took over as Chief of Staff when Jellicoe was wounded in action. **152** 'not because of your Guildhall…', Still, p.21. **153** 'Sims felt that the US Navy…', Brunciardi, *The U.S. Navy at Queenstown*, pp.39–40. **154** 'a gunnery officer of…', Jellicoe, *CONW*, p.154. **155** 'habit of speaking his mind…', Still, p.22. **156** 'resisted the urge to micromanage…', Irwin, p.3. **157** Washington, DC, Library of Congress (LC), William S. Sims Papers (Sims Papers), Box 83, Clippings, *Scientific American*, 1913–24, 'Admiral Sims in the Teamwork for Victory: How the Admiral Stood out for "Consolidation" as Against Mere "Cooperation"' (12 April 1919), 374 and 384. **158** *Ibid.* **159** 'Perhaps Sims' greatest success…', Goldrick, *After Jutland*, p.161. **160** USS *Wadsworth* (Taussig), *Conyngham* (Cdr Alfred P. Johnson), *Porter* (Lt Cdr Ward K. Wortman), *McDougal* (Lt Cdr Arthur P. Fairfield), *Davis* (Lt Cdr Rufus Zogbaum) and *Wainright* (Lt Cdr Fred H. Poteet).The last is not mentioned in the US Navy's History and Heritage web page, but is quoted in Still, p.8. **161** Taussig: his conversation with Admiral Benson was 'very unsatisfactory … He would not name a date on which we must be ready' (Taussig, p.12). **162** His sealed orders were entitled 'Protection of Commerce near the coasts of Great Britain and Ireland'. **163** 'My dear Taussig, I retain very pleasant…', Sims, *Victory*, p.53. **164** Bowman McCalla (1844–1910) joined the USN in 1861 and came to know Jellicoe well when commanding a 112-man American force as part of Admiral Seymour's relief column from Tiensin to Peking (at the time, Jellicoe was Chief of Staff to the admiral). He was wounded in the Battle of Hsiku Arsenal. **165** 'refused to wear it…', Taussig, p.125. **166** One hundred years later, I visited the site of what would become Admiral Sims's HQ with his grandson, Nat. This book was born from that meeting. **167** 'We are ready now, sir…', Sims, *Victory*, p.56. **168** Carney, Admiral Robert (1895–1990), served as Admiral 'Bull' Halsey's Chief of Staff in 1943 in the Pacific, and ten years later became Chief of Naval Operations (CNO). His connection to Bayly was through the marriage of his daughter, Betty, to Joseph Taussig. **169** 'autocrat who acquired the … "equal resonance"', Still, pp.60–61. **170** 'Gentlemen, the Admiralty…', Dunn, *Bayly*, p.146. **171** 'there was nothing about his manner…', Sims, *Victory*, p.55. **172** 'most of us … consider him…', Taussig, p.179. **173** 'a charming young woman', Taussig, p.21. **174** USS *Cassin, Ericsson, Jacob Jones, Rowan, Tucker* and *Winslow* arrived in Queenstown on 17 May. On 8 July, *Jacob Jones* picked up forty-four survivors from SS *Valetta*, two weeks later another twenty-five from *Dafila* and on 19 October 305 from the cruiser, HMS *Orama*. In August, *Tucker* forced a sub to surface, where her shellfire caused further damage, but the submarine eventually escaped. **175** The *Melville* would be designated as one of the two depot ships. **176** Two additional waves arrived in Queenstown, on 24 May (USS *Benham, Cummings, Cushing, Nicholson, O'Brien* and *Sampson*) and on 1 June (*Drayton, Jenkins, Patterson, Paulding, Trippe* and *Warrington*). The last group were known as 'Flivvers' as, like the Model-T Ford, they had been built in large numbers and rattled as badly. **177** See MAT, *Jacob Jones*, p.6. **178** The calculation is from Roblin. Uhlig (*Submarine*, p.154) states 'on 9 April 1917 the U.S. Navy had sixty-eight – some in the Pacific, some on the Asiatic station, but most in the Atlantic'. **179** 'was one of the best…', mentioned in Still. **180** 'fairly intercollegiate with eleven…', Rose, *Brittany Patrol*, p.36. **181** 'The partial rejection of the convoy…', Morison, p.357. **182** 'powerful advocate of convoy', Grove, p.13. **183** 'Mr Daniels' handling of the Navy…', Sims, *Broadside*, p.484. **184** 'has now adopted the convoy system…', Sims, *Broadside*, p.479. **185** Marder, vol. V, p.99. **186** 'Hydrophones, although not a weapon…', Messimer, p.113. **187** '*Ein U-Boot kann nämlich…*', Valentiner, p.262. **188** 'It was discovered that acoustic…', Hackmann, p.90. **189** 'a repetitious move, stop and listen procedure', Messimer, p.114. **190** 'Prior to 1917 all that…', Jellicoe, *CONW*, p.62. **191** 'smaller ships such as trawlers…', Maxwell, p.9. **192** Source: Jameson, *Formidable*, p.205. **193** 'no fewer than eleven types…', Terraine, *Business*, p.29. **194** Source: Messimer, p.115. **195** 'The last year of the war…', Manstan, p.xii, Kindle Location 198. **196** 'We are now fighting against…', Newbolt, *Operations*, vol. IV, p.61. **197** 'a grave danger in hopes…', Newbolt, *Operations*, vol. V, p.62. **198** Source: Gray, *U Boat War*, p.214. **199** 'apparent unwillingness to assist…', Stevens, p.308. **200** 'both France and Britain…', Marder, *FTDTSF*, vol. IV, p.183. **201** 'it seems on his own initiative', Winton, p.93. **202** 'passed close under our stern', Forgotten Wrecks, *Anglia and Asturias*, p.8. **203** *Glenart Castle* (6,807 tons), mined by *U.45* on 1 March 1917; *Asturias* (12,002 tons), torpedoed by *U.66* on 20 March; *Gloucester Castle* (7,999 tons), torpedoed by *UB.32* on 30 March; *Salta* (7,284 tons) sunk by mines on 10 April; and both the *Lefranc* (6,287 tons) and *Donegal*, torpedoed. **204** 'under the new designation…', Knight and Fuller, p.44. **205** 'One consequence of this heavy tanker…', Gibson and Prendergast, p.166. **206** 'At least a quarter of the 150…', Boyd, p.235. **207** 'the man spoke as though…', Heal, p.364. **208** 'read like a check list for readying…', Heal, p.368. **209** 'maximum steerage can be obtained', Heal, pp.381–82. **210** My father, George, commanded the Special Boat Squadron from March 1943 to December 1944 in the Aegean and Greek campaigns. He took a particular interest in the design of the raiding forces kayak and joked about the distinction of it being called 'the Jellicoe raider' following some of his suggestions (see Heal, p.382). **211** 'commanders were told of the re-imposition…', Heal, p.372. **212** 'delusion that submarines operating…', Heal, p.372. Also Grant, *Hunters*, p.64, quoting ADM 137/1382. **213** 'We were hardened by war…', Gray, *U Boat War*, p.173. **214** 'earned a place in naval history…', Snelling, p.183. **215** 'one of the youngest…', Dunn, *Bayly*, p.169. **216** 'had their legs all but blown off', Thomas, *Raiders*, p.196. **217** 'five diving tanks…', Thomas, *Raiders*, p.195. **218** 'a white vapour…', Snelling, p.186. **219** According to Thomas (*Raiders*, p.186), his name was Deppe. **220** 'knew diesel engines as a parson…', Thomas, *Raiders*, p.186. **221** 'I have wanted to meet the man…', Thomas, *Raiders*, p.189. **222** 'I marvelled at the bravery…', Thomas, *Raiders*, p.184. **223** 'Seven times in three days…', Spiegel, pp.9–10. **224** British officers were impressed by Spiegel's connections. He received enquiries after his health from Prince Heinrich of Prussia, the King of Spain and the Queen of Denmark. He did not get home until June 1919. **225** 'cut to pieces by…', Gray, *U Boat War*, p.190. **226** 'a nine-day voyage…', Gray, *Captains*, p.65. **227** 'two thousand miles at a snail's pace', Thomas, *Raiders*, p.197. **228** 'always most grateful…', Hashagen, p.240. **229** 'the first and only naval…', Snelling, p.151. **230** 'a nice fat tub, very broad in the beam…', Fürbringer, p.92. **231** 'the motors were hammering…', Fürbringer, p.92. **232** 'Mouths agape we watched the animal…', Fürbringer, p.93. **233** A lugsail is a four-sided sail attached to a yard that hangs at a slant. **234** It was at the extreme range of the older torpedo type which had a maximum range of 1,000 metres. **235** 'Some of *Garry*'s stokers came…', Grant, *Hunters*, p.75. **236** 'it was simply amazing…', Lightholler, Charles, *Titanic and Other Ships* (1935). **237** 'even the submarine commander…', Gibson and Prendergast, p.192. **238** 'Containers scattered around the ship…', Arthur, p.77. **239** 'floated for hours after…', Hashagen, p.38. **240** 'her three holds were fitted…', Liddle, p.181. **241** 'fair-haired boy of the Flanders' base', Thomas, *Raiders*, p.243. He died in December 1917 when he took out his new command, *UB.81*. **242** '*mit drei "Hurrahs"*….', Huber, p.22. **243** 'drifted into the cloud…', Rose, *Brittany Patrol*, p.78. **244** 'were oblivious to their narrow escape', Rose, *Brittany Patrol*, p.80. **245** 'I am sorry, sir…', Snelling, p.155. **246** See Botting, pp.52–55, Snelling, pp.142–59. Peters was awarded the VC for the attack on Oran. **247** 'I know nothing finer…', Snelling, p.158. **248** 'to my old friend…', Snelling, p.170. **249** 'this submarine was off…', Grant, *The Use of Mines*. **250** 'utterly expunged the three-masted…', Gibson and Prendergast, p.170. **251** 'The morale of the crews was…', Gibson and Prendergast, p.204. **252** 'proved adept at locating…', Watson, p.437. **253** 'within 10 nautical miles of the shore', Watson, p.438. **254** Source: ONI, *German Submarines*, June 1918, p.8. **255** 'just 39 of the 219 Atlantic…', Watson, p.438. **256** 'So far from being emptied…', Terraine, *Business*, p.88. **257** These converted U-boats (*U.151–U.157*) displaced 1,870 tons submerged and could carry eighteen torpedoes. They normally carried two 5.9in guns, sometimes also (Gibson and Prendergast, p.218) two 3.4in weapons. **258** 'only one hostile enemy war vessel', Gibson and Prendergast, p.217. **259** 'We had shown a skeptical world…', Botting, p.68. **260** 'spirited defence', Gibson & Prendergast, p.218. **261** 'A shell hit the steamer…', Gray, *U Boat War*, p.228. **262** Gibson and Prendergast (p.219) stated that the date was 12 December and that only *U.156* was involved. **263** Gibson and Prendergast (p.373) list the following U-boats sunk for October 1917: 1–11 October – *U.50* and *U.66* (mined in combined operations by subs, torpedo boats and net drifters), 3 October – *UC.14* (mined off Zeebrügge; Jellicoe added a written note that it was a German mine), 5 October – *UB.41* (when the wreck was discovered in 1989, there were clear signs of an explosion that cut her hull in two), 9 October – *U.106* (mined), 19 October – *UC.62* (torpedoed by HMS *E.45*), and 23 October – *UC.16* (sunk by explosive sweeps by the *Melampus*). **264** *Stonecrop* was also known as *Glenfoyle* or *Winona*. **265** 'I am being shelled by a submarine…', Lt Cdr Auten (*Q-Boat Adventures*), quoted in Hashagen, p.83. **266** 'it was too close for the torpedo…', Auten, quoted in Hashagen, p.85 **267** 'I lit the smoke apparatus…', Blackwood. **268** 'The fourth shot…', Gray, *U Boat War*, p.168, quoting *Q-Ships and their Story*, p.244. **269** Gibson and Prendergast (p.373) list the following sunk for September 1917: 2 September – *UC.41* (depth-charged by trawlers), 2 September – *U.28* (lost), 7 September – *U.88* (mined), 10 September – *UC.42* (blown up by German mine), 11 September – *U.49* (gunfire from SS *British Transport*), 12 September – *U.45* (torpedoed by HMS *D.7*), 22 September – *UC.72* (posted as spotted by seaplane 8695 and successfully bombed, but classified as 'mined' by Dr Innes McCartney), 26 September – *UC.33* (gunfire from and rammed by *PC.61*), 27 September – *UC.21* (caught in mine nets), 28 September – *UC.6* (bombed by seaplane 8676), and 29 September – *UC.55* (gunfire from and depth-charged by destroyers). Gray (*U Boat War*, p.224) put the number destroyed at thirteen. *UC.6* had once had to use sails to get back to Germany. On 23 July 1916, she had an engine breakdown near the Thames Estuary, using the periscope as the 'mast' and a boathook as the 'spinnaker'. **270** 'foresight [that] was both remarkable…', Terraine, *Business*, p.93. **271** *U.50*, it seems, was probably sunk by a mine on 31 August. Gerhard Berger's body was washed ashore on 23 September. *U.50* had gained notoriety after sinking the 18,099-ton *Laconia* with the loss of American lives. She had sunk just under 90,000 tons, with twenty-six ships averaging around 3,300 tons. *U.66* was sunk by a mine on 3 September (her total score of sunk or damaged ships was very similar: by her seventh sortie, *U.66* and her last commander, Kapitänleutnant von Bothmer, had sunk twenty-four ships in six sorties, with an average displacement of 3,200 tons). Von Bothmer and his predecessor, von Muhle, had been classmates when he joined the service in 1902. It seems likely that only *U.106* (Hans Hufnagel) was sunk by a mine during the period of the 'ambush'. She had only just been commissioned (28 July) and only sunk one ship, the 957-ton HMS *Contest*, an Acasta-class destroyer which had been at Jutland, while damaging the larger, 5,867-ton *City of Lincoln*. Her wreck, only discovered in 2009 off Terschelling, inside of which remain her thirty-two crew and four officers, was pronounced a war grave. **272** The convoys were initiated in December 1916. Outside of the two raids in September 1917, the loss rate between February and November 1918 was eighteen ships out of 4,207 sailings – 0.43 per cent (source: Gibson and Prendergast, p.153). The authors wrote that their success (Scandinavian Convoy and the French Coal trade) 'were derived more from route protection than from convoying proper' (p.174). **273** 'nobody connected them…', Winton, *Convoy*, p.83. **274** Jellicoe was given a commemorative model of HMS *Strongbow*, now on display at the Sea War Museum in Thyborøn, Denmark. Under escort, two had been British, one Belgian and the nine others Norwegian, Danish and Swedish. **275** Brooke was later cleared of any wrongdoing, and instead awarded a DSO. **276** Both cruisers now lie in British waters, scuttled in Scapa Flow on 21 June 1919, their wrecks being left in place. It was Spiess who had made the recommendation for surface attack when he'd been asked to report back on the viability of U-boat attacks: 'only a raid by surface ships and a wholesale massacre would produce a detererent effect' (Gibson and Prendergast, p.176). **277** 'the Germans were learning…', Terraine, *Business*, p.97. **278** 'turned away', Winton, p.90. **279** 'To the *Fanning*…', Dunn, *Bayly*, p.194. **280** 'the only submarine sunk…', Gibson and Prendergast, p.227. **281** In eight patrols over eighten months, *U.58* sank twenty-one ships with a total GRT of 30,906. The average tonnage was small, less than 1,500 tons. **282** 'abaft the propellor struts…', Taussig, p.154. **283** 'had [she] been sailing east…', Rose, *Brittany Patrol*, p.101. **284** Gibson and Prendergast (p.373) list the following U-boats sunk for November 1917: 1 November – *UC.63* (torpedoed by HMS *E.52*), 3 November – *UC.65* (torpedoed by HMS *C.15*), 13 November – *UC.51* (sunk by *Firedrake*), 17 November – *UB.18* (mined), 17 November – *U.58* (depth-charged by US destroyers *Fanning* and *Nicholson*), 18 November – *UC.47* (rammed and depth-charged by *P.57*), 19–22 November – *UC.57* (missing), 24 November – *U.48* (stranded on Goodwin Sands and scuttled by her crew after being fired on by HMS *Gypsy*), and 29 November – *UB.61* (mined off Terschelling). Many believe the *UC.51* more likely struck a mine in the English

Channel. **285** Source: Leighton, p.59. **286** 'more stranded sailors than…', Cheser, NHHC. **287** Under Allied policy, charges were kept live with the safety disengaged while in the war zone. Sims revised this rule following the sinking. He also ruled that destroyers should henceforth steam in pairs. **288** A second such honour was the naming of DD-170 as the USS *Kalk*. **289** 'I was deeply moved myself…', Robinson, *Rose*, p.182.

**6 Strategic Command, Part 2**

**1** 'usually sailed twice…', Winton, *Convoy*, p.13. **2** Winton, *Convoy*, p.14. **3** 'that was what mattered most', Warner, p.134. **4** 'achieved a major…', Davies, p.57. **5** 'protection of Britain's overseas trade…', Greig, SAMHS. **6** 'but it was pointed out…', Jellicoe, *CONW*, p.103. **7** 'differed materially', Sims, *Victory*, p.91. **8** 'these circumstances make…', Sims, *Victory*, p.93. **9** 'lost sight of the vital truth…', Winton, *Convoy*, p.10. **10** 'the problem in real life…', Uhlig, *Revolution*, p.140. **11** 'Convoy sailing for the protection…', Jellicoe, *CONW*, p.104. **12** Source: M. Seligmann, 4 November 2021, Churchill College, Jackie Fisher Presentation. **13** 'had been dangerously slow…', Marder, *FTDTSF*, vol. IV, p.346. **14** 'had the convoy system…', Hore, *Dreadnought*, p.102. **15** 'is a subjugation of private enterprise…', Newbolt, vol. V, p.7. **16** 'no successful convoy system…', Bacon, *Jellicoe*, p.350. **17** 'the great steamship owners…', Semell, p.164. **18** 'was focused too exclusively…', Marder, *FTDTSF*, vol. IV, p.128. **19** 'wedded to the system…', Roskill, *Naval Hero*, p.219. **20** 'was receiving constant consideration…', Jellicoe, *Submarine Peril*, p.96. **21** 'had the system been instituted…', Jellicoe, *Submarine Peril*, p.99. **22** 'I do not see how…', Jellicoe, *Submarine Peril*, p.110. **23** 'You will find Benson…', Temple Patterson, *JP2*, p.225, Jellicoe to Beatty, 9 November 1917. According to Colonel House, 'Jellicoe spoke highly of Benson, for whom I have a high regard' (Jackson, p.40). **24** 'owing to the withdrawal…', Jellicoe, *Submarine Peril*, p.120. **25** 'could not tolerate half-measures…', Chalmers, p.295. **26** 'J.J. was always a half-hearted man', Roskill, *Naval Hero*, p.220, Beatty to Eugénie Godfrey-Faussett, 10 May 1917. **27** 'the fetish that exists…', Chalmers, p.448, Beatty to Carson, 30 April 1917. **28** 'set him [Henderson] thinking, and not…', Terraine, *Business*, p.55. **29** 'at Sims's insistence', Morison, p.349. **30** 'gives the Admiral more credit…', Marder, *FTDTSF*, vol. IV, p.158. **31** Marder, *FTDTSF*, vol. IV, p.158. **32** 'When I found out what…', Hore, *Dreadnought*, p.100. **33** 'With a view to discouraging the enemy…', Newbolt, vol. V, p.18. **34** 'it cannot be true to say…', Black, *British Naval Staff*, p.174. **35** 'ascribe the "startling discovery"….', Black, *British Naval Staff*, p.175. **36** 'was in constant conference…', Jellicoe, *Submarine Peril*, p.viii. **37** 'very largely responsible for…', Jellicoe, *Submarine Peril*, p.viii. **38** 'rare praise indeed…', Norman C. Rivett, Naval Historical Society of Australia, June 1997. **39** 'was able to make a start with statistics…', Dewar, *The Navy From Within*, p.216. **40** 'it seemed to me that…', Dewar, *The Navy From Within*, p.225. **41** 'a docket should have been started', Dewar, *The Navy From Within*, p.216. **42** 'It seems more likely that the authorities…', Dewar, *The Navy From Within*, p.216. **43** Mentioned by Dewar in *The Navy from Within* (p.224). The result was that he did not have to take the appointment to HMS *Sapphire*; he could choose another ship 'so long as I left the Admiralty' (p.225). **44** 'The forgoing incident…', Dewar, *The Navy From Within*, p.225. **45** 'Personally, I had never heard…', Jellicoe, *Submarine Peril*, pp.36–37. **46** Breemer, *Britain's Failed ASW*. Breemer's reference to 'DeWar' actually refers to 'Dewar'. **47** 'ended Jellicoe's "honeymoon"…', Breemer, *Defeating the U-Boat*, p.50. **48** 'these disappointing successes…', Lloyd George, *Memoirs*, p.694. **49** 'assigned for this service…', Michelsen, p.103. **50** 'one of only two officers…', Still, p.47. **51** 'the principal factor in reducing…', Marder, *FTDTSF*, vol. V, p.97. **52** 'They seemed to think…', Jellicoe, *Submarine Peril*, p.119. **53** 'It is a continual fight…', letter, Jellicoe to Beatty, 12 April 1917, Temple Patterson, *JP2*, p.156. **54** 'reducing our commitments for the supply…', Temple Patterson, *JP2*, p.145. **55** 'assist in providing protection for convoys…', Temple Patterson, *JP2*, p.162. **56** 'our allies' mistakes in the past', Temple Patterson, *JP2*, p.126. **57** 'Jellicoe understood the situation…', Harris, p.229. **58** 'it was not so much lack of escorts…', Marder, *FTDTSF*, vol. IV, p.126. **59** 'one really serious impediment', Sims, *Victory*, p.99. **60** 'Any system of convoy…', Jellicoe, *CONW*, p.46. **61** 'the difficulty is to find…', Jellicoe, *Submarine Peril*, p.105. **62** 'At the Nore, Portsmouth…', Newbolt, vol. V, p.7. **63** Terraine, *Business*, p.25, states that 'all but thirty-seven' of 320 destroyers (i.e., 283) were in 'home waters'. **64** Sims maintains (*Victory*, p.91) that it was the success of protective destroyer screens that prompted him to suggest to 'Admiral Jellicoe and others', 'Why not apply this same principle to merchant ships?' I would have thought the suggestion might already have been made by others. **65** 'would not be risked again…', Jellicoe, *GF*, p.321. Jellicoe qualified this in

*CONW* (p.5), adding 'until the new submarine campaign had been given a thorough trial'. In *CONW* (p.115), he seems to contradict himself, saying that 'those who argued then, or have argued since, that we should have reduced the number of destroyers in the Grand Fleet will not, I think, meet with any support from those who served in the Fleet' (see Conference notes, Pless Castle, 9 January 1917). **66** 'Larger convoys did require more escorts…', Breemer, *Defeating the U-Boat*, p.53. **67** See Jellicoe, *Peril*, p.103, commenting on *Remarks on Submarine War*. **68** 'would be a most welcome sight', Herwig, *Total Rhetoric*. **69** 'gathered the prey of the raiders…', Brodie, p.125. **70** 'In mathematical terms…', Salgado, p.295. **71** 'at sea, mathematical odds…', Bacon, *Jellicoe*, p.358. **72** 'the oceans at once became…', Beesly, p.260. **73** In October, the last actions of the submarine war played out. On 4 October, Karl Dönitz, a young lieutenant aboard *U.68*, was cruising just to the south of Sicily when a large British convoy, coming from India, was spotted. Dönitz managed to successfully torpedo one of the steamers but was spotted by a destroyer. He escaped by diving but the trim was compromised. His submarine plunged past 230ft, 'at the time the U-boat's maximum permitted depth', and reached 302ft before he could bring her under control and get her back up. Unfortunately, he surfaced in the middle of the convoy. He was unable to dive again; they were out of compressed air. His only choice was to surrender. He was picked up out of the water by an RN sloop, *Snapdragon*, 'clad in nothing more than a shirt, a pair of underpants and one sock', but he was given a hot bath and a new set of clothes – 'the commander's tennis whites'. Earlier, Dönitz had served with Germany's second submarine ace, Walther Forstmann, aboard *U.39* and then on *UC.25*. **74** 'Although this system had…', Howe, pp.61–62. **75** 'not many individual ships…', Uhlig, *Revolution*, p.140. **76** 'the [U-boat] commander would have to wait around…', Fürbringer, p.117. **77** 'In very few convoys…', Grove, p.6. **78** 'when they found one…', Black, *Naval Warfare*, p.73. **79** 'the increase in the number…', Grove, p.5. **80** 'being aggressively counter-attacked…', Thompson, p.331. **81** 'a total of five ships…', Marder, *FTDTSF*, vol. IV, p.132. **82** Eric Grove (*The Defeat of Enemy Shipping*, p.4) wrote that the 'hold up and routing of independently routed ships' was causing 'crippling delays' that were 'as strong a reason for introducing convoy in 1917 as the need to reduce actual sinkings'. **83** 'threaten their swollen profits', Marder, *FTDTSF*, vol. IV, p.129. **84** 'on average, the total time loss…', Michelsen, p.100. **85** McKillip (p.33) says that 'the British War Economy had not yet been effectively mobilized': there was an 'estimated savings in tonnage of 4,000,000 to 5,000,000 tons per annum' from increased rationalization of British rail systems in 1917 (source: Lloyd George, *Memoirs*, p.1242). **86** 'simply been dropped…', McKillip, p.19. **87** 'intellectual exercise', Goldrick, *After Jutland*, p.131. **88** See Winton, *Convoy*, pp.28–29. **89** 'the third week of the war would have seen…', quoted in Harris, p.157. **90** The first large troop convoy was the October 1914 ANZAC convoy, when ten New Zealand troopships joined a convoy of twenty-eight Australian ships escorted by, amongst others, HMAS *Sydney* and *Melbourne*, plus a Japanese battlecruiser, *Ibuki*. **91** 'The unexpected immunity for successful U-boat…', Tarrant, p.51. **92** Source: Robinson, *Rose*, p.170. Also, Tarrant, p.51. **93** Half of these were Norwegian, which compounded Norway's losses from the Scandinavian trade route. **94** Terraine (*Business*, pp.54–55) says that the description 'controlled sailings' was used by an Admiralty with a 'reluctance to use even the word "convoy" – giving groups of colliers the escort of a few armed trawlers for which the name "warship" was scarcely more than a courtesy title'. The Norwegian trade had the protection of a flotilla leader and six destroyers. Howlett (*Unrestricted Submarine Warfare*) marks the start of escorted coal convoys from 10 January 1917. Four routes were used: Route A, Mount's Bay to Brest (with eleven armed trawlers); Route B, Weymouth to Cherbourg; Route C, Weymouth to Le Havre (with fifteen for both Weymouth routes); and Route D, from Folkstone and Dover to Calais and Boulogne. **95** Harris (p.228) cites slightly different numbers: sixteen ships out of 8,871 transits. It's not the gap between the numbers that worries me; it is the constant differences *per se*. Of 1,500 ships convoyed in March, only three were lost; for the four months to April, out of 4,000 sailings protected by thirty trawlers, a total of eight ships were lost. **96** Pierre Jules Marie Vandier (1873–1922) is often cited as being the French naval officer most influential in the convoy debate from the French Navy. After serving as Liaison Officer with the British, he became Admiral de Bon's Chief of Staff in the Eastern Mediterranean. **97** 'You, yourself will be forced…', Goldrick, *After Jutland*, p.136, citing Elizabeth Greenhalgh, *Victory Through Coalition: Britain and France During the First World War* (CUP, 2005), p.117. **98** Source: Bacon, *Jellicoe*, pp.354–55. **99** 'a gradual erosion', Black, *British Naval Staff*, p.176. **100** Halpern, p.351. Thompson copies Halpern, who himself cites Fayle, *Seaborne Trade*, vol. III, p.473. **101** HMS *Surprise*, *Torrent* and *Tornado* were mined in December 1917, while *Ulleswatter* and *Scott* were lost from other causes in August 1918. Thompson noted that all six losses occurred before June

1917, when 'stricter controls of stragglers was instituted' (p.328). **102** 'Between then and the end of April…', Thompson, p.328. **103** The initial convoy consisted of eight Norwegian and one British ship, escorted by a single destroyer, a whaler and two armed trawlers (Dunn, *Southern Thunder*, p.95). **104** 'a step on dangerous…', Dunn, *Southern Thunder*, p.116. **105** 'Steamer traffic is only found in strongly…', Log entry 19 July 1917, Messimer, p151 **106** 'a system of escorts….' Black, *British Naval Staff*, p.179. **107** 'always very scattered', Jellicoe, *CONW*, p.110 **108** 'perhaps thirty entirely strange vessels…', Sims, *Victory*, p.99 **109** 'the naval officers at that conference…', Lloyd George, *Memoirs*, p.689. **110** 'Escorts have, however, proved…', Newbolt, *Naval Operations*, vol. IV. **111** 'a system which permits of 9…', Marder, *FTDTSF*, vol.IV, p.119. **112** 'I have seen statements…', Jellicoe, *Peril*, Footnotes p.104. **113** 'a system which permits…', Marder, *FTDTSF*, vol. IV, p.119 **114** 'The conference unanimously agreed…', Dreyer, *Sea Heritage*, p.218. **115** 'four or five merchant ships…', Newbolt, vol.V, p.16. **116** 'sooner or later…', Jellicoe, *Submarine Peril*, p.105. **117** 'although he later attacked…', Black, *British Naval Staff*, p.180, Beatty to Admiralty, 5 October 1917 ADM 137/1938. **118** 'invite torpedo attack…', Marder, *FTDTSF*, vol. IV, p.143. Quoted in Dunn, *Southern Thunder*, p.120. **119** 'convoy system has not yet…', Dunn, *Southern Thunder*, p.120. **120** 'urgent requests…', Jellicoe, *CONW*, p.123. **121** 'the fact that the experiment…', Lloyd George, *Memoirs*, p.687. **122** 'a splendid prize…', quoted from *Heresies in Sea Power* by Semmel, p.165. **123** 'for some time prior to my arrival…', Heal, p.271. **124** Formerly DID (1912–13). **125** 'The Director of the Trade Division…', Lloyd George, *Memoirs*, p.680. **126** 'It would be difficult to find…', Winton, *Convoy*, p.47. **127** 'It involves the substitution of a system…', Newbolt, vol. V, p.10. **128** 'the attack on trade routes…', Winton, *Convoy*, p.50. **129** 'almost from the start…', Marder, *FTDTSF*, vol. IV, p.157. **130** 'apathy and incompetence of the naval authorities', Terraine, *Business*, p.45. **131** 'a disgrace', Boyd, p.223. **132** Jellicoe Memorandum, 'The Submarine Menace and Food Supply', GT-519 NA CAB. **133** 'two vessels in separate convoys…', CAB 23/2, Minutes 23 April 1917. **134** Jellicoe might have minimised the input as most of the convoy routing was done in the hours of darkness. **135** 'There are no destroyers at all…', Newbolt, *Naval Operations*, vol. IV, p.380. **136** Sims was an early convert even if the US Navy was not. The British Naval Attaché in Washington summed up their concerns: 'The Navy Department does not consider it advisable to attempt … convoy … In large groups of ships under convoy, fog, gales, inexperience of personnel, and general tensions on merchant vessels make the hazards of the attempt great and the probability of scattering of the convoy very strong' (Marder, *FTDTSF*, vol. IV, p.187). At this time (28 April), Sims was given command of 'all American ships operating from British bases … and then command of all U.S. forces operating in European Waters on June 14' (Harley, p.67). **137** 'the gravest doubts', Hough, *GWAS*, p.308. **138** 'as it was obviously close…', quoted in Newbolt, *Naval Operations*, vol. V, p.17, without references to the source. **139** 'War councils waste half my time', Temple Patterson, *JP2*, p.123. Jellicoe to Beatty, 13 December 1916. *Ibid.*, p.127. **140** 'little time for the work of war', Temple Patterson, *JP2*, p.154. Jellicoe to Beatty, 2 April 1917. **141** 'it was clear that the Admiralty…', Lloyd George, *Memoirs*, p.691. **142** 'that the shortage of escorts…', Marder, *FTDTSF*, vol. IV, p.159. **143** 'bunkering, discharge and taking-in…', Bacon, *Jellicoe*, p.360. **144** 'was shown as well-digested…', Morison, p.349. **145** 'detailed, and contained so many…', Winton, *Convoy*, p.64. **146** From February–May, there were nine sinkings from 4,013 sailings (Ballantyne, p.180). Gibson and Prendergast (p.153) put much of the reason for the relative safety of these ships (there were only fourteen sinkings out of 8,825 sailings from March–August 1917) down to 'the small size of these coal-carrying vessels'. **147** 'It seems to me evident that the time…', Black, *British Naval Staff*, pp.181–82, Duff to Jellicoe, 26 April 1917, ADM 137/1322. Newbolt, vol. V, p.19. **148** 'the United States having…', Newbolt, *Naval Operations*, vol. V, p.19. **149** 'it was the heavy daily losses at that time…', Hore, *Habit of Victory*, p.321. **150** 'it is difficult to believe…', Winton, *Convoy*, p.65. **151** 'a recent visit…', Marder, *FTDTSF*, vol. IV, p.190. **152** 'shared his [Jellicoe's] scepticism', Grigg, p.50. **153** 'He [Lloyd George] had worked…', Colvin, *Carson*, p.261. **154** 'without enthusiasm', Van der Vat, p.112. **155** 'the Admiralty can no longer…', Temple Patterson, *JP2*, p.160. **156** 'disaster is certain…', Herwig, *Total Rhetoric*. **157** 'we are carrying on this war…', Temple Patterson, *JP2*, p.161. **158** 'When with this help supplies…', Newbolt, *Naval Operations*, vol. IV, p.24. **159** 'the most drastic measures', CAB 21/95, Hankey Minute to Lloyd George, 'Immediate Measures to be Taken regarding the Food Shipping Problem', 29 March 1917. **160** 'cannot get at Ll. George…', Terraine, *Business*, p.54. **161** 'to extend rationing to the trenches', Breemer, p.57, *Defeating the U-Boat*, quoting CAB 23/2. **162** See Breemer, Newport Papers, 36, *Defeating the U-Boat*, p.57. **163** The amount of land used for crops had been declining from 1872–1913, from 24 to 20 million acres. There had been a parallel shift from grain to increased wheat production. Heal, p.262, citing Stewart Lygon Murray's work in Barnett, *British Food Policy*, pp.3–4. **164** 'The supply of one of the staple foods…', Goldrick, *After Jutland*, p.135. **165** 'descended upon the Admiralty…', Beaverbrook, *Men and Power* (Hutchinson, 1956), pp.155–56. **166** 'distinctly left on record…', Bacon, *Jellicoe*, p.360. **167** 'the biggest lie ever told', Carson, *The Morning Post*, 24 September 1934. **168** 'there is no foundation…', Hore, *Habit of Victory*, p.321. **169** 'a long way', Marder, *FTDTSF*, vol. IV, p.161. **170** Terraine, *Business*, p.59. **171** 'good stuff for the port and brandy…', Terraine, *Business*, p.59. **172** 'much regret that some time…', Marder, *FTDTSF*, vol. IV, p.164. **173** 'To him "British navalism" was…', Gompert, *Wilson's Decision*, p.72. **174** 'Conflict between the two was…', Olmstead, p.35. **175** Taussig did a calculation of the activities of his destroyers, noting that Wadsworth had been on operations for 126 days and had sailed 59,697 miles in 1917 from May that year (Taussig, p.174). The American destroyers were initially planned to operate '6 out and 2 in'. **176** 'without the participation…', Uhlig, *Submarine*, p.156. **177** 'After trying various methods of controlling shipping…', Harris, p.226. **178** 'despite the Admiralty's…', Harley, p.81. **179** 'the Royal Navy was finally compelled…', Harley, p.83. **180** 'The presence of the powerful High Seas fleet…', McKillip, pp.24–25. **181** 'there was a risk of sacrificing…', Brodie, p.144. **182** 'reported a conversation…', CAB 23-2, War Cabinet Meeting Minutes, 11 April 1917. **183** 'maximum number of destroyers…', Simpson, *Sims & Bayly*, p.67. **184** 'No voice condemning the Convoy…', Hough, *GWAS*, p.307. **185** 'although his heart was not in it', Tarrant, *U-Boat Offensive*, p.52. **186** 'I am not certain now…', Winton, *Convoy*, p.72. **187** 'suggested that merchant ships…', Morison, p.347. **188** 'It is interesting to note…', Jellicoe, *CONW*, p.115. **189** 'accepted the plans of the British…', Simpson, *Sims & Bayly*, p.74. **190** 'it seems to me to be…', Marder, *FTDTSF*, vol. IV, p.158. **191** 'expressed his dissent…', Lloyd George, *Memoirs*, pp.690–91. **192** 'was, by itself, hardly an endorsement…', Marder, *FTDTSF*, vol. IV, p.158. **193** 'Admiral Sims, who through…', Morison, p.351. **194** 'temporary effectiveness in protecting…', Marder, *FTDTSF*, vol. V, p.99, quoting letter from Sims to Daniels, 3 April 1918. Marder was very harsh on Sims, saying: 'Sims was absolutely wrong in his last statement. Escort was precisely the one solution. As the war showed, as the following war showed, and as all previous wars had shown, escort was not *temporarily* effective; it was *permanently* effective.' I feel that Marder is over-focusing on one instance in Sims's very large correspondence where he might have overstated himself in the enthusiasm of the moment. **195** 'who advocated instituting…', Thomas, *Raiders*, Introduction p.xvii. **196** 'lion's share', Thomas, *Raiders*, p.223. **197** 'the arguments of Sims…', Morison, p.349. **198** 'another of Sims's ideas', Owens, p.34. **199** 'it is not too much to call…', Marder, *FTDTSF*, vol. IV, pp.154–55. **200** 'behind the back of his Chief…', Hore, *Dreadnought*, p.101. **201** 'no systematic study…', Morison, p.348. **202** 'were not in the state of panic…', Jellicoe, *CONW*, p.159. **203** *The Morning Post*, 21 September 1934. **204** 'Our methods will not be effective…', Jellicoe, *CONW*, p.158. **205** 'The Admiralty had not definitely…', Jellicoe must have been referring to the all-important transatlantic trade routes. **206** It was the first test with *naval* escort vessels. An earlier one had left Sierra Leone on 17 January, escorted by armed merchant cruisers *Almanzora* and *Arlanza*. The eleven-ship convoy arrived with no casualties. The Gibraltar convoy arrived 200 miles from the Channel, where the ships were met by eight Devonport-based destroyers and a flying boat. **207** Sims (*Victory*, p.100) states that 'Eight-knot ships were selected for the experiment.' **208** The Q-ships were *Mavis* and *Rule*. **209** 'Despite fog and heavy weather…', Heal, p.278. **210** 'the chief opponents of the convoy…', Sims, *Victory*, p.101. **211** 'deep misgivings', Newbolt, vol. V, p.44. **212** 'he was prepared to take charge of thirty ships…', Dewar, *The Navy From Within*, p.220. **213** 'out of a total of seventy-three ships…', Greig, SAMHS. **214** Leighton, *SIMSADUS* (p.56), suggests thirty-five were operational in Europe by August. **215** 'nearly 100 airships…', Van der Vat, p.115. **216** Members of the committee included Capt H.W. Longden, Fleet Paymaster Manisty, Cdr J.S. Wilde, Lt G.E. Burton and Mr Norman Leslie. **217** 'the speed of…', Jellicoe, *Submarine Peril*, p.97. **218** 'remote', Gibson and Prendergast, p.175. **219** 'rarely operated beyond three…', Messimer, p.148. **220** 'the ships composing…', Jellicoe, *CONW*, p.105. **221** 'Sims and a few British…', Leighton, p.19. **222** 'an unduly large number…', Jellicoe, *Submarine Peril*, pp.100–01. **223** 'The only safety from submarines…', Muir and Davies, p.279. **224** 'sometimes by as much…', Knight and Fuller, p.20. **225** '*L'application du système*…', Kemp, *Protection des convois*, p.29. **226** In February 1918, in 'home waters', fifty attacks were made by day and forty-three by night, of which twenty-five were on moonlit nights (source: ONI, *German Submarines*, June 1918). **227** 'thus a convoy of twenty-four…',

Sims, *Victory*, p.119. **228** 'weak link in the convoy armour', Marder, *FTDTSF*, vol. V, p.104. **229** When the Germans introduced the longer-range, ocean-going UC-class subs in September 1917, the handover tactic was revisited. **230** 'by armed yachts, PQ vessels, trawlers etc', Temple Patterson, *JP2*, p.159. PQ vessels were British coastal sloops used in ASW work, a set of which were built to resemble merchant ships and were often simply referred to as Q-ships. **231** 'Far from offering protection…', Boyd, p.213. **232** 'Gun attacks are almost…', Messimer, p.153, quoting Kapitänleutnant Saalwächter, *U.94*. **233** Source: Gibson and Prendergast, p.186. **234** 'first regular', Winton, *Convoy*, p.73. **235** 'shunted to the presidency…', Simpson, p.68. **236** 'he [Bayly] was as rude to me…', Simpson, p.69. **237** 'run the show from here…', Dunn, *Bayly*, pp.160–61. **238** 'I have a suggestion…', Simpson, p.70. **239** 'We met as strangers…', Bayly to Sims, 8 March 1919, Sims Papers. **240** 'you [Jellicoe] and Admiral Sims…', Dunn, *Bayly*, p.162. **241** 'have become footnotes…', Breemer, p.48. **242** These were the *Manning*, *Algonquin*, *Yamacraw*, *Tampa*, *Seneca* and *Ossipee*. The group arrived on 27 October. One, *Tampa*, escorted eighteen convoys in this service, averaging a total of 3,566 miles/ month. She was torpedoed by *UB.91* the following September while escorting the thirty-two-ship convoy, HG-107. Her commander left the convoy after running low on fuel. Twenty-four of her crew died. The youngest was a 'fifteen-year-old, Irving Slicklen of New York City, son of a lawyer. Tall for his age, Slicklen decided to enlist one day after school in March 1918. His grandmother was so appalled she ran to the recruiting office in her bedroom slippers, followed by his father, but they couldn't get him released' (source: Carr). *Tampa*'s total loss was 130, possibly the largest single USN loss in the war. **243** 'names and positions…', Wheeler, *Reminiscences*. **244** 'began to force U-boat commanders…', Winton, *Convoy*, p.81. **245** 'the domestic aspects…', Winton, *Convoy*, p.81. **246** 'hotch-potch of nationalities', Gray, *U Boat War*, p.217. **247** 'personally antipathetic to the convoy…', Tarrant, *U-Boat Offensive*, p.64. From Notes on the *Convoy System of Naval Warfare*, Pt 2, ADM. **248** Daily coastal convoys were organised between the Humber and the port of Methil near Edinburgh (UM), the Tyne and Methil (TM and MT), the Humber and Tyne (UT and TU); Halpern, *Naval History*, p.424. **249** 'largest oceanic or coastal convoy…', Halpern, *Naval History*, p.424. **250** Source: Uhlig, *Submarine*, p.153, quoting Hezlet, Vice Admiral Sir Arthur, *The Submarine and Sea Power*, p.98. **251** 'the German submarine campaign…', Uhlig, *Submarine*, p.153, quoting Doenitz, *Memoirs: Ten Years and Twenty Days* (Naval Institute Press, 1990), p.19. **252** 'removed the initiative…', Winton, p.103. **253** 'as newer boats went…', Lautenschlager, p.112. **254** 'The convoy system alone…', Marder, *FTDTSF*, vol. IV, p. 72. **255** 'two other factors that worked…', Messimer, p.147. **256** 'it is evident that convoys…', Padfield, *Battleship Era*, p.246. **257** 'Failure of the Convoy System', October 1917, Thring papers, IWM 71/30/1. **258** 'finding the submarine…', Black, *Naval Staff*, p.207. **259** See 'Hunting Forces and Home Command', Cdr Lewis, 3 July 1917, ADM 137/1546.

### 7 After Supreme Command

**1** 'the world's ports were ransacked…', Gibson and Prendergast, p.162. **2** 'Geddes is a superman…', Temple Patterson, *JP2*, p.164. **3** 'on the best of terms with Jellicoe', Lloyd George, *Memoirs*, p.701. **4** 'had occasion to take exception…', Temple Patterson, *JP2*, p.240. **5** Source: Lloyd George, *War Memoirs*, vol. III, p.1234. **6** Grieves, Geddes's biographer, denied that the move was 'planned from the moment Geddes became First Lord' (Grieves, p.48). Indeed, he continued, Geddes had expressed his intention to Lord Derby to leave the Admiralty in December 1917. **7** 'to make up data mixed…', Winton, *Convoy*, p.102. Also Grieves, pp.41–42. **8** 'The submarine menace is no more…', Marder, *FTDTSF*, vol. IV, p.185. **9** 'The Navy Department does not consider…', Marder, *FTDTSF*, vol. IV, p.187, quoting Gaunt to Admiralty, 5 May 1917. **10** 'So long as the Belgian coast…', Jellicoe, *CONW*, p.197. **11** 'I fancy there is a scheme on foot to get rid of me…', letter, Jellicoe to Beatty, 30 June 1917, Temple Patterson, *JP2*, p.173. **12** 'ambivalent', Massie, p.741, Jellicoe to Beatty, 30 June 1916. **13** 'And you must stick at all intentions…', Beatty to Jellicoe, 2 July 1916, Temple Patterson, *JP2*, p.174. **14** 'cause great ill feeling…', Bacon, *Jellicoe*, p.376. **15** When listing the reasons why Germany was winning the war, Fisher once wrote the first reason as 'Jellicoe'; Fisher, FISR, 5/30 (4389), hand-written notes on why the Germans are doing so well. **16** 'the most significant…', Winton, p.92. **17** 'there be no question of any difference…', Temple Patterson, *JP2*, p.172, Beatty to Jellicoe, 27 June 1917. **18** 'to be very outspoken to the War Cabinet…', Jellicoe, *Submarine Peril*, p.118. **19** Colvin, Sir Edward Carson's biographer, cites examples of Lloyd George undercutting 'direct reports'. Lloyd George told Sir Douglas Haig at one War Cabinet meeting in 1917 that he didn't agree with him as he had 'a letter here from a subaltern in the trenches which gives an entirely different opinion' (Colvin, p.261). He did the same with Jellicoe, talking behind the admiral's back with officers like Dewar and Henderson, both brilliant minds, but in a manner that was lacking in integrity. In the same way, the Prime Minister's secretaries would often eat in the canteen underneath the Admiralty to pick up gossip. When he disagreed with Generals Sir Douglas Haig and Sir William Robertson over the proposed attacks through the Julian Alps or his idea to capture Jerusalem, Lloyd George said he would ask the opinions of Sir Henry Wilson and Sir John French on whether they thought what he proposed could be done (Colvin, p.281). So impressed was the Prime Minister with General Nivelle that he even put British troops under his command, without bothering to consult Haig. **20** 'He is a hopeless optimist…', Marder, *FTDTSF*, vol. IV, p.195. Jellicoe to Beatty, 12 April 1917. **21** 'Oh yes, things are bad…', Sims, *Victory*, p.23. **22** 'more converse with fighting officers…', Lloyd George, *Memoirs*, p.697; 'indefatigable if petulant', Hough, *GWAS*, p.309. **23** 'the single most important change…', Black, *British Naval Staff*, p.195. **24** Lt Cdr Joseph Kenworthy, later the 10th Baron Strabolgi, had served under Richmond on HMS *Commonwealth*. The Parliamentary Secretary to the Board of Education, Sir Herbert Llewis, had passed some of Richmond's writings (notably a paper 'On Admiralty') to the War Cabinet. Kenworthy was invited to speak with Lord Northcliffe and met with Lloyd George on two occasions (14 and 20 May), where, while praising officers like Dewar and his captain, Richmond, he criticised various aspects of the Admiralty organisation. One direct result was Dewar's appointment to the Operations Division, assigned to write the Admiralty's Weekly Appreciation of the Naval Situation for the War Cabinet. Jellicoe knew of Dewar and did not particularly like him, nor the new reporting procedure that had been put in place. Nevertheless, he was upfront: 'I hear you are a person with strong views and if your views do not agree with mine, of course yours will have to give way' (Jellicoe, *CONW*, p.65). **25** 'We [the Young Turks] were…', Black, p.196, *British Naval Staff*, quoting Kenworthy, *Sailors*, p.62. **26** 'the First Sea Lord came to see…', Marder, *FTDTSF*, vol. IV, p.198. **27** 'best man at his job…', Marder, *FTDTSF*, vol. IV, p.198. **28** 'the best possible man…', Marder, *FTDTSF*, vol. IV, pp.197–98, Carson interview, *The Morning Post*, 24 September 1934. **29** 'There is no good…', Marder, *FTDTSF*, vol. IV, p.204, quoting Haig Diary, 20 June 1917. **30** 'A most serious and startling situation…', Haig, *Diary Entry*, 20 June 1917, quoted in Marder, *FTDTSF*, vol. IV, p.204. **31** Milner, Viscount Alfred (1854–1912), joined Lloyd George's War Cabinet as Minister without Portfolio. After Kitchener's death on HMS *Hampshire*, Milner took over the Russia delegation. In 1918, he became the Secretary of State for War (for the Army). **32** 'I did not want it', Grieves, p.44. **33** 'I was convinced that Sir Edward…', Lloyd George, *Memoirs*, p.699. **34** The supply of battleships and cruisers was apportioned between the Allies: Britain, eighteen battleships and thirteen cruisers; France, five and twelve; Italy, three and three; United States, twelve and eight; and Japan, two and seven (Schoultz, p.285). **35** 'we blocked the entrance to Port Arthur but…', Schoultz, p.286. **36** 'appealed with force to that…', Newbolt, p.173. **37** 'thought of the difficulties…', Winton, *Convoy*, p.47. **38** Vice Admiral Sir Reginald Bacon was one of Jellicoe's principal biographers. Bacon, who was known in naval circles as 'Porky' Bacon, succeeded Horace Hood on 13 April 1915 as the commanding admiral at Dover. **39** *UC.44* had been lured into a clever trap by Reginald Hall, who knew that the British code for mine clearance had been compromised and was being used by the Germans to plan submarine sorties. Hall agreed with Bayly that some mines, sown by the Germans off Waterford, should be left unswept but the Germans given the impression that they had been cleared. *UC.44* went back to lay more mines and hit one of her old mines (see James, *Eyes*, p.116). **40** Geddes's brother said that Jellicoe's continued role as First Sea Lord was discussed at the War Cabinet of 21 December. General Smuts wrote to Lady Jellicoe saying that 'he had first heard of it [the dismissal] when it was first published in the press' (Bacon, *Jellicoe*, p.382). I cannot find any reference in that meeting or the meetings of 24 and 26 December when Wemyss attended in his role as Deputy First Sea Lord. Lloyd George always maintained that he 'knew the views of [my] colleagues', but not through any formal evaluation of Jellicoe' (Draft Statement, Updated, NA, ADM 116/1806. Part of the Geddes Papers drafting possible Q&As for Lloyd George's PMQs.) **41** Massie, p.743. Massie says that Geddes's letter arrived marked 'Personal and Strictly Private'. Gibson and Harper (p.327), rather theatrically, have it a little later, at 9.00 pm. 'The strokes of Big Ben's chimes floated through the still wintry night … eight … nine o'clock.' **42** 'My dear Sir John Jellicoe…', Massie, p.743. **43** 'Dear Sir, I have the honour to inform…', Massie, p.743. **44** 'A strange curtain-line…', Jameson, *The Fleet*, p.204. **45** 'a result of my own uninfluenced judgement', Geddes statement, 6 March 1918, marked 'not used'. Temple Patterson, *JP2*, p.246. **46** Source: Geddes, p.242. **47** 'I cannot find the words…', Massie, p.744. **48** 'Never a man stood higher in the estimation…',

Massie, p.744. Goodenough, Admiral Sir William (1867–1945), served with Jellicoe at Jutland, where he commanded the 2nd Light Cruiser Squadron. **49** 'No one knows better…', Massie, p.744. **50** 'his fragile constitution and unbending…', Ballantyne, p.174. **51** Duff's offer to resign, 28 December, was accepted by Geddes, even if the latter asked him to come back when he realised how much experience was lost. Carson also resigned on 22 January 1918. **52** 'had full confidence in Sir John…', Memorandum, Sea Lords to Geddes, 2 January 1918, NA, ADM 116/1807. **53** Jameson talks about Jellicoe meeting the Bishop of London as he was strolling on the Embankment. 'This is the first time, Bishop, I've been sacked in my life' (Jameson, *The Fleet*, p.204). **54** 'I advised Halsey that…', Jellicoe, *Account of Circumstances*, BL, Add. MSS 49039, in Temple Patterson, *JP2*, p.241. **55** The 2 January letter was signed by Heath, Halsey, Tothill, Paine, Oliver and Duff, i.e., the Second, Third, Fourth and Fifth Sea Lords, the DNS and the ANS. **56** 'Do? Why stand beside him…', p.276. **57** 'being run by an autocrat like a railway', Roskill, *Dismissal*, JSTOR, p.75. **58** Source: Roskill, *Dismissal*, JSTOR, pp.75–76. **59** to counter the submarine menace defence…', Wemyss, p.370. **60** 'senior members of the Staff chose…', Black, *British Naval Staff*, p.219. **61** 'full of fear for the future…', letter, Madden to Jellicoe, 27 December 1917, BL MSS 49039. **62** Grant, characterised as a 'a cautious recorder' by Terraine (*Business*, p.107). **63** Churchill commented that 'in everything that concerned machinery, invention, organization, precision, he had few professional superiors' (Churchill, *Thoughts and Adventures*, p.102). **64** 'The area was as bright…', Terraine, *Business*, p.110, quoting Churchill, *Thoughts and Adventures*, p.105. **65** 'saw in these orders the…', Terraine, *Business*, p.110. **66** 'The above statement put…', quoted from Bacon, *Dover Patrol*, in MacFarlane, p.113. **67** 'I am not able to accept…', Memorandum, Jellicoe to Keyes, 14 December 1917. **68** 'the boat was frequently illuminated…', Messimer, *Find and Destroy*, p.166, cites 'just under half' of those going through the Strait, doing so at periscope depth, i.e. just over the shallowest mines while the rest went through at depths of 65ft or more, 'which meant they were right among the mines'. **69** Jellicoe noted that thirty-five boats (and possibly another fifteen) passed through from 1 November – 9 December 1917. Messimer, *Find and Destroy*, p.164, states that the actual number between 21 November and 15 December 1917 was fifty-one. **70** See Ronald Handley, *The Dover Patrol Memorial* (Dover, 1998), pp.8–9. **71** 'since the raids…', Messimer, p.166. **72** 'The activities of the Dover Patrol…', Keyes, *Naval Memoirs*, Vol. II, p.159. **73** 'did well but [that] he…', Ranft, *Beatty Papers*, vol. I, p.511. **74** Source: Roskill, *Naval Hero*, p.126, quoting Beatty to Hood, 26 April 1915. **75** 'reputation hung on a thread', Terraine, *Business*, p.111, quoting Churchill, *Thoughts and Adventures*, p.105. **76** 'by the time of the 1918 armistice…', Gompert, *Germany's Decision*, p.67. **77** Source: Terraine, *Business*, p.106. **78** 'not having enough labourers…', Ballantyne, pp.174–75. **79** 'police in London counted…', Heal, p.260. **80** Marder (*FTDTSF*, vol. V, p.41): about four if *UB.56* is included. It was an odd mistake for him to make, as he pointed out that she was sunk on 19 December, six days before Jellicoe left the Admiralty and two weeks before Keyes arrived in Dover. Marder describes the latter's sinking as having taken place 'since the institution of the new patrol system'. Keyes only first met in Dover with his assembled officers on 2 January. **81** 'With such losses, the programme…', Marder, *FTDTSF*, vol. V, p.77, quoting Fayle, *Seaborne Trade*, vol. III. **82** Source: Gray, *U Boat War*, pp.218–19. **83** Wilhelm Werner was accused of a number of war crimes, but the *Torrington* charges never came to trial in Leipzig. He supposedly left thirty-four crew on the deck when he submerged *U.55*. The same day he sank the ss *Toro*, when fourteen crew were reported to have died the same way. After the *Belgian Prince* sinking, forty-four crew were left in lifeboats. The charge was that Werner ordered their lifejackets removed and the boats holed to make them unseaworthy. The three survivors claimed that they swum for eleven hours, and one, the American Willie Snell, claimed that he had swum 14 nautical miles. Jakobsen feels this had been Allied propaganda which survived (source: correspondence, Knud Jacobsen, 24 September 2013). **84** 'didn't feel much relief', Schultz, p.71. **85** Lines to Gibraltar, Falmouth and San Miguel were cut (Schultz, p.73). **86** *U.155*'s war diary states 40 tons; that of the *Wegadesk*, 50 tons. **87** 'not a soul on the ship…', Schultz, p.81. **88** 'As difficult as it was to use violence…', Schultz, p.85. **89** 'disappeared completely with a direct hit', Schultz, p.88. **90** *U.155*'s sortie had claimed cargoes of '9,700 tons of grain, 7,500 of flour, 5,000 tons of rice, 6,000 tons of brass ad wire, 11,000 tons of cotton, 470 tons of salt, 300 tons of salted hides, 450 tons of timber'. On board, they carried 45 tons of brass (source: Schultz, p.99). **91** 'suffering terribly…', Schultz, p.98. **92** 'very conscious of being thick headed', Marder, *FTDTSF*, vol. V, p.40. **93** 'severely damaged', Marder, *FTDTSF*, vol. V, p.42. **94** 'within two cables astern', Marder, *FTDTSF*, vol. V, p.43. **95** 'Suspicious vessels are to be regarded as enemy…', Marder, *FTDTSF*, vol. V, p.45. **96** 'painted white with large green…', Nadin-Snelling, p.111. **97** 'could only have been inflicted…', Knight and Fuller, p.46. **98** Source: *The Times*, 28 February 1918. **99** Source: *The New York Times*, 11 March 1918. Originally published in the *Liverpool Evening Express*. **100** Source: *The Times*, 14 March 1918. **101** According to Grant (*U-Boats Destroyed*, p.120), it was only one depth charge set for 100ft. **102** Source: Leighton, p.40. **103** '[He] took his U-boat…', Gray, *U Boat War*, p.244. **104** Source: Gray, *U Boat War*, p.244. **105** 'referred to it as a scheme for…', Marder, *FTDTSF*, vol. V, p.46. Letter to his sister, 'Polly' Frances Mary Tyrwhitt, 6 May 1918. **106** 'an operation which I am sure no responsible…', Memorandum 'Attacking Ostend and Zeebrügge', 18 June 1917, quoted in Hough, *GWAS*, p.314. **107** 'we are hunting hornets…', Harley, p.239. **108** 'When you have a plague of wasps…', Ballantyne, p.201. **109** 'Intercept the enemy at…', Gleaves. **110** 'The problem with bottling up…', Forstner, *Journal*. **111** 'a very limited man absolutely obsessesed…', quoted in Marder, *FTDTSF*, vol. V, p.40. **112** 'Well, Roger, you have talked…', Keyes, *Naval Memoirs*, vol. II, p.1512. **113** 'The inability of the Royal Navy…', Howlett, post 5 July 2019. **114** 'May we give the dragon's tail…', Ballantyne, p.203. **115** 'one of the most gallant…', Lloyd George, *Memoirs*, p.701. **116** 'fruitless', Grove, p.13. **117** 'In order to keep dogs…', Bacon, *Jellicoe*, p.367. **118** 'an out-and-out fisasco', Marder, *FTDTSF*, vol. V, p.56. **119** A total of eight Victoria Crosses were awarded (Halpern, *Naval History*, p.414, cites eleven VCs, while Keyes was made a KCB). **120** Source: Frost, *Zeebrügge*. **121** 'British losses were a cheap…', Frost, *Zeebrügge*. **122** 'a courageous and thrilling exploit…', Hough, *GWAS*, p.316. **123** 'about twelve', Lloyd, p.322, quoting Andrew Wiest, *Passchendaele and the Royal Navy* (Greenwood Press, New York, 1995). **124** 'unfounded', Macdonald, p.65. **125** 'the connection between the harbour…', Ballantyne, p.209. **126** 'all the great daring that…', Marder, *FTDTSF*, vol. V, p.57, quoting *Der Krieg in der Nordsee*, Vol. VII, p.267. **127** 'remained supremely confident…', Marder, *FTDTSF*, vol. V, p.62. **128** 'useless to the enemy for…', Marder, *FTDTSF*, vol. V, p.63, quoting Aspinall-Oglander, *Keyes*, pp.247–48. **129** 'the fiction … has so far not been…', Marder, *FTDTSF*, vol. V, p.63. **130** 'the last sortie…', Winton, p.104. **131** 'there was only a real decrease…', Salgado, p.288. **132** Gray (*U Boat War*) presents a confusing picture for May 1918. On p.248, he quotes sixteen submarines as having been destroyed; on p.219, he states 'of 16 boats on combat patrol, no fewer than five were lost'. Gibson and Prendergast list sixteen. **133** Most writers are certain that *UB.33*, *UB.55* and *UB.31* were mined; *UC.79* (although only Gibson and Prendergast were sure she was mined, others put an unknown) and *UC.78*'s fate was attributed to both depth-charging and mining. **134** Kapitänleutnant Johannes Remy reported *UB.70*'s position east of Gibraltar on 5 May and was not heard from again. **135** *U.32*'s complement was four officers and thirty-one men. Wikipedia's profile (possibly incorrectly) uses a figure of forty-one dead. In her eleven patrols, *U.32* had sunk thirty-seven merchant ships of 106,035 GRT. Under her previous commander, Kurt Hartwig, *U.32* had also sunk the 14,000-ton HMS *Cornwallis* in January 1917. **136** 'Contrary to the generally-accepted opinion…', Gibson and Prendergast, p.182. **137** 'made no contribution…', Grove, p.10. **138** 'It took two days of…', Thomas, *Raiders*, p.320. **139** 'cakes, candies, and dishes…', Thomas, *Raiders*, p.321. **140** Kaltenborn recognised one of Nostitz's officers. Turning to Körner, he asked: 'Weren't you in Stockholm with the battleship *Hohenzollern* in 1911.' He had evidently made quite an impression on the captain's sister: 'The world was indeed small when in the middle of a trans-Atlantic submarine raid, I could run across a reminder of a flirtation at a ball seven years before' (Thomas, *Raiders*, p.324). **141** 'become the ship's darling', Gray, *U Boat War*, p.235. **142** 'wondered how a German whaling…', Thomas, *Raiders*, p.317. **143** Other long-range voyages were also undertaken by other boats. Richard Feldt took *U.156* up to the Northern Barrage, where he fell victim to a mine on 23 September. **144** Schultz, *By U-Boat*, p.104. **145** 'Scheer had accomplished…', Weir, *Building*, p.171. **146** Of the submarines destroyed on 28 October, five were at Pola, one at Trieste; two minelayers were destroyed on 30 October at Pola and on 31 October *UB.129* was destroyed at Fiume (source: Gray, *U Boat War*, p.222). One of the Pola subs scuttled on 28 October was Wolfgang Steinbauer's *UB.48*. **147** 'The hydrophones were very good…', Raguet. **148** 'last British warship sunk…', Thomas, *Raiders*, p.346. The other warships sunk by submarines were HMS *Triumph*, *Majestic*, *Formidable* and *Cornwallis*. **149** 'some 200 of her crew…', Raguet. **150** 'should take no hostile…', Raguet. **151** 'Commence Return cruise immediately…', Botting, p.71. **152** 'To all U-boats: fire without warning…', Botting, p.73. **153** 'first, last and only submarine destroyed…', Ballantyne, p.217. **154** In May 1918, Hall helped create a specialist dive team in cooperation with the Admiralty's salvage section. It was headed up by Commander Guybon Damant and consisted of two officers and four divers. Hall's diving teams investigated twenty-two wrecks, entering eleven (source: Boyd, p.236). **155** *UB.116*'s story lives on in C.S. Forester's *U.97: A Play in Three Acts* (translated into German as *Deutschland. Die Fahrt des UB.116* and performed on stage in Nazi Germany in the early Thirties), based loosely on the story of the vessel. **156** 'First one, then another of the 15cm casemate…', Botting, p.72. **157** 'the fastest submarine…', Spiess, p.161. **158** 'they should have been fired upon at once', Thomas, *Raiders*, p.348. **159** 'When the English flag was hoisted…', Neureuther and Berger, p.203.

**8 Measuring Success and Learning Lessons**

**1** 'calculated in numbers', Koerver, *Eyes*, p.ix. **2** 'Our object was to destroy submarines…', Breemer, *Defeating the U-Boat*, p.39, quoting Jellicoe, *Submarine Peril*, p.35. **3** '*The safe arrival of merchant ships* with…', Thompson, p.330. **4** 'featured most prominently…', Moretz, p.40. **5** Titles included CB 1515-4 *Aircraft and the Submarine Campaign*, CB 1515-7 *The anti-submarine Division*, CB 1515-8 *The Convoy System*, CB 1515-14 *The Atlantic Convoy System*, CB 1515-15 *Convoy Statistics*, CB 1515-16 *Convoy Defence*, CB 1515-17 *Convoy Supplement*, CB 1515-18 *Convoy Supplement* and CB 1515-*40 Anti-Submarine Development*. **6** 'the responsibility for Coastal…', Moretz, p.262. **7** 'Sinking submarines is a bonus…', Terraine, *Business*, p.87, quoting Marder, *FTDTSF*, vol. V, p.103. **8** 'at times they complained of lack…', Michelsen, p.138. **9** 'Throughout the war, only 12…', Herwig, *Luxury*, p.219. **10** 'many of the boats never saw active…', Michelsen, p.139. **11** von Mann, Edler von Tiechler (1864–1934), Chief Inspector of Torpedo Technology before being nominated to take the position at the new U-Boat office. In October 1918, he took over from Paul von Behncke as State Secretary for the Imperial Navy and in November selected the U-boat that threatened the mutinous sailors at Kiel. **12** According to Gray (*U Boat War*, p.241), another 273 boats were ordered. **13** Letter to kaiser, 21 September; Marder, *FTDTSF*, vol. V, p.108. **14** Source: Weir, *Building*, p.175. **15** 'determination to continue…', Weir, p.275. **16** Source: Gray, *U Boat War*, p.249. **17** 'Actually the rise in ships sunk…', Grove, p.4. **18** See ADM 116/1807. Geddes correspondence, Vol. 4. 'Report by the Director Statistics', Admiralty, 21 May 1918. **19** 'gloomy reading', 'encourage potential enemies', Koerver, *Eyes*, quoting NA, ADM 116/3421, p.11. **20** 'the seafaring resources of Great Britain', Churchill, *World Crisis*, p.736. **21** 'I have urged time after time…', *FTDTSF*, vol. IV, p.68. **22** Source: Watson, p.436. **23** 'Self-satisfied, the Admiralty…', Uhlig, *Submarine*, p.152. **24** 'the shipbuilding industry…', Michelsen, p.106. **25** Source: Barnett, *How Successfully?* **26** See Jellicoe, *CONW*, pp.47–48. **27** Source: Wilson, *Avian ASW*, p.5. **28** 'dismal', Marder, *FTDTSF*, vol. IV, p.65. **29** Source: Marder, *FTDTSF*, vol. IV, p.184. **30** Source: Watson, p.449. **31** 'relieved the insurance market…', Marder, *FTDTSF*, vol. IV, p.133. **32** 'concerned with the protection…', Marder, *FTDTSF*, vol. IV, p.133. **33** 'the first elements of the problem', Marder, *FTDTSF*, vol. IV, p.134. **34** Source: Michelsen, pp.155–56. **35** 'ground maize, lentils, peas…', Watson, p.334. **36** 'offered no guarantee that…', Scriba, p.179. **37** 'how queues of 600 or 800…', Watson, p.330, quoting from Anna Kohnstern's letters. **38** 'drowning in rainwater', Koerver, *Assault*, p.197. **39** Source: Dr Helen Boak, quoting David Welch, *Germany and Propaganda in World War 1* (2000), p.128. **40** Source: Watson, pp.338–39. **41** 'look more like Mongolians…', Dr Alfred Grotjahn, diary, 17 March 1916, quoted in Scriba, p.180. **42** Source: Dr Helen Boak. **43** Source: Franken, *Bachmann*, p.845. **44** Source: Watson, p.332. **45** Padfield, *Naval Race*, cites 1,100 by the summer of 1917 (p.340). **46** 'at its lowest point in 1917…', Philips. **47** 'only permitted for…', Franken, *Bachmann*, p.858. **48** 'the beginning of the end…', Massie, *Dreadnought*, p.453. **49** Source: Marder, *FTDTSF*, vol. IV, p.63. **50** 'limited impact on overall calories', Watson, p.435. **51** Source: Holger Herwig, University of Calgary, *The Failed U-Boat War: One Good Reason (From Total Rhetoric, Unlimited War)*. **52** 'Britain increased imports…', Boyd, p.211. **53** 'to make the production…', Heal, p.392. **54** 'long-standing antagonisms…', Davis, p.5/11a. **55** 'an estimated one third…', source Dr Helen Boak, quoting Decie Denholm (ed.), *Behind the Lines, One Woman's War 1914–1918* (London, 1982), p.165. **56** '*Der Schleichhandel ist die…*', Davis, *Naval Blockades*, p.6. **57** 'per capita caloric…', Herwig, *Total Rhetoric*. **58** Source: Heal, p.389. Another study is closer to 300,000 (Hull, *Scrap of Paper*, p.168). Grebler, *Cost of the War*, p.78, used an estimate of 424,000. Heal explained that the Board of Public Health estimate was made by comparing actual civilian deaths during each of the war years with those of 1913. **59** 'German insurance companies reported…', Heal, p.390, quoting NA, FO 382/1836, f. 11663, 'Germany/Blockade', 9.1.18, Howard, *Social and Political Consequences*, p.165. **60** Dr Helen Boak, *Food and the First World War in Germany*, 29 April 2015. **61** Source: Dr Helen Boak, quoting Regulski, pp.319–20 (tuberculosis), Tobin, p.292 (Dusseldorf dysentery) and Chickering, p.144 (rickets). Full details in the article's bibliography. **62** '*Aber auch meine Eltern…*', Valentiner, p.137. **63** 'his temples had caved-in…', Valentiner, p.137. **64** 'Even the success of the German…', Holland, *100 Years*. **65** 'For now the most important…', Uhlig, *Revolution*, p.141. **66** 'British Antisubmarine craft…', Baxter, *The Atlantic Magazine*. **67** 'in the early stages…', Parkin, p.51. **68** 'It was clear beyond reasonable…', Dimbleby, p.109. **69** 'They were exasperating, futile days…', Macintyre, pp.18–19. **70** 'I might say in this connection…', Macintyre, p.58. **71** 'correctly estimated…', *Atlantic Trade Protection*, TNA, ADM 1/9466. **72** Sir Arthur Harris, Air Chief Marshal. **73** Admiral Sir Dudley Pound (1877–1943), served at Jutland (HMS *Colossus*), First Sea Lord 1939–43. **74** 'to divert [the RAF's bombers]…', Parkin, p.169.

**9 Was Jellicoe the Right Man for the Job?**

**1** 'he was better endowed…', Marder, *FTDTSF*, vol. IV, p.58. **2** 'in many ways…', Black, *British Naval Staff*, p.188. **3** 'failed … to get to grips…', Gordon, *Rules*, p.531. **4** 'reducing maritime supply…', Boyd, p.212. **5** 'I am distressed to hear of…', letter, Sims to Jellicoe, 29 December 1917, BL, Add MSS 49036. **6** 'the greatest allied triumph', Jameson, *Formidable*, p.238. **7** 'He may have been slow to decide…', Jameson, *Formidable*, p.237. **8** 'assumed the aspect of a thorn…', Leighton, p.66. **9** 'intellectually brilliant…', Jellicoe, *JUB*, p.42. **10** 'He was one of the most simple…', Bacon, *Jellicoe*, p.522. **11** 'His voluminous writings…', McKillip, p.19. **12** 'it illustrates how Britain…', Gordon, p.532. **13** Bacon (*Jellicoe*, p.378) categorically defended Haig saying that it was not pressure from him that persuaded Lloyd George to get rid of Jellicoe: 'Anything more foreign to Sir Douglas' general reserve and discretion can hardly be imagined.' He should look at the general's diaries more carefully: in the same footnote, he said there was nothing in his papers or diaries that 'gives the slightest colour to such a statement'. **14** 'the advocacy of younger officers…', Liddell Hart, p.402. **15** 'While Jellicoe was calm…', Yates, p.212. **16** 'the supreme moment in naval war', Corbett, quoted by Massie, *Castles of Steel*, p.613. **17** 'did not show the Nelson…', Bacon, *Jellicoe*, p.523. **18** Until Italy's declaration of war on 28 August 1916, Italy's exports through Switzerland of silk (for aircraft manufacture), vegetables and fruits (particularly lemons to fight scurvy) aided Germany's attempt to loosen the ever-tightening blockade. **19** 'conscientiousness combined with a distrust…', Hough, *GWAS*, p.305. **20** 'Jellicoe's determination…', Goldrick, *After Jutland*, p.57. **21** 'was a man of great ability…', Jameson, *Formidable*, p.207. **22** 'had a great objection…', Bacon, *Jellicoe*, pp.509–10. **23** 'he did not expect to last twelve months…', Brownrigg, pp.67–68. **24** In 1909, the Admiralty (Fisher and Jellicoe) had clashed with David Lloyd George and Winston Churchill over the number of dreadnoughts in the Naval Estimates. **25** Wemyss praised the portfolio but criticised their use: Jellicoe's 'knowledge of material, however, has stood his successor in good stead, and I found at hand mines, vessels, depth charges, etc, *which only required to be put to a proper use* [author's italics]' (Wemyss, p.370). **26** 'war is largely a matter…', Jellicoe, *CONW*, p.3. **27** 'Amateurs talk about tactics…', General Robert Barrow, Commandant, USMC, 1980. **28** 'laid the foundations…', Black, *Naval Staff*, p.173. **29** 'reports published regularly…', McCartney, *Paying the Prize*, p.44. **30** 'responsible for all naval air matters…', Hobbs, p.239. **31** 'No single countermeasure', Lautenschlager, p.113. **32** 'it was not until 1918…', Jellicoe, *CONW*, p.246. **33** The percentage attributed to mines varies: Spindler 22 per cent (thirty-seven out of 166 subs sunk by enemy action). **34** 'resulting at once…', Grant, *Known Sunk*. **35** Source: Bacon, *Jellicoe*, p.352. **36** 'The average [rate of sinkings]…', Taussig, p.174. **37** Winton, *Convoy*, p.42, quoting Jellicoe, 'Memorandum on Submnarine Warfare', 29 October 1916. **38** '11 submarines were sunk…', Grant, *Known Sunk*. **39** Source: Krause, pp.75–78. **40** '*SS41* reported that she…', Goldrick, *After Jutland*, p.80. **41** According to Norman Friedman (*Armaments and Innovation*), Jellicoe's letter was in December 1914. The Mk II Cruiser mine was preset to explode with a hydrostatic valve at a depth of 45ft and tested in the Firth of Forth in September 1914. **42** 'At Jellicoe's request…', McKee, p.49. **43** Beesly, *Room 40*, pp.41–45; also Michael Dockrill and David French (eds), *Strategy and Intelligence: British Policy During the First World War* (London: Hambledon Press, 1996), pp.33–45; Patrick Beesly, 'British Naval Intelligence in Two World Wars: Some Similarities and Differences', in Christopher Andrew and Jeremy Noakes (eds), *Intelligence and International Relations, 1900–1945* (Exeter: University of Exeter, 1987), pp.253–73; and David Ramsay, *'Blinker' Hall: Spymaster – The Man Who Brought America into World War I* (Brimscome Port, Gloucestershire: The History Press, 2010), pp.163–64. **44** 'the door was now opened wide…', Goldrick, *After Jutland*, p.159, quoting Naval Staff Monographs, Vol. 19, *Home Waters*, Part 9, p.159. **45** The workload on Captain Herbert Hope in ID25 overwhelmed him. In May 1917, he had to be replaced as he had 'broken down' from the strain (see Hall to Beatty, 18 May 1917, ADM 223/768, quoted in Black, *British Naval Staff*, p.187). **46** There was also direct telephone communication between the British and French Admiralties, but less confidence in sharing information. **47** Kittredge, 'Outline of Organization', 1. **48** 'given entire freedom…', Naumes, *Anglo-American ASW*, p.124. **49** Tracy Barrett Kittredge (1891–1957) served on the Staff of Admiral Sims in London from 1917–19. He had earlier established ties with Royal Navy Volunteer Reserve (RNVR) Lieutenant Commander Frank Birch. Connections among former Oxford and Cambridge students also placed Kittredge in the same circles as RNVR commanders Alastair Denniston, Nigel de Grey and other key cryptologists in Room 40 OB at the Admiralty. After the war (1921), he wrote about his experiences (*Certain Naval Lessons of the Great War*). His papers are held by Stanford University. **50** 'at the British Admiralty…', Grant, *Hunters*, p.40, quoting Dorwart, *Office of Naval Intelligence*, p.123. **51** 'Contrary to folklore, Jellicoe…', Ireland, *U-Boat Crisis*, p.24. **52** 'late adoption of convoy', Goldrick, *After Jutland*, p.278. **53** 'magic wand', Terraine, *Business*, p.61. **54** 'I am convinced convoy system…', Naumes, *Anglo-American ASW*, p.130. **55** Jellicoe, *CONW*, p.159. **56** 'still viewed arming merchant vessels…', Naumes, *Anglo-American ASW*, p.129. **57** 'Just discussed your and Sims's…', Naumes, *Anglo-American ASW*, pp.130–31. **58** 'effective in greatly reducing losses', Jellicoe, *CONW*, p.159. **59** 'I am getting very concerned…', Marder, *FTDTSF*, vol. V, p.107. **60** 'Up to May of this year submarines…', Marder, *FTDTSF*, vol. V, p.109, quoting Geddes, 'Notes for Guidance as to the Line to be Adopted in Conference with United States Navy Department and in Informal conversations', September 1918, Geddes MSS. **61** Gibson & Prendergast, p.373. The following U-boats are listed sunk for September 1917: 2 Sep, *UC.41* (depth-charged by trawlers); 2 Sep, *U.28* (lost); 7 Sep, *U.88* (mined); 10 Sep, *UC.42* (blown up by German mine); 11 Sep, *U.49* (gunfire from SS *British Transport*); 12 Sep, *U.45* (torpedoed by HMS *D.7*); 22 Sep, *UC.72* (spotted by seaplane 8695 and successfully bombed); 26 Sep, *UC.33* (gunfire from and rammed by *PC.61*); 27 Sep, *UC.21* (caught in mine nets); 28 Sep, *UC.6* (bombed by seaplane 8676); 29 Sep, *UC.55* (gunfire from and depth-charged by destroyers. Gray (*U-boat War*, p.224) put the number destroyed at thirteen. *UC.6* had once had to use sails to get back to Germany. On 23 July 1916, she had an engine breakdown near the Thames Estuary, using the periscope as the 'mast' and a boathook as the 'spinnaker'. **62** 'The English version that the submarine…', Spindler, *Value*. **63** 'the worst was definitely over…', Marder, *FTDTSF*, vol. V, p.80. **64** 'In the last twelve months, the British had made…', Fürbringer, p.117. **65** The monthly average in previous years was 1914, 1; 1915, 1.59; 1916, 1.83; and 1917, 5.17 (source: Marder, *FTDTSF*, vol. V, p.82). **66** From April–June 1918, German training schools trained twenty-seven commanding officers, fifty-five watch officers and an equal number of engineers. Officer training was for three months, the same time also for machinists and helmsmen. Watch officers also needed to be torpedo specialists. By September 1918, the force consisted of the front-line submarines plus around twenty training subs, the target ship SMS *Stettin*, mother ship SMS *Meteor*, a diving tug, fourteen steamers and seventeen older torpedo boats. **67** '*Um mich veränderte sich…*', Valentiner, pp.229–30. **68** Source: Spindler, *Value*. **69** Source: Michelsen, p.146. **70** Gleaves (*Naval Review*) quotes a slightly lower but maybe more precise number for the total losses – 515 officers and 4,849 warrant officers and men. **71** Source: Krause, p.79. **72** Source: Cayzer Archives. Higher human losses were incurred by the Clan Line by the end of the Second World War: 100 officers, thirty-three gunners and ratings and 508 lascars. The loss of ships – thirty seven – was also higher. **73** '*Rechnet man die Kräfte…*', Krause, p.80. **74** 'including ten battleships…', Herzog and Saville. **75** '54 bases, stations…', Still, p.143. **76** 'That is why I regard…', Bacon, *Jellicoe*, p.271.

**Appendices A–J**

**1** 'of the fourteen older boats…', Thomas, *Raiders*, p.39. **2** Source: Valentiner, p.81. Valentiner's claim seems rather exaggerated: over the two months, November–December 1915, he said he managed to sink 60,681 GRT. Nevertheless, in June he only narrowly missed sinking HMS *Roxburgh*, which he had hit with a single torpedo. **3** 'feeble instruments…', Terraine, *Business*, p.20. **4** 'the first boat of the Flotilla to come…', Fürbringer, pp.15–16. **5** 'only one fourth the size of the newer U-boats…', Harris, p.183. Eighteen months might have been optimistic: O'Hara estimates construction times being 'between seventeen and twenty-four months'. **6** 'astonishingly quickly', Hashagen, p.58. **7** Heimburg's next command, *UB.15*, did the same, becoming *U.XI*. **8** 'I was knocked sprawling as the boat…', Heal, p.215. **9** 'especially for the Mediterranean', O'Hara, Dickson and Worth, p.109. **10** 'It was not until *UB.48*, the precursor of the *Type VII…*', Gough, *Titans*, p.80. **11** 'first cruise of a minelayer from Flanders…', Grant, *Hunters*, pp.43–44. **12** Only twenty-seven of the first seventy-nine survived the war (Gray, *U Boat War*, p.195). **13** Source: Koerver, p.141. **14** 'gun in the dip between…', ID

1176. **15** 'the most successful…', source: Wikipedia, quoting Helgason, 'U-boat War in World War One', Uboat.net. **16** Source: Sondhaus (Kindle loc 1498). **17** Messimer, *The Merchant U-Boat*, p.64. **18** Messimer, *The Merchant U-Boat*, p.196. **19** 'shaped like that of a sleek destroyer', Botting, p.33. **20** 'thirty six men…', Valentiner, p.244. **21** 'an extremely delicate balance…', Forstner, *Journal*. **22** 'composed of practically fresh water', Forstner, *Journal*. **23** 'hydrostatic safety system which…', Forstner, *Journal*. **24** 'while the fastest surface…', Goldrick, *After Jutland*, p.45. **25** 'when on the surface one man…', Liddle, p.93. **26** 'that she reached 180 feet…', Gray, *Captains*, p.85. **27** 'seven years after the French', Koerver, *Assault*, p.148. **28** Source: correspondence, 24 August 2023, Enrico Cernuschi. **29** 'a form of propulsion which endured…', Hough, *GWAS*, p.170. **30** 'any German submarine design…', Goldrick, *After Jutland*, pp.48–49. **31** 'we went off sailing…', Thomas, *Raiders*, p.17. **32** 'I literally gasped for air…', Schultz, p.2. **33** 'it drowned any attempt at speech…', Neureuther and Bergen, p.63. **34** 'While one engine remained…', Schultz, p.86. **35** 'to absorb the poisonous carbon monoxide…', Fürbringer, p.23. **36** 'the best remedy was to wrap…', Fürbringer, p.23. **37** 'required hourly only fifteen litres…', Forstner, *Journal*. **38** 'Everything else lost its importance…', Gray, *U Boat War*, pp.149–50. **39** 'Because of the escorts…', Uhlig, *Submarine*, p.154. **40** 'had toyed with…', Herwig, *Luxury Fleet*, p.228. **41** Source: Herwig, *Luxury Fleet*, pp.228–29. **42** 'Even in 1917, Bauer…', Owen, p.43. **43** Source: Watson, p.438. **44** 'Bayly … forecast the adoption…', Simpson, *Sims & Bayly*, p.75. **45** 'we have heard submarines…', Taussig, p.17. **46** 'Too late, *Durango* awaits you…', Robinson, *Rose*, p.178. **47** 'he had sunk one ship…', Grant, *Intelligence*, p.11. **48** 'more shipping was saved…', Grant, *Intelligence*, p.12. **49** 'notably, Weg Gelb, Weg Grün…', Halpern, *Naval History*, p.345. **50** 'they *had* to give a position…', Grant, *Intelligence*, p.18. **51** The wreck of *U.51* was raised in 1968. **52** 'The scratches on the steel walls…', Neureuther and Berger, p.145. **53** 'broke out two code letters…', Clark, *When the U-Boats*, p.27. **54** 'When a steamer is stopped…', Valentiner, p.116. **55** 'but if it exceed[ed] half…', Forstner, *Journal*. **56** 'the torpedo did not come into general…', Jellicoe, *CONW*, p.7. **57** 'I took revenge for our fright…', Spiess, p.59. **58** Sims (*Victory*, p.84) noted the average cost of a torpedo at around $8,000. **59** 'the issue of the next naval war…', Jameson, *The Fleet*, p.97. **60** 'what is normally referred to…', Henry, *Depth Charge*, Kindle Location 233. **61** 'doubled', Sondhaus, Kindle Location 359. **62** 'He is so placed that his range of vision…', Forstner, *Journal*. **63** 'It was seldom effective if fired…', Sims, *Victory*, p.89. **64** 'When a dozen yards away…', Thomas, *Raiders*, p.155. **65** On another occasion, 'He was once torpedoed just outside of Bocche, and the enemy U-boat had fired a whole burst of torpedoes. And the unbelievable happened: one torpedo passed under the boat, the second jumped over it and bent the railing, the third went to the right and the fourth to the left, and a fifth shaved the stern' (von Trapp, p.147).

# Bibliography

(*Books thus marked have Forewords written by Admiral of the Fleet, Earl Jellicoe. Not all books have been used as source material.)


Antibello, John J., *Anti-Submarine Warfare in World War I. British Naval Aviation and the Defeat of the U-Boats* (Routledge, 2006)

Arthur, Max, *Lost Voices of the Royal Navy* (Hodder, 2005 edition)

Aspinall-Oglander, Cecil, *Keyes: Being the Biography of Admiral of the Fleet Lord Keyes of Zeebrugge and Dover* (Hogarth, 1951)

Bacon, Admiral Sir Reginald H., *The Concise History of the Dover Patrol* (Hutchinson, 1932)*

Bacon, Admiral Sir Reginald H., *The Life of John Rushworth Earl Jellicoe* (Cassell, 1936)

Bacon, Admiral Sir Reginald H., *The Life of Lord Fisher of Kilverstone*, vol. 1 (Hodder & Stoughton, 1919)

Ball, Christine and Hudson, Nicky, *The Effects of Rationing on the Home Front 1914–1918* (West Sussex County Council War Project)

Ballantyne, Iain, *The Deadly Trade: The Complete History of Submarine Warfare from Archimedes to the Present* (Weidenfeld & Nicolson, 2018)

Barnes, Lt Cdr Robert H., 'German Submarine Action in World War I', *United States Naval Institute Proceedings* (October 1942)

Barnett, Len, 'How Successfully did Britain Respond to German Unrestricted U-boat Warfare in 1917 and 1918?', part of Master's Degree in War Studies, King's College, London (1999, amended 2014)

Barnett, Margaret, *British Food Policy During the First World War* (Google Books, originally George Allen & Unwin, 1985)

Baxter, James Phinney, 'The Seesaw of Submarine Warfare', *The Atlantic Magazine* (August 1946)

Bayly, Admiral Sir Lewis, *Pull Together! Memoirs* (George Harrap, 1939)

Beesly, Patrick, *Room 40: British Naval Intelligence 1914–1918* (Harcourt Brace Jovanovich, 1982)

Bennett, Geoffrey, *Naval Battles of the First World War* (Pan Books, 1968)

Ben-Yehuda, Nachman, *Atrocity, Deviance and Submarine Warfare. Norms and Practices During the World Wars* (University of Michigan Press, 2013, Kindle edition)

Black, Jeremy, *Naval Warfare: A Global History since 1860* (Rowman & Littlefield, 2017)

Black, Nicholas, *The British Naval Staff in the First World War* (Boydell Press, 2009)

Blackwood, Captain Henry RN, 'Q Ship sinks U-Boat', *Naval Historical Review* (September 1966)

Blazrich, Frank A. Jnr, *The United States Navy and World War I:1914–1922, An Annotated timeline* (Naval History and Heritage Command)

Boak, Dr Helen, *Food and the First World War in Germany* (ELIW Center Research, 29 April 2015)

Botting, Douglas, *The U-boats*, part of 'The Seafarers' series of books (Time Life Books, 1979)

Boyd, Andrew, *British Naval Intelligence Through the Twentieth Century* (Seaforth, 2020)

Brady, Karl, 'U-Boat Losses off the Irish Coast', *Archaeology Ireland*, vol. 23, no. 3 (Autumn, 2009), pp.22–25

Breemer, Dr Jan S., *Before Convoys – Britain's Failed Anti-Submarine Warfare* (Road to the Great War.com, August 2017)

Breemer, Dr Jan S., *Defeating the U-boat: Inventing Antisubmarine Warfare*, Naval War College Newport Papers, no. 36 (United States Naval War College, 2010)

Brodie, Bernard, *A Layman's Guide to Naval Strategy* (Princeton University Press, 1943)

Brown, Simon, *The Story of UB.116: The First 100 Years* (Apple Books, 2018)

Brunciardi, Daire, 'The U.S. Navy at Queenstown', *History Ireland*, Issue 3, vol. XXV (May–June 2017)

Bruton, Elizabeth, *Anglo-American developments in anti-submarine warfare during World War One* (academia.edu)

Bruton, Elizabeth and Coleman, Paul, 'Listening in the Dark: Audio surveillance, communication technologies, and the submarine threat during the First World War', *History and Technology*, vol. 32, no. 3, pp.245–268

Buehrig, Edward H., 'Freedom of the Seas: 1917, 1941', *Journal of Politics* (February 1944)

Burke, Arthur E., *Torpedoes and Their Impact on Naval Warfare* (Naval Undersea Warfare Center Division, Newport, 2017)

Bywater, Hector, *Their Secret Purposes: Dramas and Mysteries of the Naval War* (Constable, 1932)

Bywater, Hector and Ferraby, H.C., *Strange Intelligence: Memoirs of Naval Secret Service* (Constable, 1931)

Chalmers, Rear Admiral W.S., *The Life and Letters of David, Earl Beatty, Admiral of the Fleet* (Hodder & Stoughton, 1951)

Chamberlin, Dr Waldo, 'German Naval Strategy in 1914', *United States Naval Institute Proceedings* (September 1940)

Charles River Editors, *Submarine Warfare in World War I: The History and Legacy of German U-boats and Allied Efforts to Counter Them* (CreateSpace, 2018)

Chatterton, E. Keeble, *The Big Blockade* (Hurst & Blackett, 1932)

Cheser, S. Matthew (with support from Prof David Kohnen, Hattendorf Centre), *The Sinking of the Jacob Jones. Toughness and Sacrifice in the North Atlantic* (History and Heritage Command, NHHC, November 2017)

Chickering, Roger, *Imperial Germany and the Great War 1914–1918* (Cambridge 3rd edn, 2014)

Clark, William Bell, *When the U-Boats Came to America* (Little, Brown and Co, 1929)

Clarke, William F., 'Elements of Cryptoanalysis' (manuscript, HW 3/15)

Clarke, William F., 'History of Room OB.40' (manuscript)

Colvin, Ian, *The Life of Lord Carson*, vol. 3 (Victor Gollancz, 1983)

Consett, Rear Admiral M.W.W.P., *The Triumph of Unarmed Forces (1914–1918)* (Williams & Norgate, 1923)

Crossley, Jim, *The Hidden Threat: Mines and Minesweeping in WWI* (Seaforth, 2011)

D'Amico, Angela and Pittenger, Richard, 'A Brief History of Active Sonar', *Aquatic Mammals*, 35(4) (2009)

Daniels, Josephus, *Our Navy at War* (Washington, Pictorial Bureau, 1922)

Davies, David, *A Brief History of Fighting Ships. Ships of the Line and the Napoleonic sea battles 1793–1815* (Robinson, 2002)

Davis, Belinda, *Food and Nutrition (Germany)* (International Encyclopedia, online, 1914–1918)

Davis, Lance E. and Engerman, Stanley L., *Naval Blockades in Peace and War: An Economic History Since 1750* (Cambridge University Press, 2007)

Dewar, Vice Admiral Kenneth G.B., *The Navy From Within* (Victor Gollancz, 1939)

Dimbleby, Jonathan, *The Battle of the Atlantic: How the Allies Won the War* (Penguin, 2015)

Dinneen, James, 'Reginald Fessenden and the Invention of Sonar: How a Radio Pioneer transformed life at sea', *Science History Institute* (19 May 2020)

Doughty, Lieutenant Commander Leonard Jr, USN, 'The Effect of Depth Charges on Submarines', *United States Naval Institute Proceedings*, vol. 61/3/385 (March 1935)

Downing, Taylor, *Secret Warriors: Key Scientists, Code Breakers and Propagandists of the Great War* (Little, Brown, 2014)

Dreyer, Admiral Sir Frederic, *The Sea Heritage: A Study in Maritime Warfare* (Museum Press, 1955)

Duncan, Francis, 'Deutschland – Merchant Submarine', United States Naval Institute Proceedings, vol. 91/4/746 (April 1965)

Dunley, Richard, *Anti-Submarine Warfare in the Pre-First World War Royal Navy: A Cultural Failure?* (University of New South Wales, Canberra, 2019)

Dunn, Steve, *Bayly's War: The Battle for the Western Approaches in the First World War* (Seaforth, 2018)

Dunn, Steve, *Blockade: Cruiser Warfare and the Starvation of Germany in World War One* (Seaforth, 2016)

Dunn, Steve, *Southern Thunder: The Royal Navy and the Scandinavian Trade in World War One* (Seaforth, 2019)

Everitt, Don, *The K Boats* (George Harrap, 1963)

Ewing, A.W., *The Man from Room 40: The Life of Sir Alfred Ewing* (Hutchinson, 1939; 1940 edn)

Fayle, C. Ernst, *Official History of the Great War (Seaborne Trade); Vol. II. The Submarine Campaign (From the Opening of the Campaign to the Appointment of a Shipping Controller); Vol. III. Seaborne Trade. Submarine Warfare*

Fisher, Admiral of the Fleet Lord, *Memories* (Hodder & Stoughton, 1919)

Forstner, Georg-Günther von, *The Journal of Submarine Commander von Forstner* (1916, trans. Anna Crafts Codman)

Friedman, Norman, 'Armaments & Innovations – Crude But Effective in Large Doses', *Naval History Magazine*, vol. 30, no. 1 (February 2016)

Friedman, Norman, 'The Great Mine Barrage', *Naval History Magazine* (October 2016)

Frost, Lt Cdr H.H., USN, 'The Attack on Zeebrugge', *United States Naval Institute Proceedings*, vol. 55/3/313 (March 1929)

Frost, Gary L., 'The Making and Selling of the Fessenden Oscillator', *Technology and Culture*, vol. 42, no. 3 (July 2001), pp.462–88

Frost, Wesley, *German Submarine Warfare. A Study of its Methods and Spirit. Including the Crime of the Lusitania. A Record of Observations and Evidence* (D. Appleton and Co., New York, 1918)

Fürbringer, Konteradmiral Werner, *FIPS. Legendary U-Boat Commander*, trans. and ed. Geoffrey Brooks (Leo Cooper, 1999)

Furer, Commander J.A., 'The 110-Foot Submarine Chasers and Eagle Boats', *United States Naval Institute Proceedings*, vol. 45/5/195 (May 1919)

Gade, John A., book review, Consett, *Triumph of Unarmed Forces, The American Historical Review*, vol. 29, no. 2 (January 1924), pp.333–35

Gannon, Paul, *Inside Room 40: The Codebreakers of World War One* (Ian Allan, 2010)

Gayer, Kapitän A. (trans. Cdr W.P. Boehler, USN ret'd), 'Summary of German Submarine Operations in Various Theatres of War from 1914–1918', *United States Naval Institute Proceedings*, vol. 52/4/278 (April 1926)

Gibson, R.H. and Prendergast, Maurice, *The German Submarine War 1914–1918* (Constable, 1931)*

Gleaves, Admiral Albert, book review, Gibson and Prendergast, *United States Naval Institute Proceedings*, vol. 58/1/347 (January 1932).

Goldstone, Lawrence, *Going Deep: John Philip Holland and the Invention of the Attack Submarine* (Pegasus Books, New York, 2017)

Goll, Nicole-Melanie, 'Our Weddigen. On the Construction of the War Hero in the k.u.k. Army. The Naval Hero Egon Lerch as an Example', in Bischof, Günter, Karlhofer, Ferdinand and Williamson, Samuel R., *Austria-Hungary, the Origins, and the First Year of World War I* (University of New Orleans Press, 2014)

Goldrick, RADM James, RAN (ret'd), *After Jutland: The Naval War in Northern European Waters, June 1916–November 1918* (Seaforth, 2018)

Goldrick, RADM James, RAN (ret'd), 'Anti-access for Sea Control: The British Mining Campaign of World War I', *Naval History* (October 2018)

Goldrick, RADM James, RAN (ret'd), 'Before (and After) Jutland', Anderson Medal Lecture (20 April 1917)

Goldrick, RADM James, RAN (ret'd), *Before Jutland: The Naval War in Northern European Waters August 1914 – February 1915* (Naval Institute Press, 2015)

Goldrick, RADM James and Hattendorf, John B., *Mahan is not Enough. The Proceedings of a Conference on the Works of Sir Julian Corbett and Admiral Sir Herbert Richmond* (Naval War College Press, 1993)

Gompert, David C., Binnendijk, Hans and Lin, Bonny, 'Germany's Decision to Conduct Unrestricted

U-boat Warfare, 1916', in *Blinders, Blunders, and Wars: What America and China Can Learn* (RAND Corporation, 2014)

Gompert, David C., Binnendijk, Hans and Lin, Bonny, 'Woodrow Wilson's Decision to Enter World War I, 1917', in *Blinders, Blunders, and Wars: What America and China Can Learn*. (RAND Corporation, 2014)

Gordon, Andrew, *The Rules of the Game: Jutland and British Naval Command* (John Murray, 1996)

Götter, Christian, 'From a Militarily to a Politically Enforced Instrument. The Development of the Allied Blockade During the First World War', *Les Cahiers Sirice*, 2021/1, no. 26, vol. 64/1/419 (January 1938), pp.59–71

Gough, Barry, *Churchill and Fisher: Titans at the Admiralty* (Seaforth, 2017)

Gould, S.W., 'Submarine Warfare in the Adriatic', *United States Naval Institute Proceedings*, vol. 70/6/496 (June 1944)

Grant, Robert M., 'Known Sunk – German Submarine War Losses, 1914–1918', *United States Naval Institute Proceedings* (January 1938)

Grant, Robert M., *U-Boats Destroyed: The Effects of Anti-Submarine Warfare 1914–1918* (Putnam, 1964)

Grant, Robert M., *U-Boat Hunters, Code Breakers, Divers and the Defeat of the U-Boats, 1914–1918* (Naval Institute Press, reprint Periscope Press, 2003)

Grant, Robert M., *U-Boat Intelligence 1914–1918* (Archon Books, 1969)

Grant, Robert M., 'The Use of Mines Against Submarines', *United States Naval Institute Proceedings*, vol. 64/9/427 (September 1938)

Gray, Edwyn, *Captains of War* (Leo Cooper, 1988); portraits of Spiegel, Weddigen and de la Perière

Gray, Edwyn, *The U Boat War 1914–1918* (Leo Cooper, 1994)

Greig, I.T., 'The Convoy System and the Two Battles of the Atlantic (1914–18 and 1939–45)', The South African Military History Society (*Die Suid-Afrikaanse Krygshistoriese Vereniging*), *Military History Journal*, vol. 6, no. 4 (December 1984)

Grieves, Keith, *Sir Eric Geddes: Business and Government in War and Peace* (Manchester University Press, 1989)

Grigg, John, *Lloyd George: War Leader* (Allen Lane, 2002)

Grove, Prof Eric, *The Defeat of the Enemy Attack on Shipping (Ch.1 Some Lessons from the First World War)* (Navy Records Society, 1997)

Hackmann, Willem D., *Seek & Destroy: Sonar, Anti-Submarine warfare and the Royal Navy 1914–1954* (HMSO, 1984)

Hackmann, Willem D., 'Sonar Research and Naval Warfare 1914–1954: A Case Study of a Twentieth-Century Establishment Science', *Historical Studies in the Physical and Biological Sciences*, vol. 16, no. 1 (University of California Press, 1986), pp.83–110

Halpern, Prof Paul G., *A Naval History of World War I* (US Naval Institute, 1995)

Halpern, Prof Paul G. (ed.), *The Keyes Papers. Vol I, 1914–1918* (The Navy Records Society, 1972)

Harley, Rear Admiral Jeffrey, *Admiral William Sowden Sims, USN and the Special Relationship: A Study in Coalition Warfare* (University of Reading, 2021)

Harris, Brayton,*The Navy Times Book of Submarines: A Political, Social and Military History* (Berkley Books, New York, 1997)

Hashagen, Ernst, trans. Lt Cdr Vesey Ross, *U-Boats Westward!* (G Putnam, 1931)

Hawkins, Nigel, *The Starvation Blockades: Naval Blockades of WWI* (Pen & Sword, Barnsley, 2002)

Heal, Chris, *Sound of Hunger: One German Family's Chronicle of Chivalry, Politics, Lies, Murder and the Aftermath of War* (Uniform, 2018)

Hendrick, Burton, *The World's Work: Admiral Sims's Own Story* (1919; serialisation of *Victory at Sea*)

Henry, Chris, *Depth Charge: Royal Naval Mines, Depth Charges and Underwater Weapons 1914–1945* (Pen & Sword, 2021)

Herwig, Holger H., *Luxury Fleet: The Imperial German Navy 1888–1918* (Humanity Books, 1987)

Herwig, Holger H., 'Total Rhetoric, Limited War: Germany's U-Boat Campaigns 1917–1918', *Journal of Military and Strategic Studies*, vol. I, no. 1 (1998)

Hill, David Jayne, 'The Correspondence Regarding the SS Sussex', *The American Journal of International Law*, vol. 10, no. 3 (July 1916), pp.556–60, published by Cambridge University Press

Hobbs, David, *The Royal Navy's Air Service in the Great War* (Seaforth, 2017)

Hoffman, Michael Harris, 'Neutral mariners and humanitarian law: a precedent for protecting neutrals in

armed conflict', The War at Sea, speech to the American Red Cross based on an article on customary law and non-international armed conflict (*The Review*, July–August 1990)
Holland, Rear Admiral William J. Jr, USN (Ret), '100 Years of Submarines', *United States Naval Institute Proceedings*, vol. 126/1/1,163 (January 2000)
Hone, Tom, *A World War One Naval Officer's Story* (WarontheRocks, September 2013)
Hore, Captain Peter, *From Dreadnought to Daring: 100 Years of Comment, Controversy and Debate in the Naval Review* (Seaforth, 2012)
Hore, Captain Peter, *The Habit of Victory: The Story of the Royal Navy 1545 to 1945* (Sidgwick & Jackson, 2005)
Hough, Richard, *First Sea Lord: An Authorized Biography of Admiral Lord Fisher* (George Allen & Unwin, 1969)
Hough, Richard, *The Great War at Sea 1914–1918 (GWAS)* (Oxford University Press, 1983)
Howlett, Alexander, *The Royal Naval Air Service and Anti-Submarine Warfare in the North Sea, 1917–1918*, King's College, London, presented at McMullen Naval History Symposium, United States Naval Academy, Annapolis (14–15 September 2017)
Howlett, Alexander, *Unrestricted Submarine Warfare, 1917–1918*, post (5 July 2019)
Hoy, Hugh Cleland, *40 O.B. or How the War Was Won* (Hutchinson & Co, 1932)
Hurd, Archibald, *The British Fleet in the First World War* (Constable & Company, 1918), 'The Menace of the Submarine', pp.187–227
Hurd, Archibald, *The Clan Line in the First World War* (private printing by Cassell, 1924)
Hurd, Archibald, 'Torpedoed in the North Sea, HMS Hawke sunk by German Submarine', *The Guardian* (17 October 1914)
Ireland, Bernard, *The U Boat Crisis and the Adoption of Convoy* (Scuttlebutt, 2017, edition 54)
Irwin, Manyley R., *U.S. Navy, Brest, France 1917: The Search for an Optimum Command Structure* (MacMullen Naval History Symposium, 2017)
Jackson, Joseph, 'Admiral William Shepherd Benson USN: The Brains of the Navy 1915–1918', *Records of the American Catholic Historical Society of Philadelphia*, vol. 56, no. 1 (March 1945), pp. 36–43, published by American Catholic Historical Society
James, Admiral Sir William, *Admiral Sir William Fisher* (Macmillan, 1943)
James, Admiral Sir William, *The Eyes of the Navy: A Biographical Study of Admiral Sir Reginald Hall* (Methuen, 1955)
Jameson, William, *The Fleet that Jack Built: Nine Men Who Made a Navy* (Harcourt, Brace and World, 1962)
Jameson, William, *The Most Formidable Thing: The Story of the Submarine from Its Earliest Days to the End of World War I* (Rupert Hart Davis, 1965)
Jellicoe, Admiral Sir John, *Memorandum on Submarine Warfare* (29 October 1916)
Jellicoe, Admiral Sir John, 'The British Navy's Titanic Task', *Current History*, vol. 5, no. 6 (March 1917), pp.1040–42. Address delivered 11 January 1917
Jellicoe, Admiral Sir John, *The Crisis in Naval War* (Cassell, 1920); citations are from 2019 paperback reprint
Jellicoe, Admiral Sir John, *The Grand Fleet 1914–1916: Its Creation, Development and Work* (Cassell, 1919); citations are from 2017 paperback reprint
Jellicoe, Admiral Sir John, *The Submarine Menace and Food Supply*, GT-519 NA CAB (22 April 1917)
Jellicoe, Admiral Sir John, *The Submarine Peril* (Cassell, 1934; there also exists a publisher's manuscript with personal annotations in author's collection)
Jellicoe, Nicholas, *Jutland: The Unfinished Battle* (Seaforth, 2016)
Karau, Mark D., *The Naval Flank of the Western Front. The German Marine Korps Flandern 1914–1918* (Seaforth, Barnsley, 2014)
Keegan, John, *The Price of Admiralty. War at Sea from Man of War to Submarine* (Hutchinson, 1988)
Kelly, Patrick, *Tirpitz and the Imperial German Navy* (Indiana University Press, 2011)
Kemp, Lt Cdr Peter K., *The Papers of Admiral Sir John Fisher*. The Navy Records Society, vol. I (1960), vol. II (1964)
Knight, E.F. and Fuller, E.G., *The Union-Castle and the War 1914–1918* (Union Castle Publication, 1920)

Koerver, Hans Joachim, *German Submarine Warfare 1914–1918 in the Eyes of British Intelligence. Selected Sources from the British National Archives, Kew* (LIS Reinisch, 2010)

Koerver, Hans Joachim, *The Kaiser's U-boat Assault on America. Germany's Great War Gamble in the First World War* (Pen & Sword, 2020)

Kohnen, Cdr David USN (ret'd), 'Sims: The US Navy's Great War Centurion', *Naval History* (April 2017)

Lake, Deborah, *Smoke and Mirrors: Q-ships against the U-boats in the First World War* (The History Press, 2009)

Lambert, Nicholas A., *Planning Armageddon: British Economic Warfare and the First World War* (Harvard University Press, 2012)

Lambert, Nicholas, *Sir John Fisher's Naval Revolution* (University of South Carolina Press, 1999)

Larson, Erik, *Dead Wake: The Last Crossing of the Lusitania* (Doubleday, 2015)

Lautenschlager, Karl, 'The Submarine in Naval Warfare, 1901–2001', *International Security*, vol. 11, no. 3 (winter, 1986/87), pp.94–140, published by The MIT Press

Lavery, Brian, *Shield of Empire: The Royal Navy and Scotland* (Birlinn, 2007)

Laws, David, *Who Killed Kitchener? The Life and Death of Britain's Most Famous War Minister* (Biteback Publishing, 2019)

Leighton, John Landon, *SIMSADUS* (1920 reprint)

Levine, Joshua, *The Hunt for the Notorious U-Boat UB.29* (Smithsonian, May 2018)

Liddell Hart, Captain Basil H., *History of the World War 1914–1918* (Faber and Faber, 1930)

Liddle, Peter R., *The Sailor's War 1914–1918* (Blandford Press, 1985)

Lilley, Terence Dawson, *Operations of the Tenth Cruiser Squadron: A Challenge for the Royal Navy and its Reserves* (University of Greenwich, 2012)

Llewellyn-Jones, Malcolm, *The Royal Navy on the Threshold of Modern Anti-Submarine Warfare, 1944–1949* (Thesis Dept of War Studies, King's College, London, 2004)

Lloyd, Nick, *Passchendaele, A New History* (Penguin, 2017)

Lloyd George, Sir David, *War Memoirs of David Lloyd George, vol.1* (Odhams Press Ltd, 1938)

Lowell Thomas, *Raiders of the Deep* (Naval Institute Press, 1928; Bluejacket Books reprint, 2004)

Lowery, Michael, *Reassessing the Fates of UB.36 and UC.36*

Lowery, Michael, *Reassessing the Losses of U.85 and UC.68*

Macdonald, Lyn, *Passchendaele, The Story of the Third Battle of Ypres 1917* (Penguin, 1978, 2014)

Macfarlane, J. Allan C., 'A Naval Travesty: The Dismissal of Admiral Sir John Jellicoe, 1917', Thesis (University of St Andrews, 2014)

Macintyre, Captain Donald, *U-Boat Killer: Fighting the U-Boats in the Battle of the Atlantic* (Cassell Military, 1956)

McCartney, Dr Innes, 'Paying the Prize for the German Submarine War: U-boats destroyed and the Admiralty Prize Fund, 1919–1932', *The Mariner's Mirror*, 104:1 (February 2018), pp.40–57

McCartney, Dr Innes, 'The Archaeology of First World War U-boat Losses in the English Channel and its Impact on the Historical Record', *The Mariner's Mirror*, 105:2 (May 2019), pp.183–201.

McCartney, Dr Innes, *The Historical Archaeology of World War I U-boats and the Compilation of Admiralty History: The Case of UC.79* (University of Bournemouth)

McKee, Fraser M., *An Explosive Story: The Rise and Fall of the Common Depth Charge* (Canadian Nautical Research, Le Marin du Nord, III, No. 1, January 1993), pp.45–58

McKillip, Lt Cdr Robert W.H., 'Undermining Technology by Strategy. Resolving the Trade Protection Dilemma in 1917', *US Naval War College Review* (summer 1991), no. 3

Manstan, Roy R., *The Listeners: U-Boat Hunters During the Great War* (Wesleyan University Press, 2018, Kindle edition)

Marder, Prof Arthur J., *Fear God and Dread Nought: Correspondence of Admiral of the Fleet, Lord Fisher of Kilverstone. Vol. I, The Making of an Admiral* (Jonathan Cape, 1952)

Marder, Prof Arthur J., *From the Dreadnought to Scapa Flow. Vol II. The Royal Navy in the Fisher Era, 1904–1919* (Oxford University Press, 1965)

Marder, Prof Arthur J., *From the Dreadnought to Scapa Flow. Vol IV. The Royal Navy in the Fisher Era, 1904–1919 (1917: The year of Crisis)* (Oxford University Press, 1969)

Marder, Prof Arthur J., *From the Dreadnought to Scapa Flow. Vol V. The Royal Navy in the Fisher Era, 1904–1919 (Victory and Aftermath January 1918 – June 1919)* (Oxford University Press, 1970)

Massie, Robert, *Castles of Steel: Britain, Germany and the Winning of The Great War at Sea* (Jonathan

Cape, 2004)

Massie, Robert, *Dreadnought, Britain, Germany and the Coming of the Great War* (Random House, 1991)

Maxwell, Diana, *Listen Up! HMS Tarlair and Memories of the Hawkscraig Admiralty Experimental Establishment Station, Aberdour, Fife, 1915–1918* (Aberdour Cultural Association, 2014)

May, Ernest R., *The World War and American Isolation 1914–1917* (Harvard University Press, 1966)

Meacham, James A., 'Four Mining Campaigns. An Historical Analysis of the Decisions of the Commanders', *Naval War College Review* (June 1967)

Messimer, Dwight R., *Find and Destroy: Antisubmarine Warfare in World War I* (US Naval Institute Press, 2001)

Messimer, Dwight R., *The Merchant U-Boat Adventures of the Deutschland, 1916–1918* (US Naval Institute Press, 1988)

Messimer, Dwight R., *Verschollen. World War I U-Boat Losses* (US Naval Institute Press, 2002)

Michelsen, Vizeadmiral D., *Der U-Bootskrieg 1914–1918* (Verlag Koehler, Leipzig, 1925)

Middleton, Drew, *Submarine: The Ultimate Naval Weapon – Its Past, Present and Future* (Playboy Press, 1976)

Miller, David, *U-Boot Katastrophen* (Geramond, 2009)

Moretz, Joseph, *Thinking Wisely, Planning Boldly: The Higher Education and Training of Royal Navy Officers, 1919–1939* (Helion & Company, 2014).

Morgan-Owen, David G., 'An "Intermediate Blockade"? British North Sea Strategy, 1912–1914', *War in History*, vol. XXII, no. 4 (November 2015), pp.478–502

Morison, Elting E., *Admiral Sims and the Modern American Navy* (Houghton Mifflin, Boston, 1942)

Muir, Augustus and Davies, Mair, *A Victorian Shipowner: A Portrait of Sir Charles Cayzer, Baronet of Gartmore* (published privately by Cayzer, Irvine and Company)

Munro, Captain D.J., *Convoys, Blockades and Mystery Towers* (Sampson Low, Marston and Co, 1930)

Nadin-Snelling, Erica, *Matron at War: The story of Katy Beaufoy (1869–1918)* (Brewin Books, 2014)

Naumes, Sean, 'These Navies and Armies and Kings and Things: Anglo American Cooperation in Anti-Submarine Warfare in World War I', *Journal of History*, Santa Clara University, vol. XIIX (2013)

Neureuther, Karl and Bergen, Claus (eds), *U-Boat Stories: Narratives of German U-Boat Sailors* (Naval and Military Press, 2005)

Newbolt, Sir Henry, *A Naval History of the War 1914–1918* (Hodder & Stoughton, 1919; see ch. 5, 'The German Submarine War', pp.183–255)

Newbolt, Sir Henry, *Submarine and Anti-Submarine* (Longmans, Green and Co, 1919)

Newbolt, Sir Henry, *The Naval History of the Great War: Based on Official Documents, Volume IV (Naval Operations)* (Longmans, Green and Co, 1928)

Nutting, Lt William Washburn, *The Cinderellas of the Fleet* (Standard Motor Construction Co, 1920)

O'Hara, Vincent, Dickson, David and Worth, Richard, *To Crown the Waves: The Great Navies of the First World War* (Naval Institute Press, 2013)

Olmstead, Justin Quinn, *Acquiring America: The Diplomatic Battle for the United States 1914–1917* (University of Sheffield, 2013)

Osborne, Eric W., *Britain's Economic Blockade of Germany 1914–1919* (Frank Cass, 2004)

Otte, T.G., *Statesman of Europe: A Life of Sir Edward Grey* (Penguin, 2020)

Owen, David, *Anti-Submarine Warfare: An Illustrated History* (Seaforth, 2007)

Padfield, Peter, *Maritime Dominion and the Triumph of the Free World: Naval Campaigns that Shaped the Modern World* (The Overlook Press, 2010)

Padfield, Peter, *The Great Naval Race. Anglo-German Naval Rivalry 1900–1914* (McKay, 1974)

Parish, Thomas, *The Submarine: A History* (Viking Books, 2004)

Parkin, Simon, *A Game of Birds and Wolves: The Ingenious Young Women Whose Secret Board Game Helped Win World War II* (Back Bay Books, Little Brown, 2020)

Parry, Cdr David, *The History of British Submarine Sonars. The Early Years: The Fessenden Oscillator is adopted and modified*

Patrick, Jeffrey L., 'On Convoy Duty in World War I: The Diary of Hoosier Guy Connor', *Indiana Magazine of History*, vol. 89, no. 4 (December 1993)

Peifer, Douglas C., 'Maritime Commerce Warfare: The Coercive Response of the Weak?', *Naval War College Review*, vol. 66, no. 2 (spring 2013)

Phillips, Christopher, 'Organization of War Economies (Great Britain and Ireland)', *International Encyclopedia Online, 1914–1918*

Ponce, Javier, 'Commerce War in the East Central Atlantic during the First World War: German Submarines Around the Canary Islands, 1916–1918', *The Mariner's Mirror*, 100:3 (August 2014), pp.335–48

Pratt, By Fletcher, 'The Destroyer Grows Up', *United States Naval Institute Proceedings*, vol. 61/5/387 (May 1935)

Preston, Anthony, *Submarine Warfare: An Illustrated History* (Brown Books, 1998)

Preston, Diana, *Wilful Murder: The Sinking of the Lusitania* (Doubleday, 2002)

Raguet, Commander Edward C., USN, 'United States Submarine Chasers at Gibraltar, November, 1918', *United States Naval Institute Proceedings*, vol. 62/12/406 (December 1936)

Ranft, B. McL., *The Beatty Papers: vol. 1, 1902–1918* (Navy Records Society, 1989)

Rawson, Geoffrey, *Earl Beatty, Admiral of the Fleet* (Jarrolds, 1930)

Rayner, J.R., 'The deadliest thing that keeps the seas: the technology, tactics and terror of the submarine in *The War Illustrated* magazine', *Journal for Maritime Research*, 19 (1) (2017), pp.1–22. ISSN 2153-3369

Redford, Duncan, *The Submarine: A Cultural History from the Great War to Nuclear Combat* (I.B. Tauris, 2015)

Robinson, Ann, *Queenstown on the Web* (27 April 2017)

Robinson, Markus F. and Robinson, Gertude, *Der Kapitän: U-Boat Ace Hans Rose* (Amberley Publishing, 2018)

Roblin, Sebastien, *World War One Taught the U.S. Navy How to Fight Submarines the Hard Way* (The National Interest)

Rose, H. Wickliffe, *Brittany Patrol: The Story of the Suicide Fleet* (W.W. Norton & Co, New York, 1937)

Roskill, Stephen, *Admiral of the Fleet Earl Beatty: The Last Naval Hero. An Intimate Biography* (Collins, 1980)

Roskill, Stephen, 'The Dismissal of Admiral Jellicoe and its Repercussions' (original typed manuscript)

Rössler, Eberhard, *The U-boat: The Evolution and Technical History of German Submarines* (Naval Institute Press, 1975)

Ryheul, Johan, *The Flandern U-boat bases and U-Bootflotille Flandern* (U-boat.net, August 2002)

Salgado, Augusto, 'The Convoy System in the Mid-Atlantic, 1917–1918', *The Mariner's Mirror*, 105:3 (August 2019), pp.288–96

Scheer, Admiral Reinhard, *Germany's High Seas Fleet in the World War* (Cassell, 1920)

Schoultz, Commodore Gustav von, *With the British Battle Fleet. War Recollections of a Russian Naval Officer* (Hutchinson, *c.* 1920)

Schultz, Paul, *By U-Boat Through the World's Oceans* (Trident Publishing, Great War Series, 2020)

Scriba, Arnulf, *Berlin in the 1914–1918 War* (Cairn Info, Musées et Archives de la ville de Bruxelles. 1E/ XLVI. 2014)

Scrimgeour, Alexander, *Scrimgeour's Small Scribbling Diary 1914–1916* (Conway, 2008)

Semmel, Bernard, *Liberalism and Naval Strategy: Ideology, Interest and Sea Power during the Pax Britannica* (HarperCollins, 1986)

Sencicle, Lorraine, 'Captain Carey, the Queen and World War I Shipping in the Channel', *The Dover Historian* (2 October 2016)

Showell, Jak Mallmann, *The U-Boat Century. German Submarine Warfare 1906–2006* (Chatham Publishing, 2006)

Simpson, Michael, 'Admiral William S. Sims and Admiral Sir Lewis Bayly Royal Navy: An unlikely Friendship and Anglo-American Co-operation 1917–1919', *Naval War College Review*,vol. 41, no. 2 (spring 1988), pp.66–80

Simpson, Richard V., *Goat Island and the U.S. Naval Torpedo Station: Guncotton, Smokeless Powder and Torpedoes* (America Through Time, 2016)

Sims, Rear Admiral William S., *How we nearly lost the War: A Broadside at the Navy Department* (The World's Work, March 1927)

Sims, Rear Admiral William S., *SIMSUSN.*

Sims, Rear Admiral William S., 'The Practical Character of the Naval College: A Lecture delivered before the Officers of the US Naval Academy' (11 November 1912)

Sims, Admiral William S. and Hendrick, Burton J., *The Victory at Sea:. The Allied Campaign Against U-Boats During the First World War 1917–1918* (Leonaur Reprint 2012, first published 1920; serialized in *Pearson's Magazine*, 1919)

Sinclair, David, *Uncharted Waters: The Cayzer Family Firm 1916–1987* (privately published, 2001)

Snelling, Stephen, *VCs of the First World War: The Naval VCs* (The History Press, 2002)

Sondhaus, Lawrence, *German Submarine Warfare in World War I: The Onset of Total War at Sea* (Rowman & Littlefield, 2017, Kindle edition)

South, Andy, *Room 40: Cryptoanalysis during World War One* (Navy General Board, navygeneralboard.com)

Spiegel und Peckelsheim, Baron Edgar von und zu, *U-Boat 202: The Diary of A German Submarine* (Amazon Books, 2020; fictional account based on Spiegel's command of *U.32*)

Spindler, Rear Admiral Arno, 'The Value of the Submarine in Naval Warfare: Based on the German Experience in the War', trans. Cdr W.P. Beehler, *United States Naval Institute Proceedings* (May 1916)

Spindler, Rear Admiral Arno, *En Sous-Marins* (*Six Years Submarine Cruising*)

Still, William N., Jnr, *Crisis at Sea: The United States Navy in European Waters in World War 1* (University Press of Florida, 2007)

Stokesbury, James L., *Navy and Empire* (William Morrow and Co, NY, 1983)

Sueter, Commander Murray Fraser RN, *The Evolution of the Submarine Boat, Mine and Torpedo* (J. Griffen and Co, 1907)

Tarrant, V.E., *The U-Boat Offensive 1914–1945* (Naval Institute Press, 1989)

Taussig, Joseph K. (ed. Still, William N. Jnr), *The Queenstown Patrol, 1917: The Diary of Commander Joseph Knefler Taussig, USN* (Naval War College Press, 1996)

Temple Patterson, A., *Jellicoe: A Biography* (Macmillan, 1969)

Temple Patterson, A., *The Jellicoe Papers, vol. I, 1893–1916 (JP1)* (Navy Records Society, 1966)

Temple Patterson, A., *The Jellicoe Papers, vol. II, 1916–1935 (JP2)* (Navy Records Society, 1968)

Termote, Tomas, *Beneath the Waves: U-Boat Flotilla in Flanders 1915–1918* (Unicorn Publishing, 2017)

Terraine, John, *Business in Great Waters: The U-Boat Wars 1916–1945* (Leo Cooper, 1989)

Thomas, Lowell, *Raiders in the Deep* (Bluejacket Books, 2004; First edition 1928)

Thompson, Julian, *The Imperial War Museum Book of the War at Sea 1914–1918* (Sidgwick & Jackson, 2005)

Trapp, Georg von, *To the Last Salute: Memories of an Austrian U-Boat Commander* (University of Nebraska, 2007)

Trask, David F., *Captains & Cabinets: Anglo-American Naval Relations, 1917–1918* (University of Missouri Press, 1972)

Tuchman, Barbara, *The Zimmermann Telegram: The Astounding Espionage Operation that Propelled America into the First World War* (Penguin, 1958)

Uhlig, Frank Jnr, 'A Real Revolution in Naval Affairs and What it Achieved', *US Naval War College Review*, vol. 52, no. 2 (spring 1999), pp.138–42

Uhlig, Frank Jnr, 'Set and Drift. A Real Revolution in Naval Affairs and what it Achieved', *Naval War College Review*, vol. 52, no. 2 (spring 1999)

Uhlig, Frank Jnr, 'The Submarine 1776–1918', *Naval War College Review*, vol. 57, no. 2 (spring 2004), pp.146–58

Vat, Dan van der, *Stealth at Sea: The History of the Submarine* (Weidenfield & Nicolson, 1994)

Vecchio, Nicholas, 'The Path to Ruin: Inflexibility, Delusion, and Discord Between the Kaiser, Chancellor, and German High Command in the Great War', *History: A Journal of Student Research*, The College at Brockport, vol. 1, article 1 (December 2016)

Warner, Oliver, *Great Sea Battles* (Weidenfeld & Nicolson, 1963)

Watson, Alexander, *Ring of Steel. Germany and Austria Hungary in World War One: The People's War* (Perseus Books, 2014)

Watt, Richard M., *The Kings Depart: The Tragedy of Germany, Versailles and the German Revolution* (Weidenfeld & Nicolson, 1968)

Weir, Garry E., *Building the Kaiser's Navy: The Imperial Navy Office and German Industry in the von Tirpitz Era, 1890–1919* (Naval Institute Press, 1919)

Weir, Garry E., 'Naval Strategy and Industrial Mobilization at the Twelfth Hour', *The Mariner's Mirror* (22 March 2013)

Wester Wemyss, Lady, *The Life and Letters of Lord Wester Wemyss, Admiral of the Fleet* (Eyre & Spottiswoode, 1935)

Wheeler, Captain William J., 'US Coast Guard, Reminiscences of World War Convoy Work', *United States Naval Institute Proceedings*, vol. 55/5/315 (May 1929)

Wilson, David A.H., 'Avian Anti-Submarine Warfare Proposals in Britain 1915–1918: The Admiralty and Thomas Mills', *International Journal of Naval History*, vol. 5, no. 1 (April 2006)

Wilson, Henry B., *An Account of Operations of the American Navy in France during the war with Germany* (Navy Department, 1919)

Wilson, Herbert Wrigley, *Hush; or the Hydrophone Service* (Mills & Boon, 1920)

Winton, John, *Convoy: The Defence of Sea Trade 1890–1990* (Michael Joseph, 1983)

Winton, John, *Jellicoe* (Michael Joseph, 1981)

Woofenden, Todd A., *Hunters of the Steel Sharks: The Submarine Chasers of WWI* (Signal Light Books, 2006)

Woofenden, Todd A., 'Taking Aim at North Sea Mines', *Naval History* (Febuary 2023)

Wragg, David, *Fisher: The Admiral who Reinvented the Royal Navy* (History Press, 2009)

Wren, Alan, *Ambush of the SS Persia, Voices from a Lost Liner* (York Publishing Services, 2020)

Yates, Keith, *Flawed Victory: Jutland 1916* (Chatham, 2000)

**French Literature**

Brézet, Francois-Emmanuel, *La Guerre Sous-Marine Allemande 1914–1945* (Perrin, 2017)

Castex, Capitaine de Frégate, *Nouveaux Aspects de la Liaison des Armes (À propos de la Guerre sous-marine allemande)* (École Supériore de Guerre, France, 1921)

Dessouly, Jean, *L'encyclopédie mondiale des Bateaux sous-marins. Tome I. Les Précurseurs – d'une guerre à l'autre*

Kemp, Lt Cdr Peter K., *La Protection des Convois Britanniques*. Presse Universitaires de France, Revue d'histoire de la deuxième guerre mondiale. 18e anneé, No. 69, *La Bataille de l'Atlantique*

Lowery, Michael, *L'Odyssée de 5 sous-marins allemands, mouilleurs de mines, coules en 1917–18 dans le Detroit du Pas-de-Calais UC26 – UC46 – UC61 – UC64 – UC79*

Noyes, Alfred, *Le Sort du Sous-marin Allemand. Notes suer L'efficacité des measures prises par la marine britanique* (Darling and Sons, London, 1916)

Villiers, Patrick, *La Lutte pour le Contrôle de la Mer en Manche-est et Pas-de-Calais pendant la Grande Guerre.* Guerre Mondiales et Conflits Contemporains. July 2012, No. 247 (Presse Universitaires France, 2012)

**German Literature**

Baseler, von Svenja, *Blut an den Händen. 1918, Zwei U-Boot-Kommandanten im Visier: Helmut Patzig und Wilhelm Werner* (SchiffClassic, 4/2022 Juni)

Bauer, Admiral Hermann, *Als Führer der U-Boote im Weltkrieg. Der Eintritt der U-Boote-Waffe in die Seekriegsführung* (Koehler & Ameland, Leipzig)

Block, Peter H., *Rauchwolke achteraus!* (Schiff Classic, August 2020)

Granier, Gerhard, *Die deutsche Seekriegsleitung im Ersten Weltkrieg : Dokumentation*, Vol. III (Bundesarchiv, Koblenz)

Franken, Klaus (ed), *Admiral Gustav Bachmann. Lebenserinnerungen und Tagebuch 1915* (Brill Schöningh, 2022)

Hillmann, Jörg und Huck, Stephan, *Schriften zur Marinegeschichte*, Band III (Brill Schöningh, 2022)

Huber, Florian, *Kein Engländer soll das Boot betreten. Die letzte Fahrt von UC.71* (Rowolt Verlag, 2019)

Kaack, Ulf, *Die deutschen U-Boote* (Geramond Verlag, 2014)

Kern, Dr Armin, *Eine teuflische Waffe. 1914/15: Österreichs U-Boote gegen Grosskampfschiffe* (SchiffClassic, 6/2022 August/September)

König, Kapitän Paul, *Die Fahrt der Deutschland* (Hearst's International Library, New York, 1916)

Krause, Günter, *U Boat Alarm! Zur Geschichte der U Boat Abwehr (1914–1945)* (Brandenburgisched Verlagshaus, 1998)

Lippisky, Stefan and Lippisky, Florian, *Deutsche U-Boote. Hundert Jahre Technik und Entwicklung* (Verlag E.S. Mittler, 2006)

Peillard, Leonce, *Geschichte des U-Boot Krieges 1939–1945* (Heyne Bücher, 1994) (Fr: *L'Histoire Générale de la Guerre sous-marine 1939–1945*)

Pemsel, Helmut, *Seeherrschaft. Eine maritime Weltgeschichte von der Dampschiffahrt bis zur Gegenwart*, Band II (Bernard und Gräfe Verlag, 1992)

Rössler, Eberhard, *Deutsche U-Boote 1898–1918. Entwicklung, Herstellung, Ausbildung. Auswendung* (Verlag E.S. Mittler, 2006)

Rössler, Eberhard, *Die Unterseeboote der Kaiserlichen Marine* (Bernard und Gräfe Verlag, 1997)

Rössler, Eberhard, *Geschichte der deutschen U-Bootbaus* (Bernard und Gräfe Verlag, 1986)

Schröder, Joachim, *Die U-Boote des Kaisers. Die Geschichte des deutschen U-Boot-Krieges gegen Großbritannien im Ersten Weltkrieg* (Bernard und Gräfe Verlag, 2003)

Simsa, Paul, *Wilhelm II und seine Flotte* (Motorbuch Verlag, 2012)

Spiess, Johannes von, *Sechs Jahre U-Boot-Fahrten* (Verlag Reimer Hobbing, Berlin) (Fr: *Six Ans de Croissieres*)

Spindler, Konteradmiral Arno, *Der Handelskrieg mit U-Booten*, vol. I (E.S. Mittler und Sohn, 1932)

Spindler, Konteradmiral Arno, *Der Handelskrieg mit U-Booten*, vol. II, Feb–Sept 1915 (E.S. Mittler und Sohn, 1933)

Spindler, Konteradmiral Arno, *Der Handelskrieg mit U-Booten*, vol. III, Oct 1915 – Jan 1917 (E..S Mittler und Sohn, 1934)

Spindler, Konteradmiral Arno, *Der Handelskrieg mit U-Booten*, vol. IV, Feb 1917 – Dec 1917

Spindler, Konteradmiral Arno, *Der Handelskrieg mit U-Booten*, vol. V, Jan–Nov 1918 (E.S. Mittler und Sohn, 1966)

Spindler, Konteradmiral Arno, *Der Lusitania Fall*

Spindler, Konteradmiral Arno, *Zur Kritik der Tirpitzchen U-boot Politik* (Nomos Verlagsgesellschaft, 1903)

Steinuth, Hans, *Lusitania* (Deutsche Verlag Anstalt, Stuttgart und Berlin)

Valentiner, Max, *U.38. Wikingerfahrte eines deutschen U-Bootes* (Ullstein Verlag, 1934)

**Government Reports and Archives**

'American Ship Casualties of the World War, Including Naval Vessels, Merchant Vessels, Merchant ships, Sailing Vessels and Fishing Craft', United States Navy Department. Naval Records. Compiled by Historical Section, Corrected 1 April 1923 (in Google books)

'Anti-U-Boat Division of the Naval Staff, 1945. Monthly Antisubmarine Report February 1945', CB 0405045 (2). London

Carricker, S. and David, D. Min., *German U-Boats 1850–2020. A reference to the 5,523 U-boats of German Production and Use* (Heritage Publishing, NC, USA, 2018; Google books)

CASS Series, 2003. Franklin, George, *Britain's Anti-Submarine Capability 1919–1939*

CASS Series, 2006. Llewellyn-Jones, Malcolm, *The Royal Navy and Anti-Submarine Warfare 1917–1949*

Colomb, Captain John, *Naval Intelligence and Protection of Commerce in War* (Royal United Services Institution, 13 May 1881)

Churchill Archives, GBR/0014/CLKE, *Papers of William F Clarke* (incl. *History of OB40, Will cryptography be of use in the Next War? Elements of Cryptography*)

Dewar, Commander K.C.B., *What is the Influence of Overseas Commerce on the operations of War?* (Royal United Services Institution Journal, 1913, and Naval Review, 1914)

*Guides to the Microfilmed Records of the German Navy, 1850–1945*, Issue 1. National Archives and Record Service, USGSA (Washington, 1984; Google books)

HW 3715 William Clarke Papers, NA History of Room OB 40

National Archives, Kew, London, 'Admiralty: Naval Intelligence Division and Operational Intelligence Centre: Intelligence Reports and Papers. Operational intelligence: Special Intelligence II', ADM 223/285

National Archives, Kew, London, Naval Staff Monograph (Historical): 'Naval Staff of Admiralty, Its Work and Development', ADM 234/434

National Archives, Kew, London, 'Reported Destruction of Submarines Aug. 1914 to Jan. 1919', ADM 239/26

National Archives, Kew, London, HW 3/16, Clarke, William F., *History of the GCCS and its Naval Section, 1919–1945*

National Archives, Kew, London – ADM 137

National Archives, Kew, London – ADM 116

National Archives, Washington, 'Daily Submarine Return' (Daily U-Boat summary reports written by Admiral Hall for Admiral Sims, USN)

Naval Staff Intelligence Division. CB 01381, 'German Views on Unrestricted Submarine Warfare', Nov 1917

Navy Department, Office of Naval Intelligence, 'German Submarines in Question and Answer', June 1918

Navy Department, Office of Naval Records and Library, 'German Submarine Activities on the Atlantic Coast of the United States and Canada (NDSA)', Government Printing Office, 1920

Orkney Library and Archives (ref D1/1017/5), 'German Submarines in Question and Answer', Intelligence Department, Royal Navy. ID 1176

US Naval War College, 'German Whitebook on Armed Merchantmen. With Facsimilies of the Secret Orders of the British Admiralty'

Wilson, Vice Admiral Henry B., *Account of the Operations of the American Navy in France During the War With Germany* (United States Atlantic Fleet, 1920)

**Other**

Forgotten Wrecks of the First World War, Maritime Archaeology Trust, Southampton, *Anglia and Asturias, Hospital Ships and the First World War*

Forgotten Wrecks of the First World War, Maritime Archaeology Trust, Southampton, *Black and Asian Seamen of the Forgotten Wrecks of the First World War*

Forgotten Wrecks of the First World War, Maritime Archaeology Trust, Southampton, *USS Jacob Jones, The First US Destroyer Sunk by Enemy Action*

The Naval Society, *The Naval Review (NR)* 1920 (Feb Vol. VIII, No. 1, May No. 2, Aug No. 3, Nov No. 4)

**Online Resources and Links**

**Websites**

archeosousmarine.net

Ballymena and the Great War

Deutsches U-Boat Museum, dubm.de

History of British Submarine Sonars

(Parry, Cdr. David) rnsubs.co.uk

Fighting ships of the World Navypedia.org

Subchasers of World War One Splinterfleet.org

South African Military History samilitaryhistory.org

Subchaser Archives subchaser.org

Torpedo *Vorhaltrechner* Project tvre.org

The Sinking of the USS *Jacob Jones* US Naval History and Heritage Command, history.navy.mil

Wartime memories project wartimememoriesproject.com

world-war.co.uk

A WW1 Naval Officer's Story (Hone, Tom) warontherocks.com/2013/09/a-wwi-naval-officers-story/6 Sept 1913

*So starben die Männer von Seiner Majestät U-31* (Althaus, Johann) Die Welt.de

Lieutenant John Thomas Carr, Purple Heart recipient jpsh.org (Peter O'Brien)

**Newspapers**

*The New York Times*, 'Sims assails Navy, Backing Mitchell' (19 November 1925)

*The New York Times*, The New York Times Current History of the European War, *German Official statements about the Arabic's sinking*, Vol. 3, No. 1 (October 1915), pp.4–8

*The New York Times*, The New York Times Current History, *Case of the Hesperian*, Vol. 3, No. 1 (October 1915), pp.8–9

**YouTube**

Brown, Simon, 'The Story of *UB.116*', youtube.com/watch?v=yGD5k-yXyMk

Grove, Dr Eric, 'Britain's Blockade', youtube.com/watch?v=ZagFa5p_q7w&t=3222s&ab_channel=WarStudie

# Index